# A History of Securities Law in the Supreme Court

# A History of Securities Law in the Supreme Court

A.C. PRITCHARD AND ROBERT B. THOMPSON

Oxford University Press is a department of the University of Oxford. It furthers
the University's objective of excellence in research, scholarship, and education
by publishing worldwide. Oxford is a registered trade mark of Oxford University
Press in the UK and certain other countries.

Published in the United States of America by Oxford University Press
198 Madison Avenue, New York, NY 10016, United States of America.

© Oxford University Press 2023

All rights reserved. No part of this publication may be reproduced, stored in
a retrieval system, or transmitted, in any form or by any means, without the
prior permission in writing of Oxford University Press, or as expressly permitted
by law, by license, or under terms agreed with the appropriate reproduction
rights organization. Inquiries concerning reproduction outside the scope of the
above should be sent to the Rights Department, Oxford University Press, at the
address above.

You must not circulate this work in any other form
and you must impose this same condition on any acquirer.

Library of Congress Cataloging-in-Publication Data
Names: Pritchard, Adam C., author. | Thompson, Robert B. (Law Professor), author.
Title: A history of securities law in the Supreme Court / A.C. Pritchard and Robert B. Thompson.
Description: New York : Oxford University Press, 2023. |
Includes bibliographical references.
Identifiers: LCCN 2022040720 (print) | LCCN 2022040721 (ebook) |
ISBN 9780197665916 (hardback) | ISBN 9780197665930 (epub) |
ISBN 9780197665947
Subjects: LCSH: Securities—United States. | United States. Supreme Court.
Classification: LCC KF1439 .P75 2023  (print) | LCC KF1439 (ebook) |
DDC 346.73/0666—dc23/eng/20221031
LC record available at https://lccn.loc.gov/2022040720
LC ebook record available at https://lccn.loc.gov/2022040721

DOI: 10.1093/oso/9780197665916.001.0001

Printed by Integrated Books International, United States of America

*For my father, who loved old things and worked patiently to bring them back to life.*
*ACP*
*To the justices who through their papers opened for all of us a window into judicial decision-making. RBT*

# Contents

| | |
|---|---|
| Introduction: The Administrative State and Capitalism | 1 |
|   A. Felix Frankfurter and the Rise of the Administrative State | 1 |
|   B. Lewis F. Powell, Jr., and the "War against Capitalism" | 4 |
|   C. The Arc of Securities Law in the Supreme Court | 8 |
|     1. The Triumph of the Administrative State | 11 |
|     2. The Era of Deference | 12 |
|     3. An Activist Court | 13 |
|     4. Lewis Powell and the Counterrevolution | 14 |
|     5. A Random Walk | 15 |
|   D. Roadmap of the Book | 17 |
| 1. The Coming of the New Deal | 20 |
|   A. The Enactment of the Federal Securities Laws | 20 |
|     1. The Securities Act of 1933 | 20 |
|     2. The Securities Exchange Act of 1934 | 25 |
|     3. The Public Utility Holding Company Act of 1935 (PUHCA) | 27 |
|     4. Roosevelt's Second Term | 31 |
|   B. A Hostile Judicial Reception | 31 |
| 2. Social Control of Finance | 37 |
|   A. Securities Regulation and Taming Big Business | 39 |
|     1. William O. Douglas and Social Control of Finance | 39 |
|     2. Douglas at the SEC | 44 |
|   B. Breaking Up Utility Empires: The Public Utility Holding Company Act of 1935 | 48 |
|     1. The PUHCA Wars | 50 |
|     2. Breaking Up the Holding Companies: A Judicial New Deal | 54 |
|   C. Reorganizations of Distressed Firms: The Chandler Act of 1938 | 58 |
|     1. The SEC's Role in Bankruptcy | 58 |
|     2. Bankruptcy and Insider Trading | 62 |
|   D. Retiring the SEC's Control | 65 |
| 3. Policing the SEC | 67 |
|   A. A Progressive Reset? | 68 |
|   B. *Chenery I & II*: The Roosevelt Court Divides | 70 |
|   C. Judicial Review of SEC Procedures | 79 |
|   D. The Skeptical Era | 82 |
|   E. The Post-Powell Period | 86 |
|   F. Conclusion | 88 |

viii CONTENTS

4. Boundaries ... 89
   A. The Early Period through the 1960s ... 90
      1. Deference to the Agency's Inclusive Definition of a Security ... 90
      2. A Glimmer of Doubt? ... 95
   B. Reining In the SEC and the Securities Laws ... 97
      1. Restrictive Holdings of the Definition of a Security ... 98
      2. Parallel Questions in the Definitions of "Sale" and "Pledge" ... 102
      3. Some Ambiguity in the Restrictive Approach to the Definition of Security ... 106
      4. The Post-Powell Period: Tension Persists ... 110
   C. Antitrust and the Securities Laws ... 112
   D. Constitutional and Geographic Boundaries ... 118
   E. Whither Boundaries? ... 125

5. Insider Trading ... 126
   A. Early Prohibitions Based on Fraud and the § 16(b) Alternative ... 127
   B. The Swinging Sixties for Insider Trading Law ... 130
      1. Bill Cary Triggers the Revolution in *Cady, Roberts* ... 130
      2. *Blau v. Lehman*: The SEC's Unsuccessful Effort to Expand § 16(b) ... 132
      3. *Capital Gains Research Bureau*: A Foothold for Fiduciary Duty ... 133
      4. *Texas Gulf Sulphur*: The Spirit of *Capital Gains* Takes Hold in the Second Circuit ... 138
      5. *Affiliated Ute*: A Purposivist Approach in Rule 10b-5 ... 139
   C. Lewis Powell Closes the Door ... 140
      1. Section 16(b) and the Transition to Textualism ... 140
      2. *Chiarella*: Fiduciary Duty Confined ... 145
      3. *Dirks*: Tipping and Personal Benefit ... 151
   D. The Post-Powell Period: Misappropriation and Tipping Revisited ... 163

6. Private Litigation ... 168
   A. A Modest Beginning ... 170
   B. Implied Private Rights of Action Unleashed ... 171
   C. Lewis Powell and the Counterrevolution ... 176
      1. Class Actions ... 178
      2. Construing Rule 10b-5 Narrowly ... 182
      3. Rolling Back Implied Rights of Action ... 188
   D. Filling Out the Elements of Explicit Private Rights of Action ... 194
   E. Arbitration and the Securities Laws ... 196
   F. Implied Rights after the Counterrevolution ... 202
      1. The Immediate Aftermath: Ping Pong ... 203
      2. The Impact of the PSLRA ... 208
      3. Summing Up ... 221

## CONTENTS ix

7. The Federal/State Flashpoint in Corporate Governance — 222
    A. Fiduciary Misbehavior and the Genesis of Federal Corporate Law — 223
    B. The Supreme Court Curtails Federal Corporate Law — 226
    C. Investment Companies — 232
    D. The Takeover Wars and Federalism — 234
        1. Implied Private Rights Under Federal Tender Offer Statutes — 234
        2. Preemption or Commerce Clause Challenges to State
           Anti-Takeover Laws — 235
    E. Post-1987, Post-Powell Drift — 245
    F. Conclusion — 250

8. Conclusion: How the Supreme Court Makes Securities Laws — 251
    A. The Tale of the Numbers — 252
    B. A Reliable Court — 255
    C. The Puzzle of Frankfurter and Douglas — 259
    D. A Purposive Court — 264
    E. A Skeptical Court and an Influential Justice — 266
    F. A Random Walk — 272
    G. A Final Word — 273

*Notes on Sources* — 275
*Appendix: Supreme Court Securities Cases, 1933–2021* — 277
*Notes* — 297
*Index* — 367

# Introduction

## The Administrative State and Capitalism

### A. Felix Frankfurter and the Rise of the Administrative State

On March 4, 1933, Franklin Delano Roosevelt (FDR) became President of a nation beleaguered by the ravages of the Great Depression, by then in its fourth year. Once inaugurated, Roosevelt immediately faced a bank run that had begun in the waning days of the Herbert Hoover administration, necessitating a "bank holiday" and emergency measures to restore the banks' liquidity. Many banks would have to be closed permanently. The incident demonstrated just how fragile public confidence in the nation's financial institutions had become. The bank crisis was averted, but FDR's new administration still faced the accumulated challenges of the Depression: an enormous slowdown in economic activity; stubborn deflation; and most demoralizing, a devastatingly high rate of unemployment. Joblessness, which stood at 3.2% in 1929, reached 24.9% by 1933. Roosevelt had been elected by a public desperate to get the economy moving again. Recovery was the top priority for the new administration.

Roosevelt had promised not just recovery, however, but also reform of the institutions that the public blamed for the economic misery. At the top of the list was finance. In the public mind, the stock market crash of October 1929 triggered the ensuing years of catastrophic decline in production and employment. The heady bull market of the 1920s had drawn many small investors into the securities markets for the first time; the stunning reversal and ongoing bear market that followed eviscerated their savings. The Dow Jones Industrial Average was at 381 in September 1929. By July of 1932 it stood at 41, with corresponding declines in stock trading and new issuances. Roosevelt viewed the speculative frenzy of the 1920s as a disaster for investors and business alike. It also created political opportunity, however, and Roosevelt capitalized on the public's simmering outrage against Wall Street with populist attacks against the moneyed interests. In his first inaugural address, Roosevelt decried "the unscrupulous money changers [who] stand indicted in the court of public opinion, rejected by the hearts and minds of men." The principal targets were investment bankers and the New York Stock Exchange.[1]

---

*A History of Securities Law in the Supreme Court.* A.C. Pritchard and Robert B. Thompson, Oxford University Press.
© Oxford University Press 2023. DOI: 10.1093/oso/9780197665916.003.0001

2  INTRODUCTION: THE ADMINISTRATIVE STATE AND CAPITALISM

High-profile Senate hearings in the last ten days of the Hoover administration, orchestrated by Ferdinand Pecora, captured the daily headlines and further fueled the populist anger. "By introducing a string of villains, [the hearings] translated economic problems into moral terms." Pecora's unrelenting cross-examination of the princes of finance had its share of a circus atmosphere, but it also uncovered a plethora of financial sins by the bankers—lax standards for screening public offerings, insider trading pools, and market manipulation—during the decade of rampant speculation. Even Hoover was outraged, perhaps because he thought the "bear raids" were part of a Democratic conspiracy against him.[2]

Roosevelt was eager to leverage the outrage generated by Pecora's efforts to advance the administration's reform campaign. Stock exchange and securities legislation was on Roosevelt's early list of "must" legislation. Sam Untermyer, who had come to prominence in Washington as the counsel for the Pujo Commission in 1912–13, had been drafted to work on a bill as early as December 1932. His bill to regulate both new offerings and stock exchange transactions ran aground even before FDR's inauguration. Untermyer's proposal to put this new regime inside the Post Office was seen as unworkable. Soon after the inauguration, an alternative drafting team produced a bill limited to securities offerings. Roosevelt's message to Congress transmitting this bill included his oft-quoted herald of a fundamental shift in the law, adding "to the ancient rule of *caveat emptor* the further doctrine: 'Let the seller also beware.' It puts the burden of telling the whole truth on the seller. It should give impetus to honest dealings in securities and thereby bring back public confidence." Within days, however, this version faced serious congressional headwinds over the draconian powers to be given to government. Just one month into FDR's term, the administration's attempt at financial reform legislation was deemed a "hopeless mess."[3]

Roosevelt's braintruster Ray Moley reached out to Harvard Law Professor Felix Frankfurter for help cleaning up. Frankfurter immediately telegraphed back to Moley, "Three of us will arrive at the Carlton Friday morning." Moley's summons afforded Frankfurter an opportunity to make himself useful to Roosevelt. Frankfurter had been advising FDR since he was elected as governor of New York but had declined to take a post in the new administration. He thought he would be more useful to Roosevelt if he maintained the independence afforded him as a law professor: "[H]aving refused the request of the President for my services as Solicitor General," Frankfurter wrote in his diary, "I could not possibly decline the President's request, these days, to do *ad hoc* jobs."[4]

Moley's call also afforded Frankfurter an opportunity to turn theory into practice. Frankfurter had devoted his academic career to the study of government regulation of business. His first public utilities lecture at Harvard, in 1914, prophesied the rise of the administrative state:

INTRODUCTION: THE ADMINISTRATIVE STATE AND CAPITALISM 3

[I]n the immediate decades ahead, during your time and mine, there will be a continuous extension of governmental activity and governmental supervision of business. This is true for various reasons. All must feel the pressure of economic and social problems, that certain evils demand answer, that there is much room for improvement, and that government is one of the most important agencies in answering these demands and in the furtherance of these improvements. This pressure, therefore, must result in increased governmental activity in its relation to business.[5]

Frankfurter was a longtime believer in governance by experts, detached from politics. Law schools had an important role to play in that project, as centers for an empirical, scientific approach to the development of social reform legislation.

Frankfurter was also a disciple of Louis Brandeis's crusade against "the curse of bigness," that is, businesses organized on a national scale, and he instilled that faith in many of the protégés he sent to Washington. Frankfurter and his fellow Brandeisians viewed big business as an enemy to be defeated; it was a moral crusade to promote individualism by supporting small businessmen, not an economic theory. This attitude put them at odds with the central planners also advising Roosevelt, who favored industrial coordination under government supervision. Roosevelt himself was of two minds. As Robert Jackson put it, Roosevelt "always was torn between the Theodore Roosevelt theory of regulated bigness and the Wilsonian-Brandeis theory of free competition and retention of the smaller units." From Brandeis's perspective, finance had facilitated the growth of giant business for its own speculative purposes. From his perch at the Supreme Court, Brandeis himself was "quiet[ly] advising [the Roosevelt administration] from the sidelines," typically using Frankfurter as his emissary.[6]

Frankfurter wrote to Justice Harlan Fiske Stone in early 1933: "I wish I had a tithe of Macauley's power and of Bagehot's financial capacity. I would write a series of studies entitled 'Enemies of Capitalism,' and instead of dealing with Marx, Lenin & Co., I should analyze the Charles W. Mitchells, the Samuel Insulls & Co...." Frankfurter had a sympathetic audience in Stone, who responded: "Perhaps the most astonishing manifestation of our times is the blindness of those who have the big stake in our present system to its evils. It is the story of the Bourbons over again." In Frankfurter's view, finance had created vast social waste. As Frankfurter wrote after the Securities Act became law:

During the height of the greatest speculative carnival in the world's history, billions of new securities were floated, of which a large part had no relation to the country's need and which inevitably became worthless; worthless not merely for millions who had sought speculative gains, but for those other

# 4 INTRODUCTION: THE ADMINISTRATIVE STATE AND CAPITALISM

millions who sought to conserve the savings of a lifetime. By all the subtle and mesmerizing arts of modern salesmanship, the sellers of securities had so extended the field of security buyers that 55 per cent of all savings . . . went into publicly marketed securities. The resulting losses cut from under the basic supports of a considerable portion of the population, and especially of those helplessly dependent on income from savings. The enormous, easy profits from their distribution stimulated the creation and sale of billions in securities, which have burdened industry and wasted or misdirected the capital resources of the nation.

Imposing social control over the world of finance was not just sound policy, but the key front in the battle to save capitalism from its real enemy. As Frankfurter wrote to Roosevelt, "the real trouble with capitalism is the capitalists." Frankfurter was preaching to the choir; Roosevelt shared the broad popular distrust of businessmen, particularly those who inhabited Wall Street. "One of my principal tasks is to prevent bankers and businessmen from committing suicide!" Roosevelt viewed his assault on the bankers as the reprise of Andrew Jackson's campaign against the Bank of the United States.[7]

## B. Lewis F. Powell, Jr., and the "War against Capitalism"

Lewis F. Powell, Jr., graduated from the Harvard Law School with an LL.M. in 1932, the year that Roosevelt was elected. A Virginia native, he had completed his LL.B. at Washington and Lee the year prior. Powell turned down an offer of $150 a month from the Davis, Polk firm in New York. He instead went to Christian, Barton and Parker in Richmond for a monthly salary of $50. No other firm in town would offer him even an office in the lean years of the Depression. He left two and a half years later to join Hunton & Williams, where he practiced (interrupted only by military service) until his nomination to the Supreme Court in 1971. Hunton & Williams was Richmond's leading firm and Powell, a consummate rainmaker, became its dominant partner.[8]

Powell recalled that "I . . . file[d] two of the earliest registration statements filed from the Richmond area under the Act of '33. This qualified me as an 'expert,' with the result that I was retained to do a good deal of securities work." Powell was the right man at the right time. In a field that values precision, Powell developed a reputation for "meticulous" work. Powell's work on registered offerings for Scott & Stringfellow (a local investment bank) led to other corporate work. Powell advised clients on the private offering exemption from registration under the Securities Act and corporate governance issues, helped them wage proxy battles, drafted charter amendments for preferred stock issues, and set up life

INTRODUCTION: THE ADMINISTRATIVE STATE AND CAPITALISM 5

insurance companies and public utilities. In sum, Powell faced the broad range of issues handled by the typical corporate lawyer of the time.[9]

Whereas Felix Frankfurter saw big business as an enemy to be defeated, Powell's experience as a corporate lawyer gave him faith in the integrity of American businessmen: "[S]ince about the middle Thirties the 'business' morals of the average American business man have been exceptionally high." Prior to that time, there had been lapses that had fueled demand for the rise of the regulatory state, Powell conceded:

> the comparative lack of morals in business during the latter part of the Nineteenth Century caused a great deal of public and private criticism of business, and resulted in the era of governmental regulation of business. This same situation developed again following the boom of the Twenties and the collapse of the early Thirties.

Those historic episodes, however, were not enough to shake Powell's faith in the businessmen he knew. That faith grew out of not only his work experience as a corporate lawyer, but also his active involvement in civic affairs at both the national and local levels.[10]

Powell's corporate practice also informed his views of the SEC. Looking back from his perch on the Supreme Court bench to his early days practicing securities law, Powell had a favorable, if measured, view of the Securities Acts:

> My first experience in corporate as distinguished from trial practice was in the representation of Virginia investment banking firms. I therefore have some familiarity with the Securities Acts, and also with the way in which they have been administered. Generally, I think these acts have been among the best of the regulatory statutes. But the SEC always has sought to expand its reach. The history of 10b-5 is an example.

Although he disagreed with the SEC's aggressive interpretations of the securities laws, Powell recognized the need for public enforcement. Shortly after handing the SEC a stinging defeat in an insider trading case, Powell wrote: "[I] have considered the SEC to be one of the better independent Agencies. It has served its basic purpose well, and the original statutes were—I thought—remarkably well drafted for their intended purposes." It was the SEC's effort to expand its authority that troubled Powell.[11]

As a young business lawyer, Powell was alarmed by the New Deal expansion of the administrative state. Powell lobbied against Roosevelt's "Court packing" plan. By 1940, Powell feared Franklin Roosevelt's vendetta against the capitalist system: "I really cannot tell you how strongly I feel that the welfare of this country

## 6 INTRODUCTION: THE ADMINISTRATIVE STATE AND CAPITALISM

requires the defeat of Mr. Roosevelt . . . and the election of a man who is sympathetic (rather than antagonistic) to the system of private profit which has enabled this country to attain its present greatness."[12]

In Powell's view, the Roosevelt administration, and FDR's appointees to the SEC, were engaged in a "war against capitalism." During World War II, Powell served as an intelligence officer. Taking a break from the invasion of North Africa to complain to a colleague about a client's loss before the SEC, Powell wrote:

> I had hoped the war . . . would temper the crusading order of SEC [*sic*], and that [the client] would receive moderate and fair treatment. It is extremely disappointing to find that agencies of the Government are still fighting an internal war against capitalism when the unified energies of all should be concentrated on fighting the very urgent and real war for physical survival. Also one of the things I *hope* we are fighting for is the survival of a just and fairly regulated capitalism. Personally, I believe capitalism (i.e.—the right to private property and moderate profit) is an essential component of democracy.

Although Powell was far from being an advocate of laissez-faire ("fairly regulated capitalism," "moderate profit"), he objected to the SEC's perceived adversarial attitude toward business. Later on, Powell worried that elites were pushing the country toward a "stultifying socialism":

> The free enterprise system is now under a wide-ranging attack from many in the media, in politics, and on the campus. Young people are no longer taught in schools and colleges that this system—and only this system—enabled America to achieve its greatness. There are many who would substitute a stultifying socialism, leading us down the road which England is following so disastrously.

Powell's faith in American business made him a strong defender of "free enterprise" against political incursion. Powell's hostility to socialism aligned with his involvement in national politics. Although he was a "Virginia Democrat" in local elections, he campaigned for Republican presidential candidates against Harry Truman and Adlai Stevenson's "left-wing socialism." He campaigned for Dwight Eisenhower, helping to organize the Virginia Democrats for Eisenhower.[13]

His efforts on behalf of Eisenhower's campaign generated an opportunity for Powell to influence the SEC directly: the Eisenhower administration offered Powell the position of the agency's chairman. Later, in a memorandum to his children, Powell explained why he declined the post:

> Walter S. Robertson, a partner in Scott & Stringfellow, and a personal client of mine, became Assistant Secretary of State for the Far East in the Eisenhower

## INTRODUCTION: THE ADMINISTRATIVE STATE AND CAPITALISM    7

Administration. He called me from the White House early in 1953 and said that the President would appoint me Chairman of the Securities & Exchange Commission if I would accept the position. Again, I conferred with clients, senior partners at Hunton & Williams and—of course—with Jo. Although I had done a good deal of SEC work, and the Chairmanship of the SEC would assure a substantial law practice thereafter, my partners wanted me to stay in Richmond. I had commenced to develop major clients of my own. . . . and also—having been away nearly four years during the war—I preferred to remain in my native city and state and concentrate on being a lawyer.

Powell enjoyed being a corporate lawyer, spurning many attractive offers that would have taken him away from his practice.[14]

Despite his preference for private practice, Powell would eventually rise to national prominence in the 1960s when he became the president of the American Bar Association. The platform afforded by that role allowed Powell to advocate for vigorous enforcement of criminal laws in response to social unrest. Powell's writing on that topic would bring him to the attention of Richard Nixon, who Powell supported in Nixon's 1968 presidential campaign as he had in 1960. The Nixon administration first reached out to Powell about the possibility of appointment to the Supreme Court in 1969 after having been rebuffed in its efforts to elevate Clement Haynsworth from the Fourth Circuit to replace Abe Fortas. Powell worried that his experience as a corporate lawyer would generate controversy. He wrote to Attorney General John Mitchell in 1969:

My own practice, both in litigation and office work over the years, has been largely for corporate and business clients. I also serve on the boards of directors of several corporations of fairly substantial size. In view of the opposition of organized labor to Judge Haynsworth because of his alleged "antilabor bias," it must be assumed that there would be similar opposition to any lawyer whose professional career has been devoted primarily to business representations.

Nixon eventually nominated Harry Blackmun to the seat, who was confirmed with minimal opposition. When Powell was subsequently nominated in 1971 to replace Hugo Black, he faced no significant opposition from labor groups. Indeed, his views on business received little attention during his confirmation hearings.[15]

Only after Powell's confirmation did his strident views defending free enterprise come under media scrutiny. The undiscovered red flag was a confidential memo entitled "Attack on the American Free Enterprise System" that Powell wrote for his friend and neighbor, Eugene B. Sydnor, Jr., then Chair of the Education Committee of the U.S. Chamber of Commerce. In the memo, written the summer

# 8 INTRODUCTION: THE ADMINISTRATIVE STATE AND CAPITALISM

before Nixon nominated Powell to the Court, Powell called for corporate America to be more aggressive in pushing back against liberal calls for government intervention. Powell proposed a campaign by corporate America, spearheaded by the Chamber, to champion the free enterprise system as essential to freedom.

> The threat to the enterprise system is not merely a matter of economics. It also is a threat to individual freedom.
>
> It is this great truth—now so submerged by the rhetoric of the New Left and many liberals—that must be reaffirmed if this program is to be meaningful.
>
> There seems to be little awareness that the only alternatives to free enterprise are varying degrees of bureaucratic regulation of individual freedom—ranging from that under moderate socialism to the iron heel of the leftist or rightist dictatorship.
>
> We in America already have moved very far indeed toward some aspects of state socialism, as the needs and complexities of a vast urban society require types of regulation and control that were quite unnecessary in earlier times. In some areas, such regulation and control already have seriously impaired the freedom of both business and labor, and indeed of the public generally.

Powell laid out a systematic campaign to defend freedom, including among other agenda items, a speakers bureau, support for academics who favored free enterprise, and scrutiny of school textbooks to uncover bias against capitalism.[16]

## C. The Arc of Securities Law in the Supreme Court

Felix Frankfurter and Lewis Powell brought very different attitudes regarding the relation between government and business when they were appointed to the Supreme Court in 1939 and 1971, respectively. Their contrasting ideologies manifested themselves in two key shifts in the Supreme Court's approach to securities law. The first, at the end of the 1930s, was the Court's embrace of agency expertise and social control of finance, overturning decades of judicial hostility to legislative interference with freedom of contract. This deferential approach to the SEC and its mission dominated the Court's jurisprudence over the next thirty-five years. The second shift, beginning in the mid-1970s, was marked by skepticism toward the SEC and securities class actions. Together, these two approaches provide the touchstones that frame the Supreme Court's securities jurisprudence.

Frankfurter and Powell, with their diametrically opposed views of the appropriate balance between the administrative state and capitalism, bookend our history of the securities laws in the Supreme Court. Frankfurter served on the Court

## INTRODUCTION: THE ADMINISTRATIVE STATE AND CAPITALISM    9

from 1939 to 1962, and his colleagues generally shared his New Deal convictions. The justices of the New Deal Court, scarred by the experience of the October 1929 crash and the ensuing depression, saw social control of finance as essential to "saving capitalism from the capitalists," as Frankfurter put it. Administration by experts was an integral part of Frankfurter's vision. As that vision played out in the 1940s and 1950s, Frankfurter's colleagues, most notably the even longer-serving Hugo Black and William O. Douglas, were more willing to defer to the SEC's expertise than Frankfurter. The result of this shared faith in the administrative state was a Court that deferred to the SEC for the first four decades of the agency's existence.

Powell, by contrast, strongly believed in free enterprise. In his view, a relatively unfettered capitalism had produced America's unmatched prosperity. Moreover, Powell was less impressed by claims of administrative expertise. He saw the SEC as an agency prone to overreaching. His appointment would usher in an era more skeptical of securities regulation. He and a majority of his colleagues in the 1970s and 1980s would be more favorably inclined toward private ordering and less trusting of the expert agency. Powell's experience as a corporate lawyer bolstered his credibility with his colleagues.[17] As the Court became more skeptical of administrative experts, it worked to limit the SEC and the securities laws. The trend was further fueled by the rise of class actions, which Powell and a number of his colleagues viewed with distrust. The SEC's decades-long winning streak would come to an abrupt halt.

The table below illustrates the differences between the two approaches. We categorize cases as Expansive if they interpret the scope of the securities law more broadly, recognize remedies and causes of action, or interpret the elements of those causes more generously to plaintiffs or the SEC. We also include cases deferring to SEC's judgment or valuation in its administrative proceedings in the Expansive category. Finally, we also include in this category decisions holding that federal securities laws preempt other bodies of law, including antitrust, arbitration, banking, insurance, and state securities law. Our rationale for including the last set in the expansive category is that these decisions expand the realm of securities law at the expense of other bodies of law.[18]

U.S. Supreme Court Securities Decisions by Outcome

| Years | Cases | Expansive | Restrictive | Neither |
|---|---|---|---|---|
| 1933–Apr. 1972 | 44 | 34 | 7 | 3 |
| May 1972–June 1987 | 45 | 15 | 29 | 1 |
| Oct. 1987–July 2021 | 45 | 20 | 20 | 5 |
| Total | 134 | 69 | 56 | 9 |

10 INTRODUCTION: THE ADMINISTRATIVE STATE AND CAPITALISM

The table crystallizes an arc that will reappear throughout the book. For decades after the adoption of the securities laws, the Court was dominated by veterans of the New Deal, committed to a broad role for government regulation of finance. Three-fourths of the securities decisions reflected expansive interpretations. That era ended with Lewis Powell's confirmation, ushering in a sustained effort to limit the reach of the securities laws. Restrictive decisions were the norm—almost two-thirds.

Since Powell's retirement in 1987, the Court's securities decisions continue to reflect each of the prior approaches, albeit without the consistency of the earlier eras. The Court's decisions sometimes reflect Frankfurter's instinct to defer, and sometimes Powell's skepticism, jumping back and forth between the two approaches. Powell's retirement left a void of expertise on the Supreme Court in the field of securities law. Since 1987, none of the justices have had prior experience with the securities laws, either as a regulator or in private practice. That absence of an experienced hand has left the Court to meander in the field of securities law, with no dominant trend other than, perhaps, a general inclination to defer to Congress. Expansive and restrictive decisions are equally balanced.

Thus, we present three distinct approaches to deciding securities cases, and three different responses to the rise of expert administrators. The different approaches reflect both the change in the country's politics and in economic perspectives. It makes a difference, for example, that Congress passed eight securities statutes in the first eight years of the New Deal, followed by very little additional legislation until a series of insider trading statutes in the 1980s, and then more fundamental revisions in 1995, 2002, and 2010. The real action in between was at the SEC and the Supreme Court. The turnover on the Court during Roosevelt's second term would transform the scope of federal authority under the Commerce Clause. The arrival of Powell and William Rehnquist in 1972 produced another great swing in the field of securities law in the opposite direction. The securities cases from the 1970s into the 1980s offer a sharp reversal from the judicial activism of the Warren Court in the 1960s, more dramatic than in other areas of law.

The work of the Supreme Court in securities law has its own unique story, but it also provides an accessible window to larger trends visible in the Court's jurisprudence. Our story demonstrates how individual justices influence the direction of the Court in a particular field. We also show justices failing to have the impact that might have been expected given their earlier key roles in the development of securities regulation. The remainder of this section summarizes the arc of the outcomes of the cases since 1933. We briefly discuss the long-running (and very restrictive) Supreme Court view toward

INTRODUCTION: THE ADMINISTRATIVE STATE AND CAPITALISM   11

administrative law prior to the New Deal, which had dominated the Court's jurisprudence over the earlier decades of the twentieth century. We also address the two intervening periods between the New Deal and Powell's counterrevolution. In the first, the Court generally ignored securities law. In the second, it plunged into an intense period of judicial activism. Overall, this history shows securities law at the center of the key shifts in the Supreme Court's jurisprudence over the twentieth century.

## 1. The Triumph of the Administrative State

The Great Depression and the New Deal legislation that followed precipitated a dramatic change in the Supreme Court's attitude toward regulation. Chapter 1 describes in more detail the lay of the land as the New Deal unfolded and securities laws were first enacted at the federal level. For the previous several decades, the Court repeatedly rebuffed federal legislation. "Freedom of Contract" constrained federal power under the Commerce Clause. The Court during Roosevelt's first term was dominated by the Four Horsemen, a quartet of dependably conservative justices—Pierce Butler, James Clark McReynolds, George Sutherland, and Willis Van Devanter—who served together on the Court from 1923 to 1937.

The 1930s conflict over the federal government's power over the economy would eventually be resolved, not by constitutional amendment, but by Roosevelt's appointment of a cadre of justices who believed in social control of finance. The eight Roosevelt appointees (more than any president other than George Washington) each had front-line experience in the battle. Frankfurter was at the center of the statutory drafting effort. Douglas headed the fledgling SEC at a critical time. Stanley Reed and Robert Jackson litigated the constitutional status of these new laws before a skeptical judiciary. Frank Murphy directed this effort as Attorney General for a time. Two other future justices—Black and James Byrnes—played key roles as Senators in securing the votes for the new legislation. Wiley Rutledge's academic experience as a corporate law professor grounded his approach to these statutes. Roosevelt would not make his first appointment until 1937, but his addition to the Court in his second and third terms of so many justices who had fought for the securities laws would eviscerate judicial resistance to government control of finance. The securities laws would be at the forefront of a jurisprudential revolution, with the fight to bring public utility holding companies and corporate reorganizations under federal control as key points of engagement.

**Figure I.1**
**A Reliable Court** (Pictured for the 1943 Term): Roosevelt filled more seats than any other president (8 of 9). His careful selection of nominees with front-line experience in passing the New Deal statutes, running the SEC, and defending the new laws against judicial attacks led to a Court protective of the evolving administrative state.

By 1946, the Court's hostility to the administrative state had been dissolved by Roosevelt's appointment of a new Court majority. The Court had affirmed—finally—the constitutionality of the Public Utility Holding Company Act (PUHCA) in the *North American* case of 1946 and by implication, the other securities laws. The securities laws, initially a critical battleground, would be rendered a constitutional fait accompli by decisions in other areas. Roosevelt's appointments assured the SEC a favorable audience at the Court well into the future. That said, a new era of government intervention into the world of finance necessitated a new approach to judicial review of agency action. The Court's relationship with the SEC would be a key laboratory for the development of a nascent administrative law in the 1940s.

## 2. The Era of Deference

After validating Congress's constitutional authority to establish social control over finance, the Court's skepticism of regulation would be replaced by

INTRODUCTION: THE ADMINISTRATIVE STATE AND CAPITALISM    13

an era of judicial deference to the SEC from 1947 to 1962. Three of Roosevelt's appointees—Black, Douglas, and Frankfurter—would serve throughout that period. They were joined by four Truman appointees, but the newcomers did not disrupt the Court's basic attitude toward the administrative state. This continuity of Democratic appointees assured ongoing support for the New Deal agenda in the postwar era.

That postwar deference may also have reflected judicial disinterest toward the securities laws. Government control of finance was not the flash point of controversy that it had been in the 1930s. Simply put, there was not much going on in securities law by the time the Court affirmed the constitutionality of PUHCA in 1946. The political momentum for reform stalled in Roosevelt's second term, with Roosevelt suffering reverses in the 1938 midterm election, a response to his failed Court-packing plan and the "Roosevelt recession" of 1937. The country's attention soon turned to the prospect of war. The war experience wiped away the public's anger against the "economic royalists"; progressives were no longer focused on "fixing capitalism." Consequently, Congress passed no major securities legislation between 1940 and 1964.[19]

The SEC went from being an activist force under Douglas to being exiled to Philadelphia in early 1942 to free up space for the war effort. The agency would not return to Washington until 1948. The SEC's first year in Philadelphia produced two of the most influential rules in the agency's history: Rule 10b-5, which today covers both insider trading and a broad space of shareholder antifraud litigation; and Rule 14a-8, authorizing shareholder proposals on company proxies. (These rules feature prominently in Chapters 5 and 6.) The agency's output, however, soon slowed. Truman's appointees to the SEC had less connection to the agency's heady New Deal era; they reflected the president's political orientation rather than any substantive policy agenda. Abe Fortas, writing to Douglas in 1949, reported on Truman's appointment of Harry McDonald to chair the SEC: "a Republican investment banker from Michigan who has political aspiration. The choice is dismally bad." The subsequent Eisenhower administration focused on budget restraint and the SEC's head count dropped precipitously, falling from 1678 in 1941 to 667 in 1955. The agency's agenda shrunk correspondingly. By the 1950s, the SEC was an administrative backwater, with Douglas bemoaning that the agency he had helped build up had been overtaken by "corruptive influences." The lack of initiative from Congress and the SEC was also reflected in the Court's docket. The Supreme Court paid scant attention to the field of securities law, deciding only a handful of cases between 1947 and 1962; none produced notable changes.[20]

## 3. An Activist Court

The fourth period, stretching from 1962 to 1972, saw a resurgence in the Court's securities docket. If the New Deal Court of the 1940s emphasized deference

14  INTRODUCTION: THE ADMINISTRATIVE STATE AND CAPITALISM

to the SEC, the Warren Court of the 1960s took on the role of partner to the agency, pushing the boundaries of the securities laws. The goal was to further the ultimate purpose of the securities laws, not simply implement their textual directives. In the 1960s, justices who recalled the SEC's glory days of the 1930s— including the long-serving Bill Douglas, who had been the Chairman of the SEC when the agency brought the New York Stock Exchange to heel—dominated the Court. Their faith in the SEC had been diminished by its passivity in the 1950s, but the liberal justices who shaped the Warren Court revitalized social control of finance, even without new legislation. New justices appointed by President Kennedy and Johnson, along with support from liberal Eisenhower appointees Earl Warren and William Brennan, would steer the Court's securities jurisprudence to a more interventionist path. The judicial attitude mirrored the popular *zeitgeist* of the nascent consumer movement, then clamoring for increased regulation of corporate social conduct.[21]

The Supreme Court dramatically expanded the law of securities fraud. Two cases had the biggest impact.[22] In *Capital Gains Research Bureau*, the Court took an expansive view of fiduciary duty under federal law. *Capital Gains* also endorsed a free-wheeling mode of statutory interpretation, emphasizing purpose over text. The Court's willingness to imply private rights of action from statutes in *J.I. Case v. Borak* transformed enforcement of securities laws, allowing class actions to flourish.

The Supreme Court's activist turn in the 1960s encouraged the progressive element of the Second Circuit, spurring the "Mother Court" of securities law to pursue an even more ambitious agenda. The regulation of insider trading, previously cabined in a technical regime, simultaneously over- and under-inclusive, was reinvented as the comprehensive antifraud provision applicable today. For the first time, fraud took in pure omission in impersonal markets, a doctrinal development that had not seemed possible in the first three decades after the enactment of the federal securities laws. The Second Circuit also pushed the line between the securities laws and state corporate law, relying on the foundation laid by *Capital Gains* to build a "federal corporation law."[23] That was a goal long sought by progressives to address perceived weaknesses in the prevailing state law, but never enacted by Congress. The courts, urged on by a resuscitated SEC, were now racing ahead of Congress.

## 4. Lewis Powell and the Counterrevolution

The Court's era of purposive interpretation would prove short-lived, brought to an abrupt halt by the last two of Richard Nixon's four appointments. The arrival of Lewis Powell and William Rehnquist at the Court in January 1972 launched the counterrevolution in securities law. Powell in particular was dubious of the

INTRODUCTION: THE ADMINISTRATIVE STATE AND CAPITALISM 15

**Figure I.2**
**The Counterrevolution:** The arrival of Lewis F. Powell, Jr., and William H. Rehnquist at the Supreme Court in January 1972 led to a sea change in securities laws. Powell's strong free market views escaped scrutiny during their confirmation hearings as senators focused their attention on Rehnquist.

SEC's claims to expertise, but Rehnquist, along with Chief Justice Warren Burger (also a Nixon appointee) shared Powell's distrust of the "private attorneys general" unleashed by the flowering of implied rights of action and class actions in the 1960s. Powell emerged as the intellectual leader of this new Court, at least in the field of securities law. As detailed in Chapter 8, the number of securities cases per term heard by the Court during Powell's tenure was double the number of the previous period. More importantly for this study, as shown in Table 1.1, the results dramatically flipped the pattern that had held constant since 1937. Powell had the support of a cadre of other like-minded justices, but the differences in how those justices voted before Powell's arrival and after his departure demonstrates how one knowledgeable and committed justice can influence the Court's jurisprudential outcome.

## 5. A Random Walk

Powell's retirement in 1987 deprived the Court of its leader in securities law. In the thirty-plus years since, no one has emerged to take his place. Perhaps because

16 INTRODUCTION: THE ADMINISTRATIVE STATE AND CAPITALISM

there was no one to set the Court's agenda, the number of securities cases declined. The cases that were decided would not point in a consistent direction, veering in either expansive or restrictive directions depending on the issue at hand. To borrow a metaphor from finance, the Court's securities cases after 1987 look more like a random walk.

The Court's post-1987 securities docket reflects a lack of both engagement and expertise. Securities decisions were more likely to turn on novel questions of statutory interpretation, as Congress, after a long period of neglect, reasserted itself in securities law. As the Court's decisions became fewer, they also became more unpredictable. Moreover, the questions selected by the Court for review were generally of less significance, sometimes bordering on trivial. The Court devoted a remarkable percentage of its securities docket to resolving statute of limitations issues. Worse yet, without an ideological consensus or a strong leader in the field of securities law, the workmanship of the Court's opinions declined, perhaps most in significant cases.

We mark a divide partway through this last period in 1994 when Harry Blackmun retired. Blackmun's retirement marks, for our study, a natural break point for two reasons. We began with the adoption of the first federal securities laws in 1933. Blackmun was the last justice to witness the rise of New Deal's administrative state during his professional lifetime, having graduated from Harvard in 1932. With his departure, the most senior remaining justice was John Paul Stevens, who served as Wiley Rutledge's law clerk for the 1947–48 term, two terms after the Court affirmed Congress's constitutional authority to enact PUHCA. For the justices who remained, the rise of the administrative state—and the SEC's role in that regime—was an accomplished fact by the time they became lawyers.

The second reason is methodological. Reading published opinions reveals only part of the story. Blackmun's departure marks the end of an important source of primary material for our research; Blackmun is the most recent justice to make his files available to the public.[24] Blackmun's papers, like many of the other justices, are available to researchers at the Library of Congress, while others can be found at various university libraries, all of which we have accessed. We tell our story, not just through analysis of published opinions, but also through the justices' internal papers: voting tallies, conference notes, correspondence among the justices, memos prepared for their own use or addressed to their clerks, and drafts of opinions as they evolve, both in chambers and in response to comments from other justices. These materials show how the justices decide cases and how they work with their colleagues and clerks to draft opinions. Taken as a whole, the justices' papers give a richer account of judicial behavior and how the Supreme Court makes law. Our approach is common in historical accounts of headline topics like constitutional law. The goal of the book is to bring those insights to an area of "private" law that has enormous significance for society as a whole.

# D. Roadmap of the Book

We organize the chapters of the book by subject, rather than strictly chronologically. Our goal is to show the main trends identified earlier as they played out in particular areas of securities law. We proceed as follows.

Chapter 1 introduces the federal securities laws and the critical role that a number of future justices had in their drafting, enactment, and litigation defense. The new laws got a chilly reception in the Supreme Court, with the SEC's first case before the justices provoking a stinging rebuke. The tide would soon turn.

Chapter 2 follows the Roosevelt administration's path—both political and legal—to establishing the federal government's authority to assert social control of finance. We highlight the role of William O. Douglas as an academic reformer of business law and then SEC Chairman taking on the New York Stock Exchange. Turning to the Court, we focus on the fight over Congress's constitutional authority to enact PUHCA. PUHCA went well beyond the disclosure requirements of the two earlier securities statutes, giving the SEC the mandate to break up the pyramid structure of those holding companies and shape the corporate governance and capital structures of the reorganized firms. PUHCA's sweeping reforms would trigger a decade-long war in the courts, as the giant utilities resisted the efforts of the SEC to dismantle them, but the Court eventually upheld the law's constitutionality. We show how the SEC's mission to establish social control of finance played out in Supreme Court decisions relating to public utility companies. We also follow the SEC along a parallel path in the field of corporate reorganizations under Chapter XI of the bankruptcy laws. These were the SEC's two most prominent fields of operation in its early days and the source of most of the Court's early securities decisions.

In Chapter 3, we examine the Court's oversight of the SEC's procedures. The Court's two decisions in the *Chenery* case in the 1940s remain black letter administrative law to this day.[25] Those decisions ultimately laid the groundwork for an administrative law affording the SEC great latitude in choosing between litigation and rulemaking in pursuing its policy agenda. That deference to the agency on questions of procedure would persist into the 1970s and 1980s, even as the SEC would struggle to overcome the Court's pushback in other areas.

Chapter 4 focuses on the Court's efforts to delineate the boundaries of the SEC's authority. Recurring decisions addressing the definition of a security and the meaning of "purchase and sale" illustrate how shifting views among the justices shaped the direction of securities law and the SEC's relations with other parts of government. We see a long era of deference to the SEC, beginning in 1940 and continuing until Lewis Powell's arrival in 1972. We then see a dramatic reversal, with Powell and his colleagues closely policing the agency

18   INTRODUCTION: THE ADMINISTRATIVE STATE AND CAPITALISM

to keep it within its statutory bounds and minimize potential interference with other bodies of law and other regulators. This area has received less attention after Powell's retirement.

Chapter 5 shows the common law development of insider trading doctrine. In the 1960s, the Court became an active participant in the creation of the securities laws, declaring that the antifraud provisions of the securities acts extended the long-standing bounds of fiduciary duty to take in anonymous trading on public markets by insiders. That judicially created prohibition, nurtured by the Second Circuit, would soon dominate the more clunky and mechanistic remedy for insider trading that Congress had put into § 16(b) of the Exchange Act. Powell's arrival on the Court would put the brakes on insider trading law's development. Powell felt that insider trading was an abuse that should be prohibited, but he worked to constrain the doctrine in a predictable framework. Powell's efforts, however, would not lead to the outright repudiation of the insider trading law developed in the sixties; that residual fiduciary duty seed would eventually flower into a much broader prohibition after Powell's retirement.

Chapter 6 addresses private rights of action under the securities laws. Private litigation got minimal attention from the Court until the sixties, when two changes spurred the development of securities class actions. The first was the Court's recognition of implied rights of action under the federal securities laws, supplementing, and in some cases supplanting, the rights explicitly created by Congress. The second was the amendment of Rule 23 of the Federal Rules of Civil Procedure, facilitating the aggregation of claims for money damages in large-scale class actions. These changes set the stage for two of the Court's most expansive securities law decisions, handed down shortly before Powell and Rehnquist were available to participate in the Court's decisions. It would not be long, however, before observers would see a dramatic shift in the Court's attitude toward private securities litigation. Elements were strictly construed to make relief harder for plaintiffs to obtain. Ultimately, the notion of implied rights of action was repudiated by the Court. The Rule 10b-5 cause of action survived their demise, however, and indeed were rejuvenated shortly after Powell retired by the last of the Court's truly activist securities law decisions, *Basic Inc. v. Levinson*. Thereafter, the Court's private right of action cases meandered between expansive and restrictive decisions, mainly reacting to Congress's statutory intervention. No clear path emerged.

Chapter 7 deals with the intersection between federal securities law and state corporate law. The Court's jurisprudence followed an arc similar to that described in the prior two chapters. Concern over the inadequacy of state fiduciary law led to a brief flowering of federal corporation law in the 1960s and early '70s. The

## INTRODUCTION: THE ADMINISTRATIVE STATE AND CAPITALISM 19

retrenchment of securities law through most of the 1970s and '80s, however, included a strong effort by the Court to preserve the role of state corporate law. Subsequent federal interventions in corporate governance have come in bits and pieces from Congress, not the Court.

Chapter 8 concludes with a more detailed look at statistics that summarize the Court's decisions in the field of securities law. We also offer our views on the trends that we observed over our period of study and contrast the different approaches to decision-making visible across nearly ninety years. Finally, we examine the influence—or lack thereof—of individual justices on the path of securities law.

Please come with us as we explore how securities law gets made in the Supreme Court.

# 1

# The Coming of the New Deal

It was an extraordinary fight, and considering the forces and resources against you, was an extraordinary achievement of a very small handful of men for decency and for honor and for the salvage of those very institutions for which the blind men of Wall Street profess to speak but which in their greed, had they a free hand, they would be speedily destroying. You and Ben in particular have shown knowledge and pertinacity and devotion and good humor and good sense.... It makes me very proud indeed of your friendships.

Letter from Felix Frankfurter, to Tom Corcoran upon the enactment of the Securities Exchange Act of 1934 (May 7, 1934) FF-LC, Reel 70

## A. The Enactment of the Federal Securities Laws

### 1. The Securities Act of 1933

Having answered Ray Moley's summons to Washington in April 1933, Frankfurter supervised as two of his protégés, Ben Cohen and James Landis, spent the weekend writing the legislation that became the Securities Act of 1933. Cohen had worked on Wall Street; Landis was Frankfurter's former student, by then a Harvard professor, after having served as Brandeis's law clerk on Frankfurter's recommendation.

On Monday, Frankfurter met with Sam Rayburn to explain the draft. Rayburn, a rural progressive from Texas with an innate distrust of Wall Street, was not yet Speaker of the House, but he was already a power in the Congress. He had asked Moley for administration assistance with the bill. As drafting continued, Frankfurter lobbied Roosevelt and Rayburn for the inclusion of detailed disclosure requirements in the statute itself. Frankfurter's argument against leaving the details for later administrative action foreshadowed some of the battles to come:

First, it would raise needless questions of constitutionality as to delegation of legislative power[.] Secondly it invites dangerous frustration of such purposes through hostile judicial interpretation[.] Thirdly it jeopardizes

## THE COMING OF THE NEW DEAL   21

effective enforcement because of the enormous discretion which it leaves to Commission and thereby invites laxity favoritism and indifference[.]

When Frankfurter supplied Rayburn with a draft of the report that Landis and Cohen had prepared for the bill, he also provided a response to the objections made by the Investment Bankers Association. The response captures his attitude toward the bankers: "The Investment Bankers Association and all their tribe . . . really think it is terrible that the securities business should be made a conservative business rather than a refined and intricate form of fleecing."[1]

Cohen and Landis's bill would bring the federal government into the regulation of the public offering of securities, curbing the investment bankers' prior domination of that process. As urged by Frankfurter, underwriters would have to disclose their compensation for selling the offering. The law also required corporate issuers to make full disclosure when offering securities. Transparency would help curb the speculative excesses seen in the 1920s. As Cohen and Landis's bill was working its way through the House, a competing bill, based on the "hopeless mess" of a draft that had precipitated Moley's call, was proceeding through the Senate. Another Frankfurter protégé, Tom Corcoran, rounded out the professor's group; he would play a key role in strategy and lobbying for the bill. Corcoran's work would establish him as a key lobbyist for Roosevelt's legislative agenda during FDR's first two terms.[2]

Frankfurter worked diligently for the Cohen and Landis version, staving off efforts to reconcile the two bills, arguing that reconciliation "would involve interminable delay and jeopardize passage because powerful and increasing financial lobbies against all regulation will exploit differences to defeat enactment." After a good deal of legislative jockeying, the Senate bill was killed in conference with the help of Senator James Byrnes, a key administration ally. (Roosevelt would later appoint him to the Court.) Within weeks Landis and Cohen's handiwork, with amendments here and there, had passed the House followed by quick passage in the Senate.[3] The Securities Act was a key part of the legendary "First Hundred Days": a legislative blitz that launched Roosevelt's New Deal. Congress readily adopted everything the administration asked for in those fear-filled days. There would be legislative battles to come, however, as Roosevelt's campaign to assert social control over finance grew more intrusive.

For Frankfurter, the Securities Act's enactment cemented his role as one of Roosevelt's key advisors. The professor's involvement in the securities laws turned out to be pervasive. Frankfurter's legendary placement of former students, first in judicial clerkships and then throughout the New Deal, widened his influence with the Roosevelt administration. That influence is most prominently illustrated by the subsequent careers of Landis, Cohen, and Corcoran. Landis's ascent began immediately as he was appointed to the Federal Trade Commission,

**Figure 1.1**
**Corcoran & Pecora:** Tommy Corcoran, on the right, played a key role, along with Ben Cohen and James Landis, in the drafting and enactment of the Securities Act, the Securities Exchange Act of 1934, and the Public Utility Holding Company Act. He is shown here with Ferdinand Pecora, who created the political momentum for the legislation by leading congressional hearing spotlighting insider dealing on Wall Street, before becoming one of the SEC's first commissioners.

which was charged with administering the new law. He became one of the inaugural commissioners of the Securities and Exchange Commission the next year and soon its second chair. Cohen and Corcoran, recurring characters in our story, emerged as key figures advancing a range of administration priorities. It all started with Frankfurter's involvement in the drafting of the Securities Act; according to Moley, that legislative campaign "was to make inevitable Felix's appointment to the Supreme Court."[4] Before that appointment, however, Frankfurter and his protégés would play vital roles in enacting the steady flow of securities legislation that would soon follow.

Frankfurter's worry that the investment bankers and corporate lawyers were conspiring to undo the Securities Act after its enactment was a recurring theme of his correspondence in late 1933 and early 1934. At first, he dismissed rumors

**Figure 1.2**
**Ben Cohen:** Ben Cohen's work with James Landis in drafting the Securities Act established his reputation as a gifted legislative draftsman. In addition to his drafting efforts on behalf of the Roosevelt administration, he played a key role in developing the strategy to defend PUHCA from judicial attack.

of a "bankers strike" as mere "newspaper talk," motivated by the newspapers' interest in "profitable but socially elicit financial advertising." Frankfurter also dismissed investment bankers' worries that their potential "liability under the present law is more than fifty times our average profit, even though we may make no untrue or misleading statement or leave out any material fact, merely because we may be unable to sustain the burden of proof that we have not made such errors." Frankfurter's response was a harbinger of modern responses to claims of excessive securities regulation: "The English seem to have done very well as the money market of the world despite their stringent controls. My patriotism is somewhat offended—and I speak as an Anglophile—that ethical and fiduciary standards which are legally enforced in England should be deemed too stringent for us. I refuse to believe it." Frankfurter believed that corporate lawyers were misrepresenting the effects of the law to their clients as part of a "concerted effort[] . . . to chloroform the Securities Act." He urged Roosevelt to resist. In Frankfurter's view, "no clarification is needed and 'clarification' isn't what is

## 24  A HISTORY OF SECURITIES LAW

wanted." Opposition to the law was "selfish and ignorant." His early government mentor, Henry Stimson, felt that Frankfurter had become infected with "an excess of crusader's zeal."[5]

Some of the criticism of the Securities Act came from an unlikely source: William O. Douglas, then a professor at the Yale Law School. Douglas was younger than Frankfurter, but he was quickly making a name for himself in progressive circles. He viewed the new legislation with considerably more skepticism than Frankfurter. Douglas concluded that disclosure alone would not prevent the recurrence of the scandals uncovered by Ferdinand Pecora's committee. Part of Douglas's critique reflected a worry that the Securities Act would chill capital formation:

> The cumulative effects of the absolute liability of the issuer, the undefined liability of stockholders, the liability of directors irrespective of the nature of their appointments, the liability of underwriters, and the increasing difficulty on the part of issuers to obtain that underwriting, make it more and more apparent that, whether rightly or wrongly, justifiably or otherwise, the Act will prevent a great amount of financing by many companies with well established businesses and will continue to deter refunding operations and reorganizations.[6]

Douglas was principally concerned, however, that the Securities Act did not go far enough in asserting government control. We cover that topic in greater detail in Chapter 2.

Douglas's critique of the Act struck the paranoid Frankfurter as echoing the reactionary drumbeat of the investment bankers and their corporate lawyers. Frankfurter confided to Landis that Douglas had fallen under the sway of the money people and their fellow travelers in the business schools: "[e]ven Bill Douglas is trying to reflect too much the people in the big offices and the business schools, among whom he likes to appear as a sound and knowing fellow." Frankfurter worried that any criticism of the law would further the conspiracy that he perceived among investment bankers and their lawyers to gut the Act:

> I happen to know in some detail what some of the leading law firms have been up to in order to create a state of mind for amendments on the plea of recovery. You know as well as I do that the notion that the Securities Act has stopped capital issues is just rubbish.

In Frankfurter's view, Douglas was lending aid and comfort to the New Deal's foes by calling for the law's amendment. "It is of course very generous of you, with everybody agin [sic] them at present, for you to champion the cause of 'the Street' and persecuted houses like J.P.Morgan [sic] and Kuhn, Loeb." Despite

Frankfurter's resistance, the move to amend the Securities Act would gather steam when the administration began drafting a law to regulate the New York Stock Exchange.[7]

## 2. The Securities Exchange Act of 1934

The New York Stock Exchange was the second bête noire of the Pecora hearings; the exchange moved to the center of the legislative stage in the second year of the New Deal. On board a ship to England, en route for a year at Oxford, Frankfurter wrote Roosevelt urging him to fight for legislation controlling the NYSE. Frankfurter quoted at length from a letter that he had received from Justice Harlan Fiske Stone, which Frankfurter considered particularly apt, as Stone was "an old-line Republican, a member of Sullivan & Cromwell before he became Coolidge's Attorney General":

> The new Securities Act promises well and undoubtedly will prevent some of the fraudulent schemes which have been common in the past, especially in marketing bonds. There is another like evil that must ultimately be reached, and that is the creation of boom markets for stocks through wash sales on the Exchange.

The NYSE claimed to be self-regulated, but at least some observers felt that self-regulation lacked teeth. As the Securities Act was working its way through Congress, Stone wrote to Frankfurter:

> Of course, the Stock Exchange should require precise information as to the total distribution made to officers and directors. The fact that it has never done so shows how little it performs what should be its real function to protect adequately those who deal in securities sold under its auspices. Many years ago, after I had unearthed a series of shockingly fraudulent performances by members of the Exchange, which should have been known to its Governors, I told the latter that the survival of the Exchange would depend primarily on their own willingness to take proper measures to protect adequately the interest of those who availed of its facilities.

Frankfurter heartily agreed with Stone that the Exchange was "long overdue" for governmental supervision. Frankfurter told Roosevelt: "There has been more than ample time for self-regulation, and self-regulation they have shown is not in them." State efforts to regulate had also failed: the NYSE had previously defeated New York legislation drafted by Pecora and Untermyer that would have required

## 26   A HISTORY OF SECURITIES LAW

registration by brokers. Also defeated was legislation requiring the exchange to incorporate, which would have facilitated more thoroughgoing regulation.[8]

Frankfurter continued his lobbying from England through telegrams and letters, with Cohen, Corcoran, and Landis on the front line in Washington. During the fall of 1933, an interagency committee, chaired by assistant secretary of commerce John Dickinson, which included Landis and Adolf Berle and two industry lawyers, produced a report suggesting a modest intervention. As FDR moved exchange regulation toward the top of the pile for 1934, Cohen had begun working on legislation with Pecora, still counsel for the Senate Finance Committee. With the help of two young lawyers at the Federal Trade Commission, a bill took shape that became known as the Fletcher-Rayburn bill. The draconian bill, introduced early in 1934, would have fundamentally changed the operation of the NYSE. Less controversially, the bill also required companies listing securities on exchanges to disclose their operations and results, a provision that tracked the existing requirements of the NYSE. Landis reported to Frankfurter: "The Stock Exchange Bill is receiving a terrific battering. All the corporate wealth of this country has gone into the attack and carried it all the way to the White House."[9]

Faced with the legislative threat to his "perfect institution," Richard Whitney, the president of the NYSE, galvanized the opposition of the brokerage community. He warned that there would be "tremendous, if not universal, withdrawal" of corporations from the exchanges. Wall Street's resistance was bolstered by the regional exchanges, which would have been crippled by the law as drafted. Corcoran, as the administration's point man in lobbying for the bill, fought tenaciously to preserve it. Landis, more pragmatic than Frankfurter, recognized that the legislation would need to be modified to be enacted. In an effort to preserve the core of the Securities Act, Landis took charge of negotiating amendments, a move that appears to have assuaged Frankfurter's concerns.[10]

The fate of the stock exchange bill, however, was still in doubt. For Frankfurter, the exchange bill was "a test of power" and the campaign against it tinged with anti-Semitism. Cohen and Corcoran "were in constant, almost daily, touch with Frankfurter. His function, so far as they were concerned, had come to be more inspirational than anything else. Felix was a patriarchal sorcerer to their apprentice, forever renewing their zeal for reform and their pride in fine workmanship." Corcoran kept Frankfurter informed of the bill's progress through a barrage of telegrams; Frankfurter sent a few telegrams of his own to key players in the fight. Corcoran was the first witness before the congressional committees when the House and Senate took up the bills. Cohen sat next to Rayburn on the House floor during the debate. Frankfurter's "happy hotdogs" were becoming entrenched in the New Deal power structure.[11]

The Exchange Act's most significant provision created a new agency to administer the securities laws: the Securities and Exchange Commission. Senator

Carter Glass, a conservative senator from Virginia with a keen interest in banking regulation, pushed for the creation of the SEC. The new agency was a concession to the securities industry, which distrusted the FTC in light of Roosevelt's appointment of Landis to that commission. As Frankfurter put it,

> Wall Street['s] . . . game, plainly enough, is like unto that of the utilities in days gone by, namely to have the 'right' kind of regulatory body. They want, that is, a regulatory body devoid of the necessary courage and resourcefulness for making the legislation effective. . . . Their game must add greatly to your amusement.

Apparently it did; Roosevelt tweaked the exchange crowd by appointing Landis as one of the SEC's first commissioners, along with the dogged Pecora. In a conciliatory move, however, Roosevelt put businessman Joseph P. Kennedy in as chairman over the more obvious candidate, Landis. Moley, more business friendly than Roosevelt's other advisors, had pushed for Kennedy's appointment as part of the "truce of God" that the administration was seeking with the business community after the bitter fight over the Exchange Act. Roosevelt's effort at rapprochement would be short-lived. He had vanquished the investment bankers and the New York Stock Exchange. Further bolstered by sweeping victories in the 1934 midterm elections, FDR's next target was the utility companies.[12]

## 3. The Public Utility Holding Company Act of 1935 (PUHCA)

When Frankfurter returned to the United States from England in the summer of 1934, he urged Roosevelt to face the "irrepressible conflict" with big business. The Exchange Act amendments relaxing the Securities Act's liability provisions had produced "[o]nly a trickling little stream of private corporation finance." SEC Chair Joe Kennedy berated the investment industry for its timidity.[13] If the capitalists were not willing to do their part to foster economic recovery, why should the administration placate business by holding back from further reforms?

Although investment banking and the NYSE had been the primary targets of the Pecora hearings, the collapse of the Insull public utility holding company was the biggest financial scandal of its day. The demise of the Insull empire cemented the public utility holding company structure's reputation for abuse. Frankfurter had a long-standing interest in public utilities, having taught his pioneering course on the subject from his earliest days at Harvard. (Future justices William F. Brennan, Jr., and Harry Blackmun had taken the class.) Frankfurter

## 28    A HISTORY OF SECURITIES LAW

laid the blame for the evils of the industry with the investment bankers, who had created elaborate holding company structures that put utilities beyond the effective reach of state regulation. With his customary impatience, the professor had been pushing Roosevelt to introduce legislation to control public utilities even before Roosevelt's inauguration; regulating holding companies was a plank in the Democratic Party's platform in 1932.[14]

Wiley Rutledge, a corporate law professor and dean at Washington University who Roosevelt would later appoint to the Court, made the case against bigness and the abuses that it facilitated in the holding company structure. He argued that the "devices of share dispersion, non-voting stock, the voting trust, etc. . . . multipl[y] the power to concentrate control almost in geometric progression." Worse yet, the intricate interconnections within the holding company empires frustrated effective regulation:

> The maze of "contracts" and of accounts is so intricate that no outsider (and probably few "insiders") can determine real costs or profits. Rate-making becomes a farce, and the balance sheet of the system a puzzle worse than Chinese. The corporate family is the only ones [sic] known which can keep alive nine generations contemporaneously.[15]

Disclosure was not enough to correct these abuses. The federal government would need to control corporate governance and capital structure too.

Frankfurter pushed FDR to make the holding company legislation a key component of the "second hundred days" legislative initiative in 1935. Frankfurter's persistence was rewarded on January 4, 1935, when Roosevelt called for the "abolition of the evil of holding companies" in his State of the Union address. Frankfurter was delighted. Holding companies, he urged, "really have no ultimate economic and social justivication [sic]. That the national interest requires their elimination I have no doubt. . . . [D]rastic regulation and taxation are indispensable, both in themselves and also for insurance against the possibility of alleviating legislation by a future Congress."[16] Frankfurter (and now Roosevelt) saw the opportunity to eliminate holding companies; it needed to be seized, and seized quickly, lest future administrations succumb to lobbying pressure from the utility industry, which was a powerful force, particularly in the South.

There was disagreement within the administration, however, on the means to achieve this end. Ben Cohen drafted one bill under the direction of Robert Healy, one of the initial SEC commissioners. Healy, while chief counsel at the FTC prior to his SEC appointment, had directed an exhaustive study of public utility companies demonstrating the ineffectiveness of local control. As Cohen described the draft in a letter to Healy:

THE COMING OF THE NEW DEAL    29

[T]he bill does not outlaw the holding company but regulates and restricts the use of the holding company form and provides a mechanism through which, over a period of time, existing holding company structures may be simplified, and their field limited to a sphere where their economic advantages may be demonstrable.

A Treasury Department team—under the direction of Robert Jackson and Herman Oliphant—favored almost immediate abolition through imposition of a stiff tax on dividends paid by operating companies to the holding companies. Roosevelt called the two sides together for a meeting and made it plain that he favored rapid abolition. Roosevelt's commitment to the legislation represented a significant victory for the Brandeisians, who were now ascendant in the Second New Deal. The influence of the central planners had ebbed. The holding companies were perhaps the most conspicuous example of the curse of bigness. Brandeis himself had been pushing behind the scenes for their abolition.[17]

The result of the meeting with Roosevelt was a clause calling for the elimination of the holding company, which would become known as the "death sentence" provision. The provision effectively limited utility holding companies to one geographic area. Companies that did not satisfy this requirement were to be broken up under the SEC's supervision. The death sentence provision departed from the disclosure paradigm of the Securities Act and the Exchange Act. The holding company legislation required registration and disclosure, but it broke new ground in giving the SEC substantive control over the utilities' capital structures and corporate governance, traditionally the province of state law. Thus, the legislation set a new high-water mark for federal oversight of business, albeit one that governed only a portion of American business— public utility holding companies. For opponents of federal economic regulation, the holding company legislation looked like a trial run for the federal control of corporate governance that progressives had been seeking since the turn of the century.

The public utilities industry, less than enthused about being the subject of the federal government's corporate experiments, predicted economic disaster. Wendell Willkie, the president of Commonwealth and Southern (and future Republican presidential nominee), was the industry's most articulate spokesman. He warned that

the utility industry would be thrown "into a chaos of liquidation and receiverships," holders of utility stocks would suffer "practically complete" losses, and a "great bureaucracy in Washington will be regulating the internal affairs of practically all utility operating companies in the United States." The

# 30 A HISTORY OF SECURITIES LAW

backers of the death sentence, Willkie charged, were trying "to 'nationalize' the power business of this country."

Although his rhetoric was shrill, Willkie's fears of a government takeover of the utility industry were not unfounded. After the enactment of the holding company legislation, Corcoran boasted to Moley: "It won't come fast, but twenty years from now the government will own and operate all the electrical utilities in the country." More to the point, the specter of socialism had political resonance with the voters after years of somewhat ineffectual collective planning by the Roosevelt administration. In a major rebuff to Roosevelt, the House rejected the death sentence provision.[18]

The industry backed its public relations attack with a massive lobbying campaign, but here the industry overreached. Allegations surfaced that a raft of telegrams opposing the bill had been sent by persons who claimed to be unaware of the messages sent in their name. A select committee chaired by then-Senator Hugo Black was appointed to investigate the utilities' lobbying against the holding company bill. Black uncovered a fictitious "grass roots" campaign against the bill, including a barrage of forged and paid-for telegraphs. "In his frenzy to uncover improper lobbying by certain utilities—and there was plenty of it—Black struck at the innocent as well as the guilty. Opposition to the bill became, *ipso facto*, an indication of bad faith." As Landis put it, "Black investigated with bare fists." Whatever its excesses, the revelations produced by Black's investigation revived the bill's prospects.[19] The utilities' lobbying campaign also provoked a stringent campaign finance prohibition in the bill, including a blanket ban on campaign contributions by holding companies and disclosure requirements for lobbying efforts.[20]

Even after the bill passed the Senate, however, it remained bottled up in conference committee. The key disagreement was over the death sentence provision. The Senate's version limited holding companies to a single "geographically and economically integrated ... system" operating in "contiguous states," while the House version required only an "integrated public-utility system." The President favored the more stringent Senate version, but Frankfurter eventually persuaded him to yield. Frankfurter drafted a compromise that used the House's "integrated public-utility system" language, but also stipulated that the system could not be "so large ... as to impair the advantages of localized management, efficient operation, or the effectiveness of regulation."[21] This stipulation was studiously vague; its meaning would be determined by the SEC, and eventually, the courts. Roosevelt signed the compromise bill—to become known by its unfortunate acronym, PUHCA—into law on August 26, 1935.

## 4. Roosevelt's Second Term

Fresh from his victory over the holding companies, Roosevelt saw himself by the end of 1935 as the leader of a new coalition against business's domination of society, particularly Wall Street.[22] Studies called for by the earlier securities laws would help fuel the legislative onslaught in Roosevelt's second term. All together Congress passed an average of one bill a year in securities and related areas over Roosevelt's first two terms. The social control over finance that the President had promised in his 1932 campaign seemed imminent. Only World War II's diversion from domestic affairs ceased the assault against Wall Street.

Congress had called for a special study of corporate bankruptcy in the Exchange Act. The study would lead to the Chandler Act, which displaced the investment bankers and the elite bar that had long dominated bankruptcy reorganization. Its placement of key substantive decisions in the hands of the experts at the SEC validated the agency's role in the rise of the administrative state.[23] The Trust Indenture Act of 1939 engineered a similar transfer of power in the adjacent space when reorganization occurred outside of bankruptcy court.[24] The Maloney Act amended the Exchange Act to require industry self-regulation of broker-dealers under the watchful eye of the SEC.[25] We chronicle the brutal fight SEC Chairman Bill Douglas led to enact the Maloney Act in Chapter 2.

Two statutes enacted in 1940 would be the last legislative installments on Roosevelt's promise to reform finance.[26] The Investment Company Act regulated mutual funds. The Pecora hearings had shined a bright light on the sales tactics used to peddle shares in these new funds in the years leading up to the stock market crash in 1929. The reform effort was further fueled by a congressional call in the holding company legislation for the SEC to study the topic. A companion bill, the Investment Advisers Act, completed the menu of New Deal securities legislation, extending federal regulation to finance professionals who managed other people's money.

## B. A Hostile Judicial Reception

Through Roosevelt's first term, his battle to tame the power of Wall Street had the strong support of both Congress and his key advisors. The New Deal vision was that administrative experts, not business leaders, should control the direction of the economy. The SEC put that theory into action. PUHCA in particular gave the agency a key role in deciding the terms of the breakup of holding companies, a question with enormous economic implications. The SEC's efforts to dismantle

# 32 A HISTORY OF SECURITIES LAW

the utility holding companies, along with its battle to tame the New York Stock Exchange, would make the agency a flash point of political and constitutional controversy in the 1930s.

Winning over Congress was one thing; the administration still faced a daunting challenge defending such a bold legislative program in the courts. This aggressive assertion of government control over the world of finance—particularly PUHCA—strained the limits of the Constitution, at least as it was understood by the mid-thirties Supreme Court. The Court had repeatedly rebuffed efforts at economic reform prior to the New Deal. The Court's protection of individual liberty to follow one's calling in business matters, commonly identified with the turn-of-the-century *Lochner* decision,[27] had loomed over economic reform movements for decades. Progressives had seen their efforts stymied by a Court suspicious of government intervention at both the state and federal level. The Court invoked the Due Process Clause's guarantee of "liberty," or limits on federal power under the Commerce Clause, to check government control of the economy. The conflict between Congress and the Court had grown sharper, with the Court striking down twenty-two acts of Congress between 1920 and 1932.[28]

Judicial hostility to legislative interference with market forces was bipartisan. To be sure, Republican appointees had dominated the Court after the Civil War. Of the forty justices confirmed between the war and 1933, Republican presidents named thirty-three. The only exceptions were two each in Grover Cleveland's non-consecutive terms, coming after twenty-four years of Republican control of the White House, and three appointed by Woodrow Wilson, two decades later. Democratic appointees, however, were also leery of government incursions into freedom of contract. Stephen Field, a Democrat appointed by Lincoln, was the Court's leading advocate of economic liberty in the 1870s and 1880s. Rufus Peckham, a Cleveland appointee, strongly pushed the *Lochner* approach. James McReynolds, appointed by Wilson while serving as Wilson's Attorney General, was one of the "Four Horsemen" of the 1930s who held the line against the New Deal legislation. McReynolds—a noted anti-Semite—fretted over Frankfurter's influence on the administration's legislative agenda: "Statutes [establishing the New Deal] carelessly drawn by young men just out of the Harvard Law School! Frankfurter's protégés, too, I suppose!"[29]

Frankfurter, for his part, was a vigorous academic critic of the jurisprudential school that McReynolds represented. Giving an address at Chatham House while on sabbatical in England in 1934, Frankfurter had this to say about the then-prevailing interpretation of the Constitution:

> Contrary to some notions, there is no provision in the Constitution of the United States which incorporates the Manchester theory of economics. . . . in

THE COMING OF THE NEW DEAL    33

case after case the Court, in opposition to the most imaginative, most humble and most powerful minds of the Court—and usually by a narrow margin of a single vote—went counter to the admonition of Justice Holmes and did read into the Constitution sectarian opinions and called them the Constitution.

In Frankfurter's view, the Constitution had more than enough flexibility to accommodate the social needs presented by challenging times:

> [T]he Constitution of the United States was the work of wise men, who knew a good deal about government and who were not so foolish as to foreclose the future by building on the dogmatic assumption that the state of society in 1787 would continue forever. . . . Roughly speaking, and subject only to certain technical limitations, it is fair to say that what mature, wise, fairminded statesmanship calls for, finds ample freedom for validity in the Constitution of the United States.[30]

The opportunity would soon come to test Frankfurter's constitutional theories. Finance was not the only sector newly subject to federal control under the New Deal; Roosevelt's agenda also swept in agriculture, labor, and other areas of the economy. There had been federal administrative agencies before—for example, the Interstate Commerce Commission and the Federal Trade Commission were by now grudgingly accepted by the Court—but the bureaus mushroomed under the New Deal.[31] The rise of the administrative state would push the limits of Congress's power under the Constitution, previously understood as creating a federal government with limited powers.

As Roosevelt's first term unfolded, challenges to the Securities Acts and PUHCA were making their way through the courts and the prognosis looked dim, particularly for PUHCA. Given that context, administration legal strategists—egged on by Frankfurter—were determined to stall in defending the New Deal legislative program. The strategy succeeded for a time, only to be dealt a string of defeats in 1935 and 1936. The bloodiest day was Monday, May 27, 1935, declared by Brandeis to be "the most important day in the history of the Court and the most beneficent."[32] Two decisions: (1) struck down the National Industrial Recovery Act ("NIRA"); and (2) held that the President could not remove members of the Federal Trade Commission without cause.[33] Both decisions were unanimous, gaining even the liberal votes of Brandeis, Benjamin Cardozo, and Stone.[34] If there were any doubt that the Court was sending Roosevelt a message, Brandeis made it perfectly clear:

> Before Tommy Corcoran could depart, a Supreme Court page tapped him on the shoulder and said that Justice Brandeis would like to see him in the Justices'

## 34 A HISTORY OF SECURITIES LAW

robing room. Brandeis wanted Corcoran to convey a message to the White House: "This is the end of this business of centralization, and I want you to go back and tell the President that we're not going to let this government centralize everything. It's come to an end."

The Old Guard feared Roosevelt's "road to socialism"; Brandeis opposed regulation that fostered "bigness." He had warned Roosevelt as early as 1934 that all of the centralization of federal power was pushing constitutional limits.[35] Even Cardozo, the most sympathetic of the justices toward the New Deal, thought the NIRA lacked an animating theory for industrial recovery. The confluence of these positions resulted in a high-profile rebuke for the Roosevelt administration.[36]

The law was not widely mourned. Even the bill's drafters doubted its constitutionality, and it had devolved into a pretext for price fixing. Not surprisingly, the law had done little to revive the economy, and Congress would probably have allowed it to die if it had not been struck down. Roosevelt, for his part, was defiant, chastising the Court for trying to turn back the clock to "the horse-and-buggy" days. SEC General Counsel John Burns, in a letter to Frankfurter, noted "how stunned and gloomy the action of the court left us. . . . It appears likely that both of our statutes will be attacked with more vigor."[37] The following term the carnage continued with Court striking down the Agricultural Adjustment Act and the Bituminous Coal Conservation Act.[38]

In between the Court took up the securities laws for the first time. The Court's initial reaction was hostile. The Supreme Court's first securities case began as a routine enforcement matter. J. Edward Jones, a dealer in oil royalties, had filed a registration statement with the SEC to issue certificates in producing such royalties. Just before the end of the twenty-day waiting period required before a registration statement can become effective under the Securities Act, the SEC filed notice of a stop order proceeding to block the offering and subpoenaed Jones to testify and produce various documents. When Jones's attorney appeared at the hearing without his client and sought to withdraw the registration statement to end the proceeding, SEC General Counsel Burns is said to have responded "You can't go up under the gun of a stop order and then seek to avoid it"; the Commission then "ordered a U.S. marshal to go forth and fetch Mr. Jones in person." The Commission's impatience led it into strategic error. At that point, Jones reversed course and announced this case to be "an excellent opportunity to test . . . the much-mooted question of the constitutionality of the securities acts."[39]

The lower federal courts upheld the SEC's refusal to permit withdrawal of the registration statement. More importantly, they affirmed the constitutionality of the Act.[40] Jones quickly appealed. To face that challenge, the administration deployed a considerable array of legal talent, bringing the leading legal

THE COMING OF THE NEW DEAL    35

lights of the New Deal to bear, including two future justices. Solicitor General Stanley Reed argued the *Jones* case before the Court. Reed regularly consulted Frankfurter regarding litigation strategy during this time. The Roosevelt administration also brought in Robert Jackson, then assistant general counsel at the Treasury, as special counsel to aid the SEC.[41]

After the case was argued in the Supreme Court, Landis, then serving as an SEC Commissioner, reported to Frankfurter that "[t]he only possibility of defeat is on a procedural point and yet I cannot see a sane bench of judges not giving us some freedom in working out our procedural technique."[42] The Court shortly gave Landis reason to question the justices' sanity. It ruled against the SEC on the withdrawal issue, thereby avoiding, for the moment, the constitutional issue. The tenor of the opinion, however, did not bode well for the SEC's relationship with the Court. The 6-3 majority consisted of the "Four Horsemen" (Butler, McReynolds, Sutherland, and Van Devanter), the key bloc overturning central parts of the New Deal, joined by Chief Justice Hughes and Owen Roberts.[43] Sutherland's opinion for the Court treated the securities registration process as little more than a license to use the mails. The statute was silent on a registrant's ability to withdraw. Under the common law, such a license would carry with it an absolute right to withdraw. The Court filled the statutory void with the common law rule, giving discretion to the individual rather than the SEC. More provocatively, Sutherland, who had a civil libertarian streak, favoring Fourth Amendment protections even for bootleggers,[44] characterized the SEC's investigation as infringing on the "constitutional safeguards of personal liberty."

Although the government avoided a direct constitutional loss, the Court denounced the SEC's "fishing bill," that is, an investigation not based on specific grounds. The Commission's action was "wholly unreasonable and arbitrary," according to the Court, stressing the need to block unauthorized powers by "lesser agencies" as well as the three primary departments of the government. The Court's opinion lumped together the SEC's investigation with the "intolerable abuses of the Star Chamber which brought that institution to an end at the hands of the Long Parliament in 1640." The Court stood vigilant to check such abuses: "Even the shortest step in the direction of curtailing one of these rights must be halted *in limine*, lest it serve as a precedent for further advances in the same direction, or for wrongful invasions of the others."

Cardozo's dissent, joined by Brandeis and Stone, ridiculed the comparison of the SEC to the Star Chamber:

> A Commission which is without coercive power, which cannot arrest or amerce or imprison though a crime has been uncovered, or even punish for contempt, but can only inquire and report, the propriety of every question in the

## 36  A HISTORY OF SECURITIES LAW

course of the inquiry being subject to the supervision of the ordinary courts of Justice, is likened with denunciatory fervor to the Star Chambers of the Stuarts. Historians may find hyperbole in the sanguinary simile.[45]

Stone grumbled to Frankfurter that the opinion "was written for morons." Frankfurter complained that the Court was "making a mockery of great fundamental constitutional experiences and traditions to invoke them with the silly irrelevance with which they were invoked" in *Jones*. Stone responded that *Jones* was an example of the Supreme Court at its worst. He observed:

> I do not suppose the heavens will fall, whether or not Mr. J. Edward Jones, in a public hearing, surrounded by all the safeguards of the Constitution, is compelled to explain the discrepancies of his statements in the public document which he had filed, but when our Court sets at naught a plain command of Congress, without the invocation of any identifiable prohibition of the Constitution, and supports it only by platitudinous irrelevancies, it is a matter of transcendent importance.

Whatever the long-term impact of Jones's victory, the decision resonated in the public debate at the time. A bitter Robert Jackson lamented that "Every tricky knave in the investment business hailed the opinion, and the enemies of the administration seized it to drive home the charge that New Deal was destroying old liberties." Frankfurter passed on to Stone this observation from the SEC's Burns: "There is hardly a crook in the country whose lawyer does not come in to read juicy extracts from Sutherland's oration. . . . [T]his decision will be a constant source of annoyance in our enforcement activities."[46]

Facing strong headwinds, the government, urged on by Frankfurter and his emissaries Cohen and Corcoran, doubled down on its strategy of delay. The constitutional challenge to PUHCA, for example, would be prolonged through three visits to the Supreme Court. The holding companies initially refused to register with the SEC, confident that PUHCA would ultimately be judged unconstitutional.[47]

The New Dealers were experimenting with the regulatory state and faced considerable constitutional uncertainty with respect to their experiments. PUHCA was the boldest of those experiments, with many provisions addressing subjects previously regulated by state law. As Roosevelt's first term came to an end, the long-standing judicial skepticism toward economic regulation showed few signs of abating, at least with regard to federal authority. The centerpieces of the New Deal's legislative program had been stuck down as beyond Congress's power. The status of the securities laws remained up in the air, but *Jones* had raised a red flag.

# 2

# Social Control of Finance

> I think an aggressive offensive against the old gang who want the old ways of life, in pursuit of the old greed is really the only effective way of dealing with them.
>
> > Felix Frankfurter (Letter to Ray Moley, May 1934)
> >
> > FF-LC, Reel 71

The New Deal vision of Felix Frankfurter and his fellow progressives looked to empower administrative experts to solve the formidable economic challenges created by the Great Depression. Large corporations had come to dominate industrialized America by the 1920s, driven by technological advances in transportation, communication, and electrification. An ever-growing field of finance had helped fuel that growth. During the boom of the 1920s, many bankers and lawyers had gotten wealthy by raising capital to build industrial behemoths. The boom era had ended with the crash of October 1929; for progressives, the task was now to manage a mature economy.

That crash had also led an angry public to believe that the wealth of the "money-changers" had come out of the small investor's pocket. As William O. Douglas wrote in 1933, "when security values shrink as they have in the last few years it is but natural to find blame laid at the door of those who got the money, who were identified with the flotation, or who were connected with the management."[1] Public resentment was further fueled by Ferdinand Pecora's hearings, which shined a spotlight on a range of self-dealing: investment bankers siphoning large fees from new issuances of securities they sold to investors; brokers fueling a speculative craze for securities trading with wash sales and stock pools; and executives whose compensation, hidden from investors, reached seemingly stratospheric heights.

Insiders seemed to be rigging the system in the industries that had grown to national scale. Wall Street raised enormous sums to finance the building of railroads in the latter part of the nineteenth century, and even more to fund the spread of electricity in the first part of the twentieth century.[2] Both industries had features of a natural monopoly based on geography. That area did not necessarily correspond to state boundaries, however, such that state regulators' ability to limit rates charged to customers seemed overmatched. Bankers had exploited

---

*A History of Securities Law in the Supreme Court.* A.C. Pritchard and Robert B. Thompson, Oxford University Press.
© Oxford University Press 2023. DOI: 10.1093/oso/9780197665916.003.0003

## 38    A HISTORY OF SECURITIES LAW

this regulatory vulnerability to organize holding companies wielding monopolistic control of American utilities. The overbuilding of railroads, by contrast, led to ruinous competition, and inevitably, corporate reorganizations to rejigger their capital structures. Those proceedings were ruled by a narrow clique of bankers and lawyers; those professionals controlled which investors prospered and which ones walked away with little or nothing. What utilities and railroad reorganizations had in common was a lack of transparency.

New Deal laws and regulations disrupted the financial status quo in these areas. Empowerment of administrative experts in pursuit of "social control of finance" necessarily meant diminished influence for the "old gang," that is, the investment bankers, lawyers, and their management clients. Commenting on the Securities Act, Douglas argued the case for protecting investors:

> the investor needs protection which bankers have not and will not give him. The reputable bankers are no exception. Even they have been known to cut corners and to be governed by the hysteria of bull markets. . . .
>
> There is a need for some agency to step in between the persons who get the money and those who supply it and to fulfill the role of protector for the latter. . . . The ideal of "rugged individualism" when applied to investors has no longer any place in the program for American high finance.[3]

Douglas was still an academic bystander when the Securities Act was working its way through Congress, but he soon came from Yale to Washington to help implement this new vision. By the time Douglas became chair of the SEC during Roosevelt's second term, the legislative architecture was in place for the SEC to become the central player in the administration's efforts to transform the economy. What was needed was leadership, and Douglas was more than willing to provide it. Douglas pushed the agency to use its authority under the Exchange Act to tackle the New York Stock Exchange's trading practices, limiting the formerly unfettered space of brokers and dealers to exploit investors. He also began an aggressive breakup of public utilities under the Public Utility Holding Company Act. Finally, Douglas pushed bankers and lawyers out of their long-held gatekeeper positions in corporate reorganizations. Along the way, he ingratiated himself as one of Roosevelt's key advisors and a regular at the White House poker game, putting him at the center of a broader regulatory push that went well beyond securities transactions. Today's securities lawyers would not fully recognize the New Deal SEC, as the Commission's remit has shrunk to the securities markets, primary and secondary. The SEC now shares other aspects of business regulation with a host of other agencies. But Douglas's SEC was at the forefront of the Roosevelt administration's effort to assert social control over finance.

This chapter tells the story of the administrative state expanding to govern American business and how this movement met and eventually overcame a recalcitrant judiciary. We follow through the eventual expiration of two of the key administrative movements chronicled here, SEC control of utility reorganizations and bankruptcy reorganizations.

We begin in Part A by placing the securities laws within the larger movement to assert social control over finance. We focus in particular on Bill Douglas's role—and the scope of his ambition—in expanding federal financial regulation. Some of these efforts, such as federal incorporation, came to nothing, while others, such as progressive taxation of corporations, were tried, only to be pushed aside by competing political imperatives. Other areas, such as corporate governance, saw the federal role gradually increase, often with a push from the Supreme Court, as we discuss in subsequent chapters.

We then turn in Parts B and C of this chapter to the New Deal's most drastic interventions in the business world: PUHCA's breakup of the public utility giants and the Chandler Act's reshaping of corporate reorganizations. Both involved intrusive government control of significant parts of the economy. In each area, Congress relied on the SEC's financial expertise, taking the agency beyond its eponymous focus to reach into the governance and structure of American corporations. These two statutes, particularly PUHCA, would dominate the Court's early securities docket. These twin allocations of authority shared not only a broad reach, but also a similar demise: Congress eventually removed both public utilities and corporate reorganizations from the SEC's statutory authority, with the agency's acquiescence. The rise and fall of this grander vision for the SEC would mirror the Court's attitude toward the agency, as we show in the chapters that follow. As the scope of the SEC's authority diminished over time, so too, did the Court's willingness to defer to the expert agency.

## A. Securities Regulation and Taming Big Business

### 1. William O. Douglas and Social Control of Finance

Ideas from academia figured prominently in the New Deal, but particularly in the debate over social control of finance. First at Columbia and then at Yale, Douglas was one of the legal realists revolutionizing legal scholarship and education in the late 1920s. In his legal scholarship, Douglas had been pushing corporate reform based on empirical research. That research was tinged with progressive values foreshadowing modern theories of stakeholder capitalism. As part of the Yale Business Failures Project, Douglas urged a broader role for employees in the corporate entity: "although workers 'do not have an investment in the business in

## 40 A HISTORY OF SECURITIES LAW

the legal or popular sense,' they possessed a 'prospective income' from it which gave them a status in the enterprise with 'a measurable degree of permanency.'"[4]

Douglas also pushed reform of a broad area of the business law curriculum, seeking to integrate insights from the newly emergent business schools into legal education. Early in his academic career, Douglas worked with his Columbia colleague Adolf A. Berle, Jr., to combine "three existing courses—Agency, Partnership, and Corporations—into one legal-realist course called Business Organizations." At Yale, "Douglas's idea was to offer an entire curriculum organized not on business theory but on the 'life cycle' of corporations. Thus, new courses on the incorporation and financing of a business would be followed by others dealing with various real-world corporate problems, such as labor management and marketing."[5]

The Yale influx into the New Deal trailed behind Frankfurter's wide-ranging placement of Harvard graduates in the Roosevelt administration, but it was prominent nevertheless.[6] Academic input was, of course, not limited just to Harvard and Yale. Columbia, too, played an important role, providing Roosevelt's braintrusters Ray Moley, who brought Frankfurter into the drafting of the securities laws; and Adolf Berle. Berle was a student of Frankfurter's at Harvard, but he was not drawn into the professor's circle. Thereafter, he had worked briefly in Brandeis's law firm. Berle had made an independent and enduring name for himself with the publication of *The Modern Corporation and Private Property* in 1932, which he coauthored with Gardiner Means. The book had Brandeisian themes, but in contrast to Brandeis's moralism, was empirically grounded. Berle and Means documented the separation between ownership and control in the industrial corporations that had come to dominate the American economy. They also laid out the theoretical justification for the agency cost critique of managerial capitalism. Management dominated public corporations, according to Berle and Means, at the expense of passive investors. Berle endorsed an incipient theory of stakeholder capitalism: "in time, the corporation would generate a conscience and a soul."[7]

Douglas's views of finance were closely aligned with those of his former colleague Berle. Douglas's initial public commentary welcoming the Securities Act soon gave way to worry that it had not gone far enough. In a law review piece published shortly after the statute's enactment, he warned that disclosure alone would not prevent the recurrence of the scandals uncovered by Ferdinand Pecora's committee, dismissing it as "of secondary importance in a comprehensive program of social control over finance." Too much authority over the interpretation of the act had been placed with the courts rather than the Federal Trade Commission (FTC), initially tasked with administering the law. Douglas hinted that consideration should be given to government regulation, not just of disclosure, but of capital allocation itself. Privately, he was more candid. He confided to Berle: "I think the Securities Act is a rather laborious and untimely effort to turn back the clock and quite antithetical to many of the other significant current developments." It was, however, a first step toward displacing the old guard:

> The Act is significant politically. It is symbolic of a shift of political power. That shift is from the bankers to the masses; from the promoter to the investor. It means that the government is taking the side of the helpless, the suckers, the underdogs. It signifies that the money-changers are being driven from the temples.

"[S]upplementary legislation" would be needed, "dealing directly with the forces which must be controlled if high finance, as Mr. Berle would say, is to be the servant not the master of society." Douglas endorsed greater "collectivism" in the interest of a "more thoroughgoing programme of stabilization."[8]

Douglas envisioned bolder reform: federal incorporation and control of corporate governance, which would lay "such solid bases for protection of investors as to make the present Act become wholly insignificant." He was anxious to involve himself in efforts that were brewing in Washington to draft legislation to displace state corporate law. In December 1933 he wrote to Jerome Frank, a leading legal realist turned activist-policymaker, then general counsel to the Agricultural Adjustment Administration: "I am particularly intrigued with your proposal for federal incorporation, as I think that only by some such beginning can genuine progress towards protection of investors get under way." Douglas would later recommend that Roosevelt make Frank an SEC commissioner. He would eventually succeed Douglas as chairman. Also in December 1933, Douglas exchanged letters with Berle who had drafted a federal incorporation bill for a House committee during the transition. Berle's update that "we are working on a federal incorporation law, which I hope will be presented to Congress in the next session" produced an effusive response from Douglas: "You can count on me to pull an oar on federal incorporation. . . . [P]erhaps we can begin to get at the really fundamental problem of the increment of power and profit inherent in our present form of organization. . . ."[9]

Although Douglas could hit a Brandeisian theme for rhetorical effect, Douglas's enthusiasm for central planning in the field of finance undercut his subsequent claim to be a follower of Brandeis's crusade against bigness. In 1934, Douglas wrote that it was "inconceivable" that the government could "turn back the clock" to "unscramble our large forms of organization."[10] Unscrambling big business was the core of Brandeis's policy agenda. Douglas's concessions to the inevitability of "bigness" made him slightly suspect in Frankfurter's view. Brandeis and his followers distrusted "bigness" in all its manifestations.

42  A HISTORY OF SECURITIES LAW

Brandeis, despite having published a frequently cited critique of state corporate law in *Ligget Co. v. Lee*,[11] opposed federal incorporation because he believed it asked too much of government. Harry Shulman, a young professor at Yale who had clerked for Brandeis, memorialized a conversation with Brandeis in December 1933:

> [Shulman] interjected a statement about the renewed agitation for federal incorporation. Both L.D.B. and Mrs. B quickly frowned upon it. I would leave a lot of power to the states, said L.D.B. and have the federal government help and direct the States by appropriate taxation. The federal government must not become too big just as corporations should not be permitted to become too big. You must remember that it is the littleness of man that limits the size of things we can undertake. Too much bigness may break the federal government as it has broken business.[12]

Brandeis's distrust of a federal leviathan would manifest itself soon enough in decisions striking down the New Deal's early efforts at central planning, as discussed in Chapter 1. Those decisions would hasten Roosevelt's shift away from central planning initiatives in his second term.

Frankfurter, like Brandeis, did not share Douglas's enthusiasm for federal incorporation, and he discouraged Roosevelt from pursuing it. In a letter to Douglas, Frankfurter echoed his mentor:

> I am much more sceptical than you are, apparently, of the large schemes of which you speak for curbing corporate abuses. . . . I am not at all for federal incorporation. . . . Where do you men get your great confidence in the effectiveness of piling on everything on the back of federal administration. I was a hot Hamiltonian when I went to Washington in 1911, but years in the government service and all the rest of the years watching its operations intently have made me less jaunty about devices for running a whole continent from Washington.

Instead of federal incorporation, Frankfurter and Brandeis favored graduated taxation rates to penalize "big corporations," leading to their eventual breakup. Frankfurter believed tax policy could "prevent all sorts of nonsense that we never could touch through a federal incorporation act." He warned Douglas:

> It's awfully easy to write these nice laws for control. I think your lawyer-banker friends would be glad to write them for you, but . . . when I think of the stuff that gets by even high-minded judges—well, I prefer to use the taxing power . . . to curb the mischief and abuses of corporate activities.

... [tax] 'em, my boy, tax 'em, and otherwise reduce the opportunities for bludgeoning that interrelation and concentration of money interests make possible.[13]

Douglas was most contrite in his response to Frankfurter's criticism—"My heart would indeed 'bleed' if I thought I was inadvertently championing the cause of 'the Street.'" He did not yield ground, however, on the need for federal incorporation. More drastically, Douglas urged complete governmental control over investment banking: "The Securities Act will be fully justified if it drives the government into the investment banking business." The law did not go far enough for Douglas: "I would apply more drastic measures at once and not wait until the reaction to the present regime sets in." Douglas would continue to pursue those issues when he became SEC chairman in 1937.[14]

Such disagreement among those jockeying for Roosevelt's ear was common, and alliances among his advisors shifted over time. Frankfurter had pushed for a broader federal control in railroad reorganization before Roosevelt's inauguration in early 1933. Douglas had espoused a more process-focused approach.[15] Some of these ideas became the statutes discussed in Parts B and C of this chapter anchoring social control of finance. Some became the template for ideas pursued decades later. For example, the Reconstruction Finance Corporation's limit on salaries of executives of railroads receiving government loans was trotted out again in connection with bailouts of banks in the financial crisis in 2008.[16] Others, such as taxing "bigness," got a tryout and then a quick hook. Federal incorporation, however, never got beyond discussion.

Federal incorporation actually made much less progress during the New Deal than earlier versions proposed during the Progressive Era of the early twentieth century. In its original incarnation, the proposal was seen as constitutional leverage for greater regulation of the corporations that had come to dominate the American economy. Three consecutive Presidents in the early twentieth century—Theodore Roosevelt, William Howard Taft, and Woodrow Wilson— endorsed it. Progressive Era legislation, however, took a different path, eventually focusing on anti-monopoly laws. Franklin Roosevelt never embraced the idea of federal incorporation and nothing came of the efforts of Berle, Frank, and Douglas during the New Deal. Without Roosevelt's support, the Borak-Mahoney federal incorporation bill introduced in 1937 went nowhere. The idea would emerge again in the 1970s, promoted by former SEC chairman William Cary, and it would again fizzle.[17] The evergreen proposal would be bandied about again during the 2020 Democratic presidential primaries.

The Roosevelt administration was more interested in pursuing a "tax on the bigness of corporations" that Frankfurter had been pushing since at least 1932. That goal intersected with a focus on "Corporate Surpluses," featured in a key

# 44 A HISTORY OF SECURITIES LAW

campaign memorandum from Roosevelt's braintrusters. Adolf Berle wrote that section of the memo, assigning much of the blame for the stock market crash and the depression that followed to corporations' unreasonable accumulation of profit. Roosevelt finally endorsed Frankfurter's tax on bigness in January 1935. Senator Burton Wheeler introduced it into Congress shortly thereafter. Robert Jackson, then general counsel of the Bureau of Internal Revenue, made the case for a graduated corporate income tax, but to little effect. The Revenue Act of 1936 instead paired a watered-down corporate income tax with a tax on unreasonable accumulation of corporate profits. For the first time, corporate earnings were fully subject to both the corporation and individual income tax, in effect increasing the government's take of corporate earnings. The more punitive approach was short-lived, however, with an economic downturn in 1937 leading to the Revenue Act of 1938 repealing the undistributed profits tax.[18]

## 2. Douglas at the SEC

Douglas wasted little time in moving to gain a spot in the newly emerging administrative state. The Exchange Act created an attractive opportunity for a man on the make. Early discussion of the proposed legislation indicated that either a new commission would be created to enforce its provisions or that the FTC would be expanded to handle the new work. Douglas's close friend, Richard Smith, a public utility lawyer in New York, took the lead in lobbying for a seat on Douglas's behalf. Now that he was pursuing a job as a regulator, Douglas downplayed his earlier criticisms of the Securities Act; the main thrust of his writing on the topic, he said, was that "it is necessary to have a very powerful commission fully equipped with a rather wide range of discretion to handle the job. The matter simply cannot be reduced to a code." Unfortunately for Douglas, his writings could not be explained away so easily. The word from Washington was that "Landis particularly is very resentful toward you, because of your writings on the Securities Act." Perhaps unsurprisingly given the rebuke he had received from Frankfurter, Douglas did not ask the Harvard professor to lobby on his behalf despite Frankfurter's well-known influence in personnel matters in the Roosevelt administration. In the end, Douglas was passed over for the newly created Securities and Exchange Commission. Ben Cohen, who had a much stronger claim to a spot based on his drafting efforts, was also passed over despite Tom Corcoran's lobbying efforts on behalf of his friend.[19]

Douglas's campaign for one of the five seats on the newly created SEC came up short, but the Exchange Act also included a provision requiring the SEC to study reorganizations and protective committees. Douglas's prior work in bankruptcy led to his appointment to head the study, at Landis's urging. The study would take

**Figure 2.1**
**The Investor's Advocate:** William O. Douglas in leading the SEC prior to joining the Supreme Court, pushed out the "old gangs" at the New York Stock Exchange, utility holding companies, and in bankruptcy reorganizations. Shown here is Douglas's first press conference where he labeled the SEC as "The Investor's Advocate."

over four years, but Douglas leveraged that work into a seat on the SEC before the study was complete, filling the opening created when Joe Kennedy resigned. Frankfurter wrote to congratulate him and urge Douglas to action: "a nice calculation on the prudence of trying to carry out the right thing is the surest road to difficulty and dissatisfaction with oneself."[20] In twenty months, Douglas was chairman, succeeding Jim Landis, who had returned to Harvard to be dean of the law school. Douglas soon answered Frankfurter's call for bold action.

In his first press conference as chairman, Douglas declared the SEC would be a counterweight to the traditional powers in finance. "We have brokers' advocates, we have got Exchange advocates, we have got investment banker advocates, and we are the investors' advocate."[21] Douglas used his time as chairman of the SEC to displace the old gang's control, both in the securities markets and in adjacent areas of finance. Public utility holding companies and corporate reorganizations topped the list of Douglas's targets.

## 46 A HISTORY OF SECURITIES LAW

### (a) Stock exchange governance reform

Concerns about stock exchange floor members exploiting their position through manipulation and sharp trading fueled a long-running debate over governance at the New York Stock Exchange. Two months into his chairmanship, after initial negotiations between the Commission and the NYSE had broken down, Douglas threatened SEC-imposed trading rules. He strongly suggested a willingness to limit or abolish the ability of exchange members to trade for their own accounts, as well as severe restrictions on short selling. Both interventions would have sharply curtailed trading volumes, the lifeblood of the exchange.

An embezzlement scandal involving former exchange president Richard Whitney—the leader of the NYSE's lobbying effort against the Exchange Act back in 1934—eroded the power of the old guard on the Exchange's Board of Governors. The SEC stepped into the void to push reforms that put a new board in charge, employed a full-time president, and increased the Exchange's internal disciplinary staff. As two prominent newspaper columnists put it: "The end of Richard Whitney was the end of the Old Guard also." Whitney's fall was dramatic; his conviction landed him in the state prison at Sing Sing. Roosevelt, who like Whitney attended both Groton and Harvard, exclaimed "Not Dick Whitney!" when he heard the news.[22]

The Exchange Act, as the name suggests, had regulated exchanges and exchange trading. Congress had punted, however, on regulating securities trading over the counter. Here, Douglas negotiated a compromise that provided for self-regulation by the brokerage community, subject to close oversight by the SEC: "Government would keep the shotgun, so to speak, behind the door, loaded, well oiled, cleaned, ready for use but with the hope it would never have to be used."[23] This approach was adopted in the Maloney Act that passed Congress in 1938.[24] The Act authorized formation of a national association of brokers or dealers who could make disciplinary rules; the SEC was empowered to review all disciplinary decisions and to abrogate or alter most association rules. Self-regulation was nominally preserved, but the SEC was clearly calling the shots.

### (b) Aggressive enforcement of PUHCA

When Douglas took over from Landis as SEC chairman, PUHCA had been tied up in court for two years. The SEC had done little enforcement. Landis fretted about the future of the SEC if the agency was too aggressive.[25] The PUHCA litigation is addressed in Part B below. The Supreme Court decision in March 1938 to uphold the registration provisions of the Act (having severed and postponed the more challenging question of the constitutionality of the death sentence provision) allowed Douglas to seize the initiative. His initial pursuit of voluntary compliance was met by an industry response demanding that the agency forego rigorous enforcement of the death sentence. Douglas's subsequent order that the major systems submit plans describing how they would comply with § 11 of PUHCA, which required that utilities be streamlined into a "single integrated public-utility system," produced few adequate proposals. An intra-agency conflict between the director of the division overseeing the new act and Douglas's top aide, Abe Fortas, lay unresolved. After Tommy Corcoran relayed an "urgent request" from the President that the division be reorganized, Douglas engineered the departure of the recalcitrant division head. He also pushed a decision to "institute proceedings practically simultaneously against all the major systems." For Douglas, enforcement would free the utility companies from the "whip hand of New York finance."[26] The Supreme Court would not validate the death sentence provision until 1946, but by then the breakup of the public utility industry was largely a fait accompli. It was perhaps the broadest breakup to that point in the history of American business.

### (c) Redefining the role of bankers and lawyers in reorganizations

Corporate reorganizations were also plagued by ongoing concerns about the role of bankers and lawyers; reformers had long sought to displace those powerbrokers from their dominant positions. The passage of the Chandler Act in 1938 and the Trust Indenture Act in 1939 came late in the New Deal, but their reforms had been percolating for many years.

Bankruptcy reorganization had been on the Roosevelt administration's original reform agenda. A bankruptcy reform movement had been growing through the 1920s and the early 1930s, with two well-known studies by New York City lawyers—one by Donovan and the other by Thatcher—highlighting the problems of the existing system.[27] Reorganization legislation was passed in the dying days of the Hoover administration for railroads, but not for other corporations.[28] The railroad reorganization bill largely codified the equity receivership process that investment bankers and reorganization lawyers had used to reorganize railroads for decades. Fiorella LaGuardia, who had introduced the House version of the railroad bill, posed the question:

> Are you going to leave the management of the reorganization and receivership of these railroads in the hands of the gang that has ruined the railroads, or are you going to take them out of the hands of that gang [JP Morgan, Kuhn, Loeb & Co., Mitchell, Whitney, Swaine and Sutherland and like ilk] and put such control and supervision in the hands of a Government agency?

LaGuardia was likely overstating the reform's impact since the bill only authorized a judge to appoint a trustee from a panel of trustees selected by the Interstate Commerce Commission. As Max Lowenthal, another Frankfurter protégé, pointed out, a judge in the Missouri Pacific railroad reorganization case filed

48 A HISTORY OF SECURITIES LAW

shortly after the bill's enactment declined to appoint any trustee and left the operations in the hands of prior management.[29] Notwithstanding the limited impact of the railroad reorganization bill, the new Congress took the same approach when it passed a parallel bill applicable to corporations more generally the following year.

Douglas's special study of reorganizations and protective committees built the case that investment bankers and lawyers had managed the reorganization process to boost their own fees at investor expense. Douglas, who had worked on corporate reorganizations while an associate at the Cravath firm, believed that the reorganization bar was "monopolized by relatively few firms" and that they had "been charging all that the traffic would bear."[30]

As with PUHCA, the Chandler Act went beyond the disclosure required by the Securities Act and the Exchange Act, mandating corporate governance changes. In this case, the debtor's management would be replaced by trustees. Trustees, in turn, were subjected to strict requirements limiting conflicts of interest.[31] These conflict restrictions and a ban on pre-bankruptcy filing solicitation of creditors diminished the bankers' traditional advantage in coordinating scattered bondholders. With the investment bankers and existing managers—the two biggest clients of the reorganization bar—thus sidelined, the old guard's power was shattered.[32] The Act also required bankruptcy courts to solicit the advice of the SEC, providing the agency a prominent place in any reorganization. The Trust Indenture Act, passed the following year (also a result of the SEC's study), brought in reorganizations occurring outside of bankruptcy.[33]

## B. Breaking Up Utility Empires: The Public Utility Holding Company Act of 1935

Roosevelt had campaigned in 1932 on federal control of utility holding companies. In a September campaign speech in Portland, Oregon, he called out the "Insull monstrosity" and other examples of how "private manipulation had outsmarted the slow-moving powers of government."[34] Candidate Roosevelt cataloged a litany of financial failings: arbitrary write-ups of assets; excessive prices paid for property; subsidiaries milked to prop up related companies. Roosevelt's vision in that speech for an agency as a "tribune of the people putting its engineering, its accounting, its legal resources into the breach . . . against private greed" was a template for Douglas's call for the SEC to serve as the investor's advocate.

The FTC had been working on a study of public utilities since 1928, eventually producing eighty-four volumes by 1935. The agency's general counsel Robert Healy, a key player in this work, became one of the initial five SEC commissioners. A Roosevelt-appointed National Power Policy Committee in 1934 brought Ben Cohen intimately into the PUHCA legislative drafting discussed in Chapter 1. Cohen was also involved in the litigation discussed below. The responsibility for overhauling the utility industry could have gone to the Federal Power Commission or the FTC; its placement within the SEC permitted reorganizations to be handled by a fresh set of lawyers and other experts who had come to Washington with the New Deal. Putting the SEC in charge also linked this effort to break up the utility holding companies with parallel moves to displace the existing Wall Street power structure.

PUHCA would be the proving ground for the New Deal securities legislation in court. Taming the power of the industry would require not just the concurrence of the legislative branch but also the Supreme Court. PUHCA was enacted at a time when the constitutional scope of federal power over the economy was still very much in doubt. Moreover, the law went a step beyond the earlier securities laws, which focused primarily on disclosure, with its "death sentence" provision requiring the dismantling of the utility holding companies. Joseph Rauh later recalled:

> I worked for Ben [Cohen] for a year on defending the Public Utility Holding Company Act. He taught me more about how to win a case that's unwinnable than anyone else could have. If you had asked anyone in 1935 if the Supreme Court would uphold the Public Utility Holding Company Act, you would have been laughed at.

PUHCA "gave the SEC power to refashion the structure and the business practices of an entire industry. Except in wartime, the federal government never before had assumed such total control over any industry."[35] At the time, PUHCA was vastly more important than the Exchange Act in regulating corporate finance. Its impact on the American economy was more dramatic even than the Sarbanes-Oxley Act of recent vintage.[36] The Roosevelt administration viewed the Court as the chief obstacle to its economic planning initiatives; PUHCA would be an important test. PUHCA provided the majority of securities cases in the Supreme Court over the first twenty years after the enactment of the securities laws, but the law's significance to the Court's docket was not merely quantitative. The Court's decisions on PUHCA were the most closely followed securities cases in the popular press, as they pitted the government against the giant utility holding companies, fighting for their survival.

The Supreme Court's ten-year journey toward affirming PUHCA's validity demonstrates the abrupt shift in the Court's balance of power. After a long delay before his first appointment, Roosevelt's appointees came to predominate in his second term. The New Deal Justices appointed by Roosevelt shared a belief

50   A HISTORY OF SECURITIES LAW

in the promise of the administrative state to tame private interest; they blamed the failures of private ordering for the Great Depression. By the early 1940s, the New Deal Court had established the power that the federal government now wields over the economy under the interstate commerce clause, including securities regulation and corporate governance. Of equal import, the Court's PUHCA decisions established a pattern of deference to administrative expertise. As a result, the SEC enjoyed a remarkable string of victories beginning in 1940 that would last, with minor exceptions, until 1973. But when Roosevelt signed PUHCA into law in 1935, the SEC faced an uphill fight to defend its authority.

## 1. The PUHCA Wars

Within three weeks of PUHCA's enactment, a furious litigation battle had begun. The government quickly found itself on the defensive. The industry brought legal action in a federal district court in Baltimore. Two debenture holders of a local subsidiary of a large holding company appeared on the same day in September to intervene in that subsidiary's ongoing bankruptcy proceeding. One asked the Court to declare PUHCA unconstitutional, while the other sought to have its constitutionality affirmed. The anti-PUHCA intervener had a lawyer he had never met: "Some Davis fellow" he testified, before the government introduced him in the courtroom to John W. Davis, the former Solicitor General and legendary Supreme Court advocate. Davis had been hired by the industry to challenge the constitutionality of the statute. He had denounced the bill that became PUHCA as "the gravest threat to the liberties of the American citizens that has emanated from the halls of Congress in my time."[37] The lawyer for the bondholder supposedly defending the Act had been a longtime opponent of utility regulation.[38] The setup suggested a less than adversarial setting for resolving an important national issue.

The district court judge quickly ruled that the Act was "void in its entirety."[39] The government responded with what turned out to be a winning litigation strategy. The team, led by Ben Cohen and several future Supreme Court justices, had to:

1. cabin the initial adverse ruling (soon to be affirmed in the court of appeals);
2. pick and pursue an alternative suit that maximized the SEC's chance to win; and
3. block any other suits (and there were many) from jumping ahead of the SEC's preferred suit.

To accomplish the first task, the SEC not only declined to seek Supreme Court review in the Baltimore case, but also developed the facts showing the lack of

SOCIAL CONTROL OF FINANCE    51

genuine adversity that would discourage the Court from granting certiorari. The goal was to avoid an immediate Supreme Court clash over the controversial death sentence provision. Frankfurter urged that "the Government's memorandum in the Baltimore case should be pitched very very coolly, not to arouse the emotional susceptibilities of most of the nine lads regarding John W. Davis."[40] The Court denied certiorari in the Baltimore case in March 1936.[41]

The SEC preferred a case with favorable facts. More importantly, the government sought to avoid resolving the contentious death sentence issue right out of the box.[42] To get control of the litigation agenda, the agency had its lawyers on the ready to file its chosen case in New York against Electric Bond & Share Co, one of the largest holding companies, after the company informed Chairman Landis that it would not register as the Act required.[43] To make Electric Bond the test case, the SEC needed to block other suits. The agency sought a stay in the federal court in Washington while it went forward with the suit in New York. Courts in jurisdictions other than the D.C. Circuit could not compel the SEC to be a party, so the SEC could control its venue as long as it did not attempt to enforce the law.[44] In January 1936, the government persuaded the trial court in the District of Columbia to grant a stay in *North American v. Landis*, but the D.C. Circuit reversed in June.[45] This time the government petitioned for certiorari, which the Supreme Court granted. The Court heard oral argument in the case a week after Roosevelt's smashing landslide in the 1936 election. Within a month, a unanimous Court reversed the court of appeals, permitting a stay of the other cases until the decision of the trial court in New York.[46] Although this was only a procedural win, the atmosphere had freshened for the agency. In contrast to the hostility expressed in *Jones* earlier that year, this opinion, written by Cardozo for a unanimous Court, was considerably more accommodating to the SEC.

> We must be on our guard against depriving the processes of justice of their suppleness of adaptation to varying conditions. Especially in cases of extraordinary public moment, the individual may be required to submit to delay not immoderate in extent and not oppressive in its consequences if the public welfare or convenience will thereby be promoted. In these Holding Company Act cases great issues are involved, great in their complexity, great in their significance.

Not only did the SEC win, but with Cardozo writing the opinion, *Jones*'s caustic tone had also disappeared.

Despite this procedural victory, PUHCA, like other New Deal legislation, remained at risk in the shadow cast by the Supreme Court's constitutional holdings in 1935 and 1936. In the weeks after *Landis*, Roosevelt, bolstered by his overwhelming electoral mandate from November, mounted a direct assault against that shadow with his "Court-packing" plan. Although the public believed

52    A HISTORY OF SECURITIES LAW

that the plan would pass, it was met by a barrage of criticism that dominated political debate for the first half of 1937.[47] The Supreme Court that would eventually uphold the constitutionality of economic regulation, including the securities laws, had not yet emerged.

The SEC's preferred case for establishing PUHCA's constitutionality, *Electric Bond*, went forward in the lower federal courts in New York.[48] Circuit Judge Julian Mack, sitting as the trial judge, heard the case. This was favorable ground for the SEC; Mack was a friend of Frankfurter and Cohen had served as Mack's law clerk.[49] Mack ruled in January 1937 that the constitutionality of the registration provisions of the legislation could be separated from the more controversial provisions permitting the SEC to impose the death sentence on a holding company. The court then upheld the constitutionality of the registration provisions. The Second Circuit affirmed in a split decision.[50]

Time was on the Roosevelt administration's side. In the period between the district court and Supreme Court decisions, the Court's direction had changed radically. The *West Coast Hotel* decision upholding the Washington state minimum wage act was announced on March 29, 1937,[51] and was quickly—if perhaps erroneously—immortalized as "the switch in time that saved nine."[52] In subsequent cases that term—argued after Roosevelt announced the Court packing plan—the Court upheld the National Labor Relations Act and the Social Security tax,[53] two core parts of the second New Deal enacted in 1935. Owen Roberts, who had sided with the Four Horsemen in 1935 and 1936, now consistently voted with the liberal justices, to the amazement of administration lawyers. Robert Jackson saw the decisions as a "full retreat by the Court from the untenable positions it had taken the year before." Frankfurter, for his part, wrote to a friend that the shift made "it very difficult for anyone to suggest that lawyers without resort to unscrupulous casuistry can reconcile the decisions of the Court in 1936 with those in 1937."[54]

Whatever the source of Roberts's change of heart, the turnover in the Court's personnel had begun, spurred by a congressional change in retirement pay for justices. In 1932 Congress had capped the pay of justices who resigned, creating a significant financial disincentive to leave the Court.[55] Justice Van Devanter had written to his sister in 1932 saying he was going to retire after that year's election but changed his mind given the loss of half of his pension. For five years, no justice left the Court: "The Court seemed to have declared the mortality table unconstitutional," complained Robert Jackson. In 1937 Congress reversed the retirement policy. Rep. Hatton Summers, a New Dealer who eventually broke with the President over Court packing, had been pushing a bill to reverse the earlier law. He reintroduced his bill on January 11, 1937. On February 5, Roosevelt announced his Court packing plan. The House passed the new retirement bill on February 10, the Senate concurred, and the President signed it on March 1.[56]

SOCIAL CONTROL OF FINANCE    53

Money well spent from Roosevelt's perspective. Two months later, the seventy-seven-year-old Van Devanter announced his departure, specifically mentioning the new legislation.[57] He was replaced by Hugo Black, who had fought so tenaciously as a senator to pass PUHCA in 1935.[58] By the middle of the following term when the Court heard arguments in *Electric Bond*, seventy-five-year-old George Sutherland, the intellectual leader of the conservative bloc, had also retired.[59] Sutherland's replacement, Solicitor General Stanley Reed, did not participate in the *Electric Bond* decision, having overseen the litigation below. Nonetheless, the addition of Black and the subtraction of two of the Four Horsemen changed the Court's balance of power. With two of the conservative justices gone, even if the swing votes Roberts and Chief Justice Charles Evans Hughes were to join the remaining two, the result would be less than a majority. The shift accelerated as Roosevelt made three more appointments during his second term and filled three more seats in his third term (eight in all). The change in personnel would transform the Court's jurisprudence.

Oral arguments before the Supreme Court in *Electric Bond* went on for three days in early February 1938; Robert Jackson and Ben Cohen argued for the government in an "electric" courtroom.[60] Six weeks later, in an opinion by Chief Justice Hughes, the Court ruled 6-1 that the registration provisions were severable and that regulation requiring the submission of information was both familiar and constitutional.[61] Thus, the decision both upheld a portion of PUHCA and implicitly affirmed the constitutionality of the Securities Act and the Exchange Act. Although the Court upheld the registration provisions, it declined to consider constitutional challenges to PUHCA's much more controversial reorganization provisions, including the "death sentence." Nonetheless, the SEC, under the leadership of then-Chairman Bill Douglas, took the Court's decision as a green light to begin enforcing PUHCA. Frankfurter telegrammed congratulations to Jackson when the decision was announced.[62]

The Supreme Court did not rule on the constitutionality of the SEC's power to break up public utility holding companies until a pair of cases in 1946, eleven years after the statute's enactment and a decade after the Court's first PUHCA decision in *Landis v. North American*. By that point, the New Deal Court had swept aside doubts about the scope of Congress's power under the Commerce Clause. The Court's decision in *Wickard v. Filburn* in 1942 put the nail in the coffin of federalism limitations on Congress's power to regulate the economy.[63] In the wake of this constitutional revolution, the PUHCA cases went from fierce battles to mere afterthoughts. The SEC ordered the breakup of the North American and Electric Bond holding companies in 1942. The SEC's action in *North American* under § 11(b)(1) of the Act was affirmed by the Second Circuit in January of 1943 and the agency's order dissolving two Electric Bond subsidiaries under § 11(b)(2) of the Act was affirmed by the First Circuit in March 1944.[64]

54   A HISTORY OF SECURITIES LAW

The involvement of Douglas, Reed, and Jackson in earlier PUHCA litigation before coming to the Court, along with the involvement of Chief Justice Stone's former firm in some of the PUHCA litigation, prevented the Court from assembling the required six-member quorum for many PUHCA cases until the 1945 term. Stone's decision to sit in the holding company cases to provide a quorum provoked conflict among the brethren.[65] Even then, Stone's sudden death, just three weeks after the *North American* decision was announced, but before the *Electric Bond* decision was handed down, destroyed the fragile quorum for the second case and sent it back for reargument the following fall.[66]

*North American* was an enthusiastic validation of the SEC's power to break up utility holding companies. Frank Murphy wrote the decision, which focused on the constitutional claims.[67] At this point in the Court's history, the Commerce Clause question was easily dispatched; the "relationship to interstate commerce is so clear and definite as to make any other conclusion unreasonable." Murphy's opinion painted with a broad, moralistic brush, noting that limits on the Commerce Clause powers do not "render the nation powerless to defend itself against economic forces that Congress decrees inimical or destructive of the national economy." Murphy was emphatic in validating Congress's power over finance: "The fact that an evil may involve a corporation's financial practices, its business structure or its security portfolio does not detract from the power of Congress under the commerce clause to promulgate rules in order to destroy that evil." Murphy's eventual opinion in the companion case put over after Stone's death concluded that "the federal commerce power is as broad as the economic needs of the nation."[68]

The lopsided victory of 1946 should not obscure the challenge posed in 1935 and 1936. At that time, securing the Supreme Court's assent to an expert administrative agency's radical transformation of an American industry—a move unprecedented in the nation's history—was highly uncertain. The administration succeeded in its strategy "to postpone review . . . and to increase the chance that the test cases would be heard by a more receptive Supreme Court."[69] The role of the SEC in regulating American finance was now assured. The question that remained was how much discretion the Court would afford the SEC; we turn now to that topic.

## 2.  Breaking Up the Holding Companies: A Judicial New Deal

Although the hurdle of PUHCA's constitutionality had been overcome, difficult questions remained for the Court. The SEC's reorganization of the holding companies raised an array of procedural questions. The resolution of those issues would have important implications for the relationship between the courts

SOCIAL CONTROL OF FINANCE    55

and the SEC. Here PUHCA provided the first testing ground for working out how judicial review fit with the newly empowered administrative state. That experiment began with largely a blank slate; the statutory infrastructure of the Administrative Procedure Act would not be enacted until 1946. The new administrative state had been built with the assistance of Black, Douglas, Frankfurter, Jackson, and Reed. Now that they were justices, would the Court afford discretion to the experts, or would judges constrain the SEC with detailed legal rules? Would the New Deal Court defer to the SEC's expertise, or would it constrain administrative discretion through narrow interpretations of the statutes that gave the SEC its authority? The Court that resolved these issues would be dominated by justices that Roosevelt had named to the Court, who all believed government power was needed to tame capitalism's excesses. Only Roberts and Stone remained from the old Court, and Stone had consistently deferred to the New Deal agenda. Despite this ideological transformation, Roosevelt's appointees split over the balance between the courts and the SEC in implementing this vision.

In the 1940s and 1950s, PUHCA cases, and claims arising under the bankruptcy statutes discussed in the next section, would dominate the Court's securities docket. Throughout the period, the Court deferred to the SEC's administrative expertise. Having brought to the Court a strong commitment to social control over finance, the justices appeared ready to ride the horse they came in on. Experts, not judges, should be answering the difficult questions involved in managing a modern economy.

Most of the PUHCA cases discussed here raised financial questions such as valuation, or weighing competing economic claims. A few, however, addressed procedures under the statute. *Chenery I*, discussed in more detail in Chapter 3, is the SEC's only loss during the period, but the agency ultimately prevailed when the case returned to the Court four years later. Chapter 3 uses the *Chenery* cases to explore the procedural concerns arising in the expanded administrative state. Those concerns gained more traction after the PUHCA breakups had been completed. Chapter 3 traces that procedural thread through the 1970s as the Court's faith in agency expertise declined. Here we focus on PUHCA cases involving economic issues.

*Otis & Co. v. SEC*, decided in 1945, showed the broad discretion accorded to the agency in carrying out its work under the Act.[70] That result was not without (private) drama, as the justices debated among themselves the appropriate level of deference to the agency. The Court upheld the SEC in negating a contractual liquidation preference for preferred shareholders in a proceeding to wind down a holding company. The contractual preference applied to "liquidation of the corporation, whether voluntary or involuntary." Applying the preference would have given all of the equity to the preferred shareholders, excluding the common

## 56 A HISTORY OF SECURITIES LAW

shareholders entirely. The SEC chose instead to ignore the contractual preference and instead valued the preferred stock on a going concern basis. This made space for an award of a small percentage of the value of the liquidated company to the common stockholders.

The SEC's approach conflicted with the Court's bankruptcy precedent. The Court had previously held in a bankruptcy proceeding—in a unanimous opinion written by Douglas—that violations of the absolute priority rule among securities holders were unfair and inequitable.[71] Was following absolute priority required for a reorganization to be "fair and equitable" under PUHCA § 11(e)? Frankfurter argued in a letter to Reed (who wrote for the majority) that there was little reason to construe the identical language "fair and equitable" one way for the Bankruptcy Act, adopted in 1934, and another way for PUHCA, adopted in 1935. Frankfurter noted that "having spent most of my professional life before I came on the Court with concern for adjudications by this Court in the light of reason, I do not think I should have less concern that the decisions of the Court be rooted in reason now that I am a member of the Court." Chief Justice Stone's reaction was not as condescending, but more dramatic, declaring at the Court's conference that affirming the SEC would be tantamount to saying that the "Commission is God."[72] The majority affirmed the SEC's divinity, holding that "[w]here pre-existing contracts provisions exist which produce results at variance with a legislative policy which was not foreseeable at the time the contract was made, they cannot be permitted to operate." The common stockholders had bargained for the risk of insolvency, but not PUHCA. The Court majority was giving the SEC a clean slate, a judicial New Deal as it were, unencumbered by the Court's interpretations of analogous laws. The holding strongly signaled that the Court would afford the SEC latitude in valuing the interests of securities holders in holding company reorganizations, not only on questions of fact, but also questions of law.

In another case challenging the SEC's valuation metrics—this time whether the SEC could use the going concern value of preferred stock over liquidation value—a unanimous Court applied *Otis* and again deferred to the agency's choice.[73] Two years later, *Niagara Hudson Power Corp. v. Leventritt* marked the complete triumph of administrative expertise over the market's valuation.[74] Harold Burton, writing for the Court, upheld the SEC's assignment of zero value to outstanding stock warrants. Notably, the warrants had no time limit for their exercise, ensuring that they would have some option value, even if currently out of the money. More damning still to the SEC's valuation, the warrants were trading—buyers were willing to pay *something*. The Court nonetheless deferred to the SEC's determination that "there is no ground for a reasonable expectation that, within the foreseeable future the warrants would be in the money. . . ." The Court's approach was clear, "[w]here the line is to be drawn is a matter for the expert judgment of the Commission." Market assessments—no matter how clear— could not trump the SEC's administrative judgment.

SOCIAL CONTROL OF FINANCE  57

A decade and a half later, Douglas and Brennan, each writing for the Court in a pair of opinions arising out of the same dispute, upheld the SEC's prediction of future valuation based on expected management performance.[75] A holding company was seeking to operate both an electric and gas facility in the same area. PUHCA permitted such an overlap only upon a showing of "substantial economic loss" if the systems were operated separately. The company showed a loss but the SEC argued that performance could be improved by "focused management."[76] In the second decision of the pair, the Court declared, "A court may believe it would have done the job differently and better; but judicial inquiry must be addressed to whether what the Commission did is fatal to its ultimate conclusion that the holding company failed to carry its burden."

Departures from the Court's hands-off approach to the SEC's administration of PUHCA were rare. Murphy wrote a draft of an opinion that would have upheld an SEC finding that the North American Company's ownership of 17% of Pacific Gas & Electric Company ("PG&E") voting securities and representation on PG&E's board were a sufficient basis to conclude that North American controlled PG&E, despite the lack of evidence of any influence by North American over PG&E's policies. That result was derailed when Frankfurter switched his earlier vote creating a 4-4 deadlock.[77] He explained to Murphy:

> After much travail I am constrained to conclude that the S.E.C. made its decision in the case on unsustainable legal criteria. That they could have reached the same result exclusively on their allowable interpretation of the facts, or that they may hereafter reach the same conclusion on such an appraisal of the facts, can not from my point of view justify our approval of erroneous criteria laid down by the Commission. You see you have educated me to keep these agencies within the legal bounds prescribed by Congress. This is for me fundamentally another *Chenery* situation.

The SEC had not lived up to the exacting standards that Frankfurter expected from the agency. Murphy was not happy with Frankfurter's switch, as it deprived him of his majority, and with Douglas recused as usual, the SEC's action would be upheld by an equally divided court. This rendered Murphy's "many long hours . . . spent on the P.G.&E. opinion" a waste, but the result was the same: the SEC won. Murphy was prepared to write off his labor, but he was more impatient with Frankfurter's explanation (or lack thereof) for his switch: "I am . . . at a loss to know what it is that has made you change your mind. If, as you say, it is the erroneous criteria used by the SEC, I ask you to reread my opinion and tell me what you think is wrong."[78]

Murphy was consistently the justice most willing to defer to the SEC's expertise, so his assignment to most of the PUHCA opinions during his tenure was surely welcomed by the agency. Murphy's trust of the experts was sufficiently great

58    A HISTORY OF SECURITIES LAW

that he was willing to construe standing narrowly in PUHCA reorganizations because of a worry that minority shareholders might harass the SEC. The Court
majority, however, was not willing to go so far.[79] In another case, the Court gave
the agency more leeway to determine whether a challenge to an enforcement
proceeding would go forward in the district court or the court of appeals.[80]

The Court treated most of these PUHCA opinions as routine, seldom going
in-depth into policy reasons. Douglas, however, wrote a 1955 opinion for the
Court in *Drexel* that showed some of the old-time religion. The Court upheld the
SEC's reservation of jurisdiction to pass on the reasonableness and allocation of
fees and expenses paid to underwriters in connection with the reorganization of
Electric Bond & Share.[81] Douglas surely drew from experience when he wrote:

> Payment of excessive fees was one of the historic abuses of the reorganization
> procedure whereby utility companies were milked, an abuse the Public Utility
> Holding Company Act sought to correct....
> ... Congress had before it the detailed record of holding company activities
> and knew that many of them had a proclivity for predatory practices. The fees
> were not only large; they were often loaded on affiliated companies and con-
> cealed in intrasystem accounts.

SEC oversight was essential to eliminate those abuses, in Douglas's view. Douglas
had now—belatedly after his many recusals—placed himself with the Court's
majority in giving the SEC free rein. Frankfurter again found himself in dissent,
this time joined by Burton.[82]

The Court majority was consistently willing to afford the agency wide latitude
to fight the abuses that had led to the enactment of the New Deal laws. With so
many of the justices involved in the drafting, implementation, or the litigation
defense of those laws, thoroughgoing support for the SEC and its mission was
almost inevitable. Frankfurter, whose guidance and lobbying for those laws had
been so essential, was waging a lonely battle to keep the SEC to what he saw as the
letter of the law. He had little to show for his efforts.

## C. Reorganizations of Distressed Firms:
### The Chandler Act of 1938

### 1. The SEC's Role in Bankruptcy

Having created the SEC to be the government's expert agency to regulate
American business in 1934, Roosevelt had a ready tool when his administration
decided to make further inroads into corporate governance during his second

term. The Chandler Act, like the earlier New Deal securities laws, put the SEC at the center of important business decisions, displacing the investment bankers' traditional authority.[83] Like PUHCA, the Chandler Act went beyond mere disclosure to give the SEC a key role in the reorganization of troubled firms.[84]

The securities laws of Roosevelt's first term dealt with public offerings, the NYSE, and the utility holding companies, all addressing abuses well known to the general public. Bankruptcy reorganization, by contrast, was a dark corner of finance, poorly understood by anyone other than the insiders who dominated the process. For reform to gain traction, it was necessary to build a case documenting the abuses of the protective committees. Only then would the political demand be there for government control.[85]

Congress's directive in the Exchange Act to study protective committees created that opportunity to help establish the case for fundamental changes in business reorganization.[86] Bill Douglas was the man for the job. For Douglas, corporate reorganization was a recurring professional focus. He had undertaken an empirical study with a New Jersey federal judge of bankruptcy filings in several districts and had been a part of the Donovan and Thatcher reform efforts referenced above.[87] Douglas's campaign to be chosen an SEC commissioner had been stymied in 1934 by Landis's opposition based on Douglas's critique of the Securities Act. Landis's antipathy for Douglas was apparently not deep rooted, however, as Landis recruited him to conduct the study of protective committees in bankruptcy. Over the next several years Douglas split his time between Washington and New Haven, assembling a talented team to work on the study, including his future Supreme Court colleague, Abe Fortas. This research would eventually catapult Douglas to the SEC and its chairmanship, just as he had planned.[88]

By the time the protective committee's study first report was ready (there would eventually be eight volumes), bankruptcy reform was gaining momentum in Congress. Douglas had now gained his coveted seat on the Commission, and would soon succeed Landis as its chairman. He and others described the work of the protective committee study as "briefs" for congressional action.[89] Three separate bills were under discussion; the SEC chose to combine its proposals with those of the Chandler Bill, which became Chapter X of that bill.[90]

The Chandler Act required a trustee in every public company reorganization. The insertion of trustees brought broad changes in the reorganization process, displacing both the investment bankers and management. As one prominent reorganization attorney put it, "In the name of 'democratization' corporate securityholders are to be enlisted in a war on corporate management. Not merely are bankers to be scourged from the temple, but corporate officers and directors are to be driven out with them." In addition, a reorganization plan had to be "fair and equitable" to be approved by the court. To ensure that standard was met, the statute directed courts to solicit the SEC's advice in reorganizations involving over \$3 million in debt, allowing courts to solicit the agency's advice in smaller reorganizations.[91] The SEC established a reorganization branch and Chairman Douglas appointed Sam Clark as its head. Clark had served on the staff of the protective committee study and was the brother of Douglas's former Yale Law dean, Charles Clark. Bringing the SEC in to advise the court ensured that the agency's experts would be the key players in the reorganization of public companies, building on the agency's role in reorganizing holding companies under PUHCA. According to Jerome Frank, who succeeded Douglas as SEC chairman, the SEC's presence had transformed reorganizations from "a battle of wits, strategy and endurance" into an administrative "study and solution of a problem in financial rehabilitation with conscious attention to the business principles and the public interests involved." By giving the SEC a central role, Congress thwarted efforts by investment bankers to call around and pick off creditors one by one to gain approval for a reorganization. The following year, Congress passed the Trust Indenture Act of 1939, which closed off the ability of investment bankers to go outside the reorganization process to gain contractual modifications for companies in distress.[92] The result was "to usher investment bankers out of the reorganization practice they had long controlled."[93]

The Chandler Act and the SEC's authority in company reorganizations did not take long to find their way to the Supreme Court. The *U.S. Realty* case of 1940 announced the triumph of the administrative state in the securities arena, just four terms after the scathing rebuke in *Jones v. SEC*.[94] Robert Jackson, soon to be the seventh of Roosevelt's eight additions to the Court, argued the case as Attorney General. By that time, the Court had already been transformed by FDR's appointees. In *U.S. Realty*, a 5-3 majority approved a broad role for the SEC in corporate bankruptcy reorganizations. Stone—long sympathetic to the goals of the Roosevelt administration, as we saw in Chapter 1—joined with four new Roosevelt appointees to make a majority. Three remaining members of the *Jones* majority (Hughes, Roberts, and McReynolds) were now in dissent.

Stone's majority opinion connects Chapter X, the core reorganization chapter of the bankruptcy code inserted by the Chandler Act, to the other New Deal securities statutes: each injects the SEC's "impartial and expert administrative assistance in the ascertainment of facts, in the detection of fraud, and in the understanding of complex financial problems" for the protection of the public. The opinion upheld the trial court's determination—following the SEC's recommendation—that the bankrupt company should be required to reorganize under the new Chapter X provided by the Chandler Act, rather than under Chapter XI. The SEC had argued that Chapter XI did not provide the safeguards of an independent trustee or the SEC as a monitor. The Court rejected the Commission's argument that public companies always must

SOCIAL CONTROL OF FINANCE    61

reorganize under Chapter X because it did not find a bright-line division between public and private companies in the statutory language. Nevertheless, the Court gave the SEC broad license to police improper uses of Chapter XI, despite the fact that the Act was equally silent on this point. The opinion below had concluded that "[a] governmental agency has no general right of intervention 'in the public interest.'"[95] The Court's majority, however, located that authority in the policy of the Act, including not just the statute's terms, but also in the equity power of the bankruptcy court. That equitable authority would come to play a dramatic role in the Court's securities cases of the 1960s, as we shall see in Chapters 5 and 6.

Douglas, having joined the Court the prior year, did not participate in the final decision. Notwithstanding his formal non-participation, Douglas's views likely shaped the debate. He wrote a memorandum, which he shared with Frankfurter and likely with Stone, who was by then drafting the Court's opinion.[96] Douglas's memo rejected the sharp line between Chapters X and XI for which the SEC had argued. Instead, Douglas urged guidelines consistent with those in the Court's ultimate opinion. Those guidelines would also appear in subsequent Chapter X opinions discussed below. Douglas's recusal from the final decision might have seemed unsurprising at the time given his recent involvement with reorganization at the SEC. By his account, however, there was no basis for disqualification:

> I sat on the case[.] I was not disqualified, having nothing to do with the matter when I was at the SEC. But I discovered later that the CJ [Hughes] was very anxious to have me withdraw. Stone told me "The Chief would like to have you out of the case." "Why?" I asked. "Because your vote will make it more difficult for him to carry the Court," said Stone. So [I] spoke to the Chief, telling him that I was not disqualified but stating that perhaps I should not participate. He said he thought that would be wise, since I had been so recently connected with the S.E.C. If the Chief had had his way, it would be another Jones decision.

Douglas's vote was not critical to the outcome; the triumph of the administrative state was already complete by the time of *U.S. Realty*. In four years, the SEC had gone from being denounced as a "Star Chamber" in *Jones* to being deemed essential to investor protection in *U.S. Realty*. This transformation was a critical part of the Roosevelt administration's overall judicial triumph.[97]

Despite his recusal in *U.S. Realty*, Douglas was having an impact on the Court's bankruptcy jurisprudence in cases not involving the SEC. In his first year on the bench, he had already written two important bankruptcy opinions for the Court, *Case v. Los Angeles Lumber* and *Pepper v. Litton*.[98] In both he succeeded in getting the cases heard over the Chief Justice's opposition; Douglas's views carried the Court in each. The *L.A. Lumber* decision overturned a pre-Chandler

# 62  A HISTORY OF SECURITIES LAW

Act reorganization that had permitted stockholders to participate in a plan in which the bondholders had not recovered their full claim. Douglas predicted the opinion "should have a healthy effect and curb the reorganization racketeers—the holding companies and the investment bankers who want to keep their preserves inviolate and under their control."[99] Douglas's determination to displace the "reorganization racketeers" was of a piece with the SEC's role in bankruptcy—the "old gang" was being squeezed out.

The agency's role, however, as with PUHCA, did not survive in the long run. Over succeeding decades, the Supreme Court heard three additional cases following up on *U.S. Realty*, each upholding the SEC's position. *General Stores Corp. v. Shlensky* in 1956 was Douglas's first participation in a Court ruling on the SEC's work in a Chapter X case, seventeen years after leaving the agency.[100] He disposed of the issue in eleven paragraphs, tracking his 1940 memo and Stone's *U.S. Realty* opinion in rejecting a bright-line approach. The opinion suggests criteria, grouped under the heading of "needs to be served" for determining when bankrupts must proceed through Chapter X. Almost a decade later in *American Tractor Rentals*, a unanimous Court rejected another effort by a bankrupt company, this one a company with a large number of public investors, to avoid Chapter X and the SEC's strong hand, even while again rebuffing the agency's effort to make the Chapter X route exclusive.[101] Three years later, in the Court's last Chapter X opinion, a splintered Court upheld an SEC objection to the settlement of a Chapter X case that involved a question of valuation and somewhat hazy questions of misconduct.[102]

Douglas's multifactor test left the door open to public corporation reorganization through Chapter XI. That space would eventually allow companies to avoid the SEC's role in reorganizations. Over time, the SEC role's in working out reorganizations for troubled companies diminished. In 1978, Congress eliminated the SEC's role in bankruptcy altogether.[103] By the 1970s, government control over industry and the delegation to an administrative agency to make the key organizing decisions had fallen out of fashion.

## 2. Bankruptcy and Insider Trading

A separate batch of reorganization cases afforded the Court the opportunity to address insider trading, long before it became a key aspect of the Court's securities jurisprudence. It was not until 1962 that the Court took a case under § 16(b) of the Exchange Act, the formulaic disgorgement remedy intended to discourage insider trading (discussed in Chapter 5). The common law rules of deceit, which the Court had used to address insider trading in 1909,[104] would not emerge again until the 1960s. In the interim, the Court dealt with insider trading only in the reorganization context.

The *Chenery I* and *II* cases are discussed at greater length in Chapter 3, but they provide an early glimpse of the SEC's approach to insider trading. In the first *Chenery* case decided in 1943, the SEC had punished insiders' purchase of preferred stock during a reorganization by substantially reducing their economic claim in the reorganized company.[105] The SEC had said it was applying "broad equitable principles" of cases such as *Pepper v. Litton*[106] and Cardozo's classic statement of fiduciary duty in *Meinhard v. Salmon*.[107] Frankfurter, writing for the majority, declined to let the agency expand the prohibited space for insider trading absent a specific showing of insider misuse or by passing a rule "expressing a more sensitive regard for what is right and wrong" than the extant common law regime when PUHCA became law.[108] When the case returned to the Court four years later, a new majority took a more generous view of the agency's power, even in the absence of rule-making.[109] This majority interpreted the Commission's order as grounded in its expertise. Managers held "a formidable battery of devices" that if used selfishly could unfairly affect the allocation of securities among existing classes in a reorganization, even absent proof of intentional wrongdoing.

The Court subsequently decided three bankruptcy cases that each provided a reprise of the core question, but did little to advance the law of insider trading beyond the two *Chenery* decisions. In *Manufacturers Trust* in 1949, *Mosser v. Darrow* in 1951, and *Wolf v. Weinstein* in 1963, the Court heard cases relating to insider trading in various bankruptcy settings.[110] The first was a Chapter XI proceeding, the second a Chapter 77B reorganization, and the last a classic Chapter X reorganization. In each case, the SEC, as an amicus, intervener, or plaintiff, challenged insider trading by officers, directors, managers, or employees of those running the reorganization. In the first two cases the plan of reorganization effectively penalized the insiders by reducing compensation or the amount they were to receive in exchange for their stock in the reorganization.

In *Manufacturers Trust*, just two years after *Chenery II*, Tom Clark's opinion for the Court attracted Frankfurter and Jackson from one side of the *Chenery* dispute, and Reed from the other. The question was decided along the lines of *Chenery I*, supported by existing precedent: "When the transactions here are drawn alongside a good faith standard of fiduciary obligations, they appear unobjectionable." Clark rejected an SEC claim that good faith and fair dealing would be inadequate because of what a director might do. The deference that the SEC got in the PUHCA context, where the agency managed reorganizations by itself, did not go as far in bankruptcy, where the agency merely offered advice to the court.

64   A HISTORY OF SECURITIES LAW

Clark's opinion did, however, nod in the direction of Second Circuit Judge Learned Hand's dissenting opinion below, which had acknowledged more nuance in the question.[111] (Burton and Black embraced Hand's reasoning in their dissent.) Hand distinguished between director freedom to buy shares in the market under the traditional rule and what would apply in a liquidation. He also went further in criticizing the failure of the common law to resolve the inevitable conflict between, on the one hand, forbidding such purchases that would dampen the directors' zeal and, on the other, permitting the directors to gain at the shareholder's expense. Hand acknowledged:

> The common law was unable to affect any compromise between the opposing considerations and chose the second. On the other hand, the Securities Exchange Act succeeded better by forbidding "quick turns" in shares by directors, yet circumscribing his freedom no further.

Clark's opinion for the Court at least left the door open to the SEC to submit "a body of evidence . . . presumably informed by expert understanding." The agency had not done so, however, in *Manufacturers Trust*.

Two years later in *Mosser v. Darrow*, the Court found the requisite evidence. Two employees hired by a trustee in an equity reorganization regularly bought company debentures, both in the over-the-counter markets and face to face, before reselling them to the trustee. The Court's opinion again attracted a majority from both sides of the *Chenery* dispute—Jackson and Frankfurter, as well as Reed. Douglas, not recused for once, signed on as well. Broad principles sufficed in Jackson's opinion for the Court to draw a bright line: "Equity tolerates in bankruptcy trustees no interest adverse to the trust. . . . The motives of man are too complex for equity to separate in the case of its trustees the motive of acquiring efficient help from motives of favoring them." That the employees, rather than the trustee, were the ones profiting, made no difference.

The third case, *Wolf v. Weinstein*, decided more than a decade later, turned on the reorganization statute's equivalent of the disgorgement provision in § 16 of the Exchange Act. Brennan, writing for the Court's majority, cited then-Chairman Douglas's 1938 testimony regarding § 249 of the Chandler Act: "We visualized a lot of administrative difficulties in defining trading so we decided to broaden the base a little bit and establish a rule of thumb." Brennan explicitly linked § 249 to § 16(b) as "cumulative" laws to address parallel practices. Douglas joined the majority as did his fellow New Dealer Black; the more recent additions of Clark, Warren, White and Goldberg joined as well. The opinion was based purely on statutory construction; equitable principles would not surface until *Capital Gains* later that year.

## D. Retiring the SEC's Control

The Court cases deferred to the SEC in both PUHCA and bankruptcy reorganization through the 1960s. That parallel path ends with the 1960s, however, as the Court heard no more cases involving the SEC in either area. Congress would eventually end the SEC's authority in both fields. What does the evolution of the SEC's role in these areas tell us about social control of finance?

The *New England Electric System* decision in 1968 was the Court's last PUHCA decision. Why the last? Like a fire that eventually burns itself out, the SEC had run through the universe of public utility conglomerates that needed to be broken up. The SEC continued to work on some cases after 1968, but none made their way to the Supreme Court. In 1982 the SEC recommended that Congress repeal PUHCA, with Congress eventually obliging in 2005.[112]

PUHCA's draconian death sentence responded to an industry in which financial opaqueness masked extensive self-dealing. That opaqueness afforded utilities an advantage over state public utility commissions charged with setting rates for monopoly power suppliers. It also covered over excessive leverage that played a role in the economy's systemic failure and the ensuing devastation that followed. The combination occurred in an industry with an unusual pyramidal structure driven by regulatory barriers to realizing economies of scale. These idiosyncratic features of the industry made it easier to impose a drastic industry-specific solution and put the SEC in charge.[113]

Decades later the power industry faced a similar financial reverse with a number of the characteristics that had beset holding companies re-emerging. Enron accumulated interest in gas and electric power distribution that by 2002 had propelled it to a top five revenue position among all American companies. It used a wide range of transactions with affiliates and byzantine accounting to prop up its balance sheet and engage in related-party transactions that misled state regulators.[114] This scandal too produced a dramatic government response. The SEC's authority would again be the focus, but the reforms took a different form than in 1935. The Enron response essentially federalized the review of auditing procedures. It also significantly expanded disclosure obligations for a large number of specific practices used by Enron. These rules were applicable to all public companies, however, rather than a particular industry.[115] By the twenty-first century, social control of finance had shifted. The focus was corporate governance, not capital structure, and even then, the principal tool was disclosure rather than a government mandate. The response to the Enron scandal added on to the disclosure requirements of the Securities Act and Exchange Act; it did not set the stage for PUHCA's revival. Politicians had lost faith in the government's ability to manage a significant sector of the economy, even under the direction of the expert SEC.

## 66  A HISTORY OF SECURITIES LAW

The Chandler Act had a different evolution. The SEC successfully displaced the investment bankers and the elite reorganization bar that had controlled the pre-New Deal reorganization process, with the agency assuming a central role in reorganizing troubled public companies. The investor protections in the new system came at a cost, in money and in extra time associated with the protections. Over time the managers, the lawyers who assumed the elite firms' role in the process, and the bankruptcy referees (judges) who themselves benefited from an expanded role within the federal judiciary, found common ground in the evolution of an alternative process: that alternative not only replaced the roman numerals of the Chandler Act, but also the SEC's role as the go-to expert in reorganization law.

The SEC had pushed for amendments to the Chandler Act as early as 1940 to make Chapter X the exclusive venue for companies with one hundred or more shareholders. After the *U.S. Realty* decision, the House Judiciary Committee reported there was no longer a pressing need for legislation. The agency renewed its effort after the *General Stores* decision in the late 1950s. In 1958, the SEC dropped the proposal in the face of opposition from the National Bankruptcy Conference, a key group of lawyers, judges, and academics.[116]

The absence of a strict mandate requiring Chapter X for public companies did not frustrate the SEC in implementing the Act. The Supreme Court continued to be amenable to the agency's views, as reflected in both *U.S. Realty* and *General Stores*. But things were changing on the ground. In 1952 Congress had deleted the "fair and equitable" requirement from Chapter XI, removing a barrier to the use of that Chapter in a larger set of reorganizations.[117] By the 1950s, Chapter XI was the venue of choice for many middle-sized firms and thereafter larger and larger firms continued to migrate toward Chapter XI. Trial courts were less willing to impose transfers. As David Skeel put it, "the smoother waters of Chapter XI . . . held a powerful allure for the bankruptcy judge just as they did for the debtor's management and lawyers."[118] When the decade-long effort to draft bankruptcy reform came to Congress in 1978, the Senate bill provided for a continued role for the SEC (that bill had been pushed by the bankruptcy judges), but the House bill, which originated in the National Bankruptcy Conference, did not. The provisions of the Senate bill improving the status of bankruptcy judges made it into the final bill; the SEC provisions were left out. In more prosperous economic times—and in the absence of villains so visible in the 1930s—the appetite for expert agency control of business had faded away.

# 3

# Policing the SEC

> With every impulse to sustain the Commission, . . . I cannot escape
> the conviction that the Commission has decided this case *ad hoc*
> without any reference to considerations that would govern it in the
> same case tomorrow. . . .
> . . . The SEC is not a Kadi sitting under a tree, dispensing judgment
> in each case, unrelated to general considerations.
> Letter from Justice Felix Frankfurter to Justice Hugo Black (Dec. 23,
> 1946), Robert Jackson Collection, Library of Congress, Box 138

The battle over PUHCA confirmed Congress's constitutional authority to allocate sweeping power to the SEC, but many questions remained concerning the relationship of the agency with the Court. As progressives saw it, judicial interference had hamstrung administrative agencies prior to the New Deal. Federal agencies had received little deference, even with respect to fact-finding. A scholar studying the work of the Federal Trade Commission in 1924 found that "a search of the opinions of Circuit Courts of Appeals and of the Supreme Court does not reveal a single case" in which "the findings of the Commission have in any way affected the decision of the court."[1] The Court's vow in the *Jones* case in 1936 to ward "off the appropriation of unauthorized power by lesser agencies" suggested that the Supreme Court would keep a tight leash on the SEC. After *Jones*, FDR's appointees began to displace the old guard. Would the rapid turnover translate into more room for the SEC to maneuver?

This chapter traces the Roosevelt Court's early development of administrative law that drew on the pre-New Deal Progressives' calls for judicial tolerance of agency discretion. Agencies would surely be afforded more latitude, but the hard question remained: What form would judicial review take in the new administrative state? In a 1936 dissenting opinion, Brandeis had urged deference to agency fact-finding, but suggested that judges might have a role to play with regard to legal questions; due process might require an "opportunity to have some court decide whether an erroneous rule of law [had been] applied" by an agency or "whether the proceeding in which the facts were adjudicated was conducted regularly."[2]

Roosevelt's third appointment, Felix Frankfurter, had a deep prior engagement with administrative law including a key role in the legislative enactments

*A History of Securities Law in the Supreme Court.* A.C. Pritchard and Robert B. Thompson, Oxford University Press.
© Oxford University Press 2023. DOI: 10.1093/oso/9780197665916.003.0004

68 A HISTORY OF SECURITIES LAW

discussed in Chapter 1. He seemed positioned to be the central player in such discussions on the Court. One of the biggest surprises of the Court's securities cases from the 1940s was Frankfurter's limited influence. His eclipse was most apparent in the switch between the two *Chenery* decisions at the center of this chapter. Roosevelt's other appointees, except Jackson, brushed aside Frankfurter's rule of law concerns. The majority was willing to provide more deference to SEC procedures than the former professor. Subsequent parts of the chapter fill in the deference that characterized most of the Court's securities decision through the early 1970s. We then focus on the more restrictive approach of the Powell era. Even though the procedural cases follow the same general arc, this area produced fewer high-profile decisions in the later period.

## A. A Progressive Reset?

Most of Roosevelt's appointees had front-line experience in the New Deal's expanded administrative state, but none had thought and written more about the role of agencies in government than Felix Frankfurter. Frankfurter had focused on administrative law throughout his time at Harvard, building on a progressive strain dating back half a century. His Dodge Lectures, presented at Yale in 1930, provided an eloquent summary of the challenges facing modern government and the necessity of administrative solutions. Dramatic changes to society wrought by the railroads and other manifestations of the Industrial Revolution changed the people's expectations of their governments: the "permeating influence of technology, large-scale industry, progressive urbanization, accentuation of groups and group interests, presses its problems on government." Administrative agencies were a necessary part of the solution, providing expertise and a continuous capacity to respond quickly to problems that legislatures could not match. Frankfurter in those pre-New Deal lectures had bitterly criticized the interventions of the Supreme Court thwarting such salutary regulatory efforts by the states.[3]

In advocating for the broad expansion of administrative power in his Dodge lectures, Frankfurter questioned the role of judges. He argued that judicial review of administrative agencies involved judges in "matters of fact and opinion not peculiarly within the special competence of judges." In doing so, Frankfurter recognized the central issue of this chapter:

> the power which must more and more be lodged in administrative experts, like all power, is prone to abuse unless its exercise is properly circumscribed and zealously scrutinized. For we have greatly widened the field of administrative discretion and thus opened the doors to arbitrariness.

The idea was not developed beyond that general admonition. Moreover, Frankfurter did not specify whether judges should be the actors to "zealously scrutinize" administrative agencies. Frankfurter's vagueness on the role that judges would play in overseeing the administrative state reflected the mainstream of progressive commentators at the time. Isaiah Leo Sharfman, for example, published a five-volume treatment of the Interstate Commerce Commission during the 1930s with views on administrative law that echoed Frankfurter's. He included a call for agencies to adopt "more meticulous procedures," but was still "quite sketchy" in spelling out what the constraints might be. Progressive writers recognized that agency procedures could not replicate judicial practices without losing the benefits of expertise and timeliness. James Landis, in his own series of lectures at Yale nearly a decade after Frankfurter, noted the "the tendency over the last few decades has been to decrease rather than increase the power of judges." He urged that that "agencies with procedures can be trusted as much as judges." Administrative agency findings of fact should be unreviewable; even agency interpretations of law should be entitled to deference, urged Landis, suggesting that "manipulative, deceptive or fraudulent" practices should be determined by the SEC, not the courts. His successor as SEC chairman, William O. Douglas, urged that administrative discretion:

> provides a realistic and sound alternative to hard and inflexible rules which proceed on the false assumption that right or wrong, black or white, constitute the only choice. But beyond that it permits of action not only case by case but by rules. A rule can be expanded, contracted or replaced in light of changed conditions or new experience. A formula fixed by legislative act tends to become more difficult to dislodge. Furthermore, the power to make rules means the power to deal with emergency situations—directly and with dispatch; in terms of minutes or hours rather than months or years. In a dynamic, fast-moving economic system responsible government must have a reserve of such powers if it is to save capitalism from its own complexities.[4]

There was a progressive consensus that administrative agencies needed considerable latitude to fulfill their promise.

In Frankfurter's first full term on the Court, in a case involving the Federal Communications Commission, he suggested that Congress should be supervising administrative agencies, not the courts: "Congress . . . must be trusted to correct whatever defects experience may reveal. Interference by the courts is not conducive to the development of habits of responsibility in administrative agencies." Later in that same term he signaled a broad deference to administrative expertise in a case arising from a ratemaking proceeding in Texas: "It is not for the federal courts to supplant the Commission's judgment even in the face

# 70    A HISTORY OF SECURITIES LAW

of convincing proof that a different result would have been better."[5] The second guessing of state agencies by federal courts under the guise of constitutional review was over.

There were signs a hands-off approach might also apply to federal administrative agencies. In the last year before the outbreak of World War II, Roosevelt fended off a legislative effort to rein in the agencies. The President had been weakened politically by reverses in the 1938 midterm elections (although retaining a party majority in both houses). The Congress which met in a lame duck session after Roosevelt had been elected to a third term in 1940 passed the Walter-Logan bill, which would have imposed more demanding judicial scrutiny of administrative agencies. That bill had its origins in reforms pushed by an American Bar Association committee chaired by Frankfurter's Harvard nemesis, Dean Roscoe Pound, a determined foe of "administrative absolutism." One of the bill's proponents in Congress, less diplomatic than Pound, had likened the SEC to "the tyrannies of the Gestapo of Germany, or the Russian Ogpu . . ." Not surprisingly, the SEC—one of the principal targets of the bill—had strongly opposed it. Roosevelt vetoed the legislation, decrying its "general philosophy of legal rigidity" and tarring it as "one of the repeated efforts by a combination of lawyers who desire to have all processes of government conducted through lawsuits and of interests which desire to escape regulations." Robert Jackson, then serving as Attorney General, provided a letter supporting the veto arguing that its provisions for judicial review were of "very doubtful [constitutional] validity." Pound characterized Roosevelt's veto message as "thoroughly in keeping with the Marxian idea of the disappearance of law. . . ."[6]

With Congress's attempted intervention rebuffed for a time, the question of judicial oversight of the administrative agencies remained for the courts to work out. Frankfurter urged that "the time has come for silly hostilities to cease, for us to give full acceptance to Administrative Law as an honorable and indispensable member of our legal household, instead of continuing to treat it as though it were a subverter."[7] Administrative law was now "honorable and indispensable"; how would that new status translate for the Court's relationship to the SEC?

## B. *Chenery I & II*: The Roosevelt Court Divides

By the time the *Chenery* case first came to the Supreme Court in the fall of 1942, the constitutionality of the securities laws was no longer in serious doubt. With Stone elevated to the center seat to replace Hughes, Roberts was the only justice who had not been nominated by Roosevelt. *Chenery I*, therefore, stands out, as it marked the SEC's first significant setback in the Supreme Court since *Jones* in 1936. The case is also notable as the Court's first brush with insider trading under

POLICING THE SEC    71

the federal securities laws. By looking to equity as the basis for an insider trading ban, it foreshadows the Court's forays into the question a generation later, when it again relied on fiduciary duty and fraud, a topic we cover in Chapter 5.[8]

The alleged insider traders were officers, directors, and controlling stockholders of the Federal Water Service Corporation who had acquired preferred stock in Federal during the course of a PUHCA reorganization. As Frankfurter characterized the rule of decision applied by the SEC, "respondents, as Federal's managers, were fiduciaries and hence under a 'duty of fair dealing' not to trade in the securities of the corporation while plans for its reorganization were before the Commission." As a sanction for the violation of that duty, the SEC refused to approve a plan put forward by the company that called for their preferred stock to be converted into common stock in the reorganized entity, thus depriving the managers of their gains from trading.[9]

The SEC's invocation of the term "fiduciary" provoked a now well-known lecture from Frankfurter on legal reasoning:

> But to say that a man is a fiduciary only begins analysis; it gives direction to further inquiry. To whom is he a fiduciary? What obligations does he owe as a fiduciary? In what respect has he failed to discharge those obligations? And what are the consequences of his deviation from duty?

Frankfurter, of course, knew the answers to these questions; the SEC had failed in its conclusory analysis. Frankfurter did not need to defer to the SEC as the expert on questions of corporate and securities law; *he* was the expert! As Frankfurter saw it, an important principle of administrative law was at stake: the agency needed to be clear about its rule of decision to facilitate judicial review of that decision. The agency was bound by its enabling statute; courts had to be able to determine whether the agency was following the statute. Here the SEC made a strategic error: it had not found that the insiders "acted covertly or traded on inside knowledge," but nonetheless concluded that they had violated "broad equitable principles" recognized in earlier judicial decisions.[10] The agency's invocation of earlier judicial decisions meant that its determination could be assessed against those decisions, which Frankfurter then proceeded to distinguish as inapposite.

The SEC would not necessarily be bound by these precedents, Frankfurter conceded, had the agency promulgated new rules reflecting its experience gained in working with the statute: "Congress certainly did not mean to preclude the formulation by the Commission of standards expressing a more sensitive regard for what is right and what is wrong than those prevalent at the time the Public Utility Holding Company Act of 1935 became law." Indeed, Frankfurter had consistently endorsed more demanding standards for fiduciaries. But once

## 72 A HISTORY OF SECURITIES LAW

the SEC had "professed to decide that case before it according to settled judicial doctrines, its action must be judged by [those] standards. . . ." Having dismantled the Commission's fiduciary duty reasoning, Frankfurter shut the door to judicially supplied alternatives by announcing the principle for which *Chenery I* is known in administrative law: "[A]n administrative order cannot be upheld unless the grounds upon which the agency acted in exercising its powers were those upon which its action can be sustained."[11]

This is now a bedrock principle of administrative law, but it may not have had the strongest of foundations at its inception. Frankfurter's majority was thin. Jackson, the fourth vote in a 4-3 decision, had written a draft concurrence in which he said, "where the administrative order depends upon legal grounds I should think it our duty to sustain an order that is right on correct legal principles even if the administrative body has assigned incorrect ones."[12] Despite these initial reservations, which seem hard to square with Frankfurter's reasoning, Jackson joined the majority without a separate concurrence.

Frankfurter's opinion broached another core issue of administrative law in suggesting an agency would be afforded greater freedom in rule-making than in formal adjudication. A court might defer to the SEC's "experience and insight" accumulated through its involvement in reorganization proceedings, but Frankfurter hinted that deference would only be given if the SEC "promulgated a general rule" proscribing the conduct in question. Indeed, in an earlier draft of the opinion, Frankfurter had gone further to suggest that the proper scope of deference to agency rule-making authority would require the invalidation of an administrative order if it had not previously adopted a rule. Chief Justice Stone suggested a more explicit endorsement of rule-making by the SEC was in order.[13] Frankfurter demurred:

> Of course I agree with you that had the SEC summarized their experience by putting the specific ruling in the *Chenery* case into a generalized rule, a totally different situation would have been created. But I thought it wiser to indicate that by innuendo rather than explicitly. To do the latter might be read by the Commission as a broad hint from us to issue a regulation. Thereby we would be stimulating new problems.[14]

Frankfurter's concern for "new problems" is cryptic. Is he suggesting that a new rule would be suspect? Or, just if it applied to this case, which might raise a retroactivity concern? Yet another possibility was that Frankfurter was worried about judicial micromanagement of agency procedure. But that was less likely given subsequent events, as we will discuss in this chapter.

The need for rule-making raised another point Jackson had made in his draft concurrence. Jackson had worried about lack of notice in generalized regulatory statues since his time as head of the Antitrust Division of the Department of Justice. In his draft, Jackson urged that the SEC's order was unsustainable because the insiders had not received notice that their conduct was illegal: "Surprise law is sometimes inevitable, but it seems almost bromidic to say that citizens are entitled to have some way of learning the general principles that they will suffer in person or property for transgressing." Thus, *Chenery I* presented two possible paths that administrative law and judicial review might take. One focused on the importance of the courts being able to review the reasons stated by an administrative agency in an adjudication; the other suggested administrative action done by rule-making would enjoy less intrusive judicial review. Frankfurter purposefully left it ambiguous in his opinion which administrative law message would control going forward.[15]

The need for advance notice provided by clear rules divided Frankfurter and Jackson from their more liberal colleagues. Black's dissent, joined by Murphy and Reed, rejected "[t]he intimation . . . that the Commission can act only through general formulae rigidly adhered to." In Black's view, PUHCA gave the SEC "wide powers to evolve policy standards, and this may well be done case by case."[16]

Frankfurter's long engagement with administrative law set him up to be the New Deal Court's leader on judicial review of agency action. Frankfurter certainly expected to be a leader and outside observers expected it as well. Moreover, Frankfurter "yearn[ed] for disciples," and he relentlessly badgered his colleagues to bring them into line with his own well-developed views. But *Chenery I* was the only majority opinion in a securities case that Frankfurter was to write in twenty-four years on the Court. In both *Chenery* cases, Frankfurter parted company with the more progressive vision of his fellow New Deal appointees, who were more willing to trust administrative expertise. By the time of *Chenery II*, Frankfurter was in the minority. Black's position would prevail in *Chenery II* and give rise to a second bedrock principle of administrative law. Frankfurter found himself increasingly isolated from what he perceived as a politically motivated coalition led by Black and Douglas.[17]

Frankfurter had two weaknesses that manifested themselves in the intramural *Chenery* debate. The first was his tendency to view those who disagreed with him as wanting either in intelligence or morals. An inveterate lobbyist of other members of the Court, he never admitted doing so, but rather perceived his own actions as helpfully 'advising' his brethren. His judicial opponents, however, were, in his view, cynically spreading their own influence. Frankfurter's contempt for what he perceived as Black and Douglas's political maneuvering is well known. Reed, who had welcomed Frankfurter's advice during his time as Solicitor General, told his clerks: "the trouble with Felix is that he never considers that he might be wrong: if you don't agree with Felix, you must be either stupid or dishonest!" Edward Prichard, Frankfurter's former student and law clerk, who

74  A HISTORY OF SECURITIES LAW

would later become a protégé of Chief Justice Fred Vinson, said that Frankfurter "did not have high regard for Vinson's judicial capabilities"; other justices also failed to live up to Frankfurter's demanding standard.[18]

To make matters worse, Frankfurter had difficulty hiding his views. Even justices who Frankfurter attempted to cultivate felt the sting of his contempt. In the words of a clerk, "he was an affronter." At times, his tactics could lead him to be overbearing toward his colleagues. According to Douglas,

> Frankfurter also indulged in histrionics in Conference. He often came in with piles of books, and on his turn to talk, would pound the table, read from the books, throw them around and create a great disturbance. His purpose was never aimless. His act was designed to get a particular Justice's vote or at least create doubts in the mind of a Justice who was thinking the other way. At times, when another was talking, he would break in, make a derisive comment and shout down the speaker.

Douglas was hardly an impartial observer, given the deep-seated antipathy that developed between the two, but his views were shared by other colleagues. Vinson, ordinarily an easy-going personality, once had to be blocked from striking Frankfurter in conference. The upshot was that Frankfurter's efforts to persuade tended to alienate. Within a few years of his appointment to the Court, Frankfurter's heavy-handed manner had left him with close connections to only Jackson and Owen Roberts.[19]

Those characteristics were starkly visible in *Chenery I* where Frankfurter had a majority. Frankfurter had been courting Reed as an ally, with some success, but Frankfurter could not hold back his impatience with Reed for having joined Black's opinion:

> Were I still at Cambridge I would be saddened to note that you underwrote an opinion like Black's dissent in the *Chenery* case. I don't think I should be less saddened because I am your colleague. I hate to see you "bogged down in the quagmire" of Populist rhetoric unrelated to fact.

This condescending introduction—so typical of Frankfurter in his relations with his colleagues—was merely the preface of an extended explication by Frankfurter on the distinction between the fiduciary duties of corporate directors and trustees and, more importantly, Frankfurter's views on administrative law. Frankfurter conceded that the SEC had the authority to depart from the common law rule, but in his view, the agency "made the purest kind of an *ad hoc* decision without any reason whatever for its conclusion except that these respondents were reorganization managers." The Commission's conclusion "affords no possible basis for a reviewing court to say that that which the Commission did was right. And so the case must be remanded to the Commission unless court review simply means rubber stamping what the Commission does." Frankfurter urged that the standards he expected from the SEC and other administrative agencies were essential to their long-term viability:

> Administrative agencies have two major functions. They exercise delegated legislation through their rule-making power, that is, they formulate general standards of conduct based on their experience and their expertness. The broadest leeway should be given to them in the exercise of this legislative function. Secondly, they exercise an adjudicatory function in disposing of specific controversies that come before them, much as courts would do if the jurisdiction in these matters were given to them. The *Chenery* case is such an exercise of the administrative adjudicatory process. And it is subject, therefore, to the requirement that the reviewing courts be enabled to know the basis of the determination of the administrative [*sic*] in order to discharge the court's function of review. I have spent most of my professional life in trying to get recognition for the indispensability of the administrative process. I do not want slipshodness and, still worse, lust for power[, to] lead to curtailment of these administrative powers by determinations without reason or by appeals to rules of law for which there is no warrant.

Frankfurter believed passionately in the administrative state—but he was equally fervent in his belief that the rule of law must apply to agencies if they were to survive. Those values would be enforced by judges, if necessary. Frankfurter had devoted much of his career to arguing for the proposition that courts should not invoke the Constitution to interfere with economic regulation by legislatures.[20] He did not equally believe in judicial restraint, however, when it came to holding administrative agencies to statutory standards—at least now that he was on the Court. Agencies were required to follow the rules set down for them by the legislature. It was the job of judges to ensure that those legislative commands were followed. This might mean ensuring that legal standards were followed in the course of adjudication, or it might mean insistence on rule-making when an agency wanted to apply a new rule that departed from common law standards.

Frankfurter's positioning of himself as the defender of the rule of law was calculated to annoy his colleagues. Reed by this time had grown tired of the professor's lectures and he believed that agencies should be given much broader latitude. In his reply, Reed argued "[y]ou [Frankfurter] say the Commission from its experience may fashion a new 'general' rule of conduct. I say, it has done just that. . . . [I]t said that fiduciary reorganization managers may not deal in stock of companies being reorganized." In Reed's view, the SEC was not

## 76 A HISTORY OF SECURITIES LAW

required to promulgate a formal rule: "A few such ad hoc decisions will result in a regulation—that is the way regulations grow." Reed was content to leave the SEC considerable space in which to grow its regulations:

> Every decision must be an ad hoc ruling, as I see it. An application of the Commission's idea as to "fair and equitable." Such application should be guided by precedents and regulations but may depart from them. If it does not go too far (arbitrary, capricious and unreasonable), it should be upheld. This is the essence of administrative law.[21]

Reed's incremental vision of administrative lawmaking anticipated minimal involvement from courts; indeed, it mirrored the rulemaking process of common law courts.

Reed's position would ultimately prevail as the New Deal Court's approach to securities law. The SEC, for its part, ameliorated some of the surprise element of its pronouncements by making liberal use of informal guidance, a practice that has developed into its current "No Action" letters. This was only a partial solution, however, as the SEC's use of informal guidance did not bind the agency going forward. More critically, the agency has generally been unwilling to offer advice on areas such as insider trading, where the prospect of potential criminal liability heightened concerns over fair notice.[22]

*Chenery* was remanded to the SEC in 1943, but it would return to the Court in 1946. In the interim, the divisions among the justices had devolved into open warfare. Jurisprudential differences were now exacerbated by sharp personal animosity. The tensions on the Court flared with the retirement of Roberts in the summer of 1945. Black refused to sign the customary letter from the justices thanking Roberts for his services, and Stone's best efforts were unable to broker a compromise.[23] The result was a very ungracious departure for the last of the Court's old guard.

These resentments spilled into public view when Chief Justice Stone died on April 22, 1946. Five of the sitting associate justices would have been delighted to be elevated to the center seat, with Douglas actively campaigning for the spot (and influence-peddler par excellence Tommy Corcoran assisting behind the scenes). Black and Jackson, however, were the primary contenders, with Jackson having been promised the spot by Roosevelt before his death. The Washington scuttlebutt was that neither would be willing to serve under the other. Moreover, Drew Pearson wrote in his prominent column that two members of the Court (implicitly, Black and Douglas), had threatened to resign if Jackson were made Chief Justice. In an effort to avoid the fallout that might follow from choosing between Black and Jackson, Truman instead appointed his Secretary of the Treasury, Fred Vinson. Truman's attempt to keep the peace among the brethren

POLICING THE SEC    77

failed. Jackson, bitter at having been passed over, wired the President from Nuremberg, where he was leading the prosecution of Nazi war criminals. Jackson also sent letters to the congressional judiciary committees, denouncing Black for having declined to recuse himself in a case involving a former law partner. That same week, Frankfurter described the Court's disarray in epochal terms: "Never before in the history of the Court were so many of its members influenced in decisions by considerations extraneous to the legal issues that supposedly control decisions."[24] Thus, it was a Court with extremely frayed personal relations and a sharp jurisprudential divide that heard *Chenery* when the case returned in the October 1946 term.

The SEC had responded to the Court's earlier remand by reaching the same result, but offering a different rationale. In *Chenery II*, Murphy, Black, and Reed, who had dissented in *Chenery I*, were now joined by new Justices Wiley Rutledge and Harold Burton to form a majority upholding the SEC's action. This majority explicitly rejected Frankfurter's suggestion in *Chenery I* that the agency should proceed by rulemaking: "[T]he choice made between proceeding by general rule or by individual, *ad hoc* litigation is one that lies primarily in the informed discretion of the administrative agency." This holding endures as a core principle of modern administrative law. Only Jackson joined Frankfurter in voting to overturn the SEC's decision. Douglas had recused himself as usual, but there could be little doubt that he would side with the liberal majority on the question of deferring to his old agency. Vinson, who had joined in the opinion below ruling against the SEC while a member of the federal appellate court, also did not participate. The Court was now committed to deference to agency discretion in choosing how to proceed; Frankfurter's concerns about judicial review of the agency performing an adjudicatory function were brushed aside.[25]

Frankfurter circulated a dissent that threatened another public blow-up. The case was argued in December and assigned to the notoriously slow Burton. After Burton failed to produce an opinion, the case was reassigned to Murphy in early June, as Murphy (or more accurately, his law clerk) had completed all of his opinions for the term. Murphy's clerk scrambled to draft an opinion in about a week's time. Frankfurter did not have time for a full-blown dissent with the Court's summer recess looming, so he circulated a draft dissent: "The Court's opinion in this case was not circulated until Tuesday, June 17th. Obviously that precluded opportunity before adjournment for the preparation, printing, circulation and consideration by the whole Court of a response adequate to the issues raised by the opinion." Frankfurter's inartful choice of language provoked a gentle scolding from Rutledge for "disclos[ing] the confidential routines of the Court." Moreover, Rutledge felt that Frankfurter's opinion put Murphy in a bad light: "[Murphy] will appear, if your circulation goes down, in the light of having caused all the delay. I do not think [that] implication is fair . . . ." Rutledge was

78  A HISTORY OF SECURITIES LAW

sufficiently distressed by Frankfurter's opinion that he wrote a draft concurrence exonerating Murphy of any blame for the lateness of the opinion. Frankfurter responded by deleting the reference to the date of circulation, instead attributing his failure to publish a full dissent to the "unavoidable lateness of the decision." Frankfurter's attempt at diplomacy fared little better, provoking an angry response from Murphy:

> I am asking Justice Frankfurter to delete all reference in his remarks to the "unavoidable lateness of the decision in this case." So far as the public is concerned, any decision rendered in the same term as that in which the case is argued is not "unavoidably" late. It is not unknown for cases to be argued early and decided late in the term. To say that such a decision is "unavoidably" late is thus to stir up needless speculation and comment by the public.

A chastened Frankfurter attempted to apologize:

> It must be due to naivete that it never occurred to me that the simple statement of an obvious fact could ever be deemed a departure, however remote, from the Court's tradition, or that it would touch anybody's sensitiveness....
>
> I am sorry even if unwittingly I should have touched the sensibilities of any of my brethren. In any event, long before the memorandum by brother Murphy reached me, I sent a revised phrasing of my notice of dissent to the printer. It says precisely what I believe it is appropriate to say, and says it in a way that does not, so far as I am able to judge, lend itself even to tortured misinterpretation.

Frankfurter had a rare gift, allowing him to offend—with his reference to "tortured misinterpretation"—even in the course of an attempted apology. His actual opinion, however, was inoffensive.[26]

It was Jackson, however, who took on the task of writing the full dissent for Frankfurter and himself. Perhaps reflecting the Court's tension, his dissent is a sarcastic attack (characterized by Frankfurter as a "rip-snorter"[27]) on the Court's reasoning and the SEC's lawlessness. "The Court's reasoning adds up to this: The Commission must be sustained because of its accumulated experience in solving a problem with which it had never before been confronted!"[28] Jackson's strident tone provoked an anxious memorandum from Vinson's law clerk, who worried that "it includes such ridicule of the majority position as possibly to intimate lack of integrity when applied to the product of able minds.... In view of publicity recently given to 'feuds' within the Court, I think the opinion may invite newspaper attention. . . ." The clerk's concern was justified; the newspaper headlines read "Jackson Says High Court Encourages Lawlessness."[29] Jackson scored polemical points, but Frankfurter passed up an opportunity to flesh out his vision of the rule of law in the administrative state.

In the months before *Chenery II* was decided, Congress finally passed the Administrative Procedure Act, a project long delayed by the war. (Attorney General Tom Clark, who would later replace Murphy on the Court, had negotiated its terms with Congress on behalf of the Truman administration.) The APA provided a partial response to Frankfurter's earlier concerns. The new statute imposed additional requirements of "substantial evidence" and judicial restraint of "arbitrary" and "capricious" actions, and sought to reverse what Congress may have perceived as "overly deferential judicial examination of agency factfinding." The Act itself reflected something of a political compromise, with the most restrictive and detailed provisions applicable to formal adjudications, leaving rulemaking with less intrusive and vague provisions. Over time administrative law would move further in Frankfurter's direction under the APA regime. Judicial deference to administrative expertise may have already begun to recede from its high point by the time of *Chenery II*.[30] At no point, however, would the Court require an agency to proceed through rulemaking, although it has hinted occasionally of a more demanding requirement.[31] That hands-off approach would have important consequences for the law of insider trading, as we discuss in Chapter 5.

## C. Judicial Review of SEC Procedures

*Chenery I* and *II* were the Court's headline SEC cases of the 1940s, and the deferential judicial stance mostly continued through succeeding decades until Lewis Powell arrived in 1972. Even the Roosevelt appointees most committed to deference joined in a rare, albeit mild, post-*Jones* rebuke to the government in *Edwards v. United States*. *Edwards* was the first criminal securities case to reach the Court.[32] Reed, writing for the Court, overturned a conviction when the defendant had not been provided a transcript of his appearance in an SEC investigation. The government asserted that the defendant had given no testimony of an incriminating nature and had offered a transcript to the court below, but Reed's opinion insisted on a right to cross-examine with the transcript as part of a certified record: "The refusal to permit the accused to prove his defense may prove trivial when the facts are developed. Procedural errors often are. But procedure is the skeleton which forms and supports the whole structure of a case." The Court rejected, however, the defendant's argument that the enactment of the Securities Act repealed by implication the mail fraud statute as it applied to the sale of securities. "The two can exist and be useful, side by side." Participants in the securities industry were put on notice that the

80 A HISTORY OF SECURITIES LAW

Justice Department had not lost any of its familiar tools for prosecuting fraudulent behavior.

The other case from the forties, *Penfield Co. v. SEC*,[33] upheld a finding of contempt and imprisonment for an officer's failure to produce documents to the SEC in connection to the agency's investigation into the corporation's sale of stock. The district court had declined to enforce the subpoena in light of a parallel criminal case, in which many of the documents had been produced to the prosecution. The circuit court reversed, however, holding that the SEC was still entitled to the documents.

Douglas, participating for the first time in a case in which the SEC was a party—eight years after leaving the agency—wrote the opinion for a unanimous Court. Douglas agreed with the court of appeals that the SEC was entitled to have its subpoena enforced:

> The records might well disclose other offenses against the Securities Act of 1933 which the Commission administers. The history of this case reveals a long, persistent effort to defeat the investigation. The fact that Young paid the fine and did not appeal indicates that the judgment of contempt may have been an easy victory for him. On the other hand, the dilatory tactics employed suggest that, if justice was to be done, coercive sanctions were necessary.

A little over a decade after *Jones*, the transformation of the Court's attitude toward the SEC was complete. The "Star Chamber" rhetoric was long gone—the Court would back the SEC's authority to do the tasks assigned to it by Congress. Frankfurter, joined by Jackson, dissented, urging deference to the district court, which had declined to impose a coercive sanction.

The Court dealt with a handful of cases involving the SEC's procedures in PUHCA cases in the 1950s and '60s, but the SEC's procedures in other areas would not receive the Court's scrutiny until the early 1970s. In *SEC v. Medical Committee for Human Rights* the SEC granted a no-action letter to Dow Chemical.[34] The company wanted to exclude from its proxy a shareholder proposal for a charter amendment banning the manufacture of napalm. The use of the chemical was a heated topic during the Vietnam War and in his pre-argument memo, Blackmun regretted the political controversy complicating the case:

> This presents an interesting question and perhaps a difficult one. Unfortunately, it is rather tainted, in my mind, because the issue of SEC proxy review has Vietnam war overtones. We are concerned with a very small institutional shareholder desiring to make a corporate issue of the manufacture of napalm by Dow chemical. I wish that this were out of the case. Everyone could then view the issue much more dispassionately.[35]

POLICING THE SEC    81

The procedural posture was unusual, a rare example of a court reviewing the SEC's decision to not oppose the company's proposed decision to exclude a shareholder proposal. The D.C. Circuit had overturned the agency's forbearance, finding that the agency had failed to adequately explain its decision. By the time the Supreme Court decided the case there was little left to the dispute. Dow had included the proposal in its proxy statement and it had received less than 3% of the shareholders' votes. Given the poor showing, the SEC's proxy rules allowed the company to exclude similar proposals from its proxy statement for the next three years.

Blackmun was inclined to defer to the SEC. "My own offhand reaction is that this is the very kind of thing which is committed to agency discretion under the Administrative Procedure Act." He did not want "a political issue and issue affecting corporate management, to wit, the determination of what products to manufacture," in court. "Surely, if Dow tomorrow decided to make traveling bags, we could hardly expect formal court review of the SEC's decision not to force that kind of proposition into a proxy statement. . . . To call for a review here would be to force rigid formality on to a minor SEC function." He doubted that "it is at all a matter of great import. The Government is complicated enough without adding this burden."[36] Blackmun's position, had it prevailed, would have maximized the SEC's discretion.

At conference, however, there was little appetite for reaching the merits. All the justices, save Douglas, thought the dispute had become moot. Marshall, writing for the Court, reasoned that there was no current controversy because it was speculative to think that the shareholder would resubmit the proposal. Even if it did, would Dow seek to exclude the proposal again instead of resubmitting it to the shareholders? In his original draft, Marshall noted that "while the decision of the Court of Appeals is no longer binding upon the parties, the careful consideration it gave to the mertis [sic] of underlying dispute may prove to be instructive to the parties, Dow and any reviewing court in the event that this litigation is renewed at some future date." Both Blackmun and Stewart objected to even this mild endorsement of the D.C. Circuit's reasoning, however, and Marshall removed the offending language.[37]

The Court's holding is unremarkable, but Douglas's shrill dissent stands out. Douglas thought the case presented a live controversy; the majority's decision not to reach the merits was one of "a growing list of monuments to the present Court's abdication of its constitutional responsibility to decide cases properly within its jurisdiction." Douglas's rhetoric recalled his crusade as SEC Chairman to assert social control of finance: "modern super-corporations, of which Dow is one, wield immense, virtually unchecked, power. Some say that they are 'private governments,' whose decisions affect the lives of us all." The initial draft had been even more intemperate in its assault on Dow: "Few corporations, however,

82   A HISTORY OF SECURITIES LAW

have been as consistent in adhering to the 'morals of the marketplace' as Dow. Its history of intransigent refusal to recognize the existence of a higher standard of corporate morality is well-known." Douglas used his published dissent to make a plea for corporations to be managed in the interest of stakeholders, presaging a twenty-first-century debate in corporate law: "The philosophy of our times, I think, requires that such enterprises be held to a higher standard than that of the 'morals of the market-place' which exalts a single-minded, myopic determination to maximize profits as the traditional be-all and end-all of corporate concern." Not satisfied with attacking Dow, Douglas also questioned a proposed SEC rule that would further limit shareholder proposals.[38] After thirty-two years on the bench, Douglas's fire to curb corporate power was undimmed. But the Court was moving further away from him, and he would dissent in the nine remaining securities cases that came to the Court during his tenure. Powell and Rehnquist had already been sworn in. Their arrival would bring a more skeptical attitude toward the SEC, as we shall see in the chapters that follow. The Court's early enthusiasm for social control of finance had faded away.

## D. The Skeptical Era

The Court's skepticism of the SEC can be seen in the procedure cases after Powell joined the Court, albeit in a diluted form. The most restrictive of the Court's opinions was *SEC v. Sloan*, decided in 1978.[39] *Sloan* involved the agency's authority under § 12(k) of the Exchange Act to "summarily . . . suspend trading in any security . . . for a period not exceeding 10 business days" if "in its opinion the public interest and the protection of investors so require."[40] In *Sloan*, the SEC had relied on this authority to issue orders summarily suspending trading in the common stock of Canadian Javelin—repeated orders, each ten days after the last, thus continuing the trading suspension indefinitely.[41]

The SEC had been issuing successive orders under this authority since 1944. The agency's interpretation, however, was hard to square with the statutory scheme. Section 12(j) of the Exchange Act authorizes the SEC to suspend securities from registration, which would have the effect of suspending trading for up to twelve months. That section, however, required the agency to give the affected company notice and a hearing.[42] By using its summary power, the SEC could avoid the notice and hearing requirements and thereby also avoid giving the company the opportunity for judicial review. Powell found it "[d]ifficult to believe Congress intended to allow the notice + hearing requirements of 12(j) to be by-passed by repetitive resort to 12(k)."[43] The SEC reinforced the impression that it was doing an end run around the statutory scheme by allowing orders to expire after Sloan sued—cutting off the opportunity for judicial review—only to renew them subsequently.[44] This was an easy application of the mootness exception for cases "capable of repetition yet evading review,"[45] which the Court had rejected in *Medical Committee*. The SEC's brazen circumvention of the statutory scheme did not sit well with the justices; even Bill Brennan, usually a dependable ally for the SEC, thought that an "[a]dmin. agency that acts as SEC did is not entitled to usual deference."[46] Harvey Pitt, general counsel of the SEC at the time, apparently drew the short straw and argued the case in the Court; he would bounce back from the defeat to later become chairman of the SEC.

The procedural questions sometimes overlapped with more substantive issues, covered in greater detail in the next three chapters. *Aaron v. SEC*, decided in 1980, is an example. The question presented was the required state of mind that the agency needed to prove to obtain a civil injunction in a fraud case. The question arose on the heels of *Ernst & Ernst v. Hochfelder*, (discussed in Chapter 6), which had rejected a private claim under Exchange Act Rule 10b-5 based on the defendant's negligence.[47] In an opinion written by Powell, the Court had held that fraud under § 10(b) required scienter. Powell's reasoning was a broad rejection of the "effect-oriented approach" that the SEC had urged, which Powell found inconsistent with the "operative language of the statute."[48] The SEC's only consolation in *Ernst & Ernst* was that Powell was forced, in order to hold his majority, to reserve the question of whether the scienter standard would apply to an action for injunctive relief brought by the SEC.[49]

*Aaron* squarely raised that question. The Second Circuit (in an opinion written by Judge William H. Timbers, former general counsel of the SEC) confined *Ernst & Ernst* to its facts in holding that the SEC only needed to show negligence when seeking an injunction under Rule 10b-5.[50] *Aaron* also raised an issue not present in *Ernst & Ernst*: the state of mind required for liability under § 17(a) of the Securities Act, which prohibited "any transaction, practice, or course of business which operates or would operate as a fraud or deceit upon the purchaser."[51] The 1960s Court had found, in *Capital Gains* (discussed in Chapter 5), that similar language in the Investment Advisers Act did not require the SEC to establish an intent to deceive.[52]

Both issues troubled Powell. He worried about the SEC as well as private litigants: "[A] suit [by the SEC] [and] an injunction are *punitive* [and] *can impose severe stigma* [and] other *penalties.*" In Powell's world, the harm to reputation from an injunction was at least as important as a monetary sanction. The SEC could overreach; the scienter standard protected defendants against unwarranted damage to their standing in the business community. Powell also agreed with his clerk that a looser interpretation of § 17 would lead the SEC to "pitch much of its enforcement effort toward that statute, but the provision is limited to those *selling* securities. . . . As a result, a certain asymmetry of enforcement policy

84  A HISTORY OF SECURITIES LAW

would develop, where negligent fraud by sellers of securities would be punishable while negligent fraud by buyers would not."[53]

Before the conference, Powell discussed the case with Potter Stewart, who had had questions about government proceedings in *Ernst & Ernst*, and the two of them settled on a resolution. Powell's discussion with Stewart was not unusual; Stewart was "by a long reach his closest colleague on the Court," and Powell regularly spoke to him about pending cases, which he did not generally do with his other colleagues. Powell brought Stewart around to the view that scienter under § 10(b) should be the same for both private and public plaintiffs, and Powell apparently came round to Stewart's view that § 17(a) could not be interpreted in the same way as § 10(b).[54] Arguably, for both justices, text prevailed over policy in *Aaron*.

At the conference, the Chief Justice led off by voting to affirm the Second Circuit. Stewart came next; he echoed Powell's concern that "injunctions are *fatal*" and proposed that the opinion should say that the "SEC should be cautious about issuing an injunction." Despite the consequences that an injunction had for defendants, Stewart found the language of § 17(a) could not be read to require a finding of scienter, although § 10(b) required a "knowing" violation. White, new to the Court back when *Capital Gains* had been decided, agreed that § 10(b) required a "knowing" violation, but § 17(a) did not. Powell and Rehnquist simply expressed their agreement with Stewart and White. Brennan, Marshall, and Blackmun made no effort to persuade their colleagues, simply voting to affirm. Finally, John Paul Stevens gave Stewart and Powell a majority, stating that he "would not have joined *Hochfelder*, but will accept it." With a majority for vacatur, the Chief Justice switched to the majority[55] and assigned the opinion to Stewart.

Stewart wrote the opinion, leaning "heavily + properly on *Ernst & Ernst*,"[56] in Powell's view. Stewart again reserved the question of whether the definition of scienter included reckless behavior, as Powell had done in *Ernst & Ernst*. Stewart distinguished *Capital Gains* on the grounds that § 206's language and legislative history differed from § 10(b)'s. Moreover, the *Aaron* Court was explicit in rejecting *Capital Gains*'s flexible/remedial interpretive principle: "generalized references to the remedial purposes of the securities laws will not justify reading a provision more broadly than its language and the statutory scheme reasonably permit."[57] The interpretive mood had dramatically changed from the 1960s.

Despite these rebuffs, *Aaron* preserved the enforcement tool of § 17(a) for the SEC, notwithstanding the misgivings of Powell and Stewart about the SEC's use of injunctions. The threat perceived by Powell was confined; Stewart took care to note that the Court did not address whether a private cause of action exists under § 17(a). Burger concurred to emphasize that in order for the SEC to show that there was a likelihood that the violation would be repeated, "it will almost always be necessary for the Commission to demonstrate that the defendant's past sins have been the result of more than negligence." Blackmun was again in dissent, joined by Brennan and Marshall, unpersuaded by the Court's attempt to distinguish *Capital Gains*.[58]

*Steadman v. SEC*, decided the following term, is a remarkable case for one reason: it is the *only* securities case in which Powell dissented, out of forty-one over sixteen terms.[59] The question was the standard of proof to be applied by the SEC in administrative proceedings to bar an investment adviser. The SEC had applied a preponderance standard. Powell worried that "[t]o bar a middle aged professional investment adviser from pursuing his vocation for life, and at the same time stigmatize him with a judgment of fraud, is more serious than most criminal penalties." For this reason, Powell favored the "clear and convincing" evidence standard borrowed from common law fraud. Despite his dissent, Powell conceded at conference that his vote to reverse was "very tentative." Without a more vigorous stand from Powell, his colleagues were not inclined to defer to his view on the relative severity of criminal and SEC sanctions. Consequently, the Court adopted the more typical civil standard of preponderance of the evidence. Stewart joined him, but not Rehnquist or Burger, who rarely departed from Powell in securities cases. White, Marshall, and Blackmun, swing voters in securities case, were also unswayed by Powell on this one. Blackmun, writing in the margin of the draft that Powell circulated, tartly observed that Powell was "Still representing t[ho]se corp[orate] clients."[60]

One final case implicated the SEC's investigative authority, hearkening back to *Penfield* nearly forty years earlier. In *O'Brien v. SEC* the Ninth Circuit required the SEC to provide notice to the targets of its nonpublic investigations that it was serving subpoenas on third parties.[61] The decision lacked any constitutional or statutory basis, and the Solicitor General argued that the Ninth Circuit's holding threatened to undermine investigations relating to over a hundred programs that used subpoenas of the type issued by the SEC. Even Powell did not want to see the SEC hobbled in its investigations. The Court voted unanimously to reverse; Powell's notes suggest that there was virtually no discussion.[62] *O'Brien* is of a piece with *Penfield* in giving the SEC wide latitude to investigate potential fraud.

The headlines provoked by *Jones* in the 1930s were not repeated by the Court's procedural cases of the 1970s and '80s. The later cases are notable, not for their salience individually, but rather, because of the deference that the SEC continued to enjoy in this area. The freedom the agency was afforded by the Court in the forties and fifties survived Powell's counterrevolution, which had such a profound effect in other areas of securities law. Powell's influence would be felt much more strongly in the subject areas of the three chapters that follow. Even amidst the Court's skepticism of the agency in the 1970s and '80s, there was still a consensus—including Powell—recognizing the importance of the SEC's

86 A HISTORY OF SECURITIES LAW

enforcement efforts. There was no revival of the hostility seen in *Jones*. The notable exception from the Court's support of the SEC's enforcement efforts was *Sloan*, in which the agency's approach seemed to fly in the face of the statutory framework. As long it stayed within statutory bounds, the Court would give the SEC room to enforce the securities laws.

## E. The Post-Powell Period

The Court's highest profile decision at the intersection of administrative law and securities law since *Chenery I and II—Free Enterprise Fund v. Public Company Accounting Oversight Board (PCAOB)*—had almost nothing to do with securities law.[63] *PCAOB* nominally involves the Sarbanes-Oxley Act of 2002, which set up the Public Company Accounting Oversight Board to regulate the accounting industry under the SEC's oversight, but it is primarily a constitutional separation of powers case. At issue was the provision of that law making PCAOB board members removable only by the SEC, and then only "for good cause shown."[64] This provision was challenged as violating the separation of powers because it deprived the President of meaningful oversight over officers exercising executive authority. Chief Justice John Roberts, for the majority, wrote a lengthy opinion surveying the Court's prior decisions involving "for cause" restrictions. Those restrictions were most notably upheld in *Humphrey's Executor*, which we saw in Chapter 1 as one of the 1935 "Black Monday" decisions rebuking Roosevelt.[65] The tenor of Roberts's discussion of those prior precedents is at best grudging, but he eventually concludes that some restrictions on the President's removal authority are permissible. The double "for cause" removal provision at issue in PCAOB, however, was too much. In a similarly lengthy opinion, Justice Stephen Breyer, joined by Justices Stevens, Ruth Bader Ginsburg, and Sonia Sotomayor, concluded that the majority was "wrong—very wrong."

Roberts's opinion for the majority is notable both for what it includes and what it omits. The notable inclusion is the Court's assumption that the members of the SEC are removable only for cause, despite the lack of a textual basis in the Exchange Act for that conclusion.[66] As Breyer points out in his dissent, the majority stretches to create a constitutional question by reading a for cause provision for the removal of SEC Commissioners into the Exchange Act. If the Court had instead read the Exchange Act to allow for at will removal of SEC Commissioners by the President, the novel constitutional question of double for cause removal could have been avoided. Why did the Court depart from its usual practice of construing statutes to avoid constitutional questions? If one reads the majority's opinion, the most reasonable conclusion to draw from its arguments is that restrictions on the President's power to remove the SEC commissioners violate the separation of powers. The holding, however, targets the new kid in town, the PCAOB. By 2010, the SEC's status in the pantheon of regulatory agencies was apparently so secure that it is unthinkable for the Court to question its independence, notwithstanding the absence of a "for cause" provision in the text of the Exchange Act. Textualism apparently had its limits.

The notable omission from the opinion is any discussion of Congress's goals in insulating the members of the PCAOB from removal. The omission is telling. Congress was not concerned about presidential interference with the Board's operations; the real threat was from Congress itself. Politics abhors a vacuum of governmental authority. By insulating the SEC from the President's removal authority, Congress made the SEC not independent, but rather, dependent on Congress. That dependence allowed Congress to strong-arm the SEC on the question of auditor independence.[67] When Arthur Andersen collapsed in the wake of the Enron scandal, the accounting firm's substantial revenue stream from consulting for Enron was diagnosed as the principal cause. Faced with a flurry of embarrassing headlines, Congress quickly got religion on the question of auditor independence. That newfound fervor found its expression in the autonomy conferred on the PCAOB, which was insulated both from the President *and* Congress. The goal was to protect accounting regulation from political interference.

None of this history is covered in the Court's opinion, nor is it addressed by the dissent. This omission of any discussion of the rationale for the PCAOB's independence might be taken as evidence of the gap between the Court's securities jurisprudence and the political economy of securities regulation. In fairness to the justices, however, it is difficult to sound judicial while discussing interest group pressures on Congress and their influence on accounting policy. Does the Court really want to introduce the question of campaign contributions into separation of powers jurisprudence? *PCAOB* reflects the Roberts Court's efforts to limit the effect of prior precedents that it considers misguided. *PCAOB* limits *Humphrey's Executor*'s insulation of expert agencies from political interference by the President, a question critical to the administrative state, not just securities law. The opinions in *PCAOB* are directed at those somewhat arid debates, paying scant attention to the substance of the securities laws.[68]

The only other cases relating to the SEC's procedures that garnered any headlines are a pair of disgorgement cases, *Kokesh* and *Liu*.[69] *Kokesh* held that disgorgement was a "penalty" for purposes of 28 U.S.C. § 2462, which imposes a five-year statute of limitations on government enforcement actions.[70] That label raised questions about the power of a court to order disgorgement as an equitable remedy, because courts of equity typically do not impose penalties. The Court further highlights the question by dropping a footnote in *Kokesh* specifically reserving it. The answer was soon forthcoming, as the Court held

88 A HISTORY OF SECURITIES LAW

in *Liu* that courts could order disgorgement of ill-gotten profits, subject to certain limitations. In particular, the Court required that the remedy not exceed the wrongdoer's net profits and that it be awarded to the victims of the violation. The decisions, taken together, constrained the SEC in ways that the agency would have preferred to avoid, but did not substantially undermine its enforcement efforts. If they had, the decisions surely would have been met by a swift congressional response—there is no constituency in Congress for fraudsters. The cases mirror the *PCAOB* decision in that they raised questions of general relevance for government enforcement, not specific to the securities laws. It is hard to read them as signaling an overarching skepticism toward the SEC's mission. That conclusion is consistent with the securities laws simply not being a principal focus for the Court after Powell's retirement.

## F. Conclusion

What can we take away from the Court' supervision of the SEC's procedures? The early arc of deference followed by Powell-era skepticism can been seen here, but in somewhat muted tones. After the Court quickly abandoned the overt hostility of *Jones*, the SEC has enjoyed a generally warm reception in the Court. The rare losses in cases like *Chenery I* and *Sloan* look like slip-ups invited by the SEC, the product of sloppy adjudication in the former, and a rather arrogant disregard of the statutory scheme in the latter. *Chenery I* had the potential to be considerably more significant for the agency, if it had evolved into a presumption favoring rulemaking, but the Court quickly moved away from that suggestion in *Chenery II*. Congress's enactment of the Administrative Procedure Act had considerably greater consequences for how the agency went about its business, but it is the D.C. Circuit, not the Supreme Court, that has scrutinized the SEC's rulemaking efforts.[71] Insofar as policy considerations affected the Court's decisions in the area, the Court has generally been sympathetic to the SEC's enforcement mission, as reflected in decisions like *Aaron* and *Steadman*. Only a clear textual mandate, such as the one at issue in *Sloan*, has resulted in a Court opinion creating an obstacle for the agency. The same cannot be said of the efforts by the SEC to *expand* its mission. We turn to that subject in our next chapter.

# 4

# Boundaries

[T]here is in the back of my mind the thought that if these bunnies
have found a hole in the fence they should be allowed to use it even
though it may seem to be against public policy to let them through.

Letter of William O. Douglas to William Brennan
(Mar. 14, 1959), WOD-LC

The SEC, like most agencies, seeks to maximize the scope of its authority. Agency personnel perceive market abuses that they think they can correct; naturally, they want to correct them. The abuse may be real, or may reflect competitors' complaints or congressional influence. Absent self-restraint from the agency, this bureaucratic instinct to expand pushes against two legal barriers. The first barrier is the question of authority. Agency power is delegated by Congress; the power the agency exercises cannot exceed that delegation. Has Congress delegated the power? The second barrier arises from the SEC's role as one cog in a larger administrative state. Some problems arguably fall within the SEC's ambit, but also potentially within another agency's authority. If there is a conflict, which agency gets to call the shots?

It frequently falls to the courts to answer these questions. Courts limit agency authority through interpretation of the agency's enabling statute to discern the powers granted by Congress. Grants of authority vary in their specificity, and judicial interpretation of those grants afford the agency more or less power. In this chapter, we examine the Supreme Court's efforts to keep the SEC within its statutory bounds. The Court was magnanimous with the agency in the first flush of New Deal enthusiasm for social control of finance. The Court became more grudging, however, as judicial faith in administrative expertise declined.

Our principal focus in this chapter is the definition of a "security," the subject of more Supreme Court opinions than any other issue under the federal securities laws. Why has this definition drawn so much judicial attention? The federal securities laws do not apply unless the instrument in question qualifies as a security. So the definition of a security necessarily limits the registration provisions of the Securities Act, with important implications for capital raising. Also implicated is the reach of the SEC's enforcement authority. More recently, defining what counts as a security has determined the reach of the Exchange Act's powerful antifraud weapons for private plaintiffs, Section 10(b) and Rule

*A History of Securities Law in the Supreme Court.* A.C. Pritchard and Robert B. Thompson, Oxford University Press.
© Oxford University Press 2023. DOI: 10.1093/oso/9780197665916.003.0005

90  A HISTORY OF SECURITIES LAW

10b-5, the focus of Chapter 6. When the Court decides whether an instrument is a security, it is defining the appropriate reach of both securities regulators and securities litigation.

We see concerns about the role of private litigation emerging as an important driver in interpreting the word "security" in the 1970s. Along the way, we take minor detours to consider the Court's approach to related boundaries in the securities law, including the distinction between public and private offerings and the definition of a "sale" of a security.

We also look at the Court's decisions reconciling the securities laws with other areas of law. The conflict between the securities laws and antitrust dragged on for decades. Drawing that line proved vexing for the Court for two reasons. First, Congress does not appear to have considered the potential overlap when it enacted the securities laws long after it adopted the principal antitrust laws. Second, the delineation between antitrust and securities law had important implications, not only for determining which agency has jurisdiction, but also to establish the boundaries of various private rights of actions arising under federal law. That boundary did not become important until the 1960s when class actions became important in both fields. We conclude the chapter with two cases in which the securities laws pushed against two very disparate boundaries. The first case drew the Court into the constitutional limits on the regulation of the securities markets. Does the First Amendment limit the SEC's power? The second is a post-1994 case implicating the territorial boundaries of the SEC's authority.

## A. The Early Period through the 1960s

### 1. Deference to the Agency's Inclusive Definition of a Security

The definition of a security involves a strategic interaction between policymakers and market participants. In order to thwart promoters from skirting the securities laws by devising new investment instruments, Congress adopted an expansive definition of a security in what is now section 2(a)(1) of the Securities Act, and a similar provision in section 3(a)(10) of the Exchange Act. The statutory list includes the commonplace, such as stocks and bonds, but also includes esoteric instruments, such as "collateral trust certificate" and "fractional undivided interest in oil, gas, or other mineral rights."

The definition's list also includes a vague category that the Court has treated as a catch-all: "investment contract." The Court's earliest decision in this area, *SEC v. C. M. Joiner Leasing Corp.*, made it clear that the reach of this catch-all would be broad.[1] The Joiner company was selling assignments of oil leases. Investors purchased the oil leases on the understanding that Joiner and its partner would

**Figure 4.1**
**Just Down the Block:** The SEC was created in 1934. The fledgling agency moved into the former building of the Interstate Commerce Commission, one block from the White House.

be responsible for drilling the wells and the investors would share in the profits from those wells. Joiner defended against the SEC's enforcement action on the ground that it was not selling the enumerated category of "fractional undivided interest[s] in oil . . . rights." Instead, the company argued, it was selling an interest in real estate. The fledgling SEC had already found success in the lower courts in applying the definition of securities to entrepreneurs nominally claiming to be merely selling animals (silver foxes, rabbits) or land (tung trees, farm lands, vineyards) but in reality offering shares in an enterprise. The Supreme Court added the Joiner enterprise to the list.

In a 7-1 decision,[2] Robert Jackson, writing for the Court, announced a new approach to reading statutes. He rejected traditional rules of statutory interpretation that he described as "com[ing] down to us from sources that were hostile toward the legislative process itself" now replaced by "a growing acceptance of statutes as a positive element of law." Highlighting a theme that would come to

92    A HISTORY OF SECURITIES LAW

dominate the Court's interpretation of the securities laws, Jackson focused on the statute's "dominating general purpose." The Court looked to the instrument's character in commerce, noting that the "exploration enterprise was woven into these leaseholds, in both an economic and legal sense." The Court rejected Joiner's argument that the specific items in the definition should govern over the general:

> We cannot read out of the statute these general descriptive designations [including investment contract] merely because more specific ones have been used to reach some kinds of documents. . . . Novel, uncommon, or irregular devices, whatever they appear to be, are also reached if it be proved as a matter of fact that they [are] "investment contracts."

Given its first opportunity to define the scope of the SEC's authority, the Court signaled that it would not constrain the agency with technical readings of the statute. Instead, the Court would look to the statute's purpose. The SEC would be given the power to accomplish the mission set for it by Congress.

The theme continued three years later in the Court's next definitional case as it once again found an "investment contract" in a "novel, uncommon, or irregular device[]" in *SEC v. W. J. Howey Co.*[3] The opinion, written by Frank Murphy, digs deeper into the policy underlying the investment contract catch-all, announcing a test broader than *Joiner's* focus on speculation. The Howey company solicited individuals who were staying at a nearby Florida resort that Howey owned and operated. The company offered rows of trees along narrow strips of land in orange groves along with service contracts (through an affiliate) to care for the trees, collect the oranges, and sell the oranges at market. The service contracts provided that the oranges would be pooled from all the strips of trees for which there was a similar service agreement "based upon a check made at the time of picking." Profits from the pooled oranges then would be distributed to the various service contract holders. Despite the presence of some individuals who purchased only the land contract and not the service contract, the Court framed the issue as whether the *offers* of orange grove and service contracts constituted offers of investment contracts, and therefore, securities. Notably, the focus on offers, rather than sales, a critical element of the analysis given the facts of the case, was not in the draft that Murphy first circulated.[4]

In the course of concluding that that the combination of land and service contracts was an investment contract, the Court rejected the lower court's reasoning that the land's intrinsic value made the scheme "non-speculative" and thus not an investment contract. Instead, the Court announced what is now known as the *Howey* test: (1) an investment of money, (2) in a common enterprise, (3) with an expectation of profits, (4) from the efforts of another. The *Howey* test, which affords the SEC and courts considerable flexibility, continues to control the definition of an investment contract to this day. Murphy derived the multipart test from judicial interpretations of state securities statutes. He described the last element as arising "solely" from the efforts of others, creating a significant loophole. Promoters assigned some small level of participation to investors in an attempt to get outside of the definition of securities. The lower courts, however, were quick to shut that door.

In *Howey*, the majority's deference to the SEC received some pushback, with Frankfurter in dissent, siding with the lower courts against a contrary agency argument. Frankfurter's approach tracked his view of agency decision-making in the *Chenery* cases discussed in Chapter 3. Although Frankfurter conceded that he might be willing to defer to a factual finding by the SEC in an administrative proceeding (which would not have been available to the SEC at the time for a violation of this type), he noted that the district court had found that the contracts were not a security and that the finding had been affirmed by the court of appeals. Frankfurter invoked "the wise rule of judicial administration under which this Court does not upset concurrent findings of two lower courts in the ascertainment of facts and the relevant inferences to be drawn from them." This focus on deference to the lower courts did not sway Frankfurter's colleagues; even Reed, who had voted with Frankfurter at conference,[5] ended up joining Murphy's majority opinion. There was a consensus on the Court that the SEC needed room to do its work without judicial interference, even when the agency pursued enforcement in court. Deference to the agency trumped deference to lower courts in the 1940s.

The same deference was visible when the Court defined the boundaries of "public" offerings, a term that divides those securities transactions that must satisfy the full registration and other disclosure requirements of the Securities Act from non-public offerings that are exempted from some or all of those requirements.[6] The disclosure requirements that accompany registration inform prospective investors about the offering and the issuing company's business. The burden of preparing these disclosures adds considerably to the expense of a securities offering. Significantly, many of these costs are fixed, that is, they do not vary with the size of the offering or the company. Generally speaking, an issuer, whatever its size, must provide the same level of mandatory disclosure in a registered public offering. In addition, companies selling securities in a public offering face substantial liability exposure for misstatements under sections 11 and 12 of the Securities Act. Moreover, a public offering commits a company to ongoing disclosure and compliance obligations under section 15(d) of the Exchange Act. Issuers selling a modest amount of securities may find that the high fixed costs of the public offering process exceed its benefits.

Despite the substantial regulatory consequences that flow from this distinction, the text of the Securities Act offers no guidance on the dividing line between

94   A HISTORY OF SECURITIES LAW

private and public offerings. The Court's first—and to date, only—case dealing with this so-called private offering exemption was *SEC v. Ralston Purina Co.* in 1953.[7] As in *Howey*, both lower courts had come down on the side of the narrower interpretation of the reach of the statute. Those courts emphasized the benign nature of the company giving bonuses to "key" employees so they might purchase stock that would spread ownership among all departments of the company.[8] In the view of the appellate court, there was "no possibility that these offerings [would] frustrate the purposes of the Act," despite the fact that the number of employees receiving offers numbered in the thousands. The Supreme Court, with Tom Clark penning his first securities opinion, worried about the company offering stock to unprotected employees who lacked full information. Forced to draw a line in the face of statutory silence, Clark turned to a phrase from the legislative history, suggesting the exemption would be limited to those for whom "there is no practical need for the Act's protective provisions."[9] Who would be in this group? The Court said "those who are shown to be able to fend for themselves." For employees, the Court provided a specific example: "executive personnel who because of their position have access to the same kind of information that the act would make available in the form of a registration statement." That formulation suggested a narrow exemption—and a correspondingly broad scope for the SEC's authority over public offerings. The Court rebuffed the SEC's argument for numerical limits on the exemption, but this did not create a substantial constraint on the SEC's authority. The Court did not go much further in delineating the exemption, but the eleven paragraphs of the opinion did mention "knowledge" and "access." These two concepts would reappear in coming decades in lower court decisions, and more importantly, SEC rulemaking as the agency fleshed out the exemption.[10] *Ralston Purina* imposed minimal constraints on the agency's effort.

The company raised a *Chenery* issue at argument in *Ralston Purina*, but Clark did not address it in his opinion. Frankfurter, who had been so passionate about constraining administrative discretion in 1943 and 1947, dissented at conference. He signed on to the majority opinion, however, after his colleagues in the minority (Vinson and Burton) failed to write a dissenting opinion.[11] The Court had settled into an era of deference to the SEC; even justices inclined to push back could not be bothered to write.

In three other definition cases of the 1950s and 1960s, the Court consistently afforded the SEC latitude without breaking much new ground. In *SEC v. Variable Annuity Life Ins. Co.*, discussed in greater detail in the next section, the Court upheld SEC jurisdiction over variable annuities, a new product being sold by insurance companies. Eight years later, the Court came down on the side of "security" in another case involving variable annuities in *SEC v. United Benefit Life Ins. Co.*,[12] essentially applying the *VALIC* precedent.[13] The Court's third definitional foray of this period, *Tcherepnin v. Knight*, involved an investment vehicle offered by a savings and loan, "withdrawable capital shares."[14] Douglas's conference notes suggest no disagreement that the shares were securities, and minimal discussion. The only comment of substance was John Harlan pointing out that the case involved "no competing regulatory scheme."[15] That factor would grow in importance in the succeeding decades in definition cases. Chief Justice Earl Warren issued the opinion for a unanimous Court a month after argument, "guided by the familiar canon of statutory construction that remedial legislation should be construed broadly to effectuate its purposes." He concluded that the shares were not only investment contracts under the *Howey* test, but also fit several other categories in the definition of a security, including "certificates of interest or participation in any profit-sharing agreement," "stock," and "transferable share(s)." If the case did not implicate alternative regulatory schemes, the Court was comfortable with an expansive domain for the securities laws—and the SEC—consistent with the laws' "remedial . . . purpose."

The line between securities law and insurance law came up again in *SEC v. National Securities, Inc.* toward the end of the sixties.[16] The question was whether the SEC was empowered to seek an injunction blocking a merger between two insurance companies; the agency contended that the shareholder proxies approving the merger were procured by fraud. The principal question was whether the proxy solicitation was part of "the business of insurance;" if it was, the McCarran-Ferguson Act protected state regulation from federal preemption. The Court had little difficulty finding that it was not part of the business of insurance, with only Hugo Black dissenting on this point. Thurgood Marshall, writing his first securities opinion for the Court, concluded that the SEC's action was intended to protect security holders from fraud, whereas the McCarran-Ferguson Act was intended to preserve state authority to regulate for the protection of policyholders.

Marshall went on, however, to hold that the merger was a sale within the meaning of Rule 10b-5. This would be the Court's first of what would eventually be many interpretations of that rule in the decades that followed. Marshall noted that the Court "enter[ed] this virgin territory cautiously" as it was "an area where glib generalizations and unthinking abstractions are major occupational hazards." Marshall's words of caution were not enough to placate John Marshall Harlan, who felt that the Court did not need to reach the Rule 10b-5 question.[17] He dissented on this point, joined by Potter Stewart. There would be less caution with respect to Rule 10b-5 in the next few years, as we detail in Chapter 6.

## 2. A Glimmer of Doubt?

Although the holdings of the cases in the 1950s and '60s continued the Court's earlier embrace of securities law, there was a new undercurrent of disillusionment

## 96   A HISTORY OF SECURITIES LAW

with the SEC. The fifties saw a slowdown at the SEC. The Eisenhower administration focused on budget restraint and the SEC's head count dropped precipitously, falling from 1678 in 1941 to 667 in 1955. The agency's agenda shrunk correspondingly.[18] *Variable Annuity Life* was the Court's first non-PUHCA securities case after a gap of six years.[19] The Court's deliberations in that case reflect its unease with this tamer version of the agency.

For the first time since 1936, the justices raised substantial doubts about the SEC as regulator. Also for the first time, the Court confronted a potential conflict with another body of law, insurance. That conflict carried with it another boundary issue, more like those discussed in section C of this chapter, and a potential conflict between state and federal law. At the time the securities laws were adopted, there was no federal insurance regulator, nor is there one today, despite the industry's enormous economic significance. That has left the field to state insurance regulators, an allocation of authority that Congress validated in the McCarran-Ferguson Act in 1945—passed by Congress to undo the Court's reinterpretation of the Commerce Clause to include the business of insurance in 1944[20] and specifically adding an exemption from the securities laws for insurance and annuity contracts.[21]

The SEC's effort to enjoin the unregistered selling of these "variable" products had been dismissed by the trial and appellate courts. The Court's initial discussion found it split 5-4 in favor of a holding that the transaction was insurance, and thereby exempted from the securities laws. That conclusion would have left variable annuities to be overseen by state insurance regulators rather than the SEC.[22] It would have been the Court's biggest pushback to expansive securities regulation since the first *Chenery* decision. Douglas, now participating in securities cases, was assigned to write the opinion. Several weeks after argument he sent a memo to the conference noting his "great difficulty" with the case and changed his vote. He described it as

> one of the most difficult cases in my 20 years here—probably the most difficult one because the issues lie so close, but I am now firmly of the view that, in spite of certain insurance aspects of the variable annuity, it is more nearly a security or an investment contract rather than insurance.[23]

Douglas's switch led Harlan, who voted with Douglas at conference, to write a dissent.[24]

William Brennan, still relatively new to the Court, had drafted a dissent of epic length while waiting on Douglas's opinion; he now found himself in the majority. Perhaps not wanting the effort to go to waste, he expressed his hope to Douglas that their two opinions could be merged into one. Douglas reported back his difficulty in making the combination "jell" and suggested a separate concurrence. The former SEC chair's letter to his junior colleague conveyed considerable angst about his former agency and perhaps surprising appreciation for regulatory arbitrage:

> [M]y basic difficulty is that I do not know which for a practical matter [the] better form of regulation is. I have seen the S.E.C. deteriorate so far and so fast since my days there that I often wonder whether some State Insurance Commissions might not in fact be better watchdogs than the Federal Agency. Moreover, there is in the back of my mind the thought that if these bunnies have found a hole in the fence they should be allowed to use it even though it may seem to be against public policy to let them through.

Brennan agreed to join Douglas's opinion and file his former dissent as a concurrence. Stewart, perhaps with tongue in cheek, as he was still in his first year on the Court, repeated Douglas's view that the case was "one of the most difficult and doubtful we have had since I have been here," but joined Brennan's concurrence. Frankfurter worried that the SEC would supplant regulation by the state now became a dissenter. Clark, who had originally sided with Harlan and Douglas when they were together, indicated late in the case that he planned to concur in the result. Further study, however, led him back to his original vote, thus joining Harlan's dissent.[25] The SEC's authority was affirmed by the Court's liberal wing, but, behind the scenes, the endorsement lacked conviction. The justices' faith in the SEC, so strong in the 1940s, had dissipated.

## B. Reining In the SEC and the Securities Laws

We saw in section A that from the inception of the federal securities laws through the 1960s, the Supreme Court held every instrument it reviewed to be a security, even when there was a competing regulatory scheme, such as state insurance regulation. Lewis Powell's appointment in the early 1970s would bring the SEC's winning streak to an end. During Powell's tenure, the Court decided five cases raising the question of the definition of a security. All five cases were private lawsuits, but the SEC, appearing as amicus, consistently urged a broad scope for the securities laws. Powell wrote four of these five opinions, with the Court rejecting the security label in three of the five. Powell also sought to confine the Act's meaning of "pledge" or "sale" to transactions relating to investments, stopping short of pensions or consumer and commercial dealings. Powell's sustained effort in this area confined the securities law during a time when both private plaintiffs and the SEC were pushing hard to expand its boundaries. There was some relaxation on the pledge/sale context in subsequent cases, but it was scarcely a return to the Court's magnanimous attitude of the forties. Powell's

## 98 A HISTORY OF SECURITIES LAW

effort to restrict the securities laws would similarly manifest itself in other areas of the securities laws, as we shall see in the chapters that follow.

## 1. Restrictive Holdings of the Definition of a Security

Powell's first foray into the definition of a security is a classic example of his efforts to rein in the activism of the Second Circuit. In *United Housing Foundation, Inc. v. Forman*, the plaintiffs had purchased "stock" in a nonprofit housing cooperative subsidized by the State of New York which allowed them to rent apartments in the cooperative.[26] The number of shares depended on the number of rooms in the desired apartment. Although denoted as stock, the shares could only be sold back to the cooperative—at the original purchase price of $25 per share—when the tenant terminated the lease. Although tenants voted on the cooperative's affairs, their votes were tied to the apartment (one vote per apartment), not the number of shares held. When the rental charges proved substantially greater than promised, creative lawyers for the disgruntled tenants filed a securities fraud class action in federal court. The Second Circuit held that the tenants had stated a claim under the securities laws, invoking the Court's repeated admonition that "Congress intended securities legislation enacted for the purpose of avoiding frauds to be construed 'not technically and restrictively, but flexibly to effectuate its remedial purposes.'"[27]

As Powell saw it, the transaction at issue in *Forman* had nothing to do with investment. Powell's exasperation with the Second Circuit's ongoing efforts to expand the securities laws comes through in an opinion he drafted to dissent from denial of certiorari:

> In this case members of Co-op City have not bought stock or real estate for investment purposes but rather have purchased living quarters generously subsidized by the State of New York. Certainly there was no profit motive, as no rational person would purchase an apartment in this nonprofit housing co-op as an investment for profit. . . . Nor can it even be suggested that the promoters of the cooperative, including the State of New York, sold shares in Co-op City as a means of raising venture capital for a profitmaking operation. Indeed, the promoter is a *nonprofit* corporation. Nothing in the instant transaction partakes of the kind of investment traditionally found to be within the scope and purpose of the securities laws.[28]

The Second Circuit's "novel" conclusion that this transaction involved a security ignored economic reality. "Novel" was not praise when Powell was describing legal decisions.

The SEC came in on the side of the plaintiffs, arguing for the broadest possible interpretation. In this case, the agency was not arguing for a strained interpretation of statutory text: "[t]he shares issued by Riverbay Corporation are securities because they are stock" and "stock" is specifically enumerated in the Exchange Act's definition of security. Powell, despite his penchant for grounding decisions in the text, was not persuaded by this statutory literalism. He seldom was inclined to defer to the SEC's expertise, and that inclination was bolstered in this case by the fact that the agency had reversed its prior position. In his view, the label "stock" did not fit this instrument. Even Blackmun, more sympathetic to plaintiffs than Powell, gave short shrift to the literalist argument "that the shares of stock are securities simply because they are called stocks. This, of course, is nonsense. Courts usually look beyond the form and examine the economic substance." Looking at that substance, Blackmun was "not too impressed with the thought of the bargain housing constituting profit within the meaning of the *Howey* test for this area of the securities law. This is real estate, not a securities transaction." At conference, Powell said less than usual, because "T[hurgood] [M]arshall has made my speech." Marshall's vote with the majority may have been motivated in part because he was anxious to avoid a lurking Eleventh Amendment question with a state agency as one of the defendants.[29] Burger and Stewart, after initially passing, fell into line with Marshall, Blackmun, Powell, and Rehnquist.

Looking through form to substance became the central theme of Powell's eventual opinion for the Court. There is no indication in Powell's papers that he ever considered the possibility that the label "stock" could be dispositive, although the argument was raised by the plaintiffs. Although it might have been the wrong result on the facts in *Forman*, a holding that the instrument was a security would have been readily sidestepped in the future by simply choosing another label (say, "housing certificates"). More importantly, it would have made the definition of security more predictable. Perhaps the message was as important as the holding for Powell. As Powell saw it, private plaintiffs, aided and abetted by the SEC, were attempting to push the securities laws into areas that Congress had never intended to reach. His instinct for predictability could not overcome that visceral reaction.

Quickly moving past the "stock" label, Powell focused on the expectation of profits prong of the *Howey* test, concluding that the motivation of the tenants was to acquire a place to live, not profit. Powell stressed that in determining whether an instrument qualified as a security, the Court must look at the economic realities of the transaction. "Because securities transactions are economic in character Congress intended the application of these statutes to turn on the economic realities underlying a transaction, and not on the name appended thereto."[30] Although Powell did look at the traditional characteristics of stock

100    A HISTORY OF SECURITIES LAW

in *Forman*, his argument was driven principally by the economic reality that the tenants were motivated to purchase the shares in order to rent an apartment. Powell's reliance on economic realities might have been thought to appeal to Douglas, a pioneer of legal realism in his days at Columbia and Yale. Douglas was unswayed, joining White in Brennan's dissent. Powell had transformed *Howey*'s invocation of economic reality into a two-way street: courts needed to consider not only what Congress intended to include, but also what it intended to leave out.

Powell's focus on "economic realities" implied that the test for an investment contract under *Howey* might be the universal test for the definition of a security. Powell wrote that the *Howey* test "in shorthand form, embodies the essential attributes that run through all of the Court's decisions defining a security." The economic realities in this case reflected expenditures on housing, not investments, and labeling the purchase "stock" could not change that fact. *Forman*'s emphasis on the economic realities, along with its elevation of substance over form for both the investment contract and stock definitions, suggested a move toward a single, unified theory for the definition of a security.

Powell's next installment defining a security, *International Brotherhood of Teamsters v. Daniel*, presented a sympathetic case for extending the coverage of the securities laws.[31] John Daniel had worked for over twenty years under a collective bargaining agreement between Teamsters Local 705 and a variety of employers. That agreement included a pension fund arrangement under which employees qualified for a pension if employed "for at least 20 consecutive, continuous and uninterrupted years immediately preceding retirement." Daniel could not meet the "continuous" service requirement because he had been laid off for a three-month period at one point during his employment. Daniel claimed that he had been deceived about the continuity requirements for vesting of the pension. More creatively, he asserted that his participation in the pension plan was the sale of a security and therefore subject to the federal securities laws.[32] Daniel's position had to overcome the obstacle that Congress had recently passed the Employee Retirement Income Security Act of 1974 (ERISA). ERISA was adopted after the period of Daniel's employment, so it gave no relief to him, but it raised the specter of regulatory overlap going forward. Notwithstanding Congress's recent intervention in the space, the district court and Seventh Circuit agreed that Daniel had stated a claim under the securities laws.[33]

Powell found the lower courts' holding "close to being absurd" with "far reaching" results. Daniel faced four barriers to his claim:

1. contributions to the pension plan were made by his employers, not him;
2. he was required to participate in the plan;

BOUNDARIES 101

3. the scheme at issue was a "defined benefit" plan, under which the benefits did not vary with the fund's performance; and

4. application of the federal securities laws to pension plans threatened to interfere with the separate federal regulatory scheme for pensions.[34]

Daniel needed to show both that his interest in the pension plan was a "security" (3 and 4 went to this question) and that there had been a "sale" of that interest to him (1 and 2 went to this point). The court of appeals found a "security" because the pension fund was similar to a mutual fund or variable annuity, and a "sale" because Daniel had made an investment decision to participate in the pension plan by foregoing alternative employment opportunities. The lower courts distinguished Congress's regulation of pension plans as "concerned with the administration of such funds . . . rather than regulation of circumstances of entry into the plan."[35]

Powell worried that the lower courts' decision could dramatically expand the scope of the securities laws: "any offer + acceptance of employment might be viewed as an investment [contract]" and, therefore, the sale of a security. He also thought that it could not be squared with the Court's focus upon economic realities in the definition of a "security." Powell's colleagues agreed; the conference vote was 8-0 to reverse, with Powell stunned to find even Blackmun in accord. (In his notes, Blackmun wrote "Clearly, Sec Act liability is preempted by ERISA".)[36] Chief Justice Warren Burger assigned the opinion to Powell.

Noting that pension plans are not specifically delineated in the definition of a security, Powell focused on whether the pension plan qualified as an investment contract. Turning to the first factor of the *Howey* test, the investment of money, Powell observed that an "investment" may include the transfer of goods or services in return for an investment. Nonetheless, the Court held that the employee's interest in the pension plan did not constitute an investment. The pension plan represented a relatively small portion of his entire compensation package: "His decision to accept and retain covered employment may have only an attenuated relationship, if any, to perceived investment possibilities of a future pension. Looking at the economic realities, it seems clear that an employee is selling his labor primarily to obtain a livelihood, not making an investment." Powell's opinion also picked up on Blackmun's concern about the potential conflict between the securities laws and ERISA. Even though ERISA did not apply to his case, Congress's enactment of that statute, in Powell's view, demonstrated that Congress believed it was filling a "regulatory void." Moreover, the presence of ERISA meant that extending the securities laws to cover pension plans would serve "no general purpose."

The legislative history of ERISA put the SEC in an awkward position. As recently as 1971, the SEC had taken the position before Congress that involuntary pension plans did not involve the sale of security. By 1979, when the case arose, it

# 102 A HISTORY OF SECURITIES LAW

was taking the opposite position. Judge Tone, concurring in the court of appeals decision, noted that:

> Apparently for the first time ever, [the SEC] takes the position in its brief before us that the employee's interest or expectancy in a plan such as this is subject to the anti-fraud provisions of the securities laws. *The Commission has been not as candid as we might have hoped in acknowledging and explaining its change in position.*

Powell observed that the SEC's lack of candor about its switch was "not unusual." The SEC's brief in the Supreme Court further undermined its credibility. Powell's clerk advised him that "[t]he *SEC has made representations to this Court in its brief* [regarding its change in position] which, put in the most charitable light, *are less than candid.*" The Solicitor General also rejected the SEC's newfound position, siding with the Department of Labor in favoring reversal.[37] The SEC's failure to hold to a consistent position was undermining its hopes for deference by the Supreme Court.

Powell was frustrated with the SEC, but his own norms of professionalism prevented public criticism. His clerk drafted a sharp rebuke of the SEC, but whatever the Court's actual practice, Powell was not prepared to announce a position of no deference to the agency. The final opinion contains much milder language.[38] Powell would not indulge the SEC's enthusiasm for expanding the federal securities laws, which he saw as a profound shift for an agency that historically held a modest view of its power, but he would not characterize the SEC as a rogue agency in the US Reports.

## 2. Parallel Questions in the Definitions of "Sale" and "Pledge"

For Powell, securities law opinions were an opportunity to shape the law, not just resolve conflicts among the lower courts. His initial draft of the *Daniel* opinion included a discussion of a related issue, the definition of "sale." Powell's desire to limit undue expansions of the regulatory footprint via a broad definition extended to transactions involving a security, but in a context that Powell felt were beyond the purview of the New Deal legislation. The meaning of the statutory terms of "sale" and "pledge" would recurringly raise this issue for the Court. Thus, Powell added to the draft of the proposed *Daniel* opinion prepared by his clerk that "[t]he SEC [*sic*] present position with respect to the term 'sale' is quite unsupportable." Specifically, Powell questioned the SEC's position that "it is possible to regard a particular financial transaction as constituting a sale under certain provisions of the Securities Act but not under others." The implicit concern here was that the SEC was trying to extend its reach by applying the antifraud rules, without risking a backlash from Congress if it applied its burdensome registration requirements to the same transactions. A "sale" is a "sale," Powell thought. Faced with objections from White and Burger, however, Powell eliminated this language and reserved the question.[39] The Court's holding is limited to the conclusion that the pension plan in question was not an investment contract, and therefore, not within the definition of a security.[40]

Powell had expressed his narrow view of "sale" in an earlier case, but that perspective, too, did not get to the printed reports. In *Bankers Trust Co. v. Mallis*, the issue was whether the pledge of stock to secure a loan was a "sale" of the stock for purposes of Rule 10b-5. For Powell, the answer was no:

> A pledge is not a transfer of title. It involves neither a purchase nor a sale, and my recollection . . . is that nothing whatever in [the Acts of '33 and '34] suggests or implies that either the pledge or the release of securities from a pledge constitutes a purchase or sale within the meaning of the Securities Acts.

The Second Circuit's contrary conclusion provoked Powell's usual reaction: "the case appears to represent an attempt to extend significantly the reach of § 10(b) far beyond the original intent of the Securities Acts." Powell appears frustrated by the Second Circuit's indifference to the Court's prior rebukes of the appellate court's expansion of the securities laws: "Our cases refute view that 10(b)5 [sic] is a license to *federalize* corp. law generally. *Santa Fe, Blue Chip, Foreman* [sic] (Act of '33). I think CA2 is *dead* wrong!" Powell characterized the Solicitor General's argument supporting the lower court's position as "absurd in the context of normal commercial transactions."[41]

Powell's attempt to link the Second Circuit's decision to the federalization of corporate law is a stretch, given the absence of any corporate governance failures. In *Mallis*, a lawyer and his client were interested in buying shares in a bank. They had located both an ostensible seller and a pair of dentists who were willing to finance the purchase. The dentists were to receive a pledge of the shares as collateral from the lawyer and his client. The shares, however, turned out to be worthless, having been received by the ostensible sellers when they sold their family company subject to earnout conditions that subsequently had not been met. Bankers Life, which held the certificates as security for its own prior loan to the ostensible sellers that would be paid off by the dentists' purchase, had received notice recalling the shares for cancellation, well before the closing with the dentists. When the dentists ended up with worthless shares to secure their loan, they sued Bankers Trust for fraud under the securities laws.

Powell was anxious to exclude pledges from being treated as a sale under the Exchange Act, but after working through complex procedural issues in the

104 A HISTORY OF SECURITIES LAW

case, the Court ended up deadlocked on the merits. Powell joined with Burger, Stewart, and Rehnquist to reverse, while Brennan, White, Marshall, and Stevens voted to affirm. Blackmun was absent from the conference.[42]

Rehnquist, who had been assigned the opinion, found a way out of the procedural morass, but then faced the reality of an equally divided court, which would affirm the decision below. Rehnquist worried that "[w]ith Harry's voting records in 10(b)(5) [sic] cases, I think affirmance showing him out would be tantamount to ratifying the CA2 opinion even though we wrote nothing." Rehnquist therefore proposed a strategic retreat, dismissing the petition for certiorari as improvidently granted (a "DIG"). As two of the votes for affirmance were willing to acquiesce in a dismissal (White and Stevens), Rehnquist got a majority for this course and the petition was dismissed.[43]

The non-result in *Mallis* meant that whether a pledge was a sale remained an open question two years later when *Rubin v. United States* made its way to the Court.[44] In the interim, the Court had decided another "sale" case, *United States v. Naftalin*, which gave a broader interpretation to sale.[45] *Naftalin* involved fraud by a broker against other brokers—a short seller placed sell orders for shares he did not own; when he failed to deliver, the brokers had to "buy in" those shares, suffering substantial losses. Consistent with Powell's (unpublished) views in *Mallis* and *Daniel*, the Eighth Circuit was unwilling to extend the Act to cover participants other than investors, citing Powell's restrictive opinion in *Ernst & Ernst*. But Powell missed the argument in *Naftalin* due to complications from surgery.[46] In his absence, Brennan wrote for a unanimous Court, finding that the statutory terms that Congress "expressly intended to define broadly" were "expansive enough to include the entire selling process." Thus, when *Rubin* arrived before the Court, neither of Powell's preliminary opinions restricting the meaning of sale were on the books and *Naftalin*, decided in his absence, took a much more expansive approach. The transaction in *Rubin*, like *Mallis*, involved a Bankers Trust transaction, this time with the bank as the victim: one of its borrowers had pledged stock in six companies and misrepresented their value. *Rubin* differed, however, in that it raised the issue under § 17(a) of the Securities Act, rather than the Exchange Act. Section 3(a)(14) of the Exchange Act defines a sale as "any contract to sell or otherwise dispose of" a security, and Section 2(a)(3) of the Securities Act defines "sale" as "every contract of sale or disposition of a security or interest in a security, for value."[47] Congress's inclusion of "every" and "interest" pushed toward a broader interpretation under the Securities Act.

Powell was unmoved by this textual distinction—his policy reasons for excluding this transaction from the scope of the securities law were the same. He agreed with his law clerk that "applying § 17(a) to commercial loans seems to extend the scope of the 1933 Act beyond its purposes. Second, there seems to be no practical need for the extension." Parties to commercial transactions had sufficient recourse in their bargaining power and the usual fraud remedies provided by state law. Burger, Stewart, and Rehnquist who had been with him in a strict view in *Mallis* (and in practically every other securities case since Powell's arrival) defected. They were less inclined to limit the Act to the issuance context particularly when criminal activity relating to securities was charged and the other members of the Court agreed. Marshall at oral argument had observed that he had some difficulty turning a blind eye to fraud, echoing the classic quotation of one of the SEC Commissioners at the time of Rule 10b-5's adoption, "Well, we are against fraud, aren't we?" Powell bowed to reality and voted to uphold the broader interpretation.[48]

Powell may have acquiesced in the holding but he still threw himself into damage control. Powell was disappointed by Burger's "simplistic" opinion for the Court, but offered suggestions for improvement. Powell did not hesitate to remind his colleagues of his superior experience when pushing them in his desired direction. Objecting to a passage in Burger's opinion characterizing a bank as lending money to "obtain" the pledge of securities, Powell invoked his work as counsel to State Planters and United Virginia Bank:

> Any bank officer who makes a loan for the purpose of obtaining an inchoate interest in collateral should be fired. Collateral may be indispensable to the extension of credit, but lending officers of the bank I represented were instructed never to make a loan on the assumption that it probably could be repaid only by liquidating the borrower's collateral.

Brennan agreed with Powell on this point;[49] Burger modified the offending language.

Powell was partially successful in discouraging Burger from citing the 1963 case of *SEC v. Capital Gains Research Bureau*, quoting language to the effect that federal security laws must be construed "not technically and restrictively but flexibly to effectuate [their] remedial purposes."

> A number of more recent decisions, for example, *Hochfelder* relied on by your opinion, have looked primarily to the plain language of the securities acts. These are highly technical and well drawn statutes, and as you make clear by the remainder of your opinion this case falls within the explicit language of §§2(3) and 17(a). Thus, the quote from *Capital Gains Research Bureau* is unnecessary and perhaps could be viewed as undercutting to some extent your reliance on the statutory language itself.

The quoted language was a staple of the SEC's briefs (and the Court's securities opinions before Powell's arrival), but it reflected the interpretive style that

106   A HISTORY OF SECURITIES LAW

Powell was anxious to expunge from the Court's securities jurisprudence. Powell also wanted a footnote reserving the status of pledges under the Exchange Act. Burger dropped the offensive language from *Capital Gains*, but he declined to include the footnote explicitly reserving the question under the Exchange Act. Predictably, the lower courts have interpreted the Exchange Act definition of "sale" to include pledges of securities. Powell might have gained more by challenging Burger on the "sale" issue, rather than the citation to *Capital Gains*, which was a matter of style rather than substance.[50] But that question of style was vital to Powell's securities law agenda.

### 3. Some Ambiguity in the Restrictive Approach to the Definition of Security

When the Court returned to the definition of a security the term after *Rubin*, Powell had more reason to be disappointed with Burger's approach to securities cases. *Marine Bank v. Weaver* is the only case involving the definition of a security during Powell's tenure in which he did not write the majority opinion.[51] The transaction at issue involved two instruments that potentially could be a security: (1) a certificate of deposit issued by a bank and (2) a unique contract negotiated between two parties for an investment in a business. The second question particularly worried Powell: "If the agreement here—unique on its facts—is a 'security,' a vast number of business [contracts] will come under Act. (Sad case!)"[52] Both instruments ultimately were held not to be securities, but the Chief Justice's opinion for the Court further muddied the water.

On the question of whether a CD is a security, Burger sensibly enough said no. Certificates of deposit are not among the enumerated categories in the definition of security. An investor who purchases a CD issued by Marine Bank benefits from its status as a federally regulated bank, with various reserve, reporting, and inspection requirements pursuant to the federal banking laws. FDIC insurance also protected depositors from loss on their deposits, making the repayment of the CD "virtually guaranteed." As a result, the Court stated that it was "unnecessary to subject issuers of bank certificates of deposit to liability under the antifraud provisions of the federal securities laws since the holders of bank certificates of deposit are abundantly protected under the federal banking laws." The alternative regulatory regime was critical to the Court's holding that an instrument that looked like an investment vehicle was not a security.

Burger confused the matter, however, in responding to a concern raised by Stevens. Stevens urged that the Court's holding not preclude later holdings that a CD is a security under the Investment Company Act (despite identical language in the definition) or that a CD might somehow become a security in secondary market trading, even though it was not one at the time of issue.[53] Despite the weakness of these arguments (and not needing Stevens for a majority), Burger obliged:

> It does not follow that a certificate of deposit or business agreement between transacting parties invariably falls outside the definition of a 'security' as defined by the Federal statutes. Each transaction must be analyzed and evaluated on the basis of the content of the instruments in question, the purposes intended to be served, and the factual setting as a whole.

This lack of predictability leaves difficulty for lawyers seeking to advise their clients on the status of the instrument.

Burger got further off track in addressing whether the privately negotiated investment was a security. He notes that the owners of the business "distributed no prospectus to the Weavers [plaintiffs] or to other potential investors, and the unique agreement they negotiated was not designed to be traded publicly." Powell objected that these facts were "immaterial," but he did not share his concerns with Burger.[54] Powell presumably would have written a cleaner opinion, focusing on the fact that the unique contract, tailored through the negotiations of the parties, was not within the realm that Congress had sought to regulate. The couple who had purchased the CD and pledged it against the debts incurred by a business owned by a second couple, was entitled to 50% of the profits of the business and the use of a barn and pastures of the business at the discretion of the borrowers. Given that only one couple was investing in the business, the case might have been resolved on a lack of "horizontal commonality," that is, no "common enterprise" among multiple investors. The Court did not take this tack, leaving unresolved the issue whether horizontal commonality is required to satisfy *Howey*'s "common enterprise" element.[55]

Powell had his own moment of doubt with regard to the definition of security three years later in a pair of cases that involved the "sale of business" doctrine, *Landreth Timber Co. v. Landreth* and its companion case, *Gould v. Ruefenacht*.[56] Under that doctrine, the sale of an entire business, if achieved by the sale of 100% of a company's stock (or perhaps just a majority), was outside the securities law. The "sale of business" doctrine was difficult to square with the specific enumeration of stock in the definition of "security." It fit with Powell's instinct, however, visible in the earlier "pledge" and "sale cases, to cabin the federal securities laws and their attendant liability exposure. The sale of an entire company, whether done by merger, sale of assets, or the sale of stock, typically would be negotiated face to face. The potential buyer could demand those disclosures relevant to him; the state common law of fraud would assure the credibility of those disclosures. The lower courts found support for the sale of business doctrine in the *Howey*

108    A HISTORY OF SECURITIES LAW

test for an "investment contract," which required an expectation of profits from the efforts of others. A purchaser of 100% of a company's stock with the control conferred by majority ownership typically could not satisfy this requirement because they would have management control. The notion that the *Howey* test applied to all financial instruments got support from Powell's opinion in *Forman*, with its focus on "economic realities," and its observation that the *Howey* test "embodies the essential attributes that run through all of the Court's decisions defining a security."

Powell had endorsed the "sale of business" doctrine a decade earlier in a draft concurrence in *Scherk v. Alberto-Culver Co.*:[57]

> It is unnecessary to say that no acquisition of an entire business, where the method employed is transfer of stock, is ever convered [*sic*] by 10(b) of the Act. There may be situations where the substance or essence of the transaction is in fact the purchase and sale of securities. But certainly in a case where one large business interest is seeking to acquire the entire business of another large interest for the purpose of operating it, if [*sic*] blinks reality to say that a security's [*sic*] transaction occurs within the language and intent of § 10(b). In this case Alberto-Culver's purpose was to acquire these business entities—their assets and going concern value—in Western Europe. Alberto-Culver desired to operate these businesses itself, and was free from the time of acquisition to convert them into such business forms as best suited its tax and business purposes. It is plain that Alberto-Culver had no interest in merely becoming a shareholder in Scherk's enterprises. In short, the purchase here was not in any realistic sense a security's [*sic*] transaction. It was the 100% acquisition of businesses by a strong, sophisticated purchaser fully capable of making all necessary investigations, and which indeed did make such investigations through American and European and [*sic*] accountants.
>
> There is nothing in the history or language structures of the Securities Acts of 1933 and 1934 which remotely suggest an intent or purpose to apply to transactions such as this or to afford protection to parties such as Alberto-Culver.

Powell objected to bringing the federal securities laws into negotiations between sophisticated commercial parties. This instinct drove his resistance to a broader reading in *Mallis* and *Rubin*, and his draft concurrence in *Scherk* underscores the point. The "sale of business" was yet another doctrinal tool that Powell could use to limit the reach of the securities laws. Powell chose not to publish his *Alberto-Culver* concurrence, however, apparently satisfied by Stewart's specific reservation of the question in the majority opinion.[58] So Powell was free to consider the question de novo without the awkwardness of having to repudiate a published opinion.

BOUNDARIES 109

Even so, he was not yet at that point. At the certiorari stage in *Landreth* and *Gould*, Powell still favored the "sale of business" doctrine. He still held that view the next spring when he reviewed the case prior to argument:

> As I had some familiarity with both of these statutes, I confess to a rather strong bias in favor of CA9's position that one must look to the substance of the transaction, rather than rely solely to [*sic*] the term "stock," to conclude that the antifraud provisions of these Acts apply. Although the SG struggles to distinguish my decision in *United Housing Foundation v. Forman*, I am not yet persuaded.
>
> To all intense [*sic*] purposes, both of these transactions involved—in effect—the transfer of assets rather than securities in the normal sense of the term. This is more obvious where 100% of the business was bought than in the case where an individual purchased only 50% of the stock. But both cases involve types of transactions that I doubt anyone, at the times these statutes were enacted, would have believed were covered by any provisions of these two federal laws.

Powell nonetheless conceded that the Solicitor General made "strong arguments." Powell also wondered whether the doctrine should be applied to the sale of a smaller percentage of stock.[59]

Wrestling with this last question evidently changed Powell's mind, with a push from his law clerk. That clerk, Lynda Guild Simpson, advised Powell that "the determination of whether stock is a 'security' in these cases will depend on extensive fact-finding as to whether control has passed and how active in management the purchaser becomes, inquiries that make the 'sale of business' doctrine more than a little elusive to apply." Moreover, she noted, "[i]t doesn't make much sense to me that the same stock is or is not a 'security' depending on how much of it was sold or who bought it." (She was unaware of the draft concurrence in *Scherk*; Powell made no mention of it.) Simpson's invocation of predictability resonated with Powell's preference for clear rules: Powell noted "Linda [*sic*] may be right." Powell believed strongly that business people needed to know how the law applied to them. He wrote in his notes prepared before argument that he saw this lack of predictability as a "serious weakness" in the "sale of business" doctrine. By the time of conference, Powell voted with his colleagues in rejecting the doctrine, after first "express[ing] my doubts at length." Stevens characterized the case as "very diffi[cult]," as he felt Congress was concerned with "just public trading"; he was "Troubled, but if LP [goes?], I do." O'Connor, too, "Agree[d] wi[th] LP."[60]

Powell was assigned the opinions for a unanimous Court.[61] In the *Landreth* opinion, he limited *Forman's* "economic reality" test to the definition of "investment contract." The "investment contract" test would not be allowed to swallow specifically enumerated categories of security. Forced to choose between predictability of application and his aversion to expanding the scope of

110    A HISTORY OF SECURITIES LAW

the securities laws, Powell opted for predictability: "uncertainties attending the applicability of the Acts would hardly be in the best interests of either party to a transaction." It helped that the expanded reach of the securities laws easily could be avoided—by structuring a transaction as an asset sale, a corporate lawyer could sidestep the securities laws. (The choice of an alternative structure might have a number of other legal consequences, principally tax issues.) There is no evidence that grappling with the sale of business doctrine caused Powell to reconsider *Forman*'s focus on economic realities and the uncertainty that it had engendered. The *Landreth* opinion acknowledges that the *Forman* rule would not apply to instruments bearing "some of the significant characteristics" of stock, naming four.

Taken together, Powell's retreat in the sale/pledge context and his rejection of the sale of business doctrine show a grudging departure away from his skepticism toward securities law and the SEC. Powell had initially focused on "economic reality" to rein in the definition of security in *United Housing Foundation v. Forman*. That emphasis conflicted with Powell's goal of predictability. Looking at economic reality suggested a case-by-case analysis of financial instruments to determine whether they were a security, a less-than-comforting prospect for corporate lawyers advising clients. This was the weakness of Burger's opinion in *Marine Bank*. When that unpredictability became unmanageable a decade later in *Landreth* and *Gould*, Powell pulled back from the full implications of "economic reality." This reversal may have provoked Blackmun's comment that "we h[a]v[e] h[a]d to eat crow here."[62] The choice for predictability over restrictiveness may have been made easier in that the expansive coverage of the securities laws in *Landreth* and *Gould* could be easily avoided by the planners in those settings by choosing an alternative structure for their transactions, that is, a sale of assets rather than a sale of the securities or a merger.

## 4. The Post-Powell Period: Tension Persists

The two definition of security cases in the time since Powell retired show the enduring tension between the Court's initial embrace of the flexible and expansive approach in *Howey*, and the instinct to exclude commercial and consumer transactions from securities regulation. *Reves v. Ernst & Young* came to the Court three terms after Powell's retirement.[63] The case raised the definition in the particular context of a note, which has its own perplexing ambiguities arising from the statutory language. Individuals were providing capital to a business, here a farmers' cooperative, and looking to receive a return on their investment from the business managed by others. Their interest was labeled a promissory note, payable upon demand and pitched as "safe and secure," but the economic reality looked like an investment. After issuing the notes, the cooperative filed for bankruptcy, leaving over a thousand holders of notes worth a total of $10 million feeling less than safe and secure. The holders of the notes filed a class action suit against the auditors of the cooperative under Rule 10b-5 of the Exchange Act.

The two reliable paths of prior "definition" jurisprudence offered little guidance. *Landreth* had expressly limited "economic reality" to the definition of investment contract; this case seemed to clearly fall within another of the specified terms in the statute, "note." The statutory treatment of note further muddied the waters. Section 3(a)(10) of the Exchange Act provides that a security includes "any note, . . . bond, debenture" and so on; section 2(a)(1) of the Securities Act provides a similar formulation. Yet the two acts, in somewhat different language, also exempt a broad swath of notes—those with "a maturity . . . not exceeding nine months." This treatment excludes short-term notes, but it ignores a necessary division between investment transactions, to which the securities acts would typically apply, and commercial or consumer transactions of longer than nine months. Applying the securities laws to this latter category would create a mess. The category would include, for example, an individual who borrows money from a bank to purchase a home, giving the bank a note and a mortgage. If the home loan were a security, the investor would be the bank and the issuer of the debt would be the individual. Banks hardly need the federal securities laws to protect them from individual homeowners. The homeowners, for their part, are protected by myriad banking and consumer finance protections. These kinds of notes fit within the class of commercial transactions that Powell had worked diligently to exclude from the remit of the securities laws prior to his retirement.

Marshall's opinion eventually reconciles in a common-sense way the disparate precedents with which he was dealing, but not before taking the reader on a somewhat bewildering journey. He starts appropriately with the congressional purpose to regulate investments, not commercial or consumer borrowing. After Stevens reminded Marshall that several members of the Court had supported the "family resemblance" test at conference—and that it was Henry Friendly's handiwork[64]—Marshall reformulated the test to incorporate Friendly's approach. (Marshall had served with Friendly on the Second Circuit.) Marshall's reformulated test begins with a rebuttable presumption that every note is a security. The test then provides a laundry list of notes that have been held to fall outside of the definition of a security. Among these non-securities are notes related to consumer financing, home mortgages, and certain short-term business loans relating to the working capital or current operations of a business. If the notes in question resemble these non-security notes the presumption is rebutted. This is the "family resemblance" portion of the test. Marshall then went on to provide factors to help determine whether a note resembled one of the excluded laundry lists of notes, which included whether an alternative regulatory regime

112   A HISTORY OF SECURITIES LAW

reduced the risk of the investment. Thus, *Reves* provides a framework for excluding consumer-related financing arrangements from the definition of a security without interfering with *Howey*'s broad application to investment contexts. It makes little sense to force consumers (the issuers in a consumer financing arrangement) to comply with the securities laws in the name of protecting lenders (the investors).

To bring this apparent investment-oriented transaction within the securities ambit required the note in question to be outside of the exemption for notes, that is, on the longer side of the nine-month dividing line in the statute. On which side of that line does a demand note fall? The Court's treatment of that question harkened to *Ralston Purina*'s approach: a bare bones statute provides no guidance so the Court looked to Congress's broader purpose. Here that purpose was "ensuring that investments of all descriptions be regulated." The Court posited that demand on a demand note could be made immediately or it could be made many years in the future. Interpreting the exception narrowly to exclude the demand notes would fit the statutory context in *Reves*. Four justices dissented on this point: Rehnquist, White, Sandra Day O'Connor, and Antonin Scalia. Their more literalist interpretation that demand notes could in some states of the world be called within nine months echoes Powell's restrictive approach to the securities law, particularly in his early years on the Court.

Since *Reves*, the Court has shown less interest in the definition of security. There has been only one case, *SEC v. Edwards*,[65] and it was a routine clarification of the "expectation of profits" prong of the *Howey* test. The only notable aspect of O'Connor's opinion for the Court was its opening paragraph: " 'Opportunity doesn't always knock . . . sometimes it rings.' " And sometimes it hangs up. So it did for the 10,000 people who invested a total of $300 million in the payphone sale-and-leaseback arrangements touted by respondent under that slogan." O'Connor gets points for her catchy introduction, but the holding of the case is the unremarkable proposition that an investment vehicle with a fixed rate of interest can be an investment contract.

## C. Antitrust and the Securities Laws

Prior to the New Deal, Congress's most ambitious interventions into the nation's economic life had been the antitrust laws, beginning with the Sherman Act in 1890. Congress had followed up with the creation of the Federal Trade Commission in 1914, giving the FTC concurrent authority with the Department of Justice to enforce the antitrust laws. A generation later, the FTC was initially given the responsibility for administering the Securities Act, potentially paving the way for an overarching federal corporate regulator. The responsibility for

BOUNDARIES 113

administering the Securities Act was shifted to the newly created SEC in 1934, however, entrenching a division between antitrust and securities law.

That division sets up a different kind of boundary question. In most of the conflicts discussed in this chapter until now, such as the overlap between securities and insurance, the two regimes could be separated. Enforcement of one statute did not preclude enforcing the other, or vice versa, although it might have created some awkwardness. The conflict between securities and antitrust has posed a more vexing question, requiring a choice of one regulator and regulatory system over another. The resolution of this conflict, however, does not fit neatly within the pattern that we see elsewhere with the expansion of securities law followed by retrenchment. The first direct conflict came in the sixties, with the Court limiting the SEC's authority at a time when the Court was otherwise exceptionally generous in interpreting the securities laws. The conflict came back to the Court in the mid-seventies, but the Court now favored the SEC at a time when it was regularly limiting the agency's reach in other areas.

In *Silver v. NYSE* the Court addressed whether the Securities Exchange Act of 1934 precluded a broker's antitrust challenge to the New York Stock Exchange's termination of his access to exchange quotes.[66] The opinion was written by Arthur Goldberg, one of John Kennedy's recent appointees. Goldberg had replaced Felix Frankfurter, and like him was a committed New Dealer, but his jurisprudential attitude could not have been more diametrically opposed to Frankfurter's. According to Goldberg's law clerk Alan Dershowitz: "The 'passive virtues,' as Professor Alexander Bickel once characterized the Supreme Court's role in not making decisions, was a vice to Arthur Goldberg. He wanted to get things done."[67] Getting things done would require judicial creativity.

Finding "no express exemption from the antitrust laws" in the Exchange Act, Goldberg adopted his own "guiding principle": "Repeal is to be regarded as implied only if necessary to make the Securities Exchange Act work, and even then only to the minimum extent necessary." Goldberg derived this principle from the purposes of the Sherman and Exchange Acts, not their texts. Applying this principle to the NYSE's action, Goldberg concluded that the NYSE violated the antitrust laws by failing to provide the broker-dealer with notice and an opportunity to be heard before terminating his connection. Remarkably, the Court was importing due process standards into antitrust law to regulate the securities exchanges. The novelty of the approach—and the complete lack of textual support—did not trouble Douglas, who praised Goldberg's "fine opinion." Goldberg responded that he was "trying to follow in the great Douglas tradition." He was surely succeeding; in 1937, Chairman Douglas had spoken of the SEC's efforts to enforce "not only the letter but the spirit of the particular statute" avoiding a "narrow legalistic conception" of the agency's work.[68] Goldberg was far from "legalistic."

114   A HISTORY OF SECURITIES LAW

Frankfurter was less impressed by his successor Goldberg's handiwork; he wrote to compliment Stewart on his *Silver* dissent:

> I cannot abstain from telling you how much your dissent in Silver v. New York Stock Exchange cheered me . . . I find in it an omen for the future, that not only John Harlan but you also still believe in law . . . I rejoice over the penetrating way in which you exposed the untenable route by which the result was reached.[69]

The Court was becoming more adventurous with the introduction of new blood, and Frankfurter, the intellectual godfather of judicial restraint, was unsettled by the change. Frankfurter's hope for the future, however, would prove misplaced. More dramatic examples of judicial freelancing would soon follow, with Stewart and Harlan generally acquiescing. We will return to that topic in subsequent chapters.

Left unresolved by the majority opinion in *Silver* was the question of when antitrust law would need to give way to the securities laws. Goldberg found no need for the Court "to define further whether the interposing of a substantive justification in an antitrust suit brought to challenge a particular enforcement of the [exchange's] rules on its merits is to be governed by a standard of arbitrariness, good faith, reasonableness, or some other measure."[70] The NYSE had failed to afford the broker-dealer notice and a hearing, which left it with no defense to the Sherman Act claim. Lower courts would have to fill out the standard for implied repeal down the road when presented with closer cases.

The Supreme Court would offer no guidance for over a decade. When a certiorari petition sought clarification of *Silver* in 1967 in a case involving the NYSE's fixed rates for trading commissions (a long-standing, but controversial, practice in the securities industry), the Court denied the petition. Only Warren dissented from the denial. Brennan and Abe Fortas joined Warren in voting to grant certiorari, falling one vote short of the necessary four, but they did not join his dissent.[71] An opportunity for an expansive interpretation of the antitrust laws was passed up; when the issue returned, it would be addressed by a more conservative Court.

*Silver*'s ambiguous holding eventually returned to the Court in two cases announced on the same day in 1975. In both cases, the Court held that the antitrust laws must give way to the securities laws, focusing on the SEC's role in overseeing the allegedly anticompetitive practices. In *Gordon v. NYSE*, the Court held that SEC oversight rendered the NYSE immune from antitrust liability for fixing commission rates among its members.[72] In *United States v. NASD*, the Court held that SEC oversight of certain sales practice restrictions for investment companies immunized those restrictions from antitrust liability.[73] In both cases, *Silver* was read narrowly to confine its abundant potential for mischief.

BOUNDARIES    115

The system of fixed commissions at issue in *Gordon* had been a feature of the NYSE from its beginnings under the buttonwood tree in 1792. Moreover, the Exchange Act gave the SEC authority under § 19(b) to ensure reasonable rates, and the exchange's fixed rates were submitted to the SEC for review under § 6(a)(4) of the Act. The fixed rate structure had been under attack, however, beginning in the 1960s, with the SEC eventually eliminating it in 1975. For Powell at least, imposing enormous liability for a practice that had enjoyed regulatory sanction would be unjust:

> it would be grossly inequitable to impose liability of this magnitude [a claimed $1.5 billion in damages, plus attorneys' fees] upon private parties who have, for nearly 40 years, followed a practice to the knowledge of the government and with the full approval of the agency established by the Congress to regulate this business.

Powell's aversion to unanticipated liability exposures would be a recurring theme in securities cases, as we shall see in Chapter 6. Even Blackmun, generally open to expanding liability, was troubled, seeing a need for a uniform approach under SEC supervision, rather than "possibly disparate results from various antitrust courts over the land." Even so, Blackmun was

> troubled . . . with SEC inaction in this area . . . for years and years. Finally, they are getting underway. The lurking question is whether their lethargy has been brought to an end because of the presence of these antitrust suits in the federal courts. Unless this factor has some weight—and I doubt that it does—I am inclined to affirm here and to say that in this area of securities regulation, the antitrust laws are inapplicable.[74]

At conference, all but Brennan agreed. Blackmun ended up writing for a unanimous Court, with Douglas and Stewart (joined by Brennan), concurring separately to urge a narrow space for SEC oversight displacing antitrust law. The SEC's belated action to undo fixed commissions may have saved the agency from further incursion into its domain by antitrust regulators.

The *NASD* case proved considerably more contentious; once again, the SEC's inaction in response to suppression of competition created controversy. The case arose under § 22 of the Investment Company Act, which regulated sales practices by "open end" mutual funds, that is, the type of fund that allows investors to redeem their shares in the mutual fund at the fund's net asset value on the date of redemption. The dispute in *NASD* revolved around secondary market transactions in fund shares; the secondary market was largely driven by efforts to avoid the sales load imposed on initial sales by the fund. Fund companies used the sales

116   A HISTORY OF SECURITIES LAW

load revenues to encourage selling efforts by broker-dealers involved in distribution. The funds limited the resale of their shares to discourage arbitrage to avoid the sales load. Those restrictions were bolstered by rules adopted by the National Association of Securities Dealers limiting brokers from participating in this secondary market.

The suit pitted two federal regulators directly against each other. The Antitrust Division of the Justice Department argued that the resale limits and the NASD rules violated the Sherman Act. The SEC, participating as amicus, urged that its regulatory authority under the Investment Company Act displaced the antitrust laws. Section 22(f) of the Act allows investment companies to put restrictions on the transferability of their shares if they are disclosed, but not if the restrictions conflict with rules promulgated by the SEC.

The difficulty was that the SEC had not bothered to adopt any rules dealing with the transferability of shares, leading Brennan to complain at conference "SEC h[a]s done little." White favored letting DOJ proceed with its suit, noting that it would be a "[t]ougher case if SEC h[a]d put out a regul[ation]." Blackmun, even though inclined to vote with the SEC, noted that "[t]he SEC also has been long aware of the activities complained of and now (perhaps finally) has determined a course of action which should eliminate some of the anticompetitive acts."[75]

Notwithstanding the SEC's inaction, Powell's opinion for the majority upheld the agency's authority in the area. In an unusual move for him, Powell deferred to the SEC's interpretation of § 22(f), which it had held since the enactment of the Investment Company Act, as a "contemporaneous interpretation by the responsible agency . . . entitled to considerable weight."[76] More surprising yet, Powell rejected the "narrower interpretation of this provision advanced by the [DOJ]" as "disserv[ing] the broad remedial function of the statute." The SEC's acquiescence in resale restrictions imposed by the funds was "precisely the kind of administrative oversight of private practices that Congress contemplated when it enacted § 22(f)." The NASD's rules were insulated from attack under the antitrust laws because they were subject to SEC oversight under the Maloney Act, which had extended the reach of the Exchange Act to brokers trading in the over-the-counter market.

White dissented, attracting three other adherents to the Brandeisian faith in antitrust (Douglas, Brennan, and Marshall).[77] He complained that a presumption against the implied repeal of the antitrust laws was being neglected, replaced by a rule of implied antitrust immunity "where a regulatory agency has authority to approve business conduct whether or not the agency is directed to consider antitrust factors in making its regulatory decisions and whether or not there is other evidence that Congress intended to displace judicial with administrative enforcement." Worse yet, White complained, "Until recently, [the SEC] has seemingly left investors and the public to the tender mercies of the industry itself." The securities laws, intended to assert social control over finance, were now being wielded to shield finance from regulation under the antitrust laws. And the SEC was providing aid and comfort to the industry!

Douglas, in his last few months on the Court, still clung to his belief in social control over finance four decades after his New Deal heyday. He wryly noted in his joinder to White's dissent, "I may be influenced by the fact that I drafted the Maloney Act."[78] Apparently, Douglas had not gained as much control over the industry as he would have liked in 1938—or the SEC was not using it the way Douglas intended.

More notable was the Court finally coming to terms with *Silver's* confusing mélange of securities law, antitrust, and due process. The *NASD* and *Gordon* cases in the seventies had limited *Silver* without overruling it. The Court's unwillingness to overrule *Silver* left the door open for the claim in *Credit Suisse Securities (USA) LLC v. Billing.*[79] This case arose out of the "laddering" scandals of 2001–2002, which involved market manipulation in the secondary market after initial public offerings. The conduct alleged violated both the anti-manipulation and antifraud provisions of the securities laws; in fact, a parallel securities class action was brought, alleging essentially the same facts, resulting in a substantial settlement.[80] The twist in *Billing* was that at least some of the conduct alleged, if proven, would violate the antitrust laws as well. The plaintiffs in *Billing* reasoned that if the conduct violated both the antitrust and the securities laws, then there was no inconsistency between the two regimes. No implied repeal of the antitrust laws would be necessary.

*Billing* found the Justice Department's Antitrust Division and the SEC on opposing sides in the lower courts. Rather than authorize the SEC to file its own brief in the Supreme Court, the Solicitor General cobbled together a compromise position. He argued the case should be remanded to the district court to determine "whether respondents' allegations of prohibited conduct can, as a practical matter, be separated from conduct that is permitted by the regulatory scheme."[81] That task would require the lower court to decide whether SEC-permitted and SEC-prohibited conduct are "inextricably intertwined."

Stephen Breyer, writing for the Court, rejected both the plaintiffs' and Solicitor General's arguments. He discerned "only a fine, complex, detailed line separate[ing] activity that the SEC permits or encourages (for which [plaintiffs] must concede antitrust immunity) from activity that the SEC must (and inevitably will) forbid (and which, on [plaintiffs'] theory, should be open to antitrust attack.)" The Court worried that only a "securities expert" could locate this line, and even then, the SEC might shift it by deciding that previously forbidden conduct was now permissible. Moreover, Breyer worried that "nuanced nature of the evidentiary evaluations necessary to separate the permissible from the impermissible" would lead to inconsistent verdicts in the hands of "different nonexpert judges and different nonexpert juries." The unpredictability of such an arrangement for market participants is obvious. Rather than disrupting the scheme of securities regulation, the Court concluded that antitrust claims should be excluded entirely. *Billing* does not explicitly overrule *Silver*, but it leaves little doubt that *Silver* need not be taken seriously going forward. Securities regulation is sufficiently pervasive in the secondary markets that antitrust claims ordinarily will be barred. The SEC bears the responsibility of policing market manipulation.

Clarence Thomas dissented, pointing to the savings clause found in the Exchange Act, which preserves "any and all" "rights and remedies."[82] For Thomas, "[w]hen Congress wants to preserve all other remedies, using the word 'all' is sufficient." Thomas's textualist position would open the door to a myriad of antitrust claims challenging practices sanctioned by the securities laws, but a decisive majority was not interested in such disruptive literalism.

*Billing* is in some ways a throwback to the judicial deference of the forties, although the New Deal justices would surely have been troubled by *Billing*'s abandonment of the Brandeisian faith in antitrust. The general theme is judicial modesty: the Court lacks confidence in the ability of judges to understand the complexity of the securities markets. This judicial modesty, however, does not translate into judicial deference to the executive branch. The Court was unimpressed with the Solicitor General's effort at compromise; his "inextricably intertwined" principle failed to address the line-drawing difficulties that the Court had found. The Court was unwilling to defer to the government's effort to push it (and lower courts) into resolving complicated disputes over competing regulatory paradigms; the Court felt that it had to make a choice, and it chose to defer to the SEC's expertise in this context.

## D. Constitutional and Geographic Boundaries

Boundary questions could arise not just from adjacent regulatory regimes created by Congress but also from a more substantial barrier: the Constitution. The early battles over PUHCA revolved around the question of Congress's constitutional power, not limits on that power. The question of potential First Amendment limits on the SEC's authority did not make it to the Court until the 1980s, after the Court began to extend limited constitutional protection to "commercial speech" in cases like *Central Hudson Gas and Electric Corp. v. Public Service Comm'n.*[83] *Central Hudson* afforded non-misleading commercial speech some freedom from government regulation; judges would review "whether the regulation directly advances the governmental interest asserted, and whether it is not more extensive than is necessary to serve that interest."

BOUNDARIES 119

The SEC's case against Christopher Lowe raised difficult line-drawing issues under the First Amendment. The agency may have felt entirely justified in exercising its regulatory authority over Lowe, who was clearly an unsavory character. Lowe had been the principal of the Lowe Management Corporation, an investment adviser registered under the Investment Advisers Act. After Lowe was convicted of misappropriating funds from a client, among other offenses, the SEC revoked the company's registration as an investment adviser and barred Lowe from associating with any investment adviser. A year later, the SEC filed an enforcement action alleging that Lowe was violating the terms of the SEC's administrative order, as well as the registration requirements of the Act, by publishing investment newsletters. The SEC asked the district court to enjoin Lowe and his affiliated companies from publishing the newsletters. The SEC, however, did not allege that the newsletters were false or misleading or that Lowe was trading in any of the securities covered in the newsletters. The district court enjoined Lowe from providing individual advice to subscribers, but refused to enjoin publication of the newsletters. The Act did not by its terms distinguish individualized advice from publishing a newsletter, but the trial court held that constitutional considerations compelled an interpretation of the Act that would allow a limited registration for the purpose of publication.[84] The Second Circuit reversed, holding that: (1) the Act's exemption for "the publisher of any bona fide newspaper, news magazine, or business of financial publication of general and regular circulation" did not apply to Lowe; and 2) "regulation of commercial activity" of this sort was "permissible under the First Amendment."[85] Moreover, the appellate court found that Lowe's criminal history made his publications "potentially deceptive commercial speech." The Second Circuit limited its holding, however, allowing Lowe to continue publishing the newsletters if they omitted any advice about specific securities.

As the case came to the Supreme Court, there were a number of directions that the Court could go. Brennan's conference notes reflect a considerable diversity of views on the central question of whether the case should be resolved on statutory or constitutional grounds. There seemed to be a firm consensus, however, that the SEC was overreaching in this case, despite Lowe's unsavory past. Burger, for example, thought that an injunction against publication would be "Prior restraint without any doubt" and Marshall "wouldn't allow SEC to do any more than could do to Wall St. Journal."[86] White, however, while agreeing that "SEC regulation simply not justified by anything shown by govt here" was "Worried what SEC can do to watch this guy—can it require him to disclose—if treated as ordinary and not commercial speech, probably not." Blackmun "would like to give SEC some power to reach this guy." He acknowledged that "Publishing newsletter like this is protected speech" but "couldn't equate them with newspapers and within exemption." Rehnquist and O'Connor, however, thought the exemption might

## 120 A HISTORY OF SECURITIES LAW

be construed to cover the newsletters. Stevens thought that "FA protected," but wanted to "write as narrowly as can . . . would say Cong[ress] may some authority (disclosure for example) + we ought at least reserve it."

Stevens took on the challenge of writing an opinion that would attract a majority. His draft came down limiting the agency's power as a matter of statutory interpretation. A long exegesis of the Act's legislative history led to the conclusion that the newsletters "fall within the statutory exclusion for bona fide publications and that none of the petitioners is an 'investment adviser' as defined in the Act."[87] White, however, was unpersuaded by Stevens's effort to avoid directly addressing the constitutional issue, in part because he wanted to preserve the SEC's authority and saw Stevens as effectively overruling *Capital Gains*:

> I do not find the legislative history compelling enough to overturn the long-standing administrative interpretation of the Act, which the Commission was implementing in Capital Gains, 375 U.S. 180. Your disposal would effectively foreclose the disclosure remedies we approved against a publisher of a capital gains "report", whom the SEC had treated as an investment advisor. I would not take that course and would not interfere with other available remedies short of enjoining publication. Also, although you purport not to decide the constitutional issue, you seem to do so . . . and far too cryptically for me. I thus will concur along the lines of the Conference vote as I understand it.

White had joined the majority in *Capital Gains*, upholding the SEC's enforcement action against a registered investment adviser. Stevens responded, conceding that his "proposed draft would foreclose disclosure remedies against an unregistered publisher who had no person-to-person relationship with his subscribers—at least until Congress amended the statute to address that specific problem."[88] Stevens was not persuaded by the invocation of *Capital Gains*, noting that "no question was raised about the defendant's status as an investment adviser." Stevens further referenced the opinion's repeated references treating the newsletter publisher as a "fiduciary" and subscribers as "clients." Stevens also noted "it may be unusual to treat the relationship between such a publisher and five thousand subscribers to a report as 'fiduciary.'" Stevens presumably was unaware that the author of the opinion, Arthur Goldberg, adopted the fiduciary analysis at White's suggestion, as we discuss in Chapter 5. The extension of the fiduciary relationship to a publisher and five thousand subscribers had not attracted any pushback in the 1960s Court.

Stevens suggested their differences might not be all that significant:

> For a holding that an unregistered publisher like Lowe has a constitutional right to publish would mean, I suppose, that he could continue to publish

BOUNDARIES 121

without disclosing his purchases and sale of securities that are the subject of his reports. . . . my proposed construction of the statute would leave Congress free to draft legislation that would require appropriate disclosures even by publishers who might not be registered.

The SEC would likely disagree that this was an insignificant difference; the agency had long considered nondisclosure of purchases and sales to be a fraudulent omission. Indeed, that was the SEC's position in *Capital Gains*. The notion that requiring such disclosure would require legislation would have been a startling conclusion. Stevens's final opinion, however, included a footnote noting that "it is incorrect to assume that the only remedies against scalping are found in the Act. The mail-fraud statute would certainly be available for many violations, and the SEC has recently had success using Rule 10b-5 against a newsletter publisher."[89] White questioned the availability of these remedies. He pointed out "the requirement of Rule 10b-5 that any disclosure violate an existing fiduciary duty," and argued that the Court's holding that Lowe was not an investment adviser "excludes the possibility that the Investment Advisers Act could supply the requisite fiduciary duty."

The exchange of letters between Stevens and White—shared with the conference—left the majority in play. Blackmun chimed in to say that he "thought the Commission's construction of the statute was a permissible one and was entitled to some deference. I am also inclined to agree with Byron that the legislative history does not support the weight your opinion would give it." Burger and Rehnquist were also on the fence. Ultimately, Blackmun, Brennan, Marshall, and O'Connor would sign on to Stevens's opinion avoiding the constitutional question, while Burger and Rehnquist joined White's concurrence.[90] The SEC's power was limited under the Investment Advisers Act, but the agency avoided a constitutional defeat that might have been much more costly in the long run.

The Court's series of commercial speech cases were part of its larger embrace of expanded constitutional rights of corporations to free speech, and later, free exercise of religion. Cases such as *First National Bank of Boston v. Bellotti*, *Citizens United v. Federal Election Comm'n*, and *Burwell v. Hobby Lobby Stores, Inc.*[91] would provoke considerable controversy and even calls for constitutional amendment. This series of cases, perhaps the Court's most intrusive constitutional interpretation relating to government regulation of business since 1937, did not implicate the securities laws. Securities law and corporate law continued as separate bodies of law, a topic we cover in Chapter 7.

The Court addressed literal boundary issues in a 2010 case arising from the extraterritorial application of securities law. *Morrison v. National Australia Bank Ltd.* concerned a so-called F-cubed securities class action in which foreign

## 122  A HISTORY OF SECURITIES LAW

plaintiffs filed suit against a foreign company having bought their shares on a foreign exchange. In this case it was Australian investors who had purchased common shares of the largest Australian bank over the Australian Stock Exchange. The district court dismissed the case for lack of subject matter jurisdiction and the Second Circuit affirmed.[92] The Second Circuit, under the leadership of Henry Friendly, had developed a two-prong test to determine whether the application of the U.S. securities laws was appropriate. Jurisdiction to adjudicate a § 10(b) claim would exist if the plaintiff could show either: (1) an effect of American securities markets or investors or (2) significant conduct relating to the fraud taking place in the United States.[93] The plaintiffs disclaimed reliance on the effects prong because the American investor who purchased National Australia's American Depository Receipts on the New York Stock Exchange was dismissed from the litigation at an early stage.[94] The conduct at issue was the inflation of the value of assets of Homeside, a wholly owned subsidiary of National Australia operating a mortgage servicing business out of Florida. The plaintiffs alleged that Homeside had exaggerated the value of its mortgage servicing contracts and that these inflated figures were passed through to National Australia's consolidated balance sheet, thereby causing National Australia's stock to trade at an artificially high value.[95] When National Australia eventually wrote down the value of Homeside's assets, the price of National Australia's stock plummeted and the plaintiffs filed suit. The Second Circuit, however, said that the federal courts lacked jurisdiction over the Australian investors' claims because conduct in Australia was the source of the alleged misrepresentations.

The plaintiffs filed a petition for certiorari, and the Supreme Court asked for the Solicitor General's views. In the government's amicus brief, the Solicitor General argued that the Second Circuit had erred in treating the question as jurisdictional.[96] Turning to the merits, the government argued that the Second Circuit was at once too restrictive and too generous in considering the § 10(b) claims. Too restrictive, because the Second Circuit had held that private plaintiffs and the SEC should be held to the same standard; the government argued that private plaintiffs should be held to a higher standard. The government urged that the correct standard for enforcement and criminal actions was what it characterized as the full reach of § 10(b): "a transnational securities fraud violates Section 10(b) when the fraud involves significant conduct in the United States that is material to the fraud's success." For private plaintiffs, additional restrictions were in order. Specifically, a private plaintiff should be required to "establish not simply that his loss resulted from the fraudulent scheme as a whole, but that the loss resulted directly from the component of the fraud that occurred in the United States."

The SEC's efforts to throw the private plaintiffs under the bus were to no avail. The Court rejected not only the plaintiffs' claim, but also the government's argument that private actions should be held to a higher standard. Antonin

Scalia—clearly a jurist on a mission—wrote for the majority. After summarily dispatching the Second Circuit's "threshold error" in treating the question as jurisdictional,[97] Scalia turned to dismantling the Second Circuit's conduct and effects test. The Second Circuit, noting the silence of § 10(b) on extraterritorial effect, had taken it upon itself to divine what Congress would have done if it had thought about the question. What would the Second Circuit's hypothetical Congress do?: (1) protect American investors; and (2) discourage fraudsters from operating out of the United States. In Scalia's view, however, the Second Circuit's test was wrong from its inception. The Second Circuit's test failed to accord due weight to the Court's long-standing presumption against giving statutes extraterritorial effect: "When a statute gives no clear indication of an extraterritorial application, it has none." The Second Circuit had gone off the tracks when it had inferred from § 10(b)'s silence on the question of extraterritorial application an invitation to engage in "judicial-speculation-made-law-divining what Congress would have wanted if it had thought of the situation before the court." That judicial speculation was bad enough, but it had led to "unpredictable and inconsistent application of § 10(b) to transnational cases." From Scalia's perspective, "[t]here is no more damning indictment of the 'conduct' and 'effects' tests than the Second Circuit's own declaration that 'the presence or absence of any single factor which was considered significant in other cases . . . is not necessarily dispositive in future cases.'" The Solicitor General's somewhat cosmetic repackaging of that test fared no better. Nor was the SEC's endorsement of that test entitled to deference, as it was premised on the judicial errors committed by the Second Circuit.

Having debunked the Second Circuit's approach, Scalia devised his own rule of decision. Unsurprisingly, he argued that his preferred test was grounded in the text of the statute. Examining the text of § 10(b), Scalia found that the focus was not on deception, but rather, the provision's requirement that deception, to be actionable, must be "in connection with the purchase or sale of securities." The purchase or sale transaction, Scalia reasoned, was the touchstone of what Congress sought to regulate; Congress sought to protect purchasers and sellers. This analysis of § 10(b)'s text led Scalia to his test for its application: "transactions in securities listed on domestic exchanges, and domestic transactions in other securities." Scalia's conclusion derived from the statutory text was bolstered by the structure of the statute.

Scalia also worried about "the probability of incompatibility with the applicable laws of other countries." On this point, the Court appears to have been swayed by the amicus briefs filed by Australia, Great Britain, and France, who protested the exposure of companies headquartered in their jurisdictions to American class actions. When the Second Circuit was developing its conduct and effects test, the United States was the only game in town for securities class

124  A HISTORY OF SECURITIES LAW

actions, so the Second Circuit's imperialism was not directly stepping on the toes of any foreign government. Many countries object, however, to the exposure of their companies to our class action regime. Most countries remain skeptical of the utility of the class action as an enforcement device. A handful, however, most notably Australia and Canada, recently have adopted securities class action regimes of their own. The conflict with American law becomes more acute when those companies are also subject to class action suit in their home jurisdictions. The threat of overdeterrence posed by double liability is obvious.

On the opposite end was Stevens's concurrence. Stevens embraced the Second Circuit's conduct and effects test, and more generally, the judiciary's role in creating the § 10(b) cause of action.

> The development of § 10(b) law was hardly an instance of judicial usurpation. Congress invited an expansive role for judicial elaboration when it crafted such an open-ended statute in 1934. And both Congress and the Commission subsequently affirmed that role when they left intact the relevant statutory and regulatory language, respectively, throughout all the years that followed.[98]

Stevens gave considerable weight to the fact the Second Circuit test was long-standing. More pointedly, while agreeing with the Court's conclusion, he decried "the Court's continuing campaign to render the private cause of action under § 10(b) toothless." (We explore the topic of implied rights of action at length in Chapter 6.)

The *National Australia* decision produced an immediate, if somewhat clumsy, reaction from Congress. Less than a month after the decision was handed down, Congress passed the Dodd-Frank Wall Street Reform and Consumer Protection Act, a wholesale reform of financial regulation responding to the 2008–2009 financial crisis. Among its reforms was one aimed at overruling the result in *National Australia*, as the bill's legislative history makes clear. Unfortunately, Congress enacted language ensuring only that the courts would have *jurisdiction* to hear cases with extraterritorial application, not that § 10(b) would have extraterritorial application. Thus, Congress repeated the Second Circuit's error of treating the scope of the law as jurisdictional, rather than a merits question. Even if the courts ignore the provision's language and follow its intent to expand the substantive scope of § 10(b), it applies only to actions brought by the SEC or the Justice Department. Congress's response is rather humorous in light of Scalia's claim that one benefit of a clear presumption against extraterritorial application is that it "preserv[es] a stable background against which Congress can legislate with predictable effects."[99] The "predictable effects" that Scalia claims for his rule are premised on an assumption of minimal competence on the part of Congress. That assumption proved unjustified in this case; keeping up with the

BOUNDARIES 125

latest Supreme Court opinions is apparently not a priority on the other side of Capitol Hill.

## E. Whither Boundaries?

What can we take away from the Court's supervision of the boundaries of the securities law? Under the definition of security, most of the Court's work has been devoted to the investment contract test. As with other areas of securities law, the Court was inclined to be generous in defining boundaries for the first three decades or so. Complications arose, however, when the securities laws began to jostle against other bodies of law, particularly antitrust. The seventies Court, under the leadership of Lewis Powell, began to push back against expansive definitions of investment contract, while being more open to the preemption of antitrust claims by the securities laws. Arguably both trends were fueled by the rise of class actions in that decade. Powell had less success in attempting to limit the definition of sale to shield what he perceived to be ordinary commercial transactions. Powell's reliance on economic realities to cabin the definition of investment contract led to difficulties of its own, creating uncertainty for enumerated categories in the definition of a security, including "stock" and "note." Consequently, the Court, again under the leadership of Powell, to pulled back from case-by-case analysis of economic reality in favor of specific tests for those categories that focused more on investor expectations. The result was greater predictability.

# 5

# Insider Trading

[The] SEC should have gone to Congress long ago. Rather, it has elected to write expansive Rules (e.g., Rule 10b-5 . . . ), and then undertake to extend the vague language of the Rule to the edge of rationality.

Letter from Lewis F. Powell, Jr., to Michael P. Dooley, Professor of
Law, University of Virginia (Oct. 25, 1980)

Insider trading law, prior to the adoption of the federal securities laws, had a limited scope. The prohibition, such as it was, was found in the common law cause of action for deceit. That cause took in affirmative misrepresentations and half-truths, but sometimes strict limits of duty, materiality, scienter, reliance, and causation confined its reach. In addition, equity courts had long supplemented the common law action of deceit to provide relief for fraud. Those equity causes arose originally in non-damages settings for which actions at law were inadequate. Even these limited causes of action were of uncertain utility in the context of government enforcement.[1]

When the Pecora hearings of 1933 highlighted the problem of manipulative trading by insiders, Congress looked beyond existing legal remedies for a solution. Section 16(a) of the Securities Exchange Act of 1934 requires all directors, officers and 10% shareholders to disclose their purchases and sales of equity securities. Section 16(b) then requires that these statutory insiders disgorge any profits from a sale and purchase (or purchase and sale) during a six-month period, whether or not those transactions are based on inside information. This broad statutory response targeted market manipulation more than trading on inside information. It was both over—and under-inclusive for dealing with information asymmetry between buyers and sellers. Nonetheless, it was the front-line response to insider trading until the 1960s. As the SEC emerged from a decade-long slumber under the vigorous leadership of Chairman Bill Cary, the agency, and then the federal courts returned to fraud concepts to regulate insider trading. The key move was a broad definition of fraud that prohibited trading based on any informational advantage. *Texas Gulf Sulphur*, a Second Circuit decision that recognized insider trading as fraud under Rule 10b-5 of the Exchange Act, was the headline securities decision of the decade.[2]

*A History of Securities Law in the Supreme Court.* A.C. Pritchard and Robert B. Thompson, Oxford University Press.
© Oxford University Press 2023. DOI: 10.1093/oso/9780197665916.003.0006

INSIDER TRADING    127

The rapid development of a broad insider trading prohibition under Rule 10b-5 would face a formidable obstacle, however, after Lewis Powell joined the Supreme Court in 1972. When the Court finally took up Rule 10b-5 insider trading law in the 1980s, Powell wrote the two foundational opinions: *Chiarella v. United States* and *Dirks v. SEC*.[3] Those decisions validated the use of fraud law to combat insider dealing, while cabining it within a fiduciary duty framework narrower than the Second Circuit's approach. Powell's opinions reflected unease with the SEC's efforts to expand Rule 10b-5 through interpretations that Powell saw as poorly grounded in the text, rather than seeking legislation. Powell reined in the SEC's regulatory imperialism, but he did not repudiate fiduciary analysis. He recognized the need to limit insiders' use of corporate information. To do that, he constructed a doctrinal framework built on common law fraud that could take in silence by a fiduciary when trading. Critically, Powell extended application of the prohibition to trading on exchanges, a departure from the common law fraud rule, which did not reach anonymous markets. That move empowered the SEC and the Justice Department to pursue the insider trading that scored the biggest jackpots. Powell's common law framework, however, left holes that bedevil the law of insider trading to this day.

In this chapter, we follow the Supreme Court (with a short detour to the Second Circuit) as it develops the modern law of insider trading. The Court, with encouragement from the SEC, proceeded down two tracks, one statutory under § 16(b), the other a quasi-common law prohibition under Rule 10b-5. The two tracks yielded very different results. The statutory path led to a prophylactic rule, relatively clear but narrow. The common law path produced a broader, but somewhat more amorphous standard, based on fraud. Neither one fully tracks the possibilities for informational advantage in the securities markets, reflecting the limits of their respective statutory foundations. As such, the SEC and others with a reformist bent who aspire to move closer to a "level playing field"—that is, limiting informational advantages if at all feasible—have been disappointed by the Court's jurisprudence. Congress resisted occasional calls for it to reenter the field and adopt a more sweeping prohibition; the legislature has been largely content to allow the courts and SEC to develop this area of law.

## A. Early Prohibitions Based on Fraud and the § 16(b) Alternative

Early twentieth-century-American cases diverged on whether silence could come within fraud. All courts agreed, however, the parties must be in privity. The privity requirement effectively blocked fraud's use in public securities markets, as it would be impossible in an anonymous market for a plaintiff to

128  A HISTORY OF SECURITIES LAW

prove reliance on an unknown insider.[4] For its part, the Supreme Court had recognized a narrow rule against insider dealing in 1909. The occasion was a common law case coming to the Court from the Philippines (then a U.S. protectorate). In *Strong v. Repide*, a shareholder of a land holding company had sued the company's managing director, who was also its majority shareholder.[5] Mrs. Strong, the shareholder-plaintiff, alleged that Repide had withheld information regarding the potential sale of the company's principal asset when buying stock from her. The director made no misrepresentations to the shareholder, but had made an active effort to conceal his identity as the purchaser. Moreover, the information withheld by the director was highly material to the company's value. The Supreme Court upheld a fraud claim against the director, holding that he had a duty to disclose based on the "special circumstances" presented by the case. Consistent with basing the obligation on the existence of a fiduciary duty, the rule was limited to existing shareholders and did not extend to prospective ones.

By the time of the first Restatement of Torts in 1938, the drafters would include silence or omissions as fraud in a business transaction in which a duty to disclose arose from "a fiduciary or other similar relationship of trust or confidence." Fiduciary duty would eventually become the dominant thread of modern insider trading law, but the Restatement commented that it was "not within the scope of the Restatement to state the rules which determine the duty of disclosure, which under the law of business association the directors owe to its shareholders." Only a few cases, such as *Strong*, had required disclosure in a corporate setting and none of those cases applied such a duty to corporate insiders trading in anonymous markets.[6] Thus, the common law as it stood when Congress enacted the securities laws in the 1930s seemed an unpromising tool for combating insider dealing.

Against that permissive backdrop, manipulative trading by insiders dominated the Pecora hearings that led up to the 1930s securities legislation.[7] The Securities Exchange Act of 1934 included § 16 designed to check trading by insiders at shareholders' expense. Instead of banning insider trading outright, Congress mandated disclosure of trades and a strict liability provision for disgorgement of profits. That remedy was prophylactic, applying whether or not the insider had used, or had access to, material nonpublic information.[8] This innovative, but draconian, approach provoked calls for modification or repeal from corporate America, but the law continues to apply to American public corporations.[9] Somewhat surprisingly, given the early controversy, nearly three decades would pass before the Supreme Court heard its first § 16(b) disgorgement case.

While the Supreme Court ignored § 16(b), the Second Circuit was busy, hearing the lion's share of § 16(b) suits in this period. The Second Circuit decided twenty-one cases, with Bill Douglas's old friend, Charles Clark,[10] an earnest advocate for regulation, sitting on fifteen. Although § 16(b) cases take a back seat to Rule 10b-5 in contemporary discussions of insider trading, these early cases set the stage for the three decisions from the sixties that are the key building blocks of this chapter—the SEC's *Cady, Roberts* ruling, the Supreme Court's decision in *Capital Gains*, and the Second Circuit's opinions in *Texas Gulf Sulphur* construing Rule 10b-5 to prohibit insider trading.

The Second Circuit's robust § 16(b) docket meant that the court filled out much of the detail for this new statute. Panels of the circuit upheld the constitutionality of the provision three times in 1943, 1947, and 1951.[11] Clark wrote the circuit's first decision, *Smolowe v. Delendo*, embracing an expansive interpretation driven by the Act's purpose, rather than its text. In *Smolowe* the court adopted the "lowest in, highest out" method of calculating damages that remains the § 16(b) standard. Clark pushed this draconian measure based on his view of the legislative purpose to squeeze out the insider's entire possible gain. Clark's unabashedly purposivist judicial philosophy shone through in his memo to his colleagues in *Smolowe*:

> I do not hold the view that when we think Congress has not done a clear job, we can throw up our hands and say we won't play; I think there is a clear judicial responsibility to make an act workable, if possible . . . Moreover, by setting such a standard for Congress, we are not refusing to interpret; we are actually interpreting, a certain way, while in the same breath we are practically admitting that probably we are going against what Congress would have intended had the M.C.s thought the matter through.[12]

Clark saw his job as a judge to implement Congress's purposes, not simply to follow textual directives.

In 1951 in *Gratz v. Claughton*, Judge Learned Hand linked Congress's purpose in passing § 16(b) to a perceived failure of state-based fiduciary duty law: "For many years a grave omission in our corporation law had been its indifference to dealings of directors or other corporate officers in the shares of their companies." A 1956 case, *Stella v. Graham-Paige Motors* again invoked the fiduciary reasoning of *Gratz* in holding that the initial transaction by which a person become a 10% shareholder counts toward creating § 16(b) liability. The interpretive theme was to read the statute broadly to stamp out the possibility of the abuses decried by Congress in 1934.[13] Would the Supreme Court follow Clark's purposivist philosophy?

The first glimmers of a broader prohibition against a fiduciary's misuse of inside information outside of § 16(b) arose in a 1951 bankruptcy case. As discussed in Chapter 2, in *Mosser v. Darrow*, the Supreme Court, at the SEC's urging, upheld liability against Darrow. Darrow was a bankruptcy trustee who allowed employees working on behalf of the trust estate to profit from trading

130   A HISTORY OF SECURITIES LAW

in bonds issued by subsidiaries of the trust. With Darrow's knowledge and consent, the employees purchased the bonds in the open market and later sold them to the trust at a mark-up. Robert Jackson, writing for the Court, held that the "transactions were as forbidden for benefit of others as they would have been on behalf of the trustee himself."[14] The rule of *Mosser* was strict, but limited in its scope: the duties imposed on trustees had long been absolute, reflecting the heightened potential for abuse in the absence of active monitoring. Moreover, *Mosser* did not suggest that any duty was owed to the bondholders who sold at a discount to the price paid by the trust. The obligation ran to the trust itself, not its security holders.

## B. The Swinging Sixties for Insider Trading Law

As the 1960s opened there was still widespread agreement that prevailing conceptions of fraud did not encompass trades occurring over anonymous securities exchanges. Affirmative lies and half-truths were covered by the traditional common law cause of action of deceit, but pure nondisclosure in exchange trading was not yet recognized as fraud.[15] Those fetters would fall away in the 1960s, as insider trading law would see a dramatic expansion. A newly activist SEC would shift the legal focus from § 16(b)'s mechanical disgorgement provision to a broadly defined fiduciary duty arising under Rule 10b-5's "catch-all" antifraud provision. The SEC drove the expansion, but the Supreme Court's purposive interpretation of fraud under the federal securities laws laid the foundation for the modern law of insider trading.

### 1. Bill Cary Triggers the Revolution in *Cady, Roberts*

John F. Kennedy's inauguration in 1961 set the stage for a securities law renaissance. Kennedy's father, Joe, had been the first chairman of the SEC. John Kennedy's transition team included James Landis, who as we saw in Chapter 1, helped draft the key securities laws. Landis had succeeded Joe Kennedy as SEC chairman. President Kennedy's choice to head the SEC, Columbia Law Professor William Cary, also had strong links to the SEC's New Deal glory days. Cary had been a student in one of Professor William O. Douglas's last corporate finance classes and later worked for Chairman Douglas at the SEC.[16]

Cary pushed the agency in a more activist direction shortly after his arrival with his opinion for the Commission in *Cady, Roberts & Co.*[17] *Cady, Roberts* announced that the agency would treat its statutory mandate to protect investors broadly, interpreting Rule 10b-5 to prohibit insider trading. The Commission had adopted Rule 10b-5 two decades earlier under § 10(b)'s authority as a general antifraud prohibition, but the rule and statute make no mention of insider trading. Moreover, testimony before Congress by prior agency chairs put coverage of insider trading outside the rule's remit.[18] Notwithstanding the textual omission, the SEC held in *Cady, Roberts* that the partner of a brokerage firm had violated Rule 10b-5 when he tipped nonpublic information to one of the traders at his firm. The partner had learned—in his role as a director of a public company—that the company was planning to reduce its dividend. In concluding that the partner had violated Rule 10b-5 by tipping, Cary laid out a broad insider trading prohibition under the antifraud rule:

**Figure 5.1**
**A New Approach to Insider Trading:** Bill Cary, shown here being sworn in as SEC Chairman by Bill Douglas, revived Douglas's activist regulatory approach. Contemporaneously with the agency's decision in *Cady Roberts*, it was also arguing before the Supreme Court for a broader understanding of fraud in *Capital Gains* and an expansive interpretation of § 16(b) in *Blau*. The SEC was rebuffed in *Blau*, but gained a sweeping victory in *Capital Gains*. *Capital Gains* validated the agency's decision in *Cady Roberts*, laying the foundation for the modern law of insider trading.

The obligation rests on two principal elements; first, the existence of a relationship giving access, directly or indirectly, to information intended to be available only for a corporate purpose and not for the personal benefit of anyone, and second, the inherent unfairness involved where a party takes advantage of such information knowing it is unavailable to those with whom he is dealing.

These elements are nowhere to be found in the text of either Rule 10b-5 or § 10(b). Cary gave notice that in interpreting "[the] elements [of § 10(b)] under the broad language of the anti-fraud provisions we are not to be circumscribed by fine distinctions and rigid classifications." The SEC intended to protect "the buying public" "from the misuse of special information." The SEC would construe the securities laws to further that purpose; statutory literalism would not be an impediment. Moreover, Cary's approach also rejected the narrow confines of insider trading under state corporate law and traditional notions of fiduciary duty, most notably, the requirement of a face-to-face transaction. "Relationship" and "unfairness" certainly overlap with fiduciary duty—the tipper in *Cady, Roberts*, as a director, occupied a classic fiduciary position—but Cary did not pigeon-hole his approach into the fiduciary framework. Indeed, Cary went so far as to proclaim the federal securities laws a far-reaching substantive corporate law.

## 2. *Blau v. Lehman*: The SEC's Unsuccessful Effort to Expand § 16(b)

Cary's broad vision of the SEC's authority and his new approach to insider trading had not yet been validated by a court.[19] Just a month after the SEC handed down *Cady, Roberts* the agency's lawyer was arguing before the Supreme Court in *Blau v. Lehman*.[20] The SEC urged that the technical language of § 16(b) be read broadly "on policy grounds" that echoed Cary's purposivist interpretation of Rule 10b-5 in *Cady, Roberts*. In *Blau* the plaintiff and the SEC asked the Court to extend § 16(b) liability to a partnership (Lehman Brothers) when one of its partners was a director with knowledge of inside information and another partner traded the stock. The district court had found, however, that the director had not shared his knowledge of the company's affairs with his Lehman partners, and therefore, that the trading decisions had not been based on inside information. The Court noted the breadth of the SEC's argument: it "suggest[s] that § 16(b)'s forfeiture of profits should be extended to include all persons realizing 'short swing' profits who either act on the basis of 'inside' information or have the possibility of 'inside' information."

The Commission's argument was weakened, however, by its concession that "such an interpretation is not justified by the literal language of § 16(b)." The statute did not prohibit insider trading across the board, but rather required disgorgement of profits made by three designated groups—directors, officers, and 10% shareholders—when they both purchased and sold within six months. The SEC's preferred construction of § 16(b) would have made it a general prohibition against insider trading, extending disgorgement to all manner of tippees.[21] Hugo Black, writing for the Court, acknowledged the SEC's "persuasive policy arguments that the [Exchange] Act should be broadened in this way to prevent 'the unfair use of information' more effectively." Amending the statute, however, was not the Court's job: "Congress can and might amend § 16(b) if the Commission would present to it the policy arguments it has presented to us, but we think that Congress is the proper agency to change an interpretation of the Act unbroken since its passage, if the change is to be made." In other words, lofty policy goals would not justify an end run around plain statutory text.

Douglas dissented, denouncing the majority for "sanction[ing], as vested, a practice so notoriously unethical as profiting on inside information."[22] Only Warren joined Douglas; even the liberal Brennan was unable to "strain the language so far."[23] The liberal bloc awaited reinforcements, as Kennedy had not yet nominated a justice to the Supreme Court. For the SEC, *Blau* offered scant hope that the Supreme Court would be receptive to Cary's free-ranging method of statutory interpretation.

### 3. *Capital Gains Research Bureau*: A Foothold for Fiduciary Duty

The SEC's opportunity came in a case coming out of the Second Circuit, *Securities and Exchange Commission v. Capital Gains Research Bureau, Inc.*[24] The case was argued at the appellate court contemporaneously with the decisions in *Blau* in the Supreme Court and *Cady, Roberts* at the SEC. The statute at issue was the antifraud provision of the Investment Advisers Act of 1940, § 206, which tracks the language of Rule 10b-5, albeit incompletely.[25] As such, the case provided an early judicial barometer for Cary's approach in *Cady, Roberts*. The SEC enforcement action against Capital Gains Research Bureau, Inc. and its owner targeted the nebulous area between misleading half-truths and pure omissions, that is, sharp dealing without affirmative misstatements.[26] Here the law of fraud remained unclear. The SEC was pursuing inside information of a more nefarious sort than in *Cady, Roberts*—not information traders learned from a confidential source, but rather information that they themselves created in order to induce others to trade in the stock. Capital Gains published a newsletter distributed to

134 A HISTORY OF SECURITIES LAW

approximately five thousand subscribers. The newsletter highlighted a number of stocks in each issue, generally predicting an increase in price. The SEC alleged that on a number of occasions the defendants had purchased shares in the recommended companies prior to distributing the newsletter. When the stocks increased in price and trading volume after the newsletter went out, Capital Gains liquidated its positions, usually within a week or two.

The lower courts—the trial court, a three-judge panel of the Second Circuit, and the in banc Second Circuit[27]—each rejected the SEC's argument that Capital Gains's failure to disclose its purchases and subsequent sales violated § 206. The courts hewed closely to the traditional common law of fraud. Leonard Moore's opinion for the Second Circuit's three-judge panel upheld the district court's denial of the injunction. Moore focused on the misrepresentation portion of the breach of duty element in the common law regime as applied to the advisor's recommendations. Moore asked whether the statement was "honest when made," looking for either misstated facts or a "belief that a recommended stock had a dismal rather than bright future.[28] If, instead of an affirmative misrepresentation, the failure to disclose the advisor's subsequent sale were pursued as a basis of liability, Moore would frame it in the language of the adjacent part of the duty element—half-truth. For example, disclosure might be required if the adviser was being paid to tout the stock.[29]

The other judges who would join Moore to form the in banc majority also construed fraud narrowly. Henry Friendly wrote his colleagues that both a "device, scheme or artifice to defraud" and a "transaction, practice or course of business which operates as a fraud or deceit" if "read in their ordinary sense" were lacking if the defendants did not believe that their sales would depress the price of the securities to the detriment of their customers.[30] Friendly invoked *Blau*—handed down by the Supreme Court the month before—as a caution "against judicial expansion of provision of the securities laws to accomplish objectives believed to be salutary." He scoffed at "the liberal use of such terms as 'fiduciaries'—making people who sell an advisory service sound like trustees of an express trust."

Moore's opinion for the panel raised a second obstacle to the SEC's interpretation—the need for rulemaking:

> [W]hat the SEC would have the court do here is to create a law which Congress has never enacted or a regulation which the SEC has never promulgated which, in effect, would prohibit investment advisers or their employees from purchasing or selling any of the many stocks covered by their services.

The SEC would have disclaimed any inference that its preferred interpretation would sweep as broadly as Moore suggested. The uncertainty over the contours of

INSIDER TRADING    135

the SEC's interpretation of § 206, however, only reinforced the need for the specificity that rulemaking could provide. And rulemaking was certainly feasible; just three days after *Capital Gains* was argued in the Second Circuit, the SEC announced a proposal to amend its rules under the Investment Advisers Act to require recordkeeping of securities transactions by investment advisers and their personnel.[31] If the SEC could require recordkeeping, it could require disclosure.

Charles Clark also sat on the three-judge panel; his dissent echoed Douglas's moralistic tone in *Blau*. The majority had "endorse[d] and in effect validate[d] a distressingly low standard of business morality," a result that "top advisers ... not only do not desire, but find rather shocking, in the doubt thus cast upon the good faith and loyalty of their profession."[32] Loyal advisers needed protection "against the stigma of unscrupulous tipsters and touts." Unlike Moore, Clark stressed that an investment adviser was a fiduciary, whose "first duty ... is loyalty to his beneficiary; if he is engaged in feathering his own nest, he cannot be giving his client that wholly disinterested advice which it is his stock in trade to provide."

The SEC's petition for rehearing in banc generated a heated debate among the Second Circuit judges on the role of text and purpose in the interpretation of the securities laws. That debate expanded on both lines of argument in Moore's decision for the panel. Clark, seizing the initiative after oral argument, launched the first memo to his colleagues just one day later. Section 206 was intended, Clark urged, "to impose fiduciary obligations on those who serve as investment advisers." Clark also rejected the argument that the SEC should have promulgated a rule, as "quite frankly judicial legislation amending the statute, since the statute is directly prohibitory." Clark urged deference to the agency:

> The SEC is indeed unfortunate in having to bring its regulatory processes before so conservative a court as ours; I wonder if any other federal appellate court would give the Commission a like run-around. I believe we should let it get on with its heavy tasks without the kind of judicial harassment it has here received.[33]

Clark retained his New Deal faith in agency expertise even after the SEC's dormant decade in the fifties.

Friendly, a prominent proponent of agency rulemaking, urged that Congress's 1960 addition of rulemaking authority to § 206 allowed "the SEC [to] accomplish everything it seeks."[34] Friendly then went on to present an extended history of that amendment, from which he concluded that the power the SEC sought in this case had previously been absent from § 206, but was now available to the agency through rulemaking pursuant to § 206(4).

The in banc majority sided with Friendly on both the narrow meaning of fraud and the need for rulemaking if the SEC wanted to expand it. All that remained was drafting a new opinion. Moore added Friendly's rendition of the

136   A HISTORY OF SECURITIES LAW

legislative history, as well as *Blau*'s caution "against the excessive judicial expansion of provisions of the securities laws to accomplish objectives believed to be salutary."[35] Purpose could not trump text.

Clark's new dissent praised the securities laws extravagantly: "this legislation was brilliantly successful in responding to a genuine social need. It is a prime demonstration of the capacity of a democratic government to meet a social crisis skillfully and positively."[36] The majority's opinion, however, would "scuttle the last of these highly useful statutes and leave it as but a shell." The securities laws, urged Clark, should be "liberally construed to effectuate the broad remedial purpose of the acts." And he rejected the suggestion that the SEC could reach the defendants' conduct through rulemaking: "the hope of regulation which will require Capital Gains to meet appropriate fiduciary standards not contained in the statute is illusory indeed."

After being rebuffed by the Supreme Court in *Blau v. Lehman*, the SEC might well have been pessimistic about its prospects in *Capital Gains*, particularly after its defeat in the Second Circuit. Yet in those few months there were important personnel changes at the Court. Byron White replaced Charles Whittaker and Arthur Goldberg replaced Felix Frankfurter; the newcomers would play a decisive role in what turned out to be a sweeping win for the SEC in the Supreme Court. Five justices voted to grant certiorari, including the two newcomers; Chief Justice Earl Warren expressed concern that the Second Circuit "gives aid + comfort to sharp dealers."[37] The result after argument was lopsided; only John Harlan voted to affirm his former colleagues on the Second Circuit.

The rookie Goldberg was assigned the opinion. Goldberg's initial circulation of his *Capital Gains* draft did not focus on the investment adviser's status as a fiduciary.[38] The language in the final opinion relating to fraud by fiduciaries was added in response to a letter from White. White, who had been a transactional lawyer rather than a litigator in his native Colorado, was relying upon the research of his law clerk, Rex Lee, as the basis for his suggestions.[39] White suggested that:

> [T]he treatment might be stronger if the investment adviser may be looked upon as a fiduciary . . . and if the content of fraud and deceit as applied to a fiduciary is considered. . . . If the fiduciary has a settled duty to disclose and if his failure to do so is termed fraudulent, there was little need for Congress in dealing with the fiduciary in the Investment Advisers Act to speak of anything but fraud in order to reach a failure to disclose a material fact or at the very least a conflict of interest.[40]

In other words, the Second Circuit majority had erred not because it restricted § 206 to common law fraud of affirmative misstatements or half-truths, but rather because material nondisclosure by a fiduciary was fraud per se—no misstatement was necessary. The Court did not search, as the appellate court did, for badges of intentional fraud tied to affirmative misstatements. In the context of action by a fiduciary, the common law (or at least equity) did not need to be stretched to treat nondisclosure as fraudulent. No specific mention of omissions in § 206's text would be required, nor would rulemaking. For this Court, silence was fraud for a fiduciary with a duty to speak.

Goldberg quickly latched on to his fellow newcomer White's suggestion, revising his opinion to emphasize the relation between fiduciary status and fraud:

> Nor is it necessary, in a suit against a fiduciary, which Congress recognized the investment adviser to be, to establish all the elements required in a suit against a party to an arms-length transaction. Courts have imposed on a fiduciary an affirmative duty of "utmost good faith, and full and fair disclosure of all material facts."[41]

Notable here is the lack of analysis supporting the conclusion that a newsletter publisher was a fiduciary.[42] Notwithstanding Goldberg's breezy treatment of this issue, the holding here would become the germ of the insider trading prohibition based on fiduciary duty that the Court would later recognize under § 10(b) and Rule 10b-5.

Having used fraud, at least in its equity sense, to free § 206 from the common law constraints that the Second Circuit had imposed on it, Goldberg announced an interpretive canon that was surely music to Bill Cary's ears: "Congress intended the Investment Advisers Act of 1940 to be construed like other securities legislation enacted for the purpose of avoiding frauds, not technically and restrictively, but flexibly to effectuate its remedial purposes." Having adopted this flexible/remedial interpretive canon from Clark's dissent, Goldberg also followed Clark in brushing aside attempts to parse the text of § 206 narrowly: "Congress, in enacting [§ 206] . . . deemed a specific proscription against nondisclosure surplusage."[43] Statutory text (or lack thereof, in this case) was no match for the flexible/remedial interpretive canon, fueled by fiduciary duty analysis.

For the SEC, *Capital Gains* was a green light to push the boundaries of its authority in other areas. Moreover, *Capital Gains* suggested that the SEC could expand its power through agency and judicial interpretation of existing statutes and regulation, without resorting to the cumbersome rulemaking process under the Administrative Procedure Act, or, still more daunting, seeking legislation. The lesson of *Chenery II* (discussed in Chapter 3)—that the agency could proceed through either rulemaking or adjudication to establish a new rule—was reaffirmed in the context of insider trading. After its victory in *Capital Gains*, the SEC would push an aggressive interpretation of § 10(b) of the Exchange Act in the lower courts. Going forward, the antifraud "catch-all" of Rule 10b-5 would be

138  A HISTORY OF SECURITIES LAW

the weapon of choice to crack down on insider trading, notwithstanding the absence of any reference to insider trading in its text.

### 4. *Texas Gulf Sulphur*: The Spirit of *Capital Gains* Takes Hold in the Second Circuit

The SEC's campaign, and *Capital Gains*'s interpretive approach, would find fertile ground in the Second Circuit. Clark was elated when he heard that his position had been vindicated by the Supreme Court. He died only four days later, but the other judges of the Second Circuit took up the SEC's cause, creating a consistent majority amenable to judicial expansion of the securities laws.[44]

The most dramatic expression of the Second Circuit's enthusiasm came five years after *Capital Gains*, in *SEC v. Texas Gulf Sulphur*, when the Second Circuit validated the SEC's expansive reading of § 10(b) of the Exchange Act.[45] That decision was a sweeping victory for the SEC, with the in banc Second Circuit adopting—and perhaps even extending—the rationale of *Cady, Roberts*. The court saw its holding as effectuating:

> the Congressional purpose that all investors should have equal access to the rewards of participation in securities transactions. It was the intent of Congress that all members of the investing public should be subject to identical market risks . . . inequities based upon unequal access to knowledge should not be shrugged off as inevitable in our way of life, or, in view of the congressional concern in the area, remain uncorrected.

*Texas Gulf Sulphur* thus announced the triumph of purpose in the federal regulation of insider trading under Rule 10b-5. The *TGS* majority included three members of the Second Circuit's five-man majority in *Capital Gains*. Just five years before, that majority had held that the antifraud provisions should be narrowly interpreted and that any expansion should come via agency rulemaking.

What had changed? *Capital Gains*. The Supreme Court's sweeping language in that opinion seems to have freed the Second Circuit, in dealing with a traditional fiduciary relationship, to embrace the expansive approach of *Cady, Roberts* in interpreting Rule 10b-5. The appellate court's rhetoric, however, suggested that it would not necessarily be cabined by fiduciary principles. Having been reversed by the Supreme Court in *Capital Gains*, the judges of the lower court abandoned the suggestion of SEC rulemaking. Rule 10b-5's prohibition of fraud was now interpreted to cover pure omissions in open market settings. Judge Sterry Waterman—who had characterized the conduct in *Capital Gains* as making "a dollar for [Capital Gains] without costing its client anything"—now wrote the opinion enthusiastically endorsing the SEC's position.[46] Swept aside were the messy debates over the nuances of affirmative misstatements, half-truths, and the traditional badges of common law fraud that had so occupied the circuit in *Capital Gains*. The Second Circuit judges now accepted—without discussion—that fraud included silence by insiders when they had a duty to speak.

*Texas Gulf Sulphur* was recognized as a sea change at the time. A lawyer representing one of the director-defendants in that case acknowledged that if the SEC's position were sustained, it would "sound the death knell to any argument that you can be safe by keeping quiet." Speaking at the same forum in 1965, Bill Cary predicted that the courts would continue the path he had blazed in *Cady, Roberts*:

> I have no doubt whatsoever that when management is engaged in trading, the courts will label nondisclosure as a violation of the third clause of 10b-5. Despite arguments to the contrary, that gaping hole will not be allowed to remain ajar, even vis a vis complainants who bought or sold on the open market.

The district judge affirmed by the Second Circuit in *Texas Gulf Sulphur* held that the statute and rule go at least as far as federal common law and a bit further: "lack of communication between defendant and plaintiff does not eliminate the possibility that 10b-5 is violated."[47] Privity was abandoned: Rule 10b-5 was interpreted to extend liability for failure to disclose to purchasers on national securities exchange.

The *Texas Gulf Sulphur* majority would cite the Supreme Court's *Capital Gains* opinion for the proposition that even negligent insider trading would be unlawful. *Capital Gains* was cited not only for that remarkable proposition, but also for the flexible/remedial interpretive presumption: "the securities laws should be interpreted as an expansion of the common law . . . to effectuate the remedial design of Congress." The Second Circuit, taking its cue from the Supreme Court's interpretive approach in *Capital Gains*, now viewed itself as the partner of the SEC in correcting market inequities. Chairman Cary's aggressive interpretive approach in *Cady, Roberts* had been validated by the leading appellate court for securities law. Despite the novelty of the Second Circuit's holding, the Supreme Court let the issue percolate, denying certiorari in *Texas Gulf Sulphur* over White's dissent.[48] But *Capital Gains* had already established that silence could be fraud under federal securities law.

## 5. *Affiliated Ute*: A Purposivist Approach in Rule 10b-5

The Supreme Court would not squarely address the central issue of Rule 10b-5's coverage of insider trading for another dozen years after *Texas Gulf Sulphur*.

# 140 A HISTORY OF SECURITIES LAW

In the interim, however, the Court reaffirmed the purposive interpretive approach of *Capital Gains* in a private Rule 10b-5 case involving nondisclosure. Harry Blackmun was eager to push the Court's expansive approach forward. After reading the briefs in *Affiliated Ute Citizens v. United States*,[49] Blackmun was looking for a way to decide for the plaintiffs, Native American tribe members.

> I am inclined to read the Securities Exchange Act broadly, and to permit it to reach this kind of fraudulent practice despite the absence of specifically alleged and proved reliance. Of course, the identity of these plaintiffs as Indians, or at least mixed bloods, makes this a little easier than it otherwise might be. There is enough here, however, to establish misrepresentation and concealment. I feel we should plump for a high standard in this area, and this is in line with the intent of Congress in enacting the legislation.[50]

Blackmun, like Brennan, had been a student in Frankfurter's legendary Public Utilities class at Harvard, and Blackmun had endorsed Frankfurter's judicial philosophy during his confirmation hearings.[51] He showed none of Frankfurter's judicial restraint, however, when it came to the law of securities fraud. Assigned to write for the majority in *Affiliated Ute*, Blackmun cited *Capital Gains* for the proposition that "Congress intended securities legislation enacted for the purpose of avoiding frauds to be construed 'not technically and restrictively, but flexibly to effectuate its remedial purposes.'" The flexible/remedial interpretive move allowed the *Affiliated Ute* Court to excuse proof of reliance under Rule 10b-5 in cases "involving primarily a failure to disclose," the equitable notion of fraud endorsed in *Capital Gains*. Thus, the Court took another step toward validating an insider trading prohibition under the rubric of Rule 10b-5, while at the same time broadening the availability of a private cause of action, a topic we address in the next chapter. By extending the *Capital Gains* interpretive approach to Rule 10b-5, *Affiliated Ute* also implicitly endorsed the Second Circuit's approach in *Texas Gulf Sulphur*. All seven of the sitting justices joined the broad *Affiliated Ute* opinion, but change was on its way. New Justices Powell and Rehnquist were already in the building, and a number of the *Affiliated Ute* majority would peel off to join the newcomers in a more restrictive approach.

## C. Lewis Powell Closes the Door

### 1. Section 16(b) and the Transition to Textualism

Three § 16(b) cases—after only one in the previous thirty-five years, and followed by only one in the next forty-five years—arose in quick succession in the early

INSIDER TRADING    141

1970s. In retrospect, the cases marked a pivot point in the Court's interpretation of the securities laws: the shift from purposivism to textualism. A long line of expansive Supreme Court securities decisions came to an end, followed by an equally one-sided series of decisions in the opposite direction.

Each of the three cases grappled with the same prong of § 16(b)—the potential disgorgement liability of 10% shareholders. As such, these cases are a step removed from the typical abuse of information by a corporate officer or director, as in *Texas Gulf Sulphur*. Congress recognized the difference in access to information between those insiders and blockholders by adding a proviso that a stockholder had to be a 10% owner at both the time of the purchase and sale for liability to apply. In these three cases the shareholder was a newcomer to the enterprise without indicia indicating a manipulative plan. In each case the Court would reject the application of § 16(b).

Two of the three cases arose out of the wave of hostile takeovers that spurred Congressional enactment of the Williams Act in 1968, a topic that we cover in Chapter 7. The third arose out of voluntary sale of a business during the same period. Both *Reliance Electric Co.* v. *Emerson Electric Co.* and *Kern County Land Co.* v. *Occidental Petroleum Corp.* involved hostile bidders who had purchased more than 10% of a target's stock only to lose out to competing bidders preferred by the target management.[52] Having lost the contest for control, the spurned bidders faced the prospect of being forced out in a cash-out merger, with the proceeds triggering § 16(b) disgorgement. The unsuccessful bidders in the two cases chose different methods of dealing with this possibility. Emerson, in the *Reliance* case, had purchased about 13% of the target. After its bid failed, Emerson sold enough shares to get below 10%, a strategy outlined in Louis Loss's Securities Regulation treatise. Occidental, in the *Kern County* case, entered into an option agreement with the company (by then controlled by the successful bidder). The agreement provided for a sale just after six months had elapsed from the purchase. Neither of these maneuvers dissuaded the target companies from suing the unsuccessful bidders to recover the profits deriving from the initial purchases and the subsequent sale. The third case, *Foremost McKesson v. Provident Securities Co.*, arose out of a sale of assets of an investment company (Provident) in exchange for (as requested by the purchaser) Foremost's convertible debentures.[53] When Provident turned around and sold the debentures to an investment bank, Foremost sued under § 16(b) to recover the purchaser's gain.

In *Reliance*, decided by the same seven justices as *Affiliated Ute*, the majority and dissent set out starkly different approaches to statutory interpretation. Potter Stewart's opinion for the Court hewed closely to the language of the statute.[54] For Stewart, the clarity of the text left no room for recourse to statutory purpose: "whatever the rationale of the proviso, it cannot be disregarded simply on the ground that it may be inconsistent with our assessment of the 'wholesome

142    A HISTORY OF SECURITIES LAW

purpose' of the Act." The Court also rejected "a judicial search for the will-o'-the-wisp of an investors 'intent'" as insufficiently objective. Finally, the majority rebuffed the SEC's policy plea for broadening coverage as properly directed to Congress, echoing Black's position in *Blau* a decade earlier: "[W]e are not free to adopt a construction that not only strains, but flatly contradicts, the words of the statute." The interpretive freedom embraced by *Capital Gains* and *Texas Gulf Sulphur* appeared to bypass § 16 entirely.

Douglas's dissent echoed his complaint from *Blau*: "In my view, this result is a mutilation of the Act, contrary to its broad remedial purpose, inconsistent with the flexibility required in the interpretation of securities legislation, and not required by the language of the statute itself."[55] Textualism should not be allowed to defeat the purpose of the act: "should the broadly remedial statutory purpose of § 16(b) require it, the literal language of the statute would not preclude an analysis in which the two transactions herein at issue are treated as part of a single 'sale.'" For Douglas, the text was at most a constraint on achieving purpose, not a directive from Congress to be applied by courts, and even the technical language of § 16(b) was not sufficiently precise to constrain.

But now the textualists were in the majority, a sharp contrast to the cases of the 1960s, when purpose had prevailed. Only Brennan and White joined Douglas's dissent. With the Court shorthanded after Black and Harlan's almost simultaneous retirements, Marshall, Blackmun, and Burger joined Stewart's opinion for a majority. Blackmun's position is the most interesting. The Court heard argument in *Reliance Electric* within a span of three weeks in which it also heard *Affiliated Ute* and *Bankers Life*, cases in which the purposivism of the 1960s remained in full flower. Blackmun seemed amenable to a similarly broad reading in *Reliance Electric* that would cover both sales, consistent with his view of the statutory purpose, although he was not free from doubt. After reading the briefs in *Reliance Electric*, Blackmun pondered the connection between § 16(b) and § 10(b):

> Section 16(b) contains a provision for exemptions from short-swing liability when the SEC so rules. Section 10(b), on the other hand, seems to relate directly to profits gained by the use of inside information. Thus, if a proper intent can be proved, § 10 leads to liability irrespective of any 10% holding.
>
> One could argue from the foregoing that the 10% rule is to be rather narrowly applied, viz, that one has to have 10% both at the time of purchase and at the time of the offending sale. This is a forceful argument.
>
> My own reaction generally, on the other hand, is that § 16(b) should be rather broadly interpreted. It was enacted and aimed at a specific abuse. We have some precedent for broad interpretation . . . the statute is not to be strictly construed. One can be over-literal in this business.

For Blackmun, the case was a challenging one, but he favored the "the liberal approach in this one and to give the greater force to the evident purpose of the statute. Even as he was writing *Affiliated Ute* and joining Douglas's broad opinion in *Bankers Life*, Blackmun was still trying to figure out where he fit in on these securities questions: "I am fairly certain the Court will divide on this and may well find myself in the minority with some strange companions."[56] Eventually he sided with Stewart; apparently the facts did not raise the same red flags as those in *Affiliated Ute* and *Bankers Life*.

The first § 16(b) case in which Powell and Rehnquist participated, *Kern County*, signaled that Powell would be influential in the area. The Court split 4-4 at conference, with White passing.[57] After sending White a memorandum on the merits, Powell—not content to wait on White's response—sent a memorandum to his law clerk the next day, instructing him to begin working on an opinion.[58] Powell explained that "[a]s I led the discussion at the Conference, I would think the chances are good that the opinion would be assigned to me if we have a majority. If I am in the minority, I will wish to dissent." As a strategic matter, Powell noted that "[t]here is obvious advantage in our circulating a draft at a fairly early date." Being first to write improved his chances of getting the crucial fifth vote. This memorandum from Powell's first insider trading case strikes a note that would become familiar in subsequent cases—Powell leading the discussion at conference and expecting to write the opinion in his area of expertise.

Powell argued in his memo to White that the statutory language compelled the conclusion that the exchange of shares was not a sale: "The concept of a purchase or sale necessarily connotes volition, i.e., a willing or conscious act on the part of the 10% owner. There was no such act in this case, and the absence of it seems to me to be dispositive." The sale of assets required only a majority vote of Kern's shareholders and California law did not provide for appraisal. Accordingly, Occidental had no alternative to the exchange: "[T]here may have been a 'shotgun wedding' but there certainly was no sale."[59] After White joined Powell's side to form a majority, Chief Justice Burger assigned the opinion to White, perhaps to keep a wavering member of the majority on board.

Although Powell agreed with White's general approach, Powell felt that the opinion did not emphasize sufficiently that the exchange of shares was involuntary. Powell wrote that he would consider a concurrence because the "[b]ar needs an answer to this question. This opinion is fact oriented [and] gives little guidance." Powell thought White unduly emphasized "whether O[ccidental] could have had insider information," an "immaterial" concern, because "Occidental could not [and] did not arrange the merger." Powell also disliked White's statement that "[w]e do not suggest that an exchange of stock pursuant to a merger may never result in § 16(b) liability."[60] Powell favored a more sweeping holding

## 144 A HISTORY OF SECURITIES LAW

offering clearer guidance. He feared that courts and lawyers would struggle to apply White's flexible standard, a concern that has proved to be justified.

Powell joined White's opinion, but drafted a concurrence, arguing that a "factually oriented 'pragmatic' approach" might be necessary in some cases, even though it risked being "inexact" and "even subjective." But "the Court need not have reached in this merger case the inquiry which is the focus of attention under the 'possibility of abuse' test, with its focus on the defendant's access to inside information." That inquiry was "immaterial" because Occidental "could neither have blocked the merger nor assured its consummation. . . . There was simply no act of volition—indeed no relevant act at all—on the part of respondent with respect to the accomplishment of the merger."[61]

Powell's "volitional" approach would have provided a more determinate test than White's possibility-of-abuse standard. Powell was willing to tolerate private planning to avoid the coverage of § 16(b); he thought that the abuses Congress sought to curb through the statute were remote, at least in the case of 10% shareholders. Powell noted in his memorandum to his clerk asking him to review the concurrence that "I know from professional experience that this is an area which creates considerable doubt and confusion. My concurrence will not help much, but it may put the question which lawyers usually are called upon to answer in a little sharper focus." Powell's file does not reveal why he decided against publishing the concurrence, to which White had "no objection whatsoever." Perhaps White's reminder that Occidental was already a 10% shareholder when it extended its tender offer caused Powell to rethink the wisdom of his concurrence; getting into this question might require the Court to resolve the issue of "whether these shares obtained by the tender offer should be treated as having been obtained all at one time or at separate times."[62] The majority was fragile enough without taking on this question. Blackmun, who had also received Powell's memo to White, joined the majority.

The question of whether the purchase that makes an individual a 10% holder is subject to § 16(b) came to the Court two years later in *Foremost-McKesson*. Provident received Foremost convertible debentures as payment for an asset and then sold those same debentures to an underwriter who would place them with the public. It had no other connection to the issuer. Could the initial receipt of the convertible debentures count as one of the two required transactions under § 16(b)?

In his notes for use at the Court's conference, Powell emphasized the statute's text. He argued that under the plain language of the proviso, "Provident was not a 10% holder *at time* of *purchase*. At *that time* it was zero holder."[63] Moreover, the purpose of the statute—to prevent the unfair use of information—would not be served by liability in this case because "[u]ntil one becomes 10% holder, Congress has concluded there is little likelihood of obtaining inf[ormation] to use unfairly.

INSIDER TRADING   145

16(b) is directed vs. *insiders*. One is not an insider under statute until he owns 10%. What information can he acquire 'simultaneously' with purchasing 10%?" Powell also argued that a statute requiring "liability w/o fault" such as § 16(b) should be "construed strictly—not expansively." The equities, "altho[ugh] irrelevant" did not favor *Foremost-McKesson*, which sold the debentures to Provident "with full knowledge . . . that they would be sold." Powell's observation that this was "[n]ot a pretty posture for a litigant who is relying on a statute designed to prevent unfairness!" may have resonated with some of his colleagues. The same could have also been said for *Kern County*; there, Tenneco later caused its subsidiary to sue to recover the disgorgement, despite having been the counterparty to the option by which the shares were sold.

Powell's final argument to his colleagues was grounded in experience: "*Proviso* distinguishes bet[ween] officers + directors—and 10% owners. There is a reason: Vast difference between managerial insiders + stockholders." Having served on numerous corporate boards, Powell was well placed to assess the access to information enjoyed by blockholders. He wrote to his law clerk:

> [i]n truth, as you know from our discussions, even one who enjoys the status of a 10% stockholder is not entitled by virtue of that status to *any* inside information. To be sure, if such a stockholder is able to place a representative on the board, the stockholder may end up obtaining the information. This would certainly be true if an individual owned 10% and also served as an officer or director. But absent a presence on the board there would be a clear violation of 10b-5 for a corporation (or its officers or directors) to disclose to any stockholder information not available to all holders.[64]

Powell subsequently would take a more forgiving view of the legality of selective disclosure in the *Dirks* case. But at this point, Powell apparently believed that Rule 10b-5 would cover any selective disclosure to stockholders that led to trading. That view allowed for a narrower scope for § 16(b) and its draconian strict liability provision. Writing for the Court, Powell got eight votes, with Blackmun, who had voted the other way at conference, signing on. (Douglas's replacement, John Paul Stevens, was not yet participating.) At least for the interpretation of § 16(b), a unanimous Court held that text controlled over purpose.[65]

## 2. *Chiarella*: Fiduciary Duty Confined

By the time the Supreme Court first heard an insider trading case based on Rule 10b-5, it had been a dozen years since *Texas Gulf Sulphur* and nineteen years since *Cady, Roberts*. In each of those cases, officers, directors, or tippees with

146 A HISTORY OF SECURITIES LAW

material inside information about their company were held to have violated Rule 10b-5 when trading stock in their company without having disclosed that information. The years in between had only muddled the arguments supporting the results. The theories advanced had included a combination of egalitarian theory focused on information available to all, traditional common law theories of deceit that fit uneasily in contexts in which parties traded across anonymous markets, and fiduciary concepts from state corporate law. The last of these had been rejected by the Court in other contexts, as we shall see in the chapters that follow.

Against that backdrop, *Chiarella v. United States* added two additional complications. First, it asked whether antifraud liability extended to inside traders who had no fiduciary obligation to the companies whose stock they traded. Vincent Chiarella was a "markup man" at Pandick Press, a printer of financial documents, giving him access to documents relating to confidential takeover plans. Pandick's clients (the tender offerors) sought to conceal the identity of the takeover targets, but Chiarella deduced them from the price histories, par values, and the number of letters in the fake names in those documents. He then purchased shares in the target before the company's shareholders got wind of the big payoff coming from the surprise offer. Chiarella's employment by Pandick Press, however, created no relationship with the target company shareholders.[66] In addition, this case was the first criminal conviction for insider trading under Rule 10b-5. The criminal context raised the stakes. Would the Supreme Court, ideologically different from the one that decided *Capital Gains*, continue to endorse the government's campaign against insider trading?

The answer was "no." The Court rejected the argument that Rule 10b-5 prohibited any informational advantage while trading in secondary markets. The Court did, however, recognize that the antifraud provisions could still take in the classic examples of insiders trading with shareholders to whom they owed a duty. The Court had now fallen under the sway of Lewis Powell in the field of securities law. With his experience as a corporate lawyer to guide him, Powell felt no need to defer to the expertise of the SEC. The SEC and prosecutors were attempting to extend § 10(b) beyond Powell's understanding of Congress's intention in 1934, and the Second Circuit was acquiescing in those efforts. As Powell saw it, courts had a responsibility to check such overreaching by the executive branch. The *Chiarella* opinion was a conscious attempt to bring precision and rigor to an area of the law in which the lower courts had strayed from Congress's mandate.[67]

Powell also worried that regulation could impair market efficiency. He saw Rule 10b-5's jurisprudence as a species of "federal common law,"[68] affording wide latitude for policy concerns. He saw efforts to impose a "parity of information" rule as undermining "incentives to perform market research in order to discover undervalued stocks and thereby bring about a more efficient allocation of resources." Powell agreed with a student author in the *Harvard Law Review*: "[t]he courts must also recognize . . . the importance of preserving incentives for legitimate economic effort, such as gathering new information or perceptively analyzing generally available facts." Powell's understanding of the market mechanisms was an informed one. In response to the government's claim that Chiarella's trading could have harmed the offerors that hired Pandick by driving up the target's stock price, Powell noted that this was unlikely given the small number of shares that Chiarella had purchased. Powell agreed, however, with the proposition that Chiarella's unusual trading patterns might have been decoded by other market participants given that he was "a single investor known to his broker to work in a printing firm [who] shows a pattern of predicting tender offers."[69] Thus, Powell distinguished demand theories of price change in securities markets from informational ones. Powell's concern with information and market efficiency would play a larger role in *Dirks*, but it was on his mind in *Chiarella*.

In *Chiarella*, Powell focused more on fiduciary principles in the corporate context, a topic familiar to him from his long years of practice. He was not advocating a return to policing insider trading only through § 16(b), although that might have been more consistent with the statutory scheme. He was more concerned by the Second Circuit's "*major extension* of 10b" to find silence to be fraud even with "no fiduciary duty."[70]

The Second Circuit's decision in *Chiarella* had approved criminal liability using language that echoed the broad scope of the Circuit's earlier decision in *Texas Gulf Sulphur*. The appellate court had narrowed *Texas Gulf Sulphur*'s reach from "anyone" to "anyone who regularly received" inside information. The Solicitor General's office, arguing to uphold *Chiarella*'s conviction, declined to defend that approach. Instead, the argument developed by Frank Easterbrook, then a deputy SG, focused on a different theory not argued at trial—misappropriation—as the basis for liability. Easterbrook's successor, Stephen Shapiro, presented two versions of the misappropriation theory to the Court. Those theories shape the opinions in *Chiarella* and the subsequent case law. One reflected fraud on the source (i.e., Pandick, Chiarella's employer and Pandick's clients), a standard application of agency law, while the other supported fraud on the investors in the companies in which Chiarella traded.

At conference there were five votes to reverse the conviction, but it was a tenuous majority.[71] White, the lone dissenter from the denial of certiorari in *Texas Gulf Sulphur*, was on board with Powell's position reversing the conviction below. Stewart and Rehnquist, who had joined Powell on almost every securities case since 1973, also agreed that Chiarella's conduct did not violate § 10(b) under any theory, including those argued by the government. In contrast, four of the other justices were willing to go as far as the government's misappropriation theory, if

148  A HISTORY OF SECURITIES LAW

not further. Brennan was not willing to endorse the Second Circuit's possession standard, but would not limit the permissible duty to that arising between a purchaser and seller to a transaction. Burger, who previously had consistently sided with Powell in securities cases, went his own way. Perhaps still smarting from a then-recent information breach involving the Court's own print office, the Chief Justice posed hypotheticals at oral argument involving court bailiffs and secretaries that would extend duty beyond those owed to shareholders or to acquiring companies. Blackmun and Marshall would not require proof of misappropriation at all where defendant knew it was wrong to use the information.[72]

Stevens cast the decisive vote. His rationale initially could have appeared problematic for Powell's position. Stevens thought that Chiarella violated a duty to his employer or to his employer's client, and that misappropriation theory might support a conviction. But, Stevens thought the government had "tried [the] case on basis of fraud to [the] wrong party."[73] Here Stevens appeared to be looking past the Second Circuit decision and the Solicitor General's misappropriation arguments in the Supreme Court. Instead, Stevens was focused on the jury instructions given at trial. Chiarella's lawyer in his reply brief before the Supreme Court had argued that the jury had not been charged with finding facts essential to the misappropriation theory that the government was now urging.[74]

Additional research by Powell's clerk confirmed "the conclusion of Mr. Justice Stevens that the jury was never presented with the theory that now forms the basis of the SG's argument—that petitioner breached a duty to the acquiring corporation that is actionable under section 10(b) and Rule 10b-5." The jury was instead instructed that it could find deceit if Chiarella had failed to disclose material information to the sellers. Accordingly, Powell (after consulting with Stevens) wrote to Stewart, White, and Rehnquist proposing an opinion reversing the Second Circuit on the ground that Chiarella owed no duty to the sellers of the securities. Powell proposed that they leave for another day the question of whether Chiarella's breach of duty to Pandick and its clients violated § 10(b).[75]

Powell seized the narrowness of the jury instructions to construct an opinion premised on a duty far narrower than the Second Circuit's. He embraced both *Cady, Roberts* and *Texas Gulf Sulphur*, characterizing them as "administrative and judicial interpretations" that premised liability on a duty "arising from a relationship of trust and confidence between parties to a transaction." Here, Powell was ignoring broader language in those prior opinions that went beyond this narrow holding. Under Powell's reconstruction of those precedents, Chiarella's acts were not fraud unless he owed an affirmative duty to disclose to such persons. The jury instructions had failed to specify any such duty. Powell's approach suggests a common law requirement that a duty to the counterparty to transaction would be the exclusive basis for liability. *Cady, Roberts*, however, had noted that the officers, directors, and controlling shareholders that it mentioned "does

**Figure 5.2**
**Insider Trading Confined:** Vincent Chiarella was the first person criminally convicted for insider trading. When the Supreme Court took up his case, Chiarella's conviction was reversed, with Lewis Powell crafting a narrow fiduciary duty theory to regulate insider trading going forward. But the Court was unable to agree on the broader misappropriation concept. Seventeen years later, the Court would accept the theory in *O'Hagan*, dramatically expanding insider trading.

not exhaust the classes of persons with such obligations." The Second Circuit in *Texas Gulf Sulphur* phrased the essence of its rule as applying to "anyone."[76] The absence of a jury instruction setting forth the misappropriation theory that Stevens could have supported meant five votes to reverse the conviction. Powell therefore resolved the case treating the court of appeals opinion as relying on a general duty between all participants in market transactions. That parity of information rule was rejected by Powell in favor of his reading of the common law as requiring a relationship between the parties to the transaction.

Powell used the common law as a guide to congressional intent when the statutory text afforded no guidance. In doing so, he was creating a federal fiduciary principle rather than incorporating state common law doctrines into the federal law of fraud.[77] Unlike the Second Circuit, however, Powell used traditional

150  A HISTORY OF SECURITIES LAW

notions of fiduciary duty as his doctrinal tool to confine the SEC's aggressive interpretations of the "vague language" of Rule 10b-5. Powell believed that vagueness was a vice to be curtailed, not an opportunity for expansive interpretation. Powell's view of fraud as encompassing a duty to speak arising out of common law fiduciary duty has come to be identified as the "traditional" or "classical" theory of insider trading liability. But Powell's opinion did not foreclose broader fiduciary duty theories, including Stevens's "misappropriation" theory—if the government pled and proved them.[78]

To make matters worse for Powell, Stevens highlighted the theory's potential in his concurrence, making five members of the Court open to possible of liability based on misappropriation. Powell responded to Stevens that he would prefer

> not emphasizing that the result may have been different if liability had been premised on a duty to the acquiring company, as I am by no means sure that 10(b) should be extended this far beyond its clear purposes at the time of its enactment in 1934. As we are talking about criminal liability, I am inclined to think we should leave it to Congress to draft a more refined and specific criminal statute. To be sure, you leave the question for another day. But with a five to four vote by the Court, I would prefer—I think—not to invite a judicial rather than a legislative consideration of the question.[79]

Powell was not eager to update his understanding of the common law past 1934, although he was amenable to a change coming from Congress. Stevens published the concurrence anyway. Powell's concessions gave him a majority in *Chiarella*, but left broader fiduciary duty theories alive, as the *New York Times* reported the next day.[80]

Powell explained to Burger his preference that Congress specify the conduct to be prohibited:

> If I were in Congress, I probably would support a carefully drawn criminal statute that would make it a crime for one to do what Chiarella did. But it is clear (at least to me) that Congress never had the slightest intention—back in 1933 and 1934—to extend the Securities Acts to this type of situation.
>     . . . Before criminal liability is imposed by the courts, I think the Congress should face up to this question, and draft a proper criminal statute that puts people on notice.
>     I add that I do not admire Mr. Chiarella any more than you do.[81]

Powell's preference for congressional action went unheeded, as Congress was unable to agree on a definition of insider trading.[82] Burger, for his part, wrote a dissent endorsing a version of what would become the misappropriation theory.

INSIDER TRADING    151

After reading Powell's draft opinion, Blackmun wrote to his law clerk about the effect on Blackmun's *Affiliated Ute* opinion: "I think it advisable, also, to point out, if it is the case, that Justice Powell is giving a narrowing interpretation to *Affiliated Ute Citizens*. I wrote that opinion, and I certainly don't want it unduly narrowed." From Blackmun's perspective, it reflected an unfortunate trend in the Court's Rule 10b-5 jurisprudence. In his first draft of his dissent, Blackmun wrote: "It seems to me that with its decision in this case the Court continues its emasculation of § 10(b) . . . I, of course, have been unsuccessful in my attempts to stop this trend." This defeatist language did not make it into the final version of Blackmun's dissent, but the published version did little to disguise his bitterness:

> The Court continues to pursue a course, charted in certain recent decisions, designed to transform § 10(b) from an intentionally elastic "catchall" provision to one that catches relatively little of the misbehavior that all too often makes investment in securities a needlessly risky business for the uninitiated investor. . . . [T]he Court fails even to attempt a justification of its ruling in terms of the purposes of the securities laws, or to square that ruling with the long-standing but now much abused principle that the federal securities laws are to be construed flexibly rather than with narrow technicality.

Blackmun attempted to invoke precedent; he argued that his *Affiliated Ute* opinion gave "strong support to the principle that a structural disparity in access to material information is a critical factor under Rule 10b-5 in establishing a duty either to disclose the information or to abstain from trading."[83] Blackmun was endorsing the parity of information theory that the SEC had pushed—successfully—in the Second Circuit. Had *Capital Gains*'s flexible interpretive approach survived past the early seventies, Blackmun's instinct to read *Affiliated Ute* broadly probably would have prevailed.

But Blackmun's invocation of purpose and remedial construction did not sway Lewis Powell, and the Supreme Court was now under Powell's influence in the field of securities law. Powell favored the technical and restrictive interpretation that *Capital Gains* had rejected. Nonetheless, he relied upon *Capital Gains*'s equitable notions of fraud in framing the insider trading prohibition under § 10(b) in *Chiarella*. To be sure, Powell's version of fiduciary duty theory was considerably more limited than those of Arthur Goldberg or Harry Blackmun.

### 3. *Dirks*: Tipping and Personal Benefit

Tipping—trading by an outsider based on information from an insider—was at issue in *Cady, Roberts*, and it had been part of the Second Circuit's holding in

152   A HISTORY OF SECURITIES LAW

*Texas Gulf Sulphur.* Powell had also included a footnote to the *Chiarella* opinion referencing tipping, but there had been no express treatment of the issue by the Court. Powell's opinion for the Court in *Dirks v. SEC* upheld the concept of tippee liability, but he rebuffed the SEC's open-ended approach.[84] Powell also addressed more squarely the relation between restrictions on the use of inside information and market efficiency that he had hinted at in *Chiarella.*

The SEC had censured Dirks, a securities analyst, for passing information to his customers about a massive fraud at Equity Funding. Dirks' sources were current and former Equity Funding employees, including a former officer who told him that various regulatory agencies had failed to act on similar charges from employees. He urged Dirks to verify the fraud and disclose it publicly. Dirks decided to investigate, openly discussing the information he had obtained with clients and investors. Dirks also shared it with a *Wall Street Journal* bureau chief who declined to write a story for fear of a defamation suit. Dirks's customers, not subject to such concerns, relied on his information to sell large quantities of Equity Funding shares before the company's collapse.[85] Equity Funding's stock price plummeted as Dirks pursued his investigation, leading the NYSE to halt trading. California insurance authorities acted, and then the SEC. Eventually, the *Wall Street Journal* published an article laying out the fraud.

On petition for certiorari, the Solicitor General—Rex Lee, who as White's law clerk had suggested the fiduciary duty idea in *Capital Gains*—authorized the SEC to file an opposition to the petition, but refused to endorse the SEC's position. Instead, Solicitor General Lee and the Justice Department filed a separate brief arguing that the information obtained by Dirks could not be considered confidential. Lee's position highlighted the enormous obstacle that Dirks's role in uncovering the Equity Funding fraud posed for the SEC's effort to sanction the analyst.[86]

The SEC was therefore left to its own devices to defend its censure of Dirks. The agency got no help from the D.C. Circuit's initial opinion, which had affirmed the censure on the ground that Dirks "breached his duty to the Commission and to the public not to misuse insider information." As Powell saw it, this "absurd" holding squarely conflicted with Powell's reasoning in *Chiarella.*[87] Although the lower court issued a more limited opinion on petition for rehearing,[88] the SEC faced an uphill battle to defend the judgment. The case was of obvious importance to the securities industry: Powell's law clerk, Jim Browning, recalled that there was "a blanket of blue and gray suits in the courtroom" with SEC staff and the local corporate bar taking up all the places in the audience for the argument.[89]

Powell had no doubt that the D.C. Circuit's judgment should be reversed. The trick was to reverse while still upholding a more carefully drawn ban on tippee trading. Powell's sense of propriety abhorred the abuse of trust that insider trading represented. A prohibition was appropriate, if that prohibition

INSIDER TRADING 153

could be applied fairly and predictably. But Powell saw the SEC's approach as unprincipled and he worried about overaggressive enforcement by the agency. Moreover, he thought that analysts were important to the operation of the securities markets. The SEC's sanction of Dirks was an assault on the analyst industry.[90] Powell charged Browning with developing a theory to thread this needle. Building on middle ground found in a commentary on the case in a legal newspaper, Browning argued that

> there was no "exploitation" by the insiders. Dirks' informants received no monetary benefit for revealing Equity Funding's secrets, nor did they have any apparent desire to make a gift of valuable information to Dirks. The informants may have had a duty not to trade on inside information without disclosure, but they did not. Therefore, even if Dirks' informants did violate a duty to the company by disclosing, their conduct did not have one of the essential elements of breach of the agency relationship: the exploitation of corporate information by an insider.
>
> We both know *Dirks* is a freak case. The situations we are concerned with are where securities analysts interview employees seeking information: is there liability? If the breach of an employee's duty alone is enough to establish tippee liability, securities analyst [*sic*] will be chilled from using any of the information he gets. If, on the other hand, exploitation of confidential information by insiders is a prerequisite to tippee liability, securities analysts will be encouraged to seek information from corporate employees.

Powell agreed that "*Dirks* is easy, but is there a general principle?"[91] He wanted to protect analysts in their work without inviting abuse by insiders.

Powell found his general principle in Browning's "exploitation" formulation, although he recast it. Powell, in an unusual step, prepared a memorandum for the conference at which the justices would decide the case, perhaps as a bid for the opinion assignment. Powell's argument built directly on *Chiarella's* foundation requiring a breach of fiduciary duty for an insider trading violation as well as its footnote 12 that suggested "The tippee's obligation has been viewed as arising from his role as a participant after the fact in the insider's breach of a fiduciary duty":

> Thus, where the tippee becomes a "participant after the fact," he shares whatever duty the insider breached by conveying the information. This analysis makes Dirks' case easy to decide. His liability depends on a finding that the former Equity Funding employees—of which *Secrist* [Dirks's principal source] was only one—who disclosed the fraud, breached their fiduciary duty to Equity Funding.

## 154 A HISTORY OF SECURITIES LAW

But even the SEC concedes there was no such breach of duty. None of these employees profited by disclosing fraud. They acted strictly in the public interest. Therefore, Dirks was not a participant after the fact in anyone's breach of duty.[92]

In sum, *Chiarella* required a breach of duty. Dirks's sources had violated no duty. Dirks therefore could not be liable for violating Rule 10b-5.

Powell was not satisfied, however, with merely exonerating Dirks. He wanted clearer rules that would protect securities analysts. His memo to the conference continued:

Deciding this case without identifying a general principle would accomplish very little.

Let me make clear the type of situation to which the principle would be applied. This case does not involve a *Texas Gulf Sulfur* [*sic*] situation where an officer or director of a corporation himself trades on inside information for personal gain. Nor do we have an insider—who to benefit a friend—discloses inside information on which the friend profits. The law is fairly well settled with respect to these straightforward cases.

The much broader, underlying problem in this case concerns the necessity of information being made available for the health of the securities markets. In this case, the SEC's opinion stated:

In the course of their work, analysts actively seek out bits and pieces of corporate information not generally known to the market for the express purpose of analyzing that information and informing their clients who, in turn, can be expected trade on the basis of the information. The value to the entire market of these efforts cannot be gainsaid: market efficiency in practice is significantly enhanced by such initiatives to ferret out an[d] analyze information, and thus the analysts' works redowns [*sic*] to the benefit of the investors.

If we sustain its opinion in this case securities analysts will be far less liable to "ferret out" information. They will be concerned constantly with the uncertainty of lawsuits, with juries determining whether the information circulated was confidential and should not have been disclosed.[93]

Breach of a duty of confidentiality did not suffice to allege an insider trading violation, in Powell's view. Powell proposed an alternative principle: "A tippee's liability should depend on the *purpose or intent* of the insider's disclosure." Powell conceded that this was "a subjective rule," but one he defended as "principled and practical." Powell recognized that the "question of 'purpose' (intent) will be determined—as it is so often in the law—by the facts." The relevant facts would include

INSIDER TRADING   155

(i) The relationship between the insider and the recipient (e.g., the analyst); what were their respective purposes? Particularly, did the insider expect to profit himself or to benefit a friend rather than to inform the market generally?

(ii) Who initiated the disclosure? Typically, the analyst seeks out the corporate executive—this is commonplace. Equally commonplace, executives brief large meeting of analysts. The circumstances of the disclosure are relevant—as in this case.[94]

This fact-intensive inquiry went against Powell's usual preference for predictability and notice, which had prevailed in *Chiarella*. But the alternatives—the SEC's blanket ban on the use of inside information, on the one hand, and turning a blind eye to abuses of office by corporate insiders, on the other—were worse. Powell wanted to leave space for securities professionals to uncover nonpublic information, even if it came from corporate insiders. Not having a ban on tipping was a non-starter for Powell—insiders would trade information for cash or give it to the stereotypical golfing buddy. But the SEC had demonstrated that it could not be trusted to determine the boundaries of legitimate and illegitimate use of inside information. Leaving it to the agency to draw the line would lead to analysts being completely frozen out.

The SEC's heavy-handedness in sanctioning Dirks made it easy for Powell to find a majority to reverse the D.C. Circuit. Holding a court would be a challenge, however, as no consensus rationale emerged from the conference. White's vote, for example, was "tentative," and seemed to be based on the fact that Dirks "didn't unload," although White thought "[h]is tippees may be guilty of violating rules." Stevens, by contrast, thought that "Dirks breached no duty. Even if he had owned stock + sold it, but [*sic*] he had no duty. A person who is an outsider has no duty." Sandra Day O'Connor believed "the ultimate solution is to require fraud to be disclosed first to SEC—+ would like to say this."[95] The risk that the *Dirks* majority would fragment was real. Powell and Browning got to work.

Browning's first draft, as edited by Powell, formulated this test for tipping liability:

> It is first necessary, in order to make out a tipping case against an insider, to prove that the insider exploited confidential information in violation of his fiduciary duties to shareholders. Whether disclosure of material nonpublic information is a breach of duty thus depends on the purpose of the disclosure. The tipper will be liable if (i) he discloses material, nonpublic information to one who trades on the information and (ii) the purpose of the disclosure was to receive some benefit in return or to make a gift of the information to the recipient to enable him to gain a market advantage over other traders. Similarly,

156  A HISTORY OF SECURITIES LAW

> a 10b-5 claim against an alleged tippee must be based on the theory that he knowingly participated with the insider in exploiting the confidential information: in essence that he was an aider and abetter [*sic*]. A recipient of such a tip would be liable if he used the information in connection with securities trading, knowing the purpose of the disclosure.

Two things jump out from this passage: (1) the insider must be tipping for the purpose of making a gift, and (2) the tippee must *know* that this was the insider's purpose. Indeed, Powell instructed Browning to omit a reference to the SEC's position that the "tippee need not have *actual* knowledge of a breach of duty of the tipper." Powell did not "wish to encourage the Commission to infer knowledge or claim constructive knowledge on suspicion."[96]

After reviewing Browning's first draft, Powell had again emphasized the importance of protecting the role of market analysts:

> As you know, it is customary for management of listed companies to convey supplemental information (some people call in [*sic*] "chumming" the market) to analysts. This is done in primarily in two ways: talks to, and questions and answer sessions with, large groups of analysts—in effect, open meetings. Similarly, information not available through required filings with the SEC often is given at stockholders meetings where most of the stock is represented by proxies, and news coverage may be scant and uninforming. The more difficult type of information gathering—difficult in terms of line drawing for our purposes—is where the analysts will visit corporate headquarters and confer with senior officers. The analyst is likely to be a specialist in the particular business. When he returns to his firm, often he will circulate "buy" or "sell" recommendations to clients and person whom the firm would like to have as clients. These recommendations are backed up by a report on the interview. The line drawing problem is one that impacts directly on both the corporate officers and the analysts. Neither can be quite sure when the "line" is crossed.

Powell's years in corporate boardrooms gave him a clear understanding of how corporate disclosure worked on the ground. This analyst context continued to be a focus as the opinion evolved through subsequent drafts. Powell recognized how much the presence of two parties (insider and analyst) complicated the legal structure he was building. For example, Powell wrote a rider for insertion into the draft opinion, laying out what he saw as the correct analytical framework as to the tippee portion of the test, shifting from a focus on the tippee's knowledge to "'notice of the violation of duty.'" In an accompanying "Note to Jim and myself," Powell reiterated the need to address the analyst context while acknowledging the difficult questions that would follow:

We would like, in addition, to make clear that the typical situation in which this question may arise is where analysts—in the normal course of their work—obtain and use confidential information. Determining whether the tipper has breached a duty and whether the tipee [*sic*] had notice, present two difficult questions. The standard we propose with respect to the tipper is his purpose or motive—essentially a subjective standard. It will be even more difficult to show whether or not the tipee [*sic*] had notice of an improper motive. These are the questions that make this case so difficult.

In a handwritten note in the margin of the memo, commenting on the appropriate standard of liability, Powell raised how the duty standard being developed in the drafts would relate to Rule 10b-5's separate requirement of scienter. Powell wrote in the margin, "I'm not sure the 'scienter' test is applicable. I'll re-read *Ernst & Ernst*." On the same day in a separate rider, Powell expanded on the relationship of the duty and scienter elements.

It is clear under our Rule 10b-5 cases that liability is imposed only when one acts with scienter (cite cases). There would be no breach of duty where corporate executive [*sic*] inadvertently or even negligently disclosed the information relied upon. The critical question, therefore is whether there was an intent or purpose to disclose material nonpublic information to one who could trade on the information to the detriment of shareholders. Ascertaining intention may be difficult, but this is a familiar question often confronted by courts. There are facts and circumstances that often justify inferences of wrongful purpose. For example, there may be a relationship exists [*sic*] the insiderand [*sic*] the recipient that a *quid pro quo* from the latter, or an intention to benefit the recipient. Also, such inference may arise where the disclosure was made at the initiative of the insider rather than by the recipient tipee [*sic*].

Where a breach of fiduciary duty by the insider is established, liability may be imposed on the tipee [*sic*] only when he has notice of such a breach. See *supra*, at __. Again, this is a question of fact that must be resolved in light of all relevant circumstances. A securities analyst, making a study of a particular corporation that includes interviews with its officers, acquires information that may form the basis of a market letter to clients. This is a typical situation, and customarily involves participants who understand their responsibilities and adhere to them. But there are cases, of course where the facts—and inferences reasonable [*sic*] drawn from them—demonstrate the requisite scienter on the part of both the tipper and the tipee [*sic*]. This is not such a case.[97]

The rider illustrates a recurring confusion about duty and scienter in the opinion's evolution. Powell was focused on the tipper's breach of a fiduciary duty

## 158   A HISTORY OF SECURITIES LAW

and the tippee's participation after the fact in that breach. To determine that breach of duty, Powell is developing a test that at various times and drafts invokes a variety of terms—purpose, intent, knowledge, should have known, good faith, notice—commonly associated with the required state of mind for deceit. Powell had written the opinion for the Court requiring scienter as the standard for Rule 10b-5 in *Ernst & Ernst* seven years before. But the multiple drafts of the opinion did not cite *Ernst*—a citation would not be added until a footnote was included just before publication in response to Blackmun's dissent.

Throughout the various drafts, Powell is clearly writing about the duty element and not scienter. Scienter is a separate element. It therefore must be proven for both affirmative lies, as well as silence when there is a duty to speak. That scienter requirement is independent of the use of those same terms to define exploitative conduct in Powell and Browning's evolving discussion of duty. The reader will be excused in thinking the line between the two elements has been blurred—for example, the first sentence and the last two sentences of this rider appear to address scienter in its independent use—but Powell's focus on duty remains foremost.[98]

Even when focusing only on the requirements for duty, various drafts use a variety of terms. The initial memorandum to the Conference referred to the tippee's knowledge of the tipper's breach. Riders connected to the first drafts shifted to "notice." After Powell's additions, Browning's fourth draft reverted to knowledge for the tippee portion of the test: "a tippee assumes a fiduciary duty to the shareholders of a corporation not to trade on material nonpublic information only when the insider breaches his fiduciary duty to the shareholders by disclosing the information to the tippee and the tippee knows of the breach." The fourth draft also contains Powell's "quid pro quo" and "intention to benefit the recipient" language from the rider quoted above.[99]

After receiving the first printed draft of the opinion, Powell added a new rider that explored the element of the tipper's purpose in greater detail. Good faith was added as a measuring stick:

> There may be situations where both the insider and the analyst recipient have acted in good faith, and yet release of the information affected markets. Whether disclosure is a breach of duty therefore depends in large part on the purpose or good faith of the insider who made the disclosure. Absent an improper purpose, there has been no breach of duty to stockholders—*e.g.*, a corporate official mistakenly thinks the information already has been disclosed or that it is not material enough to affect the market. And absent a breach by the insider, there is no derivative breach.

Disclosure of material information is clearly insufficient, and improper purpose is still the touchstone. Powell muddies the waters, however, by offering examples for which scienter would be lacking, but also for which materiality, a separate element of Rule 10b-5, would also be missing.[100]

The second printed draft adds another phrase that broadens the tippee part of the standard to reflect another familiar scienter-based term: "the tippee knows or should know that there has been a breach"—the prior draft had referred only to knowledge. The "knows or should know" language is repeated two pages later. The changes are not reflected in Powell's handwritten notes on the first printed draft, nor are they included in one of his riders. More puzzling, the memos cited above suggest that Powell favored the requirement that the tippee have actual knowledge of the tipper's breach. The change does make the language in the text more consistent, however, with the authorities cited in the appended footnote, as well as the SEC's prior position.[101] Browning's recollection—more than thirty years after the fact—was that the change was made to make the opinion more consistent with those authorities as well as the concurring opinion of Commissioner Smith in *In re Investors Management Co.*, an SEC insider trading decision heavily relied upon in the *Dirks* opinion.[102] There had also been discussion in Powell's chambers of hypothetical tippees—waiters and taxicab drivers who overheard material, nonpublic information being discussed by corporate insiders—and the proper standard to be applied to their state of mind. The change was not, however, intended to depart from the established standard of scienter for Rule 10b-5 violations, which was taken as a given.[103] The distinction was not important to the outcome of the case because the Court concluded that Secrist (the insider) had not breached a duty in providing the information to Dirks, so Dirks's knowledge was irrelevant. This opinion was focused on duty.

Powell's emphasis on "purpose" in determining whether there was a fiduciary breach proved a stumbling block in gaining a majority. Powell quickly got three votes for his initial circulation (White, Rehnquist, and Stevens), but O'Connor had reservations. She worried that looking to the insider's improper purpose in disclosing the information would require

> the fact-finder . . . to determine the subjective state of mind of the insider, and liability may be imposed only when the insider has an improper purpose, or the tippee has some independent duty not to trade. Although there may be rules of thumb, *e.g.*, the one you suggest concerning relationship between the parties, that are used to help determine subjective intent, it nevertheless appears that the focus of the inquiry is subjective motivation. Your focus on subjective purpose is consistent with, and very much like, your approach in *Ernst & Ernst v. Hochfelder*, 425 U.S. 185 (1976), although that opinion is not cited in your draft.

O'Connor found this "an inherently difficult determination to make. It requires that the tippee 'predict' what is going on in the mind of his tipper." O'Connor

160 A HISTORY OF SECURITIES LAW

contrasted the materiality determination, which she thought manageable for the tippee, with the tippee's ability to assess "whether an insider subjectively possesses a prohibited purpose." O'Connor also worried that "the purpose test might prohibit the dissemination of the information in this case. If Secrist's motivation was proven to be a desire for vengence [sic] against Equity Funding, and if the SEC determined that this was a prohibited purpose, Secrist and Dirks would violate the securities laws." Powell disagreed. O'Connor suggested that "the 'purpose' discussion may be omitted without altering your basic approach." Powell also disagreed with this point.[104]

O'Connor's alternative nonetheless appealed to Powell:

> whether the insider derives a direct or indirect benefit from his disclosure, and that benefit is primarily of a pecuniary nature. An emphasis on benefit differs from your approach only insofar as it establishes a more objective indicia of liability. If, as a factual matter, the insider did not benefit from his disclosure, then I am not inclined to be concerned with a further inquiry into his motivation. I am not sure about what will be gained from an inquiry into intent, but from my past experience on the bench, I know that a great deal of time will be lost!

Without a personal benefit, purpose would be irrelevant, according to O'Connor, streamlining the inquiry. O'Connor shrewdly couched her suggested change as "more objective" and based on her "past experience on the bench." These factors were calculated to persuade Powell, who favored predictability and respected the practical wisdom of experience. The opinion accordingly was revised to reflect O'Connor's "quite constructive" suggestions.[105]

Powell made several changes to accommodate O'Connor's personal benefit criterion. Two references to "good faith" from the May 23 rider were replaced, one with a reference to "consistently with his fiduciary duty to shareholders" and the other with "whether the insider personally expects to benefit, directly or indirectly from his disclosure." Another reference to the court determining the purpose of any one disclosure was changed to "determining whether an insider personally benefits from a particular disclosure." A sentence in the last part of the opinion that had referred to the lack of an "apparent purpose or desire to make a gift" was changed to a firmer factual statement "nor was their purpose to make a gift of valuable information to Dirks."[106]

These changes narrowed the scope of improper purposes that would count as breaches of fiduciary duty under Rule 10b-5. "Good faith" was purged. O'Connor's personal benefit standard made clear that garden variety breaches of the duty of care were out, including breaches of the duty of confidentiality. As a result, the federal fiduciary duty was aligned with the traditional terminology

INSIDER TRADING 161

in state corporate law, between breaches of care and loyalty—tipping that would breach Rule 10b-5 required a breach of the duty of loyalty.[107] In adding O'Connor's personal benefit requirement, Powell preserved the requirement that the SEC prove the tipper's *purpose* in disclosing. The new formulation simply narrowed the test—the only purpose that counted was an attempt to gain a personal benefit in exchange for disclosing the information.

A long addition responding to an SEC argument helped clarify that the personal benefit requirement—a duty question—is distinct from the question of scienter, a line that Powell had consistently drawn since the riders added in early May. The SEC had argued that if inside-trading liability does not exist when the information is transmitted for a proper purpose but is used for trading, it would be a rare situation when the parties could not fabricate some ostensibly legitimate business justification for sharing the information. In the new addendum, Powell wrote:

> We think the SEC is unduly concerned. In determining whether the insider's purpose in making a particular disclosure is fraudulent, the SEC and the courts are not required to read the parties minds. Scienter may be relevant in some cases in determining whether the tipper has violated his *Cady, Roberts* duty, but to determine whether the disclosure itself "deceive[s], manipulate[s], or defraud[s]" shareholders, *Aaron* v. *SEC*, 446 U.S. 680 (1980), courts should focus on whether the insider expects to receive a direct or indirect personal benefit from the disclosure, such as—for example—a pecuniary gain or a reputational benefit that may translate into future earnings.

Powell is again emphasizing that the personal benefit test goes to the question of duty, not state of mind. This distinction perhaps sheds light on the prior shift to "knows or should know" highlighted above; "should know" is sufficient to demonstrate participation in a breach of duty by the insider. The government, however, must also show the tippee's scienter—an intent to defraud—to satisfy each of the elements of Rule 10b-5.

O'Connor's change created a more predictable framework—and a narrower prohibition. That framework helped achieve Powell's ultimate goal of protecting the analyst community from the SEC's enforcement efforts. Powell, perhaps suspecting that the SEC would endeavor to do an end run around the personal benefit requirement, retained the purpose requirement as well—belt and suspenders. Sending the revised draft to White, Rehnquist, and Stevens, he assured them that "The reasoning of the opinion is not changed. Sandra thought my reference to the 'purpose' of the insider was unnecessarily subjective. She prefers using the more objective term: 'benefit' to insider, direct or indirect."[108]

162    A HISTORY OF SECURITIES LAW

The last set of changes to Powell's opinion came in response to Harry Blackmun's dissent. Blackmun raised the issue of scienter in its independent, freestanding role:

> Of course, an insider is not liable in a Rule 10b-5 administrative action unless he has the requisite scienter. *Aaron v. SEC*, 446 U.S. 680, 691 (1980). He must know or intend that his conduct violate his duty. Secrist obviously knew and intended that Dirks would cause trading on the inside information and that Equity Funding shareholders would be harmed. The scienter requirement addresses the intent necessary to support liability; it does not address the motives behind the intent.

Blackmun's conflation of motive with scienter and scienter with duty prodded Powell to sharpen scienter's treatment in the part of the opinion that had been added in response to O'Connor. His change emphasized that scienter and duty were separate issues. Motive was principally relevant to the latter.

> Scienter is in some cases is relevant in determining whether the tipper has violated his *Cady, Roberts* duty. But to determine whether the disclosure itself "deceive[s], manipulates[s], or defraud[s]" shareholders, *Aaron v. SEC*, 446 U.S. 680, 686 (1980), the initial inquiry is whether there has been a breach of duty by the insider. This requires courts to focus on objective criteria, *i.e.*, whether the insider receives a direct or indirect personal benefit from the disclosure, such as a pecuniary gain or a reputational benefit that will translate into future earnings.

Deception was the element of Rule 10b-5 before the Court in *Dirks*, not state of mind: without a breach of duty, there could be no deception. A footnote Powell appended at the end of the first sentence just quoted further clarifies the distinction.

> *Scienter*—"a mental state embracing intent to deceive, manipulate, or defraud"—is an independent element of a Rule 10b-5 violation. Contrary to the dissent's suggestion, motivation is not irrelevant to the issue of *scienter*. It is not enough that an insider's conduct results in harm to investors; rather, a violation may be found only where there is "intentional or willful conduct designed to deceive or defraud investors by controlling or artificially affecting the price of securities." The issue in this case, however, is not whether Secrist or Dirks acted with *scienter*, but rather whether there was any deceptive or fraudulent conduct at all, *i.e.*, whether Secrist's disclosure constituted a breach of his fiduciary duty and thereby caused injury to shareholders. Only if there was such a breach did Dirks, a tippee, acquire a fiduciary duty to disclose or abstain.

Scienter might be relevant in future insider trading cases that the SEC might bring, but that was not the issue in *Dirks*. Secrist lacked an improper motive—that is, the desire to gain a personal benefit—which meant that there was no breach of duty, and, hence, no deception. Consequently, the Court had no occasion to inquire into either Secrist's or Dirks's state of mind.[109] Scienter could be a dispositive issue, and motive might be relevant to scienter, but the antecedent question was deception. That question turned on whether the disclosure was made with an improper motive, that is, in exchange for a personal benefit, direct or indirect.

Blackmun was left to console himself with a sympathetic letter from Harvard Professor Victor Brudney praising his dissent. Blackmun's response to Brudney lamented the demise of the purposivism that had animated *Capital Gains* and *Affiliated Ute*: "I kid Lewis Powell to the effect that he is still representing his corporate clients and their appendages. I share your sadness as to the Court's action in narrowing what seems to me to be the intent of Congress."[110] Only Brennan and Marshall joined Blackmun's dissent.

## D. The Post-Powell Period: Misappropriation and Tipping Revisited

Powell wrote a third insider trading opinion, but it never made it to the United States Reports. *Carpenter v. United States* came on petition for certiorari to the Court during Powell's last term. The case raised the issue that *Chiarella* had left unresolved: Was a breach of duty to the *owner* of inside information, rather than the counterparty to the trade, sufficient for Rule 10b-5 liability?[111] Powell saw the Second Circuit's affirmative response to this question as a direct challenge to the doctrine that he had developed in *Chiarella* and *Dirks*.

The defendants in *Carpenter* were an unusual cast of characters:[112] R. Foster Winans was a reporter for the *Wall Street Journal* and one of the writers of the "Heard on the Street" column; David Carpenter was a news clerk at the *Journal*; Kenneth Felis was a stockbroker. Winans would pass securities-related information scheduled to appear in the next day's column through Carpenter to Felis, who would then, depending upon the tenor of the article, buy or sell the subject securities. *Wall Street Journal* policy deemed all news information to be company property and required nonpublic information to be treated as confidential. Ignoring this policy, the conspirators netted nearly $690,000 from the scheme. The stress of an SEC inquiry caused the conspirators to turn on each other; an indictment followed. The Second Circuit affirmed the conspirators' convictions for mail, wire, and securities fraud. With respect to the securities fraud counts, the Second Circuit upheld the convictions under the misappropriation theory

164  A HISTORY OF SECURITIES LAW

developed by the circuit in its cases after *Chiarella*. The Second Circuit also rejected the argument that the misappropriation theory did not apply because the information was purloined from the *Wall Street Journal* rather than the companies whose shares were traded.

The conspirators petitioned for certiorari, which the Court initially voted to deny. Powell's draft dissent from the denial made it clear that he would have rejected the misappropriation theory altogether. He argued that "the Second Circuit has resolved an important question of securities law in a way that appears to conflict with recent opinions of this Court." The first of these opinions was *Chiarella*, which began with the premise that

> parties to a business transaction generally do not have an affirmative duty to disclose information about the transaction. The court noted, however, that a failure to disclose material information could be fraudulent in certain circumstances. "But such liability is premised upon a duty to disclose arising from a relationship of trust and confidence *between parties to a transaction*."

Powell tied his reading of *Chiarella* closely to the common law of deceit: "[o]ne party to a business transaction is under a duty to exercise reasonable care to disclose to the other before the transaction is consummated . . . matters known to him that the other is entitled to know because of a fiduciary or other similar relation of trust and confidence between them." Thus, deceit requires that one party to a transaction owe a duty of disclosure to the other. Powell argued that *Chiarella* had incorporated this common law requirement into § 10(b), notwithstanding the concessions he had made to Stevens in that case to secure a majority.[113]

Powell then turned to *Dirks*, which "established that when outsiders have a fiduciary duty to the shareholders, they cannot purchase securities from those shareholders without first informing them of material information that might influence the decision to purchase or sell the securities." Again, the relevant disclosure duty was between the parties to the securities transaction. By contrast, in *Carpenter*, there was no fiduciary relationship between the defendants and those who had sold them securities. The only fiduciary relationship at issue was Winans's duty to the *Journal*. Powell noted, however, that previous cases did not support the proposition that the agency law duty an individual owes to his employer was sufficient to support an action under Rule 10b-5. Rather, the inquiry under Rule 10b-5 "must focus on the petitioner's relationship with the sellers of . . . securities." Because there was no such relationship, Powell concluded that the petitioners' conduct did not violate Rule 10b-5.

O'Connor and Rehnquist, both of whom had initially voted to grant certiorari, joined Powell's draft dissent. The dissent was never published, however, because Brennan and Antonin Scalia switched their votes to grant. Before *Carpenter* was argued, Powell retired. His successor, Anthony Kennedy, was not confirmed until after the argument. The Court split 4-4 on the misappropriation theory and consequently upheld the securities fraud conviction without opinion.[114] The only changes to the Court between *Chiarella* and *Carpenter* had been O'Connor replacing Stewart and Scalia replacing Burger. Burger, of course, had endorsed an even wider misappropriation argument in *Chiarella*, as discussed in the previous section. Scalia was one of the justices who changed their vote to hear the case after seeing Powell's argument in his draft dissent; he would eventually vote against the misappropriation theory when it was squarely addressed by the Court in *O'Hagan*. Given Powell's rejection of the misappropriation theory in his draft dissent, it is reasonable to conclude that if Powell had not retired when he did, the Supreme Court would have rejected the misappropriation theory in 1987.

In the aftermath of *Carpenter*, Congress considered a proposal to codify the misappropriation theory, but no legislation was forthcoming. Nevertheless, the government continued to bring misappropriation cases. The theory was accepted by the Seventh and Ninth Circuits, but rejected by the Fourth and Eighth Circuits. The last of these decisions, *United States v. O'Hagan*, provided the occasion for the Court to reconsider the misappropriation theory. A decade after Powell's retirement, the Court upheld the misappropriation theory by a 6-3 vote.[115] In her opinion for the Court, Justice Ruth Bader Ginsburg described the misappropriation theory as "complementary" to the classical theory set forth in *Chiarella*. Although the two theories are complementary in the sense that they "each address[] efforts to capitalize on nonpublic information through the purchase or sale of securities," the misappropriation theory encompasses all or almost all of the conduct proscribed by the classical theory, and more. The two theories draw on different sets of common law principles: the classical theory draws heavily on the common law of deceit, whereas the misappropriation theory draws primarily on the common law of agency. Agency law provides a more comprehensive and coherent basis for dealing with the problem of insider trading, which is, at bottom, the misuse by faithless agents of information that belongs to others, a familiar context in corporate law. From the SEC's perspective, the misappropriation theory's broad scope allows it to fill a gap left by Powell's classical theory, which, if left unfilled, would severely undermine the policy interests served by prohibitions against insider trading. This creates the peculiar result that violations of agency law—if undisclosed—are enforceable by the SEC as violations of securities law. But the Court's adoption of the misappropriation theory relieved the pressure on Congress to codify insider trading law. Consequently, it remains a common law prohibition under the auspices of Rule 10b-5.

Powell's rejection of the misappropriation theory did not survive his retirement. Powell never really had a majority to reject misappropriation in *Chiarella*,

166 A HISTORY OF SECURITIES LAW

as already discussed and only Rehnquist and Stevens remained from that Court. Powell might have swung a majority had he remained on the Court to hear *Carpenter*, but by the time of *O'Hagan*, even O'Connor voted to uphold the theory. Developing a common law prohibition on a case-by-case basis limits the potential legacy of an individual justice. Questions unanswered during Powell's tenure got a fresh look after his departure.

The SEC also fought a rearguard action against Powell's tipping doctrine, adopting Regulation FD to prohibit selective disclosure in 2000.[116] Powell confined the SEC's use of Rule 10b-5 to combat information asymmetries, but the agency had other tools at its disposal. Regulation FD prohibited selective disclosure of the sort that Powell had worked to protect in *Dirks*, but the SEC relied on its authority to regulate disclosures by public companies, not its antifraud authority. That left the *Dirks* framework intact for insider trading cases under Rule 10b-5.

The Court followed *Dirks* in the 2016 case *Salman v. United States*; that opinion broke no new ground.[117] Bassam Salman received trading tips from Michael Kara, brother of Maher Kara, who was married to Salman's sister, Suzie. Maher was an investment banker in Citigroup's healthcare investment banking group. Maher provided the information to his brother Michael for trading in an effort to assist his brother in his financial difficulties. Michael then shared the information with Salman, who was aware that Maher was the source. The Court was asked to decide whether providing information to one's brother was a "personal benefit" within the *Dirks* framework, and the justices had no difficulty concluding that it was. The *Salman* Court rejected a test adopted by the Second Circuit requiring that the government prove that the tipper received "something of a 'pecuniary or similarly valuable nature' in exchange for a gift to family or friends."[118] Instead, the Court reaffirmed the *Dirks* holding that a personal benefit can take the form of either a direct, quid pro quo benefit to the tipper, or a gift of information to a trading relative or friend. A gift to your brother counts. For tipping at least, it was business as usual.

Overall, the development of insider trading law, while somewhat late in coming, largely fits a pattern that we have seen elsewhere. When the Court finally got around to addressing the topic in *Capital Gains* and *Affiliated Ute*, it interpreted the securities laws broadly. Achieving the statutory purpose of investor protection drove the results. This pattern did not extend to § 16(b); a majority of the justices found its text too specific to bear the broad reading urged by the SEC. The Court's initial generosity in reading the antifraud provisions to cover insider trading ended with Powell's appointment to the Court.

Powell's influence in this area did not survive his departure. *O'Hagan* is at least a partial repudiation of Powell's more traditional common law approach, although Ginsberg took pains to emphasize the misappropriation theory's doctrinal compatibility with the Court's earlier precedents. The SEC has chafed under the restrictions imposed by some of those precedents, with the agency undercutting some of *Dirks*'s protection of the analyst community with its promulgation of Regulation FD. The SEC has not felt so confined, however, that it has sought a legislative fix from Congress. For the Commission, perhaps it is better to deal with the devil it knows.

# 6

# Private Litigation

I . . . know from my corporate experience in the latter years of my practice that the increase in damage suits has certain negative effects. . . .

The typical private damages action under the Securities Acts takes place several years after the alleged fraud. There are bankrupt companies today that, only a year or two ago, were widely viewed as fine investments. Jurors—and indeed judges—tend to be influenced by the present rather than conditions existing at the time of the alleged fraud. Information that may not have seemed important then can loom quite large years later. The number of suits have multiplied, and sometimes damages have been large and—as your memorandum noted—reputations destroyed.

One consequence of all of this is that many of the ablest people in our country no longer will serve on boards of directors. I know this from personal experience. Even insurance covering directors is usually limited to negligence and not fraud. Premiums are high, an expense consumers ultimately pay. Our basic economic system—the free enterprise system—is a "risk" system and investors should not expect guaranteed equity investments in particular.

In the literature in this area, is there any discussion . . . as to the public interest that may be adversely affected by opening the field wide to damage suits that have never been expressly authorized by Congress.

Memorandum from Lewis F. Powell, Jr., to Jim Browning 1-2
(Sept. 13, 1982), LFP Collection

Private securities litigation garnered little attention from the Supreme Court for the three decades after the adoption of the federal securities laws. Congress enacted a number of express private causes of action—§§ 11 and 12 of the Securities Act, and (less frequently deployed) §§ 9, 16, and 18 of the Exchange Act. Although the Securities Act causes of action, in particular, are notably plaintiff-friendly, litigants made little use of these provisions in this time.[1] As a result, the Court decided only three cases before 1962 requiring interpretation of

*A History of Securities Law in the Supreme Court.* A.C. Pritchard and Robert B. Thompson, Oxford University Press.
© Oxford University Press 2023. DOI: 10.1093/oso/9780197665916.003.0007

PRIVATE LITIGATION 169

private causes of action. The volume of private cases would increase dramatically in the decades that followed.

During the sixties the Court embraced private lawsuits as a "necessary supplement" to SEC enforcement of the securities law. Two developments would fuel the trend toward more private litigation. The first was the Court's validation in *J.I. Case v. Borak* of implied private rights of action, interpreting the securities laws to afford investors remedies for fraud beyond those provided by the common law or—at least explicitly—by statutory text.[2] *Borak* involved a proxy solicited in connection with a merger, but in the subsequent decade the Court would also recognize an implied private right of action for deception in purchase and sale transactions across anonymous markets under Rule 10b-5. The Court also relaxed the traditional elements of common law fraud needed to recover for misrepresentations in those transactional settings. The justices showed a willingness go beyond merely applying statutory directives, inserting the Court as a partner with the other branches in promoting the purpose of the New Deal securities legislation. As the Court saw it, private litigation would bolster government suits in promoting deterrence. The second development was the 1966 revision of Rule 23 of the Federal Rules of Civil Procedure, facilitating large-scale class actions for money damages. These twin developments would pave the way for large-scale securities fraud class actions.

The sixties revolution was followed in the 1970s by a repudiation of judge-made causes of action. Federal courts stopped discovering new private rights of action under the securities laws. As with insider trading, the Court's step back from purposive interpretation would be driven principally by Lewis Powell. Powell's distrust of litigation reflected his experience as a corporate lawyer, as suggested by the quote that begins this chapter. Under Powell's influence, the Court was done deferring to the SEC. Powell would wage a decade-long campaign against implied private rights of action. Under Powell's influence the Court abandoned its use of statutory purpose to expand the securities laws to help plaintiffs gain advantages not available in common law causes of action. Instead, the Court focused on statutory text. The heavy reliance on textualism was somewhat at odds with Powell's treatment of the judge-made remedy under Rule 10b-5 as a species of federal common law. We saw in Chapter 5 that Powell did not shy away from considering policy in defining Rule 10b-5's limits in the context of insider trading. Nonetheless, strict adherence to text was the tool used by Powell and other justices in the new conservative coalition to rein in the fledgling business of securities class actions. The Court repeatedly invoked statutory language to construe the elements of securities fraud to be more demanding than the lower courts' interpretations. Invocations of legislative purpose by private plaintiffs and the SEC were routinely rebuffed.

Powell's retirement would allow the pendulum to swing back, at least partially. The repudiation of implied causes of action was not complete, as the judge-made

170  A HISTORY OF SECURITIES LAW

Rule 10b-5 cause of action survived. The term after Powell's departure, the Court handed down its most far-reaching and controversial Rule 10b-5 decision, *Basic, Inc. v. Levinson*.[3] That decision, written by Harry Blackmun for a 4-2 majority, unleashed—perhaps unwittingly—a wave of "fraud-on-the-market" class actions against public companies. Those claims would become the principal cause of action in securities litigation. The absence of a statutory basis for the implied causes of action, however, would provide frequent opportunities for disagreement among the justices on their parameters.

We also follow the Court as it reverses course on a parallel track: arbitration. The Court flipped from initial hostility in the 1950s to enthusiastic embrace by the late 1980s. The arbitration decisions demonstrate the justices' long-running fault line on the proper role of judges in applying and interpreting the federal securities laws in resolving private disputes.

The class action deluge that followed *Basic* would make securities litigation a heated topic of political debate. Eventually, Congress would return to the field in 1995 with the enactment of the Private Securities Litigation Reform Act (PSLRA) over President Bill Clinton's veto.[4] The PSLRA substantially restricted securities fraud class actions through a series of procedural obstacles empowering judges to weed out non-meritorious cases. That statute would generate a significant workload for the Court in the period after our principal study, which we discuss at the end of the chapter.

## A. A Modest Beginning

The Court's first two private cases, both decided in the October 1940 term, are of a piece with the Court's other cases from this early period. *Deckert v. Independence Shares Corporation* was the first securities opinion written by the thoroughly liberal Frank Murphy, recently elevated from Attorney General to the Court by Franklin Delano Roosevelt.[5] *A.C. Frost v. Coeur D'Alene Mines Corporation* was James Clark McReynolds's last opinion before his midterm retirement from the Court, the last of the Four Horsemen to depart.[6] Both opinions were unanimous, suggesting the new private causes of action provoked little controversy among the justices.

In *Deckert*, the Court overturned a court of appeals decision that had blocked relief against third parties under the Securities Act. In permitting the plaintiff to go beyond the express remedy against the seller provided by § 12 of the Act, Murphy took a broad view of available remedies:

> The power *to enforce* implies the power to make effective the right of recovery afforded by the Act. And the power to make the right of recovery effective implies the power to utilize any of the procedures or actions normally available to the litigant according to the exigencies of the particular case.

It was of no moment that the Act did not specifically authorize suits against third parties: "That it does not authorize the bill in so many words is no more significant than the fact that it does not in terms authorize execution to issue on a judgment recovered under § 12(2)." A small step at the time, but this generous attitude toward implying remedies against additional parties for an express right of action provided by the securities laws would lend support to the Court's creation of implied rights of action a quarter-century later.

In *A.C. Frost*, the Court overturned a broad Idaho Supreme Court decision that declared an agreement in violation of the Securities Act to be void ab initio. The SEC—in its first amicus appearance at the Court—worried that such a broad holding could thwart protections for the investing public in other situations. The Court afforded deference to the agency, quoting extensively from an SEC memorandum expressing concern that holding the contract void ab initio would prevent an issuing company from recovering the sales proceeds from its underwriter in an offering in which there had been a violation. The decision preserved the statutory claim.

The holdings of these early cases fit comfortably within the dominant paradigm of the New Deal era. The Court afforded the causes of action created by Congress a plaintiff-friendly reading, consistent with their purpose to go beyond the remedies provided by the common law. In the two decades that followed, the Court would ignore private securities litigation. Moreover, Congress would not produce any federal securities legislation of any import. The sixties, however, would find the Court taking an even more plaintiff-friendly turn. We turn to that subject now.

## B. Implied Private Rights of Action Unleashed

Neither Section 10(b) of the 1934 Act, nor Rule 10b-5, the broad antifraud provision promulgated by the SEC under that section in 1942, says anything about private enforcement. (The SEC's authority to enforce the rule is clear under § 21 of the Exchange Act.) In 1947 a federal district court in *Kardon v. National Gypsum Co.* became the first court to hold that the rule supported an implied private cause of action. The Supreme Court, however, did not take up the issue of implied rights of action under the securities laws until a generation later.[7] In the interim, the Second Circuit took the lead, deciding private lawsuits that would lay the groundwork for the Supreme Court cases of the 1960s.

The postwar Second Circuit was well-situated to fill the gap in securities law. Geographically, its location in New York City, the nation's financial center, provided a steady source of securities cases. The appellate court's six long-serving members (two Roosevelt appointees joining four named by Calvin Coolidge) provided the gravitas and continuity that led to the court's recognition as the

172   A HISTORY OF SECURITIES LAW

"Mother Court" of securities law. Roosevelt's two appointees proved particularly influential on issues related to private litigation. Charles Clark, the principal drafter of the Federal Rules of Civil Procedure, had a sharply progressive attitude toward the securities laws, as we saw in Chapter 5. Jerome Frank had succeeded Douglas as SEC chair before his appointment to the appellate court. He was an influential legal realist philosopher who had served a variety of roles in the Roosevelt administration.[8] Frank's 1951 opinion in *Fischman v. Raytheon* made the Second Circuit the first appellate court to follow *Kardon* in implying a Rule 10b-5 private right of action. In another opinion, Frank emphasized the role of private litigation in encouraging investors' trust:

> An economy like ours, which thrives on the fact that thousands of persons of modest means invest in corporate shares, will be poorly served if our courts regard with suspicion all minority stockholders' suits, and, therefore, out of desire to discourage such suits, apply to them unusually strict pleading rules, thus tending to thwart judicial inquiries into the conduct of wrongdoing, controlling stockholders. The unfortunate consequences will be that those in control may be immunized from effective attacks on their misdeeds, and, as a result, the small investors will lose confidence in all corporate managements, the honest as well as the dishonest.

Other circuits followed the Second Circuit's lead in recognizing a private cause of action, relying both on Frank's opinion in *Fischman* and earlier opinions by Clark.[9]

The revolution in implied rights of action at the Supreme Court seemed almost casual in its inception. At issue in *J.I. Case Co. v. Borak* was whether a shareholder unhappy with a merger could enforce Exchange Act Rule 14a-9's antifraud prohibition in an action for rescission or damages from misstatements in a corporate proxy.[10] Absent a private right of action, the federal prohibition could only be enforced by the SEC; the shareholder would be left to his remedies under state corporate law. The SEC appeared as amicus to support the plaintiff, invoking the "broad remedial purposes" of fair corporate suffrage and discouraging abuse of the proxy process. Justice Tom Clark, writing for the Court, brushed aside the fact that § 14(a)'s "language makes no specific reference to a private right of action." He reasoned: "among [the rule's] chief purposes is 'the protection of investors,' which certainly implied the availability of judicial relief where necessary to achieve that result." Having gleaned that broad mandate from the purpose of investor protection, Clark conducted his own policy analysis to effect that purpose. Clark concluded that judicial relief was necessary: "Private enforcement of the proxy rules provides a necessary supplement to Commission action," given the volume of proxies the SEC had to review. The SEC could not handle the job all alone. That need was sufficient to trigger "the duty of the courts to be alert to provide such remedies as are necessary to make effective the congressional purpose."

Clark found the statutory hook for this judicial lawmaking in § 27 of the Exchange Act. That section confers jurisdiction on the district courts over "all suits in equity and actions at law brought to enforce any liability or duty created by this title." Even Louis Loss, generally sympathetic to a broad interpretation of the securities laws, found this reliance on § 27 question begging: "the Court reached the right result not for the wrong reason but for no reason at all."[11] The Court invoked its *Deckert* decision, discussed in section A, which had broadly interpreted similar language in the Securities Act to imply remedies. The *Borak* Court did not mention that the "right of recovery" in *Deckert* was an explicit cause of action (§ 12 of the Securities Act), albeit in an action against a party other than the defendant in the case before it.

Nor did the Court mention the explicit private rights of action created in the Exchange Act (§§ 9, 16, and 18). A structural interpretation of the Exchange Act might have suggested that Congress intended those explicit causes to be exclusive. The Court also dismissed possible interference with state law: "if the law of the State happened to attach no responsibility to the use of misleading proxy statements, the whole purpose of the section might be frustrated." Purpose was sufficient to override all objections to judicial creativity. The *Borak* Court saw itself as an active partner with the SEC and Congress in achieving the aims of the securities laws, with or without a textual basis for creating a cause of action. No justice dissented; indeed, Douglas's notes from conference do not indicate any justice even questioning the propriety of a court implying a private cause of action.[12] The revision of Rule 23 of the Federal Rules of Civil Procedure was still two years away, so there was not yet a threat of a class action for enormous money damages.

Six years passed after *Borak* before the Court returned to the task of developing private rights of action under the securities laws. The liberal stalwarts, Earl Warren and Arthur Goldberg, were now gone. Warren Burger had succeeded Earl Warren as Chief, but Harry Blackmun was not yet confirmed to replace Goldberg's successor, Abe Fortas. These changes in personnel did not alter the approach to the securities laws: *Mills v. Electric Auto-Lite*, another merger case, largely confirms and extends *Borak*.[13]

The Court was called upon in *Mills* to flesh out the necessary elements of the cause of action implied under § 14(a) in *Borak*, in this case materiality and causation. The Seventh Circuit had rejected the shareholders' claim on the grounds that the terms of the merger were fair. John Marshall Harlan, relatively conservative by sixties standards,[14] wrote for the Court, rejecting fairness as a defense: "[t]he risk that [shareholders] would be unable to rebut the corporation's

174    A HISTORY OF SECURITIES LAW

evidence of the fairness of the proposal, and thus to establish their cause of action, would be bound to discourage such shareholders from the private enforcement of the proxy rules that 'provides a necessary supplement to Commission action.'" The Court was fully committed to promoting private causes of action to further the purposes of the securities laws.

The causation standard adopted by Harlan is also generous to shareholders: if a misstatement is found to be material, the plaintiff need only prove "that the proxy solicitation itself, rather than the particular defect in the solicitation materials, was an essential link in the accomplishment of the transaction." Causation need not be direct; materiality is the key, and here too the *Mills* Court was inclined to be generous to plaintiffs. The determination of materiality "indubitably embodies a conclusion that the defect was of such a character that it might have been considered important by a reasonable shareholder who was in the process of deciding how to vote." The Court suggests that a "significant propensity to affect the voting process" would be sufficient. Under this standard, few cases would be dismissed at the early motion stage prior to discovery.

The *Mills* Court's plaintiff-friendly approach, based on its reading of statutory purpose, is underscored by the decision's final holding: plaintiffs "who have established a violation of the securities laws by their corporation and its officials, should be reimbursed by the corporation or its survivor for the costs of establishing the violation."[15] This holding provoked (modest) disagreement among the justices. Black, who viewed himself as a strict textualist,[16] dissented alone, arguing that the Exchange Act did not authorize an award of attorneys' fees. According to Black, "The courts are interpreters, not creators, of legal rights to recover and if there is a need for recovery of attorneys' fees to effectuate the policies of the Act here involved, that need should in my judgment be met by Congress, not by this Court." The majority readily rebuffed Black's objection that its holding lacked a basis in the statute:

> The Act makes no provision for private recovery for a violation of § 14(a) other than the declaration of 'voidness' in § 29(b), leaving the courts with the task, faced by this Court in *Borak*, of deciding whether a private right of action should be implied. The courts must similarly determine whether the special circumstances exist that would justify an award of attorneys' fees, including reasonable expense of litigation other than statutory costs.

Black was trying to close the stable door after the horse had left the barn. Textualism's force as an interpretive constraint had been eviscerated by *Borak*—which Black had joined. Having created the private right of action, the Court did not hesitate to rely on its own judgment in defining its elements.

PRIVATE LITIGATION    175

The Court finally addressed the Rule 10b-5 private right of action nearly a quarter-century after lower courts first recognized one. In *Superintendent of Ins. v. Bankers Life & Casualty Co.*,[17] an insurance company sold bonds on market terms. The proceeds were subsequently diverted, however, shuffled around to be used as payment for a purchaser's acquisition of shares controlling the company. Thus, corporation assets had been removed from the corporate treasury to pay the purchase price for the control block with no offsetting payment to the firm.

The case was argued in the second week of the October 1971 term; a decision was announced just over three weeks later. Douglas wrote the unanimous, vintage Douglas, opinion. The decision (along with *Affiliated Ute*, discussed below) would be the last hurrah of purposive securities interpretations. The logic of *Borak* had surely taken much of the suspense out of the question of implied causes of action (Douglas did cite *Borak*); the circuit courts were by then almost unanimous in implying a cause of action. Even so, Douglas's method of announcement was notably casual—relegated to a footnote dropped into the middle of a quotation from an appellate court opinion. Douglas, never one to be verbose, saw little need to belabor the details of a then uncontroversial proposition.

The question of remedies for corporate mismanagement under the antifraud statute of the securities laws was dispatched summarily. That the fraud was perpetrated by officers of the insurance company and their outside collaborators was "irrelevant" given the loss incurred by the company due to the wrongful conduct. Douglas quoted the House reports in 1934 for the proposition that " 'disregard of trust relationships by those whom the law should regard as fiduciaries are all a single seamless web' along with manipulation, investor ignorance, and the like." Here the insurance company's sale of bonds was in a market transaction at a fair price; the sale brought cash into the corporate coffers that duplicitous employees then purloined. Douglas's reasoning came straight out of *Capital Gains*: "Section 10(b) must be read flexibly, not technically and restrictively." Douglas did not, however, bother to cite that opinion.

The Second Circuit's *Birnbaum* decision, written by Augustus Hand almost twenty years before, could have posed a potential obstacle.[18] In *Birnbaum*, the Second Circuit held that (1) standing under Rule 10b-5 required that the plaintiff be a purchaser or seller of securities; and (2) that the cause of action was not intended to provide a remedy for corporate mismanagement. Douglas conveniently accepted the first *Birnbaum* holding—there was a sale of a security here by the corporation even if largely attenuated from the wrongdoing—while rejecting the corporate mismanagement holding, all without mentioning the Second Circuit decision. Blackmun was willing to go further and repudiate *Birnbaum* completely, but still relatively new to the Court, he deferred to Douglas.[19]

176 A HISTORY OF SECURITIES LAW

President Richard Nixon had now appointed two justices to the Court (Burger and Blackmun) with no discernible effect on the interpretation of the securities laws. Douglas's New Deal vision still held sway.

The final case of the expansionist era also involved a private right of action under Rule 10b-5. Blackmun was assigned to write the opinion for the Court in *Affiliated Ute*, argued the same month as *Bankers Life*.[20] In his cover memo to his colleagues accompanying his draft, Blackmun conceded: "I have taken a very liberal approach to Rule 10b-5. This may represent a step beyond any point the Court has heretofore reached. This undoubtedly is the most important aspect of the case and I urge your close attention to it."[21]

We touched upon *Affiliated Ute* in the last chapter in connection with insider trading, but that case's principal significance flows from its holding regarding the element of reliance under Rule 10b-5. *Mills* had focused on causation more broadly, discounting the importance of reliance in the context of Rule 14a-9 proxy fraud. *Affiliated Ute* took a similarly generous approach under Rule 10b-5 with the potential for much broader application. The Court concluded that positive proof or reliance is not a prerequisite to recovery under Rule 10b-5 in a case of omission. Instead, it looked to *Mills* and its broad conception of reliance/transaction causation for a connection between defendant's wrongful conduct and plaintiff's harm: "[a]ll that is necessary is that the facts withheld be material in the sense that a reasonable investor might have considered them important. . . ."[22] Materiality, as an objective standard, was amenable to proof on a class-wide basis, whereas individual reliance was not. Thus, by turning reliance into a common question, *Affiliated Ute* opened the door for the modern securities class action.

The Court was unanimous, albeit short-handed, on the reliance point; Powell and Rehnquist had joined the Court after oral argument and did not participate in the decision. In the meantime, *Affiliated Ute* suggested that Harry Blackmun might be prepared to take a leadership role on the Court in the field of securities law, extending the purposive interpretation that had dominated the sixties. Blackmun was "inclined to read the Securities Exchange Act broadly" and "fe[lt] we should plump for a high standard in this area, and this is in line with the intent of Congress in enacting the legislation."[23]

## C. Lewis Powell and the Counterrevolution

In early January 1972 Lewis Powell and William Rehnquist took their seats on the Supreme Court, replacing Hugo Black and John Harlan. The Supreme Court's approach to securities law was about to take a dramatic turn. The Court had now six justices appointed by Republican presidents, a departure from the

Democratic dominance for most of the previous thirty-five years.[24] Powell would rely on his experience as a corporate and securities lawyer to reshape the Court's private securities docket over the next fifteen years. This part focuses on three trend lines prominent in cases dealing with private litigation during this period:

1) worry over the adverse impacts of class actions;
2) willingness to construe the elements of Rule 10b-5 actions narrowly; and
3) hostility to implied private rights of action.

The majority of Republican appointees did not guarantee a restrictive view. Brennan, an Eisenhower appointee, took a liberal approach to securities law, consistent with his jurisprudence generally. Blackmun showed his expansionist impulses in *Affiliated Ute*, and Burger had not resisted. As the seventies wore on, Burger would write more reliably about the need to contain the number of lawsuits in federal court.[25] He would sign on to all of the key counterrevolutionary decisions of the mid-1970s. Blackmun and Brennan, however, would dissent. Blackmun would stick around to write *Basic Inc. v. Levinson* after Powell retired. But from 1972 to 1987, Powell steered the Court in a new direction.

The mid-seventies trilogy of *Blue Chip Stamps*, *Ernst & Ernst*, and *Santa Fe* showed that the Court would construe Rule 10b-5 narrowly to keep securities fraud class actions in check.[26] That restrictive approach was motivated at least in part by the private 10b-5 claim's suspect origins: it was a judicial, rather than legislative, creation. Much of the discussion of *Santa Fe* is left to the federalism discussion in the next chapter, but together these three cases are the cornerstone of the counterrevolution in private securities litigation. The Court was sending a strong message to the lower courts, particularly the Second Circuit, to reverse their expansive course in interpreting Rule 10b-5. That message was conveyed, not only in the decisions' substantive holdings, but at least as important, in their style.

How did Powell engineer this reversal? Powell's influence resulted in part from superior expertise, but he leveraged his insight with initiative and effort. He lobbied for securities cases to be included in the Court's docket; the Court heard significantly more securities cases per term during his tenure than the periods before or after. Powell did his homework, beginning with "summer memos" identifying issues in the coming term's cases and the way he thought they should be addressed. Those memos were frequently followed by outlines for his remarks at conference, and occasionally, memos lobbying his fellow justices who required extra persuasion. Powell's effort produced results: the key opinions limiting the Rule 10b-5 cause of action often were joined by at least two of the Democratic appointees from the 1960s who had signed onto the expansive opinions of that era. White and Marshall joined majorities in *Blue Chip Stamps* and *Ernst &*

178   A HISTORY OF SECURITIES LAW

*Ernst*, the clearest signals of the newly restrictive attitude. White authored—and Marshall joined—*Santa Fe*, the most emphatic rejection of the Second Circuit's effort to bring corporate governance into the domain of securities law.

## 1. Class Actions

Powell first made his influence felt at the beginning of his second full term not in a securities case, but rather in an antitrust case, *Eisen v. Carlisle & Jacquelin*, involving class action procedures.[27] The claim was based on price fixing by brokerage firms of commissions when trading in "odd lots" (generally, trades of less than one hundred shares). The case turned on complex procedural questions about the "manageability" of the class that could have derailed the Supreme Court's decision.[28]

Powell saw something much bigger than mere procedural questions. He described it, in his own preliminary memorandum about the case, as "the major *test* case involving the *contours of a proper class action case under Rule 23* [of the Federal Rules of Civil Procedure], as well as the notice requirements in a class action case compelled by Due Process." Rule 23 had been substantially amended just a few years before and its impact on securities law was still emerging. Powell, however, did not want Rule 23's interpretation to be determined by the facts of a particular case: "we must decide case on principle of general application—not on a *guess* as to what members of class will do." General principles, of course, would limit the discretion of lower courts in subsequent cases. Powell also distrusted the trial court's procedural innovation: this "requirement that a party pay his *adversary's cost* is unique in the law."[29]

Burger assigned the opinion to Powell. With a substantial majority on the procedural issues (only Douglas disagreed and his views were tentative), Powell steered clear of the difficult jurisdictional issue posed by the manageability question. Nonetheless, Powell worried about the ability of courts to manage class actions of the size and complexity seen in *Eisen*. In a suggested footnote to the opinion, he expressed his concern about class actions:

> This case's history well illustrates the array of intractable problems latent in this type of class action. With competent counsel and in a District and Circuit uniquely experienced in complex civil litigation, this suit—in which appealing policy and legal considerations are implicated on both sides—has defied rational resolution. It suggests the need for thoughtful reexamination of some of the assumptions that underlie the class action rules, with due recognition of the need for some form of class action relief, and also rules which in fact can be

administered within the framework of the adversary system with reasonable expedition and fairness to all concerned.

This footnote did not make it into the published opinion, but Burger wrote (in a private note to Powell, not shared with the conference): "I hope this will 'contain' the drift for government-by-class-action. What we need is vigorous action by appropriate regulatory agencies when these brokers get out of line." Powell's opinion reversing the district court was a step toward "containing" class actions, an issue that would occupy much of the Court's securities docket after his retirement.[30]

*Blue Chip Stamps*, decided the following term, marks the rhetorical high point of the Court's counterrevolution, particularly as to class actions. The Second Circuit's early fifties *Birnbaum* decision required that that a private plaintiff must be a purchaser or seller of securities to state a claim under Rule 10b-5.[31] The Supreme Court had yet to speak on the issue, although Douglas's opinion in *Bankers Life* had minimized its reach and multiple litigants had tried to chip away at it. The Seventh Circuit finally rejected the *Birnbaum* rule the year prior to

**Figure 6.1**
**Counting to Five:** Once Powell and Rehnquist joined the Burger Court, shown here during the 1972 term, there were four reliable votes to construe the securities laws narrowly, but success turned on Powell persuading White, Marshall, and/or Blackmun to make a majority. Those three had joined the expansive decisions of the previous decade.

180   A HISTORY OF SECURITIES LAW

*Blue Chips*, arguing "The Supreme Court has repeatedly stated that [purchase or sale of a security] should be given a broad and flexible construction."[32]

Not anymore. Called upon to resolve the circuit split, the Court chose *Birnbaum*. Unwilling to rest on the rule's long standing, Rehnquist went on—in passages written exclusively by the Justice—to highlight concerns about securities fraud class actions: "litigation under Rule 10b-5 presents a danger of vexatiousness different in degree and in kind from that which accompanies litigation in general." Rehnquist also worried that the risk from the threat of enormous discovery costs could produce "*in terrorem*" settlements.[33]

Despite Rehnquist's emphatic message, Powell was unhappy with the opinion, which "reaches correct result—but *meanders* and *wobbles* about in a most unlawyerlike manner!" Powell fretted that the opinion apologized excessively for its holding and that it paid insufficient attention to the statute's "*language*" and "*legislative history*." In light of his "special interest in this subject" Powell wrote a concurrence emphasizing the statutory language. Powell thought the rule was compelled by text, legislative intent, long history, and "*policy considerations . . . extending* standing (who may) to sue" which were particularly relevant in "a *private* cause of action . . . wholly of *judicial* creation." Those policy concerns grew out of his own experience, as Powell explained:

> In administering the 1933 Act, the SEC traditionally and consistently has encouraged and often required offerors to take conservative postures in prospectuses, especially with respect to judgmental and unfavorable matters. If a different philosophy now were to be read into the 1934 Act, inviting litigation for arguably misleading understatement as well as for overstatement of the issuer's prospects, the hazard of "going to market"—already not inconsequential— would be immeasurably increased.[34]

Powell and Rehnquist diverged in another securities case four terms later. Rehnquist again focused his concern on the impact of class actions, this time in the context of an administrative enforcement action. The question presented in *Parklane Hosiery Co. v. Shore* was whether issues resolved against a defendant in an SEC enforcement action should be given collateral estoppel effect in a subsequent private action.[35] Defendants in SEC enforcement actions are loath to contest the agency's charges in court, given the ruinous liability exposure an adverse decision would create for them in a follow-on class action by private claimants. As a result, the overwhelming majority of SEC enforcement actions are resolved through consent decrees, with defendants agreeing to pay fines and/or have injunctions entered against them, but without any admission of wrongdoing.[36]

Rehnquist worried that the Court's:

## PRIVATE LITIGATION    181

decision will have the result of coercing defendants to agree to consent orders or settlements in agency enforcement actions in order to preserve their right to jury trial in the private actions. In that event, the Court, for no compelling reason, will have simply added a powerful club to the administrative agencies' arsenals that even Congress was unwilling to provide them.

This time, unlike *Blue Chip*, Rehnquist found himself alone in dissent. Powell joined Stewart's majority opinion upholding the use of collateral estoppel despite his law clerk pointing out (and Powell agreeing) that allowing "class action plaintiffs . . . to gain a 'free ride' following a successful government enforcement suit" was inconsistent with the concept of class action plaintiffs serving as " 'private attorneys general.' " Powell conceded that Rehnquist had written a "good dissent--but I still agree with Stewart's opinion."[37] Whether Powell's close friendship with Stewart influenced his views here is impossible to say, but Rehnquist's concerns were of the sort typically raised by Powell in the Court's deliberations.

But this difference of opinion in *Parklane* was of little moment. *Blue Chip*, like Powell's decision in *Eisen*, signaled a clear change of direction to lower courts that had actively promoted the rise of class action litigation. In his thirty-three years on the Court, Rehnquist was to write only two other opinions for the Court in securities cases. Usually, it was Powell at the center of the Court's discussions.

Blackmun did not share Rehnquist's concern with "vexatious litigation." He focused more on the purpose of the statute than the risk of unleashing the lawsuit floodgates. In his pre-argument memo, Blackmun wrote:

> I have always been troubled by the Birnbaum doctrine. I think it is the product of a pragmatic approach to this area of the law. I can see why CA 2 adopted it. Nevertheless, I wonder whether its adoption was sound in the light of the statute and the entire purpose of the securities laws. If a person is injured by fraud in the making of a securities transaction, why should he not have a cause of action? I realize that giving an affirmative answer to that question in a sense opens the floodgates. On the other hand, such a plaintiff will have to prove his case. He will have to demonstrate causality and injury. This may or may not be hard to do. On net balance it may mean that many more suits will be instituted, but I would think that the floodgates can be kept under control by requiring appropriate proof. Many of the cases probably can go off on motions for summary judgment rather than initially on an evaluation of standing.
>
> What is totally persuasive for me, however, is that casting aside the Birnbaum rule will be consistent with the legislative pattern, and it will effectuate the

182   A HISTORY OF SECURITIES LAW

central purpose underlying securities regulation, namely, the protection of the investing public.

I am fortified in this by the fact that the SEC has uniformly opposed the Birnbaum doctrine as an arbitrary principle of standing.[38]

Blackmun's views here echo his position in *Affiliated Ute*: plaintiff-friendly standards were needed to serve the statutory purpose of protecting the investing public. In his dissent, Blackmun charged the majority with "preternatural solicitousness for corporate well-being and a seeming callousness toward the investing public quite out of keeping, it seems to me, with our own traditions and the intent of the securities laws." Douglas, who had written *Bankers Life* leaving *Birnbaum* undisturbed only four years prior, now joined Blackmun's call to discard its limitation on standing, as did Brennan. The split between the new conservative coalition and the purposivist bloc was hardening, and the conservatives were picking up votes.

The sharp disagreements over interpretive approach apparently did not bleed over into personal relationships. Rehnquist had clerked for Robert Jackson during the somewhat fraught fifties and was conscious of the importance of maintaining collegial relations among the brethren. He passed a note to Blackmun on the bench: "In Blue Chip, I will agree to write a short + unconvincing majority opinion if you will promise to write a short + unconvincing dissent. We will both save time." Rehnquist utterly failed in his attempt at brevity, but he may have done better at levity. Blackmun responded: "In the handwritten note you gave me on the bench on April 14, you instructed me not to exceed the length of the majority opinion. I have had this in mind, but try as I may, I have not been able to come up with 30 pages [the length of the majority opinion]."[39]

Rehnquist's verbose opinion has been a common citation in subsequent Supreme Court and lower court opinions reining in class actions. Rehnquist's message was less well received by the SEC, which had sided with the plaintiffs as amicus. The evening *Blue Chip* was handed down, Rehnquist's clerk overheard the SEC's lawyers bemoaning the agency's rare loss in the Supreme Court at the Dubliner, a watering hole of long standing.[40] SEC headquarters were only a few blocks from the Supreme Court's marble palace on Capitol Hill, but the distance was growing.

## 2. Construing Rule 10b-5 Narrowly

*Ernst & Ernst v. Hochfelder* reads Rule 10b-5 narrowly, tethering the rule to the text of § 10(b).[41] The case arose from a claim against an accounting firm for failing to uncover the long-running fraudulent scheme of a brokerage house's principal.

The plaintiffs alleged that Ernst & Ernst had aided and abetted the fraud by its negligent auditing. The question for the Court was whether negligence would suffice to state a claim under § 10(b), or would a higher state of mind be required. The Court rejected a negligence standard under Rule 10b-5, emphasizing that the scope of Rule 10b-5 "cannot exceed the power granted the [SEC] by Congress under § 10(b)." In other words, the scope of the SEC's rule would be constrained going forward by the Court's power over statutory interpretation. *Blue Chip* and *Ernst & Ernst* signaled the death knell of the Supreme Court's "flexible" construction to achieve "remedial purposes" as seen in *Borak* and *Bankers Life*. Statutory text would be used to constrain private lawsuits.

Powell's view of the case was colored by his concern about a related issue: the liability of third parties for misstatements. Powell observed in his "summer memo," written after reading the briefs during the Court's break between terms:

> As we had occasion recently to note in *Blue Chip Stamps v. Manor Drug Stores*, private causes of action for damages under Section 10(b) and Rule 10b-5 have evolved expansively by judicial interpretation. The decision of CA7, if affirmed by us, would advance this process to new frontiers. Damage liability could be imposed for negligence not only upon the contracting party (the brokerage firm in this case), but also upon a "third party" accounting firm.

Powell was at least as concerned with the identity of the defendant as he was with the standard of liability. Powell distrusted lawsuits that extended liability too far, and, in his view, professionals who assisted issuers and intermediaries in the securities markets were not well placed to police for fraud.[42]

Powell was assigned the opinion, and in a memorandum to his law clerk reviewing a draft, he noted that "[w]e do not discuss the absence of 'privity' in the common law sense between Ernst & Ernst and respondents. I view this as an important fact, and indeed one that could be controlling with me." Powell recognized, however, that the Court had not granted certiorari on this question and he did not think he could swing a majority to dismiss on absence of privity. A holding based on lack of privity would have had profound consequences for the law of securities fraud; it suggests that Powell would have had little trouble voting for the Supreme Court's controversial decision in *Central Bank*, discussed below, which foreclosed liability for aiders and abettors. Given the case's posture, Powell satisfied himself by drafting a footnote highlighting his "policy concerns."[43]

On the critical question of the required state of mind, Powell, in a somewhat impatient tone (for him) objected to his clerk's distinction between " 'knowing or intentional misconduct', on the one hand, and negligence or 'negligent misfeasance', on the other." Powell preferred the middle ground established by Judge Arlin Adams in a concurrence to a Third Circuit opinion:

184   A HISTORY OF SECURITIES LAW

Judge Adams in *Korn* [*sic*] (at p. 287) used language that I like:

"An intent to deceive, manipulate or defraud."
    Adams, p. 285, also referred to Judge Friendly's formulation as including "recklessness" that amounts to fraud. What would you think of our using the term "scienter" and defining it early in the opinion, using the Adams/Friendly terminology?[44]

This discussion suggests that Powell thought that recklessness would satisfy the scienter requirement. The first part of this suggestion was adopted, with the eventual opinion defining scienter as "a mental state embracing intent to deceive, manipulate, or defraud." The final opinion, however, did not incorporate recklessness, specifically reserving the question.

Why not resolve this critical issue? The answer is fairly mundane. Powell, despite his desire to offer guidance to the bar, had a general preference for not addressing questions unnecessary to the decision. Accordingly, he left resolution of this issue to a subsequent case.[45] Powell's jurisprudential preference to leave questions to another day conflicted with his preference for predictability. Resolution of this critical question could have made the securities laws easier to apply.

Powell could have settled the law in *Ernst & Ernst* but held back. Although Powell's opinion discouraged securities fraud class actions alleging "fraud by hindsight," the question he left unanswered—the state of mind required for fraud under § 10(b)—lingered as a central dispute in securities class actions for a generation. Powell can be forgiven for failing to anticipate that the Court would not resolve the issue; the Court's appetite for securities law cases would wane after he left the Court. It seems unlikely that Powell would have ducked the issue if he were still on the Court. If the Court had resolved the issue before Powell retired, it appears that a majority would have supported recklessness. Powell's memorandum in *Ernst & Ernst* suggests that he favored recklessness, while Brennan, Blackmun, Stevens, and Marshall favored a negligence standard, so they presumably would have voted for recklessness over a knowledge requirement.[46] In this one area where Powell's view might have led to a *more* expansive interpretation of the securities law, he never registered his vote. Here Powell's preference for predictability in the securities laws fell victim to his cautious approach to resolving cases and controversies.

Powell was proud of the work that he was doing to curb the SEC and the plaintiffs' bar and pleased by the reception that his work received among his friends in the corporate bar. Writing to his former law clerk (who had worked on the *Ernst & Ernst* opinion), Powell noted that:

[T]he Harvard Law Review . . . did a real hatchet job on *Ernst & Ernst*. That part of the Supreme Court Review must have been written by a summer intern at the

PRIVATE LITIGATION 185

SEC. The experienced corporate bar (many of whom spoke to me at the ABA meeting in Atlanta and also at the Virginia Bar meeting) view *Ernst & Ernst* as a landmark decision, the result being compelled by the language, legislative history and structure of the Act. I remain more than content with the opinion.

Powell wrote his opinions with practicing lawyers, not law students, in mind. Judges apparently were also part of that audience. Powell sent a copy of *Ernst & Ernst* to Judge Henry Friendly, telling Friendly that his "opinions and writing contributed significantly to our resolution of . . . [the] case[]." Friendly responded that he "was delighted both at the result and at your skillful handling of the problems."[47]

Blackmun again found himself in the minority. In his pre-argument memo, Blackmun lamented: "Well this is not the easiest one for me because I am not too much of an expert in securities law. I suspect that BRW and LP will have very definite ideas about this case. I am not certain that I shall be able to join them in view of my dissent in Blue Chip last spring." On the issue of scienter, Blackmun was not swayed by policy arguments favoring the higher standard.

I must confess that I do not have too much sympathy with the accountant's position on this issue. I anticipate that the Court will require scienter. Its decision in Blue Chip favors the petitioner. I have never been impressed with the practice of the accounting profession to rely generally and vaguely on "accepted accounting standards." I would be interested in WOD's reaction to this one. I am not impressed with the argument that all the accountants get is a small fee as compared with that possible liability. Accountants' fees are substantial and it seems to me should be equated with malpractice for physicians and attorneys.

Blackmun could be counted on as the Court's most consistent voice favoring expanded liability. Only Brennan joined his dissent bemoaning that Powell had interpreted Rule 10b-5 "restrictively and narrowly . . . thereby stultify[ing] recovery for the victim." Blackmun again invoked the language from *Capital Gains* "that securities legislation enacted for the purpose of avoiding frauds be construed 'not technically and restrictively, but flexibly to effectuate its remedial purposes.'"[48] But that interpretive approach was quickly dying.

*Piper v. Chris-Craft*, a case discussed in more detail in the next section in connection with implied rights of action, came to the Court shortly after *Ernst & Ernst*, raising questions of liability under Section 14(e), an antifraud provision applicable to tender offers. Powell viewed the question of scienter as central, and determined by the text:

the language of Section 10(b) and of Section 14(e) is sufficiently similar to justify the conclusion that the *Ernst and Ernst* holding with respect to § 10(b)

186  A HISTORY OF SECURITIES LAW

will govern § 14(e). My preliminary impression is that CA2 (Judge Timbers) enunciated and applied a standard of liability considerably less severe than the *scienter* standard we adopted in *Ernst and Ernst*.

In addition to the textual similarities between sections 10(b) and 14(e), Powell also identified "identical policy reasons" to those that had driven the decision in *Ernst & Ernst*: "When a *court implies* a cause of action for damages, it should hesitate—even if the first hurdle is cleared (π is within specially protected class)—to impose a low standard (threshold) of liability."[49] The Rule 10b-5 cause of action would survive the demise of implied rights of action, but the Court would construe its elements with suspicion in light of its purposivist origins. That approach would bleed over to similar causes of action.

By this point, Powell was confident in his role as the Court's securities law expert. Consider the following passage from a file memorandum he wrote in *Piper v. Chris-Craft Industries*:

> If I should vote with the majority, there is a fair possibility—I would guess— that the opinion would be assigned to me in view of my having written several SEC cases. In view of the relevance of *Ernst and Ernst* to a central issue in this case, the Conference will expect me take the lead in advising the Conference whether the standard of liability imposed by CA2 (see Judge Timber's opinion) is compatible with the standard we adopted in *Ernst and Ernst*.[50]

After only four years on the Court, Powell had established the securities laws as his domain. In this case, however, as described in the next subsection, the Chief Justice kept the *Piper* opinion for himself and the scienter issue was shunted aside.

This suspicion of implied rights of action would bleed over into elements that applied to both government and private enforcement. Materiality arises in virtually every securities fraud lawsuit, whether brought by a private litigant, the SEC, or the Justice Department. The higher the standard for materiality, the lower a corporation's risk of running afoul of the securities laws. The Court addressed this ubiquitous issue in *TSC Industries, Inc. v. Northway, Inc.*, a case decided the same year as *Ernst & Ernst*.[51] Interpreting the Rule 14a-9 private cause of action created by the Court in *Borak*, the Seventh Circuit had held that certain omissions from a proxy statement were material as a matter of law because they "might have been considered important by a reasonable shareholder." Powell saw the case through the lens of his commitment to confining implied rights of action. He saw the Seventh Circuit's formulation as an "unrealistic standard," a view no doubt colored by his perception of the case as a "strike suit." Powell instead argued at conference for his reading of the Second Circuit's standard: a "significant likelihood that a reasonable investor would consider the information important in arriving at his choice of action." Powell characterized this standard as "middle-of-road" and argued that "courts should avoid extreme standards either of laxity or liability" when dealing with a *"judicially created"* remedy. Powell's characterization seems a bit strained. Although the private right of action under Rule 14a-9 is judicially created, the materiality language is drawn from the statute and applies to both private and SEC actions. After articulating the standard, Powell then went through a careful explication of the facts in arguing that the Seventh Circuit had erred in holding that the omissions were material as a matter of law, rather than leaving them for the jury. Powell's thorough preparation paid off, as the Chief Justice, Stewart, Marshall, and Rehnquist agreed with him across the board. The Chief assigned the opinion to Marshall.[52]

Powell liked Marshall's draft opinion, with two small exceptions. Marshall wrote that "[o]ur cases have not considered, and we have no occasion in this case to consider, what showing of culpability, *if any*, is required to establish the liability under § 14(a)." The "if any" drew Powell's ire—even the suggestion of strict liability was anathema—and Marshall excised the offensive language. Powell also objected to a footnote reserving judgment "as to how the standard of materiality and its application might be altered in a case involving a contested election." Powell the corporate lawyer could not have been comfortable with the notion that the supposedly objective standard for materiality might vary with the context in which it was applied. Even Blackmun, no friend of defendants in securities cases, shared this concern.[53] Marshall removed the offending footnote. The standard adopted in *TSC* followed Judge Henry Friendly's standard from *Gerstle*[54]—Marshall had served alongside Friendly on the Second Circuit before his appointment as Solicitor General. The standard would eventually become the general standard of materiality under the securities laws. Powell had succeeded in preventing plaintiffs from winning at the summary judgment stage on materiality claims, but the Court's standard ended up making it difficult for defendants to effectively use materiality as the basis for a pre-trial dismissal.

The following year, the Court again limited the implied Rule 10b-5 cause of action in *Santa Fe Indus. v. Green*.[55] We leave the federalism aspects of that case for the next chapter, but the holding—Rule 10b-5 requires deception—confined the implied cause of action to narrow bounds. The Second Circuit had declared that a broad reading of Rule 10b-5 was "too obvious to comment." But the SEC, which had been a consistent supporter of a broad reading of Rule 10b-5, sat this one out, even though the Court's restrictive interpretation would also restrict the SEC's enforcement efforts. White, writing for the Court, rejected the lower court's approach to Rule 10b-5 "as inconsistent with that taken by the Court last term in *Ernst and Ernst*. When a statute speaks so specifically in terms of manipulation and deception . . . and when its statute reflects no more expansive intent, we are quite unwilling to extend the scope of the statute." Textualism had triumphed.

188   A HISTORY OF SECURITIES LAW

In just three terms the Court delivered a consistent message that implied rights were to be strictly construed. The contrast to the open-ended approach of *Borak*, *Mills*, *Bankers Life*, and *Affiliated Ute* is striking. There had been a change in personnel with the addition of Powell and Rehnquist, but the views of some of the incumbent justices appear to have shifted as well. White and Marshall, who signed on to expansive decisions in the 1960s, helped make the new majorities in each of the three core cases of the mid-1970s—*Blue Chip Stamps*, *Ernst & Ernst*, and *Santa Fe*. White, who had been Deputy Attorney General under Robert Kennedy before his appointment to the Court, supported government enforcement, but was skeptical of plaintiffs' attorneys masquerading as "private attorneys general." Marshall, for his part, had been close to Henry Friendly during his time on the Second Circuit, and appears to have been influenced by that association. Even with Nixon-appointee Blackmun defecting from the conservative line in each of those three cases, there was a comfortable majority that included the two remaining Democratic appointees from the sixties. The rise of class actions may have played a role in the new attitude, but Powell's presence in the Conference surely helped galvanize the response.

There were occasional deviations from the restrictive trend. In *Herman & Maclean v. Huddleston* the question was the burden of proof under the Rule 10b-5 implied right. The SEC and the Solicitor General were arguing for a preponderance of the evidence standard. Powell agreed with his law clerk that "the SG undervalues a professional's reputation" and the reputational harm from a jury finding that the defendant (in this case an accounting firm) acted with deceptive intent. Powell instead favored the common law "clear and convincing" evidence standard. Powell's influence was not brought to bear in this particular case. After writing this memorandum, Powell recused himself when he learned that his son-in-law's investment banking firm was a defendant in a similar suit.[56] With no one to advocate for the higher standard of proof at the Conference, the Court unanimously upheld the preponderance standard advocated by the SEC. Deference to agency expertise still had bite when there was not an expert justice taking the contrary position in Conference.

## 3. Rolling Back Implied Rights of Action

The implication of private rights of action under federal statutes was of paramount importance to Powell, and it became a battleground for the Court. Securities law was a key front. Powell worried that novel causes of action for securities law violations could impose crippling liability. That policy view aligned with a jurisprudential perspective that viewed lawmaking as a job for Congress. Accordingly, his work in this area shows a consistent effort to curtail causes of

PRIVATE LITIGATION 189

action not authorized by statutory text. The Court's *Borak* decision reflected a liberal attitude toward implying private rights of action, relying on a broad reading of congressional purpose. Powell, by contrast, emphasized the possible interference with regulatory schemes and the separation-of-powers issues raised by courts expanding their own jurisdiction. By the time Powell retired, the Court's approach to implied private rights of action had been transformed. His success in reshaping that body of law shows the influence that one justice—experienced and motivated—can have in a particular area.

The first case during Powell's tenure to raise the question of the implication of a private right of action from a regulatory scheme, *Securities Investor Protection Corp. v. Barbour*, decided the same month as *Blue Chip*, had generated no controversy.[57] When Congress passed the Securities Investor Protection Act in 1970 to provide investors with insurance protection in broker-dealer transactions,[58] it empowered the Securities Investor Protection Corporation (SIPC), to enforce the protections, subject to oversight by the SEC. The statute makes no mention of a private cause of action. Notwithstanding this omission, the Sixth Circuit held that investors had a private cause of action to enforce the new law.[59] The Court unanimously voted to reverse. Marshall, writing for the Court, emphasized the discretion vested by Congress in the SIPC and SEC and how private suits might interfere with the exercise of that discretion. He distinguished *Borak* on the ground that "the Court agreed with the SEC that private enforcement of the proxy rules was a necessary supplement to SEC enforcement."[60]

During that same term, Court addressed implied private rights more generally in a case outside the securities area. In *Cort v. Ash*, Brennan wrote a unanimous opinion for the court, finding no implied cause of action in a criminal statute.[61] The opinion set out a four-part test:

(1) whether the plaintiff is a member of the "class for whose especial benefit the statute was enacted";
(2) whether there is any expression of legislative intent to create or deny a private cause of action;
(3) whether a private remedy would be consistent with the purposes of the legislative scheme; and
(4) whether the cause of action is one "traditionally relegated to state law."

*Cort*'s test gave more structure than *Borak*'s summary approach, but did not necessarily portend a major reversal in the Court's jurisprudence relating to implication of private actions. The ground, however, appeared to be shifting.

The issue would soon become more fraught with a provision closer to the proxy rule at issue in *Borak*, § 14(a) of the Exchange Act. The central question in *Piper v. Chris-Craft Industries* in 1977 was whether § 14(e) of the Exchange

190   A HISTORY OF SECURITIES LAW

Act, adopted as part of the Williams Act in 1968 to prohibit fraud in connection with a tender offer, gave rise to a private right of action.[62] The facts of the case were convoluted, with two bidders, Chris-Craft and Bangor Punta, vying to take over the Piper Aircraft Corporation (controlled by the Piper family). After many twists, Bangor Punta ultimately prevailed, and Chris-Craft sought damages under § 14(e) and Rule 10b-6 of the Exchange Act, alleging that Bangor Punta, the Piper family, and First Boston (Bangor Punta's underwriter) had violated the securities laws in gaining control of Piper. On the question of whether courts should imply a cause of action for defeated tender offerors, Powell doubted that they warranted protection: "Offerors can take care of themselves (always corps. of some size)." Powell was also troubled by the damages award, which had little relation to any economic harm: "The $35 mil. judgment exceeds entire net worth (net equity) of Piper. . . ."[63]

Powell expected that the opinion would be assigned to him, as mentioned in the prior section, but that proved wrong, as Chief Justice Burger kept it for himself. Burger also sidestepped the scienter issue that had engaged Powell, instead holding that the Williams Act did not provide a cause of action for damages to a defeated bidder in a takeover contest. In determining whether it should imply a right of action, the Court applied the four-factor test that it had recently adopted in *Cort v. Ash*. The critical factor here, as Burger framed it, was that target shareholders, not rival bidders, were the particular class that Congress intended to protect by enacting the Williams Act. Thus, *Borak* was cabined using *Cort's* four-part test, but not directly challenged. Along the way, Burger took a swipe at the SEC, pointing out the SEC's change in position and questioning the agency's "presumed 'expertise' in securities fraud" as being "of limited value when the narrow legal issue is one peculiarly reserved for judicial resolution, namely whether a cause of action should be implied by judicial interpretation in favor of a particular class of litigants." This was a reverse from *Borak*, which had accepted the SEC's contention that private litigation was a "necessary supplement" to the agency's enforcement efforts. The SEC's influence on the Court was waning.

*Borak's* tenuous survival did not preclude a sharp reaction from John Paul Stevens, who had recently replaced Douglas. He urged that "[n]o one seriously questions the premise that Congress implicitly created a private right of action when it enacted § 14(e) in 1968."[64] He allowed that

> originally one might have argued that the private remedies created by the Securities Acts are limited to those expressly described in the legislation itself, history has foreclosed any such argument today. The statutes originally enacted in 1933 and 1934 have been amended so often with full congressional awareness of the judicial interpretation of Rule 10b-5 as implicitly creating a private remedy that we must now assume that Congress intended to create rights for

PRIVATE LITIGATION 191

the specific beneficiaries of the legislation as well as duties to be policed by the SEC.

Stevens's argument raised a new front in the battle over implied causes of action: If the Court was going to narrow the test for creating a right, what effect would the shift have on statutes enacted during the time that the Court was in a more generous mood? That fight would wait for another day. Applying the same four-factor test from *Cort* v. *Ash*, Stevens's reading of the legislative history led him to conclude that § 14(e) was intended to protect all shareholders, whatever their relationship to the corporation might be: "Congress would not exclude the persons most interested in effective enforcement from the class authorized to enforce the new law." Brennan joined Stevens's opinion; Blackmun agreed on the question of standing, but felt that Chris-Craft could not show causation, so he concurred in the judgment. Judges coming to disparate outcomes when applying the same *Cort* v. *Ash* test did not bode well for its future.

Powell took a cautious approach in *Piper* to the implied cause of action question, arguing only restraint in implying new causes. Two terms later, he was ready to go further, rolling back the whole business of implying private rights of action. In *TransAmerica Mortgage Advisors, Inc.* v. *Lewis*, the question was whether to imply a private right of action under § 206 of the Investment Advisers Act, which tracked closely the language of Rule 10b-5. (Recall that the Court had affirmed the implied right of action under Rule 10b-5 in *Bankers Life* earlier in the decade. When the Court's conference failed to produce the necessary four votes to grant certiorari Powell circulated a draft of a dissent that advocated a high threshold for implying a private right of action: "Recent decisions of this Court have reaffirmed that private causes of action will be inferred from securities statutes only if such an inference is consistent with the language and history of the statute and is necessary to avoid subversion of Congress' purpose in passing the statute." Rare will be the case where the implication of a private right of action is "necessary to avoid subversion of Congress' purpose"—if it were "necessary," presumably Congress would have provided for it. After Stewart and Rehnquist joined his dissent to the denial, the case was relisted for a conference in November 1978 and achieved the necessary four votes to make it to the Court's docket. Never a fan of implied rights, Powell was now campaigning to eradicate them altogether. His new attitude is captured in a memorandum to his clerk in February 1979:

I have come to think that the Court has gone much too far in inferring federal private causes of action where Congress has chosen to remain silent. Principles of federalism, where state courts traditionally have exercised jurisdiction over a particular type claim, should require that Congress confront openly the question whether there are sound reasons for also authorizing federal court suits.

192   A HISTORY OF SECURITIES LAW

One even can suspect that the draftsmen and sponsors of legislation, taking note of what can be described as the eagerness of federal courts to enhance their own jurisdiction, deliberately avoid legislative hearings and controversy simply by drafting statutes in what [Deputy Solicitor General Frank] Easterbrook calls a "neutral" fashion.[65]

Powell was ready to rethink the Court's approach to implied private rights; he wanted to put the onus on Congress to explicitly create causes of action. Federalism and separation of powers, not purpose, were the dominant themes.

He fired the first public shot a few months later in *Cannon v. University of Chicago*, involving the question of a private right of action under Title IX, which prohibits sex discrimination by universities receiving federal aid.[66] Powell dissented from the Court's recognition of an implied right, arguing that "[w]hen Congress chooses not to provide a private civil remedy, federal courts should not assume the legislative role of creating such a remedy and thereby enlarge their jurisdiction." *Borak* was singled out for special scorn, as:

both unprecedented and incomprehensible as a matter of public policy. The decision's rationale, which lies ultimately in the judgment that "[p]rivate enforcement of the proxy rules provides a necessary supplement to Commission action," ignores the fact that Congress, in determining the degree of regulation to be imposed on companies covered by the Securities Exchange Act, already had decided that private enforcement was unnecessary. More significant for present purposes, however, is the fact that *Borak*, rather than signaling the start of a trend in this Court, constitutes a singular and, I believe, aberrant interpretation of a federal regulatory statute.

Powell continued in a footnote, "[a]lthough I do not suggest that we should consider overruling *Borak* at this late date, the lack of precedential support for this decision militates strongly against its extension beyond the facts of the case." The recognition of private rights of action during the 1960s had fueled the expansion of the securities laws; Powell stood ready to limit the damage. The hardening of his views on the topic had implications that went well beyond the securities laws.

The Court took a bigger swing at *Borak* later that term in a case that Powell missed while he was out for surgery. In *Touche Ross & Co. v. Redington*, the Court, with only Marshall dissenting, found no private cause of action under § 17(a) of the Exchange Act, which requires broker-dealers to keep books and records as required by the SEC.[67] The Court's opinion, written by Rehnquist, reserved *Borak* ("We do not now question the actual holding"), but limited any further implied actions under the securities laws: "To the extent our analysis in today's decision differs from that of the Court in *Borak*, it suffices to say that in a series of cases since *Borak* we have adhered to a stricter standard for the implication of private causes of action, and we follow that stricter standard today." The opinion also cast shade on *Bankers Life*. The *Touche Ross* citation to *Cannon* sends the reader to a footnote in *Cannon* that discounted *Bankers Life* as reflecting the Court's historical "acquiesce[nce]" in the 25 years of lower courts' recognition of an implied right of action under Rule 10b-5. Stare decisis was the remaining constraint on the Court's new attitude toward implied causes of action.

Powell also missed the argument in the *TransAmerica* case after successfully lobbying to have it put on the Court's calendar—but the Court split 4-4 in his absence. When it was set for reargument the next term, Powell worried that the damages remedy that the plaintiffs were seeking "would allow circumvention of *Ernst + Ernst, Blue Stamps [sic]*, etc." Whether this result was appropriate was a question for Congress; Powell's concern was what Congress intended. Powell found Congress's intention clear from the text of the statute: the Investment Advisers Act conferred jurisdiction over suits in equity, but unlike the Securities Act and Exchange Act, omitted jurisdiction over suits at law.[68] For Powell, anxious to constrain the federal securities laws, this textual difference was dispositive.

The split in the Court that had required putting the case over for reargument persisted. This time, however, Powell joined Stewart, Blackmun, and Rehnquist in voting against the recognition of the private right of action; Burger, who had agreed with the latter three after the first argument, was now "reserv[ing] judgment." Stewart now said he agreed with Powell's intervening dissent in *Cannon*, but he had voted with the majority in that case only "because of vote in *Bakke*," which Powell notes was also true of Rehnquist.[69] The random intervention of *Bakke*—an affirmative action case—had preserved the private right in *Cannon*, but the consensus supporting implied private rights of action was eroding.

With Burger on the fence, however, *TransAmerica* was not the case for rethinking the Court's implied right of action doctrine beyond what the Court had said in *Touche Ross*. Stewart, who undertook the opinion in an effort to get a majority, did not repudiate altogether the four-factor test of *Cort v. Ash*, but he took a step toward Powell's position in emphasizing that "[t]he dispositive question remains whether Congress intended to create any such remedy."[70] Given that the statute explicitly created certain remedies, the Court saw no reason to add judicially created ones: "it is an elemental canon of statutory construction that where a statute expressly provides a particular remedy or remedies, a court must be chary of reading others into it." The Court also rebuffed the SEC's attempt to invoke the policy concerns factor from *Cort v. Ash*: "Having answered th[e] question [of whether Congress intended to create a remedy] in the negative, our inquiry is at an end." The era of deference to the SEC on private rights of action was over. White dissented for himself, Brennan, Marshall, and Stevens, but was unable to persuade Blackmun.

194   A HISTORY OF SECURITIES LAW

Powell was willing to go along with Stewart's approach, although he filed a brief concurrence noting that he saw Stewart's opinion as "compatible with my dissent in *Cannon v. University of Chicago*." Powell also lobbied Stewart (in a private letter) to define narrowly the equitable action for rescission that the Court was recognizing. At Powell's urging, Stewart added a footnote limiting the restitution available under the Act.[71]

Powell also argued (to no avail) against citing "*Borak* at all. An anomaly when decided, and in light of more recent cases (especially *Touche, Ross*, and your opinion in this case), I view *Borak* as a 'dead cock in the pit.'"[72] Powell wanted to eradicate all vestiges of the interpretive attitude that had fueled the expansion of the federal securities laws in the 1960s. With respect to the implication of private rights of action, he appears ultimately to have prevailed—the Court now requires that Congress speak in "clear and unambiguous terms" when it creates a private right of action.[73] But by not repudiating the claims recognized in *Borak* and *Bankers Life*, the Court tasked itself with the ongoing burden of defining their elements.

The Court's decision three terms later in *Herman & MacLean v. Huddelston* suggested the Court had made peace with the implied private action under Rule 10b-5.[74] The question was whether § 10(b) afforded a private cause of action for conduct that would be actionable under the explicit private cause of action provided by § 11 of the Securities Act. The Court would only need to address that question if there were in fact such a cause of action under Rule 10b-5. Although Powell was "tempted" to vote that there was no private cause of action under § 10(b), he pulled back from repudiating a cause of action that went back more than thirty years. Stare decisis had its pull, even in the face of a strongly held jurisprudential view. Having conceded the existence of the private right of action under § 10(b), Powell saw no defensible basis for carving out exceptions when the securities laws expressly provided causes of action. Marshall's unanimous opinion for the Court described the private Rule 10b-5 claim's existence as "beyond peradventure."[75]

## D. Filling Out the Elements of Explicit Private Rights of Action

In applying the Rule 10b-5 and 14a-9 implied causes of action, the Court was on its own. The absence of an express cause of action meant the Court would frequently be without a statutory text to ground a decision. That left more room for policy considerations to drive a result. We have seen that nervousness over the rise of securities class actions drove many of the decisions during the 1970s and early 1980s. Did the approach differ when the Court was called upon to interpret a cause of action expressly created by Congress?

PRIVATE LITIGATION    195

Powell, for one, did not vary much in his approach, always worrying about decisions that might create excessive liability. His dissent from the denial of certiorari in *John Nuveen & Co. v. Sanders* is of a piece with his other opinions discussed in this chapter.[76] Powell strenuously objected to the Seventh Circuit's holding in that case that reasonable care for an underwriter under § 12(a)(2) of the Securities Act required "*independent investigation* such as examination of the accountant's work papers underlying the *certified financial statements*."[77] With the statutory language somewhat vague, Powell failed to pick up enough votes to have the case heard, with only Rehnquist joining.

*Randall v. Loftsgaarden* was Sandra Day O'Connor's first securities law opinion for the Court.[78] The case raised the relatively narrow issue of whether rescission, the remedy under § 12(a)(2) of the Securities Act for fraud in a prospectus, is subject to offset. The Court said no; applying a plain language approach, it determined that tax benefits from an investment were not subject to offset as "income" within the meaning of the statute. The Court applied the same rule to the Rule 10b-5 claim raised in the case despite the lack of textual guidance, agreeing with the SEC as amicus that the common law would not require offset. Only Brennan dissented. The lop-sided result suggested greater consensus on the Court when working with a cause of action grounded in the text of a statute.

*Pinter v. Dahl* raised the issue of the application of the in pari delicto defense in a § 12(a)(1) case.[79] Dahl purchased interests in an oil and gas venture from Pinter and encouraged friends, relatives, and business associates to invest as well. When the investments soured, Dahl sued Pinter for failing to register the offering with the SEC. Pinter raised in pari delicto based on Dahl's solicitation of the other investors, but the Fifth Circuit rejected it.

Powell disagreed with this result, leading him to write his last securities law opinion during his Court tenure, a dissent from denial that persuaded his colleagues to grant review:

> [S]ophisticated investors who purchase unregistered securities place themselves in a no-lose situation. If the investment proves profitable, the buyer comes out ahead. If the venture is unprofitable, the buyer can sue to recover his investment, with interest, in a § 12[a](1) action. . . . [Dahl] faces no sanctions of any kind for his participation in the illegal transactions. Moreover, § 12[a](1) imposes liability without regard to whether the seller intended to defraud the buyer. Absent an *in pari delicto* defense, buyers will indeed obtain an "enforceable warranty" that their investment will be profitable.

Powell's complaint here seemed to concern § 12(a)(1)'s liability without fault for the sale of unregistered securities as much as the Fifth Circuit's application of the in pari delicto defense. The "enforceable warranty" he invoked exists whether or

196    A HISTORY OF SECURITIES LAW

not there is an in pari delicto defense. And under the interpretation of "seller" that Powell appeared to favor, the disappointed buyers might well seek relief from Dahl as well as Pinter, so there would be some sort of sanction. Notwithstanding the weakness in Powell's position, he continued to wield sufficient influence in this area that he was able to attract two more votes so the case could be heard. By the time the case was argued, Powell had retired. Although Powell's argument for the in pari delicto defense was rejected in a footnote, the Court did recognize a form of the defense.[80]

The more important question resolved by the Court in *Pinter* was who qualified as a "seller" within the meaning of § 12 of the Securities Act. As in *Randall*, the statutory text, while somewhat open-ended, seemed to provide a basis for consensus among the justices, with Blackmun writing for the majority and only Stevens dissenting.[81] Blackmun invoked the flexible/remedial principle from *Capital Gains* in interpreting § 12(a)(1) of the Securities Act, but he went on to ground the decision in the statutory language, rejecting the broader interpretation adopted by the court of appeals. The only substantive exchange among the justices with regard to Blackmun's opinion was a series of suggestions from Antonin Scalia to narrow the definition of "solicitation" to more clearly exclude third parties (including lawyers and accountants). Scalia also urged that there be no endorsement of an implied cause of action under § 17(a) of the Securities Act. Blackmun largely accommodated him.[82]

## E. Arbitration and the Securities Laws

Arbitration, an alternative forum for private actions, provides a parallel illustration of the development of the Court's evolving view of private litigation. Initial receptiveness to private litigation—at a time when suits were rare—manifested itself in hostility to arbitration. The Court became more receptive to arbitration in the 1980s as the volume of private litigation escalated and the Court's confidence in lawsuits' efficacy faltered.

The court's first involvement with securities arbitration occurred in *Wilko v. Swan*, the most significant of the handful of securities cases decided in the 1950s.[83] The issue was whether a pre-dispute arbitration agreement between a brokerage firm and its customer applied to a claim for misrepresentation under the Securities Act. The customer resisted enforcement of the arbitration agreement, invoking the anti-waiver provision of the Securities Act, § 14 which provides that: "Any condition, stipulation, or provision binding any person acquiring any security to waive compliance with any provision of this title or of the rules and regulations of the Commission shall be void." The SEC sided with the customer in arguing that § 14 nullified any agreement to arbitrate because it

PRIVATE LITIGATION     197

would "waive compliance" with the grant of jurisdiction to federal courts in § 22 of the Securities Act.

Stanley Reed's initial instinct was to disagree with the SEC and permit arbitration, as reflected in his handwritten notes on the certiorari memo written by his clerk: "Burden of proof stays the same in arbitration. No one knows materially false statement better than brokers. Must assume their impartiality + desire to keep business clean." Reed remained inclined to affirm the appellate court's enforcement of the agreement to arbitrate after certiorari was granted:

> Seems that § 14 forbidding waiver of any provision of title. § 22 US cts. shall have jurisdiction. But it has never been supposed that agreement to arbitrate took it out of section. Not a waiver, a method of asserting a right. Affirm.

At conference, Reed again voted to affirm, joining Frankfurter, Jackson, Clark, and Minton for a majority, with Black, Douglas, Burton, and Warren voting to reverse.[84]

Reed was assigned the opinion, but changed his mind, flipping the majority from the conference vote. His eventual opinion held that the arbitration agreement ran afoul of the anti-waiver provision. Reed's switch brought him once again into disagreement with Frankfurter, this time over the scope of judicial control over arbitration. Reed wrote that:

> This case requires subjective findings on the purpose and knowledge of an alleged violator of the Act. They must be not only determined but applied by the arbitrators without judicial instruction on the law. As their award may be made without explanation of their reasons and without a complete record of their proceedings, the arbitrators' conception of the legal meaning of such statutory requirements as 'burden of proof,' reasonable care' or 'material,' cannot be examined . . . the interpretations of the law by the arbitrators in contrast to manifest disregard are not subject, in the federal courts, to judicial review for error in interpretation.[85]

Reed then proceeded to support his position by an extensive summary of New York arbitration law.

Frankfurter disagreed, arguing that the federal district court would continue to dictate the terms of the arbitration even in the hands of the arbitrators.

> Since the arbitration proceedings would not displace the Court proceedings but merely suspend them . . . a District Court, it is plain, can define the terms of the stay. When Judge Swan says that failure to enforce the requirements of the law would "constitute grounds for vacating the award" he necessarily implies

198 A HISTORY OF SECURITIES LAW

that an order granting a stay of an action brought in the Southern District of New York to await an arbitration may provide the conditions under which, as matter of law, the arbitration must proceed. An arbitration that is subject to certain legal rules which must be observed or the award may be vacated for disregard of such rules of law necessarily must give the Court power to assure observance of the legal requirements and afford the basis for judicial determination that the arbitrators acted according to their legal duty.

Frankfurter's view of arbitration recalls his vision of administrative decision-making that we saw in Chapter 3 in *Chenery I* and *II*: the rule of law required reasoned explanation of a decision sufficient to allow (rather intrusive) judicial review. Frankfurter's framework would have saved the arbitration of securities claims, but at the cost of eliminating most of arbitration's efficiency advantages by imposing thoroughgoing judicial review of awards. More to point, Frankfurter was wrong on the law, as Reed pointed out: "I have found nothing in N.Y. cases or reports to indicate that a N.Y. Court in N.Y. arbitration proceedings . . . could instruct the panel as to legal issues . . ."[86] Frankfurter was forced to back down; his final opinion notes only that "if there were no effective means of ensuring judicial review of the legal basis of arbitration, then, of course, an agreement to settle the controversy by arbitration would be barred by § 14. . . ." Frankfurter and Reed shared common ground in believing that judges needed to control the interpretation of the securities laws; it could not be left to the arbitrators.

The intersection of arbitration and securities law would not return to the Supreme Court for twenty years. *Merrill Lynch, Pierce, Fenner & Smith, Inc. v. Ware*, decided in 1973, accepted *Wilko's* holding as settled law.[87] Blackmun, writing for a unanimous Court, held that the Exchange Act's authorization of rulemaking by exchanges did not preempt a California law exempting wage claims from arbitration. Brennan and White were initially inclined to dissent,[88] but eventually acquiesced in Blackmun's opinion rejecting the argument that the rule of *Silver v. NYSE* (discussed in Chapter 4) required preemption of the California statute.

The arbitrability issue would soon become more contentious, however, in an international case, *Scherk v. Alberto-Culver Co.*[89] In *Scherk*, a 5-4 majority held that the anti-waiver provision of the Exchange Act—not materially different from the Securities Act anti-waiver provision at issue in *Wilko*—did not bar the arbitration of a Rule 10b-5 dispute. The issue was complicated by the fact that the agreement was between sophisticated commercial parties for the acquisition of a business, and it arose in an international context where arbitration is common. Only Stewart expressed a willingness to overrule *Wilko* at conference. His opinion for the majority however, rested on the international commercial context of the negotiations and transaction. He did note that "a colorable argument could be made that even the semantic reasoning of the *Wilko* opinion does not control the case before us" given that the Rule 10b-5 cause of action was implied by the courts rather than enacted by Congress. Stewart suggested that "the [Exchange] Act itself does not establish the 'special right' that the Court in *Wilko* found significant." Blackmun resisted the distinction drawn by Stewart.

> I suspect the benefit of the rather technical distinction you draw between the "special right" in <u>Wilko</u> and its absence in this case . . . is marginal and does not really justify its inclusion. I am not entirely certain that I agree with the distinction. It seems to me that the implied right of action under the Court's decision is not different from the so-called "special right" in the <u>Wilko</u> case, since the implied right adheres to Rule 10b-5 and § 10 of the Act, and is thereby included in the sweep of § 29(a). I see no apparent reason why the two are different. . . . For me, it raises more questions than it answers and its seems that it is likely to pose problems in later cases in which the waiver provisions are asserted as a defense.[90]

Implied rights of action were becoming suspect, and that suspicion was leaking over into the arbitration debate. Blackmun was resisting.

Douglas was the only holdover from the *Wilko* Court. His draft dissent recalled the faith in the New Deal's social control over finance that characterized the Court's early securities decisions:

> Justice Brandeis starting nearly 70 years ago tried to educate the nation of the practices of the money trust. The giants of finance are the money trust today. They are the ones that fought the 1933 and 1934 Acts tooth and nail. They are the ones hopeful of short circuiting the protective devices of those Acts by using arbitration as a newly found loophole.[91]

Having been an active participant in the debates surrounding the securities laws from the beginning, Douglas saw the New Deal foundation beginning to crack in his last years on the Court.

The momentum favoring arbitration would accelerate a decade later. The first shoe to drop was *Dean Witter Reynolds, Inc. v. Byrd*, in which the Court held that state claims raised by a customer against his broker could be arbitrated while the federal securities claims proceeded in federal court.[92] The Court declined to consider the applicability of *Wilko* to Rule 10b-5 claims under the Exchange Act, but White concurred to reiterate the doubts about the implied right of action that Stewart had raised in *Scherk*:

> [t]he cause of action under § 10(b) and Rule 10b-5 . . . is implied rather than express. The phrase "waive compliance with any *provision of this chapter*," is

200 A HISTORY OF SECURITIES LAW

thus literally inapplicable. Moreover, *Wilko*'s solicitude for the federal cause of action—the "special right" established by Congress—is not necessarily appropriate where the cause of action is judicially implied and not so different from the common-law action.

The Court seemed to be moving toward a hierarchy of causes of action, with implied rights headed toward second-class status.

White's seed would bear fruit two terms later, when the Court would reject the application of *Wilko* to Rule 10b-5 claims in *Shearson/American Express, Inc. v. McMahon*.[93] In Powell's notes prepared after reading the brief, he observed that "in contrast with '33 Act's explicit right to sue, the right to sue under § 10(b) is <u>implied</u>. I could reverse CA 2 on basis of this distinction." The SEC had appeared as amicus, however, fighting a rearguard action defending implied rights under the securities laws. In an unusual move, the agency sided with the brokerage house rather than the customer in arguing that Rule 10b-5 claims could be subject to an arbitration agreement, but it nonetheless

> urge[d] the Court not to rely on a distinction between express and implied right of action in resolving the question presented in this case. . . . The implied right of action under Section 10(b) and Rule 10b-5 is as deserving of a hearing in a proper forum, and as necessary to effectuate the policies of the securities laws, as the various express rights of action.[94]

The SEC's newfound position embracing arbitration was somewhat surprising, but the agency was not going to give up its commitment to implied rights of action even in a Republican administration. Instead, the Commission argued that the Court should base the decision on (1) the Court's greater receptiveness to arbitration in the years after 1953; and (2) Congress's amendments to the Exchange Act in 1975 giving the SEC oversight over the arbitration procedures used by the self-regulatory organizations (SROs, that is, the exchanges and NASD).

The latter point was a matter of some controversy; the night before argument, the claimant's attorneys delivered to the Court a copy of a letter that John Dingell, the chairman of the House Subcommittee on Oversight and Investigations, had sent to the SEC asking for documents relating to the agency's "current position in the McMahon case."[95] The political heat over private rights of action and arbitration was ramping up. At least some members of Congress hoped to put a thumb on the scale to limit arbitration.

Powell's conference notes suggest a strongly divided Court, with some justices content to cabin *Wilko* and others advocating that it be overruled outright. Chief Justice Burger saw "no need to over-rule Wilco (sic), but could do so." White did not want to extend *Wilko* to Rule 10b-5, but did not see a need to overrule, a position shared by O'Connor. Scalia flatly asserted that *Wilko* "was wrong," and that '[a]rbitration is now widely used." Blackmun's conference notes record Scalia as saying "Wilko a pwr grab + bad dec." Only the remaining liberal bloc thought *Wilko* should apply to Rule 10b-5 claims; their reasons echoed the majority in *Wilko* and Douglas's dissent a decade prior in *Scherk*. Brennan urged "Investors need to have access to courts. Arbitration not adequate to protect investors." Marshall also believed *Wilko* should apply to Rule 10b-5 claims. Blackmun agreed with Brennan's policy concern: "Policy is to protect investors. Arbitration is not adequate." Blackmun went further than simply expressing concern for investor protection. He also asserted at conference that "SEC's position is political." In his notes from oral argument, Blackmun had written "SEC complete turnabout- + political struggle for deregulation." He was unmoved by the distinction between express causes of action under the Securities Act and the implied right of action under Rule 10b-5: "Dif btw express + implied c\a is irrel—both exist". Stevens joined this group despite having previously taken a position more sympathetic to arbitration while on the appellate court; there he had dissented from the majority's decision to bar arbitration in *Scherk*. A decade later, however, Stevens was swayed by stare decisis: "*Wilco* (sic) has been law for 35 years" and "lower courts have assumed that it should apply to claims under both the Securities Act and Exchange Act."[96]

O'Connor was assigned the opinion, and she hewed closely to the arguments of the SEC in its amicus brief, steering clear of the status of the implied right of action. She observed that

> the reasons given in *Wilko* reflect a general suspicion of the desirability of arbitration and the competence of arbitral tribunals—most apply with no greater forces to the arbitration of securities disputes that to the arbitration of legal disputes generally. It is difficult to reconcile *Wilko*'s mistrust of the arbitral process with the Court's subsequent decisions involving the Arbitration Act.

The Court was also reassured by "the 1975 Amendments to § 19 of the Exchange Act" giving the SEC "expansive power to ensure the adequacy of the arbitration procedures employed by the SROs." These reasons justified cabining *Wilko* to Securities Act claims, but they could also provide a basis for overruling it. The majority was not ready to go that far.

Blackmun, joined by Brennan and Marshall in dissent, could see the handwriting on the wall. He made little effort to disguise his bitterness at what he viewed as the SEC's betrayal of investors. Blackmun claimed the "Court effectively overrules *Wilko*" by deferring to the SEC's "newly adopted position." Blackmun who had urged deference to the SEC in the past was not inclined to defer to the agency after its change in stance during the Reagan administration. He found

202 A HISTORY OF SECURITIES LAW

plenty of ammunition for his argument in the SEC's prior releases. Investors—
and the New Deal—were being betrayed by the SEC itself. Blackmun concluded
his lengthy dissent with a Douglas-esque flourish, blasting "the Court's compla-
cent acceptance of the Commission's oversight," which he found "alarming when
almost every day brings another example of illegality on Wall Street." Blackmun
expressed "hope that Congress will give investors the relief that the Court denies
them today." Stevens's opinion was more measured, arguing only that "any mistake that the courts may have made in interpreting the statutes is best remedied
by the Legislative, not the Judicial, Branch."

After *McMahon*, *Wilko* was a dead man walking, and it did not take long for
the body to fall. Just two years later, the Court would deliver the final blow in
*Rodriguez de Quijas v. Shearson/American Express*.[97] Writing for the Court,
Kennedy quickly dispatched the statutory arguments found persuasive in *Wilko*.
He then focused on the disparate treatment that would persist if *Wilko* survived;
for Rule 10b-5 claims to be subject to arbitration while Securities Act claims
went to court, "makes little sense for similar claims, based on similar facts, which
are supposed to arise within a single federal regulatory scheme." Stevens, in a
brief dissent joined by the liberal trio of Brennan, Marshall, and Blackmun, did
not quarrel with this logic, instead arguing for a strong rule of stare decisis for
decisions involving statutory interpretation. But the New Deal faith in the efficacy of private litigation to enforce the securities laws could no longer garner a
majority.

## F. Implied Rights after the Counterrevolution

Lewis Powell's retirement in 1987 triggered another shift in the Supreme Court's
approach to securities cases. The issues were often echoes of earlier decisions,
but the outcomes were not nearly as predictable. Unlike the dominant trends of
the earlier two periods, decisions would yo-yo between expansive and restrictive results from case to case. Congress returned to the field, passing securities
legislation that would generate a significant workload for the Court. We divide
this period into two sub-parts: (1) the immediate years after Powell's retirement
and (2) decisions that follow the enactment of the PSLRA. In the first period
we focus on two decisions that illustrate how the Court of this period produced
sharply divergent results from case to case. *Basic Inc. v. Levinson* was a return to
the expansive approach that prevailed in the sixties. *Central Bank*, decided six
years later, revives the dominant restrictive approach of the Powell period. Post-
1995, we look at three issues that had emerged during Powell's time. We show
how the post-Powell Court dealt with them within the framework provided by
the PSLRA.

## 1. The Immediate Aftermath: Ping Pong

The survival of the Rule 10b-5 private cause of action left the door open for a Supreme Court decision—*Basic Inc.* v. *Levinson*—that hearkened back to the activist days of the sixties.[98] Powell had recently retired when *Basic* was argued. His departure left a void, and Blackmun, the senior justice, for a 4-2 majority, assigned himself the opinion. It was Blackmun's first securities opinion of any significance for the Court since *Affiliated Ute*, heard just before Powell and Rehnquist took their seats. *Affiliated Ute*, which had excused reliance in cases involving fraudulent omissions, had been the previous high-water mark for the implied cause of action under Rule 10b-5, the last salvo of sixties purposivism. *Basic* was a return to that old-time religion, opening the doors wide to securities fraud class actions under Rule 10b-5. The key move was creating a presumption of reliance for misrepresentations affecting securities traded in public markets— the fraud-on-the-market theory (FOTM). A plaintiff buying shares on an anonymous market would rarely be able to show actual reliance on misstatements influencing the secondary market for a company's shares. Requiring individual proof of reliance would effectively end class actions in this context. By avoiding that evidentiary issue, the presumption greatly expands the size of the class and public companies' litigation exposure. *Basic* also gave broad interpretations to materiality in a merger context.[99]

The Court was somewhat fuzzy, however, in spelling out its understanding of the required connection between the defendant's wrongdoing and the plaintiffs' harm, particularly in an open-market context. Blackmun's use of a presumption was designed to provide an indirect route to showing the necessary connection between defendant's wrongful conduct and plaintiff's injury. That would be necessary to reach transactions across impersonal markets when the alleged misrepresenting party—typically a public company—did not deal directly with the trading parties. His majority opinion noted the fundamental changes that had occurred in securities markets since the enactment of securities laws in the early 1930s and concluded "our understanding of 10b-5 reliance must encompass these differences." It includes a mini-essay assembling the law of civil procedure supporting the use of presumptions in settings such as this.

The retirement of Powell and the long delay before Anthony Kennedy was confirmed as his successor, along with the recusals of Rehnquist and Scalia, left the Court with the minimum for a quorum. The decision on how to adapt the common law to the secondary market setting apparently engaged only Blackmun and Brennan, two justices inclined to read the securities laws broadly. Blackmun, following his expansive opinion in *Affiliated Ute* more than fifteen years prior, was intent on dramatically loosening the required reliance connection, sometimes referred to as transaction causation or causation in fact. Blackmun insisted,

## 204 A HISTORY OF SECURITIES LAW

however, on preserving a sliver of traditional reliance analysis by permitting a rebuttal of the FOTM presumption. The reasons for Blackmun's insistence are not apparent from his correspondence with Brennan. In an exchange of multiple letters between the justices, Brennan advocated for a looser connection that he called "price reliance." Even if some other motivation led the plaintiff to sell, which would seem to break the transactional causation connection, Brennan's theory would nonetheless preserve a claim. The justices discussed an investor having decided to sell the stock on the investor's twenty-first birthday or selling stock in order to divest companies doing business in South Africa. Short sellers, however, might be caught up in a transaction causation requirement as well. Plaintiff's injury in selling stock trading at a reduced value even in those situations could be sufficiently linked to the fraud, in Brennan's view, because of plaintiff's reliance on the market price. Brennan worried that certain passages in Blackmun's opinion would "foreclose a pure theory of price reliance" (if the plaintiff would have traded anyway) and would be seen by subsequent courts as "support for the transactional reliance theory."[100]

Blackmun and Brennan did not resolve this difference—they agreed that the practical difficulty defendants would face in rebutting the presumption meant the result under their respective theories would be the same[101]—but their exchange exposed a gap in the theory supporting this loosened connection. Don Langevoort has argued that the Court's reliance on then-emerging economic discussion of efficient markets to support the presumption is a "hopeless fiction" and that "the only persuasive coherent interpretation of *Basic*'s presumption" is "judicial creation of an entitlement to rely on representations of fact by strangers whether or not there is any reason to trust them because doing so facilitates economic exchange."[102] Such a purposivist-driven interpretation follows naturally from Blackmun's opinion in *Affiliated Ute*, but it is a jarring departure from the approach taken during Powell's time on the Court.

Federal courts by this point were long past raising lack of privity as a barrier to private recovery. Even Powell, who was bothered by this issue while drafting the *Ernst & Ernst* opinion a dozen years before, had been unwilling to push the argument. Yet, the looser connection required between the defendant's wrong and plaintiff's loss raised new questions. After all, a secondary market investor is as likely to be on the winning end of a trade affected by the misrepresentation as the losing end. There is no *expected* loss from the misrepresentation. Respondent's brief and oral argument lamented the reach of the expanded reliance as an affront to the policy of *Blue Chip* without grounding any argument in the specifics of the secondary market setting.[103] White, in his dissent, warned of

the dangers when economic theories replace legal rules as the basis for recovery. Yet the Court today ventures into this area beyond its expertise, beyond—by its own admission—the confines of our previous fraud cases. . . . I prefer that such changes come from Congress in amending § 10(b). The Congress, with its superior resources and expertise, is far better equipped than the federal courts for the task of determining how modern economic theory and global financial markets require that established legal notions of fraud be modified. In choosing to make these decisions itself, the Court, I fear, embarks on a course that it does not genuinely understand, giving rise to consequences it cannot foresee.

Only O'Connor joined him. With Rehnquist and Scalia out, Blackmun was able to secure a majority of the short-handed Court. General warnings of unexpected consequences would not dissuade Blackmun; expansive recovery was once again the order of the day after Powell's departure.

The justices engaged in one such issue in their internal discussions, but Blackmun left it unresolved in the Court opinion. Once the FOTM presumption is in play, every investor who purchased during the time that a misrepresentation was affecting the company's stock price and did not sell it before the truth was revealed has a cause of action and potential remedies under Rule 10b-5. As a result, the question of damages takes on vital importance, given the volume of secondary trading. Brennan, in his first letter to Blackmun raising the pure price reliance theory, expressed similar concerns. He contemplated a presumption that would award the $2 difference to a seller who had received $18 when, without fraud, the price on the market would have been $20. Brennan did not think the seller was entitled to the $42 that would have been available when the bid ultimately occurred. Blackmun allayed this concern by pointing to a footnote already in the opinion that disclaimed any statement about damages. That had been inserted at the insistence of Stevens, who wanted it left for another day.[104] White, in his dissent, argued that "answers to the question of the proper measure of damages in a fraud-on-the-market case are essential for proper implementation of the fraud-on-the-market presumption." The question of damages in Rule 10b-5 "fraud-on-the-market" actions still has not been addressed by the Court. Because the damages measure relied upon by the lower courts create enormous liability, virtually all securities class actions settle, so there may never be an occasion for the Court to consider the question left unanswered in *Basic*.

The other headline case from the period prior to the PSLRA veers in the opposite direction. *Central Bank of Denver v. First Interstate Bank of Denver* shows that the restrictive approach to private actions still had legs.[105] The issue presented in *Central Bank* was whether private civil liability under § 10(b) (the authorizing statute for Rule 10b-5) extends to aiders and abettors of the violation. The issuer of the securities in the case was a public building authority that raised $26 million in bonds to finance public improvements at a planned Colorado development. Central Bank acted as indenture trustee for the bonds, which were secured

206 A HISTORY OF SECURITIES LAW

by liens on real property. The bonds had covenants requiring that the assessed value of that land must be at least 160% of bond's outstanding principal and interest and requiring the developer (AmWest) to give annual reports showing that the 160% test was being met.

Before an issue of the bonds in 1988, AmWest gave Central Bank an updated appraisal showing no change in value of land from 1986 (the date of a previous issue). But the senior underwriter of the 1986 bond issue sent Central Bank a letter questioning the 1986 valuation because property values had dropped in the region. Central Bank's in-house appraiser, asked to review the 1988 appraisal, concluded that it was too optimistic. Instead of insisting on a new independent appraisal, Central Bank agreed to delay the outside full appraisal until after the 1988 bond offering. The building authority later defaulted and the bondholders filed suit against Central Bank, alleging that the bank had aided and abetted the building authority's Rule 10b-5 violation.

Blackmun assigned the opinion to Kennedy, who had voted at conference to uphold the aiding and abetting cause of action. After further review, however, Kennedy switched his vote, flipping the result.[106] The open-ended nature of aiding and abetting liability raised concerns about strike suits for Kennedy. Recalling *Blue Chip*, he warned that uncertainty over the scope of liability could induce secondary actors to settle "to avoid the expense and risk of going to trial." The risk of having to pay such settlements could cause professionals, such as accountants, to avoid working with newer and smaller companies, and "the increased costs incurred by professionals because of the litigation and settlement costs under 10b-5 may be passed on to their client companies, and in turn incurred by the company's investors, the intended beneficiaries of the statute." Powell's successor seemed to be channeling Powell.

In an effort to increase Rule 10b-5's predictability, Kennedy's opinion adopted a two-part framework for dealing with the private right of action under § 10(b). That test was a significant departure from the free-wheeling approach of *Basic*. In the first step of the inquiry, Kennedy examined the text of § 10(b) to determine the scope of the conduct prohibited by the provision. He had little difficulty determining that the text of § 10(b) "prohibits only the making of a material misstatement (or omission) or the commission of a manipulative act." This, in Kennedy's view, was sufficient to resolve the question: aiding and abetting was not prohibited by § 10(b). Nonetheless, Kennedy set forth a second step to the inquiry:

> When the text of § 10(b) does not resolve a particular issue, we attempt to infer how the 1934 Congress would have addressed the issue had the 10b-5 action been included as an express provision in the 1934 Act. For that inquiry, we use the express causes of action in the securities Acts as the primary model for the

§ 10(b) action. The reason is evident: Had the 73d Congress enacted a private § 10(b) right of action, it likely would have designed it in a manner similar to the other private rights of action in the securities Acts.

This tracked the approach that the Court had used in *Lampf* and *Musick* (two then recently-decided cases discussed immediately below) of looking to express causes of action to infer appropriate elements under the implied cause of action under Rule 10b-5. Applying this approach, the plaintiffs' argument also failed because the explicit causes of action afforded by Congress in the Securities Act and the Exchange Act were similarly silent on the question of aiding and abetting.[107] Silence was no longer an occasion for judicial creativity, as it had been in *Deckert* in 1940 and *Borak* in 1964. In the face of silence, the Court would presume that Congress did not intend to act, rather than viewing the omission as an invitation to judicial filling-in of the interstices.

In passing, Kennedy noted one additional problem with the plaintiffs' argument, which would have important consequences in later cases: "Were we to allow the aiding and abetting action proposed in this case, the defendant could be liable without any showing that the plaintiff relied upon the aider and abettor's statements or actions." The Court left the door open for some liability for secondary participants, such as accountants, investment bankers, and lawyers, but only if they have induced investor reliance. The bottom line after *Central Bank* is that a defendant must make a misstatement (or omit a necessary statement) on which a purchaser or seller of a security reasonably relies. Kennedy did not explain further the connection between reliance and the scope of Rule 10b-5; that issue would re-emerge.

If *Central Bank* was intended to enhance predictability, Kennedy's effort failed. What did it mean to "make" a misstatement? More vexingly, what it would mean to be responsible for an omission? What sort of reliance was required? Not surprisingly, the lower courts arrived at different answers to questions of this sort.[108] The Court would return to the issue repeatedly, as we discuss in the next subsection.

The Court's other Rule 10b-5 cases in the period after Powell retired and before the passage of PSLRA also proved contentious. The Court faced the "awkward task of discerning the limitations period the Congress intended courts to apply to a cause of action it really never knew existed" in *Lampf, Pleva, Lipkind, Prupis & Petigrow v. Gilbertson*.[109] The question provoked five opinions, with Blackmun for the majority selecting the one-year discovery and three-year repose rule found in the most analogous explicit causes of action in the Exchange Act, §§ 9(e) and 18(c). Four other justices felt moved to write. Scalia concurred to note his unhappiness about "imagining" what Congress would have done. Stevens, who characterized the case as "emotionally charged," dissented (joined by David

208    A HISTORY OF SECURITIES LAW

Souter) to argue for the analogous state-law statute of limitations. O'Connor and Kennedy each wrote to object to the application of the statute of repose and complain about the retroactive application of the federal limitation period.[110] The relative consensus the Court enjoyed when construing explicit causes of action did not carry over to Rule 10b-5, despite the general agreement that the cause of action should continue. With no statutory text to guide them, the justices found plenty of room to disagree.

The Court was split, but not as splintered, when called to decide whether defendants should have a right of contribution in Rule 10b-5 cases in *Musick, Peeler & Garret v. Employers Insurance of Wasau*.[111] Kennedy, writing for the majority, acknowledged the Court's responsibility for filling out the contours of the implied right: "Having implied the underlying liability in the first place, to now disavow any authority to allocate it on the theory that Congress has not addressed the issue would be most unfair to those against whom damages are assessed." As in *Lampf*, the Court looked to the express causes of action in §§ 9 and 18 of the Exchange Act in concluding that defendants should have a right of contribution under Rule 10b-5 as well. Thomas dissented, joined by Blackmun and O'Connor, complaining that "[c]ourts should not treat legislative and administrative silence as a tacit license to accomplish what Congress and the SEC are unable or unwilling to do." The Court's clarity of the Powell era had disappeared, replaced by a seemingly random pattern of results.

## 2. The Impact of the PSLRA

In this section, we discuss some of the Court's cases from its private securities docket subsequent to the time of our study for which we were able to examine the papers of the justices. We highlight the Court's cases from the last twenty-five years that follow up on three "highlight-reel" decisions from our main period of study: *Ernst & Ernst*, *Basic*, and *Central Bank*. This subset, we believe, fairly represents the Court's overall work in private securities litigation over the last quarter-century.

The end of our period of study based on the justices' papers—1994—nearly coincides with a major intervention by Congress in the field of securities litigation: the Private Securities Litigation Reform Act of 1995. The PSLRA, and a follow-on statute intended to close off state court end runs around its restrictions, the Securities Litigation Uniform Standards Act of 1998, would feature prominently in the Court's securities docket over the next twenty-five years. The PSLRA responded to the wave of securities fraud class actions unleashed by the Court's *Basic* decision in 1988. The law contains a number of reforms making it more challenging for plaintiffs to bring a securities fraud class action, the most relevant here being a heightened pleading standard for securities fraud complaints. This pleading provision builds on the scienter requirement adopted by Powell in the *Ernst & Ernst* decision. In another response to the Court's work (and the SEC's pleas), the PLSRLA also includes an override of the *Central Bank* decision, albeit limited to SEC enforcement actions. Private plaintiffs were left to find their own workaround. The Court's response to those efforts would be heavily influenced by PSLRA's aiding and abetting provision. *Basic*, however, was left undisturbed by the PSLRA. Nonetheless, the enormous financial stakes that it created would lead to a number of Court cases grappling with its holding, culminating in a high-profile attempt to overrule the decision.

### a) *Ernst & Ernst* and the PSRLA Pleading Standard for Scienter

As discussed in Section C2, Powell pulled back in *Ernst & Ernst* from defining scienter, declining to make a choice between knowledge and recklessness. The appellate courts agreed post-*Ernst & Ernst* that allegations of recklessness satisfy the scienter requirement. Congress, however, put the question back into play when it imposed a pleading standard as part of the PSLRA, but equivocated in formulating this new standard. It required plaintiffs to show facts giving rise to a "strong inference" that the defendant acted with the "required state of mind."[112] Why "state of mind" rather than "knowledge" or "recklessness"? Two reasons. The first is that Congress also added a provision insulating forward-looking statements as part of the PSLRA. Plaintiffs claiming that defendants had made false forward-looking statements must allege that that the defendants did so knowing the statements to be false. The second, less defensible, reason was the inability of Congress to settle on a requisite state of mind for historical statements. To make matters worse, Congress not only left the text of the statute ambiguous, but individual legislators generated conflicting legislative history regarding the pleading standard in an effort to influence judicial interpretation.

Given the ambiguity, the circuit courts unsurprisingly diverged in applying the strong inference standard.[113] When the Supreme Court finally entered the fray over the interpretation of the strong inference standard in *Tellabs, Inc. v. Makor Issues & Rights, Ltd.*, it did not resolve this long-standing split among the circuits over the application of the standard.[114] Instead, it addressed a collateral, but related, issue on which the circuits also had split: In considering whether the facts alleged by the plaintiff meet the strong inference standard, how should courts assess the different possible inferences that might be drawn from the allegations in the complaint with respect to scienter? In particular, should a court consider competing inferences arising from those facts?

Prior to the Supreme Court's *Tellabs* opinion, the circuit courts split into three groups in assessing competing inferences. Four circuits adopted a "preponderance" standard, making it easier for defendants to obtain dismissal. That

## 210　A HISTORY OF SECURITIES LAW

standard required plaintiffs to show that the requisite scienter was the most plausible inference to be drawn from the facts alleged when compared with competing inferences that the defendants lacked scienter. Four other circuits required that the inference that the defendants acted with the requisite scienter be at least equally plausible with competing inferences. The Seventh Circuit, in the *Tellabs* case, and one other circuit, followed the most plaintiff-friendly approach, adopting the "reasonableness" standard that did not require any assessment of competing inferences, looking only at the plausibility of the plaintiff's allegations. Under the Seventh Circuit's reasonableness standard, a complaint should survive "if it alleges facts from which, if true, a reasonable person could infer that the defendant acted with the required intent."[115]

The Seventh Circuit standard faced an uphill fight in the Supreme Court. The government's *Tellabs* amicus brief argued that the Seventh Circuit's reasonableness standard would have made Congress's effort in enacting the strong inference standard toothless, as it would mean reverting to pre-PSLRA standards under Rule 9(b) of the Federal Rules of Civil Procedure.[116] The government's brief was notable in that it sided with the *defendants*, an unusual occurrence in its amicus practice.

The Court was not fazed by this unusual alignment. Justice Ruth Bader Ginsburg, writing for the majority, characterized her role as framing "a workable construction of the 'strong inference' standard, a reading geared to the PSLRA's twin goals: to curb frivolous, lawyer-driven litigation, while preserving investors' ability to recover on meritorious claims." Having framed the inquiry in this way, Ginsburg naturally settled on the intermediate position. She rejected the reasonableness standard adopted by the lower court, preferring instead a comparative inquiry: "A complaint will survive, we hold, only if a reasonable person would deem the inference of scienter cogent and at least as compelling as any opposing inference one could draw from the facts alleged." That conclusion was compelled by Congress's use of the word "strong." According to Ginsburg, "[t]he strength of an inference cannot be decided in a vacuum. The inquiry is inherently comparative: How likely is it that one conclusion, as compared to others, follows from the underlying facts?" At a minimum, therefore, the Court felt compelled to choose the intermediate "equal inference" standard, rejecting "reasonableness." Ties go to the plaintiff, but the plaintiff must show that the fraudulent inference is at least as likely as an innocent one.

The "preponderance" standard favored by the defendants and the government won the support of Scalia and Alito in their concurrences. Scalia provided a colorful hypothetical to illustrate his disagreement with Ginsburg:

> If a jade falcon were stolen from a room to which only A and B had access, could it *possibly* be said there was a "strong inference" that B was the thief? I think not,

PRIVATE LITIGATION    211

and I therefore think that the Court's test must fail. In my view, the test should be whether the inference of scienter (if any) is *more plausible* than the inference of innocence.

This provoked the predictable exchange between Scalia and Ginsburg over the analogy, and more fundamentally, the "meaning" of the word "strong."

Scalia also engaged in a typical debate with both the majority and Stevens (who dissented) over the appropriate approach to statutory interpretation generally, complete with the standard Scalia complaint about the use of legislative history. Scalia was particularly provoked by Stevens's free-wheeling approach to statutory interpretation. For Scalia, such discretion is "conferred upon administrative agencies, which need not adopt what courts would consider the interpretation most faithful to the text of the statute, but may choose some other interpretation, so long as it is within the bounds of the reasonable." Courts "must apply judgment, to be sure. But judgment is not discretion."

Stevens shot back that "[t]he meaning of a statute can only be determined on a case-by-case basis and will, in each case, turn differently on the clarity of the statutory language, its context, and the intent of its drafters. Stevens preferred a "probable cause" standard because "it is a concept that is familiar to judges" and "[a]s a matter of normal English usage, its meaning is roughly the same as 'strong inference.'" It is unclear who normally uses "probable cause" at all, other than criminal defense lawyers and prosecutors. Stevens, however, made no pretense: Congress intended "probable cause" in adopting the "strong inference" phrasing. Suffice to say, none of the participants in this intramural debate persuaded the others.

The bottom line from *Tellabs* was that the Supreme Court reversed a lenient Seventh Circuit decision for drawing inferences with respect to scienter, but replaced it with a standard that is nonetheless relatively generous to plaintiffs. In so doing, the Court rejected a more stringent standard adopted by a number of lower courts, which had been urged by both the government as amicus and the dissenting justices. On balance, the *Tellabs* decision was likely a net benefit to the plaintiffs' bar, but mainly, it was business as usual for securities fraud class actions. With Powell long gone, the debate was over statutory interpretation, not how to best implement the securities laws.

## b) *Basic* and Class Certification

If the motion to dismiss is the principal tool for weeding out securities fraud class actions, class certification comes second in importance. *Erica P. John Fund, Inc. v. Halliburton Co.* (*Halliburton I*) resolved a circuit split over the question of a plaintiff's burden to certify a class. The Fifth Circuit stood alone in requiring plaintiffs to prove loss causation at the class certification stage, which had proved a challenging barrier for plaintiffs in that circuit.[117] Chief Justice Roberts, writing

212   A HISTORY OF SECURITIES LAW

for a unanimous court, made short work of reversing the Fifth Circuit. The Fifth Circuit had held that plaintiffs were required to prove loss causation in order to trigger the fraud-on-the-market presumption of *Basic Inc. v. Levinson*. Recall that the Court had left open the loss causation question as it had wrangled with the reliance question in *Basic*. The Chief Justice found that the fraud-on-the-market presumption had no connection to loss causation; the presumption was about reliance, not loss causation.

> The fact that a subsequent loss may have been caused by factors other than the revelation of a misrepresentation has nothing to do with whether an investor relied on the misrepresentation in the first place, either directly or presumptively through the fraud-on-the-market theory. Loss causation has no logical connection to the facts necessary to establish the efficient market predicate to the fraud-on-the-market theory.

It is hard to see *Halliburton I* as anything more than error correction. But the case does demonstrate a willingness by the Court to take securities cases to rein in circuits imposing undue burdens on plaintiffs. *Halliburton I* is hardly a case that called out for resolution; one circuit, not a terribly significant one for securities class actions, had made an obvious mistake. The Court could have left the issue to percolate in the lower courts with the hope that the deviant court of appeals would fall in with the other circuits. Instead, the Court invested the time to bring the Fifth Circuit into line.

More momentous was the Court's next foray into class certification for securities fraud cases two years later: *Amgen*.[118] At issue in *Amgen* was "materiality," another of the traditional elements of common law fraud incorporated into a fraud claim under Rule 10b-5. In particular, the question was whether a plaintiff seeking to invoke the fraud-on-the-market presumption of reliance in certifying a class action had to show materiality at that point rather than at trial. *Halliburton I* had rejected the need to show loss causation, but there was no reason to think that loss causation was an element of that presumption. In *Amgen*, by contrast, the defendants argued that the plaintiffs should be required to prove materiality in order to invoke the fraud-on-the-market presumption—there is no question that materiality is a required element of the presumption.

The question for the Court, however, was how that element intersected with the requirements of Rule 23 of the Federal Rules of Civil Procedure. Rule 23(b)(3) requires that common questions "predominate" to certify a class. The Court created the fraud-on-the-market presumption in *Basic* to ensure that reliance would usually present a common question for Rule 23 purposes. Did the plaintiffs need to *prove* each element required to invoke the fraud-on-the-market presumption of reliance at the class certification stage?

PRIVATE LITIGATION 213

"No" said the Court, speaking through Ginsburg. As with a number of the other securities cases addressed during this later period, the question revolved around the interpretation of a rule of general applicability, in this case Rule 23, rather than the interpretation of the securities laws. The question of materiality was central to establishing the fraud-on-the-market presumption under Rule 10b-5, the Court conceded, but that only meant that it would be the plaintiff's burden to prove materiality at trial. The question of whether common questions *predominated* did not rise or fall with that issue; if the plaintiff could not show materiality, the case would fall, not just for the individual plaintiff, but for the entire class. Materiality is an objective standard under Rule 10b-5, so the proof of that element does not vary from plaintiff to plaintiff; either the misstatement is material, or it is not. Ginsburg was anxious to limit the issues that would require proof at the class certification stage. Consequently, issues that implicated the merits would not need to be proved, unless an individual claim could be established even when a class claim would fail.

Ginsburg went on to reject Amgen's suggestions that class certification should serve a gatekeeping role, kicking out meritless cases. If that task was to be undertaken, it would come at the directive of Congress, not the Court's initiative. Congress, after all, had considered the fraud-on-the-market presumption when it adopted the PSLRA in 1995, and it had not assigned courts the gatekeeper function urged by Amgen.

The responses of the concurring and dissenting justices were noteworthy for their willingness to reconsider the fraud-on-the-market presumption's status underpinning the contemporary securities fraud class action. Alito concurred, noting that Amgen had not raised the continuing viability of *Basic* in the courts below. Thomas, joined by Scalia and Kennedy, dissented, urging that "The *Basic* decision itself is questionable." Thus, at least four justices expressed a willingness to reconsider *Basic*.

That question would be front and center when the *Halliburton* case returned to the Court in the term following *Amgen*.[119] When the Court remanded *Halliburton I* to the Fifth Circuit, the appellate court rejected Halliburton's argument that it should be allowed to show that the misstatements alleged by the plaintiffs did not affect the market price of Halliburton's common stock, that is, the misstatements did not have "price impact." Halliburton petitioned for certiorari, asking the justices to allow consideration of price impact evidence at the class certification stage. More dramatically, Halliburton also urged the Supreme Court to overrule *Basic*'s FOTM presumption, thus requiring plaintiff to show actual reliance in a Rule 10b-5 case. Overruling *Basic* would have rendered Rule 10b-5 cases uncertifiable as class actions because individual questions would predominate.

Chief Justice John Roberts, writing for the Court, held that stare decisis compels the conclusion that *Basic*'s FOTM presumption be retained. He reasoned

214  A HISTORY OF SECURITIES LAW

that "special justification" is required to overrule its prior interpretations of statutes because those interpretations are always subject to reversal by Congress. Congress could have overruled *Basic* when it adopted the PSLRA, but chose not to. Indeed, it toughened the misrepresentation, scienter, and loss causation requirements for a Rule 10b-5 claim and added numerous procedural and substantive provisions to discourage vexatious litigation, but it did not touch *Basic's* treatment of the reliance element. Roberts was also unswayed by economic arguments that market efficiency is not the binary standard that *Basic* appears to have assumed. In Roberts's view, markets are efficient enough to justify *Basic's* "modest premise" that markets incorporate false information, and "*Basic* recognized that market efficiency is a matter of degree and accordingly make it a matter of proof." If *Basic* had adverse consequences, that was a policy concern best addressed by Congress.

On the second issue raised by Halliburton—"price impact"—the Court was slightly more generous, allowing the defendant to rebut the fraud-on-the-market presumption by showing that the alleged misstatement did not have a price impact. Roberts rejected, however, the argument that plaintiffs should bear the burden of proof on this issue. He reasoned that requiring plaintiffs to show price impact "would radically alter the required showing for the reliance element" by taking away the ability of the plaintiff to show reliance by demonstrating publicity and market efficiency. Once again, stare decisis controlled: "For the same reasons we declined to completely jettison the *Basic* presumption, we decline to effectively jettison half of it by revising the prerequisites for invoking it." Ginsburg concurred to predict that: "[t]he Court's judgment . . . should impose no heavy toll on securities-fraud plaintiffs with tenable claims" given that the burden of proof on price impact rested with the defendants. She was right; defendants have had little success in mounting price impact defenses. Thomas, joined by Scalia and Alito, concurred in the judgment to vacate the decision below, but his separate opinion was essentially a dissent to the Court's failure to overturn *Basic*: "Principles of *stare decisis* do not compel us to save *Basic's* muddled logic and armchair economics."

Changes in the Court during the Donald Trump administration did not disrupt the Court's general approach to FOTM cases. Amy Coney Barrett, writing for Court in *Goldman Sachs Group, Inc. v. Arkansas Teachers Retirement System* provided defendants a slight window in permitting generic evidence of lack of price movement at the time of the original misstatement to be used to rebut reliance at the class certification stage, notwithstanding the evidentiary overlap with materiality.[120] (Recall from *Amgen* that materiality would ordinarily be postponed to the merits portion of the litigation.) At the same time, the Court reaffirmed its *Halliburton II* holding that defendants carry the burden of persuasion to prove a lack of price impact by a preponderance of the evidence.

PRIVATE LITIGATION    215

Taken as a whole, the Court's post-*Basic* forays into class certification have been generally inconsequential. Plaintiffs' attorneys suffered a setback when Congress adopted the PSLRA, but the statute afforded them a substantial defense in warding off attempts to undo or reform *Basic*'s fraud-on-the market presumption when it was challenged in *Halliburton II*. Congress had spoken, and the Court was not inclined to disrupt that equilibrium. The general applicability of Rule 23 and stare decisis have been the dominant threads in the Court's decisions. Searching for the best implementation of the federal securities laws has been, at most, a secondary concern.

### c) *Central Bank* and Allocating Responsibility for Fraud

If plaintiffs generally fared well in cases addressing pleading and class certification, the same cannot be said for the Court's decisions on liability for secondary actors. The first, *Stoneridge Investment Partners, LLC v. Scientific-Atlanta, Inc.* provoked a (failed) attempt at a legislative override.[121] The second, *Janus Capital Group v. First Derivative Traders*, confirmed that the Supreme Court was serious about refusing any expansion of the implied right of action under Rule 10b-5.[122] The Court threw in a surprising twist, however, when the issue returned in the context of an SEC enforcement action, *Lorenzo v. SEC*.[123]

The *Stoneridge* plaintiffs attempted an end run around *Central Bank*: Instead of alleging that the secondary defendants had made or participated in the making of a misstatement, the plaintiffs alleged that the secondary defendants were part of a "scheme to defraud," thus invoking a separate provision in Rule 10b-5.[124] The plaintiffs' complaint alleged that the cable company Charter Communications committed a massive accounting fraud inflating its reported operating revenues and cash flow. The plaintiffs also named two equipment suppliers as defendants. The plaintiffs alleged that Charter paid the suppliers $20 extra for each cable set-top box in return for the supplier's agreement to make additional payments back to Charter in the form of "advertising fees." Charter then capitalized the $20 extra expense (shifting the accounting cost into the future) while treating the advertising fees as current income, artificially boosting Charter's current accounting revenues. The suppliers had no role in preparing or disseminating the fraudulent accounting information, nor did they approve Charter's financial statements. The plaintiffs alleged, however, that the vendors facilitated Charter's deceptions by preparing false documentation and backdating contracts. The district court granted the suppliers' motion to dismiss, relying on *Central Bank* to hold that the vendors were not primary violators under Rule 10b-5. The court of appeals affirmed, concluding that the suppliers had not engaged in any deception because they had made no misstatements, had no duty to disclose to Charter's investors, and had not manipulated Charter's shares.[125]

216    A HISTORY OF SECURITIES LAW

The case's litigation had its own minor drama. A majority of the SEC commissioners voted to file a brief siding with the plaintiffs. The agency was overruled, however, by the Solicitor General, who sided with the defendants.[126] Here, the government's argument was essentially adopted in toto by the Court, so we have deference to the government, but not to the SEC.

The Supreme Court, by a vote of 5-3 (with Stephen Breyer recused), affirmed. Kennedy, writing for the Court, rejected the appellate court's holding that there was no deception, noting that "[c]onduct itself can be deceptive." He instead hung the affirmance on the other doctrinal point from his *Central Bank* decision, the incompatibility of aiding and abetting liability with the "essential element" of reliance. In this case, investors relied on Charter for its financial statements, not the cable set-top box transactions underlying those financial statements.

Why did Kennedy focus on defendants' conduct, rather than the plaintiffs, when assessing reliance? According to Kennedy, "reliance is tied to causation, leading to the inquiry whether [suppliers'] acts were immediate or remote to the injury." Kennedy treats the reliance inquiry as a species of the tort concept of proximate cause. Kennedy's principal concern was the specter of unlimited liability, as it was in *Central Bank*: "[w]ere this concept of reliance to be adopted, the implied cause of action would reach the whole marketplace in which the issuing company does business." The plaintiff's theory threatened to inject the § 10(b) cause of action into "the realm of ordinary business operations."

Kennedy's rationale for limiting the concept of reliance would have more naturally fit in § 10(b)'s "in connection with the purchase or sale of any security" language. Kennedy nodded toward that language, but said that it did not control in this case because the "in connection with" requirement goes to the "statute's coverage rather than causation." Another reason for not putting the limit into that doctrinal category is that the Court had only recently affirmed a very broad scope for that requirement.[127] A more substantial reason is that cabining Rule 10b-5 through the "in connection with the purchase or sale" requirement would limit not only private plaintiffs, but potentially, the SEC, whose enforcement authority is limited by the reach of the statute. Kennedy conceded that the SEC's enforcement authority might reach commercial transactions like those between Charter and its suppliers, but he was reluctant to grant the same freedom to the plaintiffs' bar.

If the goal was to cabin the plaintiffs' bar, but maintain the SEC's discretion, the reliance requirement was an attractive tool. The reliance requirement, despite being an "essential element," does not flow from the language of § 10(b), but was instead derived by Blackmun from the common law of deceit. More importantly for Kennedy's purposes, reliance does not apply in enforcement actions brought by the SEC or criminal prosecutions brought by the Justice Department.[128] Using the reliance element to limit secondary party liability allowed the Court to have

PRIVATE LITIGATION    217

its cake—unfettered government enforcement—and eat it too—constrain the scope of private actions.

The importance of the SEC's enforcement efforts had been reinforced by Congress's response to *Central Bank*. Rebuffing calls to restore aiding-and-abetting liability, Congress instead affirmed that authority only for the SEC.[129] Accepting the plaintiff's argument in *Stoneridge*, Kennedy reasoned, would thus "undermine Congress' determination that this class of defendants should be pursued by the SEC and not by private litigants." Kennedy's rationale for the need to constrain private litigants echoed and amplified his policy concerns from *Central Bank*. Expanding liability would undermine the United States' international competitiveness because companies would be reluctant to do business with American issuers. Foreign issuers in particular might list their shares elsewhere to avoid these burdens.

Focusing on reliance, it is difficult to extract any consistent guiding principle from the Court's decisions. Stevens, dissenting in *Stoneridge* (as he had in *Central Bank*), hammered on this point:

> *Basic* is surely a sufficient response to the argument that a complaint alleging that deceptive acts which had a material effect on the price of a listed stock should be dismissed because the plaintiffs were not subjectively aware of the deception at the time of the securities' purchase or sale. . . .
>
> The fraud-on-the-market presumption helps investors who cannot demonstrate that they, themselves, relied on fraud that reached the market. But that presumption says nothing about causation from the other side: what an individual or corporation must do in order to have "caused" the misleading information that reached the market. The Court thus has it backwards when it first addresses the fraud-on-the-market presumption, rather than the causation required.

It is fair to say that Blackmun, who wrote the *Affiliated Ute* and *Basic* reliance decisions, would have reached a different outcome in *Stoneridge*. A generation before, Blackmun set a "high standard" in *Affiliated Ute* and *Basic*; Kennedy ratcheted it down in *Central Bank*, and again in *Stoneridge*. Kennedy brusquely rejected the argument that the plaintiffs had adequately pled reliance under common law standards: "Even if the assumption is correct, it is not controlling. Section 10(b) does not incorporate common-law fraud into federal law." More to the point, the incorporation is selective: the Court borrows the common law element of reliance, without really explaining why, but then disregards it when inconvenient. Kennedy's rejection of common law standards in *Stoneridge* suggests that the Court is charting its own common law course. *Central Bank* promised a textual, formalist approach when the Court turned to reining in the reach of the private cause of action. *Stoneridge*, with its return to a fuzzy "requisite causal

218    A HISTORY OF SECURITIES LAW

connection" notion of reliance, fails to deliver on that promise, instead returning to common law decision-making. The opinion does little more than tell us that the defendants' conduct in this case was "too remote" for plaintiffs to rely on.

*Janus Capital Group v. First Derivative Traders* provided only one real surprise: the opinion was authored by Thomas, not Kennedy.[130] Despite the change in authorship, the outcome seemed entirely predictable—the Court rebuffed efforts by the plaintiffs' bar to rope in secondary defendants under Rule 10b-5. The holding underscored the hostility of a majority to expanding the implied private right of action under the rule.

The defendants in *Janus* were Janus Capital Group, Inc. (JCG), the public company behind the Janus family of mutual funds; and Janus Capital Management LLC (JCM), its wholly owned subsidiary that acted as the investment advisor to the Janus funds. Janus Investment Fund, one of the mutual funds in the Janus family, was caught up in the market timing scandals of 2003 when the New York Attorney General accused JCG and JCM of allowing certain investors to purchase shares in the mutual fund based on stale prices. The allegations led to substantial redemptions from the mutual funds, and a sharp drop in the share price of JCG, which earned fees, through its subsidiary JCM, based upon a percentage of assets under management. A class action suit followed.

The problem for the suit was that the misstatements alleged—about policies discouraging market timing—were all in prospectuses issued by Janus Investment Fund, not JCG or JCM. The plaintiffs nonetheless alleged that JCM should be held primarily liable for the misstatements in those prospectuses, and that JCG could be held liable as the "control person" of JCM under § 20(a) of the Exchange Act. Critically, the plaintiffs did not allege that JCM should be held liable as the control person of the Janus Investment Fund, despite the fact that all of the officers of the mutual fund were also officers of JCM. This omission proved fatal to their case.

Thomas framed the issue as whether JCM had "'made' the material misstatements in the prospectuses," which *Central Bank* had set out as the requirement for primary liability. Thomas rejected the argument of plaintiffs, joined by the government as amicus, that "make" should be defined as "create." Thomas offered two principal reasons to justify that conclusion. The first was based on dictionary definitions, with the Court's citation to the 1933 edition of the *Oxford English Dictionary* and the 1934 edition of Webster's New International Dictionary trumping the government's reference to the 1958 definition of Webster's. The flavor of Thomas's dictionary argument can only be captured by a somewhat lengthy quotation:

> One "makes" a statement by stating it. When "make" is paired with a noun expressing the action of a verb, the resulting phrase is "approximately equivalent in sense" to that verb. For instance, "to make a proclamation" is the

approximate equivalent of "to proclaim," and "to make a promise" approximates "to promise." The phrase at issue in Rule 10b–5, "[t]o make any . . . statement," is thus the approximate equivalent of "to state." For purposes of Rule 10b–5, the maker of a statement is the person or entity with ultimate authority over the statement, including its content and whether and how to communicate it. Without control, a person or entity can merely suggest what to say, not "make" a statement in its own right. One who prepares or publishes a statement on behalf of another is not its maker. And in the ordinary case, attribution within a statement or implicit from surrounding circumstances is strong evidence that a statement was made by—and only by—the party to whom it is attributed. This rule might best be exemplified by the relationship between a speechwriter and a speaker. Even when a speechwriter drafts a speech, the content is entirely within the control of the person who delivers it. And it is the speaker who takes credit—or blame—for what is ultimately said.

One can agree or disagree with the Thomas's linguistic analysis. What is notable here is that the Court is not interpreting § 10(b), which presumably entails an effort to discern what the Congress meant in 1934, but instead, Rule 10b-5, which was promulgated by the SEC in 1942. The Court is refusing to defer to the SEC on the interpretation of its own rule. Why? The Court found the definition of "make" to be unambiguous; more telling perhaps, the Court had "previously expressed skepticism over the degree to which the SEC should receive deference regarding the private right of action" and "[t]his is not the first time this Court has disagreed with the SEC's broad view of § 10(b) or Rule 10b-5." Shades of Lewis Powell, but Powell had taken care to identify the limits he imposed on the private cause of action as a matter of interpreting § 10(b), not Rule 10b-5.[131] But "make" does not appear in § 10(b). The Court left a door open, but only a sliver.

The Court's final justification for its ruling seemed to put the final nail in the possibility of agency rulemaking to expand liability under the Rule 10b-5 private cause of action:

> [Plaintiff's] final theory of liability based on a relationship of influence resembles the liability imposed by Congress for control [by § 20(a)]. To adopt [that] theory of liability would read into Rule 10b-5 a theory of liability similar to—but broader in application than—what Congress has already created expressly elsewhere.

Here the Court identifies the statutory constraint missing from its linguistic analysis: Rule 10b-5 must be read to fit with § 20(b). Or to put it differently, the SEC cannot do an end run around the limitations in § 20(b) through a broad interpretation of its rulemaking authority under § 10(b).

220  A HISTORY OF SECURITIES LAW

*Janus*, like *Central Bank* and *Stoneridge* before it, provoked a vigorous dissent. Breyer, writing for four dissenters, predictably took issue with the majority's linguistic analysis, finding considerably more play in the joints of "make" as a verb. Ultimately, it is difficult to say who gets the better of this argument; you agree with one side or the other over what "make" means. Breyer also disputed that *Central Bank* and *Stoneridge* were controlling; the former addressed aiding and abetting, while the latter turned on reliance. Responding to Thomas's point that the plaintiff's broad theory of Rule 10b-5 would usurp § 20(a), Breyer worried that the majority's construction would create a loophole for "cases in which one actor exploits another as an innocent intermediary for its misstatements." Breyer contended that this possibility lurked in the facts of *Janus*: "[h]ere, it may well be that the Fund's board of trustees knew nothing about the falsity of the prospectuses." This, according to Breyer, was "the 13th stroke of the new rule's clock." In Breyer's view, potentially no one could be liable for misstatements in the prospectus. His conclusion conveniently ignores a number of other provisions in the securities laws under which Janus and its affiliates might be liable.

Breyer turned the tables on Thomas in *Lorenzo v. SEC*, exploiting Thomas's reliance on the text of Rule 10b-5, rather than § 10(b).[132] Breyer garnered six votes to uphold the SEC's sanction against Lorenzo, the vice president of an investment bank, for knowingly disseminating false information through an email to investors. The email was sent at the direction of the vice president's boss, who provided both its "central content" and approved the message. Although Lorenzo did not a "make any untrue statement of material fact" under *Janus* and thus was not a "maker" of the statement for purposes of Rule 10b–5(b), the Court nonetheless held that he could be liable under Rule 10b-5(a), which makes it illegal "[t]o employ an device, scheme or artifice to defraud," and Rule 10b-5(c), which proscribes "any act, practice, or course of business which operates or would operate as a fraud or deceit." (The Court also held that Lorenzo violated § 17(a)(1) of the Securities Act, which Rule 10b-5(a) tracks.)

The *Lorenzo* Court rejected the argument that the three subsections of Rule 10b-5 should be read as mutually exclusive, with only subsection (b) addressing misstatements: "the Rule's expansive language . . . suggests we should not hesitate to hold that Lorenzo's conduct ran afoul of subsections (a) and (c)" despite the overlap that its reading created with subsection (b). The Court worried that a narrower reading would allow "plainly fraudulent" conduct to "fall outside the scope of the Rule." A broad reading was necessary to close the potential loophole that Breyer had previously identified in *Janus*:

In instances where a "maker" of a false statement does not violate subsection (b) of the Rule (perhaps because he lacked the necessary intent), a disseminator of those statements, even one knowingly engaged in an egregious fraud, could not be held to have violated the "aiding and abetting" statute. . . . if . . . the disseminator has not primarily violated other parts of Rule 10b-5, then such a fraud, whatever its intent or consequences, might escape liability altogether.

The Court distinguished *Stoneridge* as addressing reliance, which the SEC was not required to show. In any event, "Lorenzo's conduct involved the direct transmission of false statements to prospective investors intended to induce reliance—far from the kind of concealed fraud at issue in *Stoneridge*." Thomas, not surprisingly, was miffed: "the majority's opinion renders *Janus* a dead letter." Breyer responded that "*Janus* would remain relevant (and preclude liability) where an individual neither makes nor disseminates false information—provided, of course, that the individual is not involved in some other form of fraud." Rule 10b-5 had been restored to its pre-*Central Bank* breadth, at least for the SEC, which had already had its aiding-and-abetting authority affirmed by Congress. Left unresolved was how the scheme liability upheld in *Lorenzo* would interact with the reliance requirement in private cause of action. Would the pendulum swing back again?

Taken together, the *Stoneridge-Janus-Lorenzo* trio suggests a lack of engagement with the securities laws. Neither the majorities, nor the dissents, grapple with the complicated regulatory overlap of the securities laws to determine precisely what is given up by limiting the Rule 10b-5 cause of action. In *Janus*, for example, only § 20(b) is mentioned in the majority's opinion, and then only in a footnote. What other provisions of the securities laws potentially apply, and what are the benefits and costs of those alternatives? Without Powell on the Court, there is no justice with the background—or apparently, interest—to explore how the Court's decisions fit into the broader fabric of the securities law. As a result, the Court's securities doctrine simply meanders.

## 3. Summing Up

The New Deal and sixties courts embraced private securities litigation, each in their own way, while the Court of the seventies cut back sharply on implied rights of action. The Court's more recent practice, however, lacks the overarching themes of those earlier eras. The Court has charted what amounts to a middle course, with plaintiffs and defendants each winning some and losing some. The consensus, if it can be called that, is maintenance of the status quo and deference to congressional action. Less charitably, the *Stoneridge-Janus-Lorenzo* series of cases suggests that the justices are out of their league when it comes to dealing with the complexity of the securities laws.

# 7

# The Federal/State Flashpoint in Corporate Governance

> Absent a clear indication of congressional intent, we are reluctant to federalize the substantial portion of the law of corporations that deals with transactions in securities, particularly where established state policies of corporate regulation would be overridden.
>
> *Santa Fe Indus. Inc. v. Green*, 430 U.S. 462 (1977)

The boundary between federal and state law was a political flashpoint in American securities law from the beginning. The statutes of the 1930s were the first federal incursions into what had been the exclusive space of the states, triggering immediate legal battles over the constitutionality of the new legislation. The New Deal Court overhauled the constitutional doctrine in short order, a story at the center of the opening chapters of this book. The Court then settled into a jurisprudence that not only accepted, but promoted, the federal government's social control of finance. In addition, in those early years the Court consistently deferred to the SEC as the expert agency. How would those commitments play out over time in drawing the line between federal and state law?

This chapter picks up the federalism story post-World War II. By then, the initial New Deal statutes, and the SEC as their enforcer, had become accepted features of financial regulation. Lower court judges, particularly the Second Circuit, the "Mother Court" of securities law, now grappled with the relation between federal securities law and state corporation law. A festering issue of the 1950s and '60s was concern over the ineffectiveness of state fiduciary law in addressing abuse by corporate insiders. During the sixties the rise of insider trading law and implied rights of action discussed in the previous two chapters illustrated securities law's expansive trajectory. Those parallel developments set the stage for what seemed to be a nascent federal corporate law.

We begin with this development of federal corporate law. We then track the decline of that fledgling movement in the 1970s, following an arc now familiar to the reader, as justices more skeptical of the administrative state came to hold the Court's balance of power. *Santa Fe Indus., Inc. v. Green* in 1977 illustrates this dramatic shift in focus. But it also marked the last major Supreme Court

*A History of Securities Law in the Supreme Court.* A.C. Pritchard and Robert B. Thompson, Oxford University Press.
© Oxford University Press 2023. DOI: 10.1093/oso/9780197665916.003.0008

decision relying on federalism to confine the application of federal securities law. Corporate governance at the Court settled into subdued détente between the two levels of government. Delaware, feeling the heat from the rise of federal corporate law, enhanced its fiduciary duty review of conflict transactions and applied greater scrutiny to takeovers during the 1980s. Lingering questions raised by possible federal intervention left open in *Santa Fe* were left unresolved—and unexamined—as federal suits became less frequent in transactional settings. State courts picked up more of the slack, often using federal disclosure requirements in the resolution of state law fiduciary duty claims. The Supreme Court played less of a role in delineating the realms of state and federal law.

Decisions that reached the Court during the remainder of the Powell period were in two specialized areas: investment companies and takeovers. In each space Congress had adopted specific legislation partially displacing traditional state corporate governance rules. Despite these statutory mandates, the Supreme Court decisions in these areas did little to shift the federalism line.

The last part of this chapter canvases the post-1987 treatment of federalism in securities cases. Congress played a significant role during this period, returning to the field with new legislation after a long period in which courts had been the most visible actors in federal corporate governance. The Court's federalism decisions in this period have been less momentous than cases of the *Santa Fe* period, even as federal legislation and rule-making have continued to grow. Congress has continued to share the corporate governance space with state governments, while the Court has been relatively hands off.

## A. Fiduciary Misbehavior and the Genesis of Federal Corporate Law

Concern over the erosion of investor protection in state corporate law traces back to the late nineteenth century. The economic transformation effected by the Industrial Revolution saw many American businesses grow to national scale. The "bigness" of corporations suddenly seemed inevitable to many. For others, notably progressive trustbusters, the rise of corporations doing business nationwide was an occasion for government intervention, both state and federal. The rise of nationwide businesses—coupled with courts' respect for the "internal affairs" doctrine—had a dramatic effect on state corporate law. Beginning with New Jersey in the late 1880s and quickly spreading across the country, states seeking charter fees abandoned their regulatory corporation statutes in favor of an "enabling" approach. Swept away were controls on capital, limits on duration and purpose, and most other restrictions. Corporations could pursue any lawful business—in perpetuity. Human entrepreneurs could not escape the inevitable

224    A HISTORY OF SECURITIES LAW

clutch of the reaper, but corporations—bodiless and soulless legal fictions—could go on forever.

The relaxation of state corporate law limits pushed the regulatory impulse to the federal level. Congress attacked the problems of monopoly and harsh treatment of employees by imposing substantial new regulation. Restrictions on corporations' ability to make political contributions arose for the first time. As discussed in Chapter 2, proposals for federal chartering of corporations surfaced during the progressive period at the beginning of the twentieth century as a potential answer to the monopoly problem, but they failed to gain traction. The proposals resurfaced during the New Deal as part of the effort to impose social control of finance. At that time, liberals pitched the proposals as correcting the perceived erosion of shareholder protection resulting from what Brandeis had characterized as a "race ... not of diligence but of laxity" in state corporate law.[1] Roosevelt had other priorities, so federal incorporation was shunted to the side. Then war intervened. Congress was focused on defeating the Nazis and the Japanese Empire rather than managerial overreaching. Corporate governance concerns faded to the background as American industrial strength proved pivotal in winning the war, dissipating the animosity toward big business that had propelled the New Deal reforms.

The postwar era saw concerns over abuse of corporate power re-emerge. In 1951, Judge Learned Hand observed, "For many years a grave omission in our corporation law has been the indifference to dealings of directors or other corporate officers in the shares of their companies." In a memo to his colleagues in the *Birnbaum* case a year later, Hand saw a role for federal securities fraud in reaching the core of fiduciary misbehavior: "I think we should say that for a shareholder who has control of his company to use his power against other shareholders to their detriment is a fraud upon them." The Second Circuit would, over time, take up Hand's interventionist impulse. More than a decade later, the premier chronicler of securities regulation, Professor Louis Loss, described the growth of federal corporate law as the direct consequence of Hand's widely shared perception of deficiency in state corporate law: "what we have from 10b-5 was overdue ... [t]he common law was strangely laggard in appreciating the fiduciary obligations of directors and other insiders to shareholders."[2]

For a time—the 1960s and early 1970 sit appeared that a federal corporate law was emerging not from Congress, but the courts. As discussed in Chapters 5 and 6, the Supreme Court's opinions in *Capital Gains*, in 1963; and *Borak*, decided the next year, adopted expansive interpretations of fiduciary duty and implied rights of action under the federal securities law. Taken together, the two cases suggested a Supreme Court receptive to bringing the federal securities laws to the forefront of corporate governance debates.

The Second Circuit saw those decisions as a green light to pioneer federal corporate law under the general antifraud provision of Rule 10b-5. *Texas Gulf*

CORPORATE GOVERNANCE    225

*Sulphur*, discussed in Chapter 5, confirmed *Cady, Roberts*'s suggestion that insiders' duties could be enforced under Rule 10b-5. The notion of a federal fiduciary duty was a significant incursion into corporate governance. In the same vein, a series of Second Circuit opinions expanded both standing and the scope of the Rule 10b-5 implied private cause of action. The appellate court applied the rule to a variety of conflicted management transactions:

— a corporation issuing shares to a president who controlled the board of directors;
— a controlling shareholder causing the corporation to enter an interested transaction adverse to the corporation and its minority shareholders;
— self-interested mergers.

The rule was also extended to restrict management behavior in a pre-Williams Act takeover. *Capital Gains*'s flexible approach to statutory interpretation, grounded in equity, encouraged a thousand flowers to bloom under Rule 10b-5 in the Second Circuit.[3]

Many of these cases brought the judges up against the traditional standing rule from the Second's Circuit's first important Rule 10b-5 case, *Birnbaum v. Newport Steel*. *Birnbaum* had limited standing to assert a claim under Rule 10b-5 to actual purchasers or sellers. A common thread in the Second Circuit's 10b-5 cases in the 1960s was that *Birnbaum*'s standing rule left too many abuses unchecked. Judges responded by carving out a growing number of exceptions. Would the rule survive this steady erosion? Less attention was paid to the adjacent parts of the *Birnbaum* holding in which the Second Circuit described Rule 10b-5's coverage both in positive terms—"directed solely at that type of misrepresentation of fraudulent practice usually associated with the sale or purchase of securities"—and in negative terms—"rather than at fraudulent mismanagement of corporate affairs."[4] The negative suggested an instinct to defer to state authority over corporate governance. Was the positive statement strong enough to limit the reach of the federal securities laws?

To be sure, there were occasional efforts to raise the flag of federalism in the Second Circuit. A 1964 decision, *O'Neill v. Maytag*, pointed to fiduciary duties under state law (e.g., directors' duties of loyalty and care) and sought to exclude such shareholder claims from Rule 10b-5 absent deception inducing one of the parties to buy or sell a security. In that case a purchaser and seller had engaged in a stock swap. Each party knew what it was getting and receiving from the other, but one set of directors was said to be motivated to entrench themselves. The Second Circuit panel concluded that the presence of a purchase and sale should not justify interpreting Rule 10b-5 to take in every fiduciary duty. It distinguished another Second Circuit opinion decided the same month with two of the same

226    A HISTORY OF SECURITIES LAW

judges on the panel, permitting a 10b-5 claim when interested directors deceived the board into approving issuance of stock.[5]

A steady flow of commentators described the cases applying Rule 10b-5 broadly as the emergence of federal corporate law. Chairman Cary had used the federal corporate law moniker in *Cady, Roberts* and the term quickly gained wide use. When the Supreme Court finally started to grapple with Rule 10b-5, Douglas's unanimous *Bankers Life* opinion in 1971 blew past *Birnbaum's* federalism speed bump. There was a purchase or sale—the corporation itself had sold bonds in the market for a price unaffected by fraud. Thereafter the controllers had misappropriated the proceeds to fund a transaction by which the controlling shareholder sold their controlling position to a buyer. Douglas addressed *Birnbaum's* exclusion of corporate mismanagement by limiting it to "transactions that constitute no more than internal corporate mismanagement." But true to his New Deal roots in social control of finance, Douglas linked fiduciary breaches usually addressed under state corporate law and manipulation prohibited by the federal law as "all a single seamless web," a phrase taken from the congressional hearings for the Exchange Act. Douglas threw in the familiar touchstone of the Court's sixties jurisprudence that the rules "must be read flexibly, not technically and restrictively."[6] *Bankers Life* validated the Second Circuit's expansive approach developed in the wake of *Capital Gains* and *Borak*. Rule 10b-5 appeared to be the remedy of choice for corporate mismanagement. Would federal law displace state law altogether?

## B. The Supreme Court Curtails Federal Corporate Law

In a word, no. After this expansionist glimmer from the Supreme Court, federal corporate law disappeared just as quickly. Powell and Rehnquist would arrive just after the Court handed down *Bankers Life*. Their appointment would check the expansion of federal securities law and preserve an important role for state corporate law.

The new direction first emerged, at least in retrospect, in a little-noticed securities decision early in Powell and Rehnquist's tenure. In *Bangor Punta Operations, Inc. v. Bangor & Aroostook Railroad Co.* the First Circuit had permitted the 99.3% owner of the corporation to sue the prior owner for, in essence, looting the corporation.[7] The suit—somewhat vaguely—alleged claims under the federal securities laws and antitrust laws, as well as state statutory and common law. Powell summarized the controlling issue in *Bangor Punta* this way:

> (CA1 seems to be throwing the law books away!) CA1, over-ruling DC, held that a 99% stockholder of corp may bring a derivative stockholders' suit in name of corp vs. the *former* owner of controlling stock in the corp. for mismgt.

CORPORATE GOVERNANCE 227

> CA1 allowed suit on theory that although the Resp. (present 99% owner) alleged no injury or damage to itself (+ no fraud at time it acquired the 99% interest), Resp. was entitled to sue for general benefit of public's interest in railroads. In short, Resp. was *self* appointed Atty-Gen.

Powell was dubious of the "private attorney general" concept that had animated the First Circuit: "Quite apart from purely equitable considerations, there is sound reason to leave the safeguarding of the public interest in the soundness of railroads and the quality of their service to the regulatory authorities rather than to encourage some concept of 'private attorney general' litigation." Even Blackmun, typically more receptive to representative litigation, was skeptical of the First Circuit's public interest justification:

> There is public interest, of course, in the continuing welfare of the transportation industry. Nevertheless, I get the impression that this is a rather dangerous and elusive doctrine. Would it not apply to airlines and buslines and other forms of transportation? We have had many instances of governmental subsidy to industry such as American maritime transportation, Lockheed and the like.

Marshall, however, declared at conference that "Party who stole the money should give it up," a fair summary of the reasoning that attracted a unanimous Court just two terms before in *Bankers Life*.[8] Douglas, the author of *Bankers Life*, joined Marshall in favoring recovery, as did Brennan and White. Three of the four had signed on to the most expansive of the 1960s cases, and Marshall, who joined later in the decade, showed no sign of departing from that liberal consensus. Even the private attorney general aspect of the claim evokes *Bankers Life*, which was brought by the state Superintendent of Insurance, presumably for the benefit of policy holders who may have found the cupboard bare when the time came for their policies to be paid off.

The new skepticism of public interest litigation—particularly when brought by a private plaintiff—would drive a new result. Three other members of the *Bankers Life* majority—Stewart, Burger, and Blackmun—now joined new members Powell and Rehnquist to constrain the securities laws. Powell rejected the First Circuit's distinction between public utilities and private corporations: "No such distinction exists in corp[orate] law." Instead, Powell looked to well-established practice under state corporate law, the "contemporaneous holder" rule. Powell's opinion is carefully grounded in "the settled principle of equity that a shareholder may not complain of acts of corporate mismanagement if he acquired his shares from those who participated or acquiesced in the allegedly wrongful transactions."[9] State corporate law was apparently not dead yet. Even when not controlling (at least some of the claims were based on federal law), federalism

228    A HISTORY OF SECURITIES LAW

had persuasive force. *Bangor Punta* would begin the trend, both in its result and in its reasoning; the unanimous decisions of the prior decade reflecting simpler notions of right and wrong would not re-emerge.

Federalism issues did not appear in the two cases that emphatically announced the Rule 10b-5 retrenchment. Neither *Blue Chip Stamps* decided in 1975, nor *Ernst & Ernst v. Hochfelder* a year later, arose in a transactional context that would have been governed by state corporate law. (*Blue Chip* arose from an antitrust settlement, while *Ernst & Ernst* from the collapse of a brokerage house). But the direction for securities law was clear. The Court in *Blue Chip* rebuffed the incursions made on *Birnbaum*'s actual purchaser or seller requirement, affirming the Second Circuit's standing rule full stop. Rehnquist also introduced "vexatious litigation" in *Blue Chip* as a consideration for the Court when construing judicially implied private causes of action. Powell, dealing with scienter in *Ernst & Ernst*, was equally emphatic that all of the elements of common law fraud still mattered. Since the claim in *Bankers Life* included a purchase or sale, its holding survived *Blue Chip*, even if Douglas's expansive reasoning looked increasingly suspect. The interpretive flexibility relied upon by Douglas seemed to have departed with his retirement.

The Court delivered the death blow to federal corporate law in *Santa Fe Industries v. Green*.[10] *Santa Fe*'s facts fit well enough within the federal corporate law framework of the sixties cases. Minority shareholders complained because they had been cashed out in a short form merger. Because the parent corporation owned more than 90% of the stock, compliance with the statutory merger requirements were a formality, which Delaware corporate law allowed to be skipped. The price for their stock was unilaterally set by the controlling shareholder who dictated the terms of the transaction. Appraisal, a cumbersome valuation proceeding to determine fair value, was the exclusive remedy under Delaware law. Thus, shareholders were left without a state forum to contest fiduciary duty and conflict of interest. The Second Circuit, which earlier had permitted a 10b-5 suit in another short form merger, held that the merger violated Rule 10b-5 with "no allegation or proof of misrepresentation or nondisclosure necessary." A breach of fiduciary duty was sufficient.[11]

At the Court's conference, four justices were open to bringing fiduciary duty under federal law. To Powell, however, it seemed obviously wrong. Fairness in corporate transactions was the realm of state law. If management did not misstate what they were doing, 10b-5 was irrelevant:

> The purpose of § 10b and Rule 10b(5) is to substitute full disclosure for the doctrine of *Caveat Emptor*.
>
> Nor would I have thought that § 10b was intended to create a federal commonlaw [sic] of corporations contrary to valid state statutes.

CORPORATE GOVERNANCE    229

Powell's reaction was to be expected; more critical to the outcome was White, who had signed on to expansive approaches in *Bankers Life* and *Affiliated Ute* just a few years prior. Now White agreed with Powell, as did Rehnquist, Burger, and Stewart. Burger assigned the opinion to White.[12]

White's opinion was a sweeping defense of the need to limit Rule 10b-5 to preserve the domain of state corporate law. The Court held first there could not be a breach of § 10(b) and Rule 10b-5 absent "deception, misrepresentation or nondisclosure." Second, "once full and fair disclosure had occurred" the Court was unwilling to recognize a federal fiduciary principle that would "bring within the Rule a wide variety of corporate conduct traditionally left to state regulation."

> The reasoning behind a holding that the complaint in this case alleged fraud under Rule 10b-5 could not be easily contained. . . . this extension of the federal securities laws would overlap and quite possibly interfere with state corporate law. Federal courts applying a 'federal fiduciary principle' under Rule 10b-5 could be expected to depart from state fiduciary standards at least to the extent necessary to ensure uniformity within the federal system.

The Supreme Court was drawing a line in the sand to preserve state corporate law from the Second Circuit's efforts to develop an implied federal remedy that would "cover the corporate universe." The Court acknowledged the possible need for federal fiduciary standards, but those standards would need to come from Congress. The Court quoted with approval former SEC Chair William Cary who, in calling for federal standards, recognized the anomaly if courts were to "jigsaw every kind of corporate dispute into the federal courts through the securities acts as they are presently written." In a private note, Powell commended White's opinion as "superb."[13] Powell would allow a federal fiduciary principle to survive three years later in *Chiarella* in the context of insider trading under Rule 10b-5, but its reach would be limited, applying to fraudulent nondisclosure.

*Santa Fe*'s holding was clear, but it came in a case in which there was full disclosure, the central goal of the Exchange Act. The Court had no occasion to consider what would happen if there were disclosure deficiencies *and* a conflicted corporate transaction. This was the line that the Second Circuit had tried to draw in 1964 in the *O'Neill* and *Ruckle* decisions at the dawn of the federal corporate law movement discussed earlier. The post-*Santa Fe* Second Circuit picked up on that focus. *Goldberg v. Meridor*,[14] handed down just a few months after *Santa Fe*, involved both insufficient disclosure and corporate mismanagement. The appellate court found a 10b-5 remedy for the shareholders:

> there is deception of the corporation (in effect, of its minority shareholders) when the corporation is influenced by its controlling shareholder to engage

230   A HISTORY OF SECURITIES LAW

in a transaction adverse to the corporation's interests (in effect, the minority shareholders' interests) and there is nondisclosure or misleading disclosures as to the material facts of the transaction. . . . The Supreme Court['s] . . . quarrel [in *Santa Fe*] was with this court's holding that "neither misrepresentation nor nondisclosure was a necessary element of a Rule 10b-5 action" . . . and that a breach of fiduciary duty would alone suffice. . . . Here the complaint alleged "deceit . . . upon UGO's minority shareholders. . . . the conduct attacked in Green did not violate the "'fundamental purpose' of the Act as implementing a 'philosophy of full disclosure'". . . the conduct here attacked does.

Four other circuits came to similar holdings over the next few years, two with dissents arguing that the results conflicted with *Santa Fe*. When certiorari was sought, the Court declined to hear the cases. The issue remained unresolved.[15]

As the lower courts continued to recognize a limited federal corporate law, so did the SEC. In the fall of 1977, just a few months after *Santa Fe*, the agency proposed new rules to govern going private transactions like the deal challenged in *Santa Fe*. The SEC's release began with a recognition that state laws "have not always provided an adequate remedy" specifically identifying the "cumbersome" appraisal remedy and "ineffective" other remedies. The agency boldly leveraged federal authority over disclosure to effectively regulate substance despite the obstacle created by *Santa Fe*. The SEC confidently noted "it would be appropriate for courts to construe [the provisions of section 13(e)(3) added to the Exchange Act in 1968 to cover going private] in such a way as to provide a private right thereunder." The rules were finalized in 1979, requiring a statement as to whether the board of directors reasonably believes the Rule 13e-3 transaction is fair or unfair to unaffiliated security holders.[16] How many boards would choose to describe a proposed transaction as unfair?

Another post-*Santa Fe* development later in 1977 demonstrates how state courts responded in the immediate aftermath of the Supreme Court's watershed opinion. As the federal appellate opinions and SEC rulemaking illustrate, Delaware still had reason to fear federal encroachment despite *Santa Fe*. In September its high court held that shareholders, unhappy with a going private cash-out merger dominated by a controlling shareholder, were not limited to appraisal. The state court also recognized the availability of a fiduciary duty suit where the controllers would be required to show a non-freeze-out purpose that the court would scrutinize under an entire fairness standard. Over the next decade the Delaware Supreme Court in *Weinberger*, as to conflict situations, *Van Gorkom* as to duty of care, and *Unocal* as to takeover defenses, strengthened the state's approach to fiduciary behavior in acquisitions. The state court described its work as designed "to bring our law current."[17]

CORPORATE GOVERNANCE    231

The Supreme Court did not return to the field until *Schreiber v. Burlington Northern* in 1985.[18] *Schreiber* did little more than reaffirm *Santa Fe*'s holding that allegations of unfairness with no showing of manipulative or deceptive acts failed to state a federal antifraud claim. Burlington made a hostile cash tender offer to acquire 51% of El Paso shares (that is, 25.1 million shares), which was fully subscribed in short order. At that point the target's board saw the value of a friendly deal, securing revised terms from Burlington that included golden parachutes for El Paso management, along with a new tender offer in which four million of the 25.1 million shares needed to gain control would come from El Paso itself. Shareholders who had originally tendered now faced receiving different (and arguably less valuable) consideration in the cash-out merger that followed for the remaining 49% of shares. (The revised terms had been approved by the non-Burlington members of the El Paso board). They brought breach of contract claims against Burlington and breach of fiduciary duty claims against their own directors under § 14(e), the antifraud provision of the Williams Act similar to Rule 10b-5, but applicable to tender offers. The Court did not address the harder question of whether the federal antifraud provisions would apply when both misrepresentation and unfairness by a fiduciary were present. Blackmun's conference notes suggest there was no discussion; federalism concerns were ignored.[19]

But there were some signs of movement in the lower federal courts. A post-*Schreiber* Second Circuit opinion once more identified the federal space when there were overlapping allegations of a failure to disclose and breach of fiduciary duties. The appellate court now described the prior federal claims as looting and stealing when there was irreparable injury to the company from willful misconduct of a self-serving nature. More importantly perhaps, cases of the sort left open by *Santa Fe* stopped showing up in federal courts.[20]

Class actions available in state court provided a sufficiently flexible procedural setting for litigating many shareholder claims. Subsequent state innovations provided potential "best price" remedies that could go beyond those available under federal law, along with enhanced scrutiny of defensive tactics. The state law shortcomings that troubled Learned Hand and Louis Loss in the 1950s and '60s had been ameliorated. In a post-*Santa Fe* world, state and federal spheres were demarcated more clearly. That said, state courts nevertheless free rode on the disclosure required by federal law to determine state law claims.[21] The dividing line between state corporate law and federal securities law might require further delineation by the Court, but the stakes had been greatly diminished. Federal law no longer threatened to swallow up corporate law; state courts would continue to determine much of the substance of fiduciary obligation for corporate officers and directors.

232   A HISTORY OF SECURITIES LAW

## C. Investment Companies

Post-*Santa Fe*, the Supreme Court heard more federalism/corporate governance cases for investment companies than for general corporations, which limited their impact. The last of the New Deal securities laws, both adopted in 1940, covered investment companies and investment advisers. The two laws came after the post Court-packing 1938 elections that had produced a Congress of Republicans and Southern Democrats which was generally hostile to Roosevelt's domestic agenda. Joel Seligman, author of the principal history of the SEC, termed the legislation a defeat for the administration. The result was a disclosure statute that lacked provisions for the control of investment bankers and entrenched power holders, a retreat from the aggressive approaches adopted in PUHCA and the Chandler Act passed in the prior Congress. Federal governance standards for mutual funds drew from the usual state corporate law template, with variations tilting the shareholder/director balance more toward shareholders. The investment company statute, for example, required that 40% of the board of directors must be independent directors (later increased to 75%) at a time when there were no independence requirements for corporations generally. In addition, the federal statute required shareholder approval of compensation, a requirement that would not be applied to public corporations generally until the Dodd-Frank Act was enacted in 2010.[22] In the three investment company cases to come before the high court, it recognized the impact of the different federal requirement or took a narrow approach to applying newly emerging state law rules that required demand on directors before shareholders could bring suits on behalf of the corporation.

*Burks v. Lasker* in 1979 raised the question of whether the independent directors of an investment company had the authority to dismiss a state law derivative claim. This put the Supreme Court in the middle of a contentious debate in state corporate governance: limits on the power of boards to dismiss derivative suits challenging directors' decisions. The Second Circuit held that the directors did not have the authority to dismiss the shareholder-initiated suit, invoking a federal common law rule based on the policies that it gleaned from the Investment Company Act, which was silent on the issue. The SEC argued that a federal rule should apply, but that rule would not bar the independent directors from dismissing the claim. Brennan's opinion for the Court cited the general principle that federal courts should apply state corporations law to the extent not inconsistent with federal law, noting specifically that statute's mandate of board independence as a check on director conduct. The Court's holding, however, was limited—overruling the appellate court's absolute ban of such dismissal by the directors. Powell and Stewart were "not happy with his grudging approach to authority of the disinterested Board members." Stewart's concurrence, joined

CORPORATE GOVERNANCE    233

by Powell, argued for blanket deference to state law. Blackmun's rejoinder urged that state law is not absolute. The issue of implied private actions that framed the debate in the federalism cases discussed before did not play a major role. Both courts below had assumed the existence of a private claim, so the Supreme Court assumed without deciding that there was a private cause of action.[23]

The issue of derivative suit procedures would return to the Court five years later in *Daily Income Fund v. Fox*.[24] The case involved executive compensation, for which Congress had adopted a special governance rule for investment companies. The question was whether shareholders suing for corporate harm must first make a demand on directors to redress the claim, a variation of the assertion of director control of litigation seen in *Burks*. Federal Rule 23.1 required demand, consistent with state laws on the topic. The rule was intended as a check on possible abuse ("strike suits") by minority shareholders bringing suits on behalf of the corporation. Brennan's opinion for a unanimous Court confined Rule 23.1 to suits brought on behalf of the corporation. The investment company statute specifically provided for enforcement of the compensation approval requirement by an individual shareholder or the SEC. That removed the question of the corporation's right to sue, and consequently, the directors' right under state law to control that decision. With the statute clear, the contentious question of an implied right of action was off the table.

The federalism aspect in the investment company context re-emerged in *Kamen v. Kemper Financial Services*,[25] but the case had limited implications for the larger question of the breadth of federal law to displace state governance rules. In *Kamen*, the shareholders of a mutual fund alleged that the advisor's fees had been approved based on misstatements in a proxy statement. The statute, § 20(a) of the Investment Company Act, followed §§ 10(b) and 14(a) of the Exchange Act in saying the deceptive conduct was "unlawful," without specifically providing a private cause of action.[26] As in *Burks*, the Court left that question for another day.

The question addressed in *Kamen* was whether shareholder demand on the directors was a prerequisite to filing suit. Former corporate law professor Frank Easterbrook, writing for the Seventh Circuit, adopted the universal demand requirement of the American Law Institute's Principles of Corporate Governance, ostensibly a project about state law. The ALI's principles had departed from Delaware precedent. Delaware excused demand on directors based on whether it would be futile because of director conflict or other incapacity. The ALI, by contrast, required shareholder demand in every case, subject to later review by a court.[27] Marshall, writing for a unanimous Court, characterized the Seventh Circuit's approach as "fashioning an entire body of federal corporate law."

State law would still play a role in the management of mutual funds, but Congress had the power to displace it. It was a question of statutory construction,

234    A HISTORY OF SECURITIES LAW

and the Court read the statute as elevating the shareholders' role in investment companies. As such, these decisions did not move the needle on *Santa Fe*'s federalism concerns with regard to general corporation law, which got more play in the context of implied rights.

## D. The Takeover Wars and Federalism

Hostile takeovers emerged from the periphery of the corporate landscape in the 1960s. The widespread use of tender offers spawned a new market for corporate control and the creation of diversified conglomerates. The takeover wave led to federal legislation, the Williams Act of 1968. The Williams Act extended disclosure to a new field, tender offers. It also included an antifraud provision copied from Rule 10b-5 applicable to disclosures in the tender offer context.[28] This new extension of the federal securities laws led to a series of Supreme Court cases starting in the seventies. In the first two of the Williams Act cases, the Court rebuffed aggressive uses of this new securities statute, echoing the Court's efforts to rein in implied rights of actions. These cases did not discuss federalism concerns. The last three cases addressed challenges to state laws on federalism ground—that is, preemption or Dormant Commerce Clause. Only the last decision permitted a state statute to survive. That said, the state takeover regime that eventually developed to protect managers fending off unwanted takeovers survived judicial challenge. The Supreme Court created ample space for strong state law defenses such as the poison pill and staggered boards.

### 1.  Implied Private Rights Under Federal Tender Offer Statutes

Takeovers differ from traditional corporate governance disputes discussed earlier in this chapter. The shareholder-management interaction at the center of state corporate governance remains, but joined by a new player. An outside bidder (who may well be hostile to the incumbent management) seeks to contract with the shareholders to purchase enough shares to gain voting control over the board and thereby supplant the incumbent managers. Purchases from individual shareholders are unlikely to timely produce the requisite majority, so tender offers are the principal tool for obtaining control.

Early drafts of the Williams Act unabashedly aimed to protect "proud old companies" from corporate raiders, requiring a bidder, for example, to provide twenty days advance notice before making a tender offer, giving the target extra weeks to build a defensive strategy. The bill eventually evolved into a purportedly neutral statute that, according to its sponsor, aimed to avoid tipping the balance

CORPORATE GOVERNANCE   235

either way between the bidder and target management.[29] In *Rondeau v. Mosinee Paper Co.* in 1975 and *Piper v. Chris-Craft Indus. Inc.* two years later, the Court sought to limit the reach of private rights under the statute.[30] Conspicuous by its absence from these decisions was any discussion of the balance between federal and state law. The cases were treated as purely federal questions.

The *Rondeau* decision reversed a five-year injunction based on a bidder's inadvertent late filing. Powell, no fan of hostile bidders, termed this an "an absurd penalty, where there was no showing of prejudice or injury to [Mosinee]." In *Piper*, the Court was no more accommodating to an unsuccessful bidder's effort to use alleged disclosure violations to recover damages from the ultimately successful bidder preferred by management. Burger wrote both decisions for the Court, with neutrality as his central theme. In *Rondeau* he characterized the legislative history as

> expressly disclaim[ing] an intention to provide a weapon for management to discourage takeovers bids or prevent large accumulations of stock which would create the potential for such attempts. Indeed, the Act's draftsmen commented upon the "extreme care" which was taken "to avoid tipping the balance of regulation either in favor of management or in favor of the person making the takeover bid."

In *Piper*, Burger repeated the concerns about even-handedness, but distinguished protecting investors from protecting bidders. The focus was on limiting the implied right of action. The congressional policy of "evenhandedness" has little relevance to "the quite disparate" question of whether the Williams Act "was intended to confer rights for money damages upon an injured takeover bidder." Burger's argument drew on *Cort v. Ash* and other decisions of the same time cutting back on private rights of action (discussed in Chapter 6), but he ignored the federalism arguments relied upon by White in *Santa Fe*, handed down only a month later. The dissents in both cases also illustrate this focus on private rights under the statute. Brennan and Douglas in *Rondeau*; and Stevens joined by Brennan in *Piper*, both wanted to see a more muscular interpretation of the federal statute, whether it was for the benefit of management in *Rondeau* or for the defeated bidder in *Piper*.[31]

## 2. Preemption or Commerce Clause Challenges to State Anti-Takeover Laws

State legislatures, like Congress, distrusted the tender offer trend. Their efforts to intervene to protect incumbent management compelled the Court to allocate

236    A HISTORY OF SECURITIES LAW

authority between the state and federal governments. As it happened, Lewis Powell's practice before coming to the Court had included personal involvement in state anti-takeover laws—he had lobbied to enact the first one. Virginia's anti-takeover statute predated the federal Williams Act by a few months, drawing on an early draft of the federal statute responding to the tender offer wave of the late 1960s. Powell worried that the then-existing regulatory void meant that a tender "offer may be sprung upon unwary management almost overnight." His worries became more acute when one of the great conglomerates of the 1960s, Tenneco, targeted a prominent Virginia corporation, Newport News Shipbuilding, for a takeover. Although Newport News was not a regular client, the company came to Powell when it needed legislation to ward off Tenneco.[32]

Powell's connections helped: he was a longtime supporter of Edward Lane, who sponsored the legislation. Lane introduced a bill that would apply to offers for more than 10% of a company's shares for companies that were both incorporated and doing business in Virginia. Powell lobbied for the bill on behalf of Newport News, meeting with Virginia's Attorney General (whom Powell had supported in his election campaign) and appearing before both House and Senate Committees of the General Assembly. A member of Powell's "team," Joe Carter, was sent to "pound[] the halls of the General Assembly with Cootie Holt [Newport's general counsel] begging our friends to save Newport News Ship from being taken over." The legislation passed the assembly and was signed into law by Governor Mills Godwin (another beneficiary of Powell's support). Powell thanked Lane for his leadership in enacting "a constructive bill in the overall public interest of stockholders and management of Virginia corporations and the communities they serve." Despite Powell's victory for Newport News in the legislature, the company soon abandoned its resistance and agreed to be acquired by Tenneco. Newport News's president was shown the door shortly thereafter.[33]

Powell's practice experience shaped his response to the early tender offer cases. In *Rondeau* he observed: "Suits by mgt. (like this) is a standard tactic to frustrate tender offers." But even with his belief that management needed room to respond he was not willing to discard the equitable rule requiring a showing of irreparable harm for an injunction. His concern for protecting management reappeared in a letter to Burger in *Piper*. Powell cautioned the Chief Justice against including discussion of views as to liability that

> could be construed as impliedly affirming the CA2 standard of liability, the management of target corporations may well be deterred from interposing a vigorous defense against takeover bids for fear of being sued for relatively trivial inaccuracies or overstatements. A takeover fight resembles an election contest. There must be reasonable latitude for hyperbole, for widely differing opinions

CORPORATE GOVERNANCE    237

as to value, as to management and other relevant facts. There is nothing in the Williams Act that is intended to limit expression of this kind.

Management needed freedom to defend itself against takeovers, Powell urged, because "[n]ot infrequently, the tender offeror is a predatory type company that seeks control for the purpose of liquidating (sometimes 'looting') the target company to the disadvantage of minority stockholders."[34] Previewing the cases to come, Powell did not want the Williams Act to restrain corporate incumbents from defending their positions.

*Rondeau* and *Piper* set the stage for a trilogy of cases addressing (1) whether the Williams Act preempted state take anti-takeover laws; and (2) the constitutionality of those state laws under the Dormant Commerce Clause, interpreted to encourage free trade among the states. The three cases came down over eight years. In that time, there were relatively minor changes in the makeup for the Court: O'Connor replaced Stewart, and Scalia was appointed when Rehnquist replaced Burger in the center seat. Outside the Court, the battle lines had been drawn, with the states taking the lead in protecting management from hostile takeovers. The SEC was in the opposing corner, attempting to use federal law to head off state efforts to restrict the market for corporate control.[35] In this dispute, the question was not whether one was "for" or "against" business; one had to take sides for or against management. The ultimate question was whether federal law prevented states from taking steps to protect company management against takeovers beyond what the federal government had done.

The first, *Leroy v. Great Western United Corp.* in 1979, was ultimately reversed on the narrow procedural ground of improper venue.[36] The justices expressed their views on the merits in conference, however, shedding light on where the individual justices stood on federalism in the takeover setting. Great Western made an unsolicited tender offer to the shareholders of Sunshine Mining Company, a Washington corporation with its principal mining operations in Idaho. The Fifth Circuit upheld an injunction by a Texas district court barring the director of Idaho's Department of Finance from enforcing Idaho's anti-takeover statute against Great Western. The Idaho statute added further delay and disclosure requirements beyond those imposed by the Williams Act. In addition, it required the approval of tender offers by state regulators. The Fifth Circuit concluded that the Idaho statute placed an undue burden on interstate commerce, thus violating the Dormant Commerce Clause. The appellate court also held that the statute frustrated the purposes of the Williams Act, and therefore was preempted. The SEC, supported by the Solicitor General, argued for the Fifth Circuit's decision to be upheld on the merits.[37]

If the Court were to get to the merits, at least eight justices thought the Idaho statute should be struck down, although they disagreed on the rationale. White, along with Brennan and Marshall, wanted to affirm the Fifth Circuit's decision,

238    A HISTORY OF SECURITIES LAW

which had thrown out the Idaho statute on both Dormant Commerce Clause and preemption grounds. The Chief Justice, along with Rehnquist, agreed that the statute ran afoul of the Dormant Commerce Clause as well as the Williams Act, suggesting a seeming majority to strike down the state legislation. Stewart favored only preemption, and Blackmun just described it as unconstitutional. Stevens was uncertain on jurisdiction, but felt that the case could be reversed for improper venue. If the Court were to reach the merits, Stevens thought the statute was "bad," but Powell's notes do not record Stevens's rationale. Powell conceded that "the potential availability of tender offers is valuable to shareholders in almost all corporations as an incentive to efficient management," but he worried that "the Williams Act is a weak statute that does not adequately protect shareholders of a target co." Despite his sympathies for the purposes of Idaho's law, Powell thought that it "may have gone too far, especially by *not* limiting its Act to Idaho corp[oration]s and in requiring *approval* by Idaho commission."[38] (Recall that the Virginia statute only applied to Virginia corporations.)

Apart from those views on the substance, a majority believed that the Texas district court lacked jurisdiction.[39] Stevens was assigned the opinion; his opinion reversed the Fifth Circuit's ruling, not on jurisdictional grounds, but because venue was not proper in the Texas district court. Despite Stevens's freelancing, he got a majority, perhaps because none of the other justices wanted to tackle the thorny jurisdictional issues. White (joined by Brennan and Marshall) dissented. His finding that the venue requirement had been satisfied turned on a markedly different understanding of preemption. In contrast to the majority's permitted venue only as to "participants in securities markets," White saw the Williams Act as imposing a duty on state officials not to enact inconsistent legislation, which made venue appropriate. The constitutional status of state anti-takeover provisions remained undecided with most of the justices' views seemingly hostile to state legislation. Those views, however, had not yet been publicly shared.

The opportunity for clarification arose soon enough, but once again the justices were badly splintered. *Edgar v. MITE Corp.* presented a constitutional challenge to Illinois's anti-takeover statute.[40] The Illinois law, like the Idaho statute in *Great Western*, applied to corporations that operated in the state, whether or not they were incorporated in Illinois. The Illinois statute also tracked the Idaho statute in requiring that a state regulator approve tender offers.

The final similarity between *Edgar* and *Great Western* was a procedural complication. In this case, the potential acquirer had dropped its offer by the time the case reached the Court. At first glance, the *Edgar* case looked moot. Moreover, the SEC recently had adopted rules intended to preempt statutes of this sort. The justices nonetheless decided to note probable jurisdiction. Having noted jurisdiction, however, a majority voted for mootness. Marshall was assigned to write the opinion.[41]

CORPORATE GOVERNANCE    239

Only after Marshall circulated his draft did things begin to go off track. A series of shifts among the justices resulted in a majority favoring mootness morphing into a majority striking down the Illinois law under the Dormant Commerce Clause. White's dissent evolved into the opinion that addressed both preemption and Commerce Clause reasons to strike down the state statute, but he gathered only a plurality of three for the part of his opinion holding that the Williams Act preempted the law. Three (of the six) justices who had thought that the Idaho statute was preempted in the *Great Western* discussion (Brennan, Marshall, and Rehnquist) did not register their votes on the merits in *MITE* (their views appear to have been the same as before) because they saw the case as moot.[42] Without their votes, White could not muster a majority to strike down the statute on preemption grounds.

Powell's notes at conference, at which mootness was the expected path, show that he believed that the case was moot but thought—"[i]f we reach merits"—the statute was preempted. At the point that White first circulated a draft opinion, Powell's personal notes record his intent to join White's opinion if White got a court.[43] White's preemption opinion was short of a majority even with the Virginian, but the Commerce Clause argument attracted four other votes. (Burger, Stevens, and O'Connor eventually joined the Commerce Clause section of the opinion, but Blackmun did not). Powell was willing to help form a majority, but only for the more limited portion of White's Commerce Clause holding. That part reasoned that the Illinois statute imposed an undue burden on interstate commerce relative to the state interest. Powell declined, however, to join White's argument that the statute was unconstitutional under the Dormant Commerce Clause because it directly regulated interstate commerce occurring wholly outside Illinois. The result was a majority that struck down the legislation while preserving some room for state anti-takeover legislation. White's broader reading of the Dormant Commerce Clause—which might have negated all state efforts to regulate takeovers—failed to gain a fifth vote.

> Powell explained that he joined White's undue burden reasoning because it
>
> leaves some room for state regulation of tender offers. In a period in our history marked by conglomerate corporate formations essentially unrestricted by the antitrust laws, it is far from clear to me that the Williams Act's policy of "neutrality" operates fairly or in the public interest. Often the offeror possesses resources, in terms of professional personnel experienced in takeovers as well as in capital, that vastly exceed those of the takeover target. This disparity in resources may seriously disadvantage a relatively small or regional target corporation. The Williams Act provisions seem to assume corporate entities of substantially equal resources. Moreover, in terms of general public interest, when corporate headquarters are moved away from a city and State inevitably

240   A HISTORY OF SECURITIES LAW

there are certain adverse consequences.... [T]he Williams Act should not necessarily be read as prohibiting state legislation designed to assure—at least in some circumstances—greater protection to interests that include but often are broader than those of incumbent management.

Powell noted that the "Virginia Act (that I helped write and 'lobbied' through Va Legislature) has been followed—in substance—in 36 states." Powell's criticism of the Williams Act in his draft concurrence did not make it into print, but not because of any doubts about the substance. At conference, Blackmun recorded Powell as saying "I do not like t[he] W[illiams Act . . . conglom[erate] s [and] t[ake]o[ver]s [a]r[e] a menace." Powell subsequently observed that, "I think the Williams Act has been a *disaster* as it encourages giant corps. to 'take over' smaller corps."[44] Powell seemed to equate Congress's grudging tolerance of tender offers in the Williams Act with encouragement, a reading difficult to square with the legislative history. Perhaps this was a plausible reading in a context in which the SEC was relying on the Williams Act to preserve a free market for corporate control (or at least a market controlled by the SEC, not the states).

Stevens's objection to White's preemption argument was more substantial:

I agree with you that when Congress enacted the Williams Act, it took extreme care to avoid tipping the scales . . . either in favor or [*sic*] management or in favor of possible takeovers. However, it seems to me that there is a significant difference between adopting such a policy of neutrality with respect to federal legislation that Congress was enacting, and requiring states to follow the same policy. As of now, I am not persuaded that Congress intended to prevent the states from loading the scales one way or the other. You are, of course, dead right in your analysis of the Illinois statute as being loaded in favor of management.

O'Connor, generally an advocate for federalism, thought that the "Williams Act did not preempt the state law because Congress had not expressed such an intent."[45]

The states went back to the drawing board after the twin setbacks in *MITE* and the SEC's adoption of its preemptive rules. Indiana's effort, challenged in *CTS Corp. v. Dynamics Corp. of America* in 1987 was typical of the second generation of anti-takeover statutes.[46] It required a potential acquirer (defined as anyone crossing any one of three certain threshold percentages of the company's shares) to obtain the approval of a company's "disinterested" shares (defined as shares not owned by the acquirer or management) before it would be allowed to vote its own shares. Thus, a hostile tender offeror was incentivized to seek voting approval from shareholders to gain control before pursuing the purchase route; previously, purchasing a majority of the shares had presented the fewest hurdles to acquiring control. The Indiana statute was more narrowly cast than the Illinois statute struck down in *MITE*. The Illinois statute applied to corporations with their principal executive offices in Illinois or that were incorporated in Illinois, as long as the corporation had the requisite number of shareholders in Illinois. The Indiana statute, by contrast, was limited to corporations organized under Indiana law, with their principal place of business and a substantial shareholder presence in that state.[47] It also lacked the requirement that the offer be approved by a state regulator, which had proved problematic in *MITE* and the SEC rulemaking had sought to preempt.

Those differences did not change the outcome in the Seventh Circuit. The appellate court went beyond the limited Commerce Clause holding in *MITE* to invalidate the Indiana statute on both Commerce Clause and preemption grounds. Needless to say, Powell strongly disagreed with Seventh Circuit Judge Richard Posner's enthusiasm for the economic benefits of tender offers. Powell saw the case as an opportunity to cut back on *MITE*'s preemptive dicta, but he was pessimistic about his chances of success. He was pleasantly surprised when there were four votes to note probable jurisdiction rather than affirm, but he still doubted that he could muster a majority on the merits.[48] After accounting for the views on the merits expressed in prior conference by justices who had ultimately voted for mootness in the preceding two cases, it still seemed that White could muster a majority to limit the Indiana statute on one of the two Dormant Commerce Clause holdings from *MITE*.

Powell remained anxious to curb the takeover wave that had surged again during the mid-1980s. He felt the Williams Act had been inadequate to the task: "I still adhere to my view that the Williams Act has become an economic disaster—a view that increasingly is being held by responsible economists. Indeed, hearings are now pending in the Congress to consider appropriate means of curbing takeover bids, and the bypassing in effect of antitrust laws."[49]

White's opinion in *MITE* loomed as a substantial obstacle to Powell's more mercantilist view of the market for corporate control. Powell now regretted his vote to give White a majority in *MITE*, but he nonetheless considered it controlling. In a memo shared with his clerk before oral argument, Powell described where he found himself:

> My brief concurring opinion in *MITE* summarizes my basic objections to the Williams Act and particularly the way it has been applied so expansively. But *MITE* is "the law," and I would find it difficult to sustain the complex Indiana Statute in light of the reasoning of the Court's opinion in *MITE*. If my law clerk has any ideas in this respect, they would be more than a little welcomed!

Powell needed a way around *MITE* to save the "beneficial" Indiana statute.[50]

242   A HISTORY OF SECURITIES LAW

His clerk found a path in the internal affairs doctrine. The doctrine had long prevailed in resolving conflict of laws issues, requiring other states to defer to the rules of the state of incorporation on matters of internal corporate governance. The law of the state of incorporation controlled in determining the relationship among the key actors under state corporate law: directors, shareholders, and officers. A parallel focus on internal governance underlay the deference to state law expressed in *Santa Fe*, although White did not invoke the internal affairs doctrine there. Powell's clerk identified the scope of the internal affairs doctrine as the critical issue in *CTS*:

> If you think State corporate governance should be limited strictly to laws that affect the attributes of shares and transactions by the corporation itself, you will find that Indiana has overstepped its bounds. On the other hand, if you think States legitimately can act to protect shareholders from being coerced in ways that effect major corporate changes, you will find the law satisfactory.[51]

Of course, under the internal affairs doctrine state law usually protected the autonomy of directors; director primacy has long been the foundation of state corporate law. The Indiana statute was framed to protect shareholder voting, but it was still internal under the traditional understanding of the doctrine. The second-generation statutes, limited to regulating shareholder voting in corporations incorporated in the enacting state, were more closely tethered to the traditional pattern of state corporate law. These statutes were narrower than earlier anti-takeover statutes, which had not limited their regulatory interventions to corporations organized under a particular state's law. The Indiana statute also omitted hearings before state regulators. The internal affairs doctrine could potentially be imported from the conflict of laws context to allow Powell to protect management from the threat of takeover.

Powell found himself with some unexpected allies at conference—Brennan, Marshall, and Rehnquist, who thought the Idaho and Illinois statutes in the prior cases were preempted by the Williams Act, saw no conflict between the Indiana statute and federal law. Nor did they see a problem under the Dormant Commerce Clause. Moreover, Scalia, appointed after Chief Justice Burger's retirement, saw no preemption issue and took a much narrower view of the reach of the Dormant Commerce Clause. O'Connor shared Powell's federalism streak. The result was a 6-3 majority to uphold the Indiana statute, with now Chief Justice Rehnquist giving Powell the assignment. White, Blackmun, and Stevens were in dissent. Blackmun's conference notes record Powell as saying "C[orporation]s creatures of the St[ate] etc, + supreme."[52]

After two tries, the Court had arrived at a federalism position that provided states considerable room to limit takeovers, despite the federal Williams Act and the Constitution. Powell's opinion for the Court emphasized the analogy between Indiana's voting procedure for tender offers and shareholder votes that had long been required by state corporate law for mergers or asset sales. Voting requirements are a traditional means allowing shareholders to veto bad deals. To be sure, mergers in particular pose a risk of unfair valuation because they lack the market test provided by tender offers, but Powell's analogy is at least plausible. Expropriation is a risk only with "two-tier" tender offers, in which a lower back-end price may induce shareholders to tender at the front end even if they deem the offered consideration inadequate. Powell recognized "that the percentage that really are coercive is relatively small." The opinion cloaks the weakness of this point in deference to the "empirical judgments of lawmakers." To be sure, distinguishing permissible uses of shareholder voting from impermissible uses would have been difficult for a court.[53]

More fundamentally, state authority over voting rights, as filtered through the tradition of the internal affairs doctrine, avoided the potential conflicts that might have created a Dormant Commerce Clause problem:

> So long as each State regulates voting rights only in the corporations it has created, each corporation will be subject to the law of only one State. No principle of corporation law and practice is more firmly established than a State's authority to regulate domestic corps, including the voting rights of shareholders.[54]

By implication, that tradition meant the SEC's authority in this area was questionable absent explicit legislative authorization.

Powell saw the balancing of state interests against the burden on interstate commerce as relatively straightforward. In his view:

> [The Indiana] regulations . . . will be relatively ease [*sic*] for tender offering corporations to comply with if their offers are agruably [*sic*] beneficial to the Indiana corporation and its shareholders. It is not easy to see any "burden" other than possible delay in bringing a tender offer to fruition—hardly a significant burden on a reasonable and beneficial tender proposal.

Powell discounts here the significant costs that delay can impose on an offeror, both in terms of financing and time for target management to obstruct bids or seek out a "white knight." These risks increase substantially if a tender offer must be held open for fifty days, rather than the twenty required by the Williams Act. The draft opinion asserted that:

> If a majority of the target company's shareholders think the offer is attractive, it is likely that a majority will tender their shares on the twentieth business day,

## 244  A HISTORY OF SECURITIES LAW

and that a majority of the target company's shareholders will vote to accord voting rights to the offeror so that the transaction can be consummated. Once the shares are tendered, the opportunities for incumbent management to defeat the tender offer by lobbying its own shareholders are greatly reduced.[55]

Powell seems on shaky ground here; at best his conjecture about shareholder behavior is speculation, at worst it is implausible. Why would a shareholder tender at the earliest point, rather than waiting to see if a better offer from a third party emerged while the vote was pending? An offeror would certainly take into account the risk of losing its target in determining whether to launch a bid at all. Powell's corporate law experience, grounded in the more leisurely dealmaking pace of the 1950s and 1960s, was badly out of date in the junk-bond-fueled 1980s. Powell cut this passage before circulation to the other justices.

Another discarded passage provides further evidence that Powell was out of touch with the eighties takeover market:

> It may well be that a successful tender offer will result in more effective management or may have such other benefits as providing needed diversification. Yet, we know of no convincing evidence that the type of conglomerates that may result from repetitive take over offers are in fact more efficient or that the owners of shares in the resulting conglomerate are benefited [sic].

Powell is responding to the 1960s takeovers wave, in which unrelated businesses were combined into diversified conglomerates. He was rightly skeptical that shareholders would benefit from these transactions. The takeovers of the 1980s, however, were often driven by efficiency gains from breaking up those conglomerates (or horizontal or vertical synergies), and the evidence that shareholders benefited from this process was simply overwhelming. The note was toned down in the final opinion.[56]

Despite Powell's victory, state anti-takeover statutes became an afterthought after *CTS*. Innovative lawyers pioneered new governance rules that relied on directors' authority under state law to ward off tender offers. In the years immediately before *CTS*, Martin Lipton had popularized the poison pill using traditional state law powers of the board in previously unforeseen (and indirect) ways. To implement a poison pill, the board of a target company issues to its shareholders a "right" or "warrant" to purchase a fraction of a preferred share on financial terms calibrated to make the option unattractive. But the right is a placeholder that lies dormant until a hostile bidder shows up when the right "flips" into a right available to all the shareholders—except the hostile bidder—to buy shares in the corporation (or the bidder corporation) at a bargain price. This is the "poison" that greatly dilutes the value of the bidder's previous investment

CORPORATE GOVERNANCE 245

in the company as well as the voting power of the shares it has already purchased. In addition, triggering a poison pill and issuing the new shares would dramatically increase the funds needed to purchase a majority of shares in the target company. The Delaware Supreme Court had already blessed this new tactic by the time of *CTS*, subject to enhanced judicial review. That supposedly enhanced judicial review has proved often illusory, with the result that the poison pill now blocks almost all tender offers that lack the consent of the incumbent board. The reasoning of *CTS* insulates such private ordering under state corporate common law from attack under federal law, parallel to the Court's holding as to the state statutes. When combined with a staggered board, the poison pill became unassailable, a result foreshadowed by Powell in *CTS*.[57] *CTS*, when combined with the contemporary changes in state law, proved to be the death knell of hostile takeovers and the free market for corporate control.

## E. Post-1987, Post-Powell Drift

Concern for state corporate law had a more visible role in *Virginia Bankshares, Inc. v. Sandberg* decided in 1991.[58] Plaintiff shareholders sought to pursue fiduciary claims arising from alleged mistreatment in a traditional merger context, also asserting disclosure violations in a proxy statement covered by § 14(a). The merger was intended to cash out minority shareholders in a bank with a controlling shareholder already owning 85% of the shares. With that supermajority, the vote of the minority shareholders was not necessary to approve the merger under state corporate law. The Fourth Circuit's opinion (and the jury instructions at trial) could have been written in the sixties, relying on that era's permissive interpretations of causation and recovery under § 14(a). The appellate court seemed not to have noticed how *Blue Chip*, *Ernst & Ernst*, and *Santa Fe* had narrowed the interpretation of the federal securities laws in the seventies.

The Court heard the case on David Souter's first day on the bench in October and he was assigned the opinion. The writing apparently proved challenging, however, as the decision did not come down until the last day of the term. All nine justices had little difficulty concluding that statements of opinion could be the basis for a fraud claim, at least when the opinion was based on verifiable facts. They also agreed that the directors' opinion was material based on the directors' fiduciary responsibilities to the shareholders and access to information.

The divisive issue was whether the plaintiff could establish transaction causation (sometimes categorized as reliance). This was an issue that Harlan had dealt with in *Mills v. Electric Auto-Lite Co.* somewhat vaguely—but expansively— adopting an "essential link" standard.[59] Causation brought the Court back to a discussion of the relationship between federal and state law: the vote of the minority shareholders was not necessary to approve the merger under Virginia corporate law. If their votes did not count, how were they harmed by the violation of federal disclosure standards? The plaintiff offered two theories when the case got to the Supreme Court. The first was that the merging companies would have wanted to avoid the bad public relations of a negative vote from the shareholders. Harlan's opinion in *Mills* had raised, without deciding, the possibility that management soliciting for practical reasons, even if it did not need to do so, could meet the "essential link" standard. For a post-*Blue Chip* Court worried by vexatious litigation, the public relations theory was a step too far. The majority rejected it as raising "[t]he same threats of speculative claims and procedural intractability" that lead the Court to limit Rule 10b-5 standing to actual purchasers or sellers in *Blue Chip*.

Scalia, who acknowledged a willingness to accept an expansion beyond the common law to cover opinions nonetheless, wrote separately to say implied causes of action should be interpreted narrowly. For him, the task was not statutory interpretation, but rather, more akin to damage control.

> I recognize the Court's disallowance . . . of an action for misrepresentation of belief is entirely contrary to the modern law of torts . . . I have no problem with departing from modern tort law in this regard, because I think the federal cause of action at issue here was never enacted by Congress . . . and hence the more narrow we make it (within the bound of rationality) the more faithful we are to our task.

Kennedy, in dissent, charged the majority with engaging in "a sort of guerrilla warfare to restrict a well-established implied right of action."

The second theory was based on a loss of state remedies to provide the necessary connection between the nondisclosure and the plaintiff's harm for misstatements in a proxy. Souter's first draft implied a substantial narrowing of federal law, providing a remedy only if state law did not: "the would-be plaintiff makes no case for the equity of providing a federal cause of action when state corporate law addresses the same subject by providing a remedy for the harm the plaintiff claims." This would have been a startling departure from *Borak*, which had brushed aside the possibility of overlapping state and federal remedies. White had joined the Court's opinion in *Borak* at a time when he had little more experience than Souter did at the time of *Virginia Bankshares*. The veteran now pointed out that "If there is a §14(a) violation that causes damages, I doubt, for example, that recovery would be barred if state law also provided a remedy." O'Connor agreed with White. Souter stepped back, refocusing the test on the transaction causation required when the vote outcome is not affected by the alleged deception. He suggested a revision on the

CORPORATE GOVERNANCE 247

"narrower ground . . . that equity does not require duplication of surviving state law remedies, and that respondents demonstrate no cognizable causation by reference to state law on ratification of avoidable transactions when they show no loss of state remedy." The change secured Souter the votes of White, Rehnquist, and O'Connor.[60]

White's coaching of his rookie colleague was not done. Souter's next draft began the discussion of state law remedies with:

> The occasion of this case does not, however, require to pass upon the wisdom of providing a federal back-up under § 14(a) for lost state remedies, since there is no indication in the law or facts before us that the proxy solicitation resulted in any such loss.

White, a plain-speaking Westerner, offered a shorter version of the opening clause: "This case does not however require us to decide whether § 14(a) provides a cause of action for lost state remedies. . . ."[61] Sometimes less is more. Souter adopted his senior colleague's suggestion.

The reference to duplication of surviving state law remedies was dropped entirely in the final opinion; the relationship between federal remedies and lost state remedies was reserved for another day. Kennedy, in dissent, joined by Marshall, Blackmun, and Stevens, found no difficulty in the later question as "the whole point of federal proxy rules is to support state law principles of corporate governance." Kennedy fought a rear-guard action to dismiss the causation issue as improvidently granted, but Souter was able to hold his majority for the narrowed holding.[62] The majority opinion's invocation of *Blue Chip* to reject the reputational causation argument, its recognition that omission would sometimes come within misrepresentation of facts and thus covered by existing materiality standards, and its leaving lost state remedies for another day, captures neatly the Court's approach after Powell's departure. The Court accepted key holdings from both the sixties and seventies; sometimes the result would be expansive, other times restrictive, with Kennedy in Powell's seat contributing to the inconsistencies.

A year later the Second Circuit found that the loss of appraisal rights tied to nondisclosure would trigger a federal remedy, upholding prior circuit precedent decided both before and after *Santa Fe*: "that the causal nexus between the merger and the proxy is absent when the minority shareholders' vote cannot affect the merger decision does not necessarily mean a causal link between the proxy and some other injury may not exist."[63] The Supreme Court has yet to decide that issue. Also ignored by the Court has been the adjacent question, discussed earlier, regarding the applicability of Rule 10b-5 when there is both nondisclosure and corporate mismanagement. These questions have slipped into borderline irrelevance.

248 A HISTORY OF SECURITIES LAW

The Court has resolved, however, an issue of a lost *federal* remedy with enormous economic implications for state shareholder litigation. *Matsushita Elec. Indus. Co. Ltd. v. Epstein* involved competing shareholder class actions arising out of a tender offer, one in state court and the other in federal court.[64] The question for the Court was whether a judgment from the Delaware Court of Chancery approving a class action settlement purporting to bar federal law claims was entitled to full faith and credit in federal court. The twist was that the claims that would be barred by the state court judgment included claims based on the Exchange Act, and the Exchange Act provides for exclusive federal jurisdiction.[65] In other words, the state court purported to bar claims that it could not have adjudicated on the merits. No matter, said the Supreme Court, per Thomas. It read the Full Faith and Credit Act[66] to require that a federal court give the same preclusive effect to a state court judgment as a state court would. And it found no implied repeal of the Full Faith and Credit Act in the Exchange Act's grant of exclusive federal jurisdiction. (The latter holding echoed the Court's confined reading of the jurisdictional provision in connection with the Federal Arbitration Act that we saw in *Shearson/American Express, Inc. McMahon*[67] in Chapter 6.) The Court's decision gave certainty to class action judgments, thereby encouraging settlement by allowing defendants to obtain "universal peace." It created the possibility, however, of a "reverse auction," with faithless plaintiff attorneys competing to settle their cases first to ensure a fee at the expense of their rivals.

After *Virginia Bankshares* and *Matsushita*, the Court's federalism cases reflect Congress's more active role in securities law after 1995. That year, the Private Securities Litigation Reform Act added a bevy of new substantive and procedural restrictions on private law suits under Rule 10b-5. When opportunistic plaintiffs' lawyers shifted to bringing more suits under state law, Congress added new legislation—the Securities Litigation Uniform Standards Act (SLUSA)—to preclude state law class actions in connection with the purchase or sale of "covered" (that is, nationally traded) securities. A quartet of twenty-first-century Supreme Court cases under this act, reflect congressional "sensitivity to state prerogatives," but they do not move the larger federalism debate very much. In *Merrill, Lynch v. Dabit* a unanimous Court held SLUSA precluded a state law class action alleging manipulation of stock prices influencing holders' decisions about covered stocks. A few months later the Court declined to find SLUSA's removal provision overrode a generic federal procedural rule blocking appeal when a trial court remands a case to state court.[68] The appellate court, in an opinion by Frank Easterbrook, had upheld appellate jurisdiction, describing the case as "the very sort of maneuver that SLUSA is designed to prevent." If so, the design was poor. All the justices agreed on the procedural disposition.[69]

Two cases during the last decade permitted suits to continue in state court, notwithstanding SLUSA, because Congress intended to "purposefully maintain

CORPORATE GOVERNANCE    249

state legal authority, especially over matters that are primarily of state concern." In *Chadbourne & Parke LLP v. Troice*, the Court found the "covered securities" in that case as too tangential to the "uncovered" CDs at the center of the Ponzi scheme for preclusion to be triggered.[70] The majority analogized the case to two other "in connection with" cases, one of which declined to apply securities law to an ordinary state law breach of contract claim, with the other declining to embrace a broad interpretation that would "convert any common law fraud case that happens to involve securities."[71] Kennedy's dissent, joined by Alito, cites staples of the 1960s and thereafter such as *Capital Gains*, *Silver*, *Affiliated Ute*, and *O'Hagan*. The restrictive and expansive wings of the Court seemed to have traded citation books in this case. The more recent case, *Cyan, Inc. v. Beaver County Employees Retirement Fund* most clearly illustrates how these SLUSA cases turn on the specific statutory language.[72] The Securities Act, in contrast to the Exchange Act, explicitly provides for claims under that Act to be brought in state as well as federal courts.[73] The failure of SLUSA to undo this grant of jurisdiction meant the statute had no effect on federal-law claims brought in state court. Only state claims brought in state court fall under SLUSA's axe. The failure of SLUSA to take these federal claims out of state court was likely a legislative oversight, but the Court was no longer in the business of effecting statutory purpose absent textual support. If Congress had made a mistake, the Court was not going to fix it.

After tackling litigation reform in 1995, Congress turned to corporate governance. The federal incursions into corporate governance began with the Sarbanes-Oxley Act in 2002 and were followed by the Dodd-Frank Act of 2010. Those laws, each adopted in response to the crisis du jour, were Congress's first intrusions into corporate governance traditionally left to the states since 1940. For public companies, federal law now (1) specifies board structure, including audit, nominating and compensation committees, and a majority of independent directors; and 2) requires precatory shareholder voting on executive compensation ("say on pay"). Moreover, companies are now obliged to explain their ethics policies for officers and directors, and if they combine the chair and CEO position, why. These incursions are reinforced by the SEC's long-standing proxy proposal rules providing shareholders access to the company's proxy to make corporate governance recommendations.

Questions arising from Congress's recent corporate governance interventions have not yet made their way to the Supreme Court. In 2010 the SEC adopted a rule providing a federal path to ease the ability of shareholders to nominate directors. While the rule was pending, the Dodd-Frank Act specifically granted the agency authority over the area. The D.C. Circuit subsequently set aside the rulemaking, not for interfering with state law, but as "arbitrary and capricious" in violation of the Administrative Procedure Act for insufficient consideration of the rule's economic consequences.[74] The government did not seek certiorari.

# F. Conclusion

Constitutional challenges to the New Deal securities statutes to keep the federal government from interfering with state authority over corporate governance failed, with the Court upholding a fundamental reorientation of federal power. Congress's failure to enact a federal incorporation statute in the 1930s, however, left room for the Supreme Court of the seventies to declare federalism-based limits on judicially implied private litigation rights in *Santa Fe*. In the subsequent four decades, Congress made new inroads into corporate governance at the expense of state law. The legislative effort targeted discrete issues, still far short of full federal preemption of state corporate law. The line between state and federal authority has become more precise; Congress has become more explicit in creating private actions. The result has been a much narrower role for the Supreme Court. The one exception still marked by a very blurred line is insider trading—the subject of Chapter 5—where Lewis Powell's decision in the *Chiarella* case in 1980 made some insider trading a violation of federal law but suggested that coverage was limited. The more recent *O'Hagan* and *Zandford* cases went past *Chiarella's* limits to federalize a broader prohibition. Both of those cases overturned lower court decisions that had relied on breach of fiduciary duty being a matter of state law.[75] The federal corporate law of the type created by the Supreme Court and Second Circuit in the 1960s, however, has yet to experience a renaissance. Given the current Supreme Court's deference to Congress in this area, any move to displace state law in the field of corporate governance is likely to come from the legislature, not the Court.

# 8

# Conclusion

## How the Supreme Court Makes Securities Laws

This book has examined how the Supreme Court makes securities law. For our study, we dug into the justices' internal correspondence, conference notes, memos, and opinion drafts. Those sources highlight what might be obscured if one read only published opinions—for example, the flip in result in *Variable Annuity* and *Central Bank* when the justice assigned to write the opinion changed his mind in the course of writing. We also see critical interventions from justices *not* writing the opinion—White's suggestion of fiduciary duty in *Capital Gains* and O'Connor's suggestion of personal benefit in *Dirks*. At a deeper level, we also see that text and statutory structure mattered to the justices in interpreting the securities laws, but for the justices most interested in securities law, policy mattered at least as much.

In this chapter we expand on two threads visible throughout the book. One is how the Court's view of the securities laws and the SEC changed over time. After decades favoring expansive readings, the Court shifted to skepticism under the influence of Powell, followed by a period of relative equipoise after Powell retired. The second is the influence that individual justices have had on the path of securities law. Lewis Powell stands out in this regard. The flip side of this coin is the lack of influence from other justices who might have been expected to be leaders in the field, most notably Felix Frankfurter—closely involved in drafting the key securities laws—and Bill Douglas, a former chairman of the SEC. Those two appointees had the most direct experience with securities law, but they had surprisingly little impact on the field during their time on the Court. The New Deal period shows, however, that it is not just the individuals that matter, but also how the justices interacted as a group. The common bond of the nine Roosevelt appointees (except Stone who was elevated to Chief Justice) was their work building the New Deal's expansion of the administrative state and then defending it from legal attack. This shared front-line experience overshadowed the lack of effective involvement of Frankfurter and Douglas. Powell dominated his era, but that period also demonstrates the critical importance of counting to five in Supreme Court lawmaking. In almost every securities case during the early years of Powell's tenure there were four reliable votes for a restrictive

*A History of Securities Law in the Supreme Court.* A.C. Pritchard and Robert B. Thompson, Oxford University Press.
© Oxford University Press 2023. DOI: 10.1093/oso/9780197665916.003.0009

252 A HISTORY OF SECURITIES LAW

interpretation (Powell, Rehnquist, Stewart, and Burger). But securing a majority entailed persuading justices like White, Marshall, or Blackmun, who in the prior period had joined in some of the most expansive opinions of our study. Attracting the median justice was key in *Ernst & Ernst* and *Santa Fe*, pivotal cases from the seventies that occupy a central place in our story.

Powell's ability to secure a consistent majority is set in sharp relief by developments after his retirement. Without a justice having knowledge or specific interest in securities law, the Court produced a seemingly random pattern of results. Thus, our narrative provides three distinct illustrations of the Court at work: one driven by ideological consensus, the second dominated by an individual with expertise unmatched by his colleagues, and the third seemingly random. These patterns not only tell us about the development of securities law, but offer insights into other parts of the Court's docket, particularly regulatory areas.

## A. The Tale of the Numbers

The table included in the Introduction summarized the federal securities cases decided by the Supreme Court: 134 since the enactment of the Securities Act in 1933. There we introduced the three distinct periods in the Court's approach to securities issues. That table crystallized the overall trends that we have seen throughout the book. For three and a half decades after the adoption of the securities laws, starting with Roosevelt's first appointment in 1937, the Court was dominated by New Deal veterans, committed to social control of finance. That ended with Lewis Powell's arrival in 1972, ushering in a decade and a half of profound skepticism toward the SEC and a sustained effort to limit the reach of the securities laws. Restrictive decisions were the norm for this era. Powell's retirement in 1987 left a void on the Supreme Court in the field of securities law. Since 1987, there has been no justice with meaningful prior experience with the securities laws, either as a regulator or in private practice. That absence of an experienced hand left the Court to meander in the field of securities law, with no dominant trend other than, perhaps, a general desire to defer to Congress. Expansive and restrictive decisions are equally balanced.

Here we add several tables that illuminate the trend of decisions. For these tables, we include cases in which the SEC is a party or amicus; criminal cases arising under the securities law, and private litigation in which the claim, or the principal defense, is based on the securities laws. (We provide a complete list in the Appendix.) Part of the explanation for the change in outcomes reflects significant changes in the subject matter of the Court's decisions over time.

## U.S. Supreme Court Decisions by Category

| Years | Cases | Securities Act | Exchange Act | PUHCA & Bankruptcy | Definition of "Security" | Misc.* |
|---|---|---|---|---|---|---|
| 1933–April 1972 | 44 | 7 | 9 | 15 + 6 | 5 | 2 |
| May 1972– June 1987 | 45 | 2 | 29 | 0 | 5 | 9 |
| Oct. 1987– July 2021 | 45 | 5 | 31 | 0 | 2 | 7 |
| Total | 134 | 14 | 69 | 21 | 12 | 18 |

* Miscellaneous includes Trust Indenture Act, Investment Advisers Act, Investment Company Act, and Securities Investor Protection Act.

The trend in the Court's cases reflects the shift in political attitudes toward social control of finance. The Roosevelt administration's two most expansive governmental intrusions into business, PUHCA and the Chandler Act, dominated the early period, but disappeared from the Court's docket by the late 1960s. Instead of being harbingers of broader governmental intervention into corporate governance, in hindsight these laws look like regulatory blips before the securities laws settled into the disclosure-focused paradigm familiar to modern securities lawyers. That contemporary version of securities law emphasizes antifraud enforcement, both public and private.

PUHCA, which tasked the SEC with restructuring an industry vital to the economy, faded in importance as all of the nation's public utility conglomerates were broken up by the 1950s. The SEC had largely accomplished its job executing PUHCA's "death penalty." A generation later, narrow interpretations and deregulation undid much of the work accomplished by the SEC in breaking up the holding companies. New utility conglomerates emerged with diverse business interests and sprawling operations. PUHCA's purpose—the Brandeisian assault on "bigness"—was largely repudiated, and the Act itself was repealed in 2005. The Chandler Act, which put the SEC at the center of corporate reorganizations, was replaced by the 1978 Bankruptcy Reform Act, which did not provide any role for the SEC beyond disclosure.[1] The repeal of these two laws deprived the SEC of the roles that had given it an important say in corporate structure. The agency's remaining responsibilities were the disclosure-focused regulation of the Securities Act and the Exchange Act, along with overseeing market structure.

254   A HISTORY OF SECURITIES LAW

The Sarbanes-Oxley Act, included here under the Exchange Act category, has recently increased the role of the securities laws in corporate governance, but the Court had heard only two cases involving that law in the twenty years since its adoption. Moreover, its incremental governance reforms, responding to particular scandals, hardly portend a move toward federal incorporation as PUHCA and the Chandler Act arguably did.

As the social control of finance cases wound down, private litigation filled the gap in the Court's securities docket. Private suits had been 30% of the Court's securities docket in the early period but jumped to more than two-thirds in the latter two periods. The sharp increase in the number of private litigation cases flowed from the Court's recognition of the implied rights of action under Rule 10b-5 and Rule 14a-9 beginning in the 1960s. The restrictive trend in the Court's decisions during the Powell era jumps out here. Once again, after Powell's retirement, the Court shifts toward a rough equipoise in private securities litigation.

The SEC has been a key player in securities litigation before the Supreme Court. The agency's results shed additional light on the trends reflected in the last table. As the PUHCA and Chandler Act cases dried up, SEC enforcement actions grew as a percentage of the Court's securities docket.

## SEC Win/Loss Rate in the Supreme Court

| Years | Cases | Expansive | Restrictive | Neither |
|---|---|---|---|---|
| 1933—Apr. 1972 | 30 | 24 | 3 | 3 |
| May 1972–June 1987 | 8 | 3 | 5 | 0 |
| Oct. 1987–July 2021 | 7 | 3 | 3 | 1 |
| Total | 45 | 29 | 12 | 4 |

Includes all cases in which the SEC is a party or intervenor.

The expansive trend we saw from 1933 to 1972 is even more dramatic when we focus just on cases involving the SEC. When the SEC was a litigant in the Supreme Court, the agency came away with only three restrictive decisions in its first thirty-eight years with expansive decisions outnumbering restrictive by a factor of eight. Powell's appointment flipped the trend, with restrictive decisions outpacing expansive. Since Powell's retirement, decisions in which the SEC is a party have been equally split, consistent with the overall numbers.[2] The United States fares even better in its criminal securities cases before the Court, albeit in modest numbers.

## U.S. Criminal Securities Law Win/Loss Rate in the Supreme Court

| Years | Cases | Expansive | Restrictive | Neither |
|---|---|---|---|---|
| 1933–Apr. 1972 | 1 | 1 | 0 | 0 |
| May 1972–June 1987 | 3 | 2 | 1 | 0 |
| Oct. 1987–July 2020 | 2 | 2 | 0 | 0 |
| Total | 6 | 5 | 1 | 0 |

The SEC regularly appears as an amicus in securities cases brought by private litigants. The SEC's participation rate, which was more than 96% of the Court's securities cases through 1972 (forty-two of forty-four), drops to about two-thirds for cases since then. The SEC's position in these cases is overwhelmingly expansionist across all periods; we identified only six cases in which the SEC argued for a more restrictive view, none before 1973.[3]

## SEC as Amicus in Private Securities Litigation in the Supreme Court

| SEC Amicus | Cases | Expansive | Restrictive | Neither |
|---|---|---|---|---|
| 1933–Apr. 1972 | 12 | 8 | 4 | 0 |
| May 1972–June 1987 | 23 | 9 | 13 | 1 |
| Oct. 1987–July 2021 | 27 | 14 | 11 | 2 |
| Total | 62 | 31 | 28 | 3 |

The SEC's support for private plaintiffs does seem to make a difference. When the SEC participates at the Supreme Court, the case results are roughly balanced, but when the SEC stays on the sidelines, the ratio skews dramatically toward restrictive decisions. The exception is the Powell era. Powell was suspicious of the SEC's support for private class actions: "SEC usually favors *all* π. I can't recall a case in which this was not so."[4] Powell's influence with his colleagues meant that the SEC's influence was attenuated.

## B. A Reliable Court

Why did the Court read the federal securities laws so generously for so long after the end of the New Deal? The answer lies in Franklin Delano Roosevelt's

256    A HISTORY OF SECURITIES LAW

strategic skill as a judge picker. Presidents regularly have set out to mold the Supreme Court to implement the administration's goals, with varying degrees of success. For Roosevelt, the challenge was more salient than for his successors, both because he initially faced a Court hostile to the New Deal agenda and because his agenda was more aggressive than his successors. To his great frustration, he had no vacancies arise until into his second term. Roosevelt viewed the Court as just another political branch, and he looked for justices who would vote his way.[5] And his appointees did vote his way. The New Deal Court delivered in validating political control over finance, a legislative priority for his administration. Looking back, perhaps the most striking feature of the New Deal Court's work in the field of securities law is how reliable the Court was in accomplishing Roosevelt's agenda—FDR's legacy was continued for twenty-five years after his death.

The eight men Roosevelt added to the Court (filling one seat twice) each accepted Roosevelt's new role for government in the nation's economy. Stone's elevation to Chief Justice was no exception to this pattern. Although a Republican holdover, Stone had long railed against judicial activism by the old Court and he shared his new colleagues' belief in judicial deference to political control over finance. Roosevelt's appointments quickly eviscerated the old Court's resistance to New Deal initiatives. By the early forties, the Court had baldly announced it was granting Congress essentially unlimited latitude in economic regulation. That repudiation of the Court's earlier skepticism toward incursions on freedom of contract persists as a bedrock constitutional principle to this day.

Amidst the drama of that sweeping constitutional victory for the New Deal, it is easy to overlook the new deference to administrative agencies like the SEC that came with it. The Court gave the SEC an unfettered hand as it asserted governmental control over finance. After the *Jones* case in 1936, private ordering was swept aside with the Court's blessing. More than three decades would pass before the Supreme Court made any sustained effort to rein in the SEC and the reach of the securities laws. Frankfurter, an apostle of administrative law before his appointment to the Court, could not muster consistent support for his effort to bring judicial scrutiny to bear on the agency. *Chenery I* proved to be a short-lived aberration in a string of nearly three dozen wins for the SEC and/or an expansive view of securities laws.

The SEC's long win streak is all the more remarkable in light of the fact that no individual justice was leading the fight for Roosevelt's priorities in finance. The two justices who might have led the Court based on their deep experience and scholarship in the area, Frankfurter and Douglas, exercised very little influence. We explore that topic below. Murphy, who had a political tussle with the electric utilities while serving as governor of Michigan, ended up with a recurring role in the PUHCA cases that dominated the 1940s. Given his relative lack of experience in the field of finance and the low regard that his brethren had for his abilities, it is hard to ascribe a leadership role to Murphy in this area.[6] His role instead arose due to numerous recusals by his brethren, most notably Douglas, limiting the pool of available opinion writers. Murphy's PUHCA opinions reflect a broad consensus—forged in experiences that the New Deal Justices brought to the Court—that judges should defer to the SEC and allow the expert agency to develop securities law. That broad consensus favoring social control of finance shows up not only in the outcomes of the Court's cases, but also in the vote margins. The table below shows the voting balance in securities cases for our three periods.

## Votes in U.S. Supreme Court Securities Cases

| Years | Cases | Unanimous | 8-1, 7-2, 7-1, 6-2, 6-1, 5-2 | 6-3, 5-4, 5-3, 4-3, 4-2 |
|---|---|---|---|---|
| 1933–Apr. 1972 | 44 | 17 | 19 | 8 |
| May 1972–June 1987 | 45 | 17 | 11 | 17 |
| Oct. 1987–July 2021[7] | 45 | 20 | 8 | 17 |
| Total | 134 | 54 | 38 | 42 |

The Court's securities decisions provoked little disagreement before 1972. Only eight decisions (less than 20% of the total) generated any substantial opposition, notwithstanding the bitter personal acrimony among the justices during the forties. During the Powell period, by contrast, the number of close decisions more than doubles.

Why did Roosevelt have such success translating his appointments into favorable outcomes? His appointees shared several key characteristics. First, most had had prior advocacy positions in the executive branch, which proved to be a reliable barometer of a justice's future leanings. Most obviously, Douglas headed the SEC. On the legal side, Jackson served as both Solicitor General and Attorney General, among other high-level positions at Treasury and Justice. He had been detailed from Treasury, at FDR's direction, to lead the initial litigation defense of PUHCA in 1935. Reed served as general counsel to the Reconstruction Finance Corporation and then Solicitor General. He and Jackson both played key roles arguing significant

258 A HISTORY OF SECURITIES LAW

securities cases before the Court. Murphy had made his name as an Assistant U.S. Attorney prosecuting war graft; after a variety of stops, he would rise all the way to Attorney General before his appointment to the Court.[8] Black lacked executive branch experience, but his record in the Senate—including his bitter attack on the utility industry in the fight over PUHCA—provided a reliable predictor of his future judicial attitudes. Frankfurter was the most skeptical of the justices toward the SEC, but he mocked the hostility expressed by the Old Guard in *Jones* and never came close to matching it. He had served briefly in government before undertaking an academic career, and his recurring informal service to FDR produced at least some bonding effect similar to that produced by holding a formal office in the executive branch. Only Rutledge came from an appellate court, the typical path for modern justices, after serving as a corporate law professor and dean, but he wholeheartedly bought into the New Deal agenda. The bottom line: Roosevelt's appointees enthusiastically endorsed his vision of government management of the economy ravaged by the Great Depression.

Second, Roosevelt clearly had a "litmus test": He picked nominees who had already proved their loyalty on the Court-packing plan, the administration's frontal assault on the old Court. Reed helped draft the bill. Jackson was a key administration witness in the congressional hearings. Black was a principal lieutenant to the Senate's majority leader, Joe Robinson, in this debate, and stood with the administration even when the bill's prospects began to erode in the Senate. Byrnes, also a senator, likewise supported the plan. Douglas quickly enlisted in the administration's efforts to push the plan. Frankfurter—with Roosevelt's blessing—was silent in the face of overwhelming pressure to speak against the plan, including from his own wife. Privately critical of the plan to Cohen and Corcoran, he offered strategic counsel behind the scenes, suggesting his approval to Roosevelt in a characteristically sycophantic letter. Frankfurter's public silence may have ensured his appointment.[9] A willingness to stomach the deeply controversial Court-packing plan demonstrated genuine commitment to constraining judicial interference with the prerogatives of the political branches.

Third, Roosevelt knew his nominees personally. They were trusted advisors, both in defending the New Deal against judicial attack and on the question of Court appointments. By and large they were a mutual admiration society before their appointment to the Court. Frankfurter and Douglas each pushed for the appointment of the other to the Court. Later, they would become bitter enemies. Jackson pushed for Frankfurter's nomination. Both Jackson and Murphy pushed for Douglas. Murphy, Black, and Douglas pushed for Rutledge, although Frankfurter lobbied for Learned Hand. Frankfurter had urged the appointment of Reed as Solicitor General. And the justices' relationships with the President did not end when they were appointed to the Court. Frankfurter, Douglas, Murphy, and Jackson continued to advise the President, and Douglas and Jackson were regulars in the President's poker game.[10]

Fourth, Roosevelt's appointees were not just politically astute, but ambitious. Douglas was plotting to seek the vice presidency in 1944 and in 1948. Black believed his prior Klan association knocked him out of the vice presidency in 1944. Murphy, the former Governor of Michigan, retained presidential ambitions after moving to Washington. Jackson had been talked of as Roosevelt's choice as a successor had FDR adhered to George Washington's limit of serving only two terms. Contradicting the Roosevelt administration on a key aspect of the New Deal agenda likely would not have played well for any of them.[11] Only Frankfurter was immune to the siren song of political ambition; his Austrian birth meant he could never attain the top rung of political life.

This combination of executive branch experience, trial by fire during the Court-packing battle, political advising, and political ambition produced justices who were of one mind with Roosevelt on the central question of government control over the economy. Appointments in the intervening decades have seen Presidents coming to regret their choices. Eisenhower's appointments of Warren and Brennan stand out in this regard. Roosevelt did not live long enough to see the decades of service by Black, Frankfurter, and Douglas, but his nominees certainly gave him no cause for similar regret during his lifetime, or after. Roosevelt's justices transformed the Court, removing it as an obstacle to social control of finance.

## C. The Puzzle of Frankfurter and Douglas

Given the general consensus on the Court favoring the New Deal effort to curb Wall Street, why did Felix Frankfurter—one of its foremost apostles before his judicial appointment—exercise so little influence? Frankfurter rejected the label "New Deal Justice,"[12] and in the field of securities law at least, he did little to advance the cause. Among justices participating in ten or more securities cases, only Douglas, Harlan, and Stevens found themselves more often in dissent than Frankfurter. Frankfurter wrote only one majority opinion for the Court in a securities case during his twenty-three years, the *Chenery I* decision in Chapter 3. Even that result was reversed four years later. Frank Murphy would end up writing six in a career that that spanned less than ten years.

**Figure 8.1**
**The Professor:** Felix Frankfurter had extensive experience in administrative and securities law at Harvard before his appointment to the Supreme Court, but his efforts as justice to educate his colleagues—and his professorial tone—tended to alienate them.

Given Frankfurter's scholarly interest in administrative law and public utilities, and the key role he had played lobbying for the securities legislation, he might have been expected to lead the Court in the field. As it played out, Frankfurter's vision of administrative law had little attraction for his colleagues. Frankfurter is remembered as an advocate of judicial restraint, but his conservatism principally manifested itself with respect to constitutional issues. He was more willing to assert himself when interpreting statutes. He wrote to Black early in their tenure:

> Judges, as you well know, cannot escape the responsibility of filling in gaps which the finitude of even the most imaginative legislation renders inevitable.... I think one of the evil features, a very evil one, about all this assumption that judges only find the law and don't make it, often becomes the evil of a lack of candor. By covering up the limited lawmaking function of judges, we miseducate the people and fail to bring out into the open the real responsibility of judges for what they do, leaving it to the primary lawmaking agency, the legislature, to correct what judges do if they don't like it, or to give them more specific directions than what they do often do by what is put on the statute books.[13]

## SUPREME COURT AND SECURITIES LAWS 261

Frankfurter was under no illusion that judges did not make law; he differed from his colleagues only on the extent of the creativity that should be brought to the inevitable task of "filling in the gaps." ·

The principal explanation for Frankfurter's lack of influence was not jurisprudential differences, but his personality. His persona, so attractive to the disciples that gathered at his feet at Harvard, alienated his colleagues, who regarded themselves as his professional equals, rather than students to be taught. A cogent example is a letter he wrote to Murphy after the death of Chief Justice Stone. At the time, the justices were engulfed in turmoil over a fierce intra-court battle to replace Stone in the center seat.

> Dear Frank:
>
> Today ends another epoch in the history of the Court—the quinquennium of the 1941–1945 terms. Of course there have been many shortcomings in the past and some striking instances of what Chief Justice Hughes so aptly called "self-inflicted wounds." But if I were transplanted into a classroom and had to tell my students what I thought about the period just closed, I would have to say the following— assuming, of course, that I lived up to Holmes' injunction "never lie to the young!":
>
> 1. Never before in the history of the Court were so many of its members influenced in decisions by considerations extraneous to the legal issues that supposedly control decisions.
> 2. Never before have members of the Court so often acted contrary to their convictions on the governing legal issues in decisions.
> 3. Never before has so large a proportion of the opinions fallen short of requisite professional standards.
>
> It would relieve me of much unhappiness if I did not feel compelled to have these convictions. But they are based on a study of the history of the Court which began from the day I left the Law School, just forty years ago and on first-hand and detailed knowledge of what has been going on inside the Court during the last thirty-five years.
>
> Of all earthly institutions this Court comes nearest to having, for me, sacred aspects. Having been endowed by nature with zestful vitality, I still look forward hopefully to the era which will open on the first Monday of October next.

Frankfurter's professorial tones—reflecting fervent hopes, but so condescendingly conveyed—failed to peel Murphy away from the liberal orbit of Black and Douglas, as he had earlier failed to persuade Reed.

The professorial tone showed up, not only in his correspondence with his colleagues, but also at their weekly conferences. Unsurprisingly, Frankfurter's colleagues resented his efforts at instruction. According to Brennan, "we would

262  A HISTORY OF SECURITIES LAW

be inclined to agree with Felix more often in conference, if he quoted Holmes less frequently to us." Here is a response from Vinson to Frankfurter, after a series of memos from Frankfurter regarding multiple opinions in a case: "Thanks for the lecture even though you misjudged my position and set up a strawman to attack. I would have preferred to have had it face-to-face. It started in that manner—it will only be continued in that way." Frankfurter also managed to alienate Vinson's successor, Earl Warren, to the point where the two were sniping at each other in open court. The acrimony with Douglas was particularly intense, notwithstanding their friendly relations before coming to the Court—Douglas refused even to attend Frankfurter's funeral. As Reed remarked to his law clerks, "the trouble with Felix is that he never considers that he might be wrong: if you don't agree with Felix, you must be either stupid or dishonest!"[14] Frankfurter the man blunted the power of Frankfurter the intellect.

Douglas's lack of influence is murkier. His academic interests were more focused than Frankfurter's: bankruptcy and corporate law. Moreover, he had active administrative experience with the SEC at the highest level. Somewhat surprisingly, Douglas's tenure at the SEC provides the readiest explanation for his lack of influence: his consistent recusals in securities cases. All told, Douglas participated in only thirty-seven of the fifty-two securities cases decided by the Court during his tenure, while other justices recused themselves in only a handful of cases. Having been chair of the SEC when the agency launched its enforcement of PUHCA, he did not sit on a PUHCA case for his first dozen years on the Court, as the breakup of the utility holding companies dragged on. By the time he participated as a justice, the SEC had fought and won the great battles of that front. Douglas did not write a PUHCA opinion until 1954, the tail end of the Court's PUHCA jurisprudence. He also recused himself from all securities cases for his first six years on the Court. In the first securities case decided during his tenure, *U.S. Realty*, Douglas recused himself despite having no basis for disqualification, simply because of pressure from Chief Justice Hughes, who he thought was wielding recusal as a strategic weapon. For other cases, Douglas recused based on tangential contact. The notes in his files indicate that his secretary, Edith Waters, collected the information on his ties to the case at the time that Douglas was at the Commission. In one case, the investigation had not started until three years after Douglas left the Commission, but the mere mention of a possible earlier investigation at the staff level was sufficient to trigger recusal even though it had never reached the commissioners. In the *Joiner* case heard in 1943, the case had been opened only recently, but mention of an earlier informal staff investigation that was closed in February 1936 (Douglas had become a commissioner on January 23) was enough to cause Douglas to recuse himself.[15] Rutledge worried that Douglas's recusals were depriving the court of expertise. He did not write a securities opinion until 1947.

Douglas left little guidance on his recusal policy, other than to say it was up to each justice. Perhaps Douglas's political ambition made him sensitive to any potential charge of conflict of interest. The pattern of nonparticipation suggests that Douglas was finished with securities law. His autobiography does not mention even a single securities case for his entire time on the Court.[16] Perhaps the field had done all it could for him in getting him to the SEC, which he leveraged to his spot on the high court. With the large issues of the government's role in the economy resolved, perhaps he now wanted to make his mark on the public stage in areas like civil liberties. Douglas's remaining ambitions in corporate law—federal incorporation and socialized investment banking—could be achieved only through legislative, not judicial, action.

Douglas's nonparticipation in securities cases does not appear to have affected their results; Douglas would have joined in the broad deference given to the SEC. Even after he stopped recusing, Douglas was not an active participant in securities cases. Indeed, most of his securities opinions show up in the last four years of his tenure, most notably his short but wide-ranging opinion for the Court in *Bankers Life*. That case marked the apogee of Rule 10b-5 as a regulator of securities transactions, but it is remarkable for its opacity. Even less significant are a string of dissents Douglas wrote in the 1970s after the Court's majority had taken a more restrictive turn in securities law. By then, his abilities had begun to wane.[17]

Douglas's lack of influence in securities cases may also reflect his personality and inability to get along with colleagues. Cavalier work habits, colleagues' resentment of his political ambitions, and even the fallout from his first divorce seemed to isolate him from the brethren, despite early shared experiences. According to Brennan, the master of coalition-building, Douglas had no interest in cultivating allies. Charles Clark, Douglas's dean at Yale and an ardent progressive during his later time on the Second Circuit, had it right in predicting that Douglas would chafe under the confines of the bench: "Douglas is one of the ablest and sincerest persons I know, and it is a grand thing to have so young and vigorous a person on the bench, unless indeed one believes that he could have done more elsewhere. . . . It is hard to think of so vigorous a personality as Douglas confined so young."[18]

Thus, the two justices appointed by Roosevelt with the most direct securities experience played rather minor roles in the Court's securities law jurisprudence. Felix Frankfurter had overseen the drafting of the Securities Act, brokered the key compromise for PUHCA and advised the new administration on litigation strategy, but he squandered any leadership role with a condescending attitude toward colleagues that made it difficult for anyone to follow. In the *Chenery* cases, Frankfurter did frame the point at which the New Deal alliance frayed, arguing for judicial control of the SEC, but he could not swing a majority in *Chenery II*. That debate would reappear with the efforts of Lewis Powell to rein in the SEC's fight against insider trading and it continues to this day. Bill Douglas's achievements in the field of securities law were even more striking: He drove the SEC expansion into bankruptcy reorganizations, brought the New York Stock Exchange to heel, and oversaw the agency's aggressive role in breaking up the public utility holding companies. Douglas seemingly lost all interest in securities law upon his

264  A HISTORY OF SECURITIES LAW

appointment to the Court, although he did write a number of influential bankruptcy opinions. The bottom line is that neither Frankfurter nor Douglas had any significant impact on the Court's securities jurisprudence during their tenure.

The ineffectiveness and/or abdication of these leading figures, however, did not affect the outcomes. No other justice stepped into the void, but Roosevelt's other appointees did not need forceful leadership. They were already bonded to the cause from their political and advocacy roles. Roosevelt's justices were committed to government control of finance, and the Court's decisions reflected that commitment.

When Truman had his opportunity to make appointments to the Court, his picks did nothing to disturb the established pattern. His appointees—Burton, Vinson, Clark, and Minton—wrote a total of four securities' opinions between them. Only Clark's had any significance (*Ralston Purina* and *J.I. Case*). Perhaps more surprisingly, Eisenhower's appointees did nothing to alter the Court's course in securities cases. Warren, "who had passionately denounced the New Deal," which he viewed as "immoral" and lawless, soon fell into step with the Court's liberals.[19] Brennan, a Democrat, signed on to the New Deal faith unreservedly. Whitaker was a non-entity during his brief service. The more traditional Republicans, Harlan and Stewart, were simply outnumbered, particularly after Kennedy appointed liberal reinforcements. The result was judicial deference to the SEC, an attitude that would last until the 1970s. Only then would Stewart join the majority coalition led by Powell to restrict the reach of the securities laws.

## D. A Purposive Court

A generation after the enactment of the securities law, their constitutional validity was beyond question, but faith in the expertise of administrative agencies had faded. The SEC was included among that tarnished group after a long fallow period during the 1950s. This loss of faith manifested itself on the Court in diametrically opposing ways, depending on the observer's ideological lens. Liberal justices looked at the SEC's diminished stature and saw the need to supplement the agency's efforts, while conservative justices saw the need to rein the agency in to bounds it could more readily handle. These conflicting ideologies would first rise, and then fall as justices came and went from the Supreme Court in the 1960s and '70s. The shift in the Court's ideological center to the left would set the stage for a revolution in the securities laws in the 1960s, followed by an abrupt about-face in the 1970s led by Nixon's appointees.

John F. Kennedy's appointment of Bill Cary to chair the SEC in 1961 reinvigorated the agency. The President's subsequent appointments of Byron White and Arthur Goldberg to the Court set the stage for a move beyond mere deference to the Commission. For a decade—1962 to 1972—the Supreme Court took the initiative in actively promoting the underlying goals of the securities laws. During this decade, the Court looked to statutory purpose, making it paramount in the task of interpretation. The sixties Supreme Court, aided by the Second Circuit, transformed the federal securities laws. Two trends would emerge, both driven at least in part by the perception that state courts had been lax in enforcing fiduciary duty standards. Insider trading regulation, seemingly confined by the 1934 Congress to the technical approach of § 16(b), moved to Rule 10b-5's broader and more malleable antifraud space. Of greater economic significance for public companies and their shareholders, the Supreme Court embraced implied rights of action in Rules 10b-5 and 14a-9. Coupled with the revised Rule 23 of the Federal Rules of Civil Procedure, the newly discovered private rights of action enabled a private securities enforcement regime parallel to government enforcement. That regime would have enormous consequences for public companies and the professionals who serve them. This new activism by federal courts—the advent of a federal corporate law—promoted a goal sought by progressives since the turn of the century.

The purposive era, however, was fleeting. The trend's lack of staying power can be explained, in part, by turnover among the justices. Arthur Goldberg brought a New Deal sensibility to the Court with a "strong hostility to the concentrated economic power [he] had witnessed while growing up in the urban industrial America of the early twentieth century." *Capital Gains* and *Silver* suggested that Goldberg might become the leader of the Court in the field of securities—he wrote three of the Court's five securities opinions during his tenure—but his stay proved too short for him to have any lasting impact. The Court's path might have been quite different if Lyndon Johnson had accepted Warren's recommendation and nominated Goldberg to succeed Warren or if Johnson's nomination of Abe Fortas to be Chief Justice in 1968 had not been derailed. Goldberg considered Fortas his jurisprudential "clone," and Fortas had worked with Douglas at the SEC and taught securities law at Yale.[20] Blackmun, who eventually replaced Fortas, turned out to be generally expansive on securities law issues. Blackmun did not emerge as a leader in the field, however, and he was not likely to vote in a more liberal direction than Fortas or Goldberg if either had remained. Moreover, Fortas or Goldberg might have provided a stronger balance to Powell's dominating influence.

Despite the demise of purposivism in securities law at the Supreme Court, some threads from the sixties survived. Powell himself, although typically insisting on the priority of statutory text, grafted insider trading on to Rule 10b-5 despite minimal textual support. More significant still, the Court's adoption of the misappropriation theory in the 1997 *O'Hagan* case gave insider trading law a scope nearly as broad as *Texas Gulf Sulphur*'s high-water mark. Congress has repeatedly passed on codifying the insider trading prohibition. Congress also passed on the opportunity to repudiate securities class actions when it adopted the PSLRA. The Roberts Court has continued to validate securities class actions in the twenty-first century. The seeds planted by the sixties Court in cases like *Capital Gains* and *J.I. Case* may not have produced a full-blown federal corporate law of the sort sought by William Cary and other progressives, but they survive at the center of securities regulation today.

## E. A Skeptical Court and an Influential Justice

The purposive trend dominated securities law when Lewis F. Powell, Jr., was sworn in as an Associate Justice on January 7, 1972. Harry Blackmun was hard at work on his *Affiliated Ute* opinion, purposivism's swan song. Powell's swearing in coincided with an immediate sea change in the path of the federal securities laws. Although the Burger Court has been described as "the counter-revolution that wasn't" in constitutional law,[21] that was not true of securities law. By the time Powell retired from the Court in June 1987, federal securities law had been confined. The threat to state corporate law had been rebuffed.

**Figure 8.2**
**Corporate Lawyer:** Lewis Powell translated his long experience advising Virginia corporations into outsized influence in the Court's securities cases.

SUPREME COURT AND SECURITIES LAWS   267

We have seen how Powell's influence dramatically altered the Court's dynamic in dealing with securities cases. In this section, we explore some of the reasons for Powell's profound impact on the Court's securities jurisprudence between 1972 and 1987. Powell worked diligently to maximize his influence with his colleagues, coming well prepared to conferences in securities cases, having mastered the often-complicated facts and reduced a carefully thought-out analysis to writing. Powell believed in hard work and organization, and his thorough preparation may have given him an edge in the Court's deliberations. In a frequently technical area where the other justices were unlikely to have strongly held views, Powell's superior knowledge and preparation were a powerful force. And, unlike Frankfurter, Powell maintained collegial relations with his fellow justices. Powell might vent his frustration with his colleagues in the privacy of his chambers, but he took care to keep that frustration out of his opinions. Powell "preferred understatement in responding to dissents."[22] This restraint no doubt enhanced his influence with his colleagues.

Powell's influence is confirmed by our statistical analysis. The chart below demonstrates Powell's outsized impact on the Court's securities law agenda in the seventies and eighties. It also allows some comparison to other eras.

## Supreme Court Justices and Securities Cases, 1933–2021

| | Tenure | Cases | Majority | Dissent | Majority % |
|---|---|---|---|---|---|
| Samuel Alito | 2006– | 26 | 22 (2, 2) | 4 (0) | 85% |
| Hugo Black | 1937–1971 | 38 | 31 (1) | 7 (5) | 82% |
| Harry A. Blackmun | 1970–1994 | 60 | 48 (6) | 12 (7) | 80% |
| William J. Brennan, Jr. | 1956–1990 | 69 | 49 (7) | 20 (4) | 71% |
| Stephen Breyer | 1994–2022 | 34 | 31 (6, 1) | 3 (2) | 91% |
| Warren E. Burger | 1969–1986 | 48 | 47 (6, 1) | 1 (1) | 98% |
| Harold H. Burton | 1945–1958 | 13 | 10 (1) | 3 (1) | 77% |
| Tom C. Clark | 1949–1967 | 17 | 16 (3) | 1 | 94% |
| William O. Douglas | 1939–1975 | 37 | 25 (6) | 12 (7) | 68% |
| Felix Frankfurter | 1939–1962 | 24 | 17 (1) | 7 (5) | 71% |
| Ruth Bader Ginsburg | 1993–2020 | 35 | 27 (4) | 8 (2) | 77% |
| John M. Harlan (II) | 1955–1971 | 16 | 8 (1) | 8 (7) | 50% |
| Robert H. Jackson | 1941–1954 | 10 | 8 (2, 1) | 2 (1) | 80% |
| Elena Kagan | 2010– | 18 | 17 (4) | 1 | 94% |
| Anthony M. Kennedy | 1988–2018 | 39 | 34 (5) | 5 (2) | 87% |
| Thurgood Marshall | 1967–1991 | 60 | 47 (9) | 13 (3) | 78% |

| | Tenure | Cases | Majority | Dissent | Majority % |
|---|---|---|---|---|---|
| Frank Murphy | 1940–1949 | 14 | 14 (6) | 0 | 100% |
| Sandra Day O'Connor | 1981–2006 | 31 | 27 (3) | 4 (1) | 87% |
| Lewis F. Powell, Jr. | 1971–1987 | 41 | 40 (11, 3) | 1 (1) | 98% |
| Stanley F. Reed | 1938–1957 | 19 | 17 (3) | 2 | 89% |
| William H. Rehnquist | 1971–2005 | 60 | 56 (3) | 4 (3) | 93% |
| John Roberts | 2005– | 26 | 26 (4) | 0 | 100% |
| Owen J. Roberts | 1930–1945 | 11 | 8 (0) | 3 (1) | 73% |
| Wiley B. Rutledge | 1943–1949 | 10 | 10 (*1*) | 0 | 100% |
| Antonin Scalia | 1986–2016 | 38 | 34 (3,6) | 4 (2) | 89% |
| Sonia Sotomayor | 2009– | 21 | 17 (3) | 4 (2) | 81% |
| David H. Souter | 1990–2009 | 19 | 15 (3) | 4 | 79% |
| John Paul Stevens | 1975–2010 | 57 | 40 (5,4) | 17 (13) | 70% |
| Potter Stewart | 1958–1981 | 48 | 41 (7) | 7 (1) | 85% |
| Harlan F. Stone | 1925–1946 | 11 | 9 (1) | 2 (1) | 82% |
| Clarence Thomas | 1991– | 37 | 28 (2,3) | 9 (8) | 76% |
| Earl Warren | 1953–1969 | 16 | 15 (1) | 1 | 94% |
| Byron R. White | 1962–1993 | 71 | 61 (4) | 10 (5) | 86% |

Only justices who participated in ten or more securities cases are included. Number of written opinions in parentheses; concurring opinions in italics.[23]

Not only did Powell write some of the most important cases during his tenure, he dominated in sheer numbers, writing eleven majority opinions in the forty-one securities cases in which he participated on the merits. As the chart demonstrates, this far exceeds the production of any other justice of that era. The chart also shows that Powell rarely found himself in the minority. Of the forty-one securities cases in which Powell participated, he dissented only once. Frankfurter, by contrast, found himself in the majority only 70% of the time, Douglas only 68%. Powell's consistent success is more remarkable when one considers that Powell always took the most pro-business position of any justice in securities cases. One looks in vain for more restrictive positions than Powell's in either published opinions or internal conference notes.[24] By contrast, in Powell's more widely noticed constitutional law opinions, he often found the middle ground in multi-factor balancing tests with stronger roots in political expediency than in constitutional principle. Not surprisingly, this gave Powell a reputation among general Court followers as a "swing vote." That does not describe Powell's work in the field of securities law. He was a fixture in the majority, but it was a consistently conservative majority.

SUPREME COURT AND SECURITIES LAWS   269

Powell's leadership is reflected not only in his many majority opinions and extraordinary winning percentage, but also in his influence over the Court's docket. Powell, more than any other justice, was responsible for the substantial number of securities law cases the Court heard during his tenure.[25] From 1936 to 1971, the Court decided forty-four securities cases, an average of one and a half per term. The Court averaged three securities cases per term for the fifteen full terms that Powell sat on the Court. Powell voted to grant certiorari in forty of the forty-five securities cases granted during his time on the Court (and three cases heard the term following his retirement). Powell enhanced his influence over the Court's docket with his willingness to write dissents from the denial of certiorari. Powell drafted and circulated five such dissents during his time on the Court, persuading the Court to grant certiorari in four of those cases. Other justices wrote only four dissents from denial in securities cases during Powell's tenure, and our research uncovered none that resulted in a grant of certiorari. Since Powell's retirement, no securities case has resulted in a published dissent from the denial of certiorari.

Bolstering Powell's influence was the absence of an effective counterweight. Lewis Powell has been the only securities lawyer appointed to the Court since the adoption of the federal securities laws. Although other justices had private practice experience in varied fields, none could match Powell's hands-on experience with the federal securities laws. Unlike many areas of the Court's docket that Powell was confronting for the first time, he knew securities law and was confident of his views. Most of the other justices simply lacked interest in what can be a highly technical field. Blackmun showed flashes of emotional commitment, but little more than that. His liberal impulses were not backed by Powell's expertise, and Blackmun knew it. Blackmun's conference notes from *CTS* describe Powell as "our C lawyer!"[26] Blackmun's opinion in *Affiliated Ute* marked the end of the purposive era for securities law in the Supreme Court. He would not write another significant securities opinion for the Court until *Basic Inc. v. Levinson*—the term after Powell retired, and with the minimum quorum of six participating.

During Powell's time on the Court there was a reliable group of four justices taking a restrictive position: Powell, Rehnquist, Stewart, and Burger. Each of the latter three took a position different from Powell in only one securities case during the 1970s and '80s. O'Connor and Scalia did not change the balance when they replaced Stewart and Burger. The fifth vote, however, varied. The Court's majority in securities cases, including critical ones such as *Ernst & Ernst* and *Santa Fe*, each depended on gaining votes from those who had joined in expansive decisions prior to Powell's arrival. This sometimes included both White and Marshall, or one of those and Blackmun.

Rehnquist regularly sided with Powell but wrote only three majority opinions in securities cases. Two of those were blockbusters—*Blue Chip Stamps* (adopting

# 270 A HISTORY OF SECURITIES LAW

the *Birnbaum* standing rule) and *Touche Ross* (blocking creation of more implied private rights of action). The tone of each is more of a direct challenge to the Court's prior doctrine and the language more colorful (e.g., fear of "vexatious litigation"). Rehnquist gravitated to more structural questions like federalism and separation of powers, and both of these cases might be characterized as falling in that category. He did not engage, however, in any sustained way with the intricacies of securities doctrine that fascinated Powell.

Powell's experience as a securities lawyer gave him credibility when he urged his colleagues to reject the SEC's efforts to reshape the securities markets, as he so often did. Agency expertise carried no weight when the SEC came into court with newly developed positions that conflicted with Powell's understanding of well-established securities practice. The deference that the SEC had enjoyed in the Supreme Court before Powell's confirmation evaporated. As a result, the SEC's winning percentage plummeted, particularly in the highest profile cases.

The SEC's precipitous decline in the Court did not go unnoticed. Shortly after the agency's high-profile loss in *Chiarella*, the *Wall Street Journal* noted that the Supreme Court was disagreeing with the SEC with much greater frequency and gave "the credit—or blame—for the court's position to Justice Lewis Powell, former corporate lawyer who has written many of the majority opinions in these cases." Powell evidently hoped the SEC was getting the message—he sent his law clerk to discuss the Court's securities cases with the *Journal* reporter doing the story.[27] What explains Powell's perceived hostility to the agency?

As a corporate lawyer, Powell's relationship with the SEC had not always been smooth. Like most securities lawyers, Powell found the agency to be unreasonable at times. Taking a break from the invasion of North Africa to complain to a colleague about a client's loss before the agency, Powell wrote:

> I had hoped the war ... would temper the crusading arder [*sic*] of SEC, and that [the client] would receive moderate and fair treatment. It is extremely disappointing to find that agencies of the Government are still fighting an internal war against capitalism when the unified energies of all should be concentrated on fighting the very urgent and real war for physical survival. Also one of the things I *hope* we are fighting for is the survival of a just and fairly regulated capitalism. Personally, I believe capitalism (i.e.—the right to private property and moderate profit) is an essential component of democracy.[28]

Although Powell was far from being an advocate of laissez-faire ("fairly regulated capitalism," "moderate profit"), he objected to the SEC's perceived heavy-handedness again and again during his time on the Court. Having worked with the SEC from its earliest days, Powell recoiled from the agency's aggressively expansionist tack in the 1960s and 1970s.

SUPREME COURT AND SECURITIES LAWS    271

Powell's conservative stance in securities cases was not the product of grand theory; he and his colleagues decided securities cases one at a time, not as part of an overarching agenda. Powell did not subscribe to normative libertarianism or economic analysis. Rather, Powell's nearly forty years of experience in corporate boardrooms led him to trust the character of the average American businessman. That trust was reinforced by working alongside those clients in civic affairs. In Powell's world, free enterprise and the businessmen who made it work were the foundation of strong communities. Free enterprise was a resource to be nurtured, not a menace to be tamed. Character, not the threat of lawsuits, was the safeguard of the integrity of American capitalism. That trust in American business led Powell to read the securities laws—in all good faith—as setting down predictable rules that would allow business to proceed without undue interference or liability risk. These narrow readings reversed the trend in the Second Circuit and other lower courts to expand the securities laws. The securities laws experienced a counterrevolution, not as the result of a coup, but because of the commitments and intuitions derived from one person's experience before becoming a justice.

Powell's experience did not always push him to oppose regulation. Powell was not naïve; he recognized that there were abuses in American business. His distaste for the corruption of insider trading led him to read the common law of fraud broadly in *Chiarella* to make room for a prohibition under section 10(b). The SEC's "parity of information" position would have cracked down on information asymmetry more completely, but it strayed too far from the common law baseline for Powell, outstripping any possible intention of the 1934 Congress.

A more significant departure from free market dogma was Powell's profound suspicion of takeovers. Federal preemption of state regulation of takeovers, pushed by the SEC, was the most promising avenue for preserving a free market in corporate control. Powell's distrust of that market led him to tolerate state anti-takeover laws, which invariably protected management. In this, Powell's attitudes mirrored Brandeis, who had pushed for policies favoring the small businessmen that he had represented while a practicing lawyer.[29] Like Brandeis, Powell's instincts were grounded in experience, not economic theory. Powell wanted to preserve space for local businesses and their leaders to contribute to the community in the way that he and his clients had done. Powell's support for state efforts to discourage takeovers was consistent with his federalist principles, which helped him swing a Court majority. Powell shut the door to an open market in corporate control in *CTS*. Corporate managers could sleep better as a result.

Powell's securities law legacy, however, does not rest solely on the attitudes that he brought to that work. Powell's presence ensured that the Court would pay attention to the highly technical field of securities law. That focus has declined

272  A HISTORY OF SECURITIES LAW

since his retirement. Powell's extensive experience in the area, bolstered by his willingness to write at the certiorari stage when other justices did not recognize the importance of a securities issue, made him a force to be reckoned with. These advantages were magnified by Powell's hard work and thorough preparation. No other justice could (or perhaps, would) match his mastery of the facts of the cases and the relevant law. In sum, Powell was the Court's leader in securities law for a decade and a half, largely based on his experience in the field.

## F.  A Random Walk

The Court has scaled back its securities docket since Powell left the Court. In the thirty-five terms since Powell's retirement, the Court has heard forty-five securities cases, an average of slightly more than one per term, a sharp decline from the average of three per term during Powell's tenure. Fewer grants of certiorari suggest less interest, no doubt encouraged by a lack of familiarity with the field. Moreover, the decisions have been equally balanced between expansive and restrictive results. The randomness of this period is reflected in the opinions of Powell's successor Anthony Kennedy. Kennedy wrote the Court's decision in *Central Bank*, a major restriction on the reach of private litigation, but he also wrote a scathing dissent to the Court's restrictive approach in *Virginia Bankshares*. There he labeled Souter's majority opinion as "guerilla warfare to restrict a well-established implied private right of action." Perhaps the challenges of tracking a consistent path are most evident in Kennedy's opinion in *Gustafson*, which struggles to reconcile various statutory sections of the Securities Act.[30]

These phenomena are consistent with the absence of a dominant force on the Court—either individual or ideological—in the field of securities law during the last three plus decades. That conclusion is supported by the numbers—none of the justices serving after Powell has come close to his number of majority opinions in the area. On the current Court, Chief Justice Roberts has been with the majority in every case, but his handful of majority opinions have been animated by other concerns, for example, separation of powers in the *PCAOB* case, stare decisis in *Halliburton II*. His presence in the majority seems motivated more by a desire to maintain his prerogative to assign opinions rather than any overarching principle. (This supposition is bolstered by the fact that his three predecessors—Warren, Burger, and Rehnquist—were all in the majority more than 90% of the time.) If you are not committed to a normative position, it is easy to vote with the majority.

Turning to the Court's securities law output during this period, that work has been at times trivial, and at others, mediocre. The Court seems fixated on procedural questions: class certification, statutes of limitations, and jurisdictional boundaries. These topics are generally removed from the core of securities law. When the Court ventures into more significant areas, the opinions have been occasionally impenetrable—*Virginia Bankshares*—and sometimes bizarre—*Gustafson*. In insider trading cases, the Court simply regurgitates the party line offered by the SEC—*O'Hagan*—or the reasoning of prior cases—*Salman*.[31] The Court's most consequential decision of the period—*Basic Inc. v. Levinson*—unleashed a flood of securities class actions against public corporations. Notwithstanding the enormous economic consequences of that decision, the Court refused to consider the question of damages, a critical factor in the cost imposed by those cases and their deterrent value. Overall, the Court's output in securities cases has not been very useful since Powell retired.

## G. A Final Word

A familiar arc recurs in the evolution of American securities law before the high court. An initial judicial willingness to support the SEC and a broad construction of securities law evolved into a more ambitious jurisprudence during the 1960s. The Court assumed a more prominent role than the SEC in providing remedies to private litigants that decade, becoming a full partner with the legislative and executive branches in making law. The 1970s brought a counterrevolution across a variety of securities topics.

Yet this narrative of the Court's development of securities law does not exhaust the lessons provided by this slice of the Court's docket. Securities law offers an illuminating window into the Supreme Court's administrative law jurisprudence over the last century. The securities cases provide one of the most accessible illustrations of key transitions of American law. The expansion of federal legislative power over the economy in response to the Great Depression was highlighted by the securities laws passed in the first two terms of Franklin Roosevelt's New Deal. Roosevelt and Congress embraced social control of finance, and eventually, so did the Supreme Court. The flip between the *Jones* opinion in 1936 and the *US Realty* opinion in 1940 reflects a sea change. The New Deal Court would fill statutory silence by expanding federal power, not restricting it. The evolution in the Court's approach to statutory interpretation jumps out in its securities cases.

The bellwether status of securities law is not confined to these revolutionary changes of the late 1930s. At two later times, securities law again provides compelling illustrations of crucial shifts in Supreme Court jurisprudence. The Warren Court of the 1960s is well-known for its liberalism, which manifested itself with a vengeance in securities law. Between 1962 and 1972 (thus surviving the retirement of the eponymous Chief Justice by a few years), the securities

274   A HISTORY OF SECURITIES LAW

opinions of the Court demonstrate an ambitiously purposive approach to statutory interpretation. In that decade, the Court outpaced both Congress and the SEC in providing remedies for a variety of perceived wrongs in the markets. The Court took its place alongside the SEC and the Congress as a full partner in making securities law.

The period that followed featured an equally remarkable shift in the opposite direction. The reversal of the SEC's winning streak is the most dramatic evidence of the change in the Supreme Court jurisprudence that took place between 1968 and 1992. During this time, Republican presidents made all ten of the appointments to the Court. Richard Nixon's well-known commitment to appointing strict constructionists to the Supreme Court produced more tangible results in securities law than in constitutional law, the field which gave impetus to his agenda.

Studying the Court's securities jurisprudence also makes a second contribution to a broader understanding of the Court over the last century. The periods just described offer distinct case studies of interactions in a multi-member court with an evolving composition. To be sure, there are other variations than the four documented here, but these patterns in securities cases shed light on path of the Court's twentieth-century jurisprudence.

First, the New Deal Court of the 1940s shows a Court driven by a collective vision firmly held by a supra-majority of the justices. Roosevelt was able to fill eight seats, a number only surpassed by George Washington. His appointments shared a strong commitment to the growing administrative state. No individual justice dominated the field. Frankfurter and Douglas, who had leading roles in the creation and early development of the securities laws, had surprisingly little impact on the Court's securities jurisprudence. The sixties provide a second example. Justices appointed by the four presidents who succeeded Roosevelt forged a shared philosophy of judicial construction focused on purpose rather than text. Another dramatic transformation of securities law after 1972 illustrates the third pattern: the impact that one knowledgeable justice, committed to shaping a particular field, can have on the Court when the other justices do not care as much. In the last thirty-plus years, the Court's securities jurisprudence illustrates a fourth pattern, reflecting indifference and ignorance of the details of a field among all of the justices. As a result, the law slides along without guidance from the Court.

The internal details we unearthed from the justices' papers provide a more nuanced account of how the Supreme Court makes law than would be revealed from merely reading the final opinions. Our account reveals interesting characters and some surprising twists. The patterns of securities jurisprudence over the last century sheds light, not just on the development of securities law, but also how the Supreme Court works.

# Notes on Sources

We relied heavily on the papers of the justices, which typically include correspondence among the justices, memos from clerks and the justices, and general correspondence. The justices' papers are found in a variety of academic libraries as well as the Library of Congress. We are indebted for invaluable help from too many librarians to list here, but John Jacob, formerly the archivist of the Lewis F. Powell, Jr. Archives at Washington & Lee University, deserves a special note of gratitude for assistance above and beyond the call of duty.

Most of these judicial sources are referenced in full, but we adopt the following conventions for certain frequently used sources in the interest of brevity.

HAB-LC: Harry Blackmun Collection, Manuscript Room, Library of Congress.

WOD-LC: William O. Douglas Collection, Manuscript Room, Library of Congress.

FF-Harvard and FF-LC: Felix Frankfurter's papers are divided between the Harvard Law School Library and the Library of Congress.

LFP Collection: Papers of Lewis F. Powell, Jr., Lewis F. Powell, Jr. Archives, Law Library, Washington & Lee University.

We also refer to the following books repeatedly:

Moley, After Seven Years: Raymond Moley, After Seven Years (1939).

Moley, First New Deal: Raymond Moley, The First New Deal (1966).

Murphy, Wild Bill: Bruce Alan Murphy, Wild Bill: The Legend and Life of William O. Douglas (2003).

Seligman, Transformation of Wall Street: Joel Seligman, The Transformation of Wall Street: A History of the Securities and Exchange Commission and Modern Corporate Finance (3rd ed. 2003).

Other books are cited in full the first time they appear in the endnotes to a chapter and in abbreviated form thereafter.

We interviewed a number of law clerks to the justices in the course of our research and those interviews are cited by the name of the clerk, the justice for whom they clerked, and term. We are indebted to them for sharing their recollections. We add the caveat, however, that those interviews were conducted

## NOTES ON SOURCES

many decades after the decisions in question and subject to the limits of human recall. The notes to those interviews are in Pritchard's files.

Finally, the pictures in the book, listed in order of appearance, come from the following sources.

Introduction
A Reliable Court: Collection of the Supreme Court of the United States
Powell & Rehnquist Cartoon by Jeff MacNelly: Jeff MacNelly Archive

Chapter 1
Corcoran & Pecora: CPA Media Pte Ltd./Alamy Stock Photo
Ben Cohen: colaimages/Alamy Stock Photo

Chapter 2
William O. Douglas's first press conference at the SEC: Library of Congress

Chapter 4
SEC Building 1934–1942: Library of Congress

Chapter 5
Bill Cary Being Sworn in by Bill Douglas: Associated Press
Vincent Chiarella: *The New York Times*

Chapter 6
The Burger Court: Collection of the Supreme Court of the United States

Chapter 8
Professor Frankfurter: Alamy
Justice Powell: Library of Congress

APPENDIX

# Supreme Court Securities Cases, 1933–2021

| Case Name | Cite | Year | Expansive/ Restrictive | Substantive Context | Vote | Majority Writer | Dissenting | Government Role | Description |
|---|---|---|---|---|---|---|---|---|---|
| Jones v. SEC | 298 U.S. 1 | 1936 | Restrictive | Securities Act | 6-3 | Sutherland | **Cardozo** Brandeis Stone | SEC plaintiff | Registrant's withdrawal of registration stops SEC's §8 and §19 investigation |
| Landis v. North American Co. | 299 U.S. 248 | 1936 | Neither | PUHCA | 8-0 | Cardozo | | SEC plaintiff | Stay of PUHCA litigation upheld |
| Electric Bond & Share Co. v. SEC | 303 U.S. 419 | 1938 | Expansive | PUHCA | 6-1 | Hughes | **McReynolds** | SEC plaintiff | PUHCA registration provisions upheld |
| SEC v. United States Realty & Improv. Co. | 310 U.S. 434 | 1940 | Neither | Bankruptcy | 5-3 | Stone | **Roberts** Hughes McReynolds | SEC plaintiff | SEC can intervene in Ch. 11; SEC loses on argument that Ch. 10 exclusive for large companies |
| Deckert v. Independence Shares Corp. | 311 U.S. 282 | 1940 | Expansive | Securities Act | 8-0 | Murphy | | None | Plaintiff can pursue assets held by third party under §12(2) |
| A. C. Frost & Co. v. Coeur D'Alene Mines | 312 U.S. 38 | 1941 | Expansive | Securities Act | 8-0 | McReynolds | | SEC amicus | Illegality of contract to deliver securities does not render contract null & void |
| Edwards v. U.S. | 312 U.S. 473 | 1941 | Expansive | Securities Act | 7-0 | Reed | | U.S. prosecutor | Criminal defendant entitled to transcript of testimony before SEC |
| SEC v. Chenery Corp. (I) | 318 U.S. 80 | 1943 | Restrictive | PUHCA | 4-3 | Frankfurter | **Black** Reed Murphy | SEC admin | SEC sanction against insiders in public utility holding company merger not supported by agency's rationale |

| Case Name | Cite | Year | Expansive/ Restrictive | Substantive Context | Vote | Majority Writer | Dissenting | Government Role | Description |
|---|---|---|---|---|---|---|---|---|---|
| SEC v. C.M. Joiner Leasing Corp | 320 U.S. 344 | 1943 | Expansive | Definition of security | 7-1 | Jackson | Roberts | SEC plaintiff | Assignments of oil and gas leases were a security |
| Otis & Co. v. SEC | 323 U.S. 624 | 1945 | Expansive | PUHCA | 5-3 | Reed | **Stone** Roberts Frankfurter | SEC admin | SEC not required to apply charter preference in holding company reorganization |
| American Power & Light Co. v. SEC | 325 U.S. 385 | 1945 | Restrictive | PUHCA | 7-1 / 5-3 | Murphy | **Murphy** Black Reed | SEC admin | Holding company shareholder is a person aggrieved with standing |
| North American Co. v. SEC | 327 U.S. 686 | 1946 | Expansive | PUHCA | 6-0 | Murphy | | SEC admin | §11(b)(1) proceeding constitutional |
| SEC v. W. J. Howey Co. | 328 U.S. 293 | 1946 | Expansive | Definition of security | 6-1 | Murphy | **Frankfurter** | SEC plaintiff | Offer of orange grove and service agreement was a security |
| American Power & Light Co. v. SEC (II) | 329 U.S. 90 | 1946 | Expansive | PUHCA | 6-0 | Murphy | | SEC admin | §11(b)(2) proceeding constitutional |
| Penfield Co. of California v. SEC | 330 U.S. 585 | 1947 | Expansive | Enforcement | 7-2 | Douglas | **Frankfurter** Jackson | SEC plaintiff | Contempt and imprisonment appropriate for officer's failure to produce documents in corporation's sale of stock |
| SEC v. Chenery Corp. (II) | 332 U.S. 194 | 1947 | Expansive | PUHCA | 5-2 | Murphy | **Jackson** Frankfurter | SEC admin | SEC sanction against insiders in public utility holding company merger upheld under agency's new rationale |
| SEC v. Central-Illinois Securities Corp. | 338 U.S. 96 | 1949 | Expansive | PUHCA | 7-0 | Rutledge | | SEC admin | SEC valuation of preferred stock at going-concern value rather than liquidation value entitled to deference |

| Case | Citation | Year | Direction | Subject | Vote | Majority | Concurrence/Dissent | SEC Role | Holding |
|---|---|---|---|---|---|---|---|---|---|
| Manufacturers Trust Co. v. Becker | 338 U.S. 304 | 1949 | Restrictive | Bankruptcy | 6-2 | Clark | **Burton** Black | SEC amicus | Rejects SEC argument that director cannot profit from claims purchased during bankruptcy |
| Niagara Hudson Power Co. v. Leventritt | 340 U.S. 336 | 1951 | Expansive | PUHCA | 6-2 | Burton | **Frankfurter** Black | SEC admin | SEC did not violate fair and equitable standard in assigning no value to out-of-the-money stock warrants |
| Mosser v. Darrow | 341 U.S. 267 | 1951 | Expansive | Bankruptcy; Insider Trading | 7-1 | Jackson | **Black** | SEC intervenor | Trustee personally liable for profits from trading in securities of subsidiaries by employees who purchased bonds for resale to bankruptcy estate |
| SEC v. Ralston Purina Co. | 346 U.S. 119 | 1953 | Expansive | Enforcement | 6-2 | Clark | **Vinson** Burton | SEC plaintiff | Non-public offering not available to unsophisticated employees |
| Wilko v. Swan | 346 U.S. 427 | 1953 | Expansive | Arbitration | 7-2 | Reed | **Frankfurter** Minton | SEC amicus | Agreement to arbitrate violated grant of jurisdiction to federal courts |
| General Protective Committee v. SEC | 346 U.S. 521 | 1954 | Expansive | PUHCA | 9-0 | Douglas | | SEC plaintiff | SEC can split provisions of reorganization plan between §11(e) and §24(a) |
| SEC v. Drexel & Co | 348 U.S. 341 | 1955 | Expansive | PUHCA | 6-2 | Douglas | **Frankfurter** Burton | SEC plaintiff | SEC can review fees and expenses in approving reorganization |

| Case Name | Cite | Year | Expansive/Restrictive | Substantive Context | Vote | Majority Writer | Dissenting | Government Role | Description |
|---|---|---|---|---|---|---|---|---|---|
| SEC v. La. Pub. Ser. Comm'n | 353 U.S. 368 | 1957 | Expansive | PUHCA | 9-0 | PC (Whitaker) | | SEC plaintiff | SEC order denying reopening of divestment proceeding not subject to judicial review |
| SEC v. Variable Annuity Life Ins. Co. | 359 U.S. 65 | 1959 | Expansive | Definition of a security | 5-4 | Douglas | **Harlan** Frankfurter Clark Whittaker | SEC plaintiff | Variable annuities are securities under Securities and Investment Company Acts; not contracts of insurance that would be exempt and state regulated |
| Blau v. Lehman | 368 U.S. 403 | 1962 | Restrictive | Exchange Act 16(b) | 6-2 | Black | **Douglas** Warren | SEC amicus | Partnership not liable where no deputization of partner to serve as director of public company |
| Wolf v. Weinstein | 372 U.S. 633 | 1963 | Expansive | Bankruptcy; Insider Trading | 7-2 | Brennan | **Harlan** Stewart | None | Bankruptcy ban on officer reimbursement while trading is cumulative to §16(b) |
| Silver v. New York Stock Exchange | 373 U.S. 341 | 1963 | Restrictive | Antitrust | 7-2 | Goldberg | **Stewart** Harlan | SEC amicus | New York Stock Exchange exclusion of non-member violates the Sherman Act absent fair procedure; Exchange Act does not preempt |
| SEC v. Capital Gains Research Bureau | 375 U.S. 180 | 1963 | Expansive | Inv. Advisors Act | 7-1 | Goldberg | **Harlan** | SEC plaintiff | Investment advisor engaged in fraud by failing to disclose purchases prior to publishing recommendation of stock |

| Case | Cite | Year | Type | Subject | Vote | Majority | Dissent | SEC role | Holding |
|---|---|---|---|---|---|---|---|---|---|
| J. I. Case Co. v. Borak | 377 U.S. 426 | 1964 | Expansive | Proxy | 9-0 | Clark | | SEC amicus | Implied private cause of action under §14(a) recognized |
| SEC v. American Trailer Rentals | 379 U.S. 594 | 1965 | Expansive | Bankruptcy | 9-0 | Goldberg | | SEC plaintiff | District court should have granted SEC motion to transfer proceedings to Ch. X for reorganization |
| SEC v. New England Electric Sys. (I) | 384 U.S. 176 | 1966 | Expansive | PUHCA | 7-2 | Douglas | Harlan Stewart | SEC plaintiff | Holding company can control additional system only if serious impairment of economies otherwise |
| SEC v. United Ben. Life Ins. Co. | 387 U.S. 202 | 1967 | Expansive | Definition of security | 9-0 | Harlan | | SEC plaintiff | Deferred annuity contract was a security; not exempt as a contract of insurance |
| Tcherepnin v. Knight | 389 U.S. 332 | 1967 | Expansive | Definition of security | 8-0 | Warren | | SEC amicus | Savings & loan shares withdrawable as cash were securities |
| SEC v. New England Electric Sys. (II) | 390 U.S. 207 | 1968 | Expansive | PUHCA | 7-0 | Brennan | | SEC admin | SEC view on economics of system upheld after remand |
| Protective Committee for Indep. Stockholders of TMT Trailer Ferry v. Anderson | 390 U.S. 414 | 1968 | Expansive | Bankruptcy | 5-3 | White | Harlan Stewart Fortas | SEC amicus | Ch. X plan overturned, agreeing with SEC position of determination of insolvency in accord with proper valuation standards |
| SEC v. National Securities, Inc. | 393 U.S. 453 | 1969 | Expansive | 10b-5 | 6-3 | Marshall | Black Harlan Stewart | SEC plaintiff | SEC suit for fraud in merger between insurance companies not preempted by McCarran-Ferguson Act |

| Case Name | Cite | Year | Expansive/ Restrictive | Substantive Context | Vote | Majority Writer | Dissenting | Government Role | Description |
|---|---|---|---|---|---|---|---|---|---|
| Mills v. Electric Auto-Lite Co. | 396 U.S. 375 | 1970 | Expansive | Proxy | 8-0 | Harlan | **Black** | SEC amicus | Materiality standard; reliance established if merger is essential link; plaintiff entitled to expenses and attorneys' fees |
| Investment Co. Institute v. Camp | 401 U.S. 617 | 1971 | Expansive | Inv. Co. Act; Banking; | 6-2 | Stewart | **Harlan Blackmun** | SEC respondent | Bank underwriting investment fund violates Glass-Stegall: overturning SEC exemption |
| Superintendent of Ins. v. Bankers Life & Casualty Co. | 404 U.S. 6 | 1971 | Expansive | 10b-5 | 7-0 | Douglas | | SEC amicus | Looting of company by managers was in connection with purchase or sale |
| SEC v. Medical Committee for Human Rights | 404 U.S. 403 | 1972 | Neither | Proxy | 6-1 | Marshall | **Douglas** | SEC admin | Case moot; SEC affirmed staff no action on shareholder proposal for Dow proxy |
| Reliance Electric Co. v. Emerson Electric Co. | 404 U.S. 418 | 1972 | Restrictive | Exchange Act 16(b) | 4-3 | Stewart | **Douglas** Brennan White | SEC amicus | Shareholder who sells down to below 10% and then sells the rest only liable for first transaction |
| Affiliated Ute Citizens v. U.S. | 406 U.S. 128 | 1972 | Expansive | 10b-5 | 7-0 | Blackmun | | SEC amicus U.S. defendant | Reliance presumed for material omission |
| Caplin v. Marine Midland Grace Trust Co. | 406 U.S. 416 | 1972 | Restrictive | Trust Indenture Act | 5-4 | Marshall | **Douglas** Brennan White Blackmun | SEC intervenor | Chapter X trustee does not have standing to assert claims under trust indenture |
| Kern County Land Co. v. Occidental Petroleum Corp. | 411 U.S. 582 | 1973 | Restrictive | Exchange Act 16(b) | 6-3 | White | **Douglas** Brennan Stewart | None | Unsuccessful bidder who was cashed out not subject to § 16(b) |

| | | | | | | | | | |
|---|---|---|---|---|---|---|---|---|---|
| Merrill Lynch, Pierce, Fenner & Smith v. Ware | 414 U.S. 117 | 1973 | Restrictive | Arbitration | 8-0 | Blackmun | | SEC amicus | Exchange Act does not preempt state law exempting wage claim from arbitration. |
| Scherk v. Alberto-Culver Co. | 417 U.S. 506 | 1974 | Restrictive | Arbitration | 5-4 | Stewart | **Douglas** Brennan White Marshall | None | Exclusive jurisdiction provision did not bar arbitration of 10b-5 claim under international arbitration agreement |
| Bangor Punta Operations, Inc. v. Bangor & Aroostook R.R. Co. | 417 U.S. 703 | 1974 | Restrictive | 10b-5; Anti-trust | 5-4 | Powell | **Marshall** Douglas Brennan White | None | Company cannot sue for mismanagement after acquiring shares from alleged wrongdoer |
| Securities Investor Protection Corp. v. Barbour | 421 U.S. 412 | 1975 | Restrictive | SIPA | 8-1 | Marshall | **Douglas** | SEC respondent | Rejecting implied right to compel SIPC to take action |
| Blue Chip Stamps v. Manor Drug Stores | 421 U.S. 723 | 1975 | Restrictive | 10b-5 | 6-3 | Rehnquist | **Blackmun** Douglas Brennan | SEC amicus | Plaintiff must have purchased or sold to have standing |
| United Housing Foundation v. Forman | 421 U.S. 837 | 1975 | Restrictive | Definition of security | 6-3 | Powell | **Brennan** Douglas White | SEC amicus | "Stock" affording right to rent apartment in housing cooperative not a security |
| Rondeau v. Mosinee Paper Co. | 422 U.S. 49 | 1975 | Restrictive | Tender Offer | 6-3 | Burger | **Brennan** Douglas Marshall | None | Inadvertent failure to file disclosure did not give rise to irreparable harm needed for injunctive action |
| Gordon v. New York Stock Exchange | 422 U.S. 659 | 1975 | Expansive | Antitrust/ Exchange Act | 9-0 | Blackmun | | SEC amicus | SEC oversight preempts antitrust liability for NYSE fixing commissions among its members |

| Case Name | Cite | Year | Expansive/ Restrictive | Substantive Context | Vote | Majority Writer | Dissenting | Government Role | Description |
|---|---|---|---|---|---|---|---|---|---|
| U.S. v. National Association of Securities Dealers | 422 U.S. 694 | 1975 | Expansive | Antitrust/ Inv. Co. Act | 5-4 | Powell | **White** Douglas Brennan Marshall | SEC amicus | SEC oversight preempts antitrust liability for sales restrictions imposed by investment companies on mutual fund shares |
| Foremost-McKesson, Inc. v. Provident Sec. Co. | 423 U.S. 232 | 1976 | Restrictive | Exchange Act 16(b) | 8-0 | Powell | | None | Transaction pushing shareholder above 10% does not count as one of the required two transactions for short-swing profits rule |
| Ernst & Ernst v. Hochfelder | 425 U.S. 185 | 1976 | Restrictive | 10b-5 | 6-2 | Powell | **Blackmun** Brennan | SEC amicus | 10b-5 requires fraudulent intent, not mere negligence |
| Radzanower v. Touche Ross & Co. | 426 U.S. 148 | 1976 | Restrictive | 10b-5 | 8-1 | Stewart | **Stevens** | SEC amicus | Venue provisions of Exchange Act did not repeal venue provision of National Bank Act |
| TSC Industries, Inc. v. Northway, Inc. | 426 U.S. 438 | 1976 | Restrictive | Proxy | 8-0 | Marshall | | SEC amicus | Materiality standard requires substantial likelihood that information would affect shareholder action |
| Piper v. Chris-Craft Indus., Inc. | 430 U.S. 1 | 1977 | Restrictive | Tender Offer | 7-2 | Burger | **Stevens** Brennan | SEC amicus | Rejecting implied private cause of action for bidder under §14(e) |
| Santa Fe Indus., Inc. v. Green | 430 U.S. 462 | 1977 | Restrictive | 10b-5 | 8-1/ 6-3 | White | **Brennan** | None | 10b-5 requires misrepresentation |
| E.I. duPont de Nemours and Co. v. Collins | 432 U.S. 46 | 1977 | Expansive | Inv. Co. Act | 7-1 | Burger | Brennan | SEC admin | SEC approval of investment company merger upheld |

| Case | Citation | Year | Orientation | Topic | Vote | Author | Dissent | Government | Holding |
|---|---|---|---|---|---|---|---|---|---|
| SEC v. Sloan | 436 U.S. 103 | 1978 | Restrictive | Enforcement | 9-0 | Rehnquist | | SEC admin | SEC cannot repeatedly use §12(k) to suspend trading |
| Coopers & Lybrand v. Livesay | 437 U.S. 463 | 1978 | Restrictive | 10b-5; Securities Act | 9-0 | Stevens | | None | Orders relating to class certification are not independently appealable |
| Parklane Hosiery Co. v. Shore | 439 U.S. 322 | 1979 | Expansive | 10b-5; Proxy | 8-1 | Stewart | Rehnquist | SEC amicus | Applying offensive collateral estoppel in private action to contested findings made in prior administrative proceeding |
| International Brotherhood of Teamsters v. Daniel | 439 U.S. 551 | 1979 | Restrictive | Definition of security | 8-0 | Powell | | SEC amicus | Non-compulsory, non-contributory pension not a security |
| Burks v. Lasker | 441 U.S. 471 | 1979 | Restrictive | Inv. Co. Act | 8-0 | Brennan | | SEC amicus | Federal courts should apply state corporate law to directors' decision to terminate derivative suit on behalf of an investment company if not inconsistent with federal law. |
| U.S. v. Naftalin | 441 U.S. 768 | 1979 | Expansive | Securities Act 17(a) | 8-0 | Brennan | | U.S. prosecutor | §17(a) protects brokers deceived by customer as well as investors |
| Touche Ross & Co. v. Redington | 442 U.S. 560 | 1979 | Restrictive | Exchange Act 17(a) | 7-1 | Rehnquist | Marshall | SIPC | No implied private action under §17(a) against broker's auditors |
| Leroy v. Great Western United Corporation | 443 U.S. 173 | 1979 | Neither | Tender Offer | 6-3 | Stevens | White Brennan Marshall | SEC amicus | Federal injunction sought again state law limiting takeovers lacked proper venue |

| Case Name | Cite | Year | Expansive/ Restrictive | Substantive Context | Vote | Majority Writer | Dissenting | Government Role | Description |
|---|---|---|---|---|---|---|---|---|---|
| Transamerica Mortgage Advisors, Inc. v. Lewis | 444 U.S. 11 | 1979 | Restrictive | Inv. Advisers Act | 5-4 | Stewart | **White** Brennan Marshall Stevens | SEC amicus | No private cause of action under §206 |
| Chiarella v. U.S. | 445 U.S. 222 | 1980 | Restrictive | Insider Trading | 6-3 | Powell | **Burger Blackmun** Marshall | U.S. prosecutor | Fraud based on silence requires duty to disclose |
| Aaron v. SEC | 446 U.S. 680 | 1980 | Restrictive | 10b-5 | 6-3 | Stewart | **Blackmun** Brennan Marshall | SEC plaintiff | SEC must show scienter for injunction under 10b-5, but not §17(a)(2) & (3) |
| Rubin v. US | 449 U.S. 424 | 1981 | Expansive | Securities Act 17(a) | 9-0 | Burger | | U.S. prosecutor | Pledge of stock is sale for §17(a) |
| Steadman v. SEC | 450 U.S. 91 | 1981 | Expansive | Inv. Co. Act | 7-2 | Brennan | **Powell** Stewart | SEC admin | Preponderance sufficient for SEC action to bar investment advisor |
| Marine Bank v. Weaver | 455 U.S. 551 | 1982 | Restrictive | Definition of security | 9-0 | Burger | | SEC amicus | Certificate of deposit and unique one-on-one business agreement not a security |
| Edgar v. MITE | 457 U.S. 624 | 1982 | Expansive | Tender Offer | 6-3 | White | **Marshall** Brennan **Rehnquist** | SEC amicus | State anti-takeover law imposes undue burden on interstate commerce; (no decision on pre-emption or dormant commerce clause) |
| Herman & MacLean v. Huddleston | 459 U.S. 375 | 1983 | Expansive | 10b-5 | 8-0 | Marshall | | SEC amicus | 10b-5 cause of action not precluded by availability of §11 claim; proof is by preponderance |

| Case | Citation | Year | Direction | Topic | Vote | Majority | Dissent | SEC Role | Holding |
|---|---|---|---|---|---|---|---|---|---|
| Dirks v. SEC | 463 U.S. 646 | 1983 | Restrictive | Insider Trading | 6-3 | Powell | **Blackmun** Brennan Marshall | SEC admin | 10b-5 insider trading incudes tippee liability if awareness of personal benefit to insider from disclosing |
| Daily Income Fund v. Fox | 464 U.S. 523 | 1984 | Expansive | Inv. Co. Act | 9-0 | Brennan | | SEC amicus | Derivative suit requirements do not apply to shareholder suit for excessive compensation to advisor |
| SEC v. O'Brien | 467 U.S. 735 | 1984 | Expansive | Enforcement | 9-0 | Marshall | | SEC respondent | SEC not required to serve notice to target in non-public investigation that it was serving subpoena on third parties |
| Landreth Timber Co. v. Landreth | 471 U.S. 681 | 1985 | Expansive | Definition of security | 8-1 | Powell | **Stevens** | SEC amicus | Sale of 100% of stock of a company is sale of security |
| Gould v. Ruefenacht | 471 U.S. 701 | 1985 | Expansive | Definition of security | 8-1 | Powell | **Stevens** | SEC amicus | Sale of 60% of stock of a company is sale of security |
| Schreiber v. Burlington Northern, Inc. | 472 U.S. 1 | 1985 | Restrictive | Tender Offer | 7-0 | Burger | | None | Allegations of unfairness but not showing a misleading statement or manipulation fails to state § 14(e) claim |
| Lowe v. SEC | 472 U.S. 181 | 1985 | Restrictive | Inv. Advisers Act | 8-0 | Stevens | | SEC admin | Newsletter exempt from registration requirements |
| Bateman Eichler, Hill Richards, Inc. v. Berner | 472 U.S. 299 | 1985 | Expansive | Insider Trading | 8-0 | Brennan | | SEC amicus | In pari delicto does not bar tippee from suing tipper for false tips |
| Randall v. Loftsgaarden | 478 U.S. 647 | 1986 | Expansive | 10b-5; Securities Act 12(2) | 8-1 | O'Connor | **Brennan** | SEC amicus | §12(2) rescission not subject to offset |

| Case Name | Cite | Year | Expansive/ Restrictive | Substantive Context | Vote | Majority Writer | Dissenting | Government Role | Description |
|---|---|---|---|---|---|---|---|---|---|
| CTS Corp. v. Dynamics Corp. of Am. | 481 U.S. 69 | 1987 | Restrictive | Tender Offer | 6-3 | Powell | **White** Blackmun Stevens | SEC amicus | Second generation state anti-takeover statute applicable only to instate corporations sustained as internal corporate affairs |
| Shearson/ American Express, Inc. v. McMahon | 482 U.S. 220 | 1987 | Restrictive | 10b-5; Arbitration | 5-4 | O'Connor | **Blackmun** Brennan Marshall **Stevens** | SEC amicus | Limiting *Wilko* to Securities Act |
| Basic Inc. v. Levinson | 485 U.S. 224 | 1988 | Expansive | 10b-5 | 4-2 | Blackmun | **White** O'Connor | SEC amicus | Reliance presumed based on fraud on the market; adopt materiality standard from *TSC* for 10b-5; forward-looking information assessed on probability x magnitude |
| Pinter v. Dahl | 486 U.S. 622 | 1988 | Restrictive | Securities Act | 7-1 | Blackmun | **Stevens** | SEC amicus | §12(a)(1) liability only for persons who solicit for sellers or their own financial interest |
| Rodriguez de Quijas v. Shearson/ American Express, Inc. | 490 U.S. 477 | 1989 | Restrictive | Securities Act; Arbitration | 5-4 | Kennedy | **Stevens** Brennan Marshall Blackmun | None | Pre-dispute arbitration agreement enforceable; *Wilko* overruled |
| Reves v. Ernst & Young | 494 U.S. 56 | 1990 | Expansive | Definition of security | 5-4 | Marshall | **Rehnquist** White O'Connor Scalia | SEC amicus | Demand notes are securities under family resemblance test; not exempt under short-term maturity exemption |

| Case | Cite | Year | Direction | Statute | Vote | Majority | Dissent | Amicus | Holding |
|---|---|---|---|---|---|---|---|---|---|
| Kamen v. Kemper Financial Services, Inc. | 500 U.S. 90 | 1991 | Restrictive | Inv. Co. Act | 9-0 | Marshall | | SEC amicus | State law demand futility rule applies to derivative suit on behalf of investment company not ALI's universal demand rule |
| Virginia Bankshares, Inc. v. Sandberg | 501 U.S. 1083 | 1991 | Restrictive | Exchange Act; Proxy | 5-4 | Souter | Kennedy Blackmun **Stevens** Marshall | SEC amicus | Opinions actionable under §14(a) if based on verifiable facts; no transaction causation when vote outcome not affected by alleged deception |
| Gollust v. Mendell | 501 U.S. 115 | 1991 | Expansive | Exchange Act 16(b) | 9-0 | Souter | | SEC amicus | Standing available to shareholder of parent company for §16(b) claim of subsidiary |
| Lampf, Pleva, Lipkind, Prupis & Petigrow v. Gilbertson | 501 U.S. 350 | 1991 | Restrictive | 10b-5 | 5-4 | Blackmun | **Stevens** Souter **Kennedy** O'Connor | SEC amicus | Borrowing statute of limitations for 10b-5 claims from the express causes of action |
| Musick, Peeler & Garrett v. Employers Ins. of Wausau | 508 U.S. 286 | 1993 | Expansive | 10b-5 | 6-3 | Kennedy | **Thomas** Blackmun O'Connor | SEC amicus | Contribution claim available under 10b-5 |
| Central Bank of Denver N.A. v. First Interstate Bank of Denver | 511 U.S. 164 | 1994 | Restrictive | 10b-5 | 5-4 | Kennedy | **Stevens** Blackmun Souter Ginsburg | SEC amicus | No aiding and abetting in suits by private plaintiff |
| Gustafson v. Alloyd Co., Inc. | 513 U.S. 561 | 1995 | Restrictive | Securities Act | 5-4 | Kennedy | **Thomas** Scalia **Ginsburg** Breyer | SEC amicus | Prospectus for $12 claims limited to documents used in public offering |

| Case Name | Cite | Year | Expansive/ Restrictive | Substantive Context | Vote | Majority Writer | Dissenting | Government Role | Description |
|---|---|---|---|---|---|---|---|---|---|
| Plaut v. Spendthrift Farm, Inc. | 514 U.S. 211 | 1995 | Restrictive | 10b-5 | 7-2 | Scalia | **Stevens** Ginsburg | SEC amicus | Statute retroactively reviving claims barred by statute of limitations unconstitutional after limitation period has lapsed |
| Matsushita Elec. Indus. Co. Ltd. v. Epstein | 516 U.S. 367 | 1996 | Restrictive | Claim preclusion | 6-3 | Thomas | **Stevens Ginsburg** Souter | None | State court judgment settling state & federal clams precludes federal claims under full faith & credit notwithstanding claims could not be brought in federal court |
| U.S. v. O'Hagan | 521 U.S. 642 | 1997 | Expansive | Insider Trading | 6-3 | Ginsburg | **Scalia Thomas** Rehnquist | U.S. prosecutor | Recognizing 10b-5 insider trading liability under misappropriation theory; Rule 14e-3 within SEC's rule-making authority as applied |
| Wharf (Holdings) Ltd. v. United Intern. Holdings, Inc. | 532 U.S. 588 | 2001 | Expansive | 10b-5 | 9-0 | Breyer | | SEC amicus | Secret reservation not to sell was a misrepresentation; option was a security; oral agreement could support a 10b-5 claim |
| SEC v. Zandford | 535 U.S. 813 | 2002 | Expansive | 10b-5 | 9-0 | Stevens | | SEC plaintiff | Brokers sale of securities with undisclosed intent to misappropriate proceeds was fraud in connection with purchase or sale |
| SEC v. Edwards | 540 U.S. 389 | 2004 | Expansive | Definition of security | 9-0 | O'Connor | | SEC plaintiff | Instrument with fixed rate return was an investment contract |

| Case | Citation | Year | Direction | Statute | Vote | Majority | Dissent/Concur | Amicus | Holding |
|---|---|---|---|---|---|---|---|---|---|
| Dura Pharmaceuticals, Inc. v. Broudo | 544 U.S. 336 | 2005 | Restrictive | 10b-5 | 9-0 | Breyer | | None | Plaintiffs must plead loss causation |
| Merrill Lynch, Pierce, Fenner & Smith v. Dabit | 547 U.S. 71 | 2006 | Expansive | SLUSA | 8-0 | Stevens | | SEC amicus | State law suit by "holders" pre-empted |
| Kircher v. Putnam Funds Trust | 547 U.S. 633 | 2006 | Neither | SLUSA | 9-0 | Souter | | None | Decision to remand suit previously removed not appealable |
| Credit Suisse Securities (US) LLC v. Billing | 551 U.S. 264 | 2007 | Expansive | Exchange Act/Antitrust | 7-1 | Breyer | Thomas | U.S. amicus | Antitrust claims precluded by securities laws |
| Tellabs Inc. v. Makor Issues & Rights, Ltd. | 551 U.S. 308 | 2007 | Neither | PSLRA | 8-1 | Ginsburg | Stevens | SEC amicus | Allegations in complaint as to inference of fraud under PSLRA's strong inference provision must be at least as compelling and cogent as competing inferences |
| Stoneridge Investment Partners, LLC v. Scientific-Atlanta, Inc. | 552 U.S. 148 | 2008 | Restrictive | 10b-5 | 5-3 | Kennedy | Stevens Souter Ginsburg | U.S. amicus | Investors did not rely on acts of third-party vendors that facilitated fraud by public company |
| Jones v. Harris Associates L.P. | 559 U.S. 335 | 2010 | Expansive | Inv. Co. Act | 9-0 | Alito | | SEC amicus | Reasonableness of advisor fees assessed under multi-factor test |
| Merck & Co., Inc. v. Reynolds | 559 U.S. 633 | 2010 | Expansive | 10b-5 | 9-0 | Breyer | | SEC amicus | Rejects inquiry notice; statute of limitations begins to run when a reasonably diligent plaintiff would have known facts establishing violation |

| Case Name | Cite | Year | Expansive/ Restrictive | Substantive Context | Vote | Majority Writer | Dissenting | Government Role | Description |
|---|---|---|---|---|---|---|---|---|---|
| Morrison v. National Australia Bank Ltd. | 561 U.S. 247 | 2010 | Restrictive | 10b-5 | 8-0 | Scalia | | SEC amicus | No private cause of action for foreign investors purchasing securities of foreign company on foreign exchange |
| Free Enterprise Fund v. PCAOB | 561 U.S. 477 | 2010 | Restrictive | Sarbanes-Oxley Act | 5-4 | Roberts | **Breyer** Stevens Ginsburg Sotomayor | U.S. defending law | Sarbanes-Oxley unconstitutionally limits removal of PCAOB members |
| Matrixx Initiatives v. Siracusano | 563 U.S. 27 | 2011 | Expansive | 10b-5 | 9-0 | Sotomayor | | SEC amicus | Statistical significance not required to establish materiality if reasonable investors would rely |
| Erica P. John Fund, Inc. v. Halliburton Co. (I) | 563 U.S. 804 | 2011 | Expansive | 10b-5 | 9-0 | Roberts | | SEC amicus | Plaintiff not required to show loss causation to certify a class |
| Janus Capital Group v. First Derivative Traders | 564 U.S. 135 | 2011 | Restrictive | 10b-5 | 5-4 | Thomas | **Breyer** Ginsburg Sotomayor Kagan | SEC amicus | Investment adviser to a related mutual fund did not "make" the statements of the mutual fund for 10b-5 liability |
| Credit Suisse Sec. (USA) LLC v. Simmonds | 566 U.S. 221 | 2012 | Restrictive | Exchange Act 16(b) | 8-0 | Scalia | | SEC amicus | Statute of limitations for §16(b) not tolled by failure to disclose transactions pursuant to §16(a); splits 4-4 on repose question |
| Gabelli v. SEC | 568 U.S. 442 | 2013 | Restrictive | Inv. Co. Act. | 9-0 | Roberts | | SEC plaintiff | Discovery rule does not toll SEC enforcement actions seeking a civil penalty |

| Case | Cite | Year | Type | Statute | Vote | Majority | Dissent | Amicus | Holding |
|------|------|------|------|---------|------|----------|---------|--------|---------|
| Amgen Inc. v. Connecticut Ret. Plans and Trust Funds | 568 U.S. 455 | 2013 | Expansive | 10b-5 | 6-3 | Ginsberg | **Scalia Thomas** Kennedy | SEC amicus | Class action plaintiff need not show materiality to certify a class under fraud-on-the-market presumption |
| Chadbourne & Parke LLP v. Troice | 571 U.S. 377 | 2014 | Restrictive | SLUSA | 7-2 | Breyer | **Kennedy** Alito | SEC amicus | SLUSA did not preclude a state-law class action based on misrepresentations concerning uncovered certificates of deposit not traded on a national exchange |
| Lawson v. FMR LLC | 571 U.S. 429 | 2014 | Expansive | Sarbanes-Oxley Act | 6-3 | Ginsburg | **Sotomayor** Kennedy Alito | SEC amicus | Sarbanes-Oxley Act extends whistleblower protection to employees of privately held contractors and subcontractors |
| Halliburton Co. v. Erica P. John Fund, Inc. (II) | 573 U.S. 258 | 2014 | Expansive | 10b-5 | 6-3 | Roberts | **Thomas** Scalia Alito | SEC amicus | *Basic* not overruled; defendant can raise lack of price impact as defense to class certification |
| Omnicare, Inc. v. Laborers Dist. Council Const. Ind. Pen. Fund | 575 U.S. 175 | 2015 | Expansive | Securities Act | 9-0 | Kagan | | SEC amicus | Opinions actionable under §11 if subjectively false or material facts conflicting with what reasonable investor would take from the statement |
| Merrill Lynch, Pierce, Fenner & Smith Inc. v. Manning | 578 U.S. 374 | 2016 | Restrictive | Exchange Act | 8-0 | Kagan | | None | Exclusive jurisdiction for securities claims does not block state law claims for short selling |
| Salman v. US | 580 U.S. 39 | 2016 | Expansive | Insider Trading | 8-0 | Alito | | U.S. prosecutor | Gift of material non-public information to brother is a personal benefit to the tipper |

| Case Name | Cite | Year | Expansive/ Restrictive | Substantive Context | Vote | Majority Writer | Dissenting | Government Role | Description |
|---|---|---|---|---|---|---|---|---|---|
| Kokesh v. SEC | 581 U.S. 455 | 2017 | Restrictive | Enforcement, Disgorgement | 9-0 | Sotomayor | | SEC plaintiff | Disgorgement action is a penalty that must be brought within 5 years |
| Cyan, Inc. v. Beaver Cty. Empl. Ret. Fund | 138 S. Ct. 1061 | 2018 | Neither | Securities Act; SLUSA | 9-0 | Kagan | | U.S. amicus | SLUSA did not deprive state courts of jurisdiction over § 11 claims |
| Lucia v. SEC | 138 S. Ct. 2044 | 2018 | Restrictive | Appointments Clause | 7-2 | Kagan | **Sotomayor** Ginsburg | SEC admin | Administrative law judges are officers of United States; must be appointed by SEC |
| Lorenzo v. SEC | 139 S. Ct. 1094 | 2019 | Expansive | 10b-5 | 6-2 | Breyer | **Thomas** Gorsuch | SEC admin | Transmission of false statements fits within other parts of Rule 10b-5 even if not "made" per 10b-5(b) |
| Liu v. SEC | 140 S. Ct. 1936 | 2020 | Neither | Exchange Act Enforcement; Disgorgement | 8-1 | Sotomayor | **Thomas** | SEC plaintiff | Disgorgement is equitable relief permitted subject to equitable limits |
| Goldman Sachs Group, Inc. v. Arkansas Teachers Ret. Syst. | 141 S. Ct. 1951 | 2021 | Neither | 10b-5 | 8-1/ 6-3 | Barrett | **Sotomayor Gorsuch** Thomas Alito | SEC amicus | Defendants can argue that statements are too generic to have price impact at certification; Defendants bear burden of persuasion to show lack of price impact to defeat class certification |

## Supreme Court Dissents from Denial of Certiorari, 1933–2021

| Case Name | Cite | Year | Substantive Context | Writer | Joining | Description |
|---|---|---|---|---|---|---|
| Kaplan v. Lehman Bros. | 389 U.S. 954 | 1967 | Antitrust | Warren | | Brokerage commission price fixing |
| Kline v. SEC | 394 U.S. 976 | 1969 | Insider trading | White | | Petition from Second Circuit's *Texas Gulf Sulphur* decision |
| Sennott v. Rodman & Renshaw | 414 U.S. 926 | 1973 | Exchange Act | Douglas | Blackmun | Broker liable for executing fraudulent trades? |
| Yeomans v. Kentucky | 423 U.S. 983 | 1975 | 11th Amendment | Brennan | | Does sovereign immunity under the 11th Amendment apply in securities cases? |
| Dupuy v. Dupuy | 434 U.S. 911 | 1977 | Rule 10b-5 | White | | What standard of care is required for plaintiffs in Rule 10b-5 cases? |
| Nuveen v. Sanders | 450 U.S. 1005 | 1981 | Securities Act | Powell | Rehnquist | Did due care defense require review of accountant's work papers by commercial paper dealers? |
| Mordaunt v. Incomco | 469 U.S. 1115 | 1985 | Definition of a security | White | Burger Brennan | Commonality under "common enterprise" for investment contract test |
| Whitman v. U.S. | 574 U.S. 1003 | 2014 | 10b-5 | Scalia | Thomas | Deference to agency rule inappropriate in a criminal proceeding; petitioner did not seek review on this question |

# Notes

## Introduction

1. Moley, First New Deal 127–164. Thomas K. McCraw, Prophets of Regulation 169 (1984). The Roosevelt speech is reprinted in Moley, First New Deal 121.
2. Donald A. Ritchie, The Pecora Wall Street Expose, 219, 223–24 in Congress Investigates, 1792–1974 (Arthur M. Schlesinger, Jr., and Roger Bruns, eds. 1975); Michael Perino, The Hellhound of Wall Street 190–91 (2010).
3. Moley, After Seven Years 176–79. Sam Rayburn, a House committee chair and later Speaker who would be a key player in each of the three securities laws passed during FDR's first term, questioned the government's power to revoke securities as "not based on sound principle": "Now we have passed a lot of laws since we met here on the 5th of March. But I do not think we have given anybody this much power yet." Federal Securities Acts Hearings, House Commerce Committee, 73rd Congress, 1st Sess. (1933) p. 135.
4. Moley, After Seven Years 179. The Carlton refers to the stately hotel, two blocks north of the White House on 16th Street, now known as the St. Regis.
   Memorandum from Felix Frankfurter, Professor, Harvard Law Sch. (Mar. 15, 1933) FF-LC, Reel 60. Letter from Felix Frankfurter, Professor, Harvard Law Sch., to President Franklin D. Roosevelt (Mar. 14, 1933) FF-LC, Reel 60. Felix Frankfurter, Diary (May 8, 1933) FF-LC, Box 1, Reel 1.
5. Felix Frankfurter, Lecture Notes, at 5 (Sept. 28, 1914), FF-Harvard, Part 3, Reel 21.
6. Louis Brandeis, *A Curse of Bigness*, Harper's Weekly, Jan. 10, 1914, at 18. What passed for economics in Brandeis's thinking can charitably be described as muddled, and less charitably as anti-consumer. See Thomas K. McCraw, Prophets of Regulation 100–01, 104–07, 136 (1984) (describing Brandeis's analytical confusion on the subject of monopoly). H.N. Hirsch, The Enigma of Felix Frankfurter 104 (1981). Robert H. Jackson, That Man: An Insider's Portrait of Franklin Delano Roosevelt 122 (John Q. Barrett ed. 2003). Peter H. Irons, The New Deal Lawyers 20 (1982). Letter from Raymond Moley to Felix Frankfurter, Professor, Harvard Law Sch. (Oct. 31, 1935) FF-LC, Reel 51. Brandeis's use of Frankfurter as his mouthpiece was a long-standing practice. David W. Levy & Bruce Allen Murphy, Preserving the Progressive Spirit in a Conservative Time: The Joint Reform Efforts of Justice Brandeis and Professor Frankfurter, 1916–1933, 78 Mich. L. Rev. 1252, 1257, 1279 (1980).
7. Letter from Felix Frankfurter, Professor, Harvard Law Sch., to Justice Harlan Fiske Stone (undated) FF-Harvard, Part 3, Reel 3. Mitchell and Insull were two of the targets skewered by Pecora. Letter from Justice Harlan Fiske Stone to Felix Frankfurter, Professor, Harvard Law Sch. (Feb. 17, 1933) FF-Harvard Part 3, Reel

298 NOTES

3. Felix Frankfurter, The Federal Securities Act: II, Fortune, Aug. 1933, at 53, 54. Letter from Felix Frankfurter, Professor, Harvard Law Sch., to President Franklin D. Roosevelt (May 18, 1934) FF-LC, Reel 60. Moley, First New Deal 72. Arthur M. Schlesinger, Jr., The Age of Roosevelt: The Coming of the New Deal 503, 248 (1958).

Frankfurter had a similarly dim view of the lawyers and accountants who served the capitalists. Letter from Felix Frankfurter, Professor, Harvard Law Sch., to James M. Landis, Comm'r, Fed. Trade Comm'n (Feb. 8, 1934) FF-LC, Reel 70 ("I have long had strong suspicions that these fancy accounting firms occupy a role towards financial and business immoralities comparable to that of the eminent law firms.").

8. Memorandum from Lewis F. Powell, Jr., to Joe Carter, Managing Partner, Hunton & Williams (Aug. 1977), LFP Collection. Telephone Interview with Lawrence E. Blanchard, Jr., Former Attorney, Hunton & Williams (Mar. 22, 2002) (describing Powell as a "master of making connections") (notes on file with authors). John C. Jeffries, Justice Lewis F. Powell: A Biography (2001) at 187.

9. Memorandum from Lewis F. Powell, Jr., to Joe Carter. Telephone Interview with Lawrence E. Blanchard, Jr. Memorandum from Lewis F. Powell, Jr., to James J. Ward and James E. Galleher 2 (Oct. 5, 1940) (advising that "an offering to ten or fifteen institutions would clearly seem to be private, other things being consistent, whereas, an offering to from twenty to twenty-five institutions may not be such a clear case"). Letter from Lewis F. Powell, Jr., to Edwin B. Horner 1–2 (Mar. 22, 1957). Letter from Lewis F. Powell, Jr., to Edwin Hyde 1–2 (June 1, 1956). Letter from Lewis F. Powell, Jr., to Martin Victor, Attorney, Sullivan & Cromwell 1 (Nov. 15, 1946). Letter from Edwin B. Horner to Lewis F. Powell, Jr. 1 (Nov. 8, 1971) ("I remember vividly in your office the day you said, 'You cannot start a life insurance company. You have done enough funny things.' But at your desk First Colony was created."). Letter from Lewis F. Powell, Jr., to John W. Riely (discussing the formation of Commonwealth Natural Resource Corporation), LFP Collection.

10. Letter from Lewis F. Powell, Jr., to Morton G. Thalhimer 1 (Nov. 27, 1951), LFP Collection.

11. Memorandum from Lewis F. Powell, Jr., to Jim Browning, at 1 (Sept. 13, 1982). Letter from Justice Lewis F. Powell, Jr., to Michael P. Dooley, Professor of Law, University of Virginia 1 (Oct. 25, 1980), LFP Collection.

12. Letter from Lewis F. Powell, Jr., to Senator Burton K. Wheeler 1 (Mar. 25, 1937) ("I am doing what I can in a quiet way to stimulate activity against this attack on the Supreme Court."). Letter from Lewis F. Powell, Jr., to Henry C. Riely 2 (Oct. 5, 1940), LFP Collection.

13. Letter from Lewis F. Powell, Jr., to George Gibson 1 (Nov. 25, 1942). Letter from Lewis F. Powell, Jr., to Virginius Dabney 3 (June 3, 1975). Memorandum from Lewis F. Powell, Jr., to Joe Carter, at 28 ("It was necessary to keep a sensible balance between community and public service activities and a lawyer's obligations to clients and partners."). Powell's work on behalf of local Democrats was limited to financial support and some speeches on behalf of politicians who were friends. Letter from Lewis F. Powell, Jr., to Colgate W. Darden, Jr. 1 (Mar. 15, 1976) ("Although I was always a Virginia Democrat in state politics . . . I was never actually a participant in party

affairs or decision-making."). Letter from Lewis F. Powell, Jr., to Senator Harry F. Byrd 1 (Oct. 15, 1952) ("Stevenson will be more successful than Truman in obtaining the passage of pet left-wing legislation such as the FEPC, socialized medicine, continued deficit spending, higher taxes and the like. In short, the trend toward socialism will inevitably be accelerated if Stevenson is elected."). Memorandum from Lewis F. Powell, Jr., to Jody, Penny, Molly and Lewis III [Powell], at 9 (Dec. 15, 1981) (stating that Powell and others organized a group called "Democrats for Eisenhower" in the 1952 and 1956 elections). Letter from Lewis F. Powell, Jr., to Webster S. Rhoads 1 (Oct. 13, 1952) ("I am now in this campaign up to my neck. With the indulgence of my partners and my clients, I am averaging only three or four hours per day practicing law. The remainder of my time, usually until about midnight, is devoted to the campaign."). Letter from Lewis F. Powell, Jr., to Senator Harry F. Byrd 3 (Oct. 10, 1956) ("[I]f Stevenson should be elected the trend toward an American brand of socialism will be greatly accelerated [*sic*]. In short, we know that Virginia should support Eisenhower and conversely we all should do everything in our power to defeat Stevenson and Kefauver."), LFP Collection.

14. Memorandum from Lewis F. Powell, Jr., to Jody, Penny, Molly, and Lewis III [Powell], at 10–11; Letter from Lewis F. Powell, Jr., to Walter S. Robertson, Attorney, Scott & Stringfellow 1 (Feb. 26, 1953) (removing his name from consideration for Chairman of the SEC); Letter from Walter S. Robertson, Attorney, Scott & Stringfellow to Lewis F. Powell, Jr. 1 (Mar. 2, 1953) (expressing his regret as to Powell's decision). Shortly after the offer of the SEC chairmanship, Ralph Demmler, appointed chairman after Powell declined, asked Powell if he would be interested in being a commissioner. Powell again declined (without telling Demmler of the earlier offer). Letter from Lewis F. Powell, Jr., to Ralph H. Demmler, Attorney, Reed, Smith, Shaw & McClay 1 (Apr. 23, 1953); Letter from Ralph H. Demmler, Attorney, Reed, Smith, Shaw & McClay to Lewis F. Powell, Jr. 1 (Apr. 27, 1953), LFP Collection.

15. Letter from Lewis F. Powell, Jr., to Winthrop Rockefeller, Governor of Arkansas 1 (Sept. 19, 1968) ("We are making a major effort here in Virginia to carry the state for Nixon."). Letter from Lewis F. Powell, Jr., to Private James Harvie Wilkinson, III 2 (Oct. 20, 1968) ("I am afraid Virginia is going for Humphrey. . . . The idiot vote—and lots of otherwise sensibl(e votes—will go to Wallace; the Negro bloc and the straight-ticket Democrats will, of course, go for Humphrey."). Virginia went for Nixon. Letter from Lewis F. Powell, Jr., to Richard M. Nixon 1 (Oct. 27, 1960) ("I appreciate very much your letter concerning my support in the campaign. I want you to know that I think, regardless of the outcome, that you are making a magnificent effort against the most formidable odds. I have also been proud of the way in which you have stood by your principles, and not endeavored to 'out promise' your opponent."). Letter from Lewis F. Powell, Jr., to John N. Mitchell, Attorney General, U.S. Department of Justice 1 (Dec. 12, 1969). Fred P. Graham, *Powell Proposed Business Defense*, N.Y. Times, Sept. 29, 1972, at 31, LFP Collection.

16. Jack Anderson, *Powell's Lesson to Business Aired*, Wash. Post, Sept. 28, 1972, at F7. Powell, Lewis F. Jr., "The Memo" (1971). *Powell Memorandum: Attack On American Free Enterprise System* 1. https://scholarlycommons.law.wlu.edu/powellmemo/1.

300 NOTES

17. Telephone Interview with John Buckley, Powell clerk OT '73 (June 5, 2002) (notes on file with authors).

18. In many of these cases defendants are invoking the federal securities laws as a defense to claim based on one of those other bodies of law—e.g., the Exchange Act blocking an antitrust claim—so the numbers presented here do not map onto a pro-plaintiff/pro-defendant dichotomy.

19. Broad amendments to the initial securities laws were introduced in both houses of Congress in May 1940 that would have continued the earlier legislative pattern, but the coming war diverted congressional attention. The legislative interest would wane further during the immediate postwar period. With the arrival of a Republican administration, Congress and the SEC became still more timid. Louis Loss, Securities Regulation (2d ed. 1961) at 199. This legislative silence continued into the early 1960s, broken by a Special Study requested by Congress that led to the Securities Acts Amendments of 1964.

20. Alan Brinkley, The End of Reform 7, 20, 23 (1995). SEC Exchange Act Release No. 3230, Published May 21, 1942. Seligman, Transformation of Wall Street 241, 267. Letter from Abe Fortas to the Hon. William O. Douglas (Nov. 3, 1949), WOD-LC. Louis Loss & Joel Seligman, Securities Regulation 3d ed. at 298, n. 23. Ralph De Bedts, The New Deal's SEC 202 (1964).

21. President Kennedy named Byron White and Arthur Goldberg to replace Charles Whittaker and Felix Frankfurter, moving the court from 5-4 in justices appointed by Eisenhower to 5-4 in justices appointed by Roosevelt, Truman, and Kennedy. Lyndon Johnson swapped Abe Fortas for Arthur Goldberg and Thurgood Marshall for Tom Clark, keeping the breakdown at 5-4, with a majority of justices appointed by Democratic presidents. Marshall's appointment was the critical one moving the Court in a more liberal direction, as Clark was relatively conservative. Warren had been strongly opposed to the New Deal, but he was also strongly suspicious of big business based on his political experiences Jim Newton, Justice for All: Earl Warren and the Nation He Made 70–71, 346 (2006). Dodd Vogel, The "New" Social Regulation in Historical and Comparative Perspective, in Regulation in Perspective 155–56, 164 (Thomas K. McCraw ed., 1981).

22. SEC v. Capital Gains Research Bureau, 375 U.S. 180 (1963); J.I. Case Co. v. Borak, 377 U.S. 426 (1964).

23. Arthur Fleischer, Jr., "*Federal Corporation Law: An Assessment*," 78 Harv. L. Rev. 1146 (1965).

24. The papers of John Paul Stevens have become partially available but not for cases past Blackmun's retirement.

25. SEC v. Chenery Corp., 318 U.S. 80 (1943), 332 U.S. 194 (1947).

# Chapter 1

1. Telegrams from Felix Frankfurter to Franklin D. Roosevelt and Sam Rayburn (Apr. 14, 1933), FF-LC, Reel 115. Letter from Felix Frankfurter, Professor, Harvard Law

Sch., to Sam Rayburn, U.S. Rep. (Apr. 24, 1933) FF-LC, Reel 115. Memorandum Commenting upon a Memorandum Prepared by Counsel for the Investment Bankers' Association in re H.R. 5480 (undated) FF-LC, Reel 84. Letter from Felix Frankfurter, Professor, Harvard Law Sch., to Raymond Moley (May 10, 1933) FF-LC, Reel 51.

2. Letter from Felix Frankfurter to James M. Landis (Mar. 27, 1933), FF-LC, Reel 115. Frankfurter would have gone further, adding restrictions on selling efforts. Id. ("I still think we ought also to cover the mischief of peddling securities from door to door or over the telephone, as was so widely practiced prior to 1929."). Felix Frankfurter, Diary (May 8, 1933) FF-LC, Box 1, Reel 1.

3. Telegram from Felix Frankfurter, Professor, Harvard Law Sch., to Raymond Moley (Apr. 27, 1933) FF-LC, Reel 115; Letter from Felix Frankfurter, Professor, Harvard Law Sch., to Raymond Moley (Apr. 28, 1933) FF-LC, Reel 115 Telegram from Felix Frankfurter, Professor, Harvard Law Sch., to President Franklin Roosevelt (Apr. 14, 1933) FF-LC, Reel 11). Telegram from Felix Frankfurter, Professor, Harvard Law Sch., to President Franklin D. Roosevelt (May 8, 1933) FF-LC, Reel 115. Moley, After Seven Years 182–83 (noting that Byrnes helped Senate Majority Leader Joe Robinson bury the Senate bill in conference in favor of the Frankfurter bill). For a firsthand account of the maneuvering over the legislation, see James M. Landis, The Legislative History of the Securities Act of 1933, 28 Geo. Wash. L. Rev. 29 (1959).

4. Frankfurter picked clerks for Brandeis, Cardozo, and Stone; Corcoran clerked for Holmes on Frankfurter's recommendation. Joseph P. Lash, From the Diaries of Felix Frankfurter 36 (1975). Frankfurter denied exercising influence over personnel matters, despite the overwhelming evidence to the contrary. Letter from Felix Frankfurter, Professor, Harvard Law Sch., to Drew Pearson (May 17, 1933) FF-LC, Reel 53. Moley, After Seven Years 180.

5. Letter from Felix Frankfurter, Professor, Harvard Law Sch., to Arthur Perry (Sept. 18, 1933) FF-LC, Reel 84. Letter from Felix Frankfurter, Professor, Harvard Law Sch., to Justice Harlan Fiske Stone (Sept. 28, 1933) FF-LC, Reel 64; Letter from Felix Frankfurter, Professor, Harvard Law Sch., to George Brownell (Dec. 1, 1933) FF-LC, Reel 69 ("The leading law firms of New York and Boston . . . began a systematic campaign to undermine the essentials of the Act by attributing to it the congealing of capital investment. . . . [T]here isn't a particle of doubt that lawyers of responsibility and high standing infused clients with fears and worse than that—I know what I am talking about—actually discouraged clients, at times, from doing any financing for the present, so that the campaign against the Act, when Congress next meets, should show that the Act had prevented financing,"). Letter from Felix Frankfurter, Professor, Harvard Law Sch., to President Franklin D. Roosevelt (Dec. 19, 1933) FF-LC, Reel 155. Letter from Felix Frankfurter, Professor, Harvard Law Sch., to Henry Stimson (Dec. 19, 1933) FF-LC, Reel 84. Letter from Felix Frankfurter, Professor, Harvard Law Sch., to James M. Landis, Comm'r, Fed. Trade Comm'n (Jan. 10, 1934) FF-LC, Reel 70. Letter from Felix Frankfurter, Professor, Harvard Law Sch., to James M. Landis, Chairman, SEC (Apr. 30, 1935) FF-LC, Reel 45. Letter from Henry L. Stimson to Felix Frankfurter (Jan. 26, 1934), FF-LC, Reel 84.

302 NOTES

6. William O. Douglas & George E. Bates, The Federal Securities Act of 1933, 43 Yale L.J. 171, 171 & 192 (1933) ("There is nothing in the Act which would control the speculative craze of the American public, or which would eliminate wholly unsound capital structures. There is nothing in the Act which would prevent a tyrannical management from playing wide and loose with scattered minorities, or which would prevent a new pyramiding of holding companies violative of the public interest and all canons of sound finance."). Douglas conceded some virtue in the ambiguities in the Securities Act, as they "would give the enforcing agency a powerful weapon . . . with which to control financial practices deemed inimical to the public interest." Id. at 211. His bottom line, however, was that the Act required amendment to correct its "ambiguities and inconsistencies" lest it "paralyz[e] . . . legitimate activity." William O. Douglas & George E. Bates, Some Effects of the Securities Act upon Investment Banking, 1 U. Chi. L. Rev. 283, 306 (1933).
7. Letter from Felix Frankfurter, Professor, Harvard Law Sch., to James M. Landis, Comm'r, Fed. Trade Comm'n (Mar. 17, 1934), FF-LC, Reel 70 ("I wrote him a letter the other day, in a half-saucy, half-severe strain. . . ."). Letter from Felix Frankfurter, Professor, Harvard Law Sch., to William O. Douglas, Professor, Yale Law Sch. (Jan. 16, 1934) WOD-LC. Letter from Felix Frankfurter, Professor, Harvard Law Sch., to William O. Douglas, Professor, Yale Law Sch. (Feb. 5, 1934) WOD-LC. Letter from James M. Landis, Comm'r, Fed. Trade Comm'n, to Felix Frankfurter, Professor, Harvard Law Sch. (Dec. 13, 1933) FF-LC, Reel 70 ("As you know, the Securities Act has been opened pretty widely for discussion.").
8. Letter from Felix Frankfurter, Professor, Harvard Law Sch., to President Franklin D. Roosevelt (Oct. 1, 1933 FF-LC), Reel 155. Letter from Justice Harlan Fiske Stone to Felix Frankfurter, Professor, Harvard Law Sch. (May 15, 1933) FF-LC, Reel 64. Letter from Felix Frankfurter, Professor, Harvard Law Sch., to President Franklin D. Roosevelt (Feb. 14, 1934) FF-LC, Reel 155. Perino, Hellhound 38–39. Richard N. Sheldon, The Pujo Committee, 1912, 171, 192, in Congress Investigates, 1792–1974 (Arthur M. Schlesinger, Jr., and Roger Bruns, eds., 1975).
9. Joseph Lash, Dealers and Dreamers 159–71(1988). Seligman, Transformation of Wall Street 85–87. Letter from James M. Landis to Felix Frankfurter (Mar. 6, 1934), FF-LC, Reel 70.
10. April 12, 1934 Letter from Richard Whitney, New York Stock Exchange, to President Roosevelt (requesting meeting on "unsound" securities legislation), available at http://www.sechistorical.org/collection/papers/1930/1934_04_12_Whitney_to_FDR.pdf. Arthur M. Schlesinger, Jr., The Age of Roosevelt: The Coming of the New Deal 463 (1958). Seligman, Transformation of Wall Street 89–93. Letter from Ben Cohen to Felix Frankfurter, Professor, Harvard Law Sch. (May 11, [1934]), FF-LC, Reel 70. Letter from James M. Landis, Comm'r, Fed. Trade Comm'n, to Felix Frankfurter, Professor, Harvard Law Sch. (Mar. 6, 1934) FF-LC, Reel 70. Letter from Felix Frankfurter, Professor, Harvard Law Sch., to James M. Landis, Comm'r, Fed. Trade Comm'n (Mar. 17, 1934) FF-LC, Reel 70 ("What you tell me as to the likely direction of amendments to the Securities Act is, of course, extremely interesting and sounds like sense."). The 1933 Act had provided liability in some ways greater

NOTES 303

than that of the English Act. Eustace Seligman, "Amend the Securities Act," Atlantic Monthly, Mar. 1934. The Exchange Act made some changes such as permitting the defendant to limit damages by showing a lack of causation.

11. Letter from Felix Frankfurter, Professor, Harvard Law Sch., to Raymond Moley (Apr. 24, 1934) FF-LC, Reel 71. Letter from Felix Frankfurter, Professor, Harvard Law Sch., to Tom Corcoran (May 7, 1934) FF-LC, Reel 70 ("[T]he talk against the Jews in the government comes from the powerful financial and business interests, who have given battle and will continue to give battle to the Administration on things like the Seucrites [sic] Act and stock exchange legislation. It's Wall Street that is using the Jewish stick precisely as it has used and will use any other stick. . . ."). Moley, After Seven Years 285. Telegram from Felix Frankfurter, Professor, Harvard Law Sch., to John Dickinson (Mar. 4, 1934) FF-LC, Reel 70. Lash, Dealers and Dreamers at 168.

12. Schlesinger, Coming of the New Deal 465, 507. Lash, Dealers and Dreamers 168–69. Letter from Felix Frankfurter to Franklin Delano Roosevelt (Feb. 22, 1934), FF-LC, Reel 60. Moley, First New Deal 382–83. Letter from Tom Corcoran to Felix Frankfurter, Professor, Harvard Law Sch. (May 11, 1934) FF-LC, Reel 70 ("If Ray [Moley] is any barometer of what's going on in the White House mind, the plan of battle is to avoid any further attempt at reforms that might bring down more criticism during the present Congress, arrange a 'truce of God', reorganize the machinery down here to help along business recovery this summer, and in every other way postpone all other considerations to the necessarily primary objective of winning the Congressional elections.").

13. Michael Parrish, Securities Regulation and the New Deal 244 (1970). Joseph P. Kennedy, Speech to the American Arbitration Association 4 (Mar. 19, 1935) WOD-LC. Securities Act Release No. 317 (Mar. 19, 1935).

14. Frank Partnoy, The Match King: Ivan Kreuger, The Financial Genius Behind a Century of Wall Street Scandals (2009). Felix Frankfurter, The Public & Its Government 109–10 (1930). Letter from Felix Frankfurter, Professor, Harvard Law Sch., to Ray Moley (Feb. 28, 1933) FF-LC, Reel 51 ("This time I am troubling you about legislation regarding the reorganization and extension of federal public utility control. This is a subject on which F.D.R. spoke to me when I saw him last, and as to which he desires, I am sure, early action."). DeBedts, New Deal's SEC 25.

15. Wiley B. Rutledge, Editorial, The Future of the Interstate Power Holding Company, St. Louis Post-Dispatch, May 5, 1935, Editorial Section 1.

16. Arthur M. Schlesinger, Jr., The Age of Roosevelt: 1935–1936, The Politics of Upheaval 305 (1960). Letter from Felix Frankfurter, Professor, Harvard Law Sch., to President Franklin D. Roosevelt (Jan. 24, 1935) FF-LC, Reel 155.

17. Letter from Ben Cohen to Robert E. Healy, Comm'r, Sec. Exch. Comm'n (Nov. 23, 1934) FF-LC, Reel 113; Letter from Ben Cohen to Felix Frankfurter, Professor, Harvard Law Sch. (Nov. 23, 1934) FF-LC, Reel 113 (soliciting Frankfurter's comments on the draft bill). DeBedts, New Deal's SEC 118. Letter from Ben Cohen to Robert E. Healy, Comm'r, Sec. Exch. Comm'n (Nov. 23, 1934) FF-LC, Reel 113. Schlesinger, Politics of Upheaval 305, 387. William Leuchtenburg, Franklin D. Roosevelt and the New Deal 156 (1963) ("The Public Utilities Holding Company Act was a bold stroke

## 304 NOTES

against bigness, and the Brandeisians were delighted. 'If F.D. carries through the Holding Company bill we shall have achieved considerable toward curbing Bigness.'" (quoting Brandeis)). Bruce Allen Murphy, Elements of Extrajudicial Strategy: A Look at the Political Roles of Justices Brandeis and Frankfurter, 69 Geo. L.J. 101, 120 (1980).

18. Schlesinger, Politics of Upheaval 306–16. Moley, After Seven Years 354.

19. William A. Gregory and Rennard Strickland, Hugo Black's Congressional Investigation of Lobbying and the Public Utilities Holding Company Act: A Historical View of the Power Trust, New Deal Politics, and Regulatory Propaganda, 29 Oklahoma L. Rev. 543, 553–55 (1976). Blake B. Hulnick, "Consumer Crusade: Hugo Black as Senate Investigator," Journal of Southern Legal History 24, 69–108 (2016) (putting emphasis on Southern populist anti-monopoly concerns.) Moley, After Seven Years 315. Roger K. Newman, Hugo Black: A Biography 191 (1994). Schlesinger, Politics of Upheaval 318–24.

20. PUHCA § 12(h).

21. Moley, After Seven Years 316 & n.2. Parrish, Securities Regulation 250.

22. Schlesinger, Politics of Upheaval 411, 443.

23. Pub. L. No. 75–696, 52 Stat. 840 (1938).

24. 53 Stat. 1149.

25. 1938 Amendments to the Securities Exchange Act of 1934 (the Maloney Act), Pub. L. No. 75–719, 52 Stat. 1070.

26. Investment Company Act of 1940, Pub. L. No. 76–768, 54 Stat. 789. Investment Advisers Act of 1940, Pub. L. No. 76–768, 54 Stat. 847.

27. Lochner v. New York, 198 U.S. 45 (1905). The decision struck down state limits on the working hours of bakers.

28. Schlesinger, Politics of Upheaval 455.

29. The Forgotten Memoir of John Knox 114 (Dennis J. Hutchinson & David J. Garrow, eds., 2002); see also id. at 70 (quoting McReynolds: "I also hope that you did not come under the influence of Frankfurter when you were in law school. . . . He is certainly one man not to be trusted! Even though he is dangerous to the welfare of this country, he evidently has a powerful influence at the White House.").

30. Felix Frankfurter, The Constitutional Aspect of President Roosevelt's Recovery Programme 1 (Feb. 1, 1934), FF-Harvard, Part 3, Reel 24.

31. Thomas K. McCraw, Prophets of Regulation 210 (1984).

32. Schlesinger, Politics of Upheaval (1960). John D. Fassett, New Deal Justice: The Life of Stanley Reed of Kentucky 66 (1994). William E. Leuchtenburg, The Supreme Court Reborn: The Constitutional Revolution in the Age of Roosevelt 84–89 (1995) ("The [Roosevelt] Administration put off tests of the constitutionality of the legislation of the First Hundred Days as long as possible; as a result the Supreme Court did not have the opportunity to rule on a New Deal statute until 1935."). Alpheus Thomas Mason, Brandeis: A Free Man's Life 620 (1946).

33. A.L.A. Schechter Poultry Corp. v. United States, 295 U.S. 495, 542 (1935); Humphrey's Executor v. United States, 295 U.S. 602, 632 (1935). Brandeis, as an advisor to Woodrow Wilson, played a central role in creating the FTC. Thomas K. McCraw, Rethinking the Trust Question, in Regulation in Perspective 2 (Thomas K. McCraw, ed., 1981).

NOTES 305

34. The *Schechter* decision, striking down the NIRA, sparked a rare occasion for agreement between Brandeis and McReynolds. McReynolds credited *Schechter* with restoring business confidence. The Forgotten Memoir of John Knox 72 (quoting McReynolds: "[B]usinessmen throughout the country have become more and more confident because of the Court's [*Schechter*] decision. . . . The decision stimulated industry, which had been hampered by the N.R.A. laws.").

35. Brandeis had passed the warning to Roosevelt through Adolf Berle. Letter from Adolf A. Berle to Franklin Roosevelt (Apr. 23, 1934), *in* Navigating the Rapids 95 ("Mr. Justice Brandeis has been revolving matters in his head and I think requires some attention."). Joseph P. Lash, Dealers and Dreamers 178. Brandeis had apparently sent word via Frankfurter in mid-May that the New Deal's "eleventh hour" was at hand. Jordan A. Schwarz, The New Dealers: Power Politics in the Age of Roosevelt 113 (1993).

36. Peter H. Irons, The New Deal Lawyers 104 (1982) (relating conversation with Corcoran). The Forgotten Memoir of John Knox 72 (quoting McReynolds: "[I]f it were not for the Court, this country would go too far down the road to socialism ever to return."). M. Paul Holsinger, Mr. Justice Van Devanter and the New Deal: A Note, 31 The Historian 57, 61–62 (1968) (describing Van Devanter's fears that totalitarianism would come to the United States after he visited Nazi Germany and Soviet Russia in the mid-1930s). Henry M. Holland, Jr., Mr. Justice Cardozo and the New Deal Court, 12 J. Pub. L. 383, 401 (1963).

37. Jeff Shesol, Supreme Power: Franklin Roosevelt vs. The Supreme Court 44 (2010) (reporting Charles Wyzanski's doubts shared with Frankfurter). Arthur M. Schlesinger, Jr., The Age of Roosevelt: The Coming of the New Deal 125 (1958). McCraw, Prophets of Regulation 211. Jackson suggested that the Court had done Roosevelt a favor by allowing him to avoid a congressional rejection of the NIRA's renewal. Shesol, Supreme Power 137. Frankfurter himself was not that distressed by the invalidation of the NIRA. Nelson L. Dawson, Louis D. Brandeis, Felix Frankfurter and the New Deal (1982). Schlesinger, Coming of the New Deal 167, 285. Letter from John Burns, Gen. Counsel, Sec. Exch. Comm'n, to Felix Frankfurter, Professor, Harvard Law Sch. (May 29, 1935) FF-LC, Reel 84.

38. United States v. Butler, 297 U.S. 1, 74 (1936); Carter v. Carter Coal Co., 298 U.S. 238, 311–17 (1936).

39. Royalist's Revelations, Time, July 1, 1935, at 47, *available at* https://content.time.com/time/subscriber/article/0,33009,770055,00.html.

40. SEC v. Jones, 12 F. Supp. 210, 213 (S.D.N.Y. 1935), aff'd, 79 F.2d 617 (2d Cir. 1935), rev'd, 298 U.S. 1 (1936).

41. Letter from Felix Frankfurter, Professor, Harvard Law Sch., to Stanley Reed, Solicitor Gen. (Feb. 15, 1936) FF-Harvard, Reel 2. Letter from Stanley Reed, Solicitor Gen., to Felix Frankfurter, Professor, Harvard Law Sch. (Dec. 17, 1936) FF-Harvard, Part 3, Reel 2 ("My own views have not chrystalized [*sic*]. Can you help me?"). Letter from Felix Frankfurter, Professor, Harvard Law Sch., to Stanley Reed, Solicitor Gen. (Dec. 7, 1936) FF-Harvard, Part 3, Reel 2 ("I appreciate your thoughtfulness in sending me a copy of your confidential memorandum on pending matters involving administration

306 NOTES

measures."). Frankfurter also consulted with John Burns, the SEC's general counsel. Letter from John Burns, Gen. Counsel, Sec. Exch. Comm'n, to Felix Frankfurter, Professor, Harvard Law Sch. (Oct. 18, 1935) FF-LC, Reel 115 (discussing litigation strategy with respect to constitutional issues). Letter from Robert H. Jackson, Asst. Gen. Counsel, Treasury Dept., to Herman Oliphant, Gen. Counsel, Treasury Dept. (Dec. 8, 1935), Robert Jackson Collection, Library of Congress, Box 66.

42. Letter from James Landis, Chairman, Sec. Exch. Comm'n, to Felix Frankfurter, Professor, Harvard Law Sch. (Mar. 11, 1936) FF-LC, Reel 45. Reed had not predicted a tougher go on the constitutional argument. He wrote Homer Cummings, the Attorney General that " 'I think that if we lose, it will be on the statutory construction point and not on the constitutional point. We may get a good result and I would be very much surprised if we got a bad result.' " Fassett, New Deal Justice 121.

43. Jones v. SEC, 298 U.S. 1, 28 (1936). The Court said the stop order proceeding had the effect of suspending the operation of the registration statement; the appellate court had ruled that the registration statement remained effective, since no stop order had been issued. Id. at 15. Sutherland wrote the opinion for the court despite not having heard oral argument in the case, participating via the "vouch[ing in]" approach that Chief Justice Hughes employed. Letter from Justice William O. Douglas to Justice Arthur Goldberg (Jan. 18, 1964) WOD-LC.

44. Barry Cushman, Secret Lives of the Four Horsemen, 83 Va. L. Rev. 559, 640 & n.140 (1987)(collecting cases).

45. Jones, 298 U.S. at 33 (Cardozo, J., dissenting).

46. Letter from Justice Harlan Fiske Stone to Felix Frankfurter, Professor, Harvard Law Sch., (Apr. 7, 1936) FF-LC, Reel 64. Letter from Felix Frankfurter, Professor, Harvard Law Sch., to Justice Harlan Fiske Stone (Apr. 7, 1936) FF-LC, Reel 64. Letter from Justice Harlan Fiske Stone to Felix Frankfurter, Professor, Harvard Law Sch. (Apr. 9, 1936) FF-LC, Reel 64. Robert H. Jackson, The Struggle for Judicial Supremacy 152–53 (1940). Letter from Felix Frankfurter, Professor, Harvard Law Sch., to Justice Harlan Fiske Stone, (May 18, 1936) FF-LC, Reel 64.

47. Joseph P. Lash, Dealers and Dreamers 267–68. DeBedts, New Deal's SEC 174.

# Chapter 2

1. William O. Douglas & George E. Bates, The Federal Securities Act of 1933, 43 Yale L.J. 171, 172 (1933).

2. Thomas K. McCraw, Prophets of Regulation 9 (1984).

3. William O. Douglas, Letter to the Editor, N.Y. Times, Apr. 3, 1933, FF-LC, Reel 116.

4. Quoted in John W. Hopkirk, William O. Douglas—His Work in Policing Bankruptcy Proceedings, 18 Vand. L. Rev. 663, 680 (1965).

5. Murphy, Wild Bill 73, 87.

6. Douglas's protégé Abe Fortas, a future Supreme Court justice, worked with Douglas on his reorganization study at the SEC and during Douglas's later work as chair.

NOTES  307

Thurman Arnold, also a faculty member, headed the antitrust division at the Department of Justice. Charles Clark, a former dean of the law school, was appointed to the Second Circuit, which allowed him to play a prominent role in the development of insider trading law, the subject of Chapter 5. His brother Sam was tapped by Douglas to lead the SEC's new reorganization division in 1938.

7. Moley, First New Deal 230. Jessica Wang, Neo-Brandeisianism and the New Deal: Adolf A. Berle, Jr., William O. Douglas, and the Problem of Corporate Finance in the 1930s, 33 Seattle U. L. Rev. 1221, 1231–32 (2010). Berle quoted in Arthur M. Schlesinger, Jr., The Age of Roosevelt: The Coming of the New Deal 183 (1958).

8. William O. Douglas & George E. Bates, The Federal Securities Act of 1933, 43 Yale L.J. 171, 171 (1933) ("There is nothing in the Act which would control the speculative craze of the American public, or which would eliminate wholly unsound capital structures. There is nothing in the Act which would prevent a tyrannical management from playing wide and loose with scattered minorities, or which would prevent a new pyramiding of holding companies violative of the public interest and all canons of sound finance."). William O. Douglas & George E. Bates, Some Effects of the Securities Act Upon Investment Banking, 1 U. Chi. L. Rev. 283, 306 (1933). Letter from William O. Douglas, Professor, Yale Law Sch., to A.A. Berle, Jr., Professor, Columbia Law Sch. (Dec. 29, 1933) WOD-LC. William O. Douglas, Protecting the Investor, 23 Yale Rev. 521, 522, 530 (1934).

9. William O. Douglas, Protecting the Investor, 23 Yale Rev. 521, 530 (1934). Letter from William O. Douglas, Professor, Yale Law Sch., to Jerome N. Frank, Gen. Counsel, Agric. Adjustment Admin. (Dec. 2, 1933) WOD-LC. Letter from Adolf A. Berle to William O. Douglas (Dec. 30, 1933) WOD-LC. Letter from William O. Douglas, Professor, Yale Law Sch., to A.A. Berle, Jr., Professor, Columbia Law Sch. (Jan. 3, 1934) WOD-LC.

10. This is from a speech given by Douglas while he was SEC chairman: "The disappearance of free enterprise has submerged the individual in the impersonal corporation. And when a nation of shopkeepers is transformed into a nation of clerks enormous spiritual sacrifices are made. Communities everywhere lose men of stature and independence. Man loses opportunities to develop his personality and his capacities. He is denied a chance to stand on his own before man and God. He is subservient to others and his thinking is done for him from afar. His opportunities to become a leader, to grow in stature, to be independent in mind and spirit, are greatly reduced. Widespread submergence of the individual in a corporation has as insidious an effect on democracy as has his submergence in the state in other lands." William Orville Douglas, Democracy and Finance: The Addresses and Public Statements of William O. Douglas as Member and Chairman of the Securities and Exchange Commission (1940) 15–16. "[Brandeis's] 'Other People's Money,' had been of course a Bible for me for years, as had his 'Curse of Bigness,' the philosophy of which was my own." William O. Douglas, Diary (Mar. 26, 1939) WOD-LC, Box 1780. The occasion was Douglas's nomination to replace Brandeis on the Supreme Court. William O. Douglas, Protecting the Investor, 23 Yale Rev. 521, 529–30 (1934).

11. 288 U.S. 517 (1933) (Brandeis, J., dissenting).

308  NOTES

12. Harry Shulman, Memorandum of Talk with L.D.B.—Dec. 8, 1933, FF-LC, Reel 116.

13. Letter from Felix Frankfurter, Professor, Harvard Law Sch., to President Franklin D. Roosevelt (Mar. 6, 1934) FF-LC, Reel 60 ("I notice also some talk of an Administration measure for federal incorporation. . . . Great difficulties are involved in such a measure, and I hope there won't be any urgency in pushing it. Of course many abuses have found shelter under our corporation laws. But the abuses that call for public protection and are essential to a healthy economic life can be dealt with by a number of specific improvements in federal legislation, especially through the use of the taxing power, without prematurely raising the many problems that are involved in a federal incorporation law.").

14. Letter from William O. Douglas, Professor, Yale Law Sch., to Felix Frankfurter, Professor, Harvard Law Sch. (Feb. 19, 1934) WOD-LC ("On analysis it will be seen that federal incorporation is only one device. But it is a damn convenient one. Hooked up with the commerce and taxing powers it can be made a powerful weapon for social control."). Letter from William O. Douglas to Felix Frankfurter (Apr. 6, 1934), FF-LC, Reel 31. Seligman, Transformation of Wall Street 205–09 (discussing federal incorporation). Letter from William O. Douglas, Chairman, Sec. Exch. Comm'n, to Henry A. Wallace, Sec'y, Dep't of Agric. (Apr. 11, 1938) WOD-LC (advocating a system of government investment banking). Letter from William O. Douglas, Chairman, Sec. Exch. Comm'n to Marriner S. Eccles, Chairman, Board of Governors Federal Reserve System (Aug. 10, 1938) WOD-LC ("On the whole, I am convinced that the problem of small issuers in the capital markets is a result of fundamental defects in our capital markets machinery. Consequently, I have, as you know, been interested in remedial measure such as the expansion of regional investment banking and perhaps the creation of a new type of financial organization to aid this movement.").

15. Compare the debate on the pages of the Harvard Law Review between Max Lowenthal, closely associated with Frankfurter in this debate, and Douglas. Max Lowenthal, The Railroad Reorganization Act, 47 Harv. L. Rev. 18 (1933); William O. Douglas, Protective Committees in Railroad Reorganizations, 47 Harv. L. Rev. 565 (1934).

16. Jordan A. Schwarz, The New Dealers: Power Politics in the Age of Roosevelt 77 (1994).

17. Daniel Crane, The Dissociation of Incorporation and Regulation in the Progressive Era and the New Deal, in Corporations and American Democracy (2017) (proponents saw federal chartering as a means of reinserting restrictions on corporations; from roughly the late nineteenth century to 1937, "a significant obstacle to federal corporate regulatory efforts was the limited view of federal commerce power that prevented Congress from regulating large swaths of commercial and economic life"). William Cary, Federalism and Corporate Law, 83 Yale L.J. 700 (1974).

18. Letter from Burton K. Wheeler, U.S. Sen., to Felix Frankfurter, Professor, Harvard Law Sch. (Mar. 30, 1932) FF-LC, Reel 67. Letter from Felix Frankfurter, Professor, Harvard Law Sch., to Burton K. Wheeler, U.S. Sen. (Apr. 4, 1932) FF-LC, Reel 67. Memorandum for the Secretary of the Treasury from President Franklin D. Roosevelt

(Jan. 16, 1935) FF-LC, Reel 155. Letter from Felix Frankfurter, Professor, Harvard Law Sch., to Burton Wheeler, U.S. Sen. (Mar. 12, 1935) FF-LC, Reel 67 ("I rejoice over your introduction of the tax on bigness . . ."). Schlesinger, Coming of the New Deal 332. Jackson would renew his attack on "bigness" after his appointment as Assistant Attorney General for the Antitrust Division, giving a series of anti-monopoly speeches featuring Brandeisian themes. Alan Brinkley, The End of Reform 56–60 (1995). Steven A. Bank, From Sword to Shield, The Transformation of the Corporate Income Tax, 1861–Present (2016). Joseph Thorndike, Their Fair Share: Taxing the Rich in the Age of FDR (2013).

19. Seligman, Transformation of Wall Street 84. Letter from Richard Smith to Francis T. Maloney, U.S. Rep. (Mar. 23, 1934) WOD-LC. Letter from William O. Douglas, Professor, Yale Law Sch., to Richard Smith (Apr. 9, 1934) WOD-LC. Letter from Richard Smith to William O. Douglas, Professor, Yale Law Sch. (May 26, 1934) WOD-LC. Landis's view was evidently shared by others. Letter from Richard Smith to William O. Douglas, Professor, Yale Law Sch. (June 13, 1934) WOD-LC ("I received a letter from Maloney in which he stated that he was running into opposition to you among the crowd who have resented your Articles."). Letter from William O. Douglas, Professor, Yale Law Sch., to Richard Smith (June 12, 1934) WOD-LC.

According to Corcoran, Roosevelt was afraid to put Cohen on the newly created SEC for fear that it would provoke anti-Semitism. Telegraph from Centurion [Tom Corcoran] to Felix Frankfurter, Professor, Harvard Law Sch. (May 30, 1934) FF-LC, Reel 70. The next year, however, Frankfurter recommended that Roosevelt not appoint Cohen to the SEC because Cohen was too essential to Roosevelt's legislative efforts. Memorandum for the President from Felix Frankfurter (Aug. 21, 1935) FF-LC, Reel 155. Cohen also lost out on the General Counsel position at the new agency when the SEC's first chairman, Joe Kennedy, picked John Burns instead. (This scarcely reduced Frankfurter's influence; Burns was a Harvard Law graduate, and he would soon be filling the SEC's ranks with candidates recommended by Frankfurter.) Telegram from John J. Burns, Gen. Counsel, Sec. Exch. Comm'n, to Felix Frankfurter, Professor, Harvard Law Sch. (May 10, 1935) FF-LC, Reel 84. Burns was also soliciting Frankfurter's views on the interpretation of the Exchange Act. Letter from John J. Burns, Gen. Counsel, Sec. Exch. Comm'n, to Felix Frankfurter, Professor, Harvard Law Sch. (Aug. 8, 1934) FF-LC, Reel 115.

20. Letter from Felix Frankfurter to William O. Douglas (Jan. 18, 1936), FF-LC, Reel 155.

21. Transcript of Douglas press conference Sept. 22, 1937, WOD-LC, Container # 21.

22. Alsop and Whitney, The Battle of the Market Place, Saturday Evening Post June 25, 1938, p. 82. Douglas did not succeed in getting segregation of all floor members of the exchange, but Seligman concluded that even though the significance of the reforms dissipated, "[i]n part, the enormous post-World War II expansion in securities trading occurred because Douglas-type reforms did reduce the likelihood of manipulation on the New York Stock Exchange." Seligman, Transformation of Wall Street 179. Malcom McKay, Impeccable Connections, The Rise and Fall of Richard Whitney (2014).

23. Douglas, Democracy and Finance, *supra* note 10.

310  NOTES

24. 1938 Amendments to the Securities Exchange Act of 1934 (the Maloney Act), Pub. L. No. 75-719, 52 Stat. 1070.
25. Interview with Abe Fortas, Dec. 28, 1979, Washington, D.C., as set out in Seligman, Transformation of Wall Street 781.
26. Seligman, Transformation of Wall Street 183. Douglas Address, A Call for Leadership, reprinted in Democracy and Finance at 128.
27. H. Comm. on the Judiciary, 71st Cong., Report on the Administration of Bankruptcy Estates (Comm. Print 1931) (Donovan Report); Att'y Gen., Strengthening of Procedures in the Judicial System: The Report of the Attorney General on Bankruptcy Law and Practice, S. Doc. No. 65, at 90–93 (1st Sess. 1932) (Thatcher Report).
28. Act of Mar. 3, 1933, ch. 204, §77, 47 Stat. 1474, 1474–82; Act of June 7, 1934, ch. 424, § 77B, 48 Stat. 911, 912–22.
29. Joseph P. Lash, Dealers and Dreamers, A New Look at the New Deal (1988) at 93 quoting the House Debates, Max Lowenthal, The Railroad Reorganization Act, 47 Harv. L. Rev. 18 (1933).
30. David Skeel, The Rise and Fall of the SEC in Bankruptcy, SSRN abstract #172030 (July 1998) at 8. John W. Hopkirk, William O. Douglas—His Work in Policing Bankruptcy Proceedings, 18 Vand. L. Rev. 663, 673–74 (1965) (quoting 1 Report on Protective Comm. 215–16).
31. Chandler Act, 52 Stat. 840, Pub. L. No. 75-696.
32. Skeel, Rise and Fall of SEC in Bankruptcy 29.
33. Trust Indenture Act of 1939, Pub. L. No. 73-291, 48 Stat. 881.
34. James A. Hagerty, "Portland Cheers Speech," N.Y. Times, Sept. 22, 1932.
35. Recollections of Joseph H. Rauh, in The Making of the New Deal (Katie Louchheim, ed.) 56–57 (1983). Seligman, Transformation of Wall Street 131.
36. Sarbanes-Oxley Act of 2002, Pub. L. 107-204, 116 Stat. 745 (codified at 15 U.S.C. §§ 7201–66 (2006)).
37. The intervenor made clear he had no intention of covering Davis's fees. Lash at 343. Arthur M. Schlesinger, Jr., The Age of Roosevelt: The Politics of Upheaval 311 (1966).
38. Robert H. Jackson, The Struggle for Judicial Supremacy 120 (1940).
39. In re Am. States Public Services Co., 12 F. Supp. 667 (D. Md. 1935) affirmed 81 F.2d 721 (4th Cir. 1936) cert. denied Burco, Inc. v. Whitworth, 297 U.S. 724 (1936).
40. Letter from Felix Frankfurter to John Burns (Mar. 24, 1936), FF-LC, Reel 84.
41. Burco, Inc. v. Whitworth, 297 U.S. 724 (1936).
42. *N. Am. Co.*, 299 U.S. at 252 (noting that forty-seven other cases had been filed); Seligman, Transformation of Wall Street 134.
43. William O. Douglas, Go East Young Man: The Early Years 278 (1974).
44. Seligman, Transformation of Wall Street 137.
45. N. Am. Co. v. Landis, 85 F.2d 398, 401 (D.C. Cir. 1936). The PUHCA legal and political teams overlapped with the effort to defend other parts of the New Deal. Attorney General Homer Cummings, Solicitor General Stanley Reed and SEC General Counsel John Burns, who had argued the *Jones* case late in the previous term, were back before the Court in *Landis*, now reinforced by newly appointed Assistant Attorney General Robert Jackson. Also, on the briefs as special counsel were Ben Cohen and

NOTES 311

Tommy Corcoran, Frankfurter's all-purpose pair. Lash, From the Diaries of Felix Frankfurter 36.

46. Landis v. N. Am. Co., 299 U.S. 248, 259 (1936). McReynolds concurred in the result without opinion and Stone did not participate, likely because of his prior partnership with Sullivan & Cromwell, the law firm for the company.

47. Alex Badas, Policy Disagreement and Judicial Legitimacy: Evidence from the 1937 Court-Packing Plan, 48 J. Leg. Stud. 377, 387 (2019) (citing 1937 Gallup poll showing that 86% of those surveyed thought bill would pass). Jeff Shesol, Supreme Power: Franklin Roosevelt vs. The Supreme Court 301 (2010) (plan widely opposed in press, including by papers that had endorsed Roosevelt in 1936). The plan's prospects were presumably not enhanced by endorsements from the Nazi press and Mussolini. Id. at 303.

48. SEC v. Elec. Bond & Share Co., 18 F. Supp 131 (S.D.N.Y. 1937).

49. Seligman, Transformation of Wall Street 136.

50. Elec. Bond & Share Co. v. SEC, 92 F.2d 580, 590 (2d Cir. 1937).

51. West Coast Hotel Co. v. Parrish, 300 U.S. 379, 400 (1937).

52. On the original source of the phrase, see G. Edward White, The Constitution and the New Deal 17 (2000). Scholars have questioned the extent to which Roberts "switched," given that he voted at the conference before the announcement of the Court-packing plan, albeit after Roosevelt's landslide victory. Barry Cushman, Rethinking the New Deal Court: The Structure of a Constitutional Revolution 103 (1998). At the time, however, Frankfurter viewed the switch as transparent. Letter from Felix Frankfurter, Professor, Harvard Law Sch., to President Franklin D. Roosevelt, (Mar. 30, 1937) FF-Harvard, Reel 155 ("And now, with the shift by Roberts, even a blind man ought to see that the Court is in politics, and understand how the Constitution is 'judicially' construed."). Barry Cushman, The Securities Laws and the Mechanics of Legal Change, 95 Va. L. Rev. 927 (2009) (describing Frankfurter's later view backing away from his earlier comment and concluding Roberts had not changed his vote).

53. NLRB v. Jones & Laughlin Steel Corp., 301 U.S. 1, 43 (1937); Steward Machine Co. v. Davis, 301 U.S. 548, 598 (1937).

54. A CQ Research note illustrates the change in the Court's direction between the 1935–36 term and the 1936–37 term. The number of dissents from the Four Horsemen (Butler, McReynolds, Sutherland, and Van Devanter) increased from 18 in 1935–36 to 62 in 1936–37. The number of dissents of the three Musketeers (Brandeis, Cardozo and Stone), went in the opposite direction, going from 49 dissents in 1935–36 to 15 in 1936–37.

William E. Leuchtenburg, The Nine Justices Respond to the 1937 Crisis, 22 J. Supreme Court Hist. 55, 67 (1997). Robert H. Jackson, The Struggle for Judicial Supremacy 191–92 (1940). Leuchtenburg 68 (quoting Felix Frankfurter to Sir Maurice Sheldon Amos, Dec. 11, 1937, FF-LC, Box 20).

55. The Economy Act, P.L. 72-212, 47 Stat. 382, 402 (1932). The 1932 legislation, which received media attention as to its impact on Oliver Wendell Holmes, Jr. who had recently resigned, was reversed in the last days of the Hoover administration. P.L. 72-48, 47 Stat. 1489, 1512–14 (1933); but similar budget cuts soon passed Congress in

312  NOTES

the new administration. P.L. 73-2, 48 Stat. 12 (1933) and the Roosevelt administration argued they should apply to judges, before backing off. The episode persuaded justices thinking about retirement that their anticipated benefits remained at risk of a congressional takeway. See Judge Glock, Unpacking the Supreme Court: Judicial Retirement and the Road to the 1937 Court Battle, 106 J. Am History 47 (2019). Justice Van Devanter, whose retirement decision is discussed in the text, characterized the Holmes debacle as "notice to all justices that they could no longer rely on the congressional promise" as to retirement income. Chief Justice Stone in 1937 wrote that the "disposition of Congress to tinker with the judge's retirement as a serious drawback to retirement at the Supreme Court." Jeff Shesol, Supreme Power: Franklin Roosevelt v. the Supreme Court 342 (New York 2010).

56. Willis Van Devanter to Mrs. John W. Lacy, Oct. 28, 1932, Willis Van Devanter Papers, Box 16, Library of Congress. Robert H. Jackson, The Struggle for Judicial Supremacy 187 (1940). Glock, Unpacking.

57. Letter from Willis Van Devanter to Franklin Roosevelt May 18, 1937, Willis Van Devanter Papers, Library of Congress. His announcement was publicized just as Senators were entering a committee room to vote down FDR's first court packing plan 10-8.

58. Black had fought against the Alabama business elites while working his way up as a practicing lawyer, William M. Wiecek, The Birth of the Modern Constitution: The United States Supreme Court 1941–1953 73 (2006), generally refused to represent corporations, with only two exceptions in twenty-five years of practice. Roger K. Newman, Hugo Black: A Biography 35, 54 (1994). Black announced his disdain for corporations soon after his arrival at the Court by arguing in dissent that corporations should not be treated as persons under the Fourteenth Amendment. Connecticut Gen. Life v. Johnson, 303 U.S. 77 (1938).

59. Schlesinger, Politics of Upheaval 456–57. Glock provides evidence suggesting the two retirements were linked. Glock, Unpacking. Chief Justice Hughes autobiographical notes reflect that Sutherland did not want to announce his retirement until the Van Devanter seat was filled. Daniel Danelski & Joseph Tulchin, The Autobiographical Notes of Charles Evans Hughes (1973) at 302–03.

60. Letter from Stanley Reed, Solicitor Gen., to Felix Frankfurter, Professor, Harvard Law Sch. (Dec. 19, 1937) FF-Harvard, Reel 56 ("We are filing our response in E. B. & S. tomorrow. Ben and Bob Jackson are to argue it. I think they have both earned the right. . . "). Letter from Dave G[insburg] to Felix Frankfurter, Professor, Harvard Law Sch. (Feb. 12, 1938) (describing Cohen's argument), FF-Harvard, Reel 27. While not a record, arguments over three days are unusual in the last one hundred years, and are reserved for cases of particular importance—illustrating again the perceived importance of PUHCA. National Public Radio, https://www.npr.org/sections/itsallpolitics/2011/11/15/142363047/obamacare-will-rank-among-the-longest-supreme-court-arguments-ever (Nov. 15, 2011; accessed July 24, 2020).

61. Electric Bond & Share Co. v. SEC, 303 U.S. 419, 442–43 (1938). Hughes's opinion gained the support of Butler and Roberts from the *Jones* majority as well as Brandeis and Stone from the minority and new appointee Black. McReynolds

NOTES 313

dissented without opinion. Cardozo did not participate; he died shortly after the term ended.

62. Seligman, Transformation of Wall Street 179–80. Telegram from Felix Frankfurter, Professor, Harvard Law Sch., to Robert H. Jackson, Solicitor Gen. (Mar. 30, 1938) FF-Harvard, Part 3, Reel 1.

63. 317 U.S. 111, 125 (1942) ("even if appellee's activity be local and though it may not be regarded as commerce, it may still, whatever its nature, be reached by Congress if it exerts a substantial economic effect on interstate commerce").

64. N. American Co. v. SEC, 133 F.2d 148 (2d Cir. 1943) aff'd 327 U.S. 686 (1946); Am. Power & Light Co. v. SEC, 141 F.2d 606 (1st Cir. 1944) aff'd 329 U.S. 910 (1946).

65. Sidney Fine, Frank Murphy: The Washington Years 250 (1984) ("When because of quorum problems in the 1943 term Stone stated in conference that he would sit in a holding company case despite having previously disqualified himself in a similar case, Roberts exploded and said that 'he would write and tell the world about Stone.' The chief justice 'turned white' and responded that no one would tell him in what cases he should disqualify himself. Although it was 'a very embarrassing situation' for him, he was 'willing to be the goat' and to participate in the two cases. . . ."); Alpheus Thomas Mason, Harlan Fiske Stone: Pillar of the Law 640–41 (1956) ("The Chief Justice was much disturbed that litigants, otherwise entitled to it, could not have their day in Court. His concern grew as more cases involving features of the holding company law were filed. Should not this consideration, he wondered, overbalance those that moved him initially to announce disqualification? As no former law partner or client was present in these cases, he now saw no reason to disqualify himself. When he broached the matter in conference, however, Justice Roberts objected to his sitting on the ground that similar issues were raised in all the cases, and that if he were disqualified in the one, he ought not to sit in judgment on a related case. Roberts' suggestion, apparently querying the Chief Justice's honor and implying that he would discuss in an opinion the propriety of Stone's sitting, brought on a heated debate. The accusation so angered the Chief that he had his clerk prepare a memorandum of cases on which Roberts had sat although his old firm or former clients were involved.").

66. Letter from Justice Frank Murphy to Chief Justice Fred Vinson (Oct. 9, 1946), Frank Murphy Collection, Bentley Library, University of Michigan ("I had finished most of the work on the *Engineers Public Service* and the *American Power & Light—Electric Power & Light* opinions and was about ready to circulate them when, unfortunately, the good Chief Justice died, destroying the necessary quorum."). The *Engineers Public Service* case was eventually dismissed as moot. Eng'rs Pub. Serv. Co. v. SEC, 332 U.S. 788, 788 (1947).

67. N. Am. Co. v. SEC, 327 U.S. 686 (1946). Douglas, Jackson and Reed did not participate. Id. at 711. Frankfurter wrote Reed during the time when the quorum problem remained unresolved:

[Y]ou are right in not sitting in the *North American* case. . . . I also know that the people who were eager to have you sit were not moved by the considerations that should move a court. They counted on your deciding their way, which is precisely the reason why the other side would have had a just grievance. And you do not alleviate

314 NOTES

a grievance by showing that similar grievances that others might have had in the past were equally disregarded. Nor are feelings of injustice rendered unreasonable by having those who inflict them tell those who feel them they are really quite unreasonable in feeling them. That psychological fact is, I believe, at the core of the labor problem as it is of the race problem.

Letter from Justice Felix Frankfurter to Justice Stanley Reed (Mar. 27, 1944) FF-Harvard, Reel 56.

68. American Power & Light Co. v. SEC, 329 U.S. 90 (1946).

69. John D. Fassett, New Deal Justice: The Life of Stanley Reed of Kentucky 66 (1994).

70. 323 U.S. 624 (1945).

71. Case v. Los Angeles Lumber Co., 308 U.S. 106, 114–16 (1939); see also Consol. Rock Prod. Co. v. DuBois, 312 U.S. 510, 530–31 (1941), another unanimous opinion written by Douglas.

72. Letter from Justice Felix Frankfurter to Justice Stanley Reed (Nov. 21, 1944) FF-LC, Reel 56. Handwritten Notes from Conference, No. 81, OT 1944 (undated) Frank Murphy Collection, Bentley Library, University of Michigan, Reel 131.

73. SEC v. Cent. Ill. Sec. Corp., 338 U.S. 96, 155 (1949).

74. 340 U.S. 336 (1951). The Court's opinion drew a dissent from the odd couple of Frankfurter and Black. Id. at 348 (Frankfurter, J., dissenting).

75. SEC v. New England Electric System, 384 U.S. 176 (1966); SEC v. New England Electric System, 390 U.S. 207 (1968).

76. The SEC's vague claim of management efficiencies echoed Brandeis's argument, in the famous Advance Rate Case in 1910, that principles of "scientific management" could reduce the railroad's costs, making a rate increase unnecessary. Thomas K. McCraw, Louis D. Brandeis Reappraised, 54 Am. Sch. 525, 529 (1985). The railroads' petition was denied by the ICC; a few years later they were in such desperate financial straits that the federal government was forced to take them over.

77. Pac. Gas & Elec. Co. v. SEC, 324 U.S. 826 (1945) (per curiam) (affirming judgment below by an equally divided Court).

78. Letter from Justice Felix Frankfurter to Justice Frank Murphy (Feb. 22, 1945) FF-LC, Reel 52. Letter from Justice Frank Murphy to Justice Felix Frankfurter (Feb. 23, 1945) FF-LC, Reel 52. No response was forthcoming from Frankfurter.

79. American Power & Light Co. v. SEC (American Power I), 325 U.S. 385, 386 & n.1 (1945).

80. General Protective Committee v. SEC, 346 U.S. 521 (1954).

81. SEC v. Drexel & Co., 348 U.S. 341, 348–49 (1955).

82. Frankfurter wrote:

> Congress effectively equipped the Commission with power to regulate fees in the various proceedings which required approval by the Commission. But Congress particularized. It did not vest this fee-fixing authority of the Commission in a comprehensive provision. It dealt with the problem distributively. It was explicit in relating the power to fix fees to the particular proceeding.
>
> . . . .

> The [Public Utility] Holding Company Act of 1935 is a reticulated statute, not a hodge-podge. To observe its explicit provisions is to respect the purpose of Congress and the care with which it was formulated.

Id. at 349–50 (Frankfurter, J., dissenting).

83. David A. Skeel, Jr., Debt's Dominion: A History of Bankruptcy Law in America 125 (2001) ("Within a few years, the starring role that the Wall Street bankers had played for more than fifty years was a thing of the past.").

84. Act of June 22, 1938, ch. 575, §§ 171–74, 52 Stat. 840, 890–91.

85. Ralph F. de Bedts, The New Deal's SEC: The Formative Years 109 (1964) ("In his demand for studies and more studies Landis can be likened to the field general who will not unnecessarily risk his forces until sure of overwhelming superiority. But the many studies begun by Chairman Landis—and frequently used to such good advantage by his successor, William O. Douglas—were not born of timidity.").

86. Act of June 6, 1934, ch. 404, § 211, 48 Stat. 881, 909.

87. Skeel, Debt's Dominion 109.

88. Letter from William O. Douglas, Professor, Yale Law Sch., to James Landis, Comm'r, Fed. Trade Comm'n (July 12, 1934) WOD-LC. Letter from William O. Douglas, Professor, Yale Law Sch., to Abe Fortas, Agric. Adjustment Admin. (Aug. 2, 1934) WOD-LC. Murphy, Wild Bill 107 ("To Douglas, this new appointment signaled the beginning of his rise to the top. 'Bill began telling us he would be the chairman of the SEC,' recalled Irene Hamilton.").

89. 1–8 Sec. & Exch. Comm'n, Report on the Study and Investigation of the Work, Activities, Personnel and Functions of Protective and Reorganization Committees (1936–40). Revision of the Bankruptcy Act: Hearings on H.R. 6439 Before the H. Comm. on the Judiciary, Reintroduced as H.R. 8046, 75th Cong. 199 (1937) (statement of William O. Douglas, Chairman, Sec. Exch. Comm'n). Douglas's perspective was shared by outsiders: "Part I and Part II of the report are essentially briefs-fair-minded and well documented briefs to be sure-in support of the Commission's recommendations for reform." E. Merrick Dodd, Jr., The Securities and Exchange Commission's Reform Program for Bankruptcy Reorganization, 38 Colum. L. Rev. 223, 225 (1938).

90. See Skeel, Debt's Dominion 84, 116–17.

91. Act of June 22, 1938, ch. 575, § 172, 52 Stat. 840, 890–91.

92. Trust Indenture Act of 1939, Pub. L. No. 73-291, 48 Stat. 881.

93. Robert T. Swaine, "Democratization" of Corporate Reorganizations, 38 Colum. L. Rev. 256, 259 (1938). Investor's Advocate, Time, Sept. 26, 1938, at 57, *available at* https://content.time.com/time/subscriber/article/0,33009,788825,00.html. Jerome Frank, Epithetical Jurisprudence and the Work of the Securities and Exchange Commission in the Administration of Chapter X of the Bankruptcy Act, 18 N.Y.U.L.Q. 317, 321 (1941), quoted in Jessica Wang, Imagining the Administrative State: Legal Pragmatism, Securities Regulation, and New Deal Liberalism, 17 J. Pol. History 257, 280 (2005). Skeel, Debt's Dominion 28.

94. SEC v. U.S. Realty & Improvement Co., 310 U.S. 434 (1940).

95. In re U.S. Realty & Improvement Co., 108 F.2d 794, 798 (2d Cir. 1940).

316   NOTES

96. Note from Justice Felix Frankfurter to Justice William O. Douglas (undated), appended to Memorandum from William O. Douglas on *SEC v. U.S. Realty & Improvement Co.* (undated) ("Bill, Hadn't you better send a copy of this memo to Stone? FF") WOD-LC.

97. William O. Douglas, Diary (May 27, 1940) WOD-LC, Box 1780. Douglas's account is certainly open to question; it is somewhat difficult to imagine the magisterial Hughes stooping to such a gambit, and it seems somewhat unlikely that he would use Stone as his messenger.

William Leuchtenburg, Franklin D. Roosevelt and the New Deal (1963) 154 ("This new Court—the 'Roosevelt Court' as it was called—ruled favorably on every one of the New Deal laws whose constitutionality was challenged. It expanded the commerce power and the taxing and spending power so greatly that it soon became evident that there was almost no statute for social welfare or the regulation of business that the Court would not validate.").

98. 308 U.S. 106, 113–14 (1939); 308 U.S. 295 (1939).

99. Douglas described the proceedings as to both cases in his diary. As to *L.A. Lumber* he noted:

> The CJ has a "special list" for certioraris. Those which he thinks are not even worthy of discussion in conference are placed by him on the "special list." He circulates the "special list" a day or so before conference. Case v. Los Angeles Lumber Products Co. was on his "special list." I wrote him that I wanted it discussed. So he discussed it and firmly recommended that the petition be denied. Before conference I had planted some seeds of doubt in the minds of the Brethern [*sic*]. As a result we got 4 votes necessary for a grant. The C.J. seemed quite upset. I later learned that this was the first time in the C.J.'s regime when a case had been removed from his "special list."

William O. Douglas, Diary (Oct. 18, 1939) WOD-LC, Box 1780.

As to *Pepper v. Litton*, Douglas's first opinion for the Court, he wrote: "This case had been on the C.J.'s 'special list.' I was responsible for taking it off. He was against it since it involved only a factual question, not an 'important principle.' I thought otherwise and carried the Court." William O. Douglas, Diary (Nov. 9, 1939) WOD-LC, Box 1780. William O. Douglas, Diary (Oct. 21, 1939) WOD-LC, Box 1780 ("The CJ was bent on affirming the judgment below in Case v. Los Angeles Lumber Products Co. He had McR and Reed with him. Stone assigned the opinion to me.").

100. 350 U.S. 462 (1956).

101. 379 U.S. 594 (1965).

102. 390 U.S. 414 (1968) The Court had originally voted to dismiss the case as improvidently granted but White's dissent from dismissal garnered a majority for his side. Douglas Conference Notes, Nov. 10, 1967, WOD-LC.

103. Skeel, Debt's Dominion, ch. 6.

104. Strong v. Repide, 213 U.S. 419 (1909).

105. SEC v. Chenery Corp. (Chenery I), 318 U.S. 80 (1943).

106. 308 U.S. 295 (1939).

107. 164 N.E. 545 (N.Y. 1928).

108. Chenery I, 318 U.S. at 89.

NOTES 317

109. SEC v. Chenery Corp. (Chenery II) 332 U.S. 194 (1947).
110. Manufacturers Trust Co. v. Becker, 338 U.S. 304 (1949); 341 U.S. 267 (1951); 372 U.S. 633 (1963).
111. In Re Carlton Crescent, Inc., 173 F.2d 944, 951 (Learned Hand dissenting), affirmed 338 U.S. 304 (1949). Id. at 306–07 (Burton, J. dissenting).
112. Hearings on S1879, S1871, & S1977 (statement of John S.R. Shad) (1982). Energy Policy Act of 2005, section 1263, P.L. No. 109-58, 119 Stat. 594.
113. James C. Bonbright and Gardiner C. Means, The Holding Company (McGraw-Hill 1932) ("the holding company has become the greatest of the modern devices by which business may escape the various forms of social control that have been developed, wisely or unwisely, as a means of limiting the vast power of the great captains of industry"). Melynk and Lamb, PUHCA's Gone: What's Next for Holding Companies, 27 Energy L.J. 1 (2006). Paul Mahoney, The Public Utility Pyramid, 41 J. Leg. Studies 37, 61 (2012).
114. Fortune 500 2002. Richard D. Cudahy and William D. Henderson, From Insull to Enron: Corporate (re)Regulation After the Rise and Fall of Two Energy Icons, 26 Energy L.J. 35, 91 (2005).
115. Sarbanes-Oxley Act of 2002, P. L. No. 107-204, 116 Stat. 745, Titles II, III, & IV.
116. Skeel, Debt's Dominion 153, 175.
117. Frankfurter in his dissent in *General Stores* had cited the SEC's failure to consider this legislative change as a reason not to defer to the agency's decision to transfer the reorganization to Chapter X.
118. Skeel, Debt's Dominion 164–65, 169.

# Chapter 3

1. The "Kadi" reference made its way into a published dissent a few years later. See Terminiello v. Chicago, 337 U.S. 1, 11 (1949) (Frankfurter, J., dissenting) ("This is a court of review, not a tribunal unbounded by rules. We do not sit like a kadi under a tree dispensing justice according to considerations of individual expediency."). Gerard C. Henderson, The Federal Trade Commission: A Study in Administrative Law and Procedure 336 (1924).
2. St. Joseph Stockyards Co. v. United States, 298 U.S. 38, 84 (Brandeis, J., dissenting) (1936).
3. Felix Frankfurter, The Public and Its Government 24, 89 (1930); Reuel E. Schiller, The Era of Deference: Courts, Expertise, and the Emergence of New Deal Administrative Law, 106 Mich. L. Rev. 399, 417–21 (2007) (describing Professor Frankfurter's views on the need for judicial deference to administrative experts).
4. Frankfurter, The Public and Its Government 50–51, 157–58. Isaiah Leo Sharfman, The Interstate Commerce Commission (1933–1937); James M. Landis. The Administrative Process 128 (1938). William O. Douglas, Address before the Eighth Annual Forum on Current Problems, sponsored by the New York Herald

318   NOTES

Tribune, 26 October 1938, WOD-LC, Box 686, quoted in Jessica Wang, Imagining the Administrative State: Legal Pragmatism, Securities Regulation, and New Deal Liberalism, 17 J. Policy Hist. 257, 277 (2005).

5. FCC v. Pottsville Broad. Co., 309 U.S. 134, 146 (1940); R.R. Comm'n of Texas v. Rowan & Nichols Oil Co., 310 U.S. 573, 584 (1940).

6. Walter Gellhorn, The Administrative Procedure Act: The Beginnings, 72 Va. L. Rev. 219, 221, 224 (1986). George B. Shepherd, Fierce Compromise: The Administrative Procedure Act Emerges from New Deal Politics, 90 Nw. U. L. Rev. 1557, 1600, 1610 (1996). 86 Cong. Rec. 13,942 (1940) (veto message of President Franklin D. Roosevelt), reprinted 27 A.B.A. J. 52 (1941). The House failed to get the necessary two-thirds vote to overturn the veto. Letter from Attorney General Robert H. Jackson to President Franklin Delano Roosevelt, 86 Cong. Rec. 13944 (Dec. 18, 1940). Roscoe Pound, The Place of the Judiciary in a Democratic Polity, 27 A.B.A. J. 133, 133, (1941).

7. Felix Frankfurter, Foreword, 41 Colum. L. Rev. 585, 586–87 (1941).

8. SEC v. Chenery Corp. (*Chenery I*), 318 U.S. 80 (1943). The vote was 4-3 with Jackson, Roberts, and Stone joining Frankfurter's majority. Douglas did not participate, as usual for PUHCA cases in his early years, and Rutledge had not yet taken Byrnes's seat. Jackson, in a letter to Frankfurter two days before the decision was released, suggested that the insider trading may well have helped the shareholders, a view that was also to appear in later debates about insider trading. He argued that "if, as is frequently the case, they were selling under compulsion, the bids of these directors may well have sustained their market, and they may well have benefited therefrom as against the terms they must have accepted in the absence of such bids." Letter from Justice Robert H. Jackson to Justice Felix Frankfurter (Jan. 30, 1943) FF-Harvard, Part 1, Reel 7.

9. *Chenery I*, 318 U.S. at 81–82, 85.

10. *Chenery I*, 318 U.S. at 85–87.

11. *Chenery I*, 318 U.S. at 89, 95. Felix Frankfurter, Social Issues before the Supreme Court (1933), *reprinted in* Law and Politics at 48, 50 ("[T]he law must become more sophisticated in its conception of trustees' obligations. It must sharpen and extend the duties incident to the fiduciary relations of corporate directors and officers.").

12. Draft Concurrence of Justice Jackson, *SEC v. Chenery Corp.*, No. 254, October Term, 1942, at 1, Papers of Robert H. Jackson, Library of Congress, Box 126.

13. Handwritten Note from Chief Justice Harlan Fiske Stone to Justice Felix Frankfurter (undated) FF-Harvard, Part 1, Reel 7.

14. *Chenery I*, 318 U.S. at 92; Draft Opinion, *SEC v. Chenery Corp.*, at 8–9 (undated), Hugo Black Papers, Library of Congress, Box 270: ("But whether it is 'necessary or appropriate in the public interest or for the protection of investors or consumers' that a general rule or regulation be adopted to prohibit reorganization managers from participating equally with others with respect to stock acquired by them during the course of the reorganization is for the Commission to determine. Where an administrative order is valid only if it rests upon a determination which the agency alone is authorized to make, its failure to make such a determination cannot

be remedied by the fact that the agency might properly have made such a determination. It is not for us to determine independently what is 'detrimental to the public interest or the interest of investors or consumers' or 'fair and equitable' within the meaning of §§ 7 and 11 of the Public Utility Holding Company Act of 1935.").

In his published opinion, Frankfurter merely asserted that,

> [B]efore transactions otherwise legal can be outlawed or denied their usual business consequences, they must fall under the ban of some standards of conduct prescribed by an agency of government authorized to prescribe such standards—either the courts or Congress or an agency to which Congress has delegated its authority.

*Chenery I*, 318 U.S. at 92–93. Letter from Justice Felix Frankfurter to Chief Justice Harlan Fiske Stone (Jan. 23, 1943) FF-Harvard, Part 1, Reel 7.

15. R. Hewitt Pate, Robert H. Jackson at the Antitrust Division, 68 Alb. L. Rev. 787, 795 (2005). Draft Concurrence of Justice Jackson, *SEC v. Chenery Corp.*, No. 254, October Term, 1942, at 6, Robert H. Jackson Papers, Library of Congress, Box 126.

16. *Chenery I*, 318 U.S. at 99–100 (Black, J., dissenting).

17. Joseph Lash, From the Diaries of Felix Frankfurter 64 (1988) ("'If you appoint Felix,' Ickes said to Roosevelt, 'his ability and learning are such that he will dominate the Supreme Court for fifteen or twenty years to come. The result will be that probably after you are dead, it will still be your Supreme Court.'"). Recollections of Joseph H. Rauh, in The Making of the New Deal (Katie Loucheim, ed.) 64 (1983) ("When Felix went on the bench in January 1939 he had such stature as a professor, and adviser to Presidents, an articulate writer, and a liberal that he was assumed to be the leader of the liberal wing."). Lash, From the Diaries of Felix Frankfurter 75 ("Frankfurter had come on the Court expecting that in time he would become its intellectual leader and that the authority he exercised in his seminar at Harvard would be replicated in the conferences of the Brethren. He had a yearning for disciples.").

The split—and Frankfurter's eroding influence—may have had its roots in other areas. The first tensions in the New Deal bloc began to surface in the Flag Salute cases. In the first of these cases, *Minersville School District v. Gobitis*, 310 U.S. 586, 600 (1940), Frankfurter wrote for an eight-Justice majority upholding a Pennsylvania law requiring school children to salute the American flag. Soon thereafter, however, Frankfurter felt his leadership position slipping away. H.N. Hirsch, The Enigma of Felix Frankfurter 155 (1981). Hirsch argues that this was a turning point for Frankfurter psychologically:

> This unexpected development embittered him: by the end of the 1942 term, Frankfurter had the sense of being under siege. Unexpectedly, he found himself in a position of being in opposition; his leadership had been rejected. He would react in a manner that had become a familiar part of his psychological makeup. The reaction would be particularly bitter, for this time his opponents were former allies; the challenge was in a domain where he had every reason to anticipate complete success; and he had no choice but to remain where he was and fight it out.

Id. at 176.

The erosion of Frankfurter's influence became quite obvious when *Gobitis* was overruled only three years after being handed down by *West Virginia State Board of*

Education v. Barnette, 319 U.S. 624 (1943). Frankfurter was angered by the switch of Black, Douglas, and Murphy and appalled by what he saw as their political motivation. Edward F. Prichard, Jr., Clerks of the Court on the Justices, in The Making of the New Deal: The Insiders Speak 47–71 ("Frankfurter . . . had great contempt for Murphy, Black, and Douglas, because they voted with him in the first case and then changed their minds. He always said he didn't believe they had reread the Constitution, they had just read the newspapers."). Recollections of Joseph H. Rauh, in Making of the New Deal 64 ("When Frankfurter asked Douglas whether Hugo Black had any new insight into the case, Douglas said, 'No, but he's read the papers.' Felix thought that was terrible!"). Whatever motivated the progressive trio to switch, Frankfurter's leadership role on the Court had quite publicly disappeared with the Flag Salute cases.

18. Frankfurter's self-righteous streak seemed to push him to measure "every colleague by his alignment with what he regarded as the ultimate split within the Court—between his 'disinterested' and scholarly belief in judicial self-restraint, and the 'shoddy,' 'result-oriented,' 'demagogic' jurisprudence of his opponents." Hirsch, Enigma 190. Schlesinger, Politics of Upheaval 228–29 ("Stanley Reed became the particular protector of the Harvard Law School crowd. RFC and, after Reed became Solicitor General in 1935, Justice served as the intelligence switchboard and the operational base for the web of Frankfurter-Corcoran relationships through the new agencies."). *Quoted in* John D. Fassett, New Deal Justice: The Life of Stanley Reed of Kentucky 584 (1994). Sidney Fine, Frank Murphy, The Washington Years (1984) 195 (Frankfurter had similarly low regard for Burton); Hirsch, Enigma 182 (noting that Frankfurter wrote to Hand that " 'Hugo is a self-righteous, self-deluded part fanatic, part demagogue, who really disbelieves in law, thinks it is essentially manipulation of language. Intrinsically, the best brain in the lot, but undisciplined and 'functional' in its employment, an instrument for supporting a predetermined result, not a means for responsible inquiry'").

19. John M. Ferren, Salt of the Earth: Conscience of the Court: The Story of Justice Wiley Rutledge 277 (describing how Frankfurter harangued Reed to his face and made fun of him behind his back, calling him a "vegetable"). J. Woodford Howard, Jr., Mr. Justice Murphy: A Political Biography 268 ("Justice Murphy enjoyed Frankfurter's wit and acknowledged his superior intellect. Yet he felt defensive beside them. . . . Frankfurter was an excitable and scrappy intellectual who had ill-concealed contempt for the Irishman's intellect and night life. . . ."). James E. St. Clair and Linda C. Gugin, Chief Justice Fred M. Vinson of Kentucky: A Political Biography 174 ("Although Vinson was an affable man by nature, 'he could take offense if he were affronted and Frankfurter was a good affronter.' "). William O. Douglas, The Court Years: 1939–1975 22 (1980). Howard, Jr., Mr. Justice Murphy 269 ("Justice Murphy in turn came to regard Justice Frankfurter's professorial habits as tiresome and tangential. The former law professor's campaigns for 'self-restraint' and 'law as the embodiment of reason,' he found hard not to dismiss as masks for the same use of personal convictions that Frankfurter so readily condemned in others."). Murphy, Wild Bill 301. Eugene Gressman, Psycho-Enigmatizing Felix Frankfurter, 80

NOTES 321

Mich. L. Rev. 731, 739 (1982) (reviewing Hirsch, Enigma) ("Neither I [Gressman was Murphy's law clerk] nor Murphy could discover what Frankfurter hoped to accomplish with this endless chain of condescending admonishments. . . . If the notes were really designed to reform or change Murphy's ideological commitments, they were futile. If they were designed to change a Murphy vote or position in a given case, they utterly failed. But if they were written to annoy, insult, or display Frankfurter's 'personalia' techniques, perhaps they hit their mark."). A clerk for Chief Justice Vinson reported how quickly Vinson's sentiments shifted after he joined the Court: "from deferring to Frankfurter to not being able to wait for a case to vote against him, all in six weeks." Dennis J. Hutchinson, The Man Who Once Was Whizzer White (1998).

20. Fassett, New Deal Justice 347 (noting that over the course of the 1942 and 1943 terms Reed voted most frequently with Frankfurter). Letter from Felix Frankfurter to Stanley Reed, at 1–4 (Jan. 29, 1943), FF-Harvard, Part 1, Reel 7. Felix Frankfurter, Does Law Obstruct Government? *in* The Public and Its Government 47, 50 (expressing dismay at Supreme Court's increasing tendency to strike down economic regulation: "And always by a divided Court, always over the protest of its most distinguished minds!").

21. Letter from Stanley Reed to Felix Frankfurter (Jan. 29, 1943) FF-Harvard, Part 1, Reel 7.

22. The SEC's approach has not been uniform in this regard. Market manipulation, for example, carries potential criminal liability, but the agency staff has been more willing to provide no-action letters and other informal guidance in this area.

23. Barry Cushman, Lost Fidelities, 41 Wm. & Mary L. Rev. 95, 98 (1999).

24. Fassett, New Deal Justice 405 (noting that, on Stone's death, "it is quite clear that five of the associate justices each seriously aspired to, or at least would wholeheartedly have welcomed, becoming chief justice"). Ferren, Salt of the Earth 326, 325. Murphy, Wild Bill 244. Cable from Justice Robert H. Jackson to President Harry Truman (June 8, 1946), *discussed in* Melvin I. Urofsky, Division and Discord: The Supreme Court Under Stone and Vinson 1941–1953 143–44 (1997). The case giving rise to the recusal question was Jewel Ridge Coal Corp. v. Local No. 6167, United Mine Workers of Am., 325 U.S. 161 (1945). Letter from Felix Frankfurter to Frank Murphy (June 10, 1946), FF-Harvard, Reel 52.

25. SEC v. Chenery Corp., (Chenery II) 332 U.S. 194, 203, 209 (1947).

26. St. Clair & Gugin, Chief Justice Fred M. Vinson; Telephone Interview with Eugene Gressman, Law Clerk to Justice Frank Murphy 1943–48 (Sept. 6, 2008) (notes on file with the authors). Justice Felix Frankfurter, Memorandum to the Conference in Nos. 81 and 82, Oct. Term, 1946 (June 23, 1947), Justice Frank Murphy, Memorandum to the Conference (June 18, 1947), and Justice Felix Frankfurter, Memorandum for the Conference Nos. 81 and 82 (June 18, 1947), all from Hugo Black Collection, Library of Congress, Box 283. Letter from Justice Wiley Rutledge to Justice Felix Frankfurter (June 18, 1947), FF-Harvard, Part 3, Reel 3. Draft Concurrence of Justice Rutledge, SEC v. Chenery Corp., Nos. 81 and 82, Oct. Term, 1946 (June 23, 1947), and Justice Felix Frankfurter, Memorandum to the Conference in Nos. 81

322  NOTES

and 82 (June 18, 1947), Wiley Rutledge Collection, Library of Congress, Box 155. Letter from Justice Frank Murphy to Justice Felix Frankfurter (June 18, 1947), FF-Harvard, Part 1, Reel 17 ("Thanks for your last circulation in the Chenery case. It is entirely satisfactory to me now.").

27. Letter from Justice Felix Frankfurter to Justice Robert H. Jackson (July 23, [1947]) Robert Jackson Collection, Library of Congress, Box 138.

28. SEC v. Chenery Corp., 332 U.S. 194, 213 (1947) (Jackson, J., dissenting).

29. Memo on dissenting opinion in S.E.C. v. Chenery from JT to Chief Justice Fred Vinson (Oct. 4, 1947) Fred Vinson Collection, University of Kentucky). Jackson Says High Court Encourages Lawlessness, Minneapolis Morning Tribune, Oct. 7, 1947, at 2, Robert Jackson Collection, Library of Congress, Box 138.

30. George B. Shepherd, Fierce Compromise: The Administrative Procedure Act Emerges from New Deal Politics, 90 Nw. U. L. Rev. 1557, 1661 (1996). Administrative Procedure Act, 5 U.S.C. §§ 551–59, 701–06 (2000). M. Elizabeth Magill, Agency Choice of Policymaking Form, 71 U. Chi. L. Rev. 1383, 1427 (2004). Lisa Schultz Bressman, Procedures as Politics in Administrative Law, 107 Colum. L. Rev. 1749, 1756 (2007). Reuel E. Schiller, The Era of Deference: Courts, Expertise, and the Emergence of New Deal Administrative Law, 106 Mich. L. Rev. 399, 441 (2007).

31. The bedrock holding of *Chenery II* as to agency choice would come into question after Frankfurter's retirement. NLRB v. Wyman-Gordon, 394 U.S. 759 (1969), suggested "that a doctrine policing agency choice of procedure might be on the horizon," but the doctrine thereafter evolved to emphasize the breadth of an agency's discretion to choose between rulemaking and adjudication. Magill, Agency Choice 1407.

32. 312 U.S. 473 (1941). Douglas did not participate. Id. at 484.

33. 330 U.S. 585 (1947).

34. 404 U.S. 403 (1972).

35. Harry Blackmun Memo, No. 70-61—SEC v. Medical Committee for Human Rights, at 1 (11/10/71), HAB-LC.

36. Harry Blackmun Memo, No. 70-61—SEC v. Medical Committee for Human Rights, at 2 (11/10/71), HAB-LC

37. Conference Notes, William O. Douglas, No. 70–61 – SEC v. Medical Committee (Nov. 12, 1971), WOD-LC. 1st Draft, SEC v. Medical Committee for Human Rights, at 5 (undated), Letter from Potter Stewart to Thurgood Marshall, No. 70–61, SEC v. Medical Committee (Dec. 21, 1971), Letter from Harry Blackmun to Thurgood Marshall, No. 70–61, SEC v. Medical Committee (Dec. 22, 1971), Thurgood Marshall Collection, Library of Congress.

38. 404 U.S. at 409, 410 & n.6 (Douglas, J., dissenting); Chambers Draft, SEC v. Medical Committee for Human Rights (undated), WOD-LC.

39. 436 U.S. 103 (1978).

40. 15 U.S.C. § 78*l*(k)(1)(A) (2000).

41. Preliminary Memorandum, SEC v. Sloan, to Lewis F. Powell, Jr. 2 (Oct. 14, 1977), LFP Collection.

42. 15 U.S.C. § 78*l*(j) (2000).

NOTES 323

43. Handwritten notes of Lewis F. Powell, Jr., for the Argument in SEC v. Sloan 1 (Mar. 27, 1978), LFP Collection.
44. Preliminary Memorandum, SEC v. Sloan, to Justice Lewis F. Powell, Jr., at 2, LFP Collection.
45. S. Pac. Terminal Co. v. ICC, 219 U.S. 498, 514–15 (1911).
46. Handwritten notes of Lewis F. Powell, Jr., from the Conference on SEC v. Sloan 1 (Mar. 3, 1978), LFP Collection.
47. 446 U.S. 680 (1980).
48. 425 U.S. 185 (1976).
49. Telephone Interview with Greg Palm, Powell Clerk, OT' 75 (notes on file with authors); Ernst & Ernst v. Hochfelder, 425 U.S. 185, 193 n.12 (1976). The published decision reflected a 6-2 split but Powell's handwritten notes reflect that two-members of the majority—Stewart and Marshall—thought rules might be different in a claim brought by the government. Handwritten notes of Lewis F. Powell, Jr., from the Conference on Ernst & Ernst v. Hochfelder, at 1, LFP Collection. A 4-4 split would have affirmed the decision below in favor of the plaintiff. The case was heard in December 1975 in the month between William O. Douglas's retirement and the confirmation of his successor John Paul Stevens; Douglas was still seeking to participate in the Court's docket despite his retirement, an effort rebuffed by the other justices.
50. Preliminary Memorandum, Aaron v. SEC, to Lewis F. Powell, Jr. 1 (Oct. 12, 1979), LFP Collection.
51. Aaron v. SEC, 446 U.S. 680, 687 (1980) (quoting 15 U.S.C. § 77q(a)(3)).
52. SEC v. Capital Gains Research Bureau, Inc., 375 U.S. 180, 195 (1963) (construing section 206 of the Investment Advisers Act, Pub. L. No. 76–768, 54 Stat. 789, 852 (1940), which makes it illegal for any investment adviser "(1) to employ any device, scheme, or artifice to defraud any client or prospective client; (2) to engage in any transaction, practice, or course of business which operates as a fraud or deceit upon any client or prospective client").
53. Bench Memorandum, Aaron v. SEC, to Lewis F. Powell, Jr. 1, 3, 6 (Feb. 15, 1980), LFP Collection.
54. Telephone Interview with David Stewart, Powell Clerk OT '79 (Apr. 17, 2002) (notes on file with authors); Handwritten notes of Lewis F. Powell, Jr., from the Conference on Aaron v. SEC, at 1, LFP Collection. Powell notes on his copy of Stewart's eventual draft that Stewart "reads § 17(a)(3) differently from my tentative view—but P.S. persuades me." Potter Stewart, First Draft Opinion, Aaron v. SEC 1 (circulated Apr. 16, 1980) (handwritten notes of Lewis F. Powell, Jr.), LFP Collection.
55. Handwritten notes of Lewis F. Powell, Jr., from the Conference on Aaron v. SEC, at 1-3, LFP Collection.
56. Potter Stewart, First Draft Opinion, Aaron v. SEC, at 1 (handwritten notes of Lewis F. Powell, Jr.), LFP Collection.
57. *Aaron*, 446 U.S. at 686 n.5., 694, 695.
58. Aaron, 446 U.S. at 703 (Burger, C. J., concurring); 705–10 (Blackmun, J., dissenting).
59. 450 U.S. 91 (1981).

## 324 NOTES

60. Letter from Lewis F. Powell, Jr., to Potter Stewart 1 (Feb. 12, 1981), LFP Collection. Handwritten notes of Lewis F. Powell, Jr., from the Conference on Steadman v. SEC 1 (Dec. 5, 1980), LFP Collection. Handwritten Notes of Harry Blackmun, 1st Draft, No. 79-1266, Steadman v. SEC, Powell, J., dissenting (Feb. 17, 1981), HAB-LC.
61. 704 F.2d 1065, 1069 (1983).
62. Preliminary Memorandum, SEC v. O'Brien, to Lewis F. Powell Jr. 5 (Jan. 6, 1984 Conference). Handwritten notes of Lewis F. Powell, Jr., from the Conference on SEC v. O'Brien 1 (Apr. 20, 1984), LFP Collection.
63. 561 U.S. 477 (2010).
64. 15 U.S.C. § 7211(e)(6). A second issue was raised in the case regarding the appointment of the PCAOB members by the SEC, but the Court rejected the argument summarily.
65. Humphrey's Executor v. United States, 295 U.S. 602 (1935). Roosevelt believed he should have the power to control agency personnel, a view somewhat at odds with the Progressives' commitment to civil service protections.
66. *PCAOB*, at 3148–49 ("The parties agree that the Commissioners cannot themselves be removed by the President except under the *Humphrey's Executor* standard of 'inefficiency, neglect of duty, or malfeasance in office,'" . . . and we decide the case with that understanding.").
67. Interview with Arthur Levitt, Frontline (Mar. 12, 2002), transcript available at http://www.pbs.org/wgbh/pages/frontline/shows/regulation/interviews/levitt.html.
68. The Court's other foray into separation of powers jurisprudence was even less consequential for the administration of the securities laws. Lucia v. SEC, 138 S. Ct. 2044 (2018), raised an appointment clause question: Were the administrative law judges of the SEC employees, who could be hired through ordinary civil services processes, or were they officers, who had to be appointed by the head of the department (i.e., the SEC)? The Court concluded that they were officers, the SEC promptly reappointed its ALJs, and life carried on as before.
69. 581 U.S. 455 (2017); 140 S. Ct. 1936 (2020).
70. The Court had previously held that the statute of limitations applied to SEC actions seeking monetary penalties. Gabelli v. SEC, 568 U.S. 442 (2013).
71. See, e.g., Chamber of Commerce of the U.S. v. SEC, 412 F.3d 133, (D.C. Cir. 2005); Chamber of Commerce of the U.S. v. SEC, 443 F.3d 890, 370 U.S. App. D.C. 249 (D.C. Cir. 2006); Goldstein v. S.E.C, 451 F.3d 873 (D.C. Cir. 2006).

# Chapter 4

1. 320 U.S. 344 (1943).
2. Douglas did not participate. The SEC filed suit on February 16, 1942, well after Douglas had left the Commission. Joiner acquired the land in 1940, which was also after Douglas's appointment to the Court.
3. 328 U.S. 293 (1946).

NOTES 325

4. Memorandum from Frank Murphy to the Conference re no. 843—S.E.C. v. Howey Co. (May 17, 1946), Wiley Rutledge Collection, Library of Congress, Box 141.

5. Conference Notes of Harold Burton, SEC v. W. J. Howey Co. (undated) Harold Burton Collection, Library of Congress, Box 128.

6. Section 5 of the Securities Act covers *any* sale of securities. Section 4(a)(2) then exempts transactions that do not involve a "public offering."

7. 346 U.S. 119 (1953).

8. SEC v. Ralston Purina Co, 102 F. Supp. 964, 968–69 (1952); SEC v. Ralston Purina Co., 200 F.2d 85, 88 (8th Cir. 1952), rev'd 346 U.S. 119 (1953).

9. Quoting the House Report on the Securities Act of 1933 at 5.

10. See, e.g., Doran v. Petroleum Management Corp. 545 F.2d 893 (5th Cir. 1977) (discussing a series of Fifth Circuit opinions seeking to explain the private offering exemption); Regulation D, 17 C.F.R. §230.500 et seq.

11. Letter from Tom Clark letter to Fred Vinson, S.E.C. v. Ralston-Purina, No. 512; Letter from Felix Frankfurter to Tom Clark, [June 2, 1953], Tom Clark Collection, Box A25, Folder 12, University of Texas Law Library.

12. 387 U.S. 202 (1967).

13. Douglas Conference Notes, No. 428—Securities & Exchange Comm'n v. United Benefit Life, Conference April 14, 1967, WOD-LC.

14. 389 U.S. 322 (1967).

15. Douglas Conference Notes, No. 104—Alexander Tcherepnin v. Knight (Nov. 14, 1967), WOD-LC.

16. 393 U.S. 453 (1969).

17. Letter from John M. Harlan to Thurgood Marshall, No. 41—SEC v. National Securities, Inc. (Jan. 8, 1969), Thurgood Marshall Collection, Box 51, Library of Congress.

18. Seligman, Transformation of Wall Street 267. Louis Loss & Joel Seligman, Securities Regulation 3d ed. 298, n. 23.

19. 359 U.S. 65 (1959).

20. United States v. S.E. Underwriters, 322 U.S. 533 (1944).

21. Securities Act § 3(a)(8).

22. Douglas Conference Notes, No. 237—National Assoc. of Securities v. Variable, No. 290—Securities & Exchange Com. v. Variable (1-23-1959), WOD-LC, Box 1210.

23. William O. Douglas, Memorandum to the Conference, Nos. 237 and 290 (Feb. 14, 1959), Earl Warren Collection, Box 456, Library of Congress. The opinion was Douglas's fourth securities opinion in the almost twenty years since he had left the SEC to join the Court.

24. John M. Harlan, Memorandum to the Conference, Nos. 237 and 290 (Feb/ 17, 1959), John Harlan Collection, Box 68, Princeton University.

25. Memorandum of Mr. Justice Brennan, NASD v. Variable Annuity Life Ins. Co. of America, Nos. 237 and 290 (Circulated 2-16[-1959]), John Harlan Collection, Box 68, Princeton University. Letter of William Brennan to William O. Douglas, Nos. 237 and 290 (Mar. 5, 1959), Letter of William O. Douglas to William Brennan (Mar. 14, 1959), Letter of William Brennan to William O. Douglas, Nos. 237 and 290—VALIC

326 NOTES

(Mar. 16, 1959), WOD-LC, Box 1210; Letter of Potter Stewart to John Harlan, Nos. 290 and 237—Variable Annuities (Mar. 18, 1959), Potter Stewart Collection, Box 166, Folder 1367, Yale University Library. Douglas Conference Notes, No. 237—National Assoc. of Securities v. Variable, No. 290—Securities & Exchange Com. v. Variable (1-23-1959), Letter to conference from Tom Clark, Nos. 290 and 237 (Mar. 21, 1959), WOD-LC, Box 1210.

26. 421 U.S. 837 (1975).

27. Lewis F. Powell, Jr., Second Draft Opinion Dissenting from Denial of Certiorari, United Hous. Found., Inc. v. Forman 1 (Jan. 16, 1974), LFP Collection. Community Services, Inc., et al., Appellees, 500 F.2d 1246 n. 9 (2d Cir. 1974).

28. Lewis F. Powell, Jr., Second Draft Opinion Dissenting from Denial of Certiorari, United Hous. Found., Inc. v. Forman 1 (Jan. 16, 1974 [sic]), at 4, LFP Collection. The Court granted the writ of certiorari on January 20, 1975. 419 U.S. 1120 (1975).

29. Brief of Amicus Curiae Securities and Exchange Commission at 7, United Hous. Found., Inc. v. Forman, 421 U.S. 837 (1975) (No. 74–157) (citing section 3(a)(10) of the Exchange Act, 15 U.S.C. 78c(a)(10). Offers and Sales of Condominiums or Units in a Real Estate Development, Securities Act Release No. 33–5347, 38 Fed. Reg. 1735 (Jan. 18, 1973) (concluding that condominiums are not securities). HAB Memo, No. 74-157—United Housing Foundation v. Forman; No. 74-647—New York v. Forman, at 4, 8 (4/18/75), and Conference Notes, No. 74-157—United Housing Foundation v. Forman; No. 74-647—New York v. Forman, (4/18/75), HAB-LC ("No reach 11 Am").

30. United Housing Foundation, Inc. v. Forman, 421 U.S. 837, 849 (1975).

31. 439 U.S. 551 (1979).

32. Brief for the Securities and Exchange Commission as Amicus Curiae at 6–8, Int'l Bhd. of Teamsters v. Daniel, 439 U.S. 551 (1979) (Nos. 77–753, 77–754).

33. Daniel v. Int'l Bhd. of Teamsters, 410 F. Supp. 541, 547 (N.D. Ill. 1976), aff'd, 561 F.2d 1223, 1231 (7th Cir. 1977).

34. Preliminary Memorandum, Int'l Bhd. of Teamsters v. Daniel, to Lewis F. Powell, Jr., at 1 (handwritten notes of Lewis F. Powell, Jr.). Bench Memorandum, Int'l Bhd. of Teamsters v. Daniel, to Lewis F. Powell, Jr. 1, 21–22 (Aug. 21, 1978) (identifying the plan's compulsory, noncontributory, and defined-benefit characteristics as the three primary issues in determining whether the plan was a security, and then examining whether applying the securities laws interfered with ERISA), LFP Collection.

35. Daniel, 561 F.2d at 1237, 1243 and Daniel, 410 F. Supp. at 549.

36. Bench Memorandum, Int'l Bhd. of Teamsters v. Daniel, to Lewis F. Powell, Jr., at 14 (handwritten notes of Lewis F. Powell, Jr.). J. Mark Fisher, Note, *The Application of the Antifraud Provisions of the Securities Laws to Compulsory, Noncontributory Pension Plans After* Daniel v. International Brotherhood of Teamsters, 64 VA. L. REV. 305, 307–08, 314 (1978) (handwritten notes of Lewis F. Powell, Jr., on the margins of a photocopy). Handwritten notes of Lewis F. Powell, Jr., from the Conference on Int'l Bhd. of Teamsters v. Daniel 2 (Nov. 3, 1978) (revealing that Powell had punctuated Blackmun's vote to reverse with two exclamation points), LFP Collection. Harry Blackmun Handwritten Notes, 77–753/4 Teamsters v. Daniel (18 Oct. 78), HAB-LC.

37. Daniel v. Int'l Bhd. of Teamsters, 561 F.2d 1223, 1251 (7th Cir. 1977); Preliminary Memorandum, Int'l Bhd. of Teamsters v. Daniel, to Lewis F. Powell, Jr., at 9 (quoting *Daniel*, 561 F.2d at 1251 (Tone, concurring) (emphasis added by Lewis F. Powell, Jr.) and (handwritten notes of Lewis F. Powell, Jr.). Bench Memorandum, Int'l Bhd. of Teamsters v. Daniel, from Paul [B. Stephan] to Lewis F. Powell, Jr., at 23 (handwritten notes of Paul B. Stephan) (emphasis added by Lewis F. Powell, Jr.), LFP Collection. Brief for the United States as Amicus Curiae at 8–10, Int'l Bhd. of Teamsters v. Daniel, 439 U.S. 551 (1979) (No. 77–753).

38. The initial draft explained the Court's refusal to defer to the SEC this way:

> [W]hen it becomes apparent that an agency has shaped its interpretation of a statute solely to determine the outcome of a particular case, without regard to the ongoing problems of policy and purpose that underlie that agency's regulatory function, this deference is forfeited. *Ad hoc*, unprincipled decisionmaking does not draw on developed expertise and constitutes an abuse of accorded flexibility.
>
> On a number of occasions in recent years this Court has found it necessary to reject the SEC's interpretation of various positions of the Securities Acts. In those cases, the SEC either had shifted its position, had not previously developed a position, or had developed its position without consideration of the statutory authorization under which it acts. This case falls into the same category. Our review of the SEC's past actions convinces us that until the instant litigation arose that agency never had to consider the Securities Acts applicable to non-contributory, involuntary pension plans and that its argument to the contrary here demonstrates an alarming and disheartening lack of candor.

Lewis F. Powell, Jr., First Draft Opinion, Int'l Bhd. of Teamsters v. Daniel, at 16–17, LFP Collection. Int'l Bhd. of Teamsters v. Daniel, 439 U.S. 551, 565–66 & n.20 (1979).

39. Lewis F. Powell, Jr., First Draft Opinion, Int'l Bhd. of Teamsters v. Daniel 20 (Dec. 4, 1978) (handwritten notes of Lewis F. Powell, Jr. Bench Memorandum, Int'l Bhd. of Teamsters v. Daniel, to Lewis F. Powell, Jr. 18 (Aug. 21, 1978).

> [T]he SEC has taken the position that almost every form of injustice that results from a failure to disclose information violates § 10(b) of the Securities Exchange Act. That agency has been free to do this in part because it has not enforced a concomitant registration requirement, a burden that would both swamp the agency and engender substantial political pressure to amend the securities laws. A determination that a sale means the same thing for both registration and fraud might encourage the SEC to take a more responsible position in these cases and to husband its resources for those situations where the securities laws were meant to apply.

Letter from Byron R. White to Lewis F. Powell, Jr. 1 (Dec. 26, 1978). Letter from Chief Justice Warren E. Burger to Lewis F. Powell, Jr. 1 (Jan. 2, 1979). Letter from Lewis F. Powell, Jr., to Chief Justice Warren E. Burger 1 (Jan. 11, 1979). LFP Collection.

40. Int'l Bhd. of Teamsters v. Daniel, 439 U.S. 551, 569 n.22 (1979).

41. Memorandum from Lewis F. Powell, Jr., to Nancy Bregstein 2, 3 (Oct. 25, 1977). Bench Memorandum, Bankers Trust Co. v. Mallis, to Lewis F. Powell, Jr. 1 (Nov. 18, 1977) (handwritten notes of Lewis F. Powell, Jr.), LFP Collection. We discuss *Santa Fe* and *Blue Chip* in Chapters 6 and 7.

328 NOTES

42. The plaintiffs changed their theory at oral argument, declining to defend the Second Circuit decision. Handwritten notes of Lewis F. Powell, Jr., from the Argument in Bankers Trust Co. v. Mallis 3 (Nov. 30, 1977). In addition, there was no document recording the judgment of the district court, suggesting that the Second Circuit may have lacked jurisdiction. Memorandum from Bob Comfort to Lewis F. Powell, Jr. 1 (Nov. 30, 1977). Handwritten notes of Lewis F. Powell, Jr., from the Conference on Bankers Trust Co. v. Mallis 1–2, 3 (Dec. 2, 1977), LFP Collection.

43. Brennan, Stewart, Warren, and Stevens joined Rehnquist's position on jurisdiction. Note from William H. Rehnquist to Lewis F. Powell, Bankers Trust Co. v. Mallis, LFP Collection. Bankers Trust Co. v. Mallis, 435 U.S. 381, 388 (1978). Handwritten notes of Lewis F. Powell, Jr., from the Conference on Bankers Trust Co. v. Mallis 1 (Mar. 6, 1978), LFP Collection.

44. 449 U.S. 424 (1981). Preliminary Memorandum, Rubin v. United States, to Lewis F. Powell, Jr. 1 (Apr. 11, 1980 Conference) (handwritten notes of Lewis F. Powell, Jr.), LFP Collection.

45. United States v. Naftalin, 441 U.S. 768 (1979).

46. William Brennan, First Draft Opinion, United States v. Naftalin 1 (May 8, 1979), William F. Brennan, Jr. Collection, Library of Congress.

47. 15 U.S.C. § 77r and 15 U.S.C. § 77b(3).

48. Bench Memorandum, Rubin v. United States, to Lewis F. Powell, Jr. 13 (Sept. 16, 1980) (handwritten notes of Lewis F. Powell, Jr.) (noting Powell's agreement with his clerk), LFP Collection. Milton V. Freeman, Colloquium Foreword, 61 Fordham L. Rev. S1, S1–S2 (1993). Handwritten notes of Lewis F. Powell, Jr., from the Conference on Rubin v. United States 3 (Nov. 14, 1980), LFP Collection.

49. Chief Justice Warren E. Burger, First Draft Opinion, Rubin v. United States 1 (Jan. 7, 1981) (handwritten notes of Lewis F. Powell, Jr.). Letter from Lewis F. Powell, Jr., to Chief Justice Warren E. Burger 1–2 (Jan. 8, 1981). Letter from William J. Brennan, Jr. to Chief Justice Warren E. Burger (Jan. 8, 1981), LFP Collection.

50. Letter from Lewis F. Powell, Jr., to Chief Justice Warren E. Burger 1–2 (Jan. 8, 1981) (citing SEC v. Capital Gains Research Bureau, 375 U.S. 180 (1963). Ernst & Ernst v. Hochfelder, 425 U.S. 185 (1976). Letter from Chief Justice Warren E. Burger to Lewis F. Powell, Jr. 1 (Jan. 8, 1981), LFP Collection.

Powell's efforts to root out the *Capital Gains* decision were for naught, as one of the Court's twenty-first-century opinions in this area (expanding the reach of the securities laws) invokes the case. SEC v. Zandford, 535 U.S. 813 (2002).

51. 455 U.S. 551 (1982).

52. Handwritten notes of Lewis F. Powell, Jr., from the Argument in Marine Bank v. Weaver 1 (Jan. 8, 1982), LFP Collection.

53. Letter from John Paul Stevens to Chief Justice Warren E. Burger 1 (Mar. 4, 1982), LFP Collection.

54. Chief Justice Warren E. Burger, First Draft Opinion, Marine Bank v. Weaver 1, 8 (circulated Mar. 1, 1982). (Handwritten notes of Lewis F. Powell, Jr.), LFP Collection.

55. The issue was presented to the Court shortly thereafter, but the Court declined to grant certiorari over White's dissent. Mordaunt v. Incomco, 469 U.S. 1115 (1985)

(White, J., dissenting from the denial of certiorari). Powell was absent from the Court at the time due to complications from surgery. It is inconceivable that he would have voted against hearing the case, given the clear conflict and the importance of the issue. It remains unresolved.

56. 471 U.S. 681 (1985); 471 U.S. 701 (1985).

57. 417 U.S. 506 (1974). We discuss *Alberto-Culver* at greater length in Chapter 6.

58. Lewis F. Powell, Jr., Rough First Draft Concurring Opinion, Scherk v. Alberto-Culver Co. 5–6 (June 2, 1974). Lewis F. Powell, Jr., Suggested Note to Be Added to the Opinion of the Court, Scherk v. Alberto-Culver Co. 1 (June 6, 1974). Potter Stewart, Fourth Draft Opinion, Scherk v. Alberto-Culver Co. 1 (circulated June 7, 1974) (handwritten notes of Lewis F. Powell, Jr.) ("My suggested note 8 is included."), LFP Collection.

59. Powell wrote on the certiorari pool memorandum that he was "inclined to agree" with the Ninth Circuit's application of the doctrine. Preliminary Memorandum, Landreth Timber Co. v. Landreth 1 (Sept. 24, 1984 Conference) (handwritten notes of Lewis F. Powell, Jr.). Memorandum from Lewis F. Powell, Jr., to Lynda [Guild Simpson] 2–3 (Mar. 7, 1985). *See id.* at 4 ("Is *Gould* different because he bought only 50%. What if he had bought 25%?"), LFP Collection.

60. Bench Memorandum, Gould v. Ruefenacht, to Lewis F. Powell, Jr. 8 (Mar. 5, 1985). Memorandum from Lynda [Guild Simpson] to Lewis F. Powell, Jr. 3 (Mar. 7, 1985). Telephone Interview with Lynda Guild Simpson, Powell Clerk OT'84 (July 24, 2020) (notes on file with authors). Memorandum from Lynda [Guild Simpson] to Lewis F. Powell, Jr. (Mar. 7, 1985) at 4 (handwritten notes of Lewis F. Powell, Jr.). Handwritten notes of Lewis F. Powell, Jr., for the Argument in Gould v. Ruefenacht and Landreth Timber Co. v. Landreth 1 (Mar. 21, 1985). Handwritten notes of Lewis F. Powell, Jr., from the Conference on Landreth Timber Co. v. Landreth 2 (Mar. 29, 1985), LFP Collection. Conference Notes, Harry Blackmun, No. 83–1961 Landreth Timber Company v. Landreth (3/29/85), HAB-LC.

61. Stevens evidently had a change of heart, as he subsequently dissented. Landreth Timber Co. v. Landreth, 471 U.S. 681, 697 (1985) (Stevens, J., dissenting).

62. Handwritten Note of Harry Blackmun, 1st Draft, Landreth Timber Company v. Landreth (April 25, 1985), HAB-LC.

63. 494 U.S. 56 (1990).

64. 1st Draft, Reves v. Arthur Young & Co., No. 88-1480, at 7 (Jan. 2, 1990), Thurgood Marshall Collection, Library of Congress. Letter from John Paul Stevens to Thurgood Marshall, No. 88-1480 Reves v. Arthur Young & Co. (Jan. 17, 1990), William F. Brennan Jr. Collection, Library of Congress.

65. 540 US 389 (2004).

66. 373 U.S. 341 (1963).

67. David L. Stebbene, Arthur J. Goldberg, New Deal Liberal 8 (1996); Alan M. Dershowitz, Justice Arthur Goldberg and His Law Clerks, in IN Chambers: Stories of Supreme Court Law Clerks and Their Justices, Todd C. Peppers & Artemus Ward, eds. (2012) 295–96.

68. Letter of William O. Douglas to Arthur Goldberg (Apr. 16, 1963), Arthur Goldberg Collection, Box 11, Folder 11, Northwestern University Library. Handwritten Note

330  NOTES

from Arthur [Goldberg] to Bill [Douglas] (Apr. 17, 1963), WOD-LC. William O. Douglas, Address sponsored by the Graduate School of Public Affairs of American University and the Graduate School of the Department of Agriculture, 17 April 1937, WOD-LC, Box 683.

69. Letter of Felix Frankfurter to Potter Stewart, cc: John Harlan (May 27, 1963) John Harlan Collection, Princeton University, Box 174.

70. *Silver*, 373 US at 365.

71. Kaplan v. Lehman, 389 U.S. 954 (1967) (Warren, C.J., dissenting from the denial of certiorari) (criticizing the Seventh Circuit's "blunderbuss approach" as "fall[ing] far short of the close analysis and delicate weighing process mandated by this Court's opinion in *Silver*."). Docket Sheet, Kaplan v. Lehman Brothers, No. 197, Earl Warren Collection, Box 383, Library of Congress.

72. 422 U.S. 659 (1975).

73. 422 U.S. 694 (1975).

74. Memorandum to Lewis F. Powell, Jr. 2 (Mar. 27, 1975), LFP Collection. HAB Memo, No. 74-304—Gordon v. New York Stock Exchange, Inc., at 4–5 (3/24/75), HAB-LC.

75. Conference Notes, Harry Blackmun, 73–1701, United States v. National Association of Securities Dealers, Inc., (3/19/75); Memo, HAB, No. 73-1701—United States v. National Association of Securities Dealers (3/7/75), HAB-LC.

76. *NASD*, 422 U.S. at 725.

77. *NASD*, 422 U.S. at 735 (White, J., dissenting).

78. Letter from William O. Douglas to Byron White, No. 73–1701—U.S. v. Nat. Assoc. Securities Dealers (June 19, 1975), WOD-LC.

79. 551 U.S. 264 (2007).

80. In re IPO Litigation, Stipulation and Agreement of Settlement (Civ. Action NO. 21 MC 92 (SAS) (Oct. 5, 2009 S.D.N.Y.) (approving $586 million settlement), available at http://iposecuritieslitigation.com/stipofsettlement3.09.pdf.

81. *Billing*, 551 U.S. at 284 (quoting Brief for United States as Amicus Curiae 9).

82. Securities Exchange Act § 28(a); 15 U.S.C. 78bb(a).

83. 447 U.S. 557 (1980).

84. 556 F. Supp. 1359, 1369 (E.D.N.Y. 1983).

85. 725 F. 2d 892, 896–97, 900, 901 (2nd Cir. 1984)

86. William J. Brennan, Jr., Conference Notes, No. 83–1911, LOWE v. SEC (undated), William F. Brennan, Jr. Collection, Library of Congress.

87. Lowe v. Securities and Exchange Commission, 1st Draft, at 24 (Apr. 3, 1985), Byron R. White Collection, Box II: 23, Library of Congress.

88. Letter from Byron R. White to John Paul Stevens, No. 83-1911—Lowe v. SEC (Apr. 4, 1985); Letter from John Paul Stevens to Byron R. White, No. 83-1911—Lowe v. SEC (Apr. 5, 1985), Byron R. White Collection, Box II: 23, Library of Congress.

89. Lowe v. SEC, 472 U.S. at 209 n.56.

90. Letter from Harry Blackmun to John Paul Stevens, No. 83-1911—Lowe v. SEC (April 9, 1985); Letter from William H. Rehnquist to John Paul Stevens, No. 83-1911— Lowe v. SEC (Apr. 9, 1985); Letter from Warren E. Burger to John Paul Stevens, No.

83-1911—Lowe v. SEC (May 20, 1985), Byron R. White Collection, Box II: 23, Library of Congress. Powell was out from the case due to complications from surgery.

91. 435 U.S. 465 (1978). 558 U.S. 310 (2010). 573 U.S. 682 (2014).

92. 2006 WL 3844465 (S.D.N.Y. 2006) and 547 F.3d 167 (2d Cir. 2008), respectively.

93. SEC v. Berger, 322 F.3d 187, 192–93 (2d Cir. 2003).

94. In re Nat'l Australia Bank Sec. Litig., No. 03 Civ. 6537(BSJ), 2006 WL 3844465, at *9 (S.D.N.Y., Oct. 25, 2006).

95. Morrison v. Nat'l Australia Bank Ltd., 561 U.S. 247, 251–52 (2010).

96. Brief for the United States as Amicus Curiae Supporting Respondents, Morrison v. Nat'l Australia Bank Ltd., Docket # 08-8-1191, at 9–13, 16, 26, and 30 (criticizing holding of SEC v. Berger, 322 F.3d 187 (2d Cir. 2003) that same jurisdictional standard applies to private plaintiffs and SEC).

97. *Nat'l Australia*, 561 U.S. at 253–54.

98. *Nat'l Australia*, 561 U.S. at 276 (Stevens, J. concurring).

99. Remarks of Congressman Kanjorski, Cong. Record H5237 (June 30, 2010) ("This bill's provisions concerning extraterritoriality . . . are intended to rebut [*National Australia*]'s presumption by clearly indicating that Congress intends extraterritorial application in cases brought by the SEC or the Justice Department."); H.R. 4173, 111th Cong., § 929P(b) (2010). *Nat'l Australia*, 561 U.S. at 261.

# Chapter 5

1. William L. Prosser, The Law of Torts (4th ed. 1971) at §105.

2. SEC v. Texas Gulf Sulphur Co., 401 F.2d 833 (2d Cir. 1968), *cert. den. sub nom* Coates v. SEC, 394 U.S. 976 (1969).

3. 445 U.S. 222 (1980); 463 U.S. 646 (1983).

4. See H.L. Wilgus, Purchase of Shares of Corporation by a Director from a Shareholder, 8 Mich. L. Rev. 267 (1910); Roberts Walker, Duty of Disclosure by a Director Purchasing Stock from his Stockholder, 23 Yale L.J. 637 (1923). Henry Manne, writing later in the 1960s, argued that insider trading was widespread and accepted. Henry G. Manne, Insider Trading and the Stock Market 9–33 (1966). Michael Perino has contested that history. Michael Perino, The Lost History of Insider Trading, 2019 U. Ill. L. Rev. 951–1004 (2019).

5. 213 U.S. 419 (1909).

6. Restatement of Torts § 551, and 170, comment on clause (2) (1938). The Restatement (Second) of Torts drafted during the 1960s and published in 1977 included the same core language for silence as fraud if there is a duty to speak because of fiduciary or other relationship of trust and confidence and the same comment that the Institute was not addressing duties within business associations. Tentative Drafts 10–12, containing the misrepresentation sections, were considered by the Institute during 1965–67 between *Cady, Roberts* and *Texas Gulf Sulphur* discussed later in this chapter. The notes, which listed many examples of fiduciary relationships—attorney-client;

332　NOTES

doctor-patient; priest-parishioner—included only one example relevant to corporate law, that of a majority shareholder to a minority shareholder illustrated by the Speed v. Transamerica case, 235 F.2d 369 (3d Cir. 1956). The Restatement 2nd was cited by *Chiarella* for the rule covering insiders within corporations. Chiarella v. United States, 445 U.S. 222, 228 (1980). The question of whether duties were owed to the corporation only or to individual shareholders persisted well into the postwar era. Donald C. Cook & Myer Feldman, Insider Trading Under the Securities Exchange Act (Part II), 66 Harv. L. Rev. 612, 640 (1953).

7. H.R. Rep. Nos. 1383, 1838, 73d Cong., 2d Sess. (1934); Sen. Rep. Nos. 792, 1455 at 55, 73d Cong., 2d Sess. (1934).

8. Exchange Act §16(b) applying to officers, directors and 10% shareholders, when they both purchased and sold shares of their company within a six-month period.

9. Louis Loss, Securities Regulation (2d ed. 1961) at 1087-89 ("probably the most cordially disliked provision" of the securities laws and describing industry and managers recommendations for repeal).

10. On the friendship of Douglas and Clark, see William O. Douglas, Charles E. Clark, 73 Yale L.J. 3 (1963).

11. Smolowe v. Delendo Corp., 136 F.2d 231 (2nd Cir. 1943); Park & Tilford, Inc. v. Schulte, 160 F. 2d 984 (2nd Cir. 1947); Gratz v. Claughton, 187 F. 2d 46 (2nd Cir. 1951).

12. Memo of CEC, Smolowe and Levy v. Delendo Corp. (March 24, 1943), Charles Clark Papers, Series II, Box 31, Folder 59, Yale Law School. Clark shared his views on interpretation at greater length in Charles E. Clark, A Plea for the Unprincipled Decision, 49 Va. L. Rev. 660 (1963).

13. Gratz v. Claughton, 187 F. 2d 46, 49 (2nd Cir. 1951); Stella v. Graham-Paige Motors Corp., 232 F.2d 299 (2nd Cir. 1956). The Second Circuit opinions did not uniformly expand the reach of § 16(b), despite Clark's best efforts. In Shaw v. Dreyfus, a 1949 decision, the panel majority held, over Clark's dissent, that a gift was not a sale for purposes of the rule. 172 F.2d 140 (2nd Cir. 1949). A panel without Clark, Rattner v. Lehman in 1952, declined to hold a partner liable for the trading of the partnership. 193 F.2d 564 (2nd Cir. 1952). Learned Hand's separate opinion noted his decision rested on the assumption that the partnership bought/sold without advice from the individual and "wished to say nothing" about whether the firm deputizes a partner, an issue that was presented to the Supreme Court a decade later. As we discuss below, the Supreme Court held in Blau v. Lehman that it was bound by the text of § 16(b), thus following *Rattner*.

14. 341 U.S. 267, 271–72 (1951).

15. William Painter, The Federal Securities Code and Corporate Disclosure, 221–23 (1979) ("it is extremely doubtful that prior to Cady Roberts, the Commission envisaged Rule 10b-5 as having any real application to insider trading beyond the fraud area." Professor Loss would characterize this extension as a major contribution of William Cary as SEC chair. See Recent Developments in Securities Regulation, 63 Colum. L. Rev. 856, 861 (1963).

16. Seligman, Transformation of Wall Street 293.

NOTES 333

17. 40 SEC 907 (1961).

18. William Painter, Federal Securities Code at 221–23 (citing congressional testimony of three chairs of the SEC during the 1940s and '50s).

19. The respondents in *Cady, Roberts* did not seek judicial review of the agency's order.

20. 368 U.S. 403 (1962).

21. Brief for the Securities and Exchange Commission as Amicus Curiae, Blau v. Lehman, No. 61–66, 1961 WL 102336.

22. *Blau*, 368 U.S. at 414 (Douglas, J., dissenting).

23. William O. Douglas, Conference Notes, No 66—(12/15/1961), Blau v. Lehman, WOD-LC, Box 1272.

24. 375 U.S. 180 (1963).

25. Section 206 makes it unlawful (1) "to employ any device, scheme or artifice to defraud any client or prospective client" or (2) "to engage in any transaction, practice, or course of business which operates as a fraud or deceit upon any client or prospective client." 15 U.S.C. § 80b-6(1) & (2). This provision of the Advisers Act incorporates the substance of the first and third specifications of fraud included in § 17(a) of the Securities Act of 1933 and later incorporated into Rule 10b-5, but omits the middle ground of § 17 and 10b-5 that define fraud via the black-letter elements of deceit developed at common law that spoke to the specific contexts of affirmative misrepresentations and half-truths.

26. The SEC urged "the failure to disclose to clients to whom purchase was recommended that they (defendants), too, had made purchases, constituted a scheme to defraud by failing to disclose a material fact." *Capital Gains*, 300 F.2d at 747. This part of the SEC's argument sounds like the half-truth species of fraud. What was the material fact? The SEC also argued that Capital Gains' "advice to buy was dishonest and fraudulent" because it failed to disclose the advisers' plan to sell its stock in the near future. *Capital Gains*, 300 F.2d at 748. So characterized, the SEC's allegation of fraud sounds in misleading omission, applicable to any defendant; fiduciary duty arising from a relationship does not necessarily come into play.

  A detailed history of the enforcement action can be found in Arthur Laby, SEC v. Capital Gains Research Bureau and the Investment Advisers Act of 1940, 91 B. U. L. Rev. 1051, 1056–59 (2011).

27. The Second Circuit during this period used "in banc" rather than the now more familiar "en banc" and we follow that usage here.

28. Memorandum of LPM, SEC v. Capital Gains Research (Oct. 17, 1961), Charles Clark Papers, Series II, Box 55, Folder 262, Yale Law School.

29. *Capital Gains*, 300 F.2d at 749.

30. Memorandum of HJF, SEC v. Capital Gains Research (Feb. 26, 1962), Charles Clark Papers, Series II, Box 55, Folder 262, Yale Law School.

31. At the *in banc* oral argument Judges Sterry Waterman and Edward Lumbard wondered why the SEC had not adopted "simple rules" requiring disclosure of the trading the SEC alleged to be fraudulent. Clark Argument Notes (Feb. 21, 1962), Charles Clark Papers, Series II, Box 55, Folder 262, Yale Law School. Judge Moore complained of the unfairness of not providing the defendant with notice. SEC, Investment Advisers Act

334  NOTES

of 1940, Rel. No. 120 (Oct. 16, 1961), Charles Clark Papers, Series II, Box 55, Folder 262, Yale Law School.

32. *Capital Gains*, 300 F.2d at 751 (Clark, J., dissenting).

33. Supplemental Memo on Rehearing *in Banc*, CEC, SEC v. Capital Gains Research (Feb. 23, 1962), Clark Papers, Series II, Box 55, Folder 262, Yale Law School. Clark contrasted § 10(b). Id. at 5 ("When Congress wanted to make a provision not self-executing, but dependent on the adoption of regulations, it knew how to do it expressly, as it did in § 10(b) of the Securities Exchange Act of 1934.").

34. Henry J. Friendly, The Federal Administrative Agencies: The Need for Better Definitions of Standards (1962). Memorandum of HJF, SEC v. Capital Gains Research at 1, Charles Clark Papers, Series 11, Box 55, Folder 262, Yale Law School.

35. SEC v. Capital Gains Research Bureau, Inc., 306 F.2d 606, 609–11 (2nd Cir. 1962) (in banc).

36. *Capital Gains*, 306 F.2d at 611–12 (Clark, J., dissenting).

37. SEC v. Capital Gains Research Bureau, No. 42, Docket Sheet (Jan. 18, 1963) ("Grant: Goldberg, White, Douglas, Black, C.J."), Earl Warren Collection, Box 378, Library of Congress.

38. SEC v. Capital Gains Research Bureau, First Circulation (Nov. 27, 1963), Arthur Goldberg Collection, Box 17, Folder 3, Northwestern University Library.

39. Dennis J. Hutchinson, The Man Who Once Was Whizzer White 226 (1998); REL, Memo, No. 42 OT 1963, SEC v. Capital Gains Research Bureau, Concealment by a fiduciary as fraud, Byron R. White Collection, Box 35, Folder 6, Library of Congress ("Early cases in this Court . . . indicate by dictum that a fiduciary or one who occupies a special relation to another, commits fraud when he fails to disclose a material fact.").

40. Letter from Byron R. White to Arthur Goldberg, Re: No. 42—SEC v. Capital Gains Research Bureau (Dec. 2, 1963), Arthur Goldberg Collection, Box 17, Folder 3, Northwestern University Library.

41. SEC v. Capital Gains Research Bureau, Second Circulation, at 14 (Dec. 4, 1963), Arthur Goldberg Collection, Box 17, Folder 3, Northwestern University Library (citations omitted).

42. James R. Ukropina, The Investment Advisers Act and the Supreme Court's Interpretation of its Anti-Fraud Provisions, 37 S. Cal. L. Rev. 359, 362 (1964) ("A more relevant inquiry from the outset might have been to ask whether or not a subscriber to a market letter costing $18 a year should be considered to have entered into a fiduciary relationship when he pays his subscription price.").

43. *Capital Gains*, 375 U.S. at 195, 198–99.

44. Email to Adam Pritchard from Harry Reasoner, law clerk to Charles Clark (May 13, 2012) (on file with authors). Federal Judicial Center, History of the Federal Judiciary.

45. 401 F.2d 833 (2nd Cir. 1968) (in banc), *cert. den. sub nom* Coates v. SEC, 394 U.S. 976 (1969).

46. Just over a year after *Capital Gains*, Waterman wrote for the Second Circuit in List v. Fashion Park, Inc., showing a new openness to extending fraud to nondisclosure. 340 F.2d 457 (2nd Cir. 1965). *List* involved a face-to-face transaction (for which there

was some earlier precedent to cover nondisclosure), but Waterman went further in rejecting the defendant's argument that 10b-5 did not cover complete nondisclosure. The reasoning of *List* anticipated the holding in *Texas Gulf Sulphur* that nondisclosure in an impersonal market setting could be fraud. "The doctrine for which defendant Lerner contends would tend to reinstate the common law requirement of affirmative misrepresentation . . . the effect of adopting such a doctrine would be automatically to exempt many impersonal transactions. The effect would be contrary to the intent of Congress as set forth in section 2 of the Exchange Act." *List*, 340 F.2d at 462.

47. Insider Trading in Stocks, 21 Bus. Law. 1009, 1014, 1024 (1965–66). SEC v. Texas Gulf Sulphur, 258 F. Supp. 262, 279 (S.D. N.Y. 1966).

48. *Texas Gulf Sulphur*, 401 F.2d at 855. See also Irving Kaufman Memo, Texas Gulf Sulphur (5/1/468), Henry Friendly Collection, Box 135, Folder 51, Harvard Law School ("While I am attracted to HJF's proposal of limiting §10(b) to cases where there is some kind of evil motive, or, in Loss' terms, p.1766, imposing a watered-down <u>scienter</u> requirement, it seems to me that such an explicit formulation goes against the thrust of S.E.C. v. Capitol [*sic*] Gains"); *Kline v. SEC*, 394 U.S. 976 (1969); Coates v. SEC, 394 U.S. 976 (1969) (denying petition of Texas Gulf Sulphur insider held liable for negligent insider trading).

49. 406 U.S. 128 (1972).

50. Blackmun Memo to File, Affiliated Ute Citizens v. United States, at 3, HAB-LC.

51. Seth Stern & Stephen Wermiel, Justice Brennan: Liberal Champion 24, 348 (2010).

52. 404 U.S. 418 (1972); 411 U.S. 582 (1973).

53. 423 U.S. 232 (1976).

54. *Reliance Electric*, 404 U.S. at 424 ("Read literally, this language clearly contemplates that a statutory insider might sell enough shares to bring his holdings below 10%, and later—but still within six months—sell additional shares free from liability under the statute.").

55. *Reliance Electric*, 404 U.S. at 428 (Douglas, J., dissenting).

56. Harry Blackmun Memo to File, No. 70-79—Reliance Electric Co. v. Emerson Electric Co., at 2-4 (11/9/71), HAB-LC.

57. Handwritten notes of Lewis F. Powell, Jr., from the Conference on Kern County Land Co. v. Occidental Petroleum Corp. 1 (Dec. 8, 1972), LFP Collection. Powell's notes indicate that Blackmun tentatively voted to reverse, but subsequently switched his vote.

58. Memorandum from Lewis F. Powell, Jr., to William C. Kelly, Jr. 1 (Dec. 10, 1972), LFP Collection.

59. Memorandum from Lewis F. Powell, Jr., to Byron R. White 2–3 (Dec. 9, 1972), LFP Collection.

60. Byron R. White, First Draft Opinion, Kern County Land Co. v. Occidental Petroleum Corp. 1 (circulated Mar. 6, 1973) (handwritten notes of Lewis F. Powell, Jr.), LFP Collection.

61. Lewis F. Powell Jr., Draft Concurring Opinion, Kern County Land Co. v. Occidental Petroleum 1 (Mar. 10, 1973), LFP Collection.

62. Memorandum from Lewis F. Powell, Jr., to Larry A. Hammond 1 (Mar. 10, 1973). Letter from Byron R. White to Lewis F. Powell, Jr. 1 (Mar. 12, 1973), LFP Collection.

336 NOTES

63. Handwritten notes of Lewis F. Powell, Jr., for the Conference on Foremost-McKesson v. Provident Securities Co. 1 (Oct. 10, 1975), LFP Collection.
64. Memorandum from Lewis F. Powell, Jr., to Carl Schenker 4–5 (Nov. 19, 1975), LFP Collection.
65. The Court would not decide another § 16(b) for fifteen years. Even though Powell had left the Court by then, the text of § 16(b) continued to be the focus. Gollust v. Mendell, 501 U.S. 115 (1991) was a fairly standard § 16(b) claim with a procedural twist: the shareholder bringing the claim ceased to be a shareholder in the issuing corporation when it ceased to exist as a result of a merger during the pendency of his suit. The Second Circuit, hearkening back to its sixties glory days, looked to the statute's "remedial purposes" in determining "whether the policy behind the statute is best served by allowing the claim," 909 F.2d 724, 728–29 (2nd Cir. 1990). Concluding that policy analysis in the affirmative, the appellate court allowed the claim to proceed. The Supreme Court's days of searching for legislative purpose, however, were long gone. David Souter, recently appointed to replace Brennan, was writing his first securities opinion for the Supreme Court. He focused on the language of § 16(b), which only required ownership of a security of the issuer at the time suit was "instituted." Souter concluded that Congress had conferred "standing of signal breadth, expressly limited only by conditions existing at the time an action is begun," 501 U.S. at 124. This broad approach to standing, although amply supported by the statutory text, created a constitutional issue, as it potentially exceeded the scope of standing permissible under Article III. The Court sidestepped that constitutional issue on the facts of the case, focusing on the plaintiff's continuing interest in the survivor of the merger, concluding that the plaintiff "stills stands to profit, albeit indirectly, if this action is successful." That sufficed for Article III.
66. Bench Memorandum, Chiarella v. United States, to Lewis F. Powell, Jr. 2 (Sept. 28, 1979), LFP Collection. Powell was familiar with Pandick's operation, having used their services for the Ethyl deal, a milestone in his career as a corporate lawyer. Lawrence E. Blanchard, Jr., The Albemarle-Ethyl Deal in 1962 (Aug. 1974), LFP Collection.
67. Telephone Interview with Jonathan Sallet, Powell Clerk OT'79 (May 21, 2002) (notes on file with authors).
68. Telephone Interview with James Browning, Powell Clerk OT'82 (Apr. 3, 2002) (notes on file with authors).
69. Bench Memorandum, Chiarella v. United States, to Lewis F. Powell, Jr. 2 (Sept. 28, 1979) (handwritten notes of Lewis F. Powell, Jr.), LFP Collection. There is some evidence the SEC had moved away from the broadest reading of Texas Gulf Sulphur. The American Law Institute's proposed Federal Securities Code, which had been done in the years between Texas Gulf Sulphur and Chiarella, had not embraced the Texas Gulf Sulphur view. Case Comment, The Application of Rule 10b-5 to "Market Insiders": United States v. Chiarella, 92 Harv. L. Rev. 1538, 1543 (1979) (handwritten notes of Lewis F. Powell, Jr., on the margins of a photocopy), LFP Collection. Bench Memorandum, at 12 (handwritten notes of Lewis F. Powell, Jr.) ("not in amounts purchased").

NOTES 337

70. Fiduciary duty had been argued by Chiarella's lawyer, Stanley Arkin, in briefs to the Court. Donna Nagy, *Chiarella v. United States* and Its Indelible Impact on Insider Trading Law, 15 Tenn. J.L. & Pol. 6 (2020). That theory got Arkin's client off on the facts argued to the jury in *Chiarella*, but retained space to reach trading by those who had abused a trust relationship. Preliminary Memorandum, Chiarella v. United States, to Lewis F. Powell, Jr. 1 (Apr. 13, 1979 Conference) (handwritten notes of Lewis F. Powell, Jr.), LFP Collection.

71. Marshall missed the conference, but later communicated his vote to affirm. Handwritten notes of Lewis F. Powell, Jr., from the Conference on Chiarella v. United States 1 (Nov. 7, 1979), LFP Collection.

72. *Chiarella*, 445 U.S. at 240 (separate opinion of Burger, CJ), id. at 239–40, (Brennan J. concurring in the judgment) (agreeing that mere possession was not sufficient but not limiting fiduciary duty to those between a buyer and seller). Donna Nagy, *Chiarella v. United States* and Its Indelible Impact on Insider Trading Law, 15 Tenn. J. L. & Pol. 6 (2020). *Chiarella*, 445 U.S. at 251 (dissenting opinion of Blackmun and Marshall).

73. Handwritten notes of Lewis F. Powell, Jr., from the Conference on Chiarella v. United States 1 (Nov. 7, 1979), LFP Collection.

74. Petitioner's Reply Brief at 2 (filed Oct. 31, 1979), Chiarella v. United States, 445 U.S. 222 (1980).

75. Memorandum from Jon Sallet to Lewis F. Powell, Jr. 1 (Nov. 25, 1979), LFP Collection. Letter from Lewis F. Powell, Jr., to John Paul Stevens (Nov. 28, 1979). Letter from Lewis F. Powell, Jr., to Justices Potter Stewart et al. 1 (Nov. 29, 1979), LFP Collection.

76. Chiarella v. United States, 445 U.S. 222, 228, 232–33 (1980):

> No duty could arise from [Chiarella]'s relationship with the sellers of the target company's securities, for petitioner had no prior dealings with them. He was not their agent, he was not a fiduciary, he was not a person in whom the sellers had placed their trust and confidence. He was, in fact, a complete stranger who dealt with the sellers only through impersonal market transactions.
>
> *In re Cady, Roberts & Co.*, 40 SEC 907 at *4 (1961). *TGS*, 401 F.2d at 848.

77. Telephone Interview with Jonathan Sallet.

78. 445 U.S. at 236.

79. 445 U.S. at 237 (Stevens, J., concurring). Letter from Lewis F. Powell, Jr., to John Paul Stevens 1 (Feb. 4, 1980), LFP Collection.

80. Linda Greenhouse, Supreme Court rules for Printer, N.Y. Times, Mar. 19, 1981 ("Government lawyers indicated . . . future prosecutions would be based on the misappropriation theory.").

81. Letter from Lewis F. Powell, Jr., to Chief Justice Warren E. Burger 1 (Feb. 4, 1980), LFP Collection. Powell had earlier observed that Chiarella's conduct was "egregiously dishonest," but "we should resist the temptation to make bad law." Bench Memorandum, Chiarella v. United States, to Lewis F. Powell, Jr., at 27 (handwritten notes of Lewis F. Powell, Jr.), LFP Collection.

82. Steve Thel, Section 20(d) of the Securities Exchange Act: Congress, the Supreme Court, the SEC, and the Process of Defining Insider Trading, 69 N.C. L. Rev. 1261, 1262 (1991).

338 NOTES

83. Memo from HAB to Mark, No. 78–1202—Chiarella v. United States (2/4/80), HAB-LC. *Chiarella*, 445 U.S. at 246–47, 251 (Blackmun, J., dissenting).

84. 463 U.S. 646 (1983).

85. *In re* Raymond L. Dirks, Exchange Act Release No. 17,480, 21 SEC Docket 1401, 1405, 1421–13 (Jan. 22, 1981).

86. Preliminary Memorandum, Dirks v. SEC, to Lewis F. Powell, Jr., at 8, LFP Collection. Powell noted this point made by the United States in its brief on the merits: "The Commission's erroneous imposition of liability in this case has serious consequences for federal law enforcement, which frequently depends upon private initiative to uncover criminal conduct . . . Petitioner accomplished what regulatory authorities were unable to do." Memorandum from Lewis F. Powell, Jr., to File, Dirks v. SEC at 4 (Mar. 21, 1983), LFP Collection.

87. "Bobtail" Bench Memorandum to Lewis F. Powell, Jr. 3 (Mar. 21, 1983) (handwritten notes of Lewis F. Powell, Jr.), LFP Collection.

88. Dirks v. SEC, 681 F.2d 824 (D.C. Cir. 1982).

89. Telephone Interview with James Browning.

90. A later case confirms that Powell's position on insider trading was based on ethics, not finance theory. Bateman Eichler, Hill Richards, Inc. v. Berner, 472 U.S. 299 (1985), raised the issue of whether corporate insiders and broker-dealers who induce an investor to trade by falsely representing that they are conveying inside information could raise an in pari delicto defense. The plaintiffs made the somewhat unusual admission that they had purchased stock on the basis of what they believed was nonpublic information. The information proved to be false, however, and the plaintiffs lost money. They sought to recover their losses from the broker-dealer who had communicated the false inside information, as well as an officer of the issuer that was the subject of the rumor, who had tacitly confirmed the information. The Court held that the in pari delicto defense could not be successfully asserted under the circumstances.

Powell summarized his view of the case in his notes for the post argument conference:

> I conclude Tippees did know that [the corporate officer] had breached his duty by confirming that info. was not public + that broker was trustworthy. Thus tippees were culpable.
> But tippees conduct was not as culpable as tippers. Duty of tippers was clear.
> Disallowing defense of in pari delicto furthers policy of Securities Acts. Persons who become tippers present basic problem of insiders giving out tips. They should not go free because tippees also act unlawfully.

Handwritten notes of Lewis F. Powell, Jr., from the Conference on Bateman Eichler, Hill Richards, Inc. v. Berner 1 (Apr. 4, 1985), LFP Collection. This excerpt confirms that Powell viewed the principal problem with insider trading as the abuse of trust by the corporate insider. The harm to the securities markets stemming from information asymmetry was, at most, a secondary concern.

The *Bateman Eichler* opinion, written by Brennan, is unexceptional, emphasizing that the in pari delicto defense can only be invoked when the fault of the parties is substantially equal, and where recognition of the defense would not "significantly interfere with the effective enforcement of the securities laws." *Bateman Eichler*, 472 U.S. at 310–11. Powell's only notable contribution was to persuade Brennan to delete a footnote discussing the SEC's "shingle theory." See Charles Hughes & Co. v. SEC, 139 F.2d 434, 436–37 (2d Cir. 1943) (holding that broker-dealers make an implied representation of fair dealing by the act of putting out their "shingle" as broker-dealers). Powell feared "the SEC might view [the note] as at least an implicit approval of its theory." Letter from Lewis F. Powell, Jr., to William J. Brennan, Jr. 1 (May 24, 1985), LFP Collection. Telephone Interview with James Browning.

91. Browning was in some ways an odd choice for this task because he had "considerable doubts that federal securities law should ban any insider trading." Memorandum from Jim [Browning] to Lewis F. Powell, Jr. 1 (Mar. 22, 1983). Moreover, he felt either the SEC's position prohibiting any use of inside information in trading, or the laissez faire position permitting unconstrained insider trading, were more intellectually defensible than the middle ground sought by Powell. Telephone Interview with James Browning. Leonard Chazen, "Dirks" Presents Unique Corporate, Social Issues, Legal Times, Mar. 14, 1983, at 14. Chazen would not receive attribution in the opinion, however, because of Powell's unease with citing a piece that was not in "a scholarly journal." Lewis F. Powell, Jr., Second Draft Opinion, Dirks v. SEC, at 24 (circulated May 10, 1983) (handwritten notes of Lewis F. Powell, Jr.), LFP Collection. Memorandum from Jim [Browning] to Lewis F. Powell, Jr. 6–7 (Mar. 22, 1983) and handwritten notes of Lewis F. Powell, Jr., LFP Collection.

92. Lewis F. Powell, Jr., Memorandum for Conference, Dirks v. SEC 1 (Mar. 23, 1983), LFP Collection. Telephone Interview with James Browning. *Chiarella*, 445 U.S. at 230, note 12.

93. Lewis F. Powell, Jr., Memorandum for Conference, Dirks v. SEC, at 2–3.

94. Lewis F. Powell, Jr., Memorandum for Conference, Dirks v. SEC, at 2–4.

95. Even Brennan, while voting for affirmance, described it as a "very close case." William J. Brennan, Jr., Memorandum for Conference, SEC v. Dirks 1 (Mar. 23, 1983), William J. Brennan Collection, Library of Congress. Blackmun, by contrast, took a dimmer view of Dirks' role in uncovering the fraud: "Dirks is no folk hero He is lucky t[o] get away wi[th] only censure!" Argument Notes, 82-276, HAB-LLC. Handwritten notes of Lewis F. Powell, Jr., from the Conference on Dirks v. SEC 1 (Mar. 23, 1983), LFP Collection.

96. FIRST DRAFT: Dirks v. SEC, No. 82–276 (04/30/83), at 24–25. Memo from Lewis F. Powell, Jr. to Jim [Browning], 82–276 Dirks v. SEC, at 5-6 (05/02/83), LFP Collection.

97. Memorandum from Lewis F. Powell, Jr., to Jim [Browning] 3 (May 2, 1983). Rider A, p. 14 (Dirks) (05/14/83) (quoting Loss, 3 L. Loss, Securities Regulation 1451 (1961)). *Dirks* Memo from Lewis F. Powell, Jr. (05/14/83), LFP Collection.

98. Powell wrote an additional rider, discussing the effect that the SEC's theory would have on the work of analysts. Rider A, p. 26 (Dirks) (05/14/83), LFP Collection. This rider found its way into the published opinion largely intact. See *Dirks*, 463 U.S. at 658–59.

## 340 NOTES

99. FOURTH DRAFT: *Dirks* v. *SEC*, No. 82–276 (05/20/83), at 19–20, 23, LFP Collection.

100. Rider A, p. 15 (Dirks) (05/23/83), LFP Collection.

Materiality, scienter, reliance and loss causation have long had parallel roles to duty as separate elements required to satisfy the traditional common law cause of action for deceit. Misstatements are the core of the deceit claim, but not any misrepresentation is actionable. The separate requirement for materiality means only important lies would generate liability. Similarly, even important lies would not be actionable if defendant lacked sufficient mental state in making the misstatement. Further, if there is a material misstatement made with scienter, the claims will fall away if there is not sufficient connection between the defendant's bad behavior and the plaintiff's transaction (reliance) or loss (loss causation). The confusion referenced in the text gets eliminated by the time of the final opinion.

101. Compare Chambers Draft II, Dirks v. SEC, No. 82–276, at 13 (May 25, 1983) Chambers Draft, Dirks v. SEC, No. 82–276, at 13, 15 (May 22, 1983). The footnote made it into the published opinion unchanged. See *Dirks*, 463 U.S. at 660 n.20.

102. 44 S.E.C. 633 (1971).

103. Second Telephone Interview with James Browning (May 22, 2015) (notes on file with authors).

104. Letter from Lewis F. Powell to Byron R. White et al. 1 (June 9, 1983). Letter from Sandra Day O'Connor to Lewis F. Powell, Jr. 1–2 (June 7, 1983), LFP Collection.

One of O'Connor's reservations was rather idiosyncratic: she wanted to defer the question of whether information about criminal conduct could be considered material information. While the answer to this question would almost certainly be "Yes," deferring the answer cost Powell nothing. Powell noted his agreement with O'Connor's purpose statement in the margin, ("I agree") as well as his disagreement with her latter two points ("No" and "No") (handwritten notes of Lewis F. Powell, Jr.), LFP Collection.

105. Letter from Sandra Day O'Connor to Lewis F. Powell, Jr. 2 (June 7, 1983). Letter from Lewis F. Powell, Jr., to Sandra Day O'Connor 1 (June 9, 1983), LFP Collection.

106. *Compare* Lewis F. Powell, Jr., First Draft Opinion, Dirks v. SEC 14–15, 18–19 (May 28, 1983) *with* Lewis F. Powell, Jr., Second Draft Opinion, Dirks v. SEC 14–15, 18–19 (June 9, 1983), LFP Collection.

107. *Dirks*, 463 U.S. 653 n. 10 (distinguishing "[T]he duty that insiders owe to the corporation's shareholders not to trade on inside information . . . from the common-law duty that officers and directors also have to the corporation itself not to mis-manage corporate assets, of which confidential information is one.").

108. Letter from Lewis F. Powell, Jr. to Justices White, Rehnquist, and Stevens, re: 82–276 Dirks v. SEC (June 9, 1983), LFP Collection.

109. Harry A. Blackmun, Xerox Copy of Dissenting Opinion, No. 82–276—Dirks v. SEC, at 8 n.10 (June 24, 1983), LFP Collection. Blackmun also suggested that "When the disclosure is to an investment banker or some other adviser, however, there is normally no breach because the insider does not have scienter: he does not intend that the inside information be used for trading purposes to the disadvantage

NOTES 341

of shareholders." Id. at 8 n.11. This suggestion provoked a dismissive "naïve" from Powell in the margin of Powell's copy of Blackmun's dissent, and a note that it was "Contradictory!" of what Blackmun had said in the passage quoted in the text. Id. at 8 (handwritten notes). 3rd Draft, Dirks v. SEC, No. 82–276, at 17 & n.23 (June 27, 1983), LFP Collection.

Another addition to this draft emphasizes that deception is a separate element. Id. at 20 n. 27 ("Moreover, to constitute a violation of Rule 10b-5, there must be fraud. There is no evidence that Secrist's disclosure was intended to or did in fact 'deceive or defraud' anyone.").

110. Letter from Victor Brudney to Harry A. Blackmun (July 8, 1983). Letter from Harry A. Blackmun to Victor Brudney (July 19, 1983), HAB-LC.

111. 484 U.S. 19, 24 (1987).

112. 791 F.2d 1024, 1026–27, 1036 (2d Cir. 1986).

113. Lewis F. Powell, Jr., Draft Dissent from Denial of Certiorari, Carpenter v. United States, (Dec. 10, 1986), LFP Collection. Powell had noted his plan to write in the event of a denial even before conference. Preliminary Memorandum, Carpenter v. United States, from Lewis F. Powell, Jr. 1 (Dec. 5, 1986 Conference) (handwritten notes of Lewis F. Powell, Jr.). Restatement (Second) of Torts § 551(2) (1977) (elements of deceit).

114. Letter from Chief William H. Rehnquist to Lewis F. Powell, Jr. 1 (Dec. 11, 1986). Letter from Sandra Day O'Connor to Lewis F. Powell, Jr. 1 (Dec. 11, 1986), LFP Collection. Brennan had been willing to endorse a much broader theory in *Chiarella*, so it seems unlikely that Powell had persuaded him on the merits; more likely he saw the issue as one that required resolution. Bench Memorandum, Carpenter v. United States (No. 86–422) (Oct. 7, 1987), Thurgood Marshall Papers, Box 427, Library of Congress. Certiorari was granted on December 15, 1986. United States v. Carpenter, 479 U. S. 1016, 1016 (1986). Al Kamen, Justice Powell Resigns, Was Supreme Court's Pivotal Vote, Wash. Post, June 27, 1987, at A1. Powell retired on June 26, 1987. Stuart Taylor, Jr., n, N.Y. Times, Feb. 19, 1988, at A10. Carpenter v. United States, 484 U.S. 19, 24 (1987).

115. 521 U.S. 642, 675–76 (1997).

116. SEC Rel. No. 33-7881 (2000).

117. Salman v. United States, 580 U.S. 39 (2016).

118. United States v. Newman, 773 F.3d 438 (2nd Cir. 2014).

# Chapter 6

1. See Lawrence D. Bernfeld, Class Actions and the Federal Securities Laws, 55 Cornell L. Rev. 78 (1969); Jill E. Fisch, The Trouble with Basic: Price Distortion after Halliburton, 90 Wash. U. L. Rev. 895, 900–11 (2013).

2. 377 U.S. 426 (1964).

3. 485 U.S. 224 (1987).

342   NOTES

4. Pub. L. No. 104–67, 109 Stat. 737 (1995).
5. 311 U.S. 282 (1940).
6. 312 U.S. 38 (1941).
7. Kardon v. National Gypsum Co., 73 F. Supp. 798 (E.D. Pa. 1947). The Court came close to grappling with Rule 10b-5 in Black v. Amen, 355 U.S. 600 (1958). The Court had granted certiorari to assess jurisdiction in a purported class action, but a majority voted to remand to examine whether complaint stated a claim under the Exchange Act. Letter from Felix Frankfurter to Chief Justice Earl Warren (Nov. 20, 1957), FF-Harvard, Part 3, Reel 4. The case settled, however, before the remand could issue.
8. Blue Chip Stamps v. Manor Drug Stores, 421 U.S. 723, 762 (1975) (Blackmun, J. dissenting). Gerald Gunther, Learned Hand (1994) 244 ("of unmatched quality"); Karl Llewelyn, The Common Law Tradition 48 (1960) ("the most distinguished and admired bench in the United States); Margaret V. Sachs, Judge Friendly and the Law of Securities Regulation: The Creation of a Judicial Reputation, 50 SMU L. REV. 777, 791, n.133 (1997) (collecting tributes to the Second Circuit).
    Even after Dwight Eisenhower started to appoint judges, this initial group, often continuing to hear cases after taking senior status, dominated the circuit's securities output. Two colleagues appointed to the Second Circuit in the 1950s and 1960s went on to the Supreme Court. Eisenhower appointed John Marshall Harlan in 1955 and Lyndon Johnson appointed Thurgood Marshall in 1967, after a stint as Solicitor General.
9. Fischman v. Raytheon, 198 F.2d 783 (2nd Cir. 1951); Subin v. Goldsmith, 224 F.2d 753, 767 (2nd Cir. 1955) (Frank, J, dissenting). Frank's dissent is quoted by the Sixth Circuit in Dann v. Studebaker, an important pre-*Borak* opinion on a private right of action under § 14(a), with the court noting "we are much influenced by the sound policy considerations set forth by Judge Frank in his dissent." 288 F.2d 201, 209 (6th Cir. 1961).The Ninth Circuit's 1953 opinion in Fratt v. Robinson, 203 F.2d 627 (9th Cir. 1953), for example, relied on Clark's separate opinion in Baird v. Franklin, 141 F.2d 238, 244–45 (2nd Cir. 1944) where he had passionately endorsed a private cause of action under § 6(b) of the Exchange Act. The Third Circuit in 1956 in Speed v. Transamerica affirmed a district court decision that had found a private cause of action under Rule 10b-5, 235 F.2d 369 (3rd Cir. 1956) affirming 135 F. Supp. 176 (D. Del. 1955). The district court, in turn, had relied on another Second Circuit opinion decision by Clark, which had emphasized the broad purposes of the securities laws. Charles Hughes & Co., Inc. v. SEC, 139 F. 2d 434 (2nd Cir. 1943).
10. 377 U.S. 426 (1964).
11. 5 Louis Loss, Securities Regulation 2882 (2d ed. Supp. 1969).
12. Conference Notes, No. 402—J. I Case Co. v. Borak (April 24, 1964), WOD-LC, Box 1305. White apparently had some doubts about the sweeping scope of the opinion's reasoning upon reading Clark's first circulation in the case ("Simply too broad a proposition. All reg. stats don't give private rt of action w. all necessary remedies," Handwritten Notes of Byron White, Circulation of May 28, 1964 J.I. Case v. Borak, No. 402, at 7, Byron White Collection, Box 1:48, Folder 3, Library of Congress. There is no evidence, however, that White communicated his concerns to Clark.

NOTES     343

13. 396 U.S. 375 (1970).

14. Harlan had worked as a corporate litigator before his appointment to the Second Circuit. Tinsley E. Yarbrough, John Marshall Harlan: Great Dissenter of the Warren Court 52 (1992).

15. 396 U.S. at 389–90. The Court remanded to the appellate court to determine relief after a showing of proxy fraud. The Seventh Circuit held that damages were the appropriate remedy, but that shareholders in the merger in question had not suffered any damages. Mills v. Electric Auto-Lite Co., 552 F.2d 1239 (7th Cir. 1977) cert. denied, 434 U.S. 922 (1978). The Supreme Court returned to the necessary connection required for recovery of damages in *Virginia Bankshares* discussed in section E of this chapter.

16. Roger Newman, Hugo Black: A Biography 288 (1994) (Black as textualist).

17. 404 U.S. 6 (1971).

18. Birnbaum v. Newport Steel Corp., 193 F.2d 461 (2d Cir. 1952).

19. Harry Blackmun typed notes, No. 70-60—Supt. of Ins. State of N.Y. v. Bankers Life & Casualty Co., at 2 (10/12/71), ("[M]y inclination is at odds with that of the Second Circuit. I would also expect to conclude, if we get that far, that the Birnbaum rule, which Learned Hand evolved some time ago, restricting relief under these statutes to a purchaser or seller, would have to be overruled. I would be willing to go that far."); Conference Notes, 70–60 (10/16/71), HAB-LC, Box 311.

20. 406 U.S. 128 (1972).

21. Harry A. Blackmun, Memorandum to the Conference, No. 70–78, Affiliated Ute Citizens of Utah v. U.S. (April 10, 1972). Thurgood Marshall Collection, Box 84, Library of Congress.

22. *Mills*, 396 U.S. at 382 n. 5 ("Proof of actual reliance by thousands of individuals would . . . not be feasible, and reliance on the nondisclosure of a fact is a particularly difficult matter to define or prove.") (citations omitted); *Affiliated Ute*, 406 U.S. at 153–54. The Court also cited a Second Circuit case, Chasins v. Smith Barney & Co., 438 F.2d 1167 (2nd Cir. 1970), for the proposition that causation in fact would suffice to show reliance in a case of nondisclosure.

23. Harry Blackmun typed notes, No. 70-78—Affiliated Ute Citizens v. United States, at 2 (10/18/71), HAB-LC.

24. Eisenhower was able to name a majority of the justices by the end of the 1950s when there was a dearth of securities cases. There had also been a bare majority of Republican appointees since Blackmun had joined the Court two terms before.

25. Chief Justice Burger's 1977 Report to the American Bar Association, 63 A.B.A.J. 504 (1977); Chief Justice Burger Issues Year-End Report, 62 A.B.A.J. 189 (1976). Burger was also responsible for the 1971 founding of the National Center for State Courts in an effort to coordinate and improve the administration of justice in the several States.

26. Blue Chip Stamps v. Manor Drug Stores, 421 U.S. 723 (1975); Ernst & Ernst v. Hochfelder, 425 U.S. 185 (1976); Santa Fe Indus. Inc. v. Green, 430 U.S. 462 (1977).

27. 417 U.S. 156 (1974).

28. Eisen v. Carlisle & Jacquelin, 54 F.D.R. 565, 567, 569–70 (S.D.N.Y. 1972).

344   NOTES

The district court's novel rulings excused individual notice to class members because their claims were so small that they would be unlikely to opt out and imposed 90% of the costs of the alternative notice on the defendants based on its "preliminary" assessment that the defendants were likely to be found liable. Lurking was the question of whether the class was unmanageable because there were no practical means by which any recovery could be paid to the actual class members given their small individual stakes, which could limit the right to appeal. There was a conflict among the circuits on the appealability question. Winokur v. Bell Federal Savings and Loan Association, 560 F.2d 271 (7th Cir. 1977), in which the Seventh Circuit had rejected the "death knell" doctrine, was being held for the decision in *Eisen*. Despite the conflict, Powell recommended that certiorari be denied in *Winokur*. Memorandum from Lewis F. Powell, Jr., to the Conference 3 (May 29, 1974), LFP Collection. At conference in *Eisen* a majority (Chief Justice Burger and Douglas, Brennan, White, Marshall, Blackmun, and Powell) thought there was jurisdiction over the manageability issue, but Rehnquist and Stewart strongly disagreed. Handwritten notes of Lewis F. Powell, Jr., from the Conference on Eisen v. Carlisle & Jacquelin 1–2 (Feb. 27, 1974), LFP Collection.

As discussed in the text, Powell's opinion moved the Court's decision away from the manageability issue, resulting in a deferral of the appealability issue for four years and a reversal of what the *Eisen* conference vote had suggested. Coopers & Lybrand v. Livesay, 437 U.S. 463, 477 (1978). Given the majority in favor of the "death knell" doctrine in *Eisen*, this is a surprising result, but Powell's conference notes reflect an 8–1 vote against the doctrine in *Coopers & Lybrand*, with only Brennan disagreeing, and even Brennan ended up joining Stevens's opinion for the Court. Handwritten notes of Lewis F. Powell, Jr., from the Conference on Coopers & Lybrand v. Livesay 1–3 (Mar. 24, 1978), LFP Collection. This decision's effect has been mitigated somewhat by the adoption of Federal Rule of Civil Procedure 23(f), which gives discretion to appellate courts to entertain class action certification questions. See generally 15 Charles Allen Wright et al., Federal Practice and Procedure § 3912 (2d ed. 1992).

29. Preliminary Memorandum, Eisen v. Carlisle & Jacquelin, to Lewis F. Powell, Jr. 1 (Oct. 11, 1973 Conference). This case stands out from many of the cases studied here, however, in that the Second Circuit had also balked at the district court's innovation, reversing both the ruling on notice and the imposition of costs on the defendants. Eisen v. Carlisle & Jacquelin, 391 F.2d 555, 563, 569–70 (2d Cir. 1968).

Handwritten notes of Lewis F. Powell, Jr., for the Argument in Eisen v. Carlisle & Jacquelin 2 (Feb. 25, 1974).

30. Handwritten notes of Lewis F. Powell, Jr., from the Conference on Eisen v. Carlisle & Jacquelin at 1. Lewis F. Powell, Jr., Suggested Note to Be Added to the Opinion of the Court, Eisen v. Carlisle & Jacquelin 1 (Apr. 27, 1974). Letter from Chief Warren E. Burger to Lewis F. Powell, Jr. 1 (May 22, 1974) (handwritten notes of Chief Justice Warren E. Burger), LFP Collection.

Not surprisingly, Powell's opinion was met with hostility by class action advocates. Powell clipped the article with their reactions, but made no notation of his own. Linda Charlton, Impact of Ruling by Court Studied: Lawyers See Strong Effect on

NOTES 345

Class-Action Suits by Consumer Groups, N.Y. TIMES, May 29, 1974, at 29, LFP Collection.

31. Birnbaum v. Newport Steel Corp., 193 F.2d 461, 463–64 (2d Cir. 1952).

32. The Court was wary of the SEC's efforts (as amicus) to change the rule through the courts rather than Congress. Powell noted at argument that "Brennan asked if SEC had ever asked Congress to change Rule—it has been with us for 20 yrs. Answer was 'No.'" Handwritten notes of Lewis F. Powell, Jr., from the Argument in Blue Chip Stamps v. Manor Drug Stores 4 (argued Mar. 24, 1975), LFP Collection. Despite his skeptical question, Brennan voted against the *Birnbaum* rule.

Eason v. General Motors Acceptance Corp, 490 F.2d 654, 659 (7th Cir. 1973), cert. denied, 416 U.S. 960 (1974).

33. Telephone Interview with John O'Neill, Rehnquist Clerk OT'74 (July 15, 2020) (notes on file with authors). William H. Rehnquist, First Draft Opinion, Blue Chip Stamps v. Manor Drug Stores 16 (circulated May 5, 1975), LFP Collection.

34. William H. Rehnquist, First Draft Opinion, Blue Chip Stamps v. Manor Drug Stores 1 (circulated May 5, 1975) (handwritten notes of Lewis F. Powell, Jr.). Letter from Lewis F. Powell, Jr., to William H. Rehnquist 1 (May 13, 1975). Handwritten notes of Lewis F. Powell, Jr., from the Conference on Blue Chip Stamps v. Manor Drug Stores 7 (n.d.). Lewis F. Powell, Jr., Chambers Draft Concurring Opinion, Blue Chip Stamps v. Manor Drug Stores 5 n.4 (May 1975). LFP Collection.

35. 439 U.S. 322, 324 (1979).

36. The issue of SEC leverage was highlighted in an *amicus* brief filed by the Washington Legal Foundation. "Bobtail" Bench Memorandum, Parklane Hosiery Co., Inc. v. Shore, from David W[estin] to Lewis F. Powell, Jr. 5 (Oct. 27, 1978) LFP Collection.

More recently, the SEC's practice of not requiring admissions has been criticized, and the SEC has in some cases moved to require admissions of wrongdoing. See, e.g., Stewart, "S.E.C. Has a Message for Firms Not Used to Admitting Guilt," N.Y. Times (June 21, 2013). For the most part, however, the cases in which the SEC has in fact required admissions have been limited to those in which there is little or no threat of subsequent liability, such as violations of provisions that do not support a private right of action.

37. "Bobtail" Bench Memorandum, at 14. *Parklane*, 439 U.S. at 355–56 (Rehnquist, J., dissenting). William H. Rehnquist, First Draft Dissenting Opinion, Parklane Hosiery Co., Inc. v. Shore 1 (circulated Dec. 22, 1978) (handwritten notes of Lewis F. Powell, Jr.), LFP Collection.

38. HAB Pre-argument Memo, No. 74-124—Blue Chip Stamps v. Manor Drug Stores (Mar. 20, 1975), HAB-LC.

39. Telephone Interview with John O'Neill, Rehnquist Clerk OT'74 (July 15, 2020) (notes on file with authors); Handwritten Note, Bill HR to Harry (4/14/75), HAB-LC; Letter from Harry Blackmun to Rehnquist, No. 74-124—Blue Chip Stamps v. Manor Drug Stores (May 23, 1975), HAB-LC.

40. Telephone Interview with John O'Neill, Rehnquist Clerk, OT'74 (July 15, 2020).

41. 425 U.S. 185 (1976).

346 NOTES

42. Memorandum from Lewis F. Powell, Jr., to File, Ernst & Ernst v. Hochfelder 5 (Aug. 21, 1975), LFP Collection.

Powell returned to his concern with extending third party liability later in the memorandum:

> [A] negligence standard applicable to auditors would invite litigation based on a simple averment of absence of due care, not merely in the recording of the facts as reflected by the company's books but in failing properly to discover mismanagement or fraud. Third party suits of this kind brought years after the occurrence of the alleged negligence and viewed with "hind-sight" vision, would impose a high risk of liability on accountants.

Id. at 8.

43. Memorandum from Lewis F. Powell, Jr., to Greg Palm 3 (Feb. 4, 1976), LFP Collection. Cent. Bank v. First Interstate Bank, 511 U.S. 164 (1994). Ernst & Ernst v. Hochfelder, 425 U.S. 185, 214 n.33 (1976). Lewis F. Powell, Jr., Suggested Note to Be Added to the Opinion of the Court, Ernst & Ernst v. Hochfelder 1–2 (Feb. 20, 1976), LFP Collection.

44. Telephone Interview with Christine Whitman, Powell Clerk, OT'75, Apr. 17, 2002 (notes on file with authors); Memorandum from Lewis F. Powell, Jr., to Greg Palm, at 2 (citing Kohn v. American Metal Climax, Inc., 458 F.2d 255, 285, 287 (3d Cir. 1972) (Adams, J., concurring in part and dissenting in part) (quoting SEC v. Tex. Gulf Sulphur Co., 401 F.2d 833, 868 (2d Cir. 1968) (Friendly, J., concurring)).

45. Telephone Interview with Greg Palm, Powell Clerk, OT'75 (June 6, 2002) (notes on file with authors).

46. Memorandum from Lewis F. Powell, Jr., to File, Ernst & Ernst v. Hochfelder 6–8 (Aug. 21, 1975). Handwritten notes of Lewis F. Powell, Jr., from the Conference on Ernst & Ernst v. Hochfelder (Dec. 5, 1975). Handwritten notes of Lewis F. Powell, Jr., from the Conference on Aaron v. SEC (Feb. 27, 1980), LFP Collection. Marshall joined Blackmun's dissenting opinion in Aaron v. SEC, which favored a negligence standard. See 446 U.S. 680, 703–04 (1980) (Blackmun, J., dissenting) (arguing that section 10(b) does not require scienter).

47. Letter from Lewis F. Powell, Jr., to Gregory K. Palm 1 (Jan. 1, 1977), LFP Collection. The "Hcatchet Job" refers to The Supreme Court, 1975 Term, 90 Harv. L. Rev. 56, 255 (1976). Letter from Lewis F. Powell, Jr., to Henry J. Friendly 1 (Apr. 6, 1976). Letter from Henry J. Friendly to Lewis F. Powell, Jr. 1 (Apr. 9, 1976), LFP Collection.

48. H.A.B. Memo, No. 74-1042—Ernst & Ernst v. Hochfelder (12/2/75), HAB-LC. Douglas had retired just before argument and his successor, Stevens, had not yet joined the Court.

Ernst & Ernst, 425 U.S. at 215 and 217 (Blackmun, J., dissenting).

49. Memorandum from Lewis F. Powell, Jr., to File, Piper v. Chris-Craft Indus., Inc. 2 (Aug. 26, 1976). Handwritten notes of Lewis F. Powell, Jr., from the Conference on Piper v. Chris-Craft Indus., Inc. 2 (Oct. 4, 1976). LFP Collection.

50. Memorandum from Lewis F. Powell, Jr., to File, Piper v. Chris-Craft Indus., Inc. 2 (Aug. 26, 1976). LFP Collection.

51. 426 U.S. 438 (1976).

52. Preliminary Memorandum, TSC Indus., Inc. v. Northway, Inc., to Lewis F. Powell, Jr.1, 2 (July 1, 1975) (handwritten notes of Lewis F. Powell, Jr.). Handwritten notes of Lewis F. Powell, Jr., from the Conference on TSC Indus., Inc. v. Northway, Inc. 1 (n.d.). Handwritten notes of Lewis F. Powell, Jr., from the Argument in TSC Indus., Inc. v. Northway, Inc. 1–2 (Mar. 5, 1976), LFP Collection.

53. Thurgood Marshall, Draft Opinion, TSC Indus., Inc. v. Northway, Inc. (circulated June 2, 1976) (emphasis added) (handwritten notes of Lewis F. Powell, Jr.) ("Good opinion. I'll join. But I'll write or talk to TM about notes 7 + 11."). LFP Collection. Letter from Harry F. Blackmun to Thurgood Marshall 1 (June 9, 1976), HAB-LC. Focused as they were on the summary judgment awarded to plaintiffs in this case, none of the justices appears to have given any thought to the implications that precluding pretrial materiality determinations might have on defendants who were seeking dismissal.

54. *TSC Industries*, 426 U.S. at 449 ("We agree with Judge Friendly, speaking for the Court of Appeals in *Gerstle*, that the 'might' formulation is 'too suggestive of mere possibility, however, unlikely.'").

55. Santa Fe Indus., Inc. v. Green, 430 U.S. 462 (1977); Green v. Santa Fe Industries, Inc., 533 F.2d 1283 (2d Cir. 1976).

56. Bench Memorandum, Herman & MacLean v. Huddleston, to Lewis F. Powell, Jr. 17 (Sept. 9, 1982) and (handwritten notes of Lewis F. Powell, Jr.). Memorandum from Lewis F. Powell, Jr., to Jim Browning, at 1 (Sept. 13, 1982). Letter from Lewis F. Powell, Jr., to Warren E. Burger 1 (Nov. 11, 1982), LFP Collection.

57. 421 U.S. 412 (1975).

58. 15 U.S.C. § 78ggg(b) (2000).

59. SEC v. Guar. Bond & Sec. Corp., 496 F.2d 145, 150 (6th Cir. 1974).

60. Handwritten notes of Lewis F. Powell, Jr., from the Conference on Sec. Investor Prot. Corp. v. Barbour 1–2 (Mar. 19, 1975). Douglas, by then in his last year on the Court, did not participate in the Court's conference, but would later dissent without opinion.

61. 422 U.S. 66 (1975).

62. 430 U.S. 1 (1977).

63. Handwritten notes of Lewis F. Powell, Jr., from the Conference on Piper v. Chris-Craft Indus., Inc. 1, 3 (Oct. 5, 1976), LFP Collection. Powell had previously noted that First Boston faced "the imposition on it of three times the amount of damages that would be imposed under section 11 of the 1933 Act." Memorandum from Lewis F. Powell, Jr., to File, Piper v. Chris-Craft Indus., Inc., at 3, LFP Collection.

64. *Piper*, 430 U.S. at 55 (Stevens, J., dissenting).

65. Lewis F. Powell, Jr., First Draft Opinion, Dissenting from Denial of Certiorari, TransAmerica Mortgage Advisors, Inc. v. Lewis 3 (Oct. 12, 1978). Memorandum from Lewis F. Powell, Jr., to "Clerk" 6–7 (Feb. 20, 1979), LFP Collection.

66. 441 U.S. 677 (1979).

67. 442 U.S. 560, 568–69 (1979). Powell appears to have agreed with the result: "§ 17(a) is not an anti-fraud statute. It proscribes nothing. It merely requires reports. § 18a provides remedies." Preliminary Memorandum, Touche Ross & Co. v. Redington, to Lewis F. Powell, Jr. 1 (Nov. 22, 1978 Conference) (handwritten notes of Lewis F. Powell, Jr.). John C. Jeffries, Jr., Justice Lewis F. Powell, Jr. 536 (1994).

348  NOTES

68. Handwritten notes of Lewis F. Powell, Jr., from the Argument in TransAmerica Mortgage Advisors, Inc. v. Lewis 1 (Oct. 2, 1979) (*"Last Spring Aff.*: WJB, BRW, TM, JPS. *Rev.*: WHR, HAB, PS, CJ"); and at 3 (discussing Ernst & Ernst v. Hochfelder, 425 U.S.185 (1976) and Blue Chip Stamps v. Manor Drug Stores, 421 U.S. 723 (1975)). Handwritten notes of Lewis F. Powell, Jr., for the Conference on TransAmerica Mortgage Advisor, Inc. v. Lewis 1 (Oct. 4, 1979), LFP Collection.

69. Handwritten notes of Lewis F. Powell, Jr., for the Conference on TransAmerica Mortgage Advisors, Inc. v. Lewis 1, 3 (Oct. 5, 1979) (referring to Regents of the University of California v. Bakke, 438 U.S. 265 (1978)), LFP Collection. Stewart and Rehnquist had avoided the constitutional issue in *Bakke* by agreeing with Stevens that the affirmative action plan challenged there was prohibited by Title VI of the Education Amendments, 42 U.S.C. § 2000(d) (2000), which forbids discrimination on the basis of race. *Bakke*, 438 U.S. at 421 (Stevens, J., concurring). That necessarily supposed that Bakke had a private right of action to assert his claim. The two felt obliged to uphold the private right of action in *Cannon* the following term, thus creating a five-vote majority in that case. Handwritten notes of Lewis F. Powell, Jr., from the Conference on Cannon v. Univ. of Chicago 1 (Jan. 12, 1979), LFP Collection (noting in regard to Stewart: "*Reverse* (unhappily) . . . In view of vote last term in *Bakke*, 'I'm stuck.'"); id. at 3 (noting in regard to Rehnquist, "*Reverse* reluctantly. Bakke should have won on 14th Amend., + WHR is uncomfortable with his vote on VI. But can't think of principled way to reverse his vote in *Bakke*."). Brennan noted at the time of *Bakke* that there was probably a majority that would have voted against a private right of action under Title VI, but he did not include Stewart in that majority. Lee Epstein & Jack Knight, Piercing the Veil: William J. Brennan's Account of Regents of the University of California v. Bakke, 19 Yale L. & Pol'y Rev. 341, 358 (2001).

70. TransAmerica Mortgage Advisors, Inc. v. Lewis, 444 U.S. 11, 24 (1979).

71. Letter from Lewis F. Powell, Jr. to Potter Stewart 1 (Oct. 30, 1979), LFP Collection. *TransAmerica*, 444 U.S. at 24 n.14.

72. Letter from Lewis F. Powell, Jr. to Potter Stewart 1 (Oct. 30, 1979), LFP Collection.

73. Gonzaga Univ. v. Doe, 536 U.S. 273, 325–26 (2002).

74. 459 U.S. 375 (1983). The statute of limitations had run on the plaintiffs' § 11 claim at the time they filed suit, Preliminary Memorandum, Herman & MacLean v. Huddleston, to Lewis F. Powell, Jr. 6 (Feb. 19, 1982 Conference), LFP Collection, so it was Rule 10b-5 or nothing.

75. Bench Memorandum, Herman & MacLean v. Huddleston, from Jim [Browning] to Lewis F. Powell, Jr. 20 (Sept. 9, 1982) LFP Collection; and at 1, 11 (stating that the all-inclusive language made it difficult to carve out exceptions).

76. 450 U.S. 1005, 1005 (1981) (Powell, J., dissenting from the denial of certiorari).

77. Memorandum from Paul Cane to Lewis F. Powell, Jr., (Feb. 6, 1981) (handwritten notes of Lewis F. Powell, Jr.), LFP Collection.

78. 478 U.S. 647 (1986).

79. 486 U.S. 622 (1988). The case also raised the definition of "seller" under section 12(a) (1) of the Securities Act. This issue appears to have been of less concern to Powell, although it is an important holding of the Court.

NOTES 349

80. Lewis F. Powell, Jr., Draft Dissent from Denial of Certiorari, Pinter v. Dahl 5–6 (Apr. 10, 1987), LFP Collection.

At the initial conference, only Powell and Rehnquist favored a grant, with even Rehnquist's support a tepid "Join 3." Handwritten notes of Lewis F. Powell, Jr., from the Conference on Pinter v. Dahl 1 (Apr. 3, 1987). White and O'Connor switched their votes. Handwritten notes of Lewis F. Powell, Jr., from the Conference on Pinter v. Dahl 1 (Apr. 17, 1987), LFP Collection.

81. Powell's seat remained empty as the Senate rejected Reagan's first nominee and a second was withdrawn.

82. Letter from Antonin Scalia to Harry Blackmun, No. 86–805: Pinter v. Dahl (May 5, 1988). Letter from Harry Blackmun to Antonin Scalia, No. 86–805: Pinter v. Dahl (May 6, 1988), HAB-LC.

83. 346 U.S. 427 (1953).

84. Memorandum from WDR, No. 39, 1953 Term, WILKO v. SWAN. Memorandum from EJF, No. 39, 1953 Term, WILKO v. SWAN. Conference notes of Harold Burton, #39, 10/24/53, Harold Burton Collection, Library of Congress. Conference notes of William O. Douglas, No. 39—Wilko v. Swan, Conference 10–24-53, WOD-LC.

85. Memorandum to The Conference, RE: No. 39, Wilko v. Swan. Dec. 1, 1953, Stanley Reed Collection, University of Kentucky.

86. Memorandum for Reed and Jackson, J.J., from F.F., Dec. 2, 1953, FF-Harvard, Part 3, Reel 2; Handwritten Note from SR to RHJ & FF, FF-Harvard, Part 2, Reel 5.

87. 414 U.S. 117 (1973).

88. Conference notes of Lewis F. Powell, Jr., No. 72–312, Merrill Lynch, Pierce, Fennner & Smith v. Ware, 10/12/73, LFP Collection.

89. 417 U.S. 506 (1974).

90. Conference notes of Lewis F. Powell, Jr., No. 73–381, Scherk v. Alberto-Culver, 4/26/74, LFP Collection; Letter from Harry Blackmun to Potter Stewart, NO. 73-781—Scherk v. Alberto-Culver Co. (June 4, 1974), HAB-LC.

91. Draft Dissent, No. 73–781 Scherk v. Alberto-Culver Co., at 6, WOD-LC. The published version takes a more measured tone. Scherk v. Alberto-Culver Co., 417 U.S. 506, 533 (1974) (Douglas, J., dissenting) "(Up to this day, it has been assumed by reason of *Wilko* that they were all protected by our various federal securities Acts. If those guarantees are to be removed, it should take a legislative enactment. I would enforce our laws as they stand, unless Congress makes an exception.").

92. 470 U.S. 213 (1985).

93. 482 U.S. 220 (1987).

94. LFP Notes 2/21, 86–44 Shearson/Am Express v. McMahon et al. (CA 2), LFP Collection. Brief for the Securities and Exchange Commission as Amicus Curiae Supporting Petitioners, Shearson/American Express, Inc. v. McMahon, No. 86–44.

95. Letter from John D. Dingell to John S.R. Shad, Chairman, SEC (Feb. 11, 1987), LFP Collection.

96. Conference Notes, No. 86–44, Shearson/American Express v. McMahon (3/6/87), HAB-LC. Argument Notes, 86–44 Shearson/AmX v. McMahon (1 March 87), HAB-LC. Alberto-Culver Co. v. Scherk, 484 F. 2d 611, 615 (7th Cir. 1973) (Stevens, J.,

350 NOTES

dissenting). Lewis F. Powell, Jr. Conference Notes, No. 86–44, Shearson/American Express v. McMahon (3/6/87), LFP Collection.

97. 490 U.S. 477 (1989).

98. 485 U.S. 224 (1988).

99. If each member of the plaintiff class were required to allege that they had read and relied on the misstatement in making their decision to purchase, it would defeat the commonality requirement for class actions. Fed. R. Civ. P. 23(b)(3) (class action maintainable if "the court finds that the questions of law or fact common to the members of the class predominate over any questions affecting individual class members"). The FOTM presumption allows plaintiffs to skip the step of alleging personal reliance on the misstatement, instead allowing them to allege that the *market* relied on the misrepresentation in valuing the security. The plaintiffs in turn are deemed to have relied upon the distorted price produced by a deceived market. In the last few months prior to his retirement, Powell had voted to grant certiorari in *Basic*. Handwritten notes of Lewis F. Powell, Jr., from the Conference on Basic, Inc. v. Levinson 1 (Feb. 20, 1987), LFP Collection. Somewhat surprisingly, the "fraud-on-the-market" presumption of reliance went unremarked on by Powell. Strict reliance does not appear to have been an important issue for Powell. Handwritten notes of Lewis F. Powell, Jr., from the Conference on John Nuveen & Co. v. Sanders (Oct. 31, 1980) (noting that Powell would not grant certiorari on the question "whether [a] person who never saw [the] prospectus could sue" under Section 12[a](2) because the "[m]arket may be affected"), LFP Collection.

100. The exchange of letters between Brennan and from Blackmun dated January 14, 15, 22, and 27, 1988 is taken from No. 86-279—Basic, Inc. v. Levinson, HAB-LC.

101. Letter from William F. Brennan Jr. to Harry Blackmun, No. 86-279—Basic, Inc. v. Levinson (Jan. 27, 1988), HAB-LC.

102. Donald C. Langevoort, *Basic* at 20: Rethinking Fraud on the Market, 2009 Wisc. L. Rev. 151, 159.

103. The materiality issue—on which the Court proved to be unanimous—garnered most of the attention in the parties' briefs and in the attention of the justices at oral argument. The reliance part of respondent's oral argument included only one short interruption from any of the justices. The SEC filed an amicus brief, but did not participate in argument. Langevoort credits the agency's intervention on behalf of the petitioner as crucial and its brief as guiding the Court's opinion. Donald C. Langevoort, *Basic* at 20: Rethinking Fraud on the Market, 2009 Wisc. L. Rev. 151, 159.

104. Harry Blackmun, Conference Notes, Basic v. Levinson, No. 86-279 (Nov. 4, 1987), HAB-LC. Letter from Harry A. Blackmun to William J. Brennan, Jr., No. 86-279, Basic v. Levinson (Jan. 15, 1988), Thurgood Marshall Collection, Library of Congress ("there are at least two theories of damages that a plaintiff could propose, and this opinion does not lend particular support to either. . . . [T]he plaintiff could argue that he would not have sold had he known about the merger discussion, and thus that he should receive the difference between the price at

NOTES 351

which he sold ($18) and the eventual merger price ($42). Alternatively, one could argue that a plaintiff should recover the difference between the price he sold ($18) and what the price would have been had defendants not misrepresented the facts ($20).").

105. 511 U.S. 164 (1994).

106. Harry A. Blackmun, Conference Notes, No. 92–854, Central Bank of Denver v. First Interstate Bank (Dec. 3, 1993), (noting Kennedy's vote), HAB-LC. Letter from Harry A. Blackmun to Chief Justice Rehnquist, No. 92–854, Central Bank of Denver v. First Interst. Bank, (Dec. 7, 1993) (informing the Chief that Kennedy would write for the majority) HAB-LC. Letter from Anthony M. Kennedy to Harry A. Blackmun, Re: Central Bank v. First Interstate, No. 92–854 (Feb. 17, 1994) ("After working through the cases, particularly *Blue Chip Stamps*, *Ernst & Ernst*, *Pinter*, and *Musick*, I came to the conclusion that our precedents require us to confine the 10b-5 cause of action to primary violators, without extension to aiders and abettors."). HAB-LC.

107. Whether the question is resolved under the first or the second step of this inquiry has potentially significant consequences. When the Court interprets § 10(b), it is defining not only the limits of the private cause of action, but also the reach of the SEC's authority. When it constructs the hypothetical cause of action in the second step, only the private cause of action is implicated.

108. The Ninth Circuit, for example, found that substantial participation in the making of a misstatement would suffice, even without public attribution of that statement to the defendant. In re Software Toolworks Inc. Sec. Litig., 50 F.3d 615, 628–29 (9th Cir. 1994). The Second Circuit adopted a narrower approach, finding participation in the making of a statement insufficient; public attribution of the statement to the defendant was required. Wright v. Ernst & Young, LLP, 152 F.3d 169, 175 (2d Cir. 1998).

109. 501 US 350, 359 (1991).

110. Letter from John Paul Stevens to Harry Blackmun, 90–333—Lampf Pleva Lipkind Prupis & Petigrow v. Gilbertson (May 3, 1991), HAB-LC.

The Court's retroactivity holding provoked Congressional intervention. 15 U.S.C. § 78aa-1 (restoring applicable prior statute of limitations for cases filed prior to *Lampf Pleva*).

111. 508 US 286 (1993).

112. Exchange Act § 21D(b)(2).

113. The Second Circuit relied on one snippet from the legislative history and held that the PSLRA codified its pre-PSLRA pleading approach based on motive and opportunity and on recklessness. Novak v. Kasaks, 216 F.3d 300, 311 (2000). The Ninth Circuit also relied on the PSLRA's legislative history, but concluded that the statute raised the standard above that of the Second Circuit. In re Silicon Graphics Inc. Sec. Litig., 183 F.3d 970, 974 (9th Cir. 1999).

114. 551 U.S. 308 (2007).

115. In re Credit Suisse First Boston Corp., 431 F.3d 36 (1st Cir. 2005); Ottman v. Hanger Orthopedic Group, Inc., 353 F.3d 338 (4th Cir. 2003); Helwig v. Vencor, Inc., 251

352  NOTES

F.3d 540 (6th Cir. 2001); Gompper v. VISX, Inc., 298 F.3d 893 (9th Cir. 2002); 437 F.3d 588 (7th Cir. 2006).

116. Brief for the United States as Amicus Curiae Supporting Petitioners, Tellabs, Inc. v. Makor Issues & Rights, Ltd., No. 06–484, 2007 WL 460606, at *23 (arguing that "the court of appeals' standard appears to be equivalent to the standard that it (and some other courts of appeals) had applied *before* the enactment of the Reform Act, under which a complaint was sufficient if the plaintiff pleaded facts that supported at least a *reasonable* inference of state of mind.").

117. 563 U.S. 804 (2011).

118. Amgen, Inc. v. Connecticut Ret. Plans and Trust Funds, 568 U.S. 455 (2013).

119. Halliburton Co. v. Erica P. John Fund, Inc., 573 U.S. 258 (2014).

120. 141 S. Ct. 1951 (2021).

121. 552 U.S. 148 (2008).

122. 564 U.S. 135 (2011).

123. 139 S. Ct. 1094 (2019).

124. Exchange Act Rule 10b-5(a).

125. In re Charter Communications, Inc. Sec. Litig., 443 F.3d 987, 990–93 (8th Cir. 2006).

126. The vote was 3-2. See Paul Atkins, Just Say 'No" to the Trial Lawyers, Wall St. J., Oct. 9, 2007, at A17. Chairman Christopher Cox voted with the majority, despite having introduced a bill that in 1995 when he was a congressman that would have reversed *Basic*. Seligman, Transformation of Wall Street 663–64. The SEC had filed a brief in a Ninth Circuit case raising similar issues arguing that ""[t]he reliance requirement is satisfied where a plaintiff relies on a material deception flowing from a defendant's deceptive act, even though the conduct of other participants in the fraudulent scheme may have been a subsequent link in the causal chain leading to the plaintiff's securities transaction." SEC Reply Br. at 12, Simpson v. AOL Time Warner, Inc., No. 04–55665 (Feb. 7, 2005) <http://www.sec.gov/litigation/briefs/homestore_020 405.pdf> (last visited July 3, 2008). Brief for the United States as Amicus Curiae Supporting Affirmance (Aug. 15, 2007).

127. Merrill Lynch, Pierce, Fenner & Smith v. Dabit, 547 U.S. 71 (2006); SEC v. Zandford, 535 U.S. 813 (2002).

128. Geman v. SEC, 334 F.3d 1183, 1191 (10th Cir. 2003) ("The SEC is not required to prove reliance or injury in enforcement cases."); United States v. Haddy, 134 F.3d 542, 549–51 (3d Cir. 1998) (government need not prove reliance in criminal case).

129. PSLRA § 104, 109 Stat. 757 (codified at 15 U.S.C. § 78t(e)). Congress subsequently expanded the SEC's authority by reducing the state of mind requirement from knowledge to recklessness. See H.R. 4173, 111th Cong., § 929O (amending § 20(e) of the Exchange Act).

130. 564 U.S. 135 (2011).

131. Most famously in Ernst & Ernst v. Hochfelder, 425 U.S. 185, 214 ("despite the broad view of the Rule advanced by the Commission in this case, its scope cannot the power granted the Commission by Congress under § 10(b)").

132. 139 S. Ct. 1094 (2019).

NOTES 353

# Chapter 7

1. Louis K. Liggett Co. v. Lee, 288 U.S. 517, 558 (1933) (Brandeis, J., dissenting).
2. Gratz v. Claughton, 187 F.2d 46, 49 (2d Cir. 1951). Memo of Learned Hand in Birnbaum (Dec. 14, 1951 p. 2), Learned Hand Collection, Harvard Law School, Box 214. In spite of these concerns Hand concurred in the court's narrow holding in that case based on his view of an SEC staff description of rule passed by the Commission. Remarks of Louis Loss, American Bar Association Conference, 22 Bus. Law. 908, 918 (1967).
3. Ruckle v. Roto American Corp, 339 F.2d 24 (2nd Cir. 1964) (majority of directors caused corporation to improperly issue stock to insider to perpetuate their own control without disclosure to the entire board); Schoenbaum v. Firstbrook, 405 F.2d 215 (2nd Cir. 1968) (corporation issuing stock to controlling shareholder liable for deceiving the shareholders other than the controlling shareholders); Vine v. Beneficial Fin. Co., 374 F.2d 627 (2nd Cir. 1967); Crane Co. v. Westinghouse Air Brake Co., 419 F.2d 787 (2nd Cir. 1969).

   These federal corporate law cases were not limited to the Second Circuit. Pappas v. Moss, 393 F.2d 865 (3rd Cir. 1968) (derivative suit challenging directors selling to themselves, could be brought under Rule 10b-5); Dasho v. Susquehanna Corp., 380 F.2d 262 (7th Cir. 1967) (directors pairing their individual sale of stock to bidder at an excessive price with transfer of control).
4. Birnbaum v. Newport Steel Corp., 193 F.2d 461, cert denied, 343 U.S. 956 (1952); Crane Co. v. Westinghouse Air Brake Co., 419 F.2d 787 (2nd Cir. 1969); A.T. Brod & Co. v. Perlow, 375 F.2d 393, (2nd Cir. 1967); Ruckle v. Roto Am. Corp, 339 F.2d 24 (2nd Cir. 1964).
5. O'Neill v. Maytag, 339 F.2d 764 (2nd Cir. 1964) (no Rule 10b-5 claim for exchange of stock as part of internal struggle for control where no deception); Ruckle v. Roto American Corp., 339 F.2d 24 (2nd Cir. 1964). Future Supreme Court Justice Thurgood Marshall sat on both panels as did Chief Judge J. Edward Lumbard. Later cases extended deception to include not just of the directors who under state law had the power to act for the corporation in the transaction in question, but also of the shareholders who would be harmed from the transaction taking place. Schoenbaum v. Firstbrook, 405 F.2d 215 (2nd Cir. 1968) (allegation that shares issued to controlling shareholder at too low a price, if established, would show deception of the stockholders of the corporation other than the controlling shareholder).
6. 40 SEC at 912 n.10 (1961). Cary's executive assistant at the SEC later developed the idea of federal corporate law in a Harvard Law Review article bearing that title. Arthur Fleischer, Jr., "Federal Corporation Law": An Assessment, 78 Harv. L. Rev. 1146, 1148 (1965); Stanley A. Kaplan, Foreign Corporations and Local Corporate Policy, 21 Vand. L. Rev. 433, 476–77 (1968) ("[T]here has been an extraordinarily rapid burgeoning of so-called 'federal common law of corporations,' based upon implied civil liability under section 10(b) of the Securities Exchange Act of 1934; this law is pervading, and all but absorbing, a large portion of internal fiduciary obligations."); Louis Lowenfels, The Demise of the Birnbaum Doctrine: A New Era

354 NOTES

for Rule 10b-5, 54 Va. L. Rev. 268 (1968) ("a vast body of federal corporate common law has mushroomed under" Rule 10b-5). Superintendent of Insurance of New York v. Bankers Life and Casualty Company, 404 U.S. 6, 9 (1971). The quote is from *Capital Gains*, but Douglas did not cite the case.

*Bankers Life* had an immediate effect. The Second Circuit at that moment was considering an in banc review of a corporate mismanagement case that a panel had ruled outside of Rule 10b-5. After *Bankers Life*, without the need for full court review, the opinion was assigned to a new panel to write a contrary decision consistent with the Supreme Court's new holding. Drachman v. Harvey, 453 F.2d 722 (2nd Cir. 1972) *rev'd on rehearing*, 453 F.2d 736 (2d Cir. 1972) (in banc).

7. 417 U.S. 703 (1974).

8. Preliminary Memorandum, Bangor Punta Operations, Inc. v. Bangor & Aroostook R.R. Co. 1 (Jan. 4, 1974 Conference) (handwritten notes of Lewis F. Powell, Jr.). Memorandum from Lewis F. Powell, Jr., to John Buckley 3 (May 20, 1974), LFP Collection. Harry Blackmun Memorandum, No. 73-718—Bangor Punta Operations, Inc. v. Bangor & Aroostock RR Co., at (4/8/74), HAB-LC. Powell's reaction was "wow! This sounds like Robin Hood." Marshall's dissent, with its "typical juvenile style" provoked even more scorn. According to Powell (an avid hunter), Marshall fired, at random, a load of birdshot—some remotely relevant but most of them irrelevant. He seems to overlook the fact entirely that the parties for whom he sheds tears (the minority stockholders and creditors) may bring suit on their own behalf. nothing precludes them, and they have asserted no injury.

   Handwritten notes of Lewis F. Powell, Jr., from the Conference on Bangor Punta Operations, Inc. v. Bangor & Aroostook R.R. Co., at 2, LFP Collection. Powell's uncharacteristically exasperated tone may have reflected just end-of-the-term tension as the published responses are more measured.

9. Handwritten notes of Lewis F. Powell, Jr., from the Conference on Bangor Punta Operations, Inc. v. Bangor & Aroostook R.R. Co. 2 (Apr. 17, 1974), LFP Collection. *Bangor Punta*, 471 U.S. at 710. One complication was the fact that the claim was not, in fact, a derivative claim, but instead had been brought directly by the affected corporation, which caused Powell and his clerk some difficulty in drafting the opinion. Telephone Interview with John Buckley Powell Clerk, OT '73 (June 5, 2002) (notes on file with authors). In the end, they simply relied on the overarching principle that a court of equity should not confer windfall gains on parties who have not suffered damages.

10. 430 U.S. 462 (1977).

11. Del. Code Ann. tit. 8, § 253 (1974). Vine v. Beneficial Financial Co., 374 F.2d 627 (2nd Cir. 1967). Green v. Santa Fe Indus., Inc., 533 F.2d 1283, 1287, 1299 (2nd Cir. 1976).

12. Memorandum from Lewis F. Powell, Jr., to File, Santa Fe Indus., Inc. v. Green 9 (Dec. 27, 1976) (citations omitted). Handwritten notes of Lewis F. Powell, Jr., from the Conference on Santa Fe Indus., Inc. v. Green 1–2 (Jan. 21, 1977), LFP Collection. Marshall, who was not at the conference, later changed his mind, writing to White that he would join the opinion (making it 6-3) if it were limited to Section 10b (preserving a similar federalism question under § 13 which had different language).

Letter from Thurgood Marshall to Byron R. White 1 (Mar. 11, 1977), Thurgood Marshall Collection, Library of Congress.

13. Santa Fe Indus., Inc. v. Green, 430 U.S. 462, 473–74, 478–79 (1977). The Court had said as much in dicta in 1969. SEC v. National Securities, Inc., 393 U.S. 453, 462–63 (1969) ("Presumably, full disclosure would have avoided the particular Rule 10b-5 violations alleged in the complaint."). *Santa Fe*, 430 U.S. at 480 n.17 citing William Cary, Federalism and Corporate Law, Reflections Upon Delaware, 83 Yale L.J. 663, 700 (1974). Handwritten Note, Letter from Lewis F. Powell, Jr. to Byron White, No. 75–1753 Santa Fe Industries v. Green (Mar. 11, 1977), Byron White Collection, Box I: 37, Folder 1, Library of Congress.

14. Goldberg v. Meridor, 567 F.2d 209, 217–18 (2nd Cir. 1977) cert. denied 434 U.S. 1069 (1978).

15. Kas v. Financial General Bankshares, Inc., 796 F.2d 508 (D.C. Cir. 1986); Healey v. Catalyst Recovery of Pas., Inc., 616 F.2d 641, 646 (3rd Cir. 1980); Alabama Farm Bureau Mutual Casualty Co. v. American Fidelity Life Ins. Co., 606 f.2d 602, 613–14 (5th Cir. 1979) cert. denied, 449 U.S., 820 (1980); Kidwell ex rel. Penfold v. Meikle, 597 F.2d 1273, 1291–92 (9th Cir. 1979); see also Wright v. Heizer, 560 F.2d 236, 249–51 (7th Cir. 1977) cert. denied 434 U.S. 1066 (1978).

16. Proposed Rules, 42 FR 60090 (Nov. 17, 1977). Final Rules, 44 FR 46741 (Aug. 9, 1979).

17. Singer v. Magnavox, 380 A.2d 969 (Del. 1977); Weinberger v. UOP, Inc., 467 A.2d 701, 712 (Del. 1983); Smith v. Van Gorkom, 488 A.2d 858 (1985); Unocal v. Mesa Petroleum Corp., 493 A.2d 946, 957 (1985).

An exchange in 2019 between then Delaware Chief Justice Leo Strine and prominent Delaware litigator Gil Sparks captures this development in Delaware law:

> *Strine*: What you are saying is there were some real societal pressures on Delaware and whether this tradition of the business judgment rule could be maintained. And that *Weinberger* was one of the critical decisions in saying if we are going to maintain it, we have to do it with credibility . . . in a way that had genuine integrity.

> *Sparks*: Right . . . and it was Delaware's response to a system when you entered the 80s and the takeover era, our law had not caught up with it. . . . Big question was whether you would test these under the entire fairness concept . . . or the business judgment rule."

Oral History of A. Gilcrest Sparks, III, University of Pennsylvania 2019.

18. 472 U.S. 1 (1985).

19. Harry Blackmun, Conference Notes, No. 83–2129, Schreiber v. Burlington Northern, Inc. (Jan. 11, 1985), HAB-LC.

Powell was recovering from complications from surgery and did not participate in the decision. His notes on the preliminary memorandum indicate his agreement with the lower court, which was affirmed. Preliminary Memorandum, Schreiber v. Burlington N., Inc., to Lewis F. Powell, Jr. 1 (Sept. 24, 1984) (handwritten notes of Lewis F. Powell, Jr.), LFP Collection.

20. Field v. Trump, 850 F.2d 938, 948–49 (2nd. Cir. 1988).

21. In re The Topps Co. Shareholders Litig., 926 A.2d 58 (Del. Ch. 2007); In re Netsmart Technologies, Inc. Securities Litigation, 924 A.2d 171, 206 (Del. Ch. 2007) ("Federal

356 NOTES

regulations and exchange rules address disclosure of this kind in a detailed manner that balances costs of disclosing. . . . Those bodies of authority should not be lightly added to by our law.").

22. Seligman, Transformation of Wall Street 222. In 2004, the SEC increased the independence requirement to 75% by rule. SEC, Rel. No. IC-26520 (2004); 15 U.S.C. § 78n-1 (2000).

23. 441 U.S. 471, 473 (1979). Auerbach v. Bennett, 393 NE2d 994, 47 NY2d 619, 419 NYS2d 920 (NY 1979). Lasker v. Burks, 567 F.2d 1208, 1209 (2nd Cir. 1978). Brief for the Securities and Exchange Commission as Amicus Curiae, Burks v. Lasker, 441 U.S. 471 (1979) (No. 77-1724). William J. Brennan, Jr., First Draft Opinion, Burks v. Lasker 1 (circulated Apr. 18, 1979) (handwritten notes of Lewis F. Powell, Jr.), LFP Collection. The complaint challenged the directors' purchase of Penn Central commercial paper, an investment that did not turn out so well given the losses that befell that company. Potter Stewart, First Draft Concurring Opinion, Burks v. Lasker 1 (circulated Apr. 30, 1979), LFP Collection.

24. 464 U.S. 523 (1984).

25. 500 U.S. 90 (1991).

26. *Kamen*, 500 U.S. 95 n.4, 99-100.

27. Aronson v. Lewis, 743 A.2d 805 (Del. 1984). American Law Institute, Principles of Corporate Governance § 7.08.

28. Pub. L. No. 90-439, 82 Stat. 454 (1968) (amending the Securities Exchange Act of 1934 § 14(d)-(e), 15 U.S.C. § 78n(d)-(e) (2000)).

29. *Piper*, 430 U.S. 1, 30 ("As originally introduced, the disclosure proposals embodied in S. 2731 were avowedly pro-management in the target company's efforts to defeat takeover bids."). 113 Cong. Rec. 854 (1967) (remarks of Sen. Williams). Seligman, Transformation of Wall Street 431-32.

30. 422 U.S. 49 (1975); 430 U.S. 1 (1977).

31. Preliminary Memorandum, Rondeau v. Mosinee Paper Corp., to Lewis F. Powell, Jr. 1 (Dec. 6, 1974 Conference) (handwritten notes of Lewis F. Powell, Jr.), LFP Collection.

32. Telephone Interview with Michael Dooley (Professor, University of Virginia School of Law) (Feb. 22, 2002) (notes on file with authors). Va. Code Ann. §§ 13.1-725 to 13.1-728.9 (Michie 1999). Lewis F. Powell, Jr., Trends in Antitrust, Address at the Conference of Financial Executives, at 15. Note from Lewis F. Powell, Jr., to Joe [Carter] 1 (Apr. 18, 1981), LFP Collection. Telephone Interview with Joe Carter (former partner, Hunton & Williams) (May 21, 2002) (notes on file with authors).

33. Letter from Lewis F. Powell, Jr., to Ed[ward E. Lane] 1 (July 28, 1953) (congratulating Lane on his election); Letter from Lewis F. Powell, Jr., to Ed[ward E. Lane] 1 (May 13, 1957) (pledging to support Lane "in the coming election, as I always have in the past"); Letter from Lewis F. Powell, Jr., to [F.] Carlyle [Tiller] 1 (June 21, 1957) (forwarding "checks for Ed Lane" from Powell and two of his partners); Letter from Lewis F. Powell, Jr., to Ed[ward E. Lane] 1 (Nov. 10, 1965) (congratulating Lane on his reelection), LFP Collection.

The Virginia statute required bidders make extensive disclosure weeks before the bid, some backed up with an antifraud prohibition with both criminal and civil

NOTES    357

liability provisions (including a private right of action). The law also provided for a hearing before a state and some substantive hurdles. The Fourth Circuit struck down the amendment as imposing an undue burden on interstate commerce. Telvest, Inc. v. Bradshaw, 697 F.2d 576, 582 (4th Cir. 1983). A successor statute was upheld by the Fourth Circuit on the basis of Powell's opinion in *CTS* (discussed later in this chapter). WLR Foods, Inc. v. Tyson Foods, Inc., 65 F.3d 1172, 1182 (4th Cir. 1995) (holding that, although "the Virginia statutes impose some incidental burden on interstate commerce, we find the burden outweighed by the interest of Virginia in regulating its corporations"). Letter from Lewis F. Powell, Jr., to Bob [Y. Button] 1 (Nov. 10, 1965). Lewis F. Powell, Jr., Billing Records (Jan. 22, 1968–Feb. 29, 1968, LFP Collection. Telephone Interview with Joe Carter. Letter from Joe Carter to Lewis [F. Powell, Jr.] 1 (Apr. 22, 1981). Note from Lewis F. Powell, Jr., to Joe Carter 1 (Apr. 18, 1981) ("As I recall, you and I drafted the Virginia statute for Newport News Shipbuilding Company, and then the company backed down on using it against Tenneco. We 'lobbied' it through the legislature, and persuaded Mills Godwin to sign it."). Letter from Lewis F. Powell, Jr., to Mills [E. Godwin] 1 (Mar. 9, 1968) (congratulating Godwin on "a most successful session of the General Assembly"). Letter from Lewis F. Powell, Jr., to Ed[ward E. Lane] 1 (Mar. 9, 1968). See also Letter from Lewis F. Powell, Jr., to Mills [E. Godwin], at 1 (thanking Godwin for his "full support" of the legislation), LFP Collection. Newport News and Tenneco Discuss a "Consolidation", Wall St. J., Apr. 25, 1968, at 7. Tenneco Agrees to Buy Biggest U.S. Shipbuilder, Wall St. J., May 23, 1968, at 11. Tenneco's Walker Mfg. and Newport News Units Shift Top Management, Wall St. J., Dec. 13, 1968, at 26.

34. Handwritten notes of Lewis F. Powell, Jr., for the Argument in Rondeau v. Mosinee Paper Corp. 1 (argued Apr. 15, 1975). Handwritten notes of Lewis F. Powell, Jr., from the Conference on Rondeau v. Mosinee Paper Corp. 2 (Apr. 18, 1975). Letter from Lewis F. Powell, Jr., to Chief Justice Warren E. Burger 2 (Dec. 30, 1976), LFP Collection.

35. Tender Offer Reform Act of 1984, H.R. 5693, 98th Cong. (1984) (proposing, at the SEC's urging, that the Williams Act be expanded to give the SEC jurisdiction over anti-takeover devices). Telephone Interview with Steve Lamb (former SEC attorney) (May 30, 2002) (notes on file with author).

36. 443 U.S. 173 (1979).

37. Preliminary Memorandum, Leroy v. Great W. United Corp., to Lewis F. Powell, Jr. 1–3 (Jan. 5, 1979 Conference), LFP Collection. Great W. United Corp. v. Leroy, 577 F.2d 1256, 1286 (5th Cir. 1978) ("[W]e agree with the district court that the Idaho takeover law is invalid.") and. at 1279 ("Idaho's statute is preempted, because the market approach to investor protection adopted by Congress and the fiduciary approach adopted by Idaho are incompatible."). Bench Memorandum, Leroy v. Great W. United Corp., to Lewis F. Powell, Jr. 14 (Apr. 6, 1979), LFP Collection. Brief for the SEC as Amicus Curiae, Leroy v. Great Western United Corp., No. 78–759 (Apr. 1979).

38. Bench Memorandum, Leroy v. Great W. United Corp., to Lewis F. Powell, Jr., at 1 (handwritten notes of Lewis F. Powell, Jr.), LFP Collection.

358  NOTES

39. Handwritten notes of Lewis F. Powell, Jr., from the Conference on Leroy v. Great W. United Corp. 2 (Apr. 20, 1979), LFP Collection. Powell thought that the Texas long-arm statute, but not the Exchange Act, conferred jurisdiction. The assertion of jurisdiction on these facts, however, would violate the Due Process Clause. He did not offer a view on the merits.
40. 457 U.S. 624, 627 (1982).
41. Preliminary Memorandum, Edgar v. MITE Corp., to Lewis F. Powell, Jr. 6–7 (May 1, 1981 Conference), LPF Collection. The SEC preempted the first generation of state antitakeover laws with its Rule 14d-2(b), 17 C.F.R. § 240.14d-2(b). This rule was referred to at the SEC as the "kneecap" rule because Chairman Harold Williams had instructed John Huber to cut the state statutes off at the kneecap. Telephone Interview with Steve Lamb.

   *Edgar* provided substantial authority for upholding the rule. Nat'l City Lines, Inc. v. LLC Corp., 687 F.2d 1122, 1132 (8th Cir. 1982) (holding that to force National City Lines to comply with both SEC and state rules "[would be] impossible and [would] frustrate[] the purposes of the Williams Act"). Memorandum from Thurgood Marshall to the Conference 2 (June 18, 1982), LFP Collection.
42. Thurgood Marshall, First Draft Opinion, Edgar v. MITE Corp. 1–11 (circulated Feb. 1, 1982), LFP Collection.

   At the end of it all, Marshall circulated the following summary of the maneuvering:

   > 1) Justice Marshall circulates opinion for the Court. 2) Justice Brennan joins. 3) Justice Rehnquist joins. 4) Justice Powell joins. 5) Justice White circulates a dissent. 6) Justice Stevens circulates a dissent. 7) Justice Blackmun joins Justice White. 8) Justice O'Connor joins Justice Stevens. 9) The Chief Justice joins Justice Marshall. 10) Justice Rehnquist changes vote. 11) The Chief Justice changes vote. 12) Justice White circulates opinion for the Court. 13) Justice Marshall circulates dissent. 14) Justice Brennan joins Justice Marshall. 15) Justice Stevens circulates concurring opinion. 16) Justice Rehnquist circulates dissent. 17) The Chief Justice joins Justice White. 18) Justice O'Connor concurs. 19) Justice Powell concurs. 20) Justice Blackmun concurs.

   Memorandum from Thurgood Marshall to the Conference, at 2, LFP Collection. Handwritten notes of William J. Brennan, Jr. from the Conference on Edgar v. MITE Corp. 1–3 (n.d.), William J. Brennan, Jr. Collection, Library of Congress.
43. Handwritten notes of Lewis F. Powell, Jr., from the Conference on Edgar v. MITE Corp. 2-3 (Dec. 2, 1981). Byron R. White, First Draft Opinion, Edgar v. MITE Corp. 1 (circulated May 28, 1982) (handwritten notes of Lewis F. Powell) ("Though I am not persuaded on 'mootness' issue, if BRW gets a court I'll join it."), LFP Collection.
44. Lewis F. Powell, Jr., Draft Concurring Opinion, Edgar v. MITE Corp. 1–2 (June 21, 1982). Byron R. White, First Draft Opinion, Edgar v. MITE Corp. 1 (circulated May 28, 1982) (handwritten notes of Lewis F. Powell). Harry Blackmun, Conference Notes, Edgar v. MITE Corp., No. 80-1188 (Dec. 2, 1981), HAB-LC. Preliminary Memorandum, Schreiber v. Burlington N., Inc., to Lewis F. Powell, Jr. 1 (Sept. 24, 1984 Conference) (handwritten notes of Lewis F. Powell, Jr.), LFP Collection.
45. Letter from John Paul Stevens to Byron R. White 1 (June 1, 1982), LFP Collection. Letter from Sandra Day O'Connor to Byron R. White 1 (Apr. 23, 1982), LFP

NOTES 359

Collection. Her published concurrence with the commerce clause holding notes it was not it necessary to reach the preemption claim.

46. 481 U.S. 69, 73–74 (1987).

47. Ind. Code § 23-1-42-4(a) (1986), *quoted in CTS*, 481 U.S. at 72–73.

48. Dynamics Corp. of Am. v. CTS Corp., 794 F.2d 250, 262–64 (7th Cir. 1986). Bench Memorandum, CTS Corp. v. Dynamics Corp. of Am., from Ronald [Mann] to Lewis F. Powell, Jr. 5 (Feb. 11, 1987) (handwritten notes of Lewis F. Powell, Jr.) (Powell's response to Posner's view that "tender offers are uniformly good for the economy" was a resounding "NO!"). Preliminary Memorandum, CTS Corp. v. Dynamics Corp. of Am., to Lewis F. Powell, Jr. 1 (Sept. 29, 1986 Conference) (handwritten notes of Lewis F. Powell, Jr.) ("If other Justices show any interest I could *Note* this case, but I expect this will be *affirmed*."), LFP Collection.

49. Memorandum from Lewis F. Powell, Jr., to File, CTS Corp. v. Dynamics Corp. of Am. 1 (Feb. 6, 1987), LFP Collection.

50. Bench Memorandum, CTS Corp. v. Dynamics Corp. of Am., from Ronald [Mann] to Lewis F. Powell, Jr., *supra* note 48, at 18 (handwritten notes of Lewis F. Powell, Jr.) ("I voted wrongly [in *MITE*]" and 4. Handwritten notes of Lewis F. Powell, Jr., to File, CTS Corp. v. Dynamics Corp. of Am. 1 (Feb. 2, 1987) (noting that the district court and the Seventh Circuit found the Indiana statute significantly different from the Illinois statute in *MITE*), LFP Collection.

51. Bench Memorandum, CTS Corp. v. Dynamics Corp. of Am., from Ronald [Mann] to Lewis F. Powell, Jr., at 22, LFP Collection.

52. Handwritten notes of Lewis F. Powell, Jr., from the Conference on Edgar v. MITE Corp. 1–4 (Dec. 2, 1981) (noting that Brennan, Marshall, and Rehnquist found preemption by the Williams Act). Handwritten notes of Lewis F. Powell, Jr., from the Conference on Leroy v. Great Western 1–3 (Apr. 20, 1979) (same). LFP Collection. Handwritten notes of Lewis F. Powell, Jr., from the Conference on CTS Corp. v. Dynamics Corp. of Am. 1–2 (Mar. 4, 1987), LFP Collection. Harry Blackmun Conference Notes, CTS Corp. v. Dynamics Corp. of Am., No. 86–71 (Mar. 4, 1987), HAB-LC.

53. Memorandum from Lewis F. Powell, Jr., to Ronald [Mann], at 4 ("Virginia required, as did many other states, a two-thirds vote on a merger. In addition, the state prescribes the requisite vote on a sale of all corporate assets and a liquidation."). Memorandum from Lewis F. Powell, Jr., to Ronald [Mann] 2 (Mar. 20, 1987). Lewis F. Powell, Jr., Draft Rider A, p. 39, CTS Corp. v. Dynamics Corp. of Am. 1 (Mar. 20, 1987), LFP Collection.

[This] beneficial free market system depends at its core upon the fact that a corporation—except in the rarest situations—is organized under, and governed by, the laws of the state of its incorporation. These law [*sic*] govern the voting rights of shareholders that directly apply to a variety of corporate transactions including takeover bids.

54. Lewis F. Powell, Jr., Draft Opinion, CTS Corp. v. Dynamics Corp. of Am., at 37, LFP Collection.

55. Memorandum from Lewis F. Powell, Jr., to Ronald [Mann] 3 (Mar. 18, 1987), LFP Collection.

360  NOTES

Powell, of course, was aware of the strategic advantages afforded management by delay. In *MITE*, his law clerk had written that "forcing delay is a known weapon in tender offer battles." Bench Memorandum, Edgar v. MITE Corp., from John Wiley to Lewis F. Powell, Jr. 9 (Nov. 25, 1981). Powell's response? "Of course—but 'tender offers' are not inevitably good." *Id.* (handwritten notes of Lewis F. Powell, Jr.).

Lewis F. Powell, Jr., Draft Opinion, CTS Corp. v. Dynamics Corp. of Am. 28 n.7 (Mar. 19, 1987), LFP Collection.

56. Lewis F. Powell, Jr., Rider A, p. 43, CTS Corp. v. Dynamics Corp. of Am. 2 n.* (Mar. 20, 1987), LFP Collection. Ronald Gilson & Bernard Black, The Law and Finance of Corporate Acquisitions (1995). Gregg A. Jarrell et al., The Market for Corporate Control: The Empirical Evidence Since 1980, J. Econ. Perspectives, Winter 1988, at 49.

57. Unocal Corp. v. Mesa Petroleum Co. 493 A.2d 946 (Del. 1985). Lucian Arye Bebchuk et al., The Powerful Antitakeover Force of Staggered Boards: Theory, Evidence, and Policy, 54 STAN. L. REV. 887, 891 (2002) (finding that staggered boards double a target's likelihood of remaining independent). *CTS*, 481 U.S. at 85–86 (discussing potential delay in effecting takeovers resulting from classified boards).

58. 501 U.S. 1083 (1991).

59. 396 U.S. 375 (1970).

60. 1st Draft, Virginia Bankshares, Inc. v. Sandberg, No. 89–1448 (June 3, 1991). Letter from Byron R. White to David Souter, No. 89–1448, Virginia Bankshares v. Sandberg (June 6, 1991). Letter from Sandra Day O'Connor to David Souter, No. 89–1448, Virginia Bankshares v. Sandberg (June 7, 1991). Letter from David Souter to Byron White, No. 89–1448, Virginia Bankshares v. Sandberg (June 11, 1991). Letter from William H. Rehnquist to David Souter, No. 89–1448, Virginia Bankshares v. Sandberg (June 12, 1991). Letter Byron R. White to David Souter, No. 89–1448, Virginia Bankshares v. Sandberg (June 12, 1991). No. 89–1448, Letter from Sandra Day O'Connor to David Souter, Virginia Bankshares v. Sandberg (June 13, 1991), Byron White Papers, Box II: 157, Library of Congress.

61. 2nd Draft, Virginia Bankshares, Inc. v. Sandberg, No. 89–1448 (June 24, 1991). Letter from Byron White to David Souter, No. 89–1448, Virginia Bankshares v. Sandberg (June 25, 1991), Byron White Papers, Box II: 157, Library of Congress.

62. Letter from Anthony M. Kennedy to David Souter, No. 89–1448, Virginia Bankshares v. Sandberg (June 23, 1991), Byron White Papers, Box II: 157, Library of Congress.

63. Wilson v. Great Am. Indus., Inc., 979 F.2d 924, 931 (2d Cir. 1992) (citing to other holdings in 10b-5 cases that "deprivation of a state remedy in no way lessens federal interest in preventing the violation.")

64. 516 US 367 (1996).

65. Exchange Act § 27.

66. 28 U.S.C. § 1738.

67. 482 US 220 (1987).

68. Kircher v. Putnam Funds Trust, 547 U.S. 633 (2006).

69. Kircher v. Putnam Funds Trust, 403 F.3d 478, 484 (7th Cir. 2005), vacated and remanded, 547 U.S. 633 (2006). The circuit court's ruling on the procedural issue in the case is found at 373 3d 847 (7th Cir. 2004).

NOTES 361

Scalia concurred in the judgment, taking a different route to finding the Seventh Circuit's procedure was not permitted.

70. Chadbourne & Parke LLP v. Troice, 571 U.S. 377 (2014).
71. SEC v. Zandford, 535 U.S. 813 (2002); Wharf (Holdings) Ltd. v. United Intern. Holdings, Inc., 532 U.S. 588 (2001)
72. 138 S. Ct. 1061 (2018).
73. Compare § 22 of the Securities Act to § 27 of the Exchange Act.
74. Exchange Act Rule 14a-11. Dodd-Frank Wall Street Reform and Consumer Protection Act, P.L. No. 111–203, § 971, 124 Stat. 1915). Business Roundtable v. SEC, 647 F.3d 1144 (D.C. Cir. 2011).
75. United States v. O'Hagan, 521 U.S. 642 (1997); SEC v. Zandford, 535 U.S. 813 (2002).

# Chapter 8

1. The story of this evolution, and William O. Douglas's unintentional contribution to it, is well told by Skeel, Debt's Dominion 125–28.
2. The private claim against the US in *Affiliated Ute* is excluded here as is the government's antitrust claim in United States v. National Association of Securities Dealers, 422 U.S. 694 (1975).
3. The SEC took the more restrictive view in Merrill Lynch, Pierce, Fenner & Smith v. Ware, 414 U.S. 117 (1973), Marine Bank v. Weaver, 455 U.S. 551 (1982), Shearson/ American Express, Inc., v. McMahon, 482 U.S. 220 (1987), Pinter v. Dahl, 486 U.S. 622 (1988), Kamen v. Kemper Financial Services, Inc., 500 U.S. 90 (1991), Credit Suisse Securities (USA) LLC v. Simmonds, 566 U.S. 221 (2012).

   In Stoneridge Investment Partners, LLC v. Scientific-Atlanta, Inc., 552 U.S. 148 (2008), the Solicitor General rejected the SEC position and filed a brief favoring the restrictive interpretation. In Cyan, Inc. v. Beaver Cty. Emp. Ret. Fund, 138 S. Ct. 1061 (2018), the Solicitor General filed a brief at the invitation of the Court, but the SEC did not join the brief. We do not include either case in the SEC cases here.
4. Bench Memorandum, Herman & MacLean v. Huddleston, from Jim [Browning] to Lewis F. Powell, Jr., at 17 (handwritten notes of Justice Lewis F. Powell, Jr.), LFP Collection.
5. Schlesinger, The Politics of Upheaval 452–53. Moley, First New Deal 386.
6. Sidney Fine, Frank Murphy: The New Deal Years 445 (1979). J. Woodford Howard, Jr., Mr. Justice Murphy: A Political Biography 268 (1968) ("Justice Murphy enjoyed Frankfurter's wit and acknowledged his superior intellect. Yet he felt defensive beside them.... Frankfurter was an excitable and scrappy intellectual had ill-concealed contempt for the Irishmen's intellect and night life...").
7. The *Goldman Sachs* case, with two holdings, one 6-3 and the other 8-1, is recorded here in the 6-3 category as the Court reported that the parties' disagreement on the other claim had "largely evaporated."

362 NOTES

8. Draft Autobiography Robert Jackson Papers, Box 189, at 43 Library of Congress. Eugene Gressman, Controversial Image of Mr. Justice Murphy, 47 Geo. L.J. 631, 641 (1959).

Byrnes's Senate service would likely have served as an equally accurate predictor of his judicial judgments, had he stayed long enough on the Court to render any.

9. Joseph P. Lash, From the Diaries of Felix Frankfurter 53 (1975). John D. Fassett, New Deal Justice: The Life of Stanley Reed of Kentucky 174 (1994). Barry Cushman, Rethinking the New Deal Court 18 (1998). John M. Ferren, Salt of the Earth, Conscience of the Court: The Story of Wiley Rutledge 133–35 (2004) (describing a prominent radio address given by Black).

Black may have owed his seat on the Court—indirectly—to the Court packing plan. Roosevelt had promised the first Court vacancy to the Senate majority leader Joe Robinson, but Robinson died at the height of the fight over the plan. Jeff Shesol, Supreme Power: Franklin Roosevelt vs. The Supreme Court 486–89 (2010). Roosevelt, according to his son, James, "hopping mad, almost" at the Senate over the defeat of his plan, wanted to stick it to the Senators. Id. at 514–15. The appointment of the liberal Black, sure to be confirmed by his fellow Senators because of Senatorial courtesy, allowed Roosevelt to tweak the conservative Southern Democrats who had opposed the plan. Willliam E. Leuchtenburg, The Supreme Court Reborn: The Constitutional Revolution in the Age of Roosevelt 135 (1995) (describing the support of Byrnes, Black, and Minton as senators). Seligman, Transformation of Wall Street 155. Shesol, Supreme Power 333–34, 385. Lash, Diaries 63.

10. Shesol, Supreme Power 317.

After his appointment, Douglas wrote in his diary:

I saw Brandeis at his apartment and he told me something which gave me as great a thrill as the nomination itself. He said "You were my personal choice for my successor." He was most gracious and held my hand with great warmth as he said it. I was deeply touched. That, I felt, was the greatest compliment ever paid me. Whether he had communicated that thought to the President, I do not know. I suspect he had done so, indirectly through Felix who was most anxious that I receive the nomination.

William O. Douglas, Diary (Mar. 26, 1939), WOD-LC, Box 1780. Robert H. Jackson, Diary (Jan. 2, 1939), Robert H. Jackson Collection, Library of Congress, Box 81. Ferren, Salt of the Earth 137, 151. J. Woodford Howard, Jr., Mr. Justice Murphy: A Political Biography 192 (1968) (describing Murphy's support). Sidney Fine, Frank Murphy: The Washington Years 194 (1984). Ferren, Salt of the Earth 216–17. Peter H. Irons, The New Deal Lawyers 12 (1982). Lash, Diary of Felix Frankfurter 77. Schlesinger, Coming of the New Deal 579.

11. Bruce Murphy, Wild Bill 217–30, 251–65. William E. Leuchtenberg, Franklin D. Roosevelt and the New Deal 207–08 (1995). Sidney Fine, Frank Murphy 133. Robert Jackson, Oral History at 4, Box 258, Robert Jackson Papers, Library of Congress.

12. Copy of handwritten note, Felix Frankfurter to Owen Roberts (Feb. 4, 1943), FF-Harvard, Part 3, Reel 3, ("I wince whenever I hear any responsible person talk of "New Deal" and "Old Deal" court or Justices. I'm incurably academic and cannot rid myself of the conviction that it is of the very essence of the function of this Court

NOTES    363

that when a man comes on it, he leaves all party feelings as well as affiliations behind. I certainly do not and have not since January 30, 1939 for one split second felt like or deemed myself, or deemed it right for anyone else to think of me, as a "New Deal" Justice.").

13. Letter from Felix Frankfurter to Hugo Black (Dec. 15, 1939), FF-Harvard, Part 3, Reel 13.

14. Freedman, Justice Frankfurter and Judicial Review, in Freedman, Beaney & Rostow, Perspectives on the Court 6 (1967). Letter from Fred Vinson to Felix Frankfurter (Dec. 3, 1948), FF-Harvard, Part 3, Reel 4. Bernard Schwartz, Felix Frankfurter and Earl Warren: A Study of a Deteriorating Relationship, 1980 The Supreme Court Review, 115, 123 (1980). Howard Ball & Phillip Cooper, Fighting Justices: Hugo L. Black and William O. Douglas and Supreme Court Conflict, 38 Am. J. Legal Hist. 1, 12 (1994). Fassett, New Deal Justice 584.

15. Memorandum from Edith Walters (e.w.) for the A.C. Frost & Co. v. Coeur d'Alene's Mines Corp. conference (Dec. 21, 1940), WOD-LC. The memo notes that the regional office looked into some shareholder complaints between May and August 1937 and that the agency's general counsel decided it was not a matter for action by the Commission and was never taken to a Commission meeting.

Memorandum from Edith Walters (e.w.) for the SEC v. C.M. Joiner & Co. conference (Oct. 15, 1943) (reporting information gathered from Orval duBois), WOD-LC.

16. William O. Douglas, The Court Years: 1939–1975, 31, 417–21 ("Index of Supreme Court Cases in This Volume.") (1980). Bruce Murphy, Wild Bill 351. Walter Dellinger, then a clerk to Black (and later Acting Solicitor General in the Clinton administration), asked Douglas in 1968 if he would go on the Court if he had to do it over again. Douglas replied, "Absolutely not!" He explained that "the Court as an institution is too peripheral, too much in the backwater on the Court. You're just too far out of the action here." Id.

17. Ferren, Salt of the Earth 282. Superintendent of Ins. v. Bankers Life & Casualty Co., 404 U.S. 6 (1971).

Douglas's rate of dissent skyrocketed in cases of all kinds in the 1970s. Howard Ball & Phillip Cooper, Fighting Justices: Hugo L. Black and William O. Douglas and Supreme Court Conflict, 38 Am. J. Legal Hist. 1, 19 (1994).

18. See, e.g., James F. Simon, Independent Journey: The Life of William O. Douglas 201–02 (1980) (describing a small group that gathered to celebrate Frankfurter's appointment to the court that included Douglas, Jackson, Murphy, and Harry Hopkins in Harold Ickes's office at the Department of the Interior). Howard Ball & Phillip Cooper, Fighting Justices: Hugo L. Black and William O. Douglas and Supreme Court Conflict, 38 Am. J. Legal Hist. 1, 14 (1994). Letter from Charles Clark to Arthur B. Darling (Mar. 20, 1939), Charles E. Clark Papers, Series I, Box 1, Folder 2, Yale University Library, Manuscripts and Archives. In that same letter Clark also noted how the Supreme Court appointment disrupted Douglas's likely pick to be the next dean at Yale Law: "There was one blow to my plans which came in today when Bill Douglas was named to the Supreme Court, for I had expected, as seemed rather likely, that he would succeed me as dean."

364  NOTES

19. Jim Newton, Justice for All: Earl Warren and the Nation He Made 5, 70–71 (2006).

20. David L. Stebbene, Arthur J. Goldberg: New Deal Liberal 8, 372 (1996).

Johnson had persuaded Goldberg to resign from the Court in 1965 to become Ambassador to the United Nations, presumably to have a lead role in administration policy regarding the Vietnam War. The opening enabled LBJ to appoint Fortas to the Court, from where the justice continued to advise the President. When Earl Warrant tendered his letter of resignation in June 1968, Johnson nominated Fortas to the center position. A Senate filibuster by Republicans and southern Democrats blocked the nomination during an election year and the newly elected Nixon named Warren Burger as chief.

Within just a few months of his inauguration, Nixon was presented with a second opening when Fortas resigned after it came out that he had been retained as a consultant by the Wolfson Family Foundation while serving on the Court. Laura Kalman, Abe Fortas: A Biography 51, 365–73 (1990). The Wolfson Family Foundation was established by Louis Wolfson, whose later conviction for violating the Securities Act's registration provisions would be affirmed by the Second Circuit. United States v. Wolfson, 405 F.2d 779 (2nd Cir. 1968). Wolfson's petition for certiorari was denied by the Supreme Court, with Fortas recusing himself. Wolfson v. United States, 394 U.S. 946 (1969). Soon thereafter, the extent of Fortas's connection to Wolfson came to light in an article in *Life* magazine. Kalman 365. When it did, only Fortas's mentor Douglas, who had lobbied for his appointment to the Court, Kalman 244, discouraged him from resigning. Kalman 373. Kalman, 245 ("clone").

21. The Burger Court: The Counter-Revolution that Wasn't (Vincent Blasi, ed., 1983).

22. Telephone Interview with John Buckley, Powell Clerk, OT'73 (June 5, 2002) (notes on file with authors).

23. In addition to the opinions listed here, William O. Douglas (1), Earl Warren (1), William F. Brennan, Jr. (1), Byron White (3), and Lewis Powell (1), each wrote published dissents from denial of certiorari, and Antonin Scalia (1) wrote a statement with respect to denial of certiorari. These dissent statements are not included in the numbers here, but are listed in the Appendix.

24. Steadman v. SEC, 450 U.S. 91, 104 (1981) (Powell, J., dissenting). Chief Justice Burger has the same percentage of votes in the majority as Powell over this period, but his percentage is inflated by his frequent practice of reserving his vote until a majority emerged so he could assign the opinion.

The only exception would be Rehnquist's dissent in Parklane Hosiery Co. v. Shore, 439 U.S. 322, 337 (1979) (Rehnquist, J., dissenting), which we discuss in Chapter 6.

25. H.W. Perry quotes an anonymous Justice on this point: "[T]here was a time when four members simply weren't interested in hearing Securities and Exchange Commission cases. . . . Now I believe the Court is more disposed to hearing those cases." H.W. Perry, Jr., Deciding to Decide: Agenda Setting in the United States Supreme Court 261 (1991). Perry also quotes an anonymous justice for the proposition that "Justice [unnamed] is intensely interested in the securities area." Id. at 262. Although this is speculation, the unnamed justice was almost certainly Powell.

NOTES 365

It was also not unusual for Powell to note on certiorari memoranda that he would "write if not granted." E.g., Preliminary Memorandum, Int'l Bhd. of Teamsters v. Daniel, to Lewis F. Powell, Jr. 1 (Feb. 17, 1978 Conference) (handwritten notes of Lewis F. Powell, Jr.). Preliminary Memorandum, Dirks v. SEC, to Lewis F. Powell, Jr. 1 (Nov. 12, 1982 Conference) (handwritten notes of Lewis F. Powell, Jr.). Preliminary Memorandum, Shearson/American Express, Inc. v. McMahon, to Lewis F. Powell, Jr. 1 (Sept. 29, 1986 Conference) (handwritten notes of Lewis F. Powell, Jr.), LFP Collection.

Powell failed to gain four votes for certiorari in John Nuveen & Co. v. Sanders, 450 U.S. 1005, 1005 (1981) (Powell, J., dissenting from the denial of certiorari), but Powell's other draft dissents from denial in certiorari cases garnered the necessary four votes. Lewis F. Powell, Jr., Draft Dissent from Denial of Certiorari, United Hous. Found., Inc. v. Forman 1 (Jan. 16, 1974). Lewis F. Powell, Jr., Draft Dissent from Denial of Certiorari, TransAmerica Mortgage Advisors, Inc. v. Lewis 1 (Oct. 12, 1978). Lewis F. Powell, Jr., Draft Dissent from Denial of Certiorari, Carpenter v. United States 1 (Dec. 10, 1986). Lewis F. Powell, Jr., Draft Dissent from Denial of Certiorari, Pinter v. Dahl 1 (Apr. 10, 1987), LFP Collection.

It is apparently not unusual for dissents from denials to result in a grant of certiorari. See Perry, Deciding 171 (quoting an anonymous Justice: "Many times a dissent from denial will pick up a fourth vote."). Perry got estimates that ten to thirty dissents from denial per term picked up additional votes. Id. at 173. Powell does not appear to have carried over this willingness to write at the certiorari stage to other areas. He was less likely to write dissents from denial than most of his colleagues. See id. at 186–87 (reporting that Brennan, White, Marshall, Blackmun, and Stewart all wrote more dissents from denial than Powell, during the period 1976–80).

26. Douglas of course worked with the securities laws during his time at the SEC, but his experience in private practice as a young lawyer focused on reorganization work. Owen Roberts had long experience as a corporate lawyer before his appointment to the Court, William M. Wiecek, The Birth of the Modern Constitution: The United States Supreme Court, 1941–1953 64 (2006), but he that experience predated the enactment of the federal securities laws and he was marginalized by Roosevelt's appointees. He wrote no majority opinions in securities cases during his time on the Court.

Email from Chris Whitman, Powell Clerk OT'75 to Adam Pritchard (Apr. 18, 2002) (stating that Powell was hazy on some distinctions in torts and civil rights cases). Harry Blackmun Conference Notes, CTS Corp. v. Dynamics Corp. of Am., No. 86–71 (Mar. 4, 1987), HAB-LC.

27. Stephen Wermiel & Stan Crock, High Court Rulings are Putting SEC on Shorter Leash, Wall St. J., Oct. 2, 1980, at 30.

Since 1975, the SEC has made its views known to the Supreme Court in 18 cases. The justices have ruled against the SEC in 12 of them. The contrast couldn't be sharper with the period from 1934, when the commission was established, to 1974. In sixty appearances as a party or friend of the court, the SEC won forty-eight Supreme Court cases.

366  NOTES

Letter from Stephen Wermiel, Wall Street Journal, to Lewis F. Powell, Jr. 1 (July 17, 1980) ("I had a pleasurable chat with John Sallet and wanted to express my thanks to you for your kind assistance."), LFP Collection. Telephone Interview with Jonathan Sallet, Powell Clerk OT'80 (May 21, 2002) (notes on file with authors). When the story did not immediately appear, Powell wrote to Wermiel to inquire. Letter from Lewis F. Powell, Jr., to Stephen Wermiel, Wall Street Journal 1 (Aug. 8, 1980), LFP Collection.

Other coverage was less favorable. The *New York Times* quoted Arthur Miller: "This is a pro-business Court . . . [and Powell in particular] has a Virginia plantation mentality. I have a hunch that possibly he thinks the Civil War went the wrong way." Louis Kohlmeier, Justice Powell: For Business, a Friend in Court, N.Y. Times, Mar. 14, 1976, at F5.

28. Letter from Lewis F. Powell, Jr., to George Gibson 1 (Nov. 25, 1942), LFP Collection.

29. Thomas K. McCraw, Rethinking the Trust Question, in Regulation in Perspective 54 (Thomas K. McCraw, ed., 1981) (Brandeis advocated for small producers and retailers "seeking to use the power of government to redress or reverse economic forces that were threatening to render them obsolete. And in Brandeis they found a great advocate.")

30. Central Bank of Denver, N.A. v. First Interstate Bank of Denver, N.A., 511 U.S. 164 (1994); Virginia Bankshares, Inc. v. Sandberg, 501 U.S. 1083, 1115, 1121 (1991); Gustafson v. Alloyd Co., Inc., 513 U.S. 561 (1995).

31. United States v. O'Hagan, 521 U.S. 642 (1997). One of your authors, Pritchard, as Senior Counsel to the SEC, helped the government develop its line in *O'Hagan*. Salman v. United States, 580 U.S. 39 (2016).

# Index

*For the benefit of digital users, indexed terms that span two pages (e.g., 52–53) may, on occasion, appear on only one of those pages.*

accounting, 86–87
administrative law, 17, 67–88, 273
Administrative Procedure Act, 79, 249
administrative proceedings, 85
analysts, 152–53, 155, 156, 157, 158, 161, 166–67
anti-takeover statutes, 235–45
antitrust, 90, 112–18
arbitration, 170, 196–202

bankruptcy, 17, 31, 44–45, 47–48, 56, 58–64, 93
Barrett, Amy Coney, 214
Berle, Adolf, 26, 40, 41, 43–44
bigness, 3, 29, 34, 41–42, 43–44, 223–24
Black, Hugo L., 8–9, 11, 30, 53, 73, 76–77, 133, 174, 257–58
Blackmun, Harry A., 7, 16, 80–81, 99, 115, 139–40, 142–43, 151, 162–63, 176, 181–82, 185, 196, 198, 199, 201–2, 203–4, 205, 227, 265
Brandeis, Louis D., 3, 29, 33–34, 41–42, 67, 271
Brennan, William J., Jr., 13–14, 64, 96–97, 104, 189, 203–4, 261–62
Breyer, Stephen G., 117–18, 220–21
Browning, James, 151–63
Burger, Warren Earl, 14, 84–85, 105–7, 150, 179, 235
Burns, John, 34, 36
Burton, Harold H., 56, 77–78
Butler, Pierce, 11
Byrnes, James F., 11, 21, 258

Cardozo, Benjamin N., 35–36, 51
Cary, William, 130–32
causes of action
    express, 9, 170–71, 173, 194–96
    implied, 14, 169–70, 171–94, 199–200, 202–21, 234–35
Chamber of Commerce, US, 7–8
Chandler Act of 1938, 47–48, 58–64, 66, 253–54
Chiarella, Vincent, 145–51
Clark, Charles, 59–60, 128–29, 135, 171–72, 263

Clark, Tom Campbell, 63–64, 79, 93–94, 172–73, 264
class actions, 14, 178–82, 211–15, 231, 248, 265–66
Cohen, Benjamin I., 20–31, 48–49, 53
commerce clause, 32, 235–45
commercial speech, 118–20, 121
Corcoran, Thomas, 20–31, 33–34
court-packing plan, 51–53, 258
criminal cases, 79–80, 145–51, 252

Davis, John W., 50–51
deference
    agencies, 8–9, 14–15, 39, 49–50, 54–56, 57–58, 63, 67–68, 70–80, 81, 93, 94, 99, 102, 118, 121, 122–23, 135, 146, 171, 188, 193, 201–2, 216, 219, 256–57
    lower courts, 80, 93
Delaware, 230, 233, 244–45, 248
derivative suits, 232–33
Dirks, Raymond, 151–63
disgorgement, 87–88
Dodd-Frank Act of 2010, 124–25, 232, 249
Douglas, William O., 8–9, 11, 13, 17, 24–25, 37, 38, 39–48, 58, 59, 61–62, 64, 69, 74, 76–77, 80, 81–82, 96–97, 113, 117, 130, 142, 175–76, 199, 226, 258–59, 261–64

Easterbrook, Frank, 147, 191–92, 233, 248
Eisenhower, Dwight, 6–7, 264
Employment Retirement Income Security Act of 1974, 100–1
extraterritoriality, 121–25

federal corporate law, 14, 18–19, 103, 222–50
federal incorporation, 41, 43, 224
federalism, 18–19, 149–50, 222–50, 271
Federal Trade Commission, 21–22, 26–27, 48–49, 112–13
fiduciary duty, 18, 39–44, 63–64, 120, 121, 126–67, 223–31
First Amendment, 118–21

# 368 INDEX

Fortas, Abraham, 13, 59, 265
Frank, Jerome, 41, 59–60
Frankfurter, Felix, 2–4, 8–9, 20–31, 32–33, 35,
   36, 37, 42–43, 44–45, 50–51, 52, 56, 57,
   67–70, 93, 114, 197–98, 257–62, 263–64
fraud-on-the-market presumption, 169–70,
   203–5, 211–15, 217
Friendly, Henry, 111–12, 121–22, 134, 135–36,
   184, 185, 187, 188, 210, 213

going private, 230
Goldberg, Arthur J., 113–14, 136–37, 265
Great Depression, 1, 11, 37, 49–50, 257–58, 273

Hand, Learned, 224, 258–59
Harlan, John Marshall, 173–74, 245–46
Hoover, Herbert, 2
hostile takeovers. *See* tender offers
*Howey* test, 92–93, 94–95, 99–100, 101, 107–12

implied private rights of action, 14, 169–70,
   171–94, 199–200, 202–21, 234–35
insider trading, 18, 62–64, 70–79, 126–67, 250,
   265–66, 271
   bankruptcy, 62–64
   classical theory, 145–51
   common law, 127–28, 130, 134, 136–37, 139,
      145–46, 149–50, 164, 165
   misappropriation theory, 149–50, 163–66
   tender offers, 145–51
   tipping, 151–63, 166
insurance, 95–97
internal affairs, 242
interpretation. *See* statutory interpretation
Investment Advisers Act of 1940, 31, 119–21,
   133–38, 191
Investment Company Act of 1940, 31, 115–17,
   232–34
investment contract, 90–93, 94–95, 99–100,
   101, 107–12

Jackson, Robert H., 3, 29, 36, 43–44, 52, 53, 60,
   64, 70, 72, 76–77, 78–79, 91–92, 93, 257–59
Justice, Department of, 116

Kennedy, Anthony M., 202, 205–7, 208, 216–18,
   246, 247, 272
Kennedy, John F., 264–65
Kennedy, Joseph P., 27

Landis, James M., 20–31, 35, 44–45, 59, 69, 130
litigation, private
   loss causation, 211–12

materiality, 159–60, 173–74, 176, 186–87,
   203, 213–14, 247
misrepresentation, 134, 204, 205, 225, 228,
   229–30, 245, 246
reliance, 127–28, 140, 176, 203–5, 207, 212–
   14, 216–18, 220, 221, 245–46
scienter, 83–84, 157–58, 159, 161, 162–63,
   183–84, 185–86, 209–11
Loss, Louis, 224

Maloney Act of 1938, 46, 116, 117
manipulation, 2, 46, 117–18, 126, 175, 187, 248
Marshall, Thurgood, 81, 95, 99, 110–12, 186–87,
   189, 227, 238–39
McReynolds, James C., 11, 32, 171
mismanagement, 225, 226
Moley, Raymond, 2, 20, 21, 37
Murphy, Frank, 11, 54, 57–58, 77–78, 92–93,
   170, 251, 256–57, 258–59

New York Stock Exchange, 25–27, 113–15
Nixon, Richard M., 7, 14–15, 274

O'Conner, Sandra Day, 112, 159–61, 195, 201,
   240
offerings, public, 93–94

Pecora, Ferdinand, 2, 21–22, 25–26, 27, 37
Pitt, Harvey, 82–83
pledge, definition, 97–98, 102–6, 107–8, 110
Pound, Roscoe, 70
Powell, Lewis F., Jr., 4–8, 9, 14, 17–18, 83–86,
   98–106, 107–10, 115, 143–63, 176–94,
   195–96, 226–29, 235–37, 239–40, 241–44,
   251–52, 255, 266–72
preemption, 235–45
private attorney general, 14–15, 181, 188, 227
Private Securities Litigation Reform Act of
   1995, 170, 208–21, 248
proxy regulation, 80–82
Public Utility Holding Company Act of 1935,
   12, 14–15, 27–30, 33, 46–47, 48–58, 65–66,
   70–79, 253–54

railroads, 37–38, 47–48
Rayburn, Sam, 20–21, 26
Reed, Stanley F., 11, 75–76, 79–80, 197, 257–59,
   261–62
Regulation FD, 166
Rehnquist, William H., 14, 104, 180–81, 182,
   269–70
Roberts, John G., Jr., 86–87, 211–12, 213–14,
   272

INDEX 369

Roberts, Owen Josephus, 52, 76
Roosevelt, Franklin Delano, 1–2, 4, 5–6, 11, 26–27, 28, 29, 30, 31, 43–44, 46, 48, 51–52, 70, 255–56, 257–59, 274
Rule 10b-5, 5, 18, 83–85, 95, 121–24, 129, 137–38, 139–40, 145–63, 171–72, 175–94, 200–2, 203–21, 254, 264–65
rulemaking, 72–73, 75–76, 77, 135–36
Rutledge, Wiley B., 11, 28, 77–78, 257–59

sale, definition, 101, 102–6
sale of business doctrine, 107–10
Scalia, Antonin, 121–24, 210–11, 246
Scharfman, Isaiah Leo, 69
SEC enforcement, 5, 34–36, 46–47, 57–58, 83–86, 87–88, 90–91, 119, 122, 124–25, 126–67, 180–81, 187–88, 208–9, 216–17, 253, 254
Second Circuit, US Court of Appeals for, 14, 18, 52, 83, 98, 121–23, 128–93, 133–36, 138–39, 146, 147, 171–72, 175–76, 179–80, 187, 224–26, 229–30, 231, 247
Securities Act of 1933, 34–36, 40–41, 83–85, 104–5, 170–71, 195–97, 248–49
    Section 11, 194, 202
    Section 12, 168–69, 170–71, 173, 195–96
    Section 17, 83, 84–85, 104–5, 196, 220
Securities Exchange Act of 1934, 25–27, 46, 82–86, 117–18, 198–99, 200–1, 203–8
    Rule 10b-5, 5, 18, 83–85, 95, 121–24, 129, 137–38, 139–40, 145–63, 171–72, 175–94, 200–2, 203–21, 254, 264–65
    Section 12(j) & (k), 82–83
    Section 14(a), 172–74, 186–87, 245–47, 254, 264–65
    Section 14(e), 185–86, 189–91, 231
    Section 16(b), 18, 64, 89, 127–30, 132–33, 140–45
Securities Litigation Uniform Standards Act, 248–49
security, definition, 89–97, 98–102, 106–12
Sherman Act, 112–14, 116
short-swings profits, 18, 64, 89, 127–30, 132–33, 140–45

social control of finance, 37–66, 81–82, 273
Solicitor General, 102, 117–18, 122, 147, 152
Souter, David H., 245–47
statutory interpretation
    legislative history, 84, 93–94, 101–2, 120, 121, 124–25, 135–36, 180, 191, 209, 211, 235, 240
    purposive, 13–14, 91–92, 93–95, 98, 105–6, 111–12, 113, 129, 132, 135–36, 137, 138–39, 140, 141–42, 143, 144–45, 150, 151, 166, 169, 172–74, 181–83, 185, 188–89, 191, 192, 237, 248–49, 264–65, 274
    remedial, 84, 94–95, 98, 105–6, 132, 137, 140, 141–42, 151, 172–73, 182–83, 185, 187–88, 196
    textualism, 84, 86–87, 99, 123, 127, 132, 133, 137, 140–45, 149–50, 166, 169, 180, 182–83, 185–86, 187, 193, 194, 195, 196, 206–8, 209, 218–19, 265–66, 274
Stevens, John Paul, 16, 120–21, 124, 148, 150, 190–91, 211, 217, 238, 240
Stewart, Potter, 84, 97, 141–42, 181, 193, 198–99
Stone, Harlan Fiske, 3, 21, 25–26, 36, 56, 60–61, 261
Sutherland, George, 11, 35, 53

tender offers, 146, 185–86, 189–91, 231, 234–45
Thomas, Clarence, 118, 218–19, 248
Truman, Harry S, 13, 76–77, 264

utility holding companies, 37–38

Van Devanter, Willis, 11, 52–53
Vinson, Fred, 74, 76–77, 261–62

*Wall Street Journal,* 163–64, 270
Warren, Earl, 13–14, 94–95, 114, 264
White, Byron, 116–17, 120–21, 136–37, 199–200, 204–5, 229, 239, 246–47
Whitney, Richard, 26, 46
Williams Act, 141, 190–91, 231, 234–45
Willkie, Wendell, 29–30